INTERACTIONS

A THEMATIC READER

Third Edition

INSTRUCTOR'S EDITION

ANN MOSELEY

Texas A&M University-Commerce

JEANETTE HARRIS

University of Southern Mississippi

HOUGHTON MIFFLIN COMPANY   Boston   New York

For my husband, Fred—A. M.
For Henry—J. H.

Sponsoring Editor: Renee Deljon
Senior Associate Editor: Ellen Darion
Development Editor: Jennifer Huber
Senior Project Editor: Fred Burns
Production/Design Coordinator: Carol Merrigan
Manufacturing Manager: Florence Cadran
Marketing Manager: Nancy Lyman

Cover design: Diana Coe
Cover image: Jose Ortega-SIS

Acknowledgments begin on page 513.

Printed in the U.S.A.
Library of Congress Catalog Card Number: 96-76937

ISBNs: Student Text: 0-395-78294-5
       Instructor's Edition: 0-395-78295-3

123456789-CS-00   99 98 97 96

Contents

RHETORICAL TABLE OF CONTENTS   xxi

PREFACE   xxvi

INTRODUCTION   1

UNIT ONE: *The Self*   15

My Name   SANDRA CISNEROS   17
Unhappy with her Spanish name, a young girl selects a new name for herself.

The Misery of Silence   MAXINE HONG KINGSTON   20
A Chinese-American writer tells of the problems she encountered growing up in two very different cultures.

Lives on the Boundary   MIKE ROSE   25
An Italian-American college professor remembers his life growing up in a poor section of Los Angeles.

On Being 17, Bright, and Unable to Read
DAVID RAYMOND   33
A high-school student describes what it is like to have a learning disability.

Old at Seventeen   DAVID VECSEY   37
The author tells of a time when he realized his childhood was over.

The Right to Know   MARGARET R. BROWN   41
A young woman who was adopted as a child argues that adopted children have a right to know their birth parents.

What Do Women Want?   SARA DAVIDSON   **45**
In this essay Davidson answers the question posed by her title.

The New American Man   ROBERT BLY   **50**
Bly accuses American men of becoming "soft males" in this essay
about the developing nature of men.

Getting Started   JANET CAMPBELL HALE   **54**
The speaker in this poem sets lofty goals for herself.

The Stars of the Whole Sky   SHOZO MACHIDA   **57**
A Japanese student tells of the plans he has made for his life.

*Unit One: Critical Thinking and
Writing Assignments* **60**

EXPLORING IDEAS TOGETHER   60
WRITING ESSAYS   60

UNIT TWO: *Self with Family* **63**

Generations   JOYCE MAYNARD   **66**
On a visit to her dying grandmother, Maynard discovers that each
generation is in some ways like the one before it.

**No Snapshots in the Attic: A Granddaughter's
Search for a Cherokee Past**   CONNIE MAY FOWLER   **71**
Fowler's search for her Native American and European heritage
leads her back to the ancient oral tradition of storytelling.

Two Kinds   AMY TAN   **80**
In this excerpt from Tan's bestselling book *The Joy Luck Club,* a
daughter rebels against her mother's expectations for her.

Fatherhood   BILL COSBY   92

Popular television personality Bill Cosby focuses on the special
relationship between a father and a daughter.

The Old Man   LARRY KING   95

King recalls conflicts that he and his father had when he was a
teenager.

Never in My Life   WALTER McDONALD   100

This poem focuses on the difficulty a father and a son have in
expressing their feelings for each other.

Sibling Imprints   FRANCINE KLAGSBRUN   104

Drawing on her experiences with her own brother, Klagsbrun
argues that sibling love and rivalry have a long-lasting effect on
individual personality and development.

The Letter   RUDOLFO ANAYA   111

A letter shatters the stability of a teenager's life by revealing that he
is an adopted child.

Hold the Mayonnaise   JULIA ALVAREZ   117

This author describes the process of adjustment she underwent as a
Latina stepmother to two blond stepdaughters.

Wanted: A Mother   ORVILLE RAWLINS   121

Initially ashamed of being the son of an illiterate, unmarried maid,
the writer of this essay learns to appreciate his mother's love and
self-sacrifice.

The Family Values Debate   JAMES Q. WILSON   127

A political science professor and sociologist asserts that the family is
undergoing "worldwide, long-term change" and discusses the
debate about family values going on among both public
policymakers and ordinary citizens.

Unit Two: Critical Thinking and
Writing Assignments 135

EXPLORING IDEAS TOGETHER   135
WRITING ESSAYS   135

UNIT THREE: *Self with Friends and Mates* 137

Liked for Myself   MAYA ANGELOU   139
As an unhappy young girl, Angelou experiences a transformation
when she realizes that a teacher whom she admires likes her for
herself.

Oil and Water   VALERIE OWEN   145
A student tells of two very different people who became good
friends.

What Friends Are For   PHILLIP LOPATE   148
In defining friendship, Lopate also categorizes and describes
friendships he has known.

Death of a Friend: The Delicacy and Strength
of Lace   LESLIE MARMON SILKO AND JAMES WRIGHT   157
Close friends correspond through letters as one of them faces a
terminal illness.

Where's Dietz?   MIKE TAIBBI   164
In memorializing a friend who has recently died, Taibbi explores
the reluctance of male friends to express their feelings.

Drifting Away   DIANE COLE   168
The writer explains how she and a close childhood friend drifted
apart and analyzes her reaction to the situation.

Finding a Wife   GARY SOTO   173

Soto, a Mexican-American writer who married his Japanese-American neighbor, concludes from his own experiences that it is easy to find a wife.

The Right to Marry   JOANNE JACOBS   178

This editorial argues that homosexual relationships should be recognized as legal marriages.

The Lies That Bind   PAUL THALER   181

In this essay from *The New York Times Magazine,* Thaler supports the idea that the "truth" often hurts and is therefore less important for a successful relationship than is usually supposed.

Distance   RAYMOND CARVER   186

By exploring several kinds of "distance," this short story suggests that youthful romance does not last.

The Good Marriage   JUDITH S. WALLERSTEIN AND SANDRA BLAKESLEE   196

By analyzing successful marriages, a sociology professor and a science writer try to answer the question "How and why does love last?"

On Death and Love   JANET CAMPBELL HALE   206

A poet explores the relationship between love and death.

Unit Three: Critical Thinking and Writing Assignments   209

EXPLORING IDEAS TOGETHER   209
WRITING ESSAYS   209

UNIT FOUR: *Self with Work*   211

American Dreams: Stanley Cygan, 90
STUDS TERKEL   213
An interview with a ninety-year-old Polish immigrant.

Work and Play   ROBERT MURRAY DAVIS   217
The author remembers the lessons his father taught him about both work and play.

My Mother Enters the Workforce   RITA DOVE   221
The poet laureate of the United States pays tribute to her mother in this poem.

The Case Against Chores   JANE SMILEY   224
Smiley goes against every convention by arguing that children should not be given chores.

Initiation   REBECCA MAY   228
A young woman who wants to enter the medical profession gains a new perspective on her chosen career.

Spokesperson   JANE ARMSTRONG   232
The author discovers that her job as director of a family planning clinic has obscured her identity as a person.

The Family Farm   DAVID MAS MASUMOTO   236
In this essay Masumoto explains his decision to join his parents on the family farm.

The Workman's Compensation   REG THERIAULT   240
A longshoreman defends the practice of taking it easy on the job.

Out of College, Out of Work   STEPHEN SHERRILL   244
A young man discovers that having a college degree does not guarantee a job.

20 Hot Job Tracks *U.S. NEWS AND WORLD REPORT* 248
A look at the most promising career choices for this decade.

The Work Ahead *HARPER'S MAGAZINE* 270
A forecast of the professions that will experience the greatest
growth over the next decade.

*Unit Four: Critical Thinking and
Writing Assignments* 273

EXPLORING IDEAS TOGETHER 273
WRITING ESSAYS 273

UNIT FIVE: *Self with Society* 275

The Scholarship Jacket MARTA SALINAS 277
Through scholastic and cultural pride, Salinas and her family
overcome small town prejudices and gain her the scholarship jacket
she has earned.

In Praise of the F Word MARY SHERRY 283
A mother argues in this editorial that students who don't measure
up to standards should flunk.

The Big Squeeze DAVID SAMUELS 287
Samuels reports on the increasing costs of a college education.

The Resegregation of a Southern School
DOUGLAS A. BLACKMON 294
A journalist returns to his home in the Mississippi Delta and finds
that the schools have become resegregated.

The Recoloring of Campus Life SHELBY STEELE 301
Steele argues that "universities should emphasize commonality as a
higher value than 'diversity' and 'pluralism.'"

What Is Behind the Growth of Violence on
College Campuses?   DOROTHY SIEGEL   307
A vice president for student services at a state university in
Maryland analyzes the causes of campus crime.

Kids Who Kill   GORDON WITKIN   315
This article from *U.S. News and World Report* begins with an
example of juvenile violence and then analyzes the causes of
gun-related violence among young people.

in the inner city   LUCILLE CLIFTON   319
An African-American poet describes life in "the inner city"—her
home.

Slow Descent into Hell   JON D. HULL   321
This essay from *Time* provides a detailed description of the lives of
several homeless men in a large city.

So How Did I Get Here?   ROSEMARY L. BRAY   328
A successful African-American journalist describes how welfare
helped her and her family when she was a child and how she
became independent of the system.

Nobody Ever Died of Old Age
SHARON R. CURTIN   335
The author discusses the aging process itself as well as the attitude
that society—especially young people—have toward the aged.

We Don't Want to Grow Old   KARLA COLE   340
A student argues that her generation—the generation of the "baby
boomers"—is fascinated with the idea of youth and doesn't want to
grow older or more mature.

*Unit Five: Critical Thinking and
Writing Assignments*   343
EXPLORING IDEAS TOGETHER   343
WRITING ESSAYS   343

UNIT SIX: *Self with Environment*   345

Weather Reports   KATHLEEN NORRIS   347
A poetic narrative of a year the author spent in her grandparents' home on the border between North and South Dakota.

Wild Geese   MARY OLIVER   352
This poem expresses the poet's belief that humans share an intimate relationship with nature.

Song of the Sky Loom   NATIVE AMERICAN (TEWA)   354
This Native American (Tewa) chant portrays the harmonious relationship the Tewas have with nature.

The Gift   LOUIS DOLLARHIDE   356
This short story tells how a woman and a panther survive a flood.

A Fable for Tomorrow   RACHEL CARSON   361
In a frightening fantasy, the author describes a "strange blight" that kills plant and animal life.

Down with the Forests   CHARLES KURALT   365
As he counts the number of paper products he uses while eating breakfast, Kuralt begins to worry about the fate of our national forests.

Dice or Doves?   CINDY CAMBURN   368
A resident of the Mississippi Gulf Coast discovers the environmental cost of "progress."

Waste   WENDELL BERRY   372
The author explains the relationship between the waste of material goods and the waste of human lives.

America's "Garbage Crisis": A Toxic Myth
PATRICIA POORE   377
Poore challenges the idea that garbage is "a serious environmental hazard."

What's Best for the West?   DAVID DIAMOND   381

Is a Lab Rat's Fate More Poignant Than
a Child's?   JANE McCABE   386
A mother argues that animal research is essential to the life of her
daughter, who has cystic fibrosis.

We Must Find Alternatives to Animals
in Research   ROGER CARAS   389
A naturalist argues that we must replace animal research with other
methods.

Unit Six: Critical Thinking and
Writing Assignments   392

   EXPLORING IDEAS TOGETHER   392
   WRITING ESSAYS   392

UNIT SEVEN: Self with Technology   395

At the Electronic Frontier   MIGUEL ALGARIN   398
A poet describes what it is like to be a "child of the Electronic
Frontier."

Living with My VCR   NORA EPHRON   400
A well-known writer describes her love-hate relationship with her
VCR.

Television Addiction   MARIE WINN   405
The author argues that excessive television viewing is just another
form of addiction.

Technology and the Hearing Impaired
TAMMY HOLM   409
A student writer explains how technology both hurts and helps
those with hearing impairments.

Lonely Hearts, Classy Dreams, Empty Wallets
AMY WALDMAN   413

Waldman describes how home shopping networks prey on lonely people's hunger for companionship.

Error Error Error   DAVE BARRY   416

A newspaper columnist tells of a humorous encounter with his computer.

Getting a Degree by E-mail   MARY LORD   420

This article explains how students can pursue a college degree by enrolling in "online courses."

Gender Gap in Cyberspace   DEBORAH TANNEN   424

An expert in male-female communication patterns describes how men differ in their use of electronic mail.

The Beep Goes On   CAROL ORLOCK   429

Orlock expresses both her hopes and fears for the future as a technology-dependent society.

Unit Seven: Critical Thinking and Writing Assignments   434

EXPLORING IDEAS TOGETHER   434
WRITING ESSAYS   434

UNIT EIGHT: Self with Heroes   437

Larger Than Life   PHIL SUDO   439

The author defines the word *hero* and comments on its meaning in society today.

I Have a Dream   MARTIN LUTHER KING, JR.   443

A famous civil rights leader claims for African-Americans the rights promised in the Constitution and Declaration of Independence.

Extraordinary People   HERBERT BUCHSBAUM   450

Buchsbaum describes three extraordinary young people, all of
whom have won the Nobel Peace Prize by endangering themselves
to fight for human rights and freedom in their countries.

On Heroes and the Media
JEAN PICKER FIRSTENBERG   457

A film critic traces the development of the hero in the media.

Lenny Skutnik—Accidental Hero
RICHARD SHEREIKIS   461

A college professor describes Skutnik's heroic rescue of an air crash
victim in 1982 and his response to the fame that followed.

The Man in the Water   ROGER ROSENBLATT   468

A Washington, D.C., writer describes the unselfish heroism of an air
crash victim whose anonymity has made him an Everyman figure.

Fall of the Legends   MIKE LUPICA   473

Lupica gives examples of legendary sports figures who have "fallen"
in the eyes of the public and analyzes the causes of such downfalls.

Heroines and Role Models   MAXINE F. SINGER   478

Singer distinguishes between heroines and female role models in
this university commencement address.

Mother Teresa and Her Endless Fight
ELLEN GOODMAN   482

A tribute to Mother Teresa's selfless and heroic dedication to the
poor, this column was written just after she was awarded the Nobel
Peace Prize in 1979.

Having Our Say   SARAH DELANY AND
A. ELIZABETH DELANY   486

African-American women born in the late nineteenth century, the
Delany sisters describe their heroic struggle for professional
success—"Bessie" as a dentist and "Sadie" as a teacher.

Selena: Dreaming of You   ILAN STAVANS   493
Both before and after the death of Tejana singer Selena, her fans not
only idealized her but almost idolized her.

A Hero's Journey: Neil Armstrong's Walk on
the Moon   THOMAS TALLEY   498
This student views Armstrong as a world hero who has given us a
new way to look at ourselves and our world.

Christa McAuliffe: An Ordinary Hero
MIKE PRIDE   502
The editor of Christa McAuliffe's hometown newspaper shows how
this "ordinary" schoolteacher "stood for what was best in us."

Those Winter Sundays   ROBERT HAYDEN   506
A poet recalls the father who performed "love's austere and lonely
offices" for him when he was a child.

A Song of Greatness (from the Chippewa)
MARY AUSTIN   508
An ancient Chippewa chant celebrates the greatness within each
individual.

*Unit Eight: Critical Thinking and
Writing Assignments*   510

EXPLORING IDEAS TOGETHER   510
WRITING ESSAYS   510

ACKNOWLEDGMENTS   513

INDEX   519

Rhetorical Table of Contents

NARRATION

The Misery of Silence   MAXINE HONG KINGSTON   20
Lives on the Boundary   MIKE ROSE   25
On Being 17, Bright, and Unable to Read   DAVID RAYMOND   33
Old at Seventeen   DAVID VECSEY   37
What Do Women Want?   SARA DAVIDSON   45
Generations   JOYCE MAYNARD   66
Two Kinds   AMY TAN   80
Fatherhood   BILL COSBY   92
The Old Man   LARRY KING   95
Sibling Imprints   FRANCINE KLAGSBRUN   104
The Letter   RUDOLFO ANAYA   111
Hold the Mayonnaise   JULIA ALVAREZ   117
Wanted: A Mother   ORVILLE RAWLINS   121
Liked for Myself   MAYA ANGELOU   139
Oil and Water   VALERIE OWEN   145
Drifting Away   DIANE COLE   168
Finding a Wife   GARY SOTO   173
Distance   RAYMOND CARVER   186
American Dreams: Stanley Cygan, 90   STUDS TERKEL   213
Initiation   REBECCA MAY   228
Spokesperson   JANE ARMSTRONG   232
The Scholarship Jacket   MARTA SALINAS   277
The Resegregation of a Southern School   DOUGLAS A. BLACKMON   294
Slow Descent into Hell   JON D. HULL   321
So How Did I Get Here?   ROSEMARY L. BRAY   328
The Gift   LOUIS DOLLARHIDE   356
A Fable for Tomorrow   RACHEL CARSON   361
Down with the Forests   CHARLES KURALT   365
Living with My VCR   NORA EPHRON   400

Extraordinary People   HERBERT BUCHSBAUM   450

Lenny Skutnik—Accidental Hero   RICHARD SHEREIKIS   461

The Man in the Water   ROGER ROSENBLATT   468

Having Our Say   SARAH AND A. ELIZABETH DELANY   486

DESCRIPTION

My Name   SANDRA CISNEROS   17

What Do Women Want?   SARA DAVIDSON   45

The Stars of the Whole Sky   SHOZO MACHIDA   57

No Snapshots in the Attic: A Granddaughter's Search for a
   Cherokee Past   CONNIE MAY FOWLER   71

Two Kinds   AMY TAN   80

The Old Man   LARRY KING   95

Sibling Imprints   FRANCINE KLAGSBRUN   104

Wanted: A Mother   ORVILLE RAWLINS   121

Liked for Myself   MAYA ANGELOU   139

Death of a Friend: The Delicacy and Strength of Lace   LESLIE MARMON
   SILKO AND JAMES WRIGHT   157

Finding a Wife   GARY SOTO   173

Distance   RAYMOND CARVER   186

20 Hot Job Tracks   U.S. NEWS AND WORLD REPORT   248

The Scholarship Jacket   MARTA SALINAS   277

Slow Descent into Hell   JON D. HULL   321

Nobody Ever Died of Old Age   SHARON R. CURTIN   335

Weather Reports   KATHLEEN NORRIS   347

A Fable for Tomorrow   RACHEL CARSON   361

Down with the Forests   CHARLES KURALT   365

Waste   WENDELL BERRY   372

The Man in the Water   ROGER ROSENBLATT   468

Selena: Dreaming of You   ILAN STAVANS   493

ILLUSTRATION AND EXEMPLIFICATION

No Snapshots in the Attic: A Granddaughter's Search for a
   Cherokee Past   CONNIE MAY FOWLER   71

Sibling Imprints   FRANCINE KLAGSBRUN   104

The Family Values Debate   JAMES Q. WILSON   127
What Friends Are For   PHILLIP LOPATE   148
The Lies That Bind   PAUL THALER   181
The Good Marriage   JUDITH S. WALLERSTEIN AND
   SANDRA BLAKESLEE   196
In Praise of the F Word   MARY SHERRY   283
The Big Squeeze   DAVID SAMUELS   287
The Resegregation of a Southern School   DOUGLAS A. BLACKMON   294
What Is Behind the Growth of Violence on College Campuses?
   DOROTHY SIEGEL   307
Kids Who Kill   GORDON WITKIN   315
Slow Descent into Hell   JON D. HULL   321
Technology and the Hearing Impaired   TAMMY HOLM   409
The Beep Goes On   CAROL ORLOCK   429
Larger Than Life   PHIL SUDO   439
Extraordinary People   HERBERT BUCHSBAUM   450
On Heroes and the Media   JEAN PICKER FIRSTENBERG   457
Fall of the Legends   MIKE LUPICA   473
Heroines and Role Models   MAXINE F. SINGER   478

COMPARISON AND CONTRAST

The New American Man   ROBERT BLY   50
Two Kinds   AMY TAN   80
Hold the Mayonnaise   JULIA ALVAREZ   117
The Family Values Debate   JAMES Q. WILSON   127
Oil and Water   VALERIE OWEN   145
What Friends Are For   PHILLIP LOPATE   148
Where's Dietz?   MIKE TAIBBI   164
The Right to Marry   JOANNE JACOBS   178
Work and Play   ROBERT MURRAY DAVIS   217
Out of College, Out of Work   STEPHEN SHERRILL   244
The Big Squeeze   DAVID SAMUELS   287
We Don't Want to Grow Old   KARLA COLE   340
Is a Lab Rat's Fate More Poignant Than a Child's?   JANE McCABE   386
Television Addiction   MARIE WINN   405
Gender Gap in Cyberspace   DEBORAH TANNEN   424

Lenny Skutnik—Accidental Hero   RICHARD SHEREIKIS   461
Heroines and Role Models   MAXINE F. SINGER   478

CLASSIFICATION AND DIVISION

The Family Values Debate   JAMES Q. WILSON   127
What Friends Are For   PHILLIP LOPATE   148
The Good Marriage   JUDITH S. WALLERSTEIN AND
    SANDRA BLAKESLEE   196
The Work Ahead   HARPER'S MAGAZINE   270
On Heroes and the Media   JEAN PICKER FIRSTENBERG   457

PROCESS

Finding a Wife   GARY SOTO   173
The Good Marriage   JUDITH S. WALLERSTEIN AND
    SANDRA BLAKESLEE   196
Nobody Ever Died of Old Age   SHARON R. CURTIN   335
Technology and the Hearing Impaired   TAMMY HOLM   409
Getting a Degree by E-mail   MARY LORD   420

CAUSE AND EFFECT

The Misery of Silence   MAXINE HONG KINGSTON   20
No Snapshots in the Attic: A Granddaughter's Search for a
    Cherokee Past   CONNIE MAY FOWLER   71
Hold the Mayonnaise   JULIA ALVAREZ   117
The Family Values Debate   JAMES Q. WILSON   127
Oil and Water   VALERIE OWEN   145
Death of a Friend: The Delicacy and Strength of Lace   LESLIE MARMON
    SILKO AND JAMES WRIGHT   157
Where's Dietz?   MIKE TAIBBI   164
Drifting Away   DIANE COLE   168
The Lies That Bind   PAUL THALER   181
The Good Marriage   JUDITH S. WALLERSTEIN AND
    SANDRA BLAKESLEE   196
Initiation   REBECCA MAY   228

Spokesperson   JANE ARMSTRONG   232
In Praise of the F Word   MARY SHERRY   283
The Big Squeeze   DAVID SAMUELS   287
The Resegregation of a Southern School   DOUGLAS A. BLACKMON   294
The Recoloring of Campus Life   SHELBY STEELE   301
What Is Behind the Growth of Violence on College Campuses?
   DOROTHY SIEGEL   307
Kids Who Kill   GORDON WITKIN   315
We Don't Want to Grow Old   KARLA COLE   340
A Fable for Tomorrow   RACHEL CARSON   361
Down with the Forests   CHARLES KURALT   365
Dice or Doves?   CINDY CAMBURN   368
Living with My VCR   NORA EPHRON   400
Lenny Skutnik—Accidental Hero   RICHARD SHEREIKIS   461
The Man in the Water   ROGER ROSENBLATT   468
Fall of the Legends   MIKE LUPICA   473
Selena: Dreaming of You   ILAN STAVANS   493
A Hero's Journey: Neil Armstrong's Walk on the Moon   THOMAS
   TALLEY   498
Christa McAuliffe: An Ordinary Hero   MIKE PRIDE   502
A Song of Greatness (from the Chippewa)   MARY AUSTIN   508

DEFINITION

My Name   SANDRA CISNEROS   17
Fatherhood   BILL COSBY   92
The Family Values Debate   JAMES Q. WILSON   127
What Friends Are For   PHILLIP LOPATE   148
The Good Marriage   JUDITH S. WALLERSTEIN AND
   SANDRA BLAKESLEE   196
Television Addiction   MARIE WINN   405
Larger Than Life   PHIL SUDO   439
On Heroes and the Media   JEAN PICKER FIRSTENBERG   457
Lenny Skutnik—Accidental Hero   RICHARD SHEREIKIS   461
Heroines and Role Models   MAXINE F. SINGER   478
A Hero's Journey: Neil Armstrong's Walk on the Moon   THOMAS
   TALLEY   498

ARGUMENT AND PERSUASION

The Right to Know   MARGARET R. BROWN   41
The New American Man   ROBERT BLY   50
The Family Values Debate   JAMES Q. WILSON   127
The Right to Marry   JOANNE JACOBS   178
The Lies That Bind   PAUL THALER   181
The Case Against Chores   JANE SMILEY   224
The Family Farm   DAVID MAS MASUMOTO   236
The Workman's Compensation   REG THERIAULT   240
In Praise of the F Word   MARY SHERRY   283
The Big Squeeze   DAVID SAMUELS   287
The Recoloring of Campus Life   SHELBY STEELE   301
So How Did I Get Here?   ROSEMARY L. BRAY   328
Down with the Forests   CHARLES KURALT   365
Dice or Doves?   CINDY CAMBURN   368
Waste   WENDELL BERRY   372
America's "Garbage Crisis": A Toxic Myth   PATRICIA POORE   377
What's Best for the West?   DAVID DIAMOND   381
Is a Lab Rat's Fate More Poignant Than a Child's?   JANE McCABE   386
We Must Find Alternatives to Animals in Research   ROGER CARAS   389
Television Addiction   MARIE WINN   405
Lonely Hearts, Classy Dreams, Empty Wallets   AMY WALDMAN   413
I Have a Dream   MARTIN LUTHER KING, JR.   443
On Heroes and the Media   JEAN PICKER FIRSTENBERG   457

Preface

OVERVIEW OF THE TEXT

Like the first two editions of *Interactions: A Thematic Reader,* this third edition is designed to help students discover meaning in what they read and to convey meaning in what they write. This text's readings and accompanying apparatus, thoroughly class-tested and proven effective through the two previous editions, move students from a consideration of self to an awareness of how the self interacts with other people and phenomena. We hope that the diverse selections in this thematic reader will foster a stimulating context for reading and writing. By providing a number of perspectives on individual and societal identity, the focus on the self helps students find their own voices.

FEATURES OF THE THIRD EDITION

The following features of the third edition of *Interactions* deserve special attention:

- Thematic focus on the self
- Strong reading/writing connections
- Emphasis on critical thinking and writing
- Emphasis on collaborative learning
- Variety of genres and writing styles
- Diversity and timeliness of readings
- New unit on work
- At least one student essay in each unit

READING SELECTIONS

The readings, 30 percent of which are new to this edition, are organized into eight thematic units. In Unit One, "The Self," students are guided through an exploration of themselves as they react and interact with the readings. Unit Two, "Self with Family," and Unit Three, "Self with Friends and Mates," encourage students to examine their relationships with those people closest to them—their family members, friends, and mates. (Users of previous editions will notice that the closely linked topics of friends and mates are now addressed in the same chapter.) In the new Unit Four, "Self with Work," students are asked to think about not only their own career plans but also the role of work in their lives and how the concept of work has changed in our society. Units Five through Eight help students to examine their relationship to society, the environment, technology, and heroes. These units encourage students to consider and respond critically to larger issues that concern them.

As in previous editions, the readings represent a wide range of voices, topics, and sources. Almost half the selections are by women, and a substantial number are by culturally diverse writers. This authorial diversity allows students to hear different voices and to identify with familiar ones. The many genres represented—essays, poetry, fiction, editorials, speeches—provide various models and styles of writing.

APPARATUS

The text's *Introduction* explains the interdependence of reading and writing, stressing the connections students can make between their lives and what they read. It introduces them to writing techniques such as freewriting, brainstorming, mapping, clustering, and journals. Finally, it emphasizes the importance of considering audience and purpose in all of their reading and writing activities.

Headnotes precede and provide context for each selection, helping students understand and enjoy the selection.

Before You Read activities involve students in important prereading and prewriting techniques. Before each selection students are asked to

THINK critically about the selection's primary theme in relation to their own beliefs, values, or previous experiences.

EXAMINE specific elements of the text such as the title, the format, or potentially difficult vocabulary. This section often defines selected words in the context in which they will appear in the readings or provides additional information about word parts and origins. It may also ask students to examine headings within the selection as well as first and last paragraphs or sentences.

WRITE a reaction, in the form of a journal entry, to the topic they are going to read.

As You Read activities help students interact with the selection and make it their own by determining the main idea, annotating the text, or focusing on specific information or relating what they read to their own personal experiences.

After You Read sections echo the format of the *Before You Read* sections, encouraging students to THINK about the ideas and opinions presented in the reading, EXAMINE specific features of the text, and WRITE a response to what they have read. These activities are more analytical than those for prereading, taking students several steps further in developing their critical thinking capacities.

CRITICAL THINKING AND WRITING ASSIGNMENTS

This section includes two types of assignments. In **Exploring Ideas Together,** students collaborate on a topic suggested by the readings in the unit, synthesizing and analyzing information orally or in group writings. In **Writing Essays,** students individually elaborate on ideas derived from the readings, making connections with the readings themselves and/or with their own observations and experiences.

SUPPORT FOR INSTRUCTORS

The Instructor's Resource Manual for *Interactions* offers instructors supplemental instructional material:

- Background information on the selection's author and/or topic
- Suggestions for activities based on the *Before You Read, As You Read,* and *After You Read* sections
- Strategies for teaching vocabulary not covered in the text
- Additional reading and writing activities
- Two additional tables of contents, one emphasizing genre and one identifying alternate themes

ACKNOWLEDGMENTS

We would like to thank our colleagues at Texas A&M University-Commerce and the University of Southern Mississippi who offered helpful suggestions and responded to the manuscript. We are also indebted to the following persons for their suggestions in revising *Interactions:*

Kirk Adams, Tarrant County Junior College, Texas
Judy Forshee, Orange County Community College, New York
Judy Hanley, Wright College, Illinois
Ann Judd, Seward County Community College, Kansas
Andrea Lowenstein, New York
Julia Nichols, Okaloosa-Walton Community College, Florida
Ruth Ray, Wayne State University, Michigan
Jayne Decker Tabet, University of Maine, Farmington, Maine
Linda Weeks, Dyersburg State University, Tennessee
Linda Woodson, University of Texas at San Antonio, Texas

Finally, we would like to thank our students, who inspired the first edition of *Interactions* and who continue to teach us how to teach.

—A.M. and J.H.

Introduction

This book is about you—about the individual self that you are and how you *interact* with other people and the world. Each unit explores a different relationship. Beginning with the first unit, which focuses on your relationship to yourself, the book moves from close, intimate relationships with family and friends to more distant, abstract relationships with the society and the environment in which you live. We hope that you will enjoy the readings in this book and that you will learn more about yourself and your relationships from them.

But this book has another purpose as well: to help you become a better reader and writer. We believe that you can do this by reading, discussing, and writing about the selections in this book. In fact, because reading and writing are closely related, you cannot improve one without improving the other.

Reading, like writing, is a process of constructing meaning. When you read, you do not merely take meaning from the text by recognizing the words on the page; you *create* meaning. That is, your ideas and the information and experiences you already have *interact* with the ideas and information you discover in the text. We do not really know exactly what happens when a person reads, but we do know that discovering meaning in what you read is more likely if you view reading as a process that includes what you do *before you read, as you read,* and *after you read.*

BEFORE YOU READ

Before reading, you should be aware of the relationships that exist among reader, writer, and text. Although you may think of reading and writing as lonely tasks, neither readers nor writers operate in isolation. A writer produces a text for a reader, and a reader reads a text produced by a writer. Each must consider the other. That is, writers need to consider the purposes, knowledge, and reading skills of those who will read what they write. And readers need to consider the purpose(s) of the writer who produced what they are reading.

Becoming aware of the writer's *purpose* and intended *audience* for a given reading selection, as well as your own purposes for reading and writing about the selection, will make you not only a better reader but also a better writer. For example, in the following paragraph from *How to Study in College,* Walter Pauk writes to an audience of college freshmen to convince them of the importance of establishing a study schedule that suits their particular needs.

> It is important for each individual to choose the type of schedule that fits his or her circumstances best. Some students work better with a detailed schedule, whereas others work better with a brief list of things to do. Circumstances also influence the type of schedule a student should make. There are on-campus students, commuting students, married students, employed students, night-class students, and part-time students, and each has different scheduling requirements. Every student should *adapt* the principles of schedule building to his or her personal circumstances, rather than *adopt* some ideal model which fits hardly anybody.

Although the following paragraph by Annie Dillard is also about schedules, its purpose and intended audience are quite different from the purpose and audience of the paragraph you just read.

> The most appealing daily schedule I know is that of a certain turn-of-the-century Swedish aristocrat. He got up at four and set out on foot to hunt black grouse, wood grouse, woodcock, and snipe. At eleven he met his friends who had also been out hunting alone all morning. They converged "at one of these babbling brooks," he wrote. He outlined the rest of his schedule. "Take a quick dip, relax with a schnapps and a sandwich, stretch out, have a smoke, take a nap or just rest, and then sit around and chat until three. Then I hunt some more until sundown, bathe again, put on white tie and tails to keep up appearances, eat a huge dinner, smoke a cigar and sleep like a log until the sun comes up again to redden the eastern sky. This is living. . . . Could it be more perfect?"

In this paragraph, Dillard is addressing a general reader to provide an entertaining description of the daily work schedule of a Swedish aristocrat. As you will see when you read more of Dillard's essay on page 8, this paragraph contributes to her overall purpose of showing how a schedule for living a day or a lifetime creates order and meaning out of chaos.

As a writer, you will write more readable texts if you are aware of the reader(s) for whom you are writing. And as a reader, you will have a better understanding if you are aware of the writer who produced the text you are reading. In fact, one of the major differences between experienced and inexperienced readers and writers is not level of skill (how many words are in your vocabulary or how many words a minute you can read or how much grammar you know) but awareness of purpose and audience.

Before you read, you should also clearly understand your own purpose for reading. In performing different reading tasks, your purposes will vary widely. If you are looking for an apartment, you will "read" the want ads by scanning them very quickly, looking for certain words or phrases ("furnished," "2 bedrooms," "washer/dryer connections," and so on). You do not need to read every word or to remember everything you read in such cases. Rather, because you are searching for specific information, you will read in a highly selective fashion. If you are reading a letter from a friend, instructions for operating a new video player, an article in a magazine, a best-selling novel, or a biology text, you will read in very different ways because in each case your purpose for reading is different.

When you are assigned a selection to read in a textbook, you do not always have a real purpose for reading (other than complying with the teacher's assignment). In fact, you often have no idea what you are going to read until you have begun to read it. In this text, we give you some information about each selection so that you will know in a very general way what it is about before you begin reading.

We also ask questions or suggest activities that will help you relate what you are about to read to your own experiences. To help you recall experiences in your past that are related to what you are about to read, you may freewrite, write a journal entry, brainstorm, draw an idea map, or talk about a topic before you read about it.

In its purest form, *freewriting* is writing whatever comes into your head on any topic without worrying about form or correctness. Because this technique is a "loosening" process, it is important to keep writing even if you write only meaningless phrases such as "I can't think of anything to write." A related kind of freewriting is *focused freewriting*, which helps prepare you to read or write about a given topic by writing as rapidly and as freely as possible about it in order to recall as many related details as you can. As in any freewriting, however, you should not be concerned with formal matters of organization, sentence structure, spelling, or punctuation. Here is an example of a five-minute focused freewriting on the subject of schedules:

Lets see, schedules, schedules. What kind of schedules do I know about? I check plane schedules when I visit dad or get ready to go back to campus. I had to follow a really strict schedule when I worked at McDonald's last summer. Boy did the boss get mad when I was too late! Just looked at the spring schedule to figure out what classes I want to take next semester. I really don't think I like schedules I'm not sure if I even have a schedule. Guess I better start thinking about one.

When you freewrite, you are letting associations lead you from one idea to another—drifting back in time to retrieve information and sensations that are buried in your long-term memory. These long-buried, half-forgotten ideas and experiences can often be recalled once you begin writing. Once you begin to read, these retrieved ideas interact with the information that you encounter and enrich your understanding of what you are reading.

A *writing journal* entry differs from freewriting in that it explores a topic rather than giving immediate reactions. Thus, producing a journal entry will take more time and thought than freewriting. Like freewriting, however, a journal entry is personal and unstructured, and most instructors simply respond to journal entries with personal comments of their own rather than evaluating such entries for organization, spelling, and punctuation. Thus, journal entries allow you to examine a topic and to discover not only what you think but also how you feel. Notice how the following journal entry on schedules differs from the freewriting on the same topic:

My life seems to be run by schedules. Each morning when I get up I first have to think what day it is and then I know what schedule I have to follow. I have one schedule for Mondays, Wednesdays, and Fridays and another schedule for Tuesdays and Thursdays. On MWF days I go to class from 9:00 to 12:00 and work at the libary from 1:00 to 5:00. On TTH days I go to class from 9:30 to 12:15 but I've got a lab from 2:00 to 4:30 so I have to work at the libary from 6:00 until 10:00. Since I usully go to church on Sundays, Saturday is the only day that I have that isn't run by a schedule. Perhaps it's the freedom of that day that makes it so great to me. I can play handball, go to the movies, or just sleep in if I want. If it wasn't for this day, I couldn't face another week of "schedules."

Notice that this journal entry has more structure than the freewriting and that the ideas are more closely connected. In fact, a journal entry often looks like a paragraph or an essay, but you do not write a journal entry for a grade and should not worry about editing for such misspelled words as *library*. In a journal entry, you often express ideas that you can later use in paragraphs and essays to be written for other audiences. For the journal assignments that precede each reading selection in this book, you may wish to make entries on separate sheets of paper, or you may want to keep an ongoing journal in a notebook or a computer file.

Brainstorming works in much the same way as freewriting. Instead of writing connected ideas, however, you merely make a list when you brainstorm. For example, in brainstorming about the subject of schedules, you might produce the following list:

time	*travel schedules*
planning	*plane*
school	*train*
rigid	*work schedules*
class schedules	*McDonald's timesheet*
MWF	*weekly schedule*
last semester's	*daily schedule*
organized	*flexible*

After you have generated a fairly lengthy list, you can connect the related ideas. Or you might select one of the items, such as "work schedules" or "class schedules," that interests you and brainstorm again, this time focusing on this new narrowed topic.

Mapping or clustering ideas is a means of visualizing relationships. If you are mapping a topic before you read about it, you begin with the topic itself in the center of a blank piece of paper, and then branch out from the topic with related ideas. As illustrated in the map on the following page, you can continue this branching process as long as you can think of related ideas, examples, and details. A map is a good way of generating ideas because after you get your map started, you can select one idea from the map that interests you or that triggers other ideas and continue to develop that idea while ignoring the rest. Thus, this technique encourages you to delve deep into your memory to discover specific ideas.

Discussions can also help you recall information and experiences from your past, so occasionally we suggest that you talk with your classmates about a certain topic. For example, you could discuss the topic of schedules with a small group of your classmates, comparing your experiences and attitudes. You will find that such conversations stimulate your thinking and enable you to remember things that you have not thought about for a long time. After discussing the topic of schedules, you will be better prepared to read about it.

All these methods for retrieving information are valuable to you as both a reader and a writer because they enable you to make connections

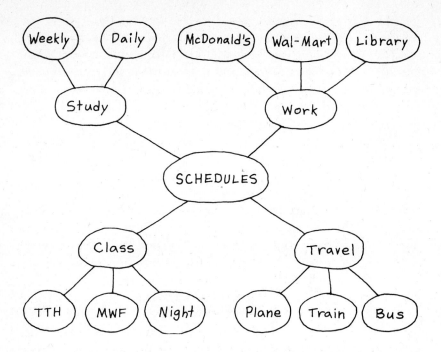

and see relationships that you would not otherwise recognize. In fact, what you do before you read an assignment can be the key to understanding what you read. The purpose of reading is not merely to "get the facts" or "remember what you read" but to construct meaning from the text—to make what you read your own by seeing relationships between what you already know and the new information that you encounter as you read. The most effective beginning of this process is recalling what you know about a subject before you even begin to read the new material.

AS YOU READ

As you read, you should be aware of the need to distinguish between *main ideas* and *supporting ideas*. Readers, like writers, need to recognize what is primary, or most important, and what is secondary, or less important. Writers develop and expand their main ideas with supporting details, and readers seek to understand a writer's purpose and meaning by identifying main ideas and the relationships among supporting details. Ideally, when writers write clearly and when readers comprehend what they read, they agree, at least to an extent, on the main idea.

The way in which experienced writers structure what they write reflects the importance of the main idea. Every sentence has a main idea, which we call the *subject and verb;* well-structured paragraphs have a main idea, which we often call a *topic sentence;* and larger pieces of discourse, such as essays or reports, have a main idea, which we call a *thesis.* Even books have at their core a main idea that controls the content so that all of the separate ideas in the book relate to it.

The three-paragraph passage below is part of Annie Dillard's essay "Schedules." Before reading this excerpt, you might like to know that the "Swedish aristocrat" mentioned in the second paragraph was the father of Isak Dinesen, the author of the novel *Out of Africa,* which was made into a successful movie starring Meryl Streep and Robert Redford; that Louis Pasteur was the French scientist who discovered the process of pasteurization to destroy bacteria in certain foods; and that Thomas Mann was a German novelist who won the Nobel Prize for literature. You should also think about how schedules are related to *you* and your life.

As you read this passage, which serves as an introduction to an essay about Dillard's own writing schedules, notice that it is a miniature essay in itself. We have underlined the main ideas, or topic sentences, of each paragraph for you. Use these main ideas to help you formulate in your mind a thesis sentence that states the main idea of the entire passage.

> I have been looking into schedules. Even when we read physics, we inquire of each least particle, "What then shall I do this morning?" How we spend our days is, of course, how we spend our lives. What we do with this hour, and that one, is what we are doing. <u>A schedule defends from chaos and whim.</u> It is a net for catching days. It is a scaffolding on which a worker can stand and labor with both hands at sections of time. <u>A schedule is a mock-up of reason and order</u>—willed, faked, and so brought into being; <u>it is a peace and a haven set into the wreck of time</u>; it is a lifeboat on which you find yourself, decades later, still living. Each day is the same, so you remember the series afterward as a blurred idyll.
>
> <u>The most appealing daily schedule I know is that of a certain turn-of-the-century Swedish aristocrat.</u> He got up at four and set out on foot to hunt black grouse, wood grouse, woodcock, and snipe. At eleven he met his friends who had also been out hunting alone all morning. They converged "at one of these babbling brooks," he wrote. He outlined the rest of his schedule. "Take a quick dip, relax with a schnapps and a sandwich, stretch out, have a smoke, take a nap or just rest, and then sit around and chat until three. Then I hunt some more until sundown, bathe again, put on white tie and tails to keep up appearances, eat a huge dinner, smoke a cigar and sleep like a log until the sun comes up again to redden the eastern sky. This is living. . . . Could it be more perfect?"

There is no shortage of good days. <u>It is good lives that are hard to come by</u>. A life of good days lived in the senses is not enough. The life of sensation is the life of greed; it requires more and more. The life of the spirit requires less and less; time is ample and its passage sweet. Who would call a day spent reading a good day? But a life spent reading—that is a good life. A day that closely resembles every other day for the past ten or twenty years does not suggest itself as a good one. But who would not call Pasteur's life a good one, or Thomas Mann's?

Because each of you has a different background and has had different experiences with reading and the subject of schedules, no two of you will understand this passage in exactly the same way. Most of you, however, probably formulated a thesis similar to this sentence: "A good schedule can bring order and meaning to a lifetime as well as to a day." The additional information in the passage provides more specific details and elaboration on how a schedule creates order and meaning. Notice that the second paragraph, which you read earlier in this chapter, focuses on a daily schedule, whereas the third paragraph focuses on longer schedules—yearly or lifelong ones.

As in the Dillard essay, you will often find the thesis statement expressed in the introductory paragraph ("A schedule defends from chaos and whim" or "A schedule is a mock-up of reason and order . . ."). And, as in the second paragraph of this essay, you will often find the topic sentence of a paragraph expressed in the first sentence ("The most appealing daily schedule I know is that of a certain turn-of-the century Swedish aristocrat"). But you cannot count on finding all main ideas expressed in exactly the same place in everything you read. Sometimes the main idea occurs as the second sentence, a middle sentence, or the last sentence. For example, the main idea of the third paragraph, "Good lives are more important than good days," is most clearly suggested by the second sentence. And the main idea may not be stated at all but merely implied. In such instances, you must infer the main idea from the information given.

As both a reader and a writer, you need to be aware of the importance of main ideas and to understand how all discourse is a series of relationships between main ideas and the more specific details that support and develop them. As a writer, you need to be able to formulate your own main ideas. As a reader you need to identify the main ideas of the authors you read.

By underlining the main ideas in the Dillard essay, we have begun to suggest that the act of reading, like the act of writing, is messy. Reading and writing are not the neat, orderly processes they seem to be when you look at words marching across a white page. The final product may appear to be neat, but reading and writing involve much more than the image of words on a page suggests. Both involve thinking about what has been and what will be; both involve going forward and going backward; and both involve anticipation and correction.

Even if a writer produces a series of words without erasing, deleting, crossing out, or otherwise revising what he or she has written, the process is messy because the writer's mind is busily shuttling back and forth—finding words, sorting through images, predicting how a reader will respond, rejecting certain choices, and selecting others. Readers go through a similarly messy process. They too must predict, accept, reject, correct, reread, and make choices. Good readers and good writers know that neither process is simple or neat.

Although the messiness of these processes is often hidden from view, discreetly tucked away inside the reader's or writer's mind, there are times when the mess needs to show—times when it needs to spill out on the clean white page. Writers often need to rewrite what they have written. They may need to create several disorganized drafts before they can produce something they want to share with a reader.

Readers also need to be willing to make a mess—to underline, highlight, circle, and draw pictures, to mark between the lines, to write on the clean white margins. If you attended public schools, you had to pass your books on to other students after you finished with them, and you may, therefore, still be reluctant to write in your textbooks. But in college you purchase the books you use. They are yours to do with as you like. If you are going to get your money's worth from them and the courses you take, you must be willing to write in your books.

In this book, you will find lots of white space and plenty of room to mark the text and write in the margins. We designed the book in this way because we want you to annotate, or mark, your text (the original Latin meaning of *annotate* is "to mark," "note," or "write"). What you write is, of course, up to you. You may want to draw illustrations, to highlight with colored markers, to circle words you don't know, to number information, to underline or put asterisks beside ideas you consider important, or to write notes to yourself about what you are reading. You may want to write notes connecting your reading with your previous experiences or to write questions to ask your instructor. You may certainly read some things that do not require a written response, such as a magazine that you pick up in the doctor's office. But if you want to improve as a reader, it is essential that you communicate in writing with yourself as you read. As a college student, you will often need to write in order to construct meaning from what you read.

The more difficult the material you are reading, the more important it is that you respond to it in writing. Ideally, you should read the material through once and then annotate it on a second reading when you have a better sense of which ideas and information are significant. But even on a first reading, you will understand what you are reading better if you annotate as you read. We have annotated the following paragraphs, condensed from *The Secrets Our Body Clocks Reveal,* by Susan Perry and Jim Dawson, to illustrate how a reader might respond to a given passage.

> *Main idea* — All living organisms, from mollusks to men and women, exhibit biological rhythms. Some are short and can be measured in minutes or hours. Others last days or months. The peaking of ① body temperature, which occurs in most people every evening, is a daily rhythm. The ② menstrual cycle is a monthly rhythm. The increase in ③ sexual drive in the autumn—not in the spring, as poets would have us believe—is a seasonal, or yearly, rhythm.
>
> *Types of biological rhythms*
>
> *State of change* — The idea that our bodies are in constant flux is fairly new—and goes against traditional medical training. In the past, many doctors were taught to believe the body has a relatively *Stable* — stable, or homeostatic internal environment. Any fluctuations were considered random and not meaningful enough to be studied.

Annotations are the tracks a reader leaves in the text. They reveal something about what was going on in the reader's mind. The annotations we have made reflect our reading of these paragraphs—the ideas that were important to us, the statements that related to our knowledge from experience and reading, the words we needed to define, the information we wanted to remember. Different readers discover different meanings as they read, and even the same reader may discover different meanings upon rereading the same material. But annotating what you read enables you to understand and remember what is most useful and important to you at the time. Your annotations provide you with a record of your reading so that you can easily review the material at a later time. Even more important, annotations force you to think about what you are reading as you read.

AFTER YOU READ

When you write, you often go back and rewrite what you have written—editing and revising your ideas so that they are more accessible to your reader. When you read, you also need to "revise"—to reconstruct and add to the meaning that you created as you read. After each reading selection, we provide questions and suggestions for informal writing activities that help you in this process of revision.

Writing about what you have read is one of the most effective ways of making what you have read your own. Whether you are summarizing the selection, organizing information in outline or map form, reacting in journal entries to ideas that you have encountered, citing specific information, or writing a paragraph or an essay on a related topic, you will increase your understanding of what you have read by writing about it. For example, after reading the selection on biological rhythms by Susan Perry and Jim Dawson, you could map the relationships among the main ideas and the major supporting ideas as shown below:

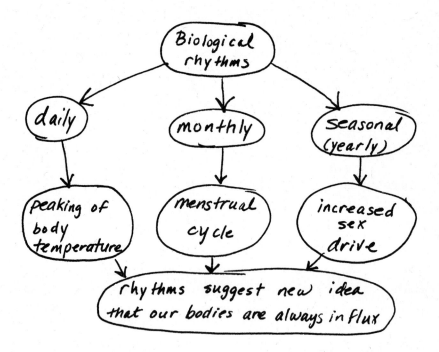

You could also respond to this reading by summarizing it, writing a journal entry about the process you used in reading it, or even writing a journal entry about your own biological rhythms.

Discussing what you have read with others also helps you to discover meaning in what you read. Therefore, we frequently suggest that you talk with your classmates about what you have read. After reading Dillard's

essay, for example, you could compare your own daily and weekly schedules with those of a group of your classmates. Talking, like writing, helps
you to see new connections, arrive at different interpretations, and discover
new meanings.

Rereading is another effective way of ensuring that your interaction
with a text is productive. Each time you read something, you gain a new
understanding of it; rereading what you have already read enables you to
build on your prior knowledge of the text as well as your own increased
knowledge of the subject. So do not hesitate to reread. Whether it is a single
word, a line or sentence, a paragraph, or even an entire selection, rereading
not only clarifies and reinforces the meaning you discover in a text but also
helps you discover new meanings.

You not only use your own experiences to discover meaning when you
read and write, but you also make sense of your experiences—and yourself—through reading and writing. As you read the selections and write the
assignments in this book, we hope you will increase your understanding of
yourself and how you interact with other people and other phenomena in
your world. In this process of self-discovery, we believe, you will also
become a more experienced reader and writer.

The Self

It is not always easy to know yourself—to know who you are and how you came to be that person. And just when you think you know yourself, you change. You get older, form different relationships, develop new interests, go to college, change jobs, or move to a new community; and the process of knowing yourself begins all over again. So your entire life is spent trying to figure out who you are and how to be happy being that person.

This book is designed to help you in this ongoing process of learning more about yourself. It does this by encouraging you to explore the important relationships in your life: with yourself; with your family; with friends and mates; with work; with the society and environment in which you exist; with the technology that increasingly dominates modern life; and with the heroes and heroines that influence who you are and how you perceive yourself. Because these relationships help define you, you need to understand them in order to understand yourself.

This first unit consists of readings that explore how and why you form different images of yourself—how factors such as your name, age, gender, family background, and physical appearance influence the way you perceive yourself. In preparing to read the selections in this first unit, think for a few moments about your image of yourself. How would you describe yourself to someone who does not know you? Compare yourself to the child you once were, analyze why you have become the person you are today, or predict the kind of person you will be in the future.

As you read the selections in this unit, keep in mind the similarities between reading and writing discussed in the Introduction. Remember that the process you go through in reading these selections is much like the process the writers went through in writing them. Both you and the writers are discovering and constructing meaning. When you read, you are adding to and modifying what you already know. You are also evaluating another person's ideas and information and opinions. Therefore, you need to be aware of the writer's purposes in writing, his or her knowledge about the subject, and the possible biases that may have influenced what was written.

Also remember that reading, like writing, is a messy process. Reading a selection through once without marking the text in any way does not usually result in your gaining much from it. So underline the sentences that are important to your understanding, circle the words you don't know, and write notes to yourself (and to the author) in the margins. Don't just read these selections; *interact* with the ideas and information in them. You will not understand yourself any better or improve yourself as a reader unless you actively engage in a dialogue with the writers and the ideas they present in their texts.

Finally, remember that you need to write in response to what you read if you really want to make the information and ideas your own. In addition to annotating the text itself, you may want to write a brief summary of some of the selections; others you may want to outline or map or merely respond to—perhaps in journal entries—by writing your reaction to what you have read. We have suggested writing activities for each selection, but you need to discover for yourself the forms of writing that best help you to understand what you read.

My Name

SANDRA CISNEROS

Sandra Cisneros, the only daughter in a large Mexican-American family, writes about conflicts related to her upbringing. She addresses such issues as poverty, cultural suppression, self-identity, and gender roles in her poetry and fiction. This reading selection is taken from The House on Mango Street, *a collection of related narrative sketches about a Mexican-American family that is struggling to adjust to life in an English-speaking culture. Loosely based on the life of the author, this selection tells of a young girl's reaction to her name, Esperanza, which means "hope."*

BEFORE YOU READ

THINK about your given name, the one you "go by." Is it a family name? Or were you named after a famous person? Do you know why your parents chose to name you as they did? Do you have a nickname? If so, what is its origin?

EXAMINE the words *esperanza* and *hope,* both of which have been used as female names. Although both words mean the same thing, they look and sound very different. The Spanish word *esperanza* is much longer and more musical; the English word *hope* is not only shorter, but almost curt sounding.

WRITE in your journal the name you would have chosen for yourself and tell why you would have chosen this name.

AS YOU READ

Think about the importance we attach to names and why.

In English my name means hope. In Spanish it means too many letters. It 1
means sadness, it means waiting. It is like the number nine. A muddy
color. It is the Mexican records my father plays on Sunday mornings when
he is shaving, songs like sobbing.

It was my great-grandmother's name and now it is mine. She was a 2
horse woman too, born like me in the Chinese year of the horse—which
is supposed to be bad luck if you're born female—but I think this is a
Chinese lie because the Chinese, like the Mexicans, don't like their women
strong.

My great-grandmother. I would've liked to have known her, a wild 3
horse of a woman, so wild she wouldn't marry until my great-grandfather
threw a sack over her head and carried her off. Just like that, as if she were
a fancy chandelier. That's the way he did it.

And the story goes she never forgave him. She looked out the window 4
all her life, the way so many women sit their sadness on an elbow. I wonder
if she made the best with what she got or was she sorry because she couldn't
be all the things she wanted to be. Esperanza. I have inherited her name,
but I don't want to inherit her place by the window.

At school they say my name funny as if the syllables were made out of 5
tin and hurt the roof of your mouth. But in Spanish my name is made out
of a softer something like silver, not quite as thick as sister's name
Magdalena which is uglier than mine. Magdalena who at least can come
home and become Nenny. But I am always Esperanza.

I would like to baptize myself under a new name, a name more like 6
the real me, the one nobody sees. Esperanza as Lisandra or Maritza or Zeze
the X. Yes. Something like Zeze the X will do.

AFTER YOU READ

THINK about the young girl's reaction to her name. Why did she want
another name? Does a person's name make a difference in the way you
perceive that person? Does your own name affect how you feel about
yourself? Do the names of others affect how you react to them? Why does
exchanging names seem important when you first meet someone? Could
you feel that you really knew someone whose name you did not know?

EXAMINE the name *Zeze the X* the girl chose for herself. Why do you think
she liked this name?

WRITE about the custom in this country of married females adopting the surnames of their husbands. Do you approve of this custom? What problems are associated with it?

The Misery of Silence

MAXINE HONG KINGSTON

Maxine Hong Kingston grew up in Stockton, California, in a Chinese immigrant community where her parents operated a laundry. Later she graduated from the University of California at Berkeley. After living in Hawaii for seventeen years, she returned to California and now teaches writing at her alma mater. Her most recent books are Tripmaster Monkey: His Fake Book *and* China Men, *both published in 1989. This selection is from her autobiography,* The Woman Warrior: Memoirs of a Girlhood Among Ghosts *(1976), in which she tells of the problems she encountered growing up as part of two very different cultures.*

BEFORE YOU READ

THINK about the effect that not speaking the language of the society in which you live would have on your image of yourself.

EXAMINE the title "The Misery of Silence." What do you associate with silence? Why do you think Kingston used the word *misery* to describe silence? When is silence a misery?

WRITE a journal entry in which you describe how you felt when you first started school or how you felt on your first day of college.

AS YOU READ

Try to imagine how it would feel if you did not speak the language of your instructor and classmates.

When I went to kindergarten and had to speak English for the first 1
time, I became silent. A dumbness—a shame—still cracks my voice
in two, even when I want to say "hello" casually, or ask an easy question
in front of the check-out counter, or ask directions of a bus driver. I stand
frozen, or I hold up the line with the complete, grammatical sentence that
comes squeaking out at impossible length. "What did you say?" says the
cab driver, or "Speak up," so I have to perform again, only weaker the
second time. A telephone call makes my throat bleed and takes up that
day's courage. It spoils my day with self-disgust when I hear my broken
voice come skittering out into the open. It makes people wince to hear it.
I'm getting better, though. Recently I asked the postman for special-issue
stamps; I've waited since childhood for postmen to give me some of their
own accord. I am making progress, a little every day.

My silence was thickest—total—during the three years that I covered 2
my school paintings with black paint. I painted layers of black over houses
and flowers and suns, and when I drew on the blackboard, I put a layer of
chalk on top. I was making a stage curtain, and it was the moment before
the curtain parted or rose. The teachers called my parents to school, and I
saw they had been saving my pictures, curling and cracking, all alike and
black. The teachers pointed to the pictures and looked serious, talked
seriously too, but my parents did not understand English. ("The parents
and teachers of criminals were executed," said my father.) My parents took
the pictures home. I spread them out (so black and full of possibilities) and
pretended the curtains were swinging open, flying up, one after another,
sunlight underneath, mighty operas.

During the first silent year I spoke to no one at school, did not ask 3
before going to the lavatory, and flunked kindergarten. My sister also said
nothing for three years, silent in the playground and silent at lunch. There
were other quiet Chinese girls not of our family, but most of them got over
it sooner than we did. I enjoyed the silence. At first it did not occur to me
I was supposed to talk or to pass kindergarten. I talked at home and to one
or two of the Chinese kids in class. I made motions and even made some
jokes. I drank out of a toy saucer when the water spilled out of the cup,
and everybody laughed, pointing at me, so I did it some more. I didn't
know that Americans don't drink out of saucers.

I liked the Negro students (Black Ghosts) best because they laughed 4
the loudest and talked to me as if I were a daring talker too. One of the
Negro girls had her mother coil braids over her ears Shanghai-style like
mine; we were Shanghai twins except that she was covered with black like
my paintings. Two Negro kids enrolled in Chinese school, and the teachers

gave them Chinese names. Some Negro kids walked me to school and home, protecting me from the Japanese kids, who hit me and chased me and stuck gum in my ears. The Japanese kids were noisy and tough. They appeared one day in kindergarten, released from concentration camp, which was a tic-tac-toe mark, like barbed wire, on the map.

It was when I found out I had to talk that school became a misery, that the silence became a misery. I did not speak and felt bad each time that I did not speak. I read aloud in first grade, though, and heard the barest whisper with little squeaks come out of my throat. "Louder," said the teacher, who scared the voice away again. The other Chinese girls did not talk either, so I knew the silence had to do with being a Chinese girl.

Reading out loud was easier than speaking because we did not have to make up what to say, but I stopped often, and the teacher would think I'd gone quiet again. I could not understand "I." The Chinese "I" has seven strokes, intricacies. How could the American "I," assuredly wearing a hat like the Chinese, have only three strokes, the middle so straight? Was it out of politeness that this writer left off strokes the way a Chinese has to write her own name small and crooked? No, it was not politeness; "I" is a capital and "you" is lowercase. I stared at that middle line and waited so long for its black center to resolve into tight strokes and dots that I forgot to pronounce it. The other troublesome word was "here," no strong consonant to hang on to, and so flat, when "here" is two mountainous ideographs. The teacher, who had already told me every day how to read "I" and "here," put me in the low corner under the stairs again, where the noisy boys usually sat.

When my second grade class did a play, the whole class went to the auditorium except the Chinese girls. The teacher, lovely and Hawaiian, should have understood about us, but instead left us behind in the classroom. Our voices were too soft or nonexistent, and our parents never signed the permission slips anyway. They never signed anything unnecessary. We opened the door a crack and peeked out, but closed it again quickly. One of us (not me) won every spelling bee, though.

I remember telling the Hawaiian teacher, "We Chinese can't sing 'land where our fathers died.'" She argued with me about politics, while I meant because of curses. But how can I have that memory when I couldn't talk? My mother says that we, like the ghosts, have no memories.

After American school, we picked up our cigar boxes, in which we had arranged books, brushes, and an inkbox neatly, and went to Chinese school, from 5:00 to 7:30 P.M. There we chanted together, voices rising and falling, loud and soft, some boys shouting, everybody reading together, reciting together and not alone with one voice. When we had a memorization test,

the teacher let each of us come to his desk and say the lesson to him
privately, while the rest of the class practiced copying or tracing. Most of
the teachers were men. The boys who were so well behaved in the American school played tricks on them and talked back to them. The girls were
not mute. They screamed and yelled during recess, when there were no
rules; they had fistfights. Nobody was afraid of children hurting themselves
or of children hurting school property. The glass doors to the red and green
balconies with the gold joy symbols were left wide open so that we could
run out and climb the fire escapes. We played capture-the-flag in the
auditorium, where Sun Yat-sen and Chiang Kai-shek's pictures hung at the
back of the stage, the Chinese flag on their left and the American flag on
their right. We climbed the teak ceremonial chairs and made flying leaps
off the stage. One flag headquarters was behind the glass door and the
other on stage right. Our feet drummed on the hollow stage. During recess
the teachers locked themselves up in their office with the shelves of books,
copybooks, inks from China. They drank tea and warmed their hands at a
stove. There was no play supervision. At recess we had the school to
ourselves, and also we could roam as far as we could go—downtown,
Chinatown stores, home—as long as we returned before the bell rang.

At exactly 7:30 the teacher again picked up the brass bell that sat on   10
his desk and swung it over our heads, while we charged down the stairs,
our cheering magnified in the stairwell. Nobody had to line up.

Not all of the children who were silent at American school found voice   11
at Chinese school. One new teacher said each of us had to get up and recite
in front of the class, who was to listen. My sister and I had memorized the
lesson perfectly. We said it to each other at home, one chanting, one
listening. The teacher called on my sister to recite first. It was the first time
a teacher had called on the second-born to go first. My sister was scared.
She glanced at me and looked away; I looked down at my desk. I hoped
that she could do it because if she could, then I would have to. She opened
her mouth and a voice came out that wasn't a whisper, but it wasn't a proper
voice either. I hoped that she would not cry, fear breaking up her voice like
twigs underfoot. She sounded as if she were trying to sing though weeping
and strangling. She did not pause or stop to end the embarrassment. She
kept going until she said the last word, and then she sat down. When it was
my turn, the same voice came out, a crippled animal running on broken
legs. You could hear splinters in my voice, bones rubbing jagged against
one another. I was loud, though. I was glad I didn't whisper.

How strange that the emigrant villagers are shouters, hollering face to   12
face. My father asks, "Why is it I can hear Chinese from blocks away? Is it
that I understand the language? Or is it they talk loud?" They turn the radio

up full blast to hear the operas, which do not seem to hurt their ears. And they yell over the singers that wail over the drums, everybody talking at once, big arm gestures, spit flying. You can see the disgust on American faces looking at women like that. It isn't just the loudness. It is the way Chinese sounds, ching-chong ugly, to American ears, not beautiful like Japanese sayonara words with the consonants and vowels as regular as Italian. We make guttural peasant noise and have Ton Duc Thang names you can't remember. And the Chinese can't hear Americans at all; the language is too soft and western music unhearable. I've watched a Chinese audience laugh, visit, talk-story, and holler during a piano recital, as if the musician could not hear them. A Chinese-American, somebody's son, was playing Chopin, which has no punctuation, no cymbals, no gongs. Chinese piano music is five black keys. Normal Chinese women's voices are strong and bossy. We American-Chinese girls had to whisper to make ourselves American-feminine. Apparently we whispered even more softly than the Americans. Once a year the teachers referred my sister and me to speech therapy, but our voices would straighten out, unpredictably normal, for the therapists. Some of us gave up, shook our heads, and said nothing, not one word. Some of us could not even shake our heads. At times shaking my head no is more self-assertion than I can manage. Most of us eventually found some voice, however faltering. We invented an American-feminine speaking personality.

AFTER YOU READ

THINK about the similarities and differences in the two schools that Kingston describes. Why did her parents send her to both schools? What did she gain from each? How did this experience affect her sense of identity?

EXAMINE Kingston's statement, "We American-Chinese girls had to whisper to make ourselves American-feminine." How did her struggle to define herself as a female contribute to the silence that characterized her childhood? How does American-feminine differ from Chinese-feminine or Hispanic-feminine? Do sex roles differ from one culture to another?

WRITE about a time when you felt isolated or shut off from the people around you. Or WRITE a paragraph in which you compare and contrast the roles of females (or males) in two different cultures.

Lives on the Boundary

MIKE ROSE

Mike Rose teaches writing at the University of California at Los Angeles and has published scholarly articles about how to teach writing and a book about remedial education entitled Lives on the Boundary. *In this book Rose writes about his own life as a member of a struggling family of poor Italian immigrants living in Los Angeles in the 1950s and 1960s. In this selection from that book, he tells about his early childhood and how different it was from the academic world he later entered.*

BEFORE YOU READ

THINK about how your own environment as you were growing up shaped your life. How was that environment similar to or different from the world in which you now live?

EXAMINE the specific images from the childhood memories Rose identifies: a gnarled lemon tree, thin rugs, a dirt alley, concrete in the sun. What do these images tell you about his life in Los Angeles when he was a child?

WRITE a journal entry in which you describe several specific images you remember vividly from your own childhood environment.

AS YOU READ

Notice the specific details Rose uses in describing his house and neighborhood.

Between 1880 and 1920, well over four million Southern Italian peas- 1
ants immigrated to America. Their poverty was extreme and hopeless—twelve hours of farm labor would get you one lira, about twenty
cents—so increasing numbers of desperate people booked passage for the
United States, the country where, the steamship companies claimed, prosperity was a way of life. My father left Naples before the turn of the century;
my mother came with her mother from Calabria in 1921. They met in
Altoona, Pennsylvania at the lunch counter of Tom and Joe's, a steamy diner
with twangy-voiced waitresses and graveyard stew.

For my mother, life in America was not what the promoters had told 2
her father it would be. She grew up very poor. She slept with her parents
and brothers and sisters in one room. She had to quit school in the seventh
grade to care for her sickly younger brothers. When her father lost his leg
in a railroad accident, she began working in a garment factory where
women sat crowded at their stations, solitary as penitents in a cloister. She
stayed there until her marriage. My father had found a freer route. He was
closemouthed about his past, but I know that he had been a salesman, a
tailor, and a gambler; he knew people in the mob and had, my uncles
whisper, done time in Chicago. He went through a year or two of Italian
elementary school and could write a few words—those necessary to
scribble measurements for a suit—and over the years developed a quiet
urbanity, a persistence, and a slowly debilitating arteriosclerosis.

When my father proposed to my mother, he decided to open a 3
spaghetti house, a venture that lasted through the war and my early years.
The restaurant collapsed in bankruptcy in 1951 when Altoona's major
industry, the Pennsylvania Railroad, had to shut down its shops. My
parents managed to salvage seven hundred dollars and, on the advice of
the family doctor, headed to California, where the winters would be mild
and where I, their seven-year-old son, would have the possibility of a
brighter future.

At first we lived in a seedy hotel on Spring Street in downtown Los 4
Angeles, but my mother soon found an ad in the *Times* for cheap property
on the south side of town. My parents contacted a woman named Mrs.
Jolly, used my mother's engagement ring as a down payment, and moved
to 9116 South Vermont Avenue, a house about one and one-half miles
northwest of Watts. The neighborhood was poor, and it was in transition.
Some old white folks had lived there for decades and were retired. Younger
black families were moving up from Watts and settling by working-class
white families newly arrived from the South and the Midwest. Immigrant
Mexican families were coming in from Baja. Any such demographic mix is

potentially volatile, and as the fifties wore on, the neighborhood would be marked by outbursts of violence.

I have many particular memories of this time, but in general these early 5 years seem a peculiar mix of physical warmth and barrenness: a gnarled lemon tree, thin rugs, a dirt alley, concrete in the sun. My uncles visited a few times, and we went to the beach or to orange groves. The return home, however, left the waves and spray, the thick leaves and split pulp far in the distance. I was aware of my parents watching their money and got the sense from their conversations that things could quickly take a turn for the worse. I started taping pennies to the bottom of a shelf in the kitchen.

My father's health was bad, and he had few readily marketable skills. 6 Poker and pinochle brought in a little money, and he tried out an idea that had worked in Altoona during the war: He started a "suit club." The few customers he could scare up would pay two dollars a week on a tailor-made suit. He would take the measurements and send them to a shop back East and hope for the best. My mother took a job at a café in downtown Los Angeles, a split shift 9:00 to 12:00 and 5:00 to 9:00, but her tips were totaling sixty cents a day, so she quit for a night shift at Coffee Dan's. This got her to the bus stop at one in the morning, waiting on the same street where drunks were urinating and hookers were catching the last of the bar crowd. She made friends with a Filipino cook who would scare off the advances of old men aflame with the closeness of taxi dancers. In a couple of years, Coffee Dan's would award her a day job at the counter. Once every few weeks my father and I would take a bus downtown and visit with her, sitting at stools by the window, watching the animated but silent mix of faces beyond the glass.

My father had moved to California with faint hopes about health and 7 a belief in his child's future, drawn by that far edge of America where the sun descends into green water. What he found was a city that was warm, verdant, vast, and indifferent as a starlet in a sports car. Altoona receded quickly, and my parents must have felt isolated and deceived. They had fallen into the abyss of paradise—two more poor settlers trying to make a go of it in the City of the Angels.

Let me tell you about our house. If you entered the front door and turned 8 right you'd see a small living room with a couch along the east wall and one along the west wall—one couch was purple, the other tan, both bought used and both well worn. A television set was placed at the end of the purple couch, right at arm level. An old Philco radio sat next to the TV, its speaker covered with gold lamé. There was a small coffee table in the center of the room on which sat a murky fish-bowl occupied by two listless guppies. If, on entering, you turned left you would see a green Formica dinner table with four chairs, a cedar chest given as a wedding present to my mother by her mother, a painted statue of the Blessed Virgin Mary, and a black trunk. It also had a plastic chaise longue between the door and the table. I would lie on this and watch television.

A short hallway leading to the bathroom opened on one side to the 9 kitchen and, on the other, to the bedroom. The bedroom had two beds, one for me and one for my parents, a bureau with a mirror, and a chest of drawers on which we piled old shirt boxes and stacks of folded clothes. The kitchen held a refrigerator and a stove, small older models that we got when our earlier (and newer) models were repossessed by two silent men. There was one white wooden chair in the corner beneath wall cabinets. You could walk in and through a tiny pantry to the backyard and to four one-room rentals. My father got most of our furniture from a secondhand store on the next block; he would tend the store two or three hours a day as payment on our account.

As I remember it, the house was pretty dark. My mother kept the blinds 10 in the bedroom drawn—there were no curtains there—and the venetian blinds in the living room were, often as not, left closed. The walls were bare except for a faded picture of Jesus and a calendar from the *Altoona Mirror.* Some paper carnations bent out of a white vase on the television. There was a window on the north side of the kitchen that had no blinds or curtains, so the sink got good light. My father would methodically roll up his sleeves and show me how to prepare a sweet potato or avocado seed so it would sprout. We kept a row of them on the sill above the sink, their shoots and vines rising and curling in the morning sun.

The house was on a piece of land that rose about four feet up from 11 heavily trafficked Vermont Avenue. The yard sloped down to the street, and three steps and a short walkway led up the middle of the grass to our front door. There was a similar house immediately to the south of us. Next to it was Carmen's Barber Shop. Carmen was a short, quiet Italian who, rumor had it, had committed his first wife to the crazy house to get her money. In the afternoons, Carmen could be found in the lot behind his shop playing solitary catch, flinging a tennis ball high into the air and running under it. One day the police arrested Carmen on charges of child molesting. He was released but became furtive and suspicious. I never saw him in the lot again. Next to Carmen's was a junk store where, one summer, I made a little money polishing brass and rewiring old lamps. Then came a dilapidated real estate office, a Mexican restaurant, an empty lot, and an appliance store owned by the father of Keith Grateful, the streetwise, chubby boy who would become my best friend.

Right to the north of us was a record shop, a barber shop presided over   12
by old Mr. Graff, Walt's Malts, a shoe repair shop with a big Cat's Paw decal in the window, a third barber shop, and a brake shop. It's as I write this that I realize for the first time that three gray men could have had a go at your hair before you left our street.

Behind our house was an unpaved alley that passed, just to the north,   13
a power plant the length of a city block. Massive coils atop the building hissed and cracked through the day, but the doors never opened. I used to think it was abandoned—feeding itself on its own wild arcs—until one sweltering afternoon a man was electrocuted on the roof. The air was thick and still as two firemen—the only men present—brought down a charred and limp body without saying a word.

The north and south traffic on Vermont was separated by tracks for   14
the old yellow trolley cars, long since defunct. Across the street was a huge garage, a tiny hot dog stand run by a myopic and reclusive man named Freddie, and my dreamland, the Vermont Bowl. Distant and distorted behind thick lenses, Freddie's eyes never met yours; he would look down when he took your order and give you your change with a mumble. Freddie slept on a cot in the back of his grill and died there one night, leaving tens of thousands of dollars stuffed in the mattress.

My father would buy me a chili dog at Freddie's, and then we would   15
walk over to the bowling alley where Dad would sit at the lunch counter and drink coffee while I had a great time with pinball machines, electric shooting galleries, and an ill-kept dispenser of cheese corn. There was a small, dark bar abutting the lanes, and it called to me. I would devise reasons to walk through it: "'Scuse me, is the bathroom in here?" or "Anyone see my dad?" though I can never remember my father having a drink. It was dark and people were drinking and I figured all sorts of mysterious things were being whispered. Next to the Vermont Bowl was a large vacant lot overgrown with foxtails and dotted with car parts, bottles, and rotting cardboard. One day Keith heard that the police had found a human head in the brush. After that we explored the lot periodically, coming home with stickers all the way up to our waists. But we didn't find a thing. Not even a kneecap.

When I wasn't with Keith or in school, I would spend most of my day   16
with my father or with the men who were renting the one-room apartments behind our house. Dad and I whiled away the hours in the bowling alley, watching TV, or planting a vegetable garden that never seemed to take.

When he was still mobile, he would walk the four blocks down to St. Regina's Grammar School to take me home to my favorite lunch of boiled wieners and chocolate milk. There I'd sit, dunking my hot dog in a jar of mayonnaise and drinking my milk while Sheriff John tuned up the calliope music on his "Lunch Brigade." Though he never complained to me, I could sense that my father's health was failing, and I began devising child's ways to make him better. We had a box of rolled cotton in the bathroom, and I would go in and peel off a long strip and tape it around my jaw. Then I'd rummage through the closet, find a sweater of my father's, put on one of his hats—and sneak around to the back door. I'd knock loudly and wait. It would take him a while to get there. Finally, he'd open the door, look down, and quietly say, "Yes, Michael?" I was disappointed. Every time. Somehow I thought I could fool him. And, I guess, if he had been fooled, I would have succeeded in redefining things: I would have been the old one, he much younger, more agile, with strength in his legs.

The men who lived in the back were either retired or didn't work that much, so one of them was usually around. They proved to be, over the years, an unusual set of companions for a young boy. Ed Gionotti was the youngest of the lot, a handsome man whose wife had run off and who spoke softly and never smiled. Bud Hall and Lee McGuire were two out-of-work plumbers who lived in adjacent units and who weekly drank themselves silly, proclaiming in front of God and everyone their undying friendship or their unequivocal hatred. Old Cheech was a lame Italian who used to hobble along grabbing his testicles and rolling his eyes while he talked about the women he claimed to have on a string. There was Lester, the toothless cabbie, who several times made overtures to me and who, when he moved, left behind a drawer full of syringes and burnt spoons. Mr. Smith was a rambunctious retiree who lost his nose to an untended skin cancer. And there was Mr. Berryman, a sweet and gentle man who eventually left for a retirement hotel only to be burned alive in an electrical fire. [17]

Except for Keith, there were no children on my block and only one or two on the immediate side streets. Most of the people I saw day to day were over fifty. People in their twenties and thirties working in the shoe shop or the garages didn't say a lot; their work and much of what they were working for drained their spirits. There were gang members who sauntered up from Hoover Avenue, three blocks to the east, and occasionally I would get shoved around, but they had little interest in me either as member or victim. I was a skinny, bespectacled kid and had neither the coloring nor the style of dress or carriage that marked me as a rival. On [18] the whole, the days were quiet, lazy, lonely. The heat shimmering over the asphalt had no snap to it; time drifted by. I would lie on the couch at night and listen to the music from the record store or from Walt's Malts. It was new and quick paced, exciting, a little dangerous (the church had condemned Buddy Knox's "Party Doll"), and I heard in it a deep rhythmic need to be made whole with love, or marked as special, or released in some rebellious way. Even the songs about lost love—and there were plenty of them—lifted me right out of my socks with their melodious longing:

> Came the dawn,
> and my heart and her love and the night
> were gone.
> But I know I'll never forget
> her kiss in the moonlight Oooo . . .
> such a kiss Oooo Oooo such a night . . .

In the midst of the heat and slow time the music brought the promise of its origins, a promise of deliverance, a promise that, if only for a moment, life could be stirring and dreamy.

But the anger and frustration of South Vermont could prove too strong 19 for music's illusion; then it was violence that provided deliverance of a different order. One night I watched as a guy sprinted from Walt's to toss something on our lawn. The police were right behind, and a cop tackled him, smashing his face into the sidewalk. I ducked out to find the packet: a dozen glassine bags of heroin. Another night, one August midnight, an argument outside the record store ended with a man being shot to death. And the occasional gang forays brought with them some fated kid who would fumble his moves and catch a knife.

It's popular these days to claim you grew up on the streets. Men tell 20 violent tales and romanticize the lessons violence brings. But, though it was occasionally violent, it wasn't the violence in South L.A. that marked me, for sometimes you can shake that ugliness off. What finally affected me was subtler, but more pervasive: I cannot recall a young person who was crazy in love or lost in work or one old person who was passionate about a cause or an idea. I'm not talking about an absence of energy—the street toughs and, for that fact, old Cheech had energy. And I'm not talking about an absence of decency, for my father was a thoughtful man. The people I grew up with were retired from jobs that rub away the heart or were working hard at jobs to keep their lives from caving in or were anchorless and in between jobs and spouses or were diving headlong into a barren tomorrow: junkies, alcoholics, and mean kids walking along Vermont looking to throw a punch. I developed a picture of human existence that rendered it short and brutish or sad and aimless or long and quiet with rewards like afternoon naps, the evening newspaper, walks around the block, occasional letters from children in other states. When, years later, I was introduced to humanistic psychologists like Abraham Maslow and Carl Rogers, with their visions of self-actualization, or even Freud with his sober dictum about love and work, it all sounded like a glorious fairy tale, a magical account of a world full of possibility, full of hope and empowerment. Sindbad and Cinderella couldn't have been more fanciful.

❀   ❀   ❀

AFTER YOU READ

THINK about the life that Rose had as a child, which he describes as "short and brutish or sad and aimless or long and quiet." Rose later escaped this life by excelling in school. What would his adult life have probably been like if he had not had the opportunity to go to college?

EXAMINE the contrast that Rose suggests between the life he knew in Los Angeles and the glamorous image of Los Angeles that most people have. How has that glamorous image been tarnished in recent years? Is there a connection between the violence and poverty that Rose experienced in his neighborhood and what has happened in Los Angeles recently? Has the poverty and violence become worse in the 1980s and 1990s than it was in the 1950s and 1960s?

WRITE a description of the place where you grew up and tell how that environment shaped who you are today.

On Being 17, Bright, and Unable to Read

DAVID RAYMOND

When David Raymond wrote this essay, he was a high school student in Connecticut. The essay, which tells of Raymond's frustrations because he could not read, was published in the New York Times. Unlike some of the other authors included in this unit, Raymond did not excel in school. In this essay he describes what it is like to have a learning disability.

BEFORE YOU READ

THINK about how you feel when you don't know the correct answer to a question a teacher asks you or cannot do what a teacher expects you to do.

EXAMINE the word *dyslexia*. The word has two parts: *dys* is a prefix meaning abnormal or impaired, and *lexia* comes from a Greek word (*lexis*) meaning speech. However, the word *dyslexia* does not mean speech impairment but rather an impairment of the ability to read.

WRITE in your journal a definition of the word *dumb*. Can you think of more than one definition?

AS YOU READ

Notice the reaction of Raymond's parents and teachers to his learning disability.

One day a substitute teacher picked me to read aloud from the textbook. 1
When I told her "No, thank you," she came unhinged. She thought I
was acting smart, and told me so. I kept calm, and that got her madder and
madder. We must have spent 10 minutes trying to solve the problem, and
finally she got so red in the face I thought she'd blow up. She told me she'd
see me after class.

Maybe someone like me was a new thing for that teacher. But she 2
wasn't new to me. I've been through scenes like that all my life. You see,
even though I'm 17 and a junior in high school, I can't read because I have
dyslexia. I'm told I read "at a fourth-grade level," but from where I sit,
that's not reading. You can't know what that means unless you've been
there. It's not easy to tell how it feels when you can't read your homework
assignments or the newspaper or a menu in a restaurant or even notes from
your own friends.

My family began to suspect I was having problems almost from the 3
first day I started school. My father says my early years in school were the
worst years of his life. They weren't so good for me, either. As I look back
on it now, I can't find the words to express how bad it really was. I wanted
to die. I'd come home from school screaming, "I'm dumb. I'm dumb—I
wish I were dead!"

I guess I couldn't read anything at all then—not even my own name— 4
and they tell me I didn't talk as good as other kids. But what I remember
about those days is that I couldn't throw a ball where it was supposed to
go, I couldn't learn to swim, and I wouldn't learn to ride a bike, because
no matter what anyone told me, I knew I'd fail.

Sometimes my teachers would try to be encouraging. When I couldn't 5
read the words on the board they'd say, "Come on, David, you know that
word." Only I didn't. And it was embarrassing. I just felt dumb. And dumb
was how the kids treated me. They'd make fun of me every chance they
got, asking me to spell "cat" or something like that. Even if I knew how to
spell it, I wouldn't; they'd only give me another word. Anyway, it was
awful, because more than anything I wanted friends. On my birthday when
I blew out the candles I didn't wish I could learn to read; what I wished
for was that the kids would like me.

With the bad reports coming from school, and with me moaning about 6
wanting to die and how everybody hated me, my parents began looking
for help. That's when the testing started. The school tested me, the
child-guidance center tested me, private psychiatrists tested me. Everybody
knew something was wrong—especially me.

It didn't help much when they stuck a fancy name onto it. I couldn't 7
pronounce it then—I was only in second grade—and I was ashamed to talk
about it. Now it rolls off my tongue, because I've been living with it for a
lot of years—dyslexia.

All through elementary school it wasn't easy. I was always having to 8
do things that were "different," things the other kids didn't have to do. I
had to go to a child psychiatrist, for instance.

One summer my family forced me to go to a camp for children with 9
reading problems. I hated the idea, but the camp turned out pretty good,
and I had a good time. I met a lot of kids who couldn't read and somehow
that helped. The director of the camp said I had a higher I.Q. than 90
percent of the population. I didn't believe him.

About the worst thing I had to do in fifth and sixth grade was go to a 10
special education class in another school in our town. A bus picked me up,
and I didn't like that at all. The bus also picked up emotionally disturbed
kids and retarded kids. It was like going to a school for the retarded. I
always worried that someone I knew would see me on that bus. It was a
relief to go to the regular junior high school.

Life began to change a little for me then, because I began to feel 11
better about myself. I found the teachers cared; they had meetings about
me and I worked harder for them for a while. I began to work on the
potter's wheel, making vases and pots that the teachers said were pretty
good. Also, I got a letter for being on the track team. I could always run
pretty fast.

At high school the teachers are good and everyone is trying to help me. 12
I've gotten honors some marking periods and I've won a letter on the
cross-country team. Next quarter I think the school might hold a show of
my pottery. I've got some friends. But there are still some embarrassing
times. For instance, every time there is writing in the class, I get up and go
to the special education room. Kids ask me where I go all the time.
Sometimes I say, "to Mars."

Homework is a real problem. During free periods in school I go into 13
the special ed room and staff members read assignments to me. When I get
home my mother reads to me. Sometimes she reads an assignment into a
tape recorder, and then I go into my room and listen to it. If we have a
novel or something like that to read, she reads it out loud to me. Then I
sit down with her and we do the assignment. She'll write, while I talk my
answers to her. Lately I've taken to dictating into a tape recorder, and then
someone—my father, a private tutor or my mother—types up what I've

dictated. Whatever homework I do takes someone else's time, too. That makes me feel bad.

We had a big meeting in school the other day—eight of us, four from 14 the guidance department, my private tutor, my parents and me. The subject was me. I said I wanted to go to college, and they told me about colleges that have facilities and staff to handle people like me. That's nice to hear.

As for what happens after college, I don't know and I'm worried about 15 that. How can I make a living if I can't read? Who will hire me? How will I fill out the application form? The only thing that gives me any courage is the fact that I've learned about well-known people who couldn't read or had other problems and still made it. Like Albert Einstein, who didn't talk until he was 4 and flunked math. Like Leonardo da Vinci, who everyone seems to think had dyslexia.

I've told this story because maybe some teacher will read it and go easy 16 on a kid in the classroom who has what I've got. Or, maybe some parent will stop nagging his kid, and stop calling him lazy. Maybe he's not lazy or dumb. Maybe he just can't read and doesn't know what's wrong. Maybe he's scared, like I was.

❀ ❀ ❀

AFTER YOU READ

THINK about Raymond's skill as a potter and his athletic ability. How did these successes improve his self-confidence?

EXAMINE Raymond's confession that he fears going to college. Do most people fear a new experience such as starting college? How does having a handicap of any kind make such experiences even more frightening? What fears do you have about college?

WRITE a paragraph or brief essay in which you discuss the effect of school performance on self-concept. Be sure you emphasize the cause and effect relationship.

Old at Seventeen

DAVID VECSEY

Originally published in the "About Men" column of the
New York Times, *this essay was written by David Vecsey*
when he was only eighteen years old. At the time, Vecsey
was a freshman at Bradley University in Peoria, Illinois.
The essay describes the author's first sense of no longer
being a child—of being old even at seventeen.

BEFORE YOU READ

THINK about the first time you were aware that you were no longer a child. When did this awareness first occur? How did it make you feel?

EXAMINE the first paragraph of the essay, in which Vecsey identifies a number of signs that indicate to men that they are getting older. What other signs of aging would you add? Would the signs of aging for women be the same?

WRITE a journal entry comparing the ways in which young women and young men recognize they are becoming adults.

AS YOU READ

Notice the details the author includes. Underline the details that help you to understand what Vecsey was experiencing. Would his story have been as convincing or as interesting if he had omitted these details?

There are signs that say you're getting older. Getting a driver's license, needing a shave every morning, going to college and reading the front page of a paper before the sports section—these all say a person is getting older. Any man who says getting older comes later, that it's a matter of balding and middle-aged spread, just can't remember, I say.

The most major signal up to now that I was getting old happened late last winter when Richie and Micah appeared at my front door early in the morning. School had been canceled because of a foot of snow. They asked me if I wanted to go on the golf course for a little while. I actually asked them, "For what?"

In the summer, the Plandome Country Club golf course is a haven for doctors and lawyers who like to wear plaid pants and hit a defenseless white ball. It's also good for catching some rays. But in the winter, it has traditionally been a haven for children who soar down "Old Glory" hill as fast as they can on a flimsy piece of wood or plastic. When I was younger, friends and I spent every waking moment out on the golf course, sledding. Now I was asking them why they wanted to go out there. Soon I'll be calling pants "trousers" and reading the *Reader's Digest* on a regular basis.

I agreed to go with them, and I put on jeans and a sweatshirt, as opposed to the snowsuit my mother used to bundle me up in when I was 8 or 9. I wisely decided to wear boots instead of sneakers. Old Glory is the most popular hill on the course, and is literally 50 yards from my house, so we were there in no time. I helped Richie carry the toboggan; I no longer own a sled.

When we reached the top of Old Glory, my first thought was that it must have shrunk, because it is no longer the mountain it used to be. It looked more like a fairway with snow on it. I watched the little kids zooming down the hill at top speeds, and I noticed something: they no longer ride Flexible Flyers or Yankee Clippers. They own sleds of the 1980's, plastic structures that look like bikes and cars and boats and things. I think some even have power steering and shocks.

Richie dropped the toboggan, and we figured out the best route to take down to the bottom. I suggested that we take a side way, so we wouldn't hit the bumps in the middle. I was greeted with sour looks of disgust. Hitting all the bumps was the idea. I was berated into going first—taking the middle path. My knees cracked and my back ached as I crouched into a sitting position on the toboggan. Micah pushed me off, and I slowly started to descend the hill. "This isn't so bad," I said, "I used to do this all the time."

Then I picked up speed. The nightmare began. Snow flew into my face   7
as I hit about 60 miles an hour. I screamed at the top of my lungs, only to
be greeted by a mouthful of snow. Out of control, I screamed at people to
get out of the way. Bodies jumped and dodged aside. Up ahead, a snow
bank headed right toward me. I was engulfed in it. Snow was everywhere—
down my shoes, down my pants, about a gallon of it down my throat.

I ached and was freezing to death. There's no way, I thought, that I   8
used to do this every day, all day. That was another little kid, a masochist,
not me. I stood up and turned around to see two sleds, each containing a
small child of about 12. They were going too fast, and they collided. The
two children lay there motionless. I ran to help, and I noticed that the
reason they were motionless was because they were laughing too hard to
move. "That was awesome, Jimmy. Let's do it again," one yelled, and they
grabbed their sleds and ran up the hill.

I decided to do the same, and headed up the hill. That is when it finally   9
looked like the massive mountain I remembered. Each step I took became
heavier and heavier. I dragged the toboggan of death behind me as I trudged
up the hill. I reached the top, where Richie and Micah anxiously awaited
their turns. They wanted to try it standing up.

I told them that, from then on, I'd prefer to observe. More sour looks.   10
They disappeared into the crowd, and I looked around. One father was
yelling at his son for going too fast, and another scolded his son for not
beating his friend in a race. A crowd of mothers huddled together over a
steaming thermos, talking about what idiots their husbands were, always
excited about last week's football game. "Who are they playing in the Super
Bowl?" one woman asked. "I think they already played it," her friend said.
"Who won?" "CBS, I think." Their conversation rolled on, and I walked
away.

A group of children formed a train by hanging onto one another's   11
ankles. It reminded me of when we used to play "hijack the sled." We'd all
start within five feet of one another at the top of the hill, but once we
picked up speed, the object was to crash into the other players, knock them
off, and take their empty sleds down the hill. The man who got to the
bottom first won. Ah, those were the days. But I'm civilized now. I'd rather
play "negotiation," in which we sit on the sleds at the top of the hill and
discuss life.

A boy of about 11 sat on his sled, holding snow up to his bloody nose.   12
His friends called him a wimp because he wouldn't go down again. A little
girl punched out a little boy for touching her sled, and he went crying to

his mom, who was busy listening to her other son complain about the cold. The mom's face turned red, partially because of the cold, but mostly because of her wrath. She grabbed both kids' wrists and dragged them to the car. Their day is history now. Never complain to a cold mother, it's bad news.

I came to the conclusion that leaving the golf course wasn't such a bad 13
idea. I'm no longer the weatherproof tot I used to be. Instead, I'm a teen-ager who would rather read or watch a movie than wrap my body around a tree while sledding. If the me of my Old Glory days met the me of my teen-age years, he would call me a lame-o and find someone else to sled with. He would be right, too, but sledding is for the younger crowd, not for us ancient 17-year-olds.

I miss that wiry little kid who used to daredevil on sleds to impress his 14
friends. Fear was no object then. But today the thought of coasting down ice and snow isn't my idea of Eden. I'll watch, thanks, with the other old people.

❀ ❀ ❀

AFTER YOU READ

THINK about what the loss of physical strength means to an individual. How would you feel if—because you were old or disabled or small—you could not perform certain acts? Is physical strength as important to people in our society as it once was? Today, is physical strength a necessity or a status symbol?

EXAMINE the paragraph structure of this essay. The essay is primarily a narrative and thus is organized chronologically. That is, Vecsey relates the events in the order in which they occurred. Do his paragraphs divide the essay into meaningful segments? Are other paragraph divisions possible? Would they be as effective? What purpose do you think paragraphs serve in this essay? In any piece of writing?

WRITE a brief narrative telling of the first time you realized you were no longer a child.

The Right to Know

MARGARET R. BROWN

Margaret Brown was a nineteen-year-old freshman biology major at St. Edward's University in Austin, Texas, when she wrote this essay, which first appeared in Newsweek *as a guest editorial. In the essay, Brown argues that it is "dreadfully wrong" to deny a child "the knowledge of his or her biological origins."*

BEFORE YOU READ

THINK about the issue of whether a child has a right to know who his or her biological parents are.

EXAMINE the term *donor insemination.* The word *donor* refers to one who gives, and *insemination* comes from the root word *semen.* Thus, donor insemination refers to the practice of a man providing semen, which is then injected into a woman's uterus so that she can become pregnant.

WRITE a journal entry in which you discuss why it is important for children to know something about their biological parents.

AS YOU READ

Try to decide whose rights are most important in cases of artificial insemination—those of the child, the mother, or the male donor.

I've had this recurring dream of floating through darkness where I am 1
whirling faster and faster through some nameless, timeless, almost
unearthly region. I get weary and want to put my feet down to stand so I
can gather myself together. But there's nothing to stand on. This is my
nightmare—I'm a person created by donor insemination, someone who
will never know half of her identity. I feel anger and confusion, and I'm
filled with questions. Whose eyes do I have? Why the big secret? Who gave
my family the idea that my biological roots are not important? To deny
someone the knowledge of his or her biological origins is dreadfully wrong.

Beginning with the selection of a sperm donor, the process is centered 2
around deception. From hair and eye color to religious and musical
preferences, a donor is carefully matched to the mother or to her husband
if she is married. Usually there is multiple insemination, a kind of pot-luck
technique of fertilization, often involving a different donor each time; so
determining the exact biological father can be next to impossible. In many
cases records are eliminated after conception (though I believe there are a
few sperm banks who release donor identities). Couples are counseled not
to tell anyone they're considering donor insemination. Some doctors
encourage the couple to lie, to say that the husband's infertility has been
treated successfully. Then friends and family will assume the child is the
natural offspring of the husband and wife.

I only recently found out my father was not really my father. My 3
parents divorced when I was 7, and I have had very little contact with him
since then. Two years ago, at 16, when I expressed interest in seeing him
again, my mother decided to tell me that my "dad" wasn't my father and
that my father's half of me came from a test tube. With no records available,
half my heritage is erased. I'll never know whose eyes I have inherited. I've
searched family photo albums to no avail.

The news has affected my sense of identity and belonging. "Who am 4
I?" is a hard question to answer when I don't know where I came from. I'd
like to have the comfort of knowing whom I resemble. It's amazing how
one can miss a sense of identity and wholeness because no one has ever
said, "You act just like your mama when she was young." I guess I act just
like my donor. And, as my thoughts, opinions and behavior are almost 180
degrees from most of my family members, I've never felt like a "piece of
the puzzle" at family gatherings—especially around my father's side of the
family. This isn't something I sensed strongly—I thought I acted differently
because I was from Tennessee and they were from Texas—but the feeling
was always there. I'll admit putting it into words is hard. As well as
grappling with who I am and where I belong, I have a more difficult obstacle

since the secret's been out: trust. I've wondered if there are other secrets being kept from me. I shouldn't have to doubt my mother. But I've found myself questioning whether I was told the truth. How can I know for sure that there was a donor as she says?

Advocates of donor babies argue that biology is not an issue in 5 parenting; the love and care a child receives is all that matters. I can understand a couple's desire for a child, and I don't deny that they can provide a great amount of love and caring, no matter how conception occurs. In a world where history is a required academic subject and libraries have special sections for genealogy, I don't see how anyone can consciously rob someone of something as basic and essential as heritage. Parents must realize that all the love and attention in the world can't mask that underlying, almost subconscious feeling that something is askew. I greatly appreciate the sacrifices my mother has made and the love my family has given me. But even while being enveloped in my father's sister's warmest embrace, I feel a strange little twinge of something deep inside me—like I'm borrowing someone else's family.

What is even more astounding, given society's present attitude toward 6 protecting children's rights—even the unborn—is that decisions about insemination are made in the interests of the parents' and the physicians' privacy, rather than those of the child. A donor is matched to the recipient's husband so the couple can pass the child off as their own. The procedure is kept secret so the couple can avoid accusations of immorality and adultery. That the child deserves the right to know of a biological father is not a consideration. One couple that Elizabeth Noble, author of "Having Your Baby by Donor Insemination," interviewed said that telling the child "would serve absolutely no useful purpose whatsoever." That assumes the child would have no thoughts on the matter of paternity because the parents don't. It seems no one thought I might want to know of the other half of my genetic makeup. But children are not commodities or possessions. They are people with an equal stake in the process.

Future donor-recipient parents must step out of their own shoes and 7 into those of the person they are creating. Parents can choose to raise a child honestly—fully respecting the child's individuality—without the self-imposed pressure to deceive. If there is honesty and openness in donor insemination, it could become a process similar to adoption—at least giving young adults a possibility to find out about their biological fathers.

So, to couples seeking babies this way, I propose that you find out who 8 your donors are, keep records and let your children know where they came from. And to a possibly brown-haired man who attended University of

Tennessee Medical School in 1974 and made a donation on my mother's behalf, I thank you for the gift of life. I think I have your eyes, your jaw and your personality. I just wish I could find out for sure.

❀ ❀ ❀

AFTER YOU READ

THINK about the statement that "advocates of donor babies argue that biology is not an issue in parenting; the love and care a child receives is all that matters." Do you agree or disagree with this point of view?

EXAMINE Brown's reasons for wanting to know her biological father. Are her reasons persuasive? Why or why not?

WRITE a summary of the reasons Brown gives to support her argument that children should have the right to know who their biological parents are.

What Do Women Want?

SARA DAVIDSON

Sara Davidson is an American novelist and journalist. This reading selection, which is taken from her book Real Property *(1980), is both an essay and a story. In it Davidson poses several riddles for her readers. An earlier book by Davidson,* Loose Change *(1977), describes what life was like for young middle-class women during the sixties.*

BEFORE YOU READ

THINK about the question, "What do women want more than anything?" How would you answer it?

EXAMINE the word *sovereignty,* which means supremacy of authority, complete independence, or power. It is another form of the word *sovereign,* which usually refers to a king, queen, or some other type of ruler or monarch. Why would women want sovereignty? Do all women want sovereignty? If women gain sovereignty, what role would men assume?

WRITE in your journal your own answer to the question expressed in the title, "What do women want?"

AS YOU READ

Look for the story's answer to the question of what women want. Underline key words and phrases that help answer this question.

D anielle Laurent was about to be married, at the age of thirty-three. "Is 1
this your first marriage?" people asked, as she drove around Jerusalem
on her motor scooter, ordering flowers and cakes.

"Yes." 2

"*Mazel tov*!" 3

Danielle was a French Jew, raised in Paris, but for seven years she had 4
been living in Jerusalem, teaching literature at the Hebrew University. Her
fiancé was a professor of physics, thirty-six, also new to marriage. A week
before the wedding, Danielle invited friends to come to the home of her
aunt, Simone, to spend the evening sewing the wedding dress.

I happened to be visiting Jerusalem and was invited. "Please, make an 5
effort," Danielle had said. "I need you."

Simone's small house in Abu Tor, overlooking King David's Tower, was 6
filled with women, professional women, ranging from twenty-six to thirty-
five. Four were American, one was Spanish, one was Romanian, two were
French and three were native Israelis. None was legally married at the time,
except Simone.

At seventy, Simone is still a beauty, tall and erect, wearing her gray hair 7
in a chignon. Simone has had two lengthy marriages, raised four children
and enjoyed a career as a concert violinist. She lived in a villa outside Paris
until her first husband died, at forty-two. Her children were away at school
by then, so Simone, long a Zionist, immigrated to Israel, where she fell in
love with her current husband, Moshe.

"I am someone who has lived by love, in love, all my life," she told me 8
as she sat on the couch, her feet propped on pillows. "I have to be an
example to the girls."

It had been Simone's idea to have the young women sew Danielle's 9
dress by hand, from fabric Simone had bought in India: white silk, with
delicate gold embroidery. As we came in, she made us wash our hands and
cover our laps with sheets, so the fabric would not be soiled.

It was peaceful, sewing together, keeping a watchful circle around 10
Danielle. But there was also a feeling of irony and self-mocking: we were
not girls of sixteen, believing in the dress as a passport to the golden land.

Simone asked that we go around the circle and take turns telling stories 11
and legends. Danielle, who was first, shook her head no. Her long dark
hair covered her eyes as she bent over her sewing. For years, Danielle had
been telling herself that what she wanted more than anything was to have
a partner, a "permanent ally," and a house full of children. All through her
twenties, she had given priority to her work, and assumed she would never
have the patience to care for infants. But around the time she turned thirty,
it became painful to walk past a children's store. She began to long, to ache

for someone to share life with. For thirteen years she had been a waif, fending for herself and traveling across three continents; now that was to change. But could she adjust? Would the love she felt abide?

"Sara, you must provide us with a story," Simone said. For a moment, 12 I could think of nothing that seemed appropriate; then I remembered an Arthurian legend I had heard from a friend, Winifred Rosen, who was adapting the tale for a children's book.

I began to relate the story, as best I could, from memory. "In the time 13 of King Arthur and the Round Table, the King was out riding in the forest when he was surprised by a strange knight in full battle dress. The knight drew his sword, but the King said, 'Wait. I'm not armed, you can't do this, it would violate our honor code.' So the knight, whose name was Sir Gromer Somer Joure, had to relent. He made the King promise that he would return to the same spot, alone and unarmed, one year later. The King's life would be spared only if he brought back the answer to this riddle: What do women want, more than anything?"

Danielle interrupted the story. "That's what Freud is supposed to have 14 asked. 'What do women want, dear God?'" Simone laughed. "The question did not originate with Freud. It recurs through the ages." She turned to me. "What did King Arthur do?"

"He rode back to the palace and met his nephew, Sir Gawain, who was, 15 you know, the most beautiful and perfect knight in all the kingdom. He told Sir Gawain his plight, and Sir Gawain said, 'Don't worry, I'll ride in one direction, you'll ride in the other, and we'll ask every man and woman we meet, what do women want?'

"So the two of them rode off, and for a year, they asked every person, 16 high and low, wise and simple, what do women want? They were given hundreds of answers."

I stopped to ask the women in Simone's sitting room, "How would 17 you answer if you had to, 'What do women want more than anything?'"

They paused in their stitching. 18

"Love." 19

"A child." 20

"Respect." 21

"To be worshiped." 22

The Romanian lady said, "I think women want to be men." 23

Simone smiled, as if she knew none of the above would have saved the 24 King.

I continued: "At the end of the year, Sir Gawain and the King each had 25 a book full of answers. But King Arthur knew he did not have the right answer, and he was prepared to meet his fate, when he saw a woman approaching. This woman was the ugliest hag in creation. She was fat and wrinkled; she had a big nose with snot dripping and hairs sprouting from her face. She gave off a terrible odor. Her teeth were like tusks. She had warts and pus oozing from her eyes. Her name was Dame Ragnell. She rode straight up to the King and said, 'Sir, I alone have the answer that will save you. I'll tell you on one condition: that you give me Sir Gawain as my husband.'

"The King was horrified. 'I can't give you Sir Gawain.' He would rather ²⁶ have died than commit his nephew to such a fate. But Sir Gawain insisted he would marry the hag, gladly, if it would save the King's life.

"So King Arthur accepted the terms. 'Now, tell me, what do women ²⁷ want more than anything?'

"Dame Ragnell said, 'Sovereignty.'" ²⁸

I paused in my story. We looked at each other, silently, covered with ²⁹ yards of white silk. Everyone seemed to sense instantly how satisfying the answer was.

"When King Arthur returned to meet Sir Gromer Somer Joure, he told ³⁰ him the answer, and his life *was* spared. Overjoyed, he rode back to the palace, but he found Dame Ragnell waiting to be married. And she wanted a grand wedding, with all the royal court. After the ceremony, Dame Ragnell gave a little tug at Sir Gawain's sleeve and croaked, 'My lord, I'm your wife now, you have certain duties . . .'"

There were groans in the room. ³¹

"Sir Gawain could barely bring himself to look at her hairy snout, but ³² he was bound by honor. He screwed up his courage, shut his eyes and turned to kiss her, and as he did, she was transformed into the most beautiful, delicate, sensuous creature he had ever dreamed of seeing. They spent the night making love, and as the sun was rising, Dame Ragnell said, 'My beauty will not hold all the time, so you must make a choice. Either have me beautiful by day, when the world can see, and ugly at night; or ugly by day and beautiful in your bed.'"

I said to the women, "Which would you choose, if you were Gawain?" ³³

The Spanish woman said, "Beautiful by day." But she was quickly ³⁴ outvoted. Danielle said, "If he was a wise man, he would have her beautiful for him alone." Simone abstained, and asked me to continue.

"What Sir Gawain said was this: 'My lady, I leave it up to you.' And at ³⁵ that, she became beautiful all the time."

Cheers broke out; cakes were passed around. Danielle clapped her ³⁶ hands. "He was a very wise man." Simone, quieting the group, said, "You know, sovereignty is not a problem when you rule alone in your kingdom, but when two sovereign people want to merge their domains . . ." She looked pointedly at her niece. "Ah, that is the riddle you have yet to answer."

❀   ❀   ❀

AFTER YOU READ

THINK about the answer Dame Ragnell gives in the story to the question of what women want. Do you agree that women want sovereignty? Why or why not?

THINK also about what men want. Do they also want sovereignty?

EXAMINE the final riddle of the story: How do two sovereign people merge their domains? Explain what is meant by this question and suggest possible answers.

EXAMINE also the structure of this essay. The Arthurian story is integrated into the modern story of the young woman who is about to be married. In effect, the modern story creates a framework, or context, for the Arthurian legend. Summarize both stories briefly. What is gained by presenting the Arthurian legend in the context of the modern story?

WRITE a paragraph or brief essay in which you argue for or against the idea that women want sovereignty.

The New American Man

ROBERT BLY

Robert Bly is a prominent American poet and critic—the author of more than fifteen books of poetry and the founder of the literary magazine Fifties (Sixties, *and so on*). *His collection of poems* The Light Around the Body *won the National Book Award for 1967. More recently, he is well-known as a spokesman for modern American males. In the following selection from his book* Iron John: A Book about Men *(1990), Bly explores the developing nature of the American man and comes to the conclusion that in recent years many American men have become what he calls "soft males."*

BEFORE YOU READ

THINK about the qualities that you associate with the ideal man. Is he soft and sensitive or firm and decisive? Is he in tune with nature or knowledgeable about technology? Can one man be all of these things?

EXAMINE the following statement: "In the seventies I began to see all over the country a phenomenon that we might call the 'soft male.'" What qualities do you associate with the term *soft male*? Are these qualities positive or negative?

WRITE in your journal your own description of the modern American male.

AS YOU READ

Compare your description of the modern American male with Bly's.

W̶e talk a great deal about "the American man," as if there were some 1
children, and admired discipline. . . . This sort of man didn't see women's
a single decade. . . .

Even in our own era the agreed-on model has changed dramatically. 2
During the fifties, for example, an American character appeared with some
consistency that became a model of manhood adopted by many men: the
Fifties male.

He got to work early, labored responsibly, supported his wife and 3
children, and admired discipline. . . . This sort of man didn't see women's
souls well, but he appreciated their bodies; and his view of culture and
America's part in it was boyish and optimistic. Many of his qualities were
strong and positive, but underneath the charm and bluff there was, and
there remains, much isolation, deprivation, and passivity. Unless he has an
enemy, he isn't sure that he is alive.

The Fifties man was supposed to like football, be aggressive, stick up 4
for the United States, never cry, and always provide. But receptive space or
intimate space was missing in this image of a man. The personality lacked
some sense of flow. . . .

The Fifties male had a clear vision of what a man was, and what male 5
responsibilities were, but the isolation and one-sidedness of his vision were
dangerous.

During the sixties, another sort of man appeared. The waste and 6
violence of the Vietnam war made men question whether they knew what
an adult male really was. If manhood meant Vietnam, did they want any
part of it? Meanwhile, the feminist movement encouraged men to actually
look at women, forcing them to become conscious of concerns and
sufferings that the Fifties male labored to avoid. As men began to examine
women's history and women's sensibility, some men began to notice what
was called their *feminine* side and pay attention to it. This process continues
to this day, and I would say that most contemporary men are involved in
it in some way.

There's something wonderful about this development—I mean the 7
practice of men welcoming their own "feminine" consciousness and nurturing it—this is important—and yet I have the sense that there is something wrong. The male in the past twenty years has become more
thoughtful, more gentle. But by this process he has not become more free.
He's a nice boy who pleases not only his mother but also the young woman
he is living with.

In the seventies I began to see all over the country a phenomenon that 8
we might call the "soft male." Sometimes even today when I look out at

an audience, perhaps half the young males are what I'd call soft. They're lovely, valuable people—I like them—they're not interested in harming the earth or starting wars. There's a gentle attitude toward life in their whole being and style of living.

But many of these men are not happy. You quickly notice the lack of energy in them. They are life-preserving but not exactly life-giving. Ironically, you often see these men with strong women who positively radiate energy. 9

Here we have a finely tuned young man, ecologically superior to his father, sympathetic to the whole harmony of the universe, yet he himself has little vitality to offer. 10

The strong or life-giving women who graduated from the sixties, so to speak, or who have inherited an older spirit, played an important part in producing this life-preserving, but not life-giving, man. 11

I remember a bumper sticker during the sixties that read "WOMEN SAY YES TO MEN WHO SAY NO." We recognize that it took a lot of courage to resist the draft, go to jail, or move to Canada, just as it took courage to accept the draft and go to Vietnam. But the women of twenty years ago were definitely saying that they preferred the softer receptive male. 12

So the development of men was affected a little in this preference. Nonreceptive maleness was equated with violence, and receptive maleness was rewarded. 13

Some energetic women, at that time and now in the nineties, chose and still choose soft men to be their lovers and, in a way, perhaps, to be their sons. The new distribution of "yang" energy among couples didn't happen by accident. Young men for various reasons wanted their women harder, and women began to desire softer men. It seemed like a nice arrangement for a while, but we've lived with it long enough now to see that it isn't working out. 14

I first learned about the anguish of "soft" men when they told their stories in early men's gatherings. In 1980, the Lama Community in New Mexico asked me to teach a conference for men only, their first, in which about forty men participated. Each day we concentrated on one Greek god and one old story, and then late in the afternoons we gathered to talk. When the younger men spoke it was not uncommon for them to be weeping within five minutes. The amount of grief and anguish in these younger men was astounding to me. 15

Part of their grief rose out of remoteness from their fathers, which they felt keenly, but partly, too, grief flowed from trouble in their marriages or 16 relationships. They had learned to be receptive, but receptivity wasn't enough to carry their marriages through troubled times. In every relationship something *fierce* is needed once in a while: both the man and the woman need to have it. But at the point when it was needed, often the young man came up short. He was nurturing, but something else was required—for his relationship, and for his life.

The "soft" male was able to say, "I can feel your pain, and I consider 17 your life as important as mine, and I will take care of you and comfort you." But he could not say what he wanted, and stick by it. *Resolve* of that kind was a different matter.

In *The Odyssey,* Hermes instructs Odysseus that when he approaches 18 Circe, who stands for a certain kind of matriarchal energy, he is to lift or show his sword. In these early sessions it was difficult for many of the younger men to distinguish between showing the sword and hurting someone. One man, a kind of incarnation of certain spiritual attitudes of the sixties, a man who had actually lived in a tree for a year outside Santa Cruz, found himself unable to extend his arm when it held a sword. He had learned so well not to hurt anyone that he couldn't lift the steel, even to catch the light of the sun on it. But showing a sword doesn't necessarily mean fighting. It can also suggest a joyful decisiveness.

The journey many American men have taken into softness, or recep- 19 tivity, or "development of the feminine side," has been an immensely valuable journey, but more travel lies ahead. No stage is the final stop.

❀   ❀   ❀

AFTER YOU READ

THINK about Bly's thesis, or main idea. Is it stated or implied? Can you identify it clearly?

EXAMINE Bly's classification of men according to decades (the men of the fifties, sixties, and so on). Underline words and phrases that describe the men of each of these decades. Do you agree with Bly's characterization of each?

WRITE an essay in which you first summarize and then compare and contrast Bly's theories about men and Davidson's theories about women.

Getting Started

JANET CAMPBELL HALE

Janet Campbell Hale is a member of the Coeur d'Alene tribe of Northern Idaho. She was born and raised on a reservation. However, rather than emphasizing her Native American background, in this poem Hale focuses on the universal dilemma of wanting to be a special type of person but failing to attain this goal because of daily concerns and affairs.

BEFORE YOU READ

THINK about your goals for your own life. What do you want to accomplish? What sort of person do you want to be?

EXAMINE the word *transcend,* which appears in the fifth line of the poem. The word means "to rise above" (or, literally, "to rise across," since *trans* means "across"). As you read the poem, determine what the speaker wants to transcend.

WRITE in your journal a list of your short-range goals and then a list of your long-term goals. Beside each goal that is within your control, write the word *I.* Beside each goal that depends upon the action or attitude of someone else, write the word *other.* Beside each goal that depends upon luck or good fortune, write the word *luck.* Then look at your list to determine how many of your goals depend primarily on your own efforts.

AS YOU READ

Try to determine whether the person in the poem has real reasons for not achieving her goals or is merely making excuses. Underline the reasons she gives and decide how valid each is.

Getting Started

It isn't that I've forgotten
Or don't intend to do
With my life what I
Know I should,
That is, transcend the petty concerns   5
And live
In truth
And in beauty
according to the
Higher aims of my existence.   10
Yet,
I have trouble
getting started
somehow
And day by day,   15
Hour by hour,
Wait,
For the spell
to be broken,
And go on,   20
Life as usual,
minute by minute,
pulse beat
by
pulse beat,   25
paying bills,
doing the laundry,
going to work,
putting band-aids
on little scraped knees,   30
watching TV,
Swept along
    and along.

AFTER YOU READ

THINK about the goals the woman has set for herself. Is it realistic to expect to live "In truth/And in beauty/according to the/Higher aims of . . . existence"? Would less ambitious, less abstract goals be more attainable?

EXAMINE through a careful rereading the details of the woman's daily life. Are these daily tasks unimportant? For example, is "putting band-aids/on little scraped knees" unimportant? Mark other daily tasks mentioned in the poem and evaluate each one in terms of its importance.

WRITE an essay in which you evaluate your goals. Are they realistic and attainable? Are they within your own control, or do they depend on others or good fortune? Are you, like the woman in the poem, focusing on future plans and failing to enjoy the life you are now living—the life that sweeps you along day by day?

The Stars of the Whole Sky

SHOZO MACHIDA

At the age of fifty-one, Shozo Machida retired from his teaching position on the island of Ogasawara (Bonin) and left his native country of Japan so that he could come to America to study English. This move was part of a plan to realize his long-range goal, "to travel all around the world for five years," and then to find "some good place" to retire. Machida explains his plans in this essay, which he wrote as a student in a freshman English course.

BEFORE YOU READ

THINK about what it would be like to move to a new country when you are fifty-one years old. What would be the most difficult thing about such a move?

EXAMINE the first paragraph of this essay, which is written in present tense. Then examine the second paragraph, which is written in past tense. Is this shift in tense justified? Why or why not?

WRITE a journal entry in which you describe something that you would like to do before you die.

AS YOU READ

Notice Machida's use of stars as a recurring theme, or motif, throughout his essay. Underline the passages in which he mentions stars.

Venus is brilliant in the west sky here in Mississippi. I'm coming back 1
home from university. For fifty-one-year-age man, the coldness and
the beauty of the stars in winter are comfortable. But sometimes it is hard
probably because there is no family waiting for me in my apartment. I am
now in Mississippi by myself to study English, which I need for my
long-range goal. I, who stay here now, am on the way to my goal, which is
looking for the peaceful place for my last living. I want to travel all around
the world for five years and to live at some good place if I can find it.

I set this goal while I was working as a teacher of the elementary school 2
in Ogasawara, a small island in Japan. After I divorced, having no family,
I lived there for twelve years. This is a very beautiful island that is situated
on latitude twenty-seven degrees north and one thousand kilometers from
Tokyo to south. It has only two thousand inhabitants who are all acquain-
tances. There is no airport and its only transportation is a ship every five
or six days. Although I was a teacher, I worked hard there not only as a
teacher but also as a caretaker of the school and a co-operator of the events
in the village. Besides teaching the children, I raised many flowers, sometimes with my pupils, in order to adorn the classrooms, the school
ceremonies, the school gardens, and their home gardens. The school was
always surrounded by many kinds of flowers. Sometimes I went to the sea
with my pupils to catch tropical fish which would be fed in the aquarium
of the school. Sometimes I gathered the children, their parents, and
villagers in the square, where we could watch the seasonal stars clearly, and
told them about the planets and constellations. All of the stars at those
times seemed extremely beautiful for me because I was satisfied with feeling
that I was useful for villagers.

After the busy but gratifying days, I often felt a kind of loneliness or 3
emptiness while I was looking at the stars lying alone on the beach. "Do
you admit of these days continuing?" or "Don't you have anything forgotten to be done?" I asked to myself. When I finished my twenty-fifth year
as a teacher, I decided to retire from my job, which had given me a great
pleasure. I remembered the forgotten dream—traveling around the
world—which would never be done after I got older and weaker. I hoped
that the god, if there was one, would forgive me to retire ten years earlier
than usual, because I had been working hard for long time, and I had no
responsibility for family; I am alone. One year later, I quit my job and left
that island, hoping to come back and see the children that I taught, the
flowers that I planted, and the stars that I watched there.

What I should do first is learning English which will help me to travel 4
or to live anywhere I want. I have traveled around sixteen countries, but

my English was not enough to communicate with people who lived there. Then I decided to study abroad, and I came to the United States last May. I have been studying English for more than six months, but it is still difficult for me to speak it so readily and fluently. My plan is to stay here for one year. It will not be long enough to get good English, but I don't give up yet. But, but, but . . .

Oh, my God! Yes, I have already realized my long-range goal. Unfor- 5 tunately, a human being can not live alone even if the place has a beautiful view and a calm weather. I am sure that I will be back after five years wandering over the world to that island or to my home town in Japan, because the villagers and my relatives are both the best intimate friends that I have ever met in my life. Perhaps I had already known these things in the corner of my heart when I began to have this dream. In addition, I am also sure of my next goal, not finding how to live longer but to die finely without giving trouble to others. Oh, I remember that I have another goal, which might be the best and the most suitable for me—dying on the road in an unknown country with an empty whiskey bottle that is reflecting the stars of the whole sky.

❀ ❀ ❀

AFTER YOU READ

THINK about Machida's statement that he hoped to be forgiven for retiring "ten years earlier than usual." In Japan most people work very hard for many years. Machida's decision to retire when he was only fifty-one goes against the expectations of his culture. How does he justify his decision?

EXAMINE Machida's syntax (sentence structure) and word choices in this essay. Notice that many of his sentences are phrased in a way different than they would be if written by a native speaker of English and that some of his word choices are unusual. Are these differences distracting to you, or do they add something valuable to the essay?

WRITE a character sketch of the author based on your reading of this essay. Use the information that the author includes about himself as well as what you infer from his description of his life.

Unit One: Critical Thinking and Writing Assignments

❈ ❈ ❈

EXPLORING IDEAS TOGETHER

1. With a group of your classmates, discuss the effects that physical appearance has on a person's self-image. Do you know an attractive person who has low self-esteem or an unattractive person who has high self-esteem? Is it important that others consider a person attractive, or is it only how the person feels about his or her own appearance that matters?

2. In a small group discuss whether a person should set extremely high, perhaps even unattainable, goals or realistic goals that can be attained. You may want to reread the poem "Getting Started" by Janet Campbell Hale and the essay "The Stars of the Whole Sky" by Shozo Machida as your group formulates and writes its answer.

3. The reading selections in this unit suggest that a person's self-concept is influenced by the following factors: name, physical appearance, age, education, successes and failures, and reactions of other people. Which of these factors do you think is most responsible for shaping a person's self-image? Support your group's opinion with examples from personal experiences as well as with information from the readings in this unit.

4. With a group of your classmates, compare and contrast the goals of males and females—what men and women typically want out of life. In discussing this issue, you may want to refer to the essays by Sara Davidson and Robert Bly and the poem by Janet Campbell Hale.

WRITING ESSAYS

1. Self-concept is, of course, influenced by a number of factors including environment, physical appearance, and personal experiences. However, some experts argue that a person's interactions with other people determine, most significantly, how a person perceives himself or herself. Write a paragraph in which you argue for or against the assertion that the most important factor in self-concept is a person's interactions with others.

2. Write an essay in which you identify and discuss one or more of the long-range goals you have set for yourself. In your essay examine your goals and show how these goals have affected your life.

3. In this unit, Maxine Hong Kingston and David Raymond discuss their feelings of isolation. Write an essay in which you describe how it feels to be different in some way.

4. Describe the environment in which you grew up in such a way that you suggest how that environment shaped your image of yourself. You may want to reread the essay by Mike Rose before beginning your essay.

5. Using Sara Davidson's and Robert Bly's essays as sources of information, explain in an essay why modern males and females have difficulty establishing satisfactory relationships.

Self with Family

O ne of the first and most important relationships that you establish is with your family. In fact, to a great extent you define yourself in terms of your family. Who you become depends on who you were—your position in your family, your relationship with different members of your family, your perception of yourself as part of your family. As you grow older, you will probably establish a new family, but that family will be a reflection of the one in which you grew up. Even if you choose consciously and deliberately to change the old patterns, they will still be there—a force you are reacting against rather than a pattern you are following.

This unit includes reading selections that will encourage you to explore the relationships within your family and to define yourself more clearly in terms of these relationships. You will read about traditional and modern families, about successful and unsuccessful families, about how families can help you and how families can hurt you. All of the selections encourage you to think about how you define a family and how a family defines you.

As you read these selections, you will, of course, think about your own family. In fact, you will understand what you read in terms of your own family experiences. Therefore, before you begin this unit, take a few minutes to write about your own family. Use one or more of the following questions to guide your writing:

1. Describe the family in which you grew up. Was it traditional or nontraditional, small or large, wealthy or poor, happy or unhappy?
2. If you have already established a family of your own, how is it similar to or different from the one in which you grew up?
3. To what member of your family are you closest? Why?
4. What member of your family do you most resemble? In what way(s)?
5. What would you change about your family if you could?
6. What would you not want to change?
7. What role(s) do you play in your family?
8. How is your family different from other families? How is your family like other families?

Now that you have written about your own family, think about the general concept of family. How do you define a family? If you are like most people, your idea of family is, as sociologist Ian Robertson has recognized, rather ethnocentric; that is, it is based on the dominant ethnic and social model of "the middle-class 'ideal' family so relentlessly portrayed in TV commercials, one that consists of a husband, a wife, and their dependent children."* In contrast, Robertson provides a definition of family that includes "many different family forms that have existed or still exist both in America and in other cultures." According to Robertson, "the family is a relatively permanent group of people related by ancestry, marriage, or adoption, who live together, form an economic unit, and take care of their young." How does this definition compare or contrast with the way you define a family? Does this definition describe your own family? Does it describe the families of your friends? Can you think of any family that it does not describe? As you read the selections in this unit, notice the different types of families represented.

Also, remember to annotate the text as you read—to circle words that you do not know, to underline ideas that you think are important or interesting, and to write questions and notes in the margins. The type of annotations you make will depend on your purpose in reading, the type of selection, and your comprehension of and interest in what you are reading. Some of the reading selections, such as Bill Cosby's "Fatherhood," are brief and humorous. These you will probably read quickly and easily without needing to annotate them extensively. However, even a very brief personal response will help you remember what you read. Other selections, such as

---

*Robertson, Ian. *Sociology,* 3rd ed. (New York: Worth, 1987), pp. 348–349.

"The Family Values Debate" by James Q. Wilson, will be more serious or more difficult and may require more work on your part. You may need to reread in order to identify main ideas or remember details, to summarize what you have read in your own words in order to understand the ideas involved, or to number the important concepts in order to see their relationship to one another. Whatever writing you do will improve your skill as a reader because it forces you to think actively and productively about the subject and how it relates to you.

Generations

JOYCE MAYNARD

Joyce Maynard published her first book, Looking Back: A Chronicle of Growing Up Old in the Sixties *(1973), when she was only eighteen years old. Since then, she has published the novels* Baby Love *(1981),* Domestic Affairs: Enduring the Pleasures of Motherhood and Family Life *(1987), and* To Die For *(1992). Her articles have appeared frequently in publications such as the* New York Times, Parents, *and* Redbook. *In this personal essay about a trip that she made to visit her dying grandmother, Maynard not only recalls some of her own family stories but also muses about the bond between mother and daughter that progresses from generation to generation, ultimately making each succeeding generation like the one before it.*

BEFORE YOU READ

THINK about some ways in which you are like some member of your own family. Consider also some ways in which you differ from other members of your family.

EXAMINE the first two paragraphs of the essay. What do these paragraphs tell you about the grandmother who is dying? About the granddaughter who is writing the essay? About the writer's mother?

EXAMINE also the following words from the selection and their definitions:

Jaundice: "She can't eat, she has been hemorrhaging, and she has severe *jaundice.*"

In reading the complete selection, you will be able to define *jaundice* from its context, for the author quotes the grandmother's statement, "I always prided myself on being different. . . . Now I *am* different. I'm yellow." As this context suggests, *jaundice* means yellowing of the skin and suggests the severe illness of Maynard's grandmother.

Pogroms, cossacks: "She tells stories of the *pogroms* and the *cossacks* who raped her when she was 12."

Both of these words reflect the Jewish grandmother's life in Russia. A *pogrom* was a persecution—sometimes a massacre—of Jews that was supported by the Russian government; a *cossack* was actually a Russian from the southern part of the country, but as used here the term means a rude Russian soldier.

Knishes: "But in the meantime, while every other relative of her generation, and a good many of the younger ones, has died . . . , she has kept making *knishes,* shopping for bargains, tending the healthiest plants I've ever seen."

This word also reflects the grandmother's Jewish background. From the Yiddish and Russian languages, a *knish* is a fried or baked dumpling stuffed with potato or another food.

WRITE a journal entry about a particular trait that you think you share with one of your parents or with some other family member. Trace this trait back as far as you can, perhaps drawing a diagram that illustrates how it has evolved from one generation to another. The trait might be simply a preference for a certain hobby or vocation, a habit or way of behaving, or an attitude or a mindset.

AS YOU READ

Underline details that show how Maynard is like her mother and how her mother is like her grandmother. How do these details help Maynard to communicate her thesis without stating it explicitly?

My mother called last week to tell me that my grandmother is dying. 1 She has refused an operation that would postpone, but not prevent, her death from pancreatic cancer. She can't eat, she has been hemorrhaging, and she has severe jaundice. "I always prided myself on being different," she told my mother. "Now I *am* different. I'm yellow."

My mother, telling me this news, began to cry. So I became the mother 2 for a moment, reminding her, reasonably, that my grandmother is 87, she's had a full life, she has all her faculties, and no one who knows her could wish that she live long enough to lose them. Lately my mother has been finding notes in my grandmother's drawers at the nursing home, reminding her, "Joyce's husband's name is Steve. Their daughter is Audrey." In the

last few years she hasn't had the strength to cook or garden, and she's begun
to say she's had enough of living.

My grandmother was born in Russia, in 1892—the oldest daughter in ₃
a large and prosperous Jewish family. But the prosperity didn't last. She
tells stories of the pogroms and the cossacks who raped her when she was
12. Soon after that, her family emigrated to Canada, where she met my
grandfather.

Their children were the center of their life. The story I loved best, as ₄
a child, was of my grandfather opening every box of Cracker Jack in the
general store he ran, in search of the particular tin toy my mother coveted.
Though they never had much money, my grandmother saw to it that her
daughter had elocution lessons and piano lessons, and assured her that she
would go to college.

But while she was at college, my mother met my father, who was ₅
blue-eyed and blond-haired and not Jewish. When my father sent love
letters to my mother, my grandmother would open and hide them, and
when my mother told her parents she was going to marry this man, my
grandmother said if that happened, it would kill her.

Not likely, of course. My grandmother is a woman who used to crack ₆
Brazil nuts open with her teeth, a woman who once lifted a car off the
ground, when there was an accident and it had to be moved. She has been
representing her death as imminent ever since I've known her—25 years—
and has discussed, at length, the distribution of her possessions and her
lamb coat. Every time we said goodbye, after our annual visit to Winnipeg,
she'd weep and say she'd never see us again. But in the meantime, while
every other relative of her generation, and a good many of the younger
ones, has died (nursed usually by her), she has kept making knishes,
shopping for bargains, tending the healthiest plants I've ever seen.

After my grandfather died, my grandmother lived, more than ever, ₇
through her children. When she came to visit, I would hide my diary. She
couldn't understand any desire for privacy. She couldn't bear it if my
mother left the house without her.

This possessiveness is what made my mother furious (and then guilt- ₈
ridden that she felt that way, when of course she owed so much to her
mother). So I harbored the resentment that my mother—the dutiful
daughter—would not allow herself. I—who had always performed especially well for my grandmother, danced and sung for her, presented her
with kisses and good report cards—stopped writing to her, ceased to visit.

But when I heard that she was dying, I realized I wanted to go to ₉
Winnipeg to see her one more time. Mostly to make my mother happy, I

told myself (certain patterns being hard to break). But also, I was offering up one more particularly fine accomplishment: my own dark eyed, dark-skinned, dark-haired daughter, whom my grandmother had never met.

I put on my daughter's best dress for our visit to Winnipeg, the way 10
the best dresses were always put on me, and I filled my pockets with animal crackers, in case Audrey started to cry. I scrubbed her face mercilessly. On the elevator going up to her room, I realized how much I was sweating.

Grandma was lying flat with an IV tube in her arm and her eyes shut, 11
but she opened them when I leaned over to kiss her. "It's Fredelle's daughter, Joyce," I yelled, because she doesn't hear well anymore, but I could see that no explanation was necessary. "You came," she said. "You brought the baby."

Audrey is just 1, but she has seen enough of the world to know that 12
people in beds are not meant to be so still and yellow, and she looked frightened. I had never wanted, more, for her to smile.

Then Grandma waved at her—the same kind of slow, finger-flexing 13
wave a baby makes—and Audrey waved back. I spread her toys out on my grandmother's bed and sat her down. There she stayed, most of the afternoon, playing and humming and sipping on her bottle, taking a nap at one point, leaning against my grandmother's leg. When I cranked her Snoopy guitar, Audrey stood up on the bed and danced. Grandma couldn't talk much anymore, though every once in a while she would say how sorry she was that she wasn't having a better day. "I'm not always like this," she said.

Mostly she just watched Audrey. Sometimes Audrey would get off the 14
bed, inspect the get-well cards, totter down the hall. "Where is she?" Grandma kept asking. "Who's looking after her?" I had the feeling, even then, that if I'd said, "Audrey's lighting matches," Grandma would have shot up to rescue her.

We were flying home that night, and I had dreaded telling her, 15
remembering all those other tearful partings. But in the end, I was the one who cried. She had said she was ready to die. But as I leaned over to stroke her forehead, what she said was, "I wish I had your hair" and "I wish I was well."

On the plane flying home, with Audrey in my arms, I thought about 16
mothers and daughters, and the four generations of the family that I know most intimately. Every one of those mothers loves and needs her daughter more than her daughter will love or need her some day, and we are, each of us, the only person on earth who is quite so consumingly interested in our child.

Sometimes I kiss and hug Audrey so much she starts crying—which is,   17
in effect, what my grandmother was doing to my mother, all her life. And
what makes my mother grieve right now, I think, is not simply that her
mother will die in a day or two, but that, once her mother dies, there will
never again be someone to love her in quite such an unreserved, unques-
tioning way. No one else who believes that, 50 years ago, she could have
put Shirley Temple out of a job, no one else who remembers the moment
of her birth. She will only be a mother, then, not a daughter anymore.

Audrey and I have stopped over for a night in Toronto, where my   18
mother lives. Tomorrow she will go to a safe-deposit box in the bank and
take out the receipt for my grandmother's burial plot. Then she will fly
back to Winnipeg, where, for the first time in anybody's memory, there was
waist-high snow on April Fool's Day. But tonight she is feeding me, as she
always does when I come, and I am eating more than I do anywhere else.
I admire the wedding china (once my grandmother's) that my mother has
set on the table. She says (the way Grandma used to say to her, of the lamb
coat), "Some day it will be yours."

❁   ❁   ❁

AFTER YOU READ

THINK about Maynard's mother's attitude toward her own mother (the
grandmother). Does the mother like the idea that she is becoming more
like the grandmother? Is Maynard's own attitude similar? Is this another
way in which Maynard and her mother are alike? Discuss with your
classmates the theory that we all become more like our parents as we
become older. How does becoming more like our parents change our
attitude toward them?

EXAMINE the specific details that Maynard uses to develop her essay. What
details provide a vivid characterization of the grandmother? What details
(see your underlining) show similarities between generations? Notice that
Maynard does not simply make a general assertion that everyone becomes
like his or her parents but uses very specific details to suggest this thesis.

WRITE a reaction to Maynard's statement that "every one of those mothers
loves and needs her daughter more than her daughter will love or need her
some day. . . ." You can substitute fathers and sons for mothers and
daughters.

No Snapshots in the Attic:
A Granddaughter's Search for
a Cherokee Past

CONNIE MAY FOWLER

The author of three novels, Sugar Cage, River of Hidden Dreams, *and* Before Women Had Wings, *Connie May Fowler is particularly concerned with family heritage.* Sugar Cage, *her first novel, was inspired by her own Cherokee grandmother, Oneida Marie Hunter May. Frustrated that her grandmother had hidden her own Native American past and by the lack of physical and factual evidence of her own personal heritage—both Native American and European—Fowler begins a physical and mental journey that leads her back to the ancient oral tradition of storytelling.*

BEFORE YOU READ

THINK about your own sense of family heritage. Do you feel that you "know" your ancestors—your grandparents and even great-grandparents that you have never met? If so, how did you learn about these ancestors? Do you feel that your life is richer for this knowledge? If you do not feel that you know your ancestors, do you believe that you have lost something valuable? Explain.

EXAMINE the title "No Snapshots in the Attic." Fowler expands this idea in the second paragraph when she declares that "our attics are empty." What does she mean by these statements? How are both statements symbolic? Besides Fowler's attic, what else is empty in her life? What, besides snapshots, might be missing from her life?

WRITE a journal entry about the ancestor who intrigues you the most. Is your interest piqued more by what you *know* or what you *do not know*

about this person? How have you acquired the information you have? Or
WRITE a journal entry about an important family object that you have in
"your attic" or other safe place. What does this object show about your
family heritage?

AS YOU READ

Follow closely the physical and mental journey that Fowler makes in search
of her Cherokee past. What roadblocks does she encounter in this search?
How does she finally achieve a sense of this past?

For as long as anyone can remember, poverty has crawled all over the 1
hearts of my family, contributing to a long tradition of premature deaths
and a lifetime of stories stymied behind the mute lips of the dead. The
survivors have been left without any tangible signs that evoke the past: no
photographs or diaries, no wedding bands or wooden nickels.

This absence of a record seems remarkable to me since our bloodline 2
is diverse: Cherokee, Irish, German, French; you would think that at least
a few people would have had the impulse to offer future generations a few
concrete clues as to who they were. But no; our attics are empty. Up among
the cobwebs and dormer-filtered light you will find not a single homemade
quilt, not one musty packet of love letters.

Lack of hard evidence of a familial past seems unnatural to me, but I 3
have developed a theory. I believe that my relatives, Indians and Europeans
alike, couldn't waste free time on preserving a baby's first bootee. There
were simply too many tales to tell about each other, living and dead, for
them to be bothered by objects that would only clutter our homes and our
minds.

The first time I noticed this compulsion to rid ourselves of handed- 4
down possessions was in the summer of my eighth year when my mother
decided to fix the front screen door, which was coming off its hinges. As
she rummaged through a junk drawer for a screwdriver, she came upon a
dog-eared photograph of her father. He stood in front of a shack, staring
into the camera as though he could see through the lens and into the eyes
of the photographer. "Oh, that old picture," my mother said disdainfully.
"Nothing but a dust catcher." She tossed the photo in the trash, pulled up
a chair, lit a cigarette and told me about how her Appalachian-born daddy
could charm wild animals out of the woods by standing on his front porch
and singing to them.

The idea that my family had time only for survival and storytelling 5
takes on special significance when I think of my grandmother, my father's
mother, Oneida Hunter May, a Cherokee who married a white man. Hers
was a life cloaked in irony and sadness, yet 30 years after she died her
personal history continues to suggest that spinning tales is a particularly
honest and noble activity.

Throughout her adult life, the only time Oneida Hunter May felt free 6
enough to claim her own heritage was in the stories she told her children.
At all other times, publicly and privately, she declared herself white. As
both a writer and a granddaughter, I have been haunted by her decision to
excise her Indian heart and I have struggled to understand it. Of course,
her story would work its way into my fiction, but how it did and what I
would learn about the truth of cultural and familial rumors when they
contradict the truth of our official histories would change the way I see the
world, the way I write, and how and whom I trust.

Until I became an adult this is what I accepted as true about my 7
grandmother: She was a Cherokee Indian who married a South Carolinian
named John May. Early in the marriage they moved to St. Augustine, Fla.
They had three children, two boys and a girl. Shortly after moving to
Florida, John May abandoned his wife and children. The family believed
he joined the circus. (When I was a child my family's yearly pilgrimage to
the Greatest Show on Earth took on special significance as I imagined that
my grandfather was the lion tamer or the high-wire artist.) Grandmama
May was short and round. While she was straightforward with the family
about her Indian ancestry, she avoided instilling in us a shred of Native
American culture or custom. Through the use of pale powder and rouge,
she lightened her skin. Her cracker-box house on the wrong side of the
tracks was filled with colorful miniature glass animals and hats and boots,
all stolen from tourist shops downtown. According to my father, she was
"run out of town on a rail" more than once because of the stealing, and
she even spent time in the city jail. Her laughter was raucous. She tended
to pick me up by putting her hands under my armpits, which hurt, and it
seemed as if every time I saw her she pinched my cheeks, which also hurt.
My grandmother mispronounced words and her syntax was jumbled. I've
since realized that her strange grammar patterns and elocution were the
results of having no formal education and of speaking in a language that
was not her native tongue.

For me, growing up was marked not only by a gradual loss of innocence 8
but by the loss of the storytellers in my life: grandparents, aunts and uncles,
parents. With them went my ability to believe and know simple truths, to

accept the face value of things without needless wrestling. As the cynicism of adulthood took hold, I began to doubt the family stories about my grandmother and I even decided my recollections were warped by time and the fuzzy judgment of childhood, and that the stories were based on oral tradition rooted in hearsay. What is this ephemeral recitation of our lives anyway? A hodgepodge of alleged fact, myth and legend made all the more unreliable because it goes unchecked by impartial inquiry. After all, don't scholars dismiss oral histories as anecdotal evidence?

I told myself I was far too smart to put much stock in my family's 9 Homeric impulses. In choosing to use my grandmother's life as a stepping-off point for a new novel; I decided that everything I knew as a child was probably exaggerated at best and false at worst. I craved empirical evidence, irrefutable facts; I turned to government archives.

I began my inquiry by obtaining a copy of my grandmother's death 10 certificate. I hoped it would provide me with details that would lead to a trail back to her early life and even to her birth. The document contained the following data: Oneida Marie Hunter May was born Aug. 14, 1901, in Dillon, S.C. She died June 8, 1963, of diabetes. But from there her history was reduced to no comment. Line 13, father's name: five black dashes. Line 14, mother's maiden name: five dashes. Line 16, Social Security number: none. The most chilling, however, because it was a lie, was line 6, color or race: white.

Her son, my uncle J. W., was listed as the "informant." Perhaps he 11 thought he was honoring her by perpetuating her longstanding public falsehood. Perhaps, despite what he knew, he considered himself white— and therefore so was she. Perhaps in this small Southern town he was embarrassed or frightened to admit his true bloodline. Did he really not know his grandparents' names? Or did he fear the names would suggest his Indian lineage? Whether his answers were prompted by lack of knowl-edge or a desire to be evasive, the result was that the "facts" of the death certificate were suspect. The information recorded for posterity amounted to a whitewash. The son gave answers he could live with, which is what his mother had done, answers that satisfied a xenophobic society.

Thinking that perhaps I had started at the wrong end of the quest, I 12 went in search of her birth certificate. I contacted the proper office in South Carolina and gave the clerk what meager information I had. I realized that without a Social Security number, my chances of locating such a document were slim, but I thought that in its thirst for data the government might have tracked Indian births. "No, I'm sorry," I was told over the phone by the clerk who had been kind enough to try an alphabetical search. "South

Carolina didn't keep detailed files on Indians back then. You could try the Cherokees, but I don't think it will help. In those days they weren't keeping good records either."

I was beginning to understand how thoroughly a person can vanish 13 and how—without memory and folklore—one can be doomed to oblivion. But I pursued history, and I changed my focus to Florida. I began reading accounts of St. Augustine's Indian population in the last century, hoping to gain insight into my grandmother's experience. There is not a great amount of documentation, and most of what does exist was written by long-dead Roman Catholic missionaries and Army generals, sources whose objectivity was compromised by their theological and military mandates. Nevertheless, I stumbled on an 1877 report by Harriet Beecher Stowe about the incarceration of Plains Indians at Castillo de San Marcos (then called Fort Marion) at the mouth of the St. Augustine harbor.

During their imprisonment, which lasted from 1875 to 1878, the 14 Indians were forced to abandon their homes, religions, languages, their dress and all other cultural elements that white society deemed "savage"—a term used with alarming frequency in writings of the time. Calling the Indians in their pre-Christian state "untamable," "wild" and "more like grim goblins than human beings," Stowe apparently approved of what they became in the fort: Scripture-citing, broken-spirited Indians dressed like their tormentors, United States soldiers. She writes, "Might not the money now constantly spent on armies, forts and frontiers be better invested in educating young men who shall return and teach their people to live like civilized beings?"

The written record, I was discovering, was fabulous in its distortion, 15 and helpful in its unabashedness. It reflected not so much truth or historical accuracy as the attitudes of the writers.

The most obvious evidence of the unreliable nature of history is the 16 cultural litany set down in tourist brochures and abstracted onto brass plaques in parks and on roadsides across America. My family has lived for three generations in St. Augustine, "The Oldest Continuously Inhabited City in America. Founded in 1565." What this proclamation leaves out is everything that preceded the town's European founding. Like my uncle's carefully edited account of my grandmother's life, St. Augustine's official version amounts to historical genocide because it wipes away all traces of the activities and contributions of a specific race. For hundreds of years this spit of land between two rivers and the sea was the thriving village of Seloy, home to the Timucuan Indians. But while still aboard a ship, before

ever stepping onto the white and coral-colored shores of the "New World,"
Pedro Menéndez renamed Seloy in honor of the patron saint of his
birthplace. Then he claimed this new St. Augustine and all of "La Florida"
to be the property of Spain; the Timucuans and their culture had been
obliterated by a man at sea gazing at their land.

These distinctions between European facts and Indian facts are not 17
trivial. The manipulation of our past is an attempt, unconscious or not, to
stomp out evidence of the success and value of other cultures. My grandmother's decision to deny her heritage was fueled by the fear of what would
happen to her if she admitted to being an Indian and by the belief that there
was something inherently inferior about her people. And the falsehoods
and omissions she lived by affected not just her; her descendants face a
personal and historical incompleteness.

But when the official chronicles are composed of dashes and distor- 18
tions and you still hunger for the truth, what do you do? For me, the answer
was to let my writer's instincts take over. I slipped inside my grandmother's
skin and tried to sort out her motives and her pain. I imagined her birth
and what her mother and father might have looked like. I gave them names,
Nightwater and Billy. I called the character inspired by my grandmother
Sparrow Hunter. She would bear a daughter, Oneida. And it would be
Oneida's offspring, Sadie Hunter, who would uncover the stories that
revealed the truth.

But I needed to know how a young Indian woman with three babies 19
to feed survives after she's been abandoned in a 1920's tourist town that
promoted as its main attraction an ancient and massive fort that had served
as a prison for Comanches, Kiowas, Seminoles, Apaches, Cheyennes,
Arapaho, Caddos and others. The writer-granddaughter listened to her
blood-born voices and heard the answers. Her grandmother made up a
birthplace and tried to forget her native tongue. She stayed out of the sun
because she tanned easily, and she bought the palest foundations and
powders available. She re-created herself. For her children and grandchildren never to be called "Injun" or "savage" must have been one of her most
persistent hopes. And what bitter irony it must have been that her children
obeyed and took on the heritage of the man who had deserted them. I was
discovering that my novel would be far better served if I stopped digging
for dates and numbers and instead strove to understand my grandmother's
pain.

My research had another effect, one far more important than causing 20
me to question our written record. It pushed me forward along the circle,

inching me back to where I had started: the oral history. My family has relentlessly nurtured its oral tradition as though instinctively each of us knew that our attics would be empty for generations but our memory-fed imaginations could be filled to overbrimming with our tales of each other. And certainly, while the stories are grandiose and often tall, I decided they are no more slanted than what is fed to us in textbooks.

I have come to view my family's oral history as beautifully double- 21 edged, for in fiction—oral or written—there is a desire to reveal the truth, and that desire betrays my grandmother's public lie. It is in the stories shared on our beloved windy porches and at our wide-planked pine tables, under the glare of naked moth-swept light bulbs, that the truth and the betrayal reside. Had my grandmother not felt compelled to remember her life before John May stepped into it and to relate to little Henry and J. W. and Mary Alice what times were like in South Carolina in the early 1900's for a dirt-poor Indian girl, then a precious link to her past and ours would have been lost forever. And while she raised her children to think of themselves as solely white, she couldn't keep secret who she really was.

Those must have been wondrous moments when she tossed aside the 22 mask of the liar to take up the cloak of the storyteller. It was a transformation rooted in our deepest past, for she transcended her ordinary state and for a brief time became a shaman, a holy person who through reflection, confession and interpretation offered to her children an opportunity to become members of the family of humankind, the family that traces its history not through DNA and documents but through the follies and triumphs, the struggles and desires of one another. So I turn to where the greatest measure of truth exists: the stories shared between mother and child, sister and brother, passed around the table like a platter of hot biscuits and gravy and consumed with hungry fervor.

My attempt to write about my grandmother's life was slow and often 23 agonizing. But turning a tangle of information and inspiration into a novel and into a facet of the truth that would shine was the process of becoming a child again, of rediscovering the innocence of faith, of accepting as true what I have always known. I had to believe in the storyteller and her stories again.

The novel my grandmother inspired is fiction, for sure, but it reinforces 24 the paradox that most writers, editors and readers know: fiction is often truer than nonfiction. A society knows itself most clearly not through the allegedly neutral news media or government propaganda or historical records but through the biased eyes of the artist, the writer. When that vision is tempered by heaven and hell, by an honesty of the intellect and gut, it allows the reader and viewer to safely enter worlds of brutal truth,

confrontation and redemption. It allows the public as both voyeur and
safely distanced participant to say, "Aha! I know that man. I know that
woman. Their struggles, their temptations, their betrayals, their triumphs
are mine."

One of my favorite relatives was Aunt Emily, J. W.'s wife. I saw her the   25
night of my father's death in 1966 and—because my aunt and uncle
divorced and because my father's death was a catastrophic event that blew
my family apart—I did not see her again until 1992. She was first in line
for the hometown book signing of my debut novel, "Sugar Cage." We had
a tearful and happy reunion, and before she left she said, "I remember the
day you were born and how happy I was that you were named for your
Grandmother Oneida."

I looked at her stupidly for a moment, not understanding what she was   26
saying. Then it dawned on me that she misunderstood my middle name
because we pronounced Oneida as though it rhymed with Anita. "Oh no,"
I told her. "My name is Connie Anita." Aunt Emily smiled and said,
"Sweetheart, the nurse wrote it down wrong on your birth certificate. All
of us except for your grandmother got a big laugh out of the mistake. But
believe me, it's what your parents said: you're Connie Oneida."

I loved that moment, for it was a confirmation of the integrity of our   27
oral histories and the frailties of our official ones. As I go forward with a
writing life, I accept that my creative umbilical cord is attached to my
ancestors. And to their stories. I've decided to allow their reflective
revelations to define me in some measure. And I have decided not to
bemoan my family's bare attics and photo albums, because as long as we
can find the time to sit on our porches or in front of our word processors
and continue the tradition of handing down stories, I believe we will
flourish as Indians, high-wire artists, animal charmers and writers all. And
the truth will survive. It may be obscured occasionally by the overblown
or sublime, but at least it will still be there, giving form to our words and
fueling our compulsion to tell the tale.

❀   ❀   ❀

AFTER YOU READ

THINK about Fowler's two different heritages: European and Native
American. Does she find these heritages to be complementary or contradictory? How does she become reconciled to both? With which does she

ultimately identify? If, like Fowler, you have a dual heritage, how have you reconciled the different elements of your ancestry?

EXAMINE this description of Fowler's grandmother as storyteller:

> It was a transformation rooted in our deepest past, for she transcended her ordinary state and for a brief time became a shaman, a holy person who through reflection, confession and interpretation offered to her children an opportunity to become members of the family of humankind, the family that traces its history not through DNA and documents but through the follies and triumphs, the struggles and desires of one another. So I turn to where the greatest measure of truth exists: the stories shared between mother and child, sister and brother, passed around the table like a platter of hot biscuits and gravy and consumed with hungry fervor.

As this passage suggests, family stories provide not only family history but also important family values. What does this passage tell you about Native American life in particular? Which images are the most effective and why?

WRITE a story about your family—one that is of some particular significance to you or your family in revealing your family's history, values, or goals. Your story might be one of those "passed around the table like a platter of hot biscuits" from family member to family member, or it might be a story that you "make up" from partial clues that you have about one of your ancestors. Like Fowler in her search for her Cherokee grandmother, you can try to "slip inside the skin" of this person and tell the story through his or her eyes.

Two Kinds

AMY TAN

As in many families, the mother and daughter in this selection by Amy Tan have difficulty understanding and communicating with each other, and ultimately the daughter rebels. "Two Kinds" is taken from Tan's best-selling book The Joy Luck Club *(1989), which describes the changing relationships between four pairs of Chinese-American mothers and daughters. Here, Jing-Mei Woo tells the story of her mother's determined campaign to force her to excel—to become a child prodigy.*

BEFORE YOU READ

THINK about the expectations that your mother or father held for you when you were growing up—and even today. Did either parent push you to excel beyond your ability or ambition? If so, was this challenge a positive one? Or did the challenge backfire, causing you to rebel and achieve less than you might have?

EXAMINE the introduction to the story. What do these first three paragraphs suggest to you about the mother's character? About her background and about her dreams for the future? Examine also the word *prodigy*, which is introduced in the second paragraph: "'Of course you can be *prodigy*, too,' my mother told me when I was nine." A prodigy is a person, especially a child, with exceptional talents and abilities. The mother's expectation that Jing-Mei Woo can become a prodigy and the daughter's reactions to this expectation provide the major tension in the story.

WRITE a journal entry discussing the expectations that your parent(s) have, or had, for you.

AS YOU READ

Try to determine how the title relates to the main idea of the story. As ideas occur to you, write them in the margins.

My mother believed you could be anything you wanted to be in 1 America. You could open a restaurant. You could work for the government and get good retirement. You could buy a house with almost no money down. You could become rich. You could become instantly famous.

"Of course you can be prodigy, too," my mother told me when I was 2 nine. "You can be best anything. What does Auntie Lindo know? Her daughter, she is only best tricky."

America was where all my mother's hopes lay. She had come here in 3 1949 after losing everything in China: her mother and father, her family home, her first husband, and two daughters, twin baby girls. But she never looked back with regret. There were so many ways for things to get better.

We didn't immediately pick the right kind of prodigy. At first my mother 4 thought I could be a Chinese Shirley Temple. We'd watch Shirley's old movies on TV as though they were training films. My mother would poke my arm and say, *"Ni kan"*—You watch. And I would see Shirley tapping her feet, or singing a sailor song, or pursing her lips into a very round O while saying, "Oh my goodness."

"*Ni kan*," said my mother as Shirley's eyes flooded with tears. "You 5 already know how. Don't need talent for crying!"

Soon after my mother got this idea about Shirley Temple, she took me 6 to a beauty training school in the Mission district and put me in the hands of a student who could barely hold the scissors without shaking. Instead of getting big fat curls, I emerged with an uneven mass of crinkly black fuzz. My mother dragged me off to the bathroom and tried to wet down my hair.

"You look like Negro Chinese," she lamented, as if I had done this on 7 purpose.

The instructor of the beauty training school had to lop off these soggy 8 clumps to make my hair even again. "Peter Pan is very popular these days," the instructor assured my mother. I now had hair the length of a boy's, with straight-across bangs that hung at a slant two inches above my eyebrows. I liked the haircut and it made me actually look forward to my future fame.

In fact, in the beginning, I was just as excited as my mother, maybe 9
even more so. I pictured this prodigy part of me as many different images,
trying each one on for size. I was a dainty ballerina girl standing by the
curtains, waiting to hear the right music that would send me floating on
my tiptoes. I was like the Christ child lifted out of the straw manger, crying
with holy indignity. I was Cinderella stepping from her pumpkin carriage
with sparkly cartoon music filling the air.

In all of my imaginings, I was filled with a sense that I would soon 10
become *perfect*. My mother and father would adore me. I would be beyond
reproach. I would never feel the need to sulk for anything.

But sometimes the prodigy in me became impatient. "If you don't hurry 11
up and get me out of here, I'm disappearing for good," it warned. "And
then you'll always be nothing."

Every night after dinner, my mother and I would sit at the Formica kitchen 12
table. She would present new tests, taking her examples from stories of
amazing children she had read in *Ripley's Believe It or Not,* or *Good
Housekeeping, Reader's Digest,* and a dozen other magazines she kept in a
pile in our bathroom. My mother got these magazines from people whose
houses she cleaned. And since she cleaned many houses each week, we had
a great assortment. She would look through them all, searching for stories
about remarkable children.

The first night she brought out a story about a three-year-old boy who 13
knew the capitals of all the states and even most of the European countries.
A teacher was quoted as saying the little boy could also pronounce the
names of the foreign cities correctly.

"What's the capital of Finland?" my mother asked me, looking at the 14
magazine story.

All I knew was the capital of California, because Sacramento was the 15
name of the street we lived on in Chinatown. "Nairobi!" I guessed, saying
the most foreign word I could think of. She checked to see if that was
possibly one way to pronounce "Helsinki" before showing me the answer.

The tests got harder—multiplying numbers in my head, finding the 16
queen of hearts in a deck of cards, trying to stand on my head without using
my hands, predicting the daily temperatures in Los Angeles, New York, and
London.

One night I had to look at a page from the Bible for three minutes and 17
then report everything I could remember. "Now Jehoshaphat had riches
and honor in abundance and . . . that's all I remember, Ma," I said.

And after seeing my mother's disappointed face once again, something 18
inside of me began to die. I hated the tests, the raised hopes and failed

expectations. Before going to bed that night, I looked in the mirror above the bathroom sink and when I saw only my face staring back—and that it would always be this ordinary face—I began to cry. Such a sad, ugly girl! I made high-pitched noises like a crazed animal, trying to scratch out the face in the mirror.

And then I saw what seemed to be the prodigy side of me—because I 19 had never seen that face before. I looked at my reflection, blinking so I could see more clearly. The girl staring back at me was angry, powerful. This girl and I were the same. I had new thoughts, willful thoughts, or rather thoughts filled with lots of won'ts. I won't let her change me, I promised myself. I won't be what I'm not.

So now on nights when my mother presented her tests, I performed 20 listlessly, my head propped on one arm. I pretended to be bored. And I was. I got so bored I started counting the bellows of the foghorns out on the bay while my mother drilled me in other areas. The sound was comforting and reminded me of the cow jumping over the moon. And the next day, I played a game with myself, seeing if my mother would give up on me before eight bellows. After a while I usually counted only one, maybe two bellows at most. At last she was beginning to give up hope.

Two or three months had gone by without any mention of my being a 21 prodigy again. And then one day my mother was watching *The Ed Sullivan Show* on TV. The TV was old and the sound kept shorting out. Every time my mother got halfway up from the sofa to adjust the set, the sound would go back on and Ed would be talking. As soon as she sat down, Ed would go silent again. She got up, the TV broke into loud piano music. She sat down. Silence. Up and down, back and forth, quiet and loud. It was like a stiff embraceless dance between her and the TV set. Finally she stood by the set with her hand on the sound dial.

She seemed entranced by the music, a little frenzied piano piece with 22 this mesmerizing quality, sort of quick passages and then teasing lilting ones before it returned to the quick playful parts.

"*Ni kan*," my mother said, calling me over with hurried hand gestures, 23 "Look here."

I could see why my mother was fascinated by the music. It was being 24 pounded out by a little Chinese girl, about nine years old, with a Peter Pan haircut. The girl had the sauciness of a Shirley Temple. She was proudly modest like a proper Chinese child. And she also did this fancy sweep of a curtsy, so that the fluffy skirt of her white dress cascaded slowly to the floor like the petals of a large carnation.

In spite of these warning signs, I wasn't worried. Our family had no 25 piano and we couldn't afford to buy one, let alone reams of sheet music and piano lessons. So I could be generous in my compliments when my mother bad-mouthed the little girl on TV.

"Play note right, but doesn't sound good! No singing sound," com- 26 plained my mother.

"What are you picking on her for?" I said carelessly. "She's pretty good. 27 Maybe she's not the best, but she's trying hard." I knew almost immediately I would be sorry I said that.

"Just like you," she said. "Not the best. Because you not trying." She 28 gave a little huff as she let go of the sound dial and sat down on the sofa.

The little Chinese girl sat down also to play an encore of "Anitra's 29 Dance" by Grieg. I remember the song, because later on I had to learn how to play it.

Three days after watching *The Ed Sullivan Show,* my mother told me what 30 my schedule would be for piano lessons and piano practice. She had talked to Mr. Chong, who lived on the first floor of our apartment building. Mr. Chong was a retired piano teacher and my mother had traded houseclean-ing services for weekly lessons and a piano for me to practice on every day, two hours a day, from four until six.

When my mother told me this, I felt as though I had been sent to hell. 31 I whined and then kicked my foot a little when I couldn't stand it anymore.

"Why don't you like me the way I am? I'm *not* a genius! I can't play 32 the piano. And even if I could, I wouldn't go on TV if you paid me a million dollars!" I cried.

My mother slapped me. "Who ask you be genius?" she shouted. "Only 33 ask you be your best. For you sake. You think I want you be genius? Hnnh! What for! Who ask you!"

"So ungrateful," I heard her mutter in Chinese. "If she had as much 34 talent as she has temper, she would be famous now."

Mr. Chong, whom I secretly nicknamed Old Chong, was very strange, 35 always tapping his fingers to the silent music of an invisible orchestra. He looked ancient in my eyes. He had lost most of the hair on top of his head and he wore thick glasses and had eyes that always looked tired and sleepy. But he must have been younger than I thought, since he lived with his mother and was not yet married.

I met Old Lady Chong once and that was enough. She had this peculiar 36 smell like a baby that had done something in its pants. And her fingers felt like a dead person's, like an old peach I once found in the back of the refrigerator; the skin just slid off the meat when I picked it up.

I soon found out why Old Chong had retired from teaching piano. He 37
was deaf. "Like Beethoven!" he shouted to me. "We're both listening only
in our head!" And he would start to conduct his frantic silent sonatas.

Our lessons went like this. He would open the book and point to 38
different things, explaining their purpose: "Key! Treble! Bass! No sharps
or flats! So this is C major! Listen now and play after me!"

And then he would play the C scale a few times, a simple chord, and 39
then, as if inspired by an old, unreachable itch, he gradually added more
notes and running trills and a pounding bass until the music was really
something quite grand.

I would play after him, the simple scale, the simple chord, and then I 40
just played some nonsense that sounded like a cat running up and down
on top of garbage cans. Old Chong smiled and applauded and then said,
"Very good! But now you must learn to keep time!"

So that's how I discovered that Old Chong's eyes were too slow to 41
keep up with the wrong notes I was playing. He went through the
motions in half-time. To help me keep rhythm, he stood behind me,
pushing down on my right shoulder for every beat. He balanced pennies on top of my wrists so I would keep them still as I slowly played
scales and arpeggios. He had me curve my hand around an apple and keep
that shape when playing chords. He marched stiffly to show me how to
make each finger dance up and down, staccato like an obedient little
soldier.

He taught me all these things, and that was how I also learned I could 42
be lazy and get away with mistakes, lots of mistakes. If I hit the wrong notes
because I hadn't practiced enough, I never corrected myself. I just kept
playing in rhythm. And Old Chong kept conducting his own private
reverie.

So maybe I never really gave myself a fair chance. I did pick up the 43
basics pretty quickly, and I might have become a good pianist at that young
age. But I was so determined not to try, not to be anybody different that I
learned to play only the most ear-splitting preludes, the most discordant
hymns.

Over the next year, I practiced like this, dutifully in my own way. And 44
then one day I heard my mother and her friend Lindo Jong both talking in
a loud bragging tone of voice so others could hear. It was after church, and
I was leaning against the brick wall wearing a dress with stiff white
petticoats. Auntie Lindo's daughter, Waverly, who was about my age, was
standing farther down the wall about five feet away. We had grown up
together and shared all the closeness of two sisters squabbling over crayons
and dolls. In other words, for the most part, we hated each other. I thought

she was snotty. Waverly Jong had gained a certain amount of fame as "Chinatown's Littlest Chinese Chess Champion."

"She bring home too many trophy," lamented Auntie Lindo that 45
Sunday. "All day she play chess. All day I have no time do nothing but dust off her winnings." She threw a scolding look at Waverly, who pretended not to see her.

"You lucky you don't have this problem," said Auntie Lindo with a sigh 46
to my mother.

And my mother squared her shoulders and bragged: "Our problem 47
worser than yours. If we ask Jing-mei wash dish, she hear nothing but music. It's like you can't stop this natural talent."

And right then, I was determined to put a stop to her foolish pride. 48

A few weeks later, Old Chong and my mother conspired to have me play 49
in a talent show which would be held in the church hall. By then, my parents had saved up enough to buy me a secondhand piano, a black Wurlitzer spinet with a scarred bench. It was the showpiece of our living room.

For the talent show, I was to play a piece called "Pleading Child" from 50
Schumann's *Scenes from Childhood*. It was a simple, moody piece that sounded more difficult than it was. I was supposed to memorize the whole thing, playing the repeat parts twice to make the piece sound longer. But I dawdled over it playing a few bars and then cheating, looking up to see what notes followed. I never really listened to what I was playing. I daydreamed about being somewhere else, about being someone else.

The part I liked to practice best was the fancy curtsy: right foot out, 51
touch the rose on the carpet with a pointed foot, sweep to the side, left leg bends, look up and smile.

My parents invited all the couples from the Joy Luck Club to witness 52
my debut. Auntie Lindo and Uncle Tin were there. Waverly and her two older brothers had also come. The first two rows were filled with children both younger and older than I was. The littlest ones got to go first. They recited simple nursery rhymes, squawked out tunes on miniature violins, twirled Hula Hoops, pranced in pink ballet tutus, and when they bowed or curtsied, the audience would sign in unison, "Awww," and then clap enthusiastically.

When my turn came, I was very confident. I remember my childish 53
excitement. It was as if I knew, without a doubt, that the prodigy side of me really did exist. I had no fear whatsoever, no nervousness. I remember thinking to myself, This is it! This is it! I looked out over the audience, at my mother's blank face, my father's yawn, Auntie Lindo's stiff-lipped smile,

Waverly's sulky expression. I had on a white dress layered with sheets of lace, and a pink bow in my Peter Pan haircut. As I sat down I envisioned people jumping to their feet and Ed Sullivan rushing up to introduce me to everyone on TV.

And I started to play. It was so beautiful. I was so caught up in how 54 lovely I looked that at first I didn't worry how I would sound. So it was a surprise to me when I hit the first wrong note and I realized something didn't sound quite right. And then I hit another and another followed that. A chill started at the top of my head and began to trickle down. Yet I couldn't stop playing, as though my hands were bewitched. I kept thinking my fingers would adjust themselves back, like a train switching to the right track. I played this strange jumble through two repeats, the sour notes staying with me all the way to the end.

When I stood up, I discovered my legs were shaking. Maybe I had just 55 been nervous and the audience, like Old Chong, had seen me go through the right motions and had not heard anything wrong at all. I swept my right foot out, went down on my knee, looked up and smiled. The room was quiet, except for Old Chong, who was beaming and shouting, "Bravo! Bravo! Well done!" But then I saw my mother's face, her stricken face. The audience clapped weakly, and as I walked back to my chair, with my whole face quivering as I tried not to cry, I heard a little boy whisper loudly to his mother, "That was awful," and the mother whispered back, "Well, she certainly tried."

And now I realized how many people were in the audience, the 56 whole world it seemed. I was aware of eyes burning into my back. I felt the shame of my mother and father as they sat stiffly throughout the rest of the show.

We could have escaped during intermission. Pride and some strange 57 sense of honor must have anchored my parents to their chairs. And so we watched it all: the eighteen-year-old boy with a fake mustache who did a magic show and juggled flaming hoops while riding a unicycle. The breasted girl with white makeup who sang from *Madama Butterfly* and got honorable mention. And the eleven-year-old boy who won first prize playing a tricky violin song that sounded like a busy bee.

After the show, the Hsus, the Jongs, and the St. Clairs from the Joy 58 Luck Club came up to my mother and father.

"Lots of talented kids," Auntie Lindo said vaguely, smiling broadly.   59

"That was somethin' else," said my father, and I wondered if he was 60 referring to me in a humorous way, or whether he even remembered what I had done.

Waverly looked at me and shrugged her shoulders. "You aren't a genius   61
like me," she said matter-of-factly. And if I hadn't felt so bad, I would have
pulled her braids and punched her stomach.

But my mother's expression was what devastated me: a quiet, blank   62
look that said she had lost everything. I felt the same way, and it seemed
as if everybody were now coming up, like gawkers at the scene of an
accident, to see what parts were actually missing. When we got on the bus
to go home, my father was humming the busy-bee tune and my mother was
silent. I kept thinking she wanted to wait until we got home before shouting
at me. But when my father unlocked the door to our apartment, my mother
walked in and then went to the back, into the bedroom. No accusations.
No blame. And in a way, I felt disappointed. I had been waiting for her to
start shouting, so I could shout back and cry and blame her for all my misery.

I assumed my talent-show fiasco meant I never had to play the piano again.   63
But two days later, after school, my mother came out of the kitchen and
saw me watching TV.

"Four clock," she reminded me as if it were any other day. I was   64
stunned, as though she were asking me to go through the talent-show
torture again. I wedged myself more tightly in front of the TV.

"Turn off TV," she called from the kitchen five minutes later.   65

I didn't budge. And then I decided. I didn't have to do what my mother   66
said anymore. I wasn't her slave. This wasn't China. I had listened to her
before and look what happened. She was the stupid one.

She came out from the kitchen and stood in the arched entryway of   67
the living room. "Four clock," she said once again, louder.

"I'm not going to play anymore," I said nonchalantly. "Why should I?   68
I'm not a genius."

She walked over and stood in front of the TV. I saw her chest was   69
heaving up and down in an angry way.

"No!" I said, and I now felt stronger, as if my true self had finally   70
emerged. So this was what had been inside me all along.

"No! I won't!" I screamed.   71

She yanked me by the arm, pulled me off the floor, snapped off the   72
TV. She was frighteningly strong, half pulling, half carrying me toward the
piano as I kicked the throw rugs under my feet. She lifted me up and onto
the hard bench. I was sobbing by now, looking at her bitterly. Her chest
was heaving even more, and her mouth was open, smiling crazily as if she
were pleased I was crying.

"You want me to be someone that I'm not!" I sobbed. "I'll never be the   73
kind of daughter you want me to be!"

"Only two kinds of daughters," she shouted in Chinese. "Those who 74
are obedient and those who follow their own mind! Only one kind of
daughter can live in this house. Obedient daughter!"

"Then I wish I wasn't your daughter. I wish you weren't my mother," 75
I shouted. As I said these things I got scared. It felt like worms and toads
and slimy things crawling out of my chest, but it also felt good, as if this
awful side of me had surfaced, at last.

"Too late change this," said my mother shrilly.   76

And I could sense her anger rising to its breaking point. I wanted to 77
see it spill over. And that's when I remembered the babies she had lost in
China, the ones we never talked about. "Then I wish I'd never been born!"
I shouted. "I wish I were dead! Like them."

It was as if I had said the magic words. Alakazam!—and her face went 78
blank, her mouth closed, her arms went slack, and she backed out of the
room, stunned, as if she were blowing away like a small brown leaf, thin,
brittle, lifeless.

It was not the only disappointment my mother felt in me. In the years 79
that followed, I failed her so many times, each time asserting my own
will, my right to fall short of expectations. I didn't get straight As. I
didn't become class president. I didn't get into Stanford. I dropped out of
college.

For unlike my mother, I did not believe I could be anything I wanted 80
to be. I could only be me.

And for all those years, we never talked about the disaster at the recital 81
or my terrible accusations afterward at the piano bench. All that remained
unchecked, like a betrayal that was now unspeakable. So I never found a
way to ask her why she had hoped for something so large that failure was
inevitable.

And even worse, I never asked her what frightened me the most: Why 82
had she given up hope?

For after our struggle at the piano, she never mentioned my playing 83
again. The lessons stopped. The lid to the piano was closed, shutting out
the dust, my misery, and her dreams.

So she surprised me. A few years ago, she offered to give me the piano, 84
for my thirtieth birthday. I had not played in all those years. I saw the offer
as a sign of forgiveness, a tremendous burden removed.

"Are you sure?" I asked shyly. "I mean, won't you and Dad miss it?" 85

"No, this your piano," she said firmly. "Always your piano. You only 86
one can play."

"Well, I probably can't play anymore," I said. "It's been years." 87

"You pick up fast," said my mother, as if she knew this was certain. 88
"You have natural talent. You could been genius if you want to."

"No I couldn't." 89

"You just not trying," said my mother. And she was neither angry nor 90
sad. She said it as if to announce a fact that could never be disproved. "Take
it," she said.

But I didn't at first. It was enough that she had offered it to me. And 91
after that, every time I saw it in my parents' living room, standing in front
of the bay windows, it made me feel proud, as if it were a shiny trophy I
had won back.

Last week I sent a tuner over to my parents' apartment and had the piano 92
reconditioned, for purely sentimental reasons. My mother had died a few
months before and I had been getting things in order for my father, a little
bit at a time. I put the jewelry in special silk pouches. The sweaters she had
knitted in yellow, pink, bright orange—all the colors I hated—I put those
in moth-proof boxes. I found some old Chinese silk dresses, the kind with
little slits up the sides. I rubbed the old silk against my skin, then wrapped
them in tissue and decided to take them home with me.

After I had the piano tuned, I opened the lid and touched the keys. It 93
sounded even richer than I remembered. Really, it was a very good piano.
Inside the bench were the same exercise notes with handwritten scales, the
same secondhand music books with their covers held together with yellow
tape.

I opened up the Schumann book to the dark little piece I had played 94
at the recital. It was on the left-hand side of the page, "Pleading Child." It
looked more difficult than I remembered. I played a few bars, surprised at
how easily the notes came back to me.

And for the first time, or so it seemed, I noticed the piece on the 95
right-hand side. It was called "Perfectly Contented." I tried to play this one
as well. It had a lighter melody but the same flowing rhythm and turned
out to be quite easy. "Pleading Child" was shorter but slower; "Perfectly
Contented" was longer, but faster. And after I played them both a few times,
I realized they were two halves of the same song.

AFTER YOU READ

THINK about the relationship Jing-Mei Woo has with her mother. From the mother's point of view, why is it so important for Jing-Mei Woo to be a success—or at least *try* to be a success? Why does Jing-Mei Woo rebel as she does? Would you have reacted the same way?

THINK also about the relationship between Jing-Mei Woo and her cousin Waverly. Jing-Mei Woo writes, "We had grown up together and shared all the closeness of two sisters squabbling over crayons and dolls. In other words, for the most part, we hated each other." What part does the competition between Jing-Mei Woo and Waverly play in Jing-Mei Woo's struggle with herself and her mother?

EXAMINE again the title "Two Kinds." To what does this title refer? Could the title refer to two kinds of children? Two kinds of attitudes? Now, examine more specifically the titles of the two piano pieces that Jing-Mei Woo plays at the conclusion of the story. How do the names of the contrasting musical pieces "Pleading Child" and "Perfectly Contented" relate to the title and to the main idea of the story?

WRITE an essay about how you reacted to a particular expectation your parent(s) had for you.

Fatherhood

BILL COSBY

As the producer, director, and star of the popular "Cosby Show," Bill Cosby has become not only a household word but also a greatly admired role model for young people. Catching the attention of viewers with his quick wit and comic antics, Cosby often follows up with liberal doses of homespun wisdom. The same combination of humor and wisdom can be found in his many best-selling books, including Fatherhood *(1986),* Love and Marriage *(1989), and* Childhood *(1991). In the following selection from* Fatherhood, *Cosby focuses on his relationship with his daughter.*

BEFORE YOU READ

THINK about the hardest truth for fathers (or mothers) to learn about their children. In your opinion, what is this truth? Look for Cosby's answer as you read.

EXAMINE Cosby's statement that "such growth is especially bittersweet with a daughter because you are always in love with her." In your opinion, is the relationship between a father and a daughter different from other parent-child relationships? Explain your response.

WRITE a journal entry in which you define the term *fatherhood*. How is fatherhood similar to or different from motherhood?

AS YOU READ

Notice that, because Cosby is addressing his book primarily to parents, he combines advice on childrearing with his personal anecdotes about his children. Locate and underline examples of this advice—which we could also call Cosby's "secrets" for fatherhood.

Some authority on parenting once said, "Hold them very close and then let them go." This is the hardest truth for a father to learn: that his children are continuously growing up and moving away from him (until, of course, they move back in). Such growth is especially bittersweet with a daughter because you are always in love with her. When she is very small, she comes to you and says, "Daddy, I have to go to the bathroom," and you proudly lead her there as if the toilet were a wedding chapel. You drop to your knees, unbutton her overalls, and lovingly put her on the seat.

And then one day it happens: she stops you from unbuttoning her and pushes you away because she wants privacy in the bathroom. It is your first rejection by this special sweetheart, but you have to remember that it means no lessening of her love. You must use this rejection to prepare yourself for others that will be coming, like the one I received on a certain day when I called my daughter at college. Someone in her dorm picked up the phone and I asked to speak to my daughter. The person left and returned about a minute later to say, "She says she's sleeping right now."

I was hurt to have my daughter put me on hold, but intellectually I knew that this was just another stage in her growth; and I remembered what Spencer Tracy had said in *Father of the Bride:* "Your son is your son till he takes him a wife, but your daughter is your daughter for all of your life." You are stuck with each other, and what a lovely adhesion it is.

There is no commitment in the world like having children. Even though they often will drive you to consider commitment of another kind, the value of a family still cannot be measured. The great French writer André Malraux said it well: "Without a family, man, alone in the world, trembles with the cold". . . .

This commitment, of course, cannot be a part-time thing. The mother may be doing ninety percent of the disciplining, but the father still must have a full-time acceptance of all the children. He never must say, "Get these kids out of here; I'm trying to watch TV." If he ever does start saying this, he is liable to see one of his kids on the six o'clock news.

Both mother and father have to work to establish an *honesty.* The child doesn't have to tell them *everything,* but he *should* be talking to his parents the same way he talks to someone who is not in charge of his life. When your son has his first wet dream, you don't want him to have it interpreted in the boys' locker room. And if your daughter's period is late, you want her to feel as comfortable going to you as to a confidante at the mall.

Sometimes I tell my son that the meaning of his name is "Trust nobody and smile." But that certainly doesn't apply to his parents: my wife and I have tried to stay tuned in to him and the girls from the very beginning.

We have shown all five of them constant attention, faith, and love. Like all parents since Adam and Eve (who never quite seemed to understand sibling rivalry), we have made mistakes; but we've learned from them, we've learned from the *kids,* and we've all grown together. The seven of us will always stumble and bumble from time to time, but we do have the kind of mutual trust that I wish the United Nations had. And, with breaks for a little hollering, we smile a lot.

❀   ❀   ❀

AFTER YOU READ

THINK about the relationship Cosby has with his daughter. How has this relationship changed over the years? Think also about Cosby's example of calling his daughter at college and finding that she doesn't have time to talk to him. How did this make Cosby feel? Do you sometimes not have time for your parents? Do they ever not have time for you?

EXAMINE Cosby's statement that "both mother and father have to work to establish an *honesty.* The child doesn't have to tell them *everything,* but he *should* be talking to his parents the same way he talks to someone who is not in charge of his life." How can parents encourage such honesty from their children?

WRITE an "advice column" for parents about how to raise children successfully. Include and briefly develop at least three items of advice in your column.

The Old Man

LARRY KING

Although Larry King is perhaps best known for his play
The Best Little Whorehouse in Texas, *he has also written
nonfiction. For example, his autobiographical book* The
Old Man and Lesser Mortals *(1974) not only tells of his
own experiences with his father but also suggests larger
truths about generational and familial conflicts and ties.
Although this book is a collection of essays, it exhibits the
unity and character development of a well-written novel.
This particular selection focuses on the relationship between King and his father as the son is asserting his
independence and breaking with certain family traditions.
King grew up in West Texas, which is the setting for this
narrative.*

BEFORE YOU READ

THINK about an argument that you had with your parents or some other
authority figure when you were younger. How did this argument make you
feel?

EXAMINE the following vocabulary words that appear in the essay:

Corporal: "The Old Man was an old-fashioned father, one who relied on
corporal punishments. . . ."

You are probably already familiar with this word as a military rank (as
in Corporal Jones), but King is using another meaning of the word in this
sentence. Here the word *corporal* refers to the body (*corpus* in Latin) and
thus means "bodily, or physical." Therefore, corporal punishment is physical punishment.

Hedonist: "Though he held idleness to be as useless and as sinful as
adventure, he had the misfortune to sire a *hedonist* son. . . ."

Even if you are not familiar with the word *hedonist,* you can probably guess its meaning from the contrast implied in the sentence: It appears that it is the opposite of hard working and cautious. Thus, a hedonist is one who believes that pleasure is the most important thing in life.

Retroactive: "I wanted to say something healing to The Old Man, to utter some gracious good-bye (the nearest thing to *retroactive* apologies a savage young pride would permit), but I simply knew no beginnings."

This is one of those words that becomes much simpler to define if you divide it into its main parts. If you see that it consists of two parts, *retro,* which means backward or behind, and *active,* then it is not difficult to figure out that *retroactive* means applying to, or going into effect, in a previous period.

King uses a number of other words in his essay that may be unfamiliar to you. Be sure to mark these words as you read. Later you may want to look them up or discuss them.

WRITE a journal entry in which you list and briefly discuss several different issues about which you and your parents (or parent figures) have argued or still argue.

AS YOU READ

Determine what you think Lawrence realizes when he and his father are saying good-bye in the bus station.

The Old Man was an old-fashioned father, one who relied on corporal   1
punishments, biblical exhortations, and a ready temper. He was not a man who dreamed much or who understood that others might require dreams as their opium. Though he held idleness to be as useless and as sinful as adventure, he had the misfortune to sire a hedonist son who dreamed of improbable conquests accomplished by some magic superior to grinding work. By the time I entered the troublesome teen-age years, we were on the way to a long, dark journey. A mutual thirst to prevail existed—some crazy stubborn infectious contagious will to avoid the slightest surrender.

The Old Man strapped, rope whipped, and caned me for smoking,   2
drinking, lying, avoiding church, skipping school, and laying out at night. Having once been very close, we now lashed out at each other in the

manner of rejected lovers on the occasion of each new disappointment. I thought The Old Man blind to the wonders and potentials of the real world; could not fathom how current events or cultural habits so vital to my contemporaries could be considered so frivolous—or worse. In turn, The Old Man expected me to obediently accept his own values: show more concern over the ultimate disposition of my eternal soul, eschew easy paths when walking tougher ones might somehow purify, be not so inquisitive or damnfool dreamy. That I could not (or would not) comply puzzled, frustrated, and angered him. In desperation he moved from a "wet" town to a "dry" one, in the foolish illusion that this tactic might keep his baby boy out of saloons.

On a Saturday in my fifteenth year, when I refused an order to dig a   3
cesspool in our backyard because of larger plans downtown, I fought back: it was savage and ugly—though, as those things go, one hell of a good fight. But only losers emerged. After that we spoke in terse mumbles or angry shouts, not to communicate with civility for three years. The Old Man paraded to a series of punishing and uninspiring jobs—night watchman, dock loader for a creamery, construction worker, chicken butcher in a steamy, stinking poultry house, while I trekked to my own part-time jobs or to school. When school was out I usually repaired to one distant oil field or another, remaining until classes began anew. Before my eighteenth birthday I escaped by joining the army.

On the morning of my induction, The Old Man paused at the kitchen   4
table, where I sat trying to choke down breakfast. He wore the faded old crossed-gallus denim overalls I held in superior contempt and carried a lunch bucket in preparation of whatever dismal job then rode him. "Lawrence," he said, "is there anything I can do for you?" I shook my head. "You need any money?" "No." The Old Man shuffled uncertainly, causing the floor to creak. "Well," he said, "I wish you good luck." I nodded in the direction of my bacon and eggs. A moment later the front door slammed, followed by the grinding of gears The Old Man always accomplished in confronting even the simplest machinery.

Alone in a Fort Dix crowd of olive drab, I lay popeyed on my bunk at   5
night, chain smoking, as Midland High School's initial 1946 football game approached. The impossible dream was that some magic carpet might transport me back to those anticipatory tingles I had known when bands blared, cheerleaders cart-wheeled sweet tantalizing glimpses of their panties, and we purple-clads whooped and clattered toward the red-shirted Odessa Bronchos or the Angry Orange of San Angelo. Waste and desolation lived in the heart's private country on the night that opening game was

accomplished on the happiest playing field of my forfeited youth. The next morning, a Saturday, I was called to the orderly room to accept a telegram— a form of communication that had always meant death or other disasters. I tore it open with the darkest fantasies to read MIDLAND 26 EL PASO YSLETA 0 LOVE DAD. Those valuable communiqués arrived on ten consecutive Saturday mornings.

With a ten-day furlough to spend, I appeared unannounced and before 6 a cold dawn on the porch of that familiar frame house in Midland. The Old Man rose quickly, dispensing greetings in his woolly long-handles. "You just a first-class private?" he teased. "Lord God, I would a-thought a King would be a general by now. Reckon I'll have to write ole Harry Truman a postcard to git that straightened out." Most of the time, however (when I was not out impressing the girls with my PFC stripe) a cautious reserve prevailed. We talked haltingly, carefully, probing as uncertainly as two neophyte premed students might explore their first skin boil.

On the third or fourth day The Old Man woke me on the sleeping 7 porch, lunch bucket in hand. "Lawrence," he said, "your mother found a bottle of whisky in your suitcase. Now, you know this is a teetotal home. We never had a bottle of whisky in a home of ours, and we been married since 19-and-11. You're perfectly welcome to stay here, but your whisky's not." I stiffly mumbled something about going to a motel. "You know better than that," The Old Man scolded. "We don't want you goin' off to no blamed motel." Then, in a weary exasperation not fully appreciated until dealing with transgressions among my own off-spring: "Good God, son, what makes you want to raise ole billy hell all the time?" We regarded each other in a helpless silence. "Do what you think is right," he said, sighing. "I've done told you how me and your mother feel." He went off to work; I got up and removed the offending liquids.

The final morning brought a wet freeze blowing down from Amarillo 8 by way of the North Pole. The Old Man's car wouldn't start; our family had never officially recognized taxis. "I'll walk you to the bus station," he said, bundling in a heavy sheepskin jumper and turning his back, I suspect, so as not to witness my mother's struggle against tears. We shivered down dark streets, past homes of my former schoolmates, by vacant lots where I played softball or slept off secret sprees, past stores I remembered for their bargains in Moon Pies and then Lucky Strikes and finally Trojans. Nostalgia and old guilts blew in with the wind. I wanted to say something healing to The Old Man, to utter some gracious good-bye (the nearest thing to retroactive apologies a savage young pride would permit), but I simply knew no beginnings.

We sat an eternity in the unreal lights of the bus station among crying ₉
babies, hung-over cowboys, and drowsing old Mexican men, in mute
inspection of those dead shows provided by bare walls and ceilings. The
Old Man made a silent offering of a cigarette. He was a vigorous fifty-nine
then, still clear eyed, dark haired, and muscular, but as his hand extended
that cigarette pack and I saw it clearly—weather cured, scarred, one finger
crooked and stiff jointed from an industrial accident—I suddenly and
inexplicably knew that one day The Old Man would wither, fail, die. In
that moment, I think, I first sensed—if I did not understand—something
of mortality; of tribes, blood, and inherited rituals.

❀   ❀   ❀

AFTER YOU READ

THINK about what young Lawrence realizes in the bus station. This
realization functions as the main idea of the essay. Can you state it in your
own words?

EXAMINE the father's attitude toward his son and the son's attitude toward
his father. How are they the same and how are they different? With which
one do you identify more closely? Why?

EXAMINE also the large number of references to specific objects, people,
and events that King includes in the essay. How do these specific details
help you to visualize the time and place in which the narrative takes place?
How do they help you understand the son's emotional reactions to his
father?

WRITE a character sketch of "The Old Man." Discuss at least three of his
major qualities, supporting each quality with specific examples from the
story. Or WRITE a personal essay in which you tell about an argument or
fight you had with a parent or some other authority figure when you were
young. Include in your narrative as many specific details as possible so that
your reader will be able to "experience" the event you are describing as
vividly as possible. In the first or last paragraph of your essay, discuss briefly
or at least imply the meaning that this event had for you.

Never in My Life

WALTER MCDONALD

Like the essay by Larry King, this poem focuses on the relationship between a father and son. The poet, Walter McDonald, often explores family relationships in his poetry. In this poem, which was originally published in the collection entitled Burning the Fence *(1981), McDonald tells of the difficulty a father and son have in communicating openly with each other. Like King, he suggests that strong feelings between a father and son often go unexpressed.*

BEFORE YOU READ

THINK about the difference between father-son and mother-daughter relationships. Do you think that females can discuss their feelings more openly than males? Why or why not?

EXAMINE the way in which the poem appears on the page. Notice that it is divided into nine stanzas and that some of the stanzas do not end with a complete sentence but continue the sentence to the next stanza. Notice too that the title of the poem is part of the first sentence of the first stanza.

WRITE a journal entry beginning with "Never in my life" in which you tell about something that you have wanted or planned to do but for some reason delayed or neglected to do.

AS YOU READ

Try to determine not only what the son tells his father but why he had so much difficulty saying it.

Never in My Life

had I heard my father mention
love. By twelve I felt something
missing, a girlfriend, or millions
of rabbits I needed to murder.
By twenty I knew, but told myself   5
it did not matter. I had never told him,

either. By thirty, after years
of emergencies and two children,
I admitted to myself it did.
By forty, after a war and another child,   10
I resolved before we died
we would say it.
I returned from Southeast Asia

to hold my wife, each child,
to bless or to be blessed by father.   15
We shook hands. Months passed
the same. One night they rushed him
to the hospital. Drugged, for days
he lived by shots and tubes.
The night his hands moved   20

I lingered in the room,
the nurse waiting with crossed arms
while I studied this man
who fought in Flanders.
Bending down   25
louder than I meant
I called his name.

The dim eyes opened,
tried focusing
without glasses.   30
Up past the failing heart,
he mumbled Humm?
I touched the blue vein
of our blood that throbbed

beneath his head's pale skin, slowly,   35
slowly pulsing. I brushed his sparse

white wisps of hair back into place,
held my hand on his cool skull
and spoke the words.
His breathing stopped.   40
I thought *I've killed him.*

At last his dry lips closed.
He breathed again. Somewhere
far back of the blur in his eyes
I imagined electrons flashing,   45
decoding this dim disturbing news
for his numbed brain.
Squinting, his eyes sank far away,

away from me and from the ceiling,
down maybe to his childhood   50
and his own dead father's doors.
The empty eyes jerked back
and focused on my face.
Fiercely I focused too
and kept the contact tight.   55

Then the drugs drowned him again
in sleep. It was enough,
was all I could receive or ever give
to him. Even in that glaze
that stared toward death,   60
I had seen him take me in,
been blessed by what I needed all my life.

❀   ❀   ❀

AFTER YOU READ

THINK about why McDonald uses the phrase "our blood" in the fifth
stanza when he is describing his father's vein. When the poet states in the
sixth stanza that he "spoke the words," what do you think he said? Do you
and your classmates agree about what you think was said? Do you think
the father heard him? Was it more important for the son to say the words
or the father to hear them?

EXAMINE the poem to identify its references to war. Can you identify the two wars from the clues that are given? Is it significant that both father and son fought in major wars? What is the difference in the kind of courage it takes to fight a war and the kind of courage it takes to express feelings openly?

WRITE a paragraph (or a poem) using the sentence you wrote earlier ("Never in my life . . .") as the topic sentence (first line). Include as many specific, vivid details as possible. Remember to include details that appeal to the senses of touch, hearing, smell, and sound as well as sight.

Sibling Imprints

FRANCINE KLAGSBRUN

A successful editor and writer, Francine Klagsbrun has edited and contributed to both the Encyclopedia Americana *and* The World Book Encyclopedia. *She has written many informative books for children and has contributed to* Ms., Seventeen, *and* Newsweek. *In the following selection, which is an excerpt from her recent book* Mixed Feelings: Love, Hate, Rivalry, and Reconciliation Among Brothers and Sisters *(1992), Klagsbrun draws on her personal experiences with her brother Robert Lifton, whose success as a businessman parallels Klagsbrun's own success as a writer.*

BEFORE YOU READ

THINK about your personal experiences with (or observations of) sibling relationships. What feelings were dominant in these sibling relationships—love, jealousy, competition, or some other feeling?

EXAMINE the title of the selection. How can siblings "imprint" one another?

WRITE a journal entry about your experiences with (or observations of) a sibling relationship.

AS YOU READ

Notice how Klagsbrun captures your attention with a clear, concrete example of the relationship she shared with her brother. She then provides thoughtful commentary and analysis of her own sibling relationship as well as of sibling relationships in general.

One Sunday afternoon of my childhood stands out in sharp relief from 1 all others. It's a grueling hot day in mid-July. We are on the way home—my father and mother, my brother Robert, and I—from a day at Jones Beach, about an hour's drive from our Brooklyn apartment. I am around six years old and my brother around ten.

We have been inching along, stuck in a massive traffic jam. Perspiring 2 from the stifling heat (air conditioners in cars as yet unknown), our bodies raw from the mixture of sunburn and dried ocean salt and itching from the tiny grains of sand we have not bothered to wipe away with our towels, Robert and I fight constantly in the back seat. Irritated, my father finally pulls off the road and rearranges the seating, my brother in back with my mother, and I with my father up front. To quiet us, he also buys each a Dixie cup—those little round containers filled with equal amounts of chocolate and vanilla ice cream.

I begin nibbling at my ice cream with the flat wooden spoon that 3 accompanies it, and in nibbling I hatch a delicious plan. I will eat slowly, so slowly that I will finish *last*. I'll have ice cream left after Robert has gulped down all of his, and just when he might be wishing for more, I'll produce mine. "Look," I'll say, "*I* still have ice cream to eat." What I will mean is that I have something he doesn't have, that this time I will have beaten him, this older brother whom I adore and idolize, but who has always bested me.

So I nibble slowly at my ice cream with my wooden spoon, and it begins 4 to melt.

"Are you finished with your ice cream?" I call out every few minutes. 5

"No, not yet," he answers. 6

On we drive, and the heat becomes more intense, and the ice cream 7 melts and melts until the chocolate runs into the vanilla, and the cup turns warm and sticky.

"Are you finished yet?" I turn around to try to see how much ice cream 8 he has left, but he holds his cup close to his chest.

"Not yet." And my ice cream is now warm liquid, the chocolate and 9 vanilla completely blended.

Then, finally, triumph. 10

"I'm finished," he says. 11

"Ha-ha," I shout in glorying delight just as I had imagined it. "*I* still 12 have *my* ice cream." I hold up my cup, crushed and leaking now, to show him. "I scream, you scream, we all scream for ice cream," I chant, and in the next moment quickly gulp down the syrupy mixture. It bears little resemblance to the cool treat it had once been, yet nothing I have ever tasted is as pleasing to me as this victory.

"Ha-ha yourself." My brother's voice, rocking with laughter, rises from 13 the back seat as I swallow the last drop. "I fooled you. I still have mine." Leaning forward, he shows me the leftover in his own cup, then proceeds to drink slowly, all the while bending close to my face so that my utter defeat will not for one second be lost on me.

Tricked! But worse. He has won again. I cannot make my mark. I 14 cannot get a leg up on him, not even with a cup of ice cream soup. I bellow with the pain only a child knows who has been totally outwitted.

"It's not fair!" I scream. "He always gets what he wants. He always has 15 more than I have. I can never win. I can never have anything of my own."

My brother roars with glee. "I scream, you scream, we all scream for 16 ice cream," he mocks as I bawl uncontrollably. My parents laugh also, scolding me for acting like a baby. Why all this fuss? It's nothing more than ice cream, after all. What difference does it make who ate it first?

But I know what the fuss is about. It's about much more than ice cream. 17 It's about coming out ahead for once. It's about establishing myself and holding my own. It's about being recognized.

Decades pass.   18

I am now a writer and my brother a businessman.   19

"You know, don't you," my husband says to me one evening when I'm 20 describing to him some of my research and findings about adult siblings, "that I make a point of trying to avoid putting myself into situations with you that you would perceive as competitive?"

"What do you mean?" I ask cautiously.   21

Although my husband is a psychiatrist, there has long been an unspo- 22 ken agreement between us that he not apply the tools of his profession to our family life. Little psychological jargon ever gets tossed around our home, and few of our discussions—or arguments—serve as sources for analytic interpretations. Now, however, I feel a worm of suspicion gnawing within. What is he trying to tell me?

"You've been talking about the influence of siblings," he says, "and I 23 was thinking that I try to steer clear of situations that would stir up in you the old feelings of competition you have with Robert."

"First of all," I reply, "Robert and I get along just fine. Secondly, my 24 old competitions with him have nothing to do with anything that goes on between us—you and me. Third of all . . ." I hesitate. "So what kinds of situations have you avoided that you think would make me feel competitive toward you?"

"Well," he says slowly, "I haven't written a book, even though I've 25 thought about doing so from time to time."

"Written a book!" I explode. "Why should you write a book? *I'm* the 26
writer in the family. You run a hospital, you hold academic appointments.
You have everything you want. Why should you move in on my turf? Why
can't I ever have anything of my own?" Echoing that long-forgotten wail
of childhood, I add with fervor, "It's not fair!"

I stop, astonished at the vehemence of my reaction.   27

"Okay," I say, trying to laugh. "You made your point. Maybe I do repeat 28
with you some of the competitive feelings I had with Robert. Let's drop
this subject."

"Sure."   29

"Want some ice cream?"   30

I have never been unaware of the importance my brother holds in my life. 31
That awareness, in fact, motivated this book, with its goal of exploring and
unraveling the mysteries of sibling attachments. But it was not until I was
well into my investigations, not until my conversation with my husband,
that I became truly conscious of the lasting imprint my relationship with
my brother has had on all aspects of my existence, including my marriage.

What I discovered in myself I have seen operating in others as well. 32
The effects of our early experiences with brothers and sisters remain with
us long after childhood has ended, long after the experiences themselves
have faded into the past, influencing us as adults in ways we rarely
recognize, from the intimate relationships we establish with lovers and
spouses, to the attitudes we carry into the workplace, to our behavior
toward our children.

The woman who, twice, married and divorced "exciting, dynamic and 33
irresponsible" men much like her younger brother is an example of the
potency of that sibling influence. So is the corporate executive who time
and again, without realizing it, stops himself from going after the top
position in his company because somewhere within he believes that only
his older brother and not he is capable of filling such a role. And so too—to
take one more example—is the lawyer who describes growing up with a
domineering older sister who physically and emotionally grabbed everything from her: clothes, toys, eventually even her friends.

"My sister dominates my life," the lawyer says, although they live miles 34
apart and have little contact. She explains: "I still can't deal with any kind
of rivalry. If I know someone else is competing with me for a client, I pull
back. But at the same time, I feel despondent if the client doesn't come to
me, as if I've lost out to my sister again. I have the same reaction to love
triangles. I get into a terrible state if I think another woman is at all

interested in a man I'm going out with. I don't want someone I care about to be taken away from me the way my sister took everything that meant something. But neither can I fight for what I want."

More aware of such inner conflicts, perhaps, than many people, she 35 says, "In every relationship that I encounter, I reenact what I had with my sister."

We usually associate such reenactments with our parents, and certainly 36 both professional and popular literature have made us conscious of the dominant and lasting impact of our parents on our lives. Yet the more closely one examines the sibling experience, the more evident it becomes that the bond between brothers and sisters leaves its own stamp, separate and apart from the mark parents make, and, in turn, demands scrutiny on its own.

Unlike the ties between parents and children, the connection among 37 siblings is a horizontal one. That is, sibs exist on the same plane, as peers, more or less equals. Although one may be stronger or more dominant than others, brothers and sisters rarely exert the kind of power and authority over one another that parents hold over their children. Nor are there rules, codes of behavior for different stages of life or biblical commandments mandating siblings to respect and honor one another as they must respect and honor parents. As a result they are freer, more open, and generally more honest with each other, than they are with parents, and less fearful of punishment or rejection. As children, they say what is on their minds, without censoring their words or concerning themselves about the long-range effects of their emotions on one another. Even as adults, many sibs speak more bluntly to each other than they dare to friends or colleagues.

The freedom siblings enjoy with one another and the peer status they 38 hold also allow them greater intimacy than they have with their mothers or fathers. In growing up, sisters and brothers often spend more time alone together than they do with parents, and they get to know each other in ways that their parents never know them. An older child reexperiences her own past in playing with a younger one. The younger learns from sharing the older's activities, and in the process comes to understand both his sib and himself.

Together, siblings become experts in penetrating each other's thoughts 39 and feelings. Studies of empathy among young children have found that toddlers as young as two or three are able to interpret for their parents baby siblings' expressions and noises and explain a baby's wishes that a mother or father doesn't understand. "He wants to go out," an older child will say, or, "She's hungry," or, "Pick her up, Mommy," and usually the information will be correct.

Siblings have a compelling need to accumulate the knowledge they 40
have of each other. Each *wants* to know what makes the other tick. Each
wants to know which buttons to press to make the other cry or cringe. Each
also wants to know how to make the other laugh and how to win the other's
love and approval. In its intensity, their mutual knowledge becomes
all-embracing—a naked understanding that encompasses the very essence
of the other's being.

Once gained, that gut understanding remains a crucial part of the 41
link between siblings for life. Even after years of separation, an adult
brother or sister may quickly, intuitively, pick up on another's thoughts,
sympathize with the other's needs, or zero in—unerringly—on the other's
insecurities.

The intimate knowledge siblings hold is not limited to themselves; it 42
also includes knowledge of their parents. Sibs are able to validate for one
another realities about their parents. They may be the only ones who know,
for instance, that beneath the wit and charm the world sees in their parents
lies a cold, mutual anger that causes the family great suffering. More
important, children often blame themselves for a parent's cruel or disturbed behavior. A brother or sister helps free the other from his guilt and
blame, helps define family conditions for the other.

Discussing the pain of growing up with an abusive, alcoholic father, 43
one man said, "My older sister was like an oasis I could escape to. I could
bounce things off her and say, 'Hey, what's happening?' and she would
reassure me that none of it was my fault, that it had nothing to do with
me. I'll always be grateful to her for that."

But even in happy homes young siblings become allies. They may fight 44
and scream at each other, but they also offer one another solace and safety
in a world that appears overwhelmingly stacked in favor of adults. They
share secrets parents never hear, and communicate with each other through
signals and codes, private languages whose meanings only they know.

One of my sweetest recollections of the past is that of lying in bed late 45
at night, speaking to my brother through the wall of our adjoining rooms.
We speak loudly, oblivious of our parents in their bedroom down the hall.
We imitate characters on the radio shows we listen to addictively, or we
talk "silly talk," making up nonsense words and sounds that send us into
peals of laughter and affirm for me that nobody is as clever and funny as
my big brother.

"Shush," my mother quiets us angrily. "Go to sleep, both of you." 46

We snort as we try to squelch the waves of giggles that envelop us, 47
dizzyingly conscious of our superiority to the parents we have excluded
from our club.

"Are you asleep?" we continue to call out to each other in stage   48
whispers until the voice down the hall sounds as though it means business,
and one of us drifts off.

Through their clubby confidences and shared secrets, through the time   49
they spend alone and the knowledge they gain, siblings learn to cooperate
and get along together. They discover the meaning of loyalty, and master
skills in defending one another against the outside even in the midst of their
own angers or vicious battles. They cultivate their ability to have fun, to
laugh and make jokes. They gain their first experiences in knowing
themselves as individuals but also as persons connected to others. In short,
they learn what it means to be "we" and not just "I."

Eventually what siblings learn with each other gets transferred to their   50
dealings with the world beyond the family, to schoolmates and friends, later
to adult peers.

With their learning and knowledge siblings also build a personal   51
history that serves as a reference point through the years. That is not to say
that brothers and sisters have identical histories. Each child in a family
experiences life differently, relates differently to parents, and creates a
different and unique environment for the other. Yet there is a family ethos
and a pool of memories—of parental attitudes, of humor and expectations,
of vacations and hard times—that transcend individual experiences and
form a common past for siblings.

The pull of memory and history and the rewards of sibling compan-   52
ionship draw adult brothers and sisters to each other in spite of their
differences.

❀   ❀   ❀

AFTER YOU READ

THINK about how one sibling can "imprint" or influence another sibling's
life. In class discussion, give examples of such imprints from the reading as
well as from your personal experience and observation.

EXAMINE the author's conversation with her husband on pp. 104–105.
What discovery does she make about herself as well as about her relationships with her brother and her husband?

WRITE a brief essay describing the relationship between siblings. Be sure
that your essay contains a clear thesis, or main point, about that relationship. Or WRITE an essay comparing the relationship that an individual
shares with a sibling to the relationship he or she shares with a friend.

The Letter

RUDOLFO ANAYA

*Novelist, short story writer, essayist, folklorist, and pro-
fessor at the University of New Mexico, Rudolfo Anaya is
best known for his award-winning novel* Bless Me, Ultima
*(1972). Anaya has also written two other novels—*Tortuga
(1979) and Albuquerque *(1992). In this selection from*
Albuquerque, *Abrán makes a surprising discovery that
causes him to question his identity.*

BEFORE YOU READ

THINK about the effect on a child of not knowing the identity of his or her
parents—or of finding out that one's parents are not who one thought they
were. How would you feel in this situation?

EXAMINE the Spanish words that you will find in this reading. A *barrio* is
a Spanish community or neighborhood that exists within or beside a larger
city; the term implies a close confederation of supportive people. The other
terms are all forms that mean "little." Abrán calls his mother *jefita,* which
means "a little female boss." In turn, Abrán's mother addresses him as *hijito*
or *mi'jito,* her little son. Meaning "little blond one," *guerito* derives from
guero, a word meaning "blond."

WRITE a journal entry predicting the contents of "the letter" in the story.
Before you write your prediction, read paragraphs 3 and 11.

AS YOU READ

Notice Abrán's reaction to the contents of the letter. Underline passages
that show his reaction.

Abrán turned south on Fourth into the Barelas barrio and home. Dusk 1
was settling over the neighborhood. He pulled into his driveway, then
stopped at the door and paused to break a sprig of yellow forsythia for his
mother.

When he entered, the aroma of food filled his nostrils. Chile, beans, 2
potatoes frying, hot tortillas. "Mamá!" he called. Always Mamá or jefita.
He never called her by her name, Sara. She was in her late fifties and proud,
she said, to be old-fashioned. Dinners were important, and they centered
around her son. I cook for you to please you, she said. Your father was like
that, the evening meal was special. It was a time for family to be together.

"Sorry I'm late," he said as he picked up the mail at the telephone table 3
and entered the kitchen. The envelope had a St. Joseph Hospital return
address. A bill? he wondered.

"Mi'jo, I'm glad to see you," his mother smiled as she turned from the 4
salad she was mixing to kiss him. He handed her the flowers. "For the
salad?" she smiled.

"For you. I met Ben Chavéz, the writer. Joe and I dropped in for a beer 5
at Jack's. And there was a fight, not bad, just . . ."

"A fight?"   6

"Not bad. An argument. The writer—"   7

"What writer?" she asked, wiping her hands and putting the sprig of 8
forsythia in a glass of water on the windowsill. The geranium was still
blooming bright red, but the forsythia made her realize spring had arrived.
She would have Abrán turn the soil in the flower bed. And the trim around
the house needed painting.

Abrán opened the letter. "Do we owe St. Joe's?"   9

"No, not that I know. So, tell me about the writer."   10

"He got in a game of pool with a bad character . . ." his voice trailed 11
off as he read the letter. When he finished he looked up at her. A dark,
penetrating look. He was looking for himself in her. She felt her heart skip
a beat, and the fear she had lived with since Abrán became her son surfaced.
It had come. The letter she had feared for so long had come.

"There's a mistake," he said softly and looked at the envelope again, 12
then at the letter.

"What does it say?" she asked, her knees weak, her mouth dry. He had 13
looked at her and did not recognize himself. Santo Niño de Atocha, it was
bound to happen. She had always known it would happen, hadn't she told
herself? She knew that one day he would look at her and not see his
reflection, and she would have to tell him that she and her husband,

Ramiro, had adopted him as a child. He was given to them, and they were made to take a vow never to tell Abrán about his past.

With trembling hands she took the letter. Cynthia Johnson. The pain 14 in her heart grew sharper.

"Sit," he said and he quickly got her a glass of water. She had glanced 15 at the letter and grown pale. He held the glass to her trembling hands and she sipped.

"It's not for me," he said. "A mistake." His voice seemed so far away. 16 Would she lose him? Why was this woman writing now?

"She says she's my mother," he said, then repeated, "a mistake." 17

"No," Sara shook her head. "Not a mistake." Her voice broke, she felt 18 tears in her eyes. "Ay, hijito, hijito," she cried.

He put his arms around her. "Who is she? Why does she call herself 19 my mother?"

He should know the truth. One day he had to know the truth, and if 20 the Johnson woman had broken the vow of silence, now was the time. Sara González had to tell her son she was not his mother. She had promised her husband that when the time came she would tell Abrán.

"There's got to be a mistake. I'll go over to the hospital in the 21 morning—"

"No. Not a mistake," she gasped and wiped her eyes with her apron. 22 She looked into his eyes. She had to be strong, she could not hide the truth from him. "I want you to know I have always loved you," she whispered.

"I know that," Abrán answered, feeling empty inside. The woman who 23 wrote the letter said she was his mother, and when he looked at Sara he knew it was true. It was his turn to feel the shock; his stomach turned and tightened. Sara was not his mother, and Ramiro was not his father. Perhaps he had always known this, but never faced it. He loved them too much, and their love for him was the love of a true father and mother.

"And I love you," he said and held her hands, and felt their strength. 24 "There's a mistake. . . ."

"We adopted you. But we loved you like our son, our own blood." 25

"Adopted?" The word rang hollow and wrenched his soul. The vague 26 dreams of his identity suddenly became a disturbing reality. The light color of his skin, his eyes, his features that were not the features of this woman he called Mother.

You resemble your father, she had told him when he asked, but he 27 remembered his father as a short, dark man. His skin was the color of the earth. Yes, I resemble my father, he agreed, and because he didn't want to trouble her, he asked no more. But in the barrio there were whispers. The old people called him güerito.

"The woman who wrote the letter is your mother." 28

He shook his head, turned and looked at the letter again. Cynthia 29 Johnson. The artist? The daughter of the well-known banker? It couldn't be. Somebody was playing a cruel joke. He was Abrán González, he had always been Abrán González. His mother was sitting in front of him, her name was Sara.

"Adopted?" he heard himself say again, and Sara's eyes told him the 30 world he once knew was slipping away. To steady himself he reached out and touched his mother's hand.

"You were given to us, mi'jito," she said and held his hands tightly. She 31 did not want to let him go. She had raised him, she knew his soul, but he was not of her blood. What would Ramiro say? Tell the boy the truth. She needed Ramiro's strength now that she felt so weak and useless.

"Ramiro worked for the family of el señor Johnson. From the time we 32 came from Guadalupe, he worked for them as the gardener. For a while I worked, cleaning the house. We knew the family; we knew Cynthia from the time she was born."

She took another drink of water and looked into Abrán's eyes. The 33 pain was as much his as hers. Would the truth separate them? She braced herself and continued.

"The girl grew. Cynthia. Cindy, the kids used to call her. When she was 34 in high school she became pregnant. You see, they are rich, they did not want the child."

Me, Abrán thought. They didn't want me. I am that woman's child, 35 the unwanted baby.

"I would not lie to you, my son. It hurts me to tell you this." 36

"Go on," he said. He felt bruised, as if he had taken a beating, as if he 37 had just come in from a long, tiring journey.

"Cynthia's father wanted the girl to have an abortion, but the girl 38 resisted. You were born, and you were given to us."

"But you've never said anything," he groaned. His life had been a lie, 39 and the woman he had called Mother was part of that lie.

"We couldn't," she grasped him. "Don't you see, we gave our word 40 that we would never reveal the truth. El señor Johnson is a very rich man. He made us promise that we would never say anything."

"And my father?" he asked. "Who is he?" 41

There was a long silence, then Sara sighed. "We never knew," she said. 42 "But Cynthia is your mother. Your blood."

He looked again at the letter. "She's dying. Cancer."   43

"That is why she wants to see you."   44

"All these years," he shook his head.   45

She reached out and touched his cheek. "Don't be harsh on me, mi'jito.   46
We did what we had to do. We promised to raise you as best we could.
Ramiro and I didn't have children; we were hungry for children! And don't
be harsh on the woman who is your mother. She provided for you."

"I should have known, I should have asked."   47

"There was nothing to tell you. We took a vow, and until now the   48
woman has never contacted us."

"She sent money?"   49

"Yes. We had enough, Ramiro always worked. After he died she made   50
sure we had what we needed. She was always generous."

"Ah, damn, jefita!" Abrán cried, a sob escaping with the pain he felt.   51
"I don't know what to say." He rose and looked out the kitchen window.
Night had settled on the barrio. His mother rose to remove the food from
the stove.

Where do I belong, Abrán wondered.   52

"I have to see her," he said.   53

"Yes," Sara nodded. "She needs you."   54

"I'll go right away."   55

"Eat first."   56

"Can't."   57

She understood. "I wish I could have made this easier," she said,   58
hugging him. "You are still my son."

"I always will be," he answered and tried to smile. He kissed her   59
forehead and went out the door into the night. But now his world was
different. In the night shadows there lurked a sense of danger. Who am I?
he asked, and he did not know the answer.

❀ ❀ ❀

AFTER YOU READ

THINK about the idea of open adoption—of allowing the birth parent(s)
and the adoptive parent(s) to know each other's identity at the time of
adoption. Do you think this practice would make it easier or more difficult
for an adopted child to adjust to and accept adoption? Would open
adoption have been advisable in Abrán's situation? Why or why not?

EXAMINE paragraphs 26, 27, 52, and 59, which focus on Abrán's confused sense of identity. Analyze the reasons for his confusion. In your opinion, what identity will Abrán ultimately embrace? Why do you feel as you do?

WRITE a letter that Abrán might have written to his birth mother after receiving her letter.

Hold the Mayonnaise

JULIA ALVAREZ

Like Rudolfo Anaya, Julia Alvarez writes about family relationships involving different cultures. In this selection, Alvarez focuses specifically on the relationship between a Latino stepmother and her American stepdaughters. Alvarez is the author of two novels, How the Garcia Girls Lost Their Accents *(1991) and* In the Time of the Butterflies *(1994).*

BEFORE YOU READ

THINK about the stereotype of "the stepmother" as found in stories such as "Hansel and Gretel." Have such stories caused you to form a negative opinion of stepmothers in general? Have you personally known any "stepmothers"? How do your personal experiences and observations compare or contrast with the stereotype?

EXAMINE the title of this selection. With what culture is mayonnaise most closely associated? Can you think of any Latino foods that use mayonnaise?

WRITE a journal entry in which you discuss your reaction—positive or negative—to a particular cultural food.

AS YOU READ

Notice how Alvarez uses mayonnaise as a symbol of American culture. How do her reactions to this food parallel her reactions to American culture in general and to her new American stepdaughters in particular?

"If I die first and Papi ever gets remarried," Mami used to tease when we   1
were kids, "don't you accept a new woman in my house. Make her life
impossible, you hear?" My sisters and I nodded obediently, and a filial
shudder would go through us. We were Catholics, so of course, the only
kind of remarriage we could imagine had to involve our mother's death.

We were also Dominicans, recently arrived in Jamaica, Queens, in the   2
early 60's, before waves of other Latin Americans began arriving. So, when
we imagined who exactly my father might possibly ever think of remarry-
ing, only American women came to mind. It would be bad enough having
a *madrastra,* but a "stepmother."

All I could think of was that she would make me eat mayonnaise, a   3
food I identified with the United States and which I detested. Mami
understood, of course, that I wasn't used to that kind of food. Even a
madrastra, accustomed to our rice and beans and tostones and pollo frito,
would understand. But an American stepmother would think it was normal
to put mayonnaise on food, and if she were at all strict and a little mean,
which all stepmothers, of course, were, she would make me eat potato salad
and such. I had plenty of my own reasons to make a potential stepmother's
life impossible. When I nodded obediently with my sisters, I was imagining
not just something foreign in our house, but in our refrigerator.

So it's strange now, almost 35 years later, to find myself a Latina   4
stepmother of my husband's two tall, strapping, blond, mayonnaise-eating
daughters. To be honest, neither of them is a real aficionado of the
condiment, but it's a fair thing to add to a bowl of tuna fish or diced
potatoes. Their American food, I think of it, and when they head to their
mother's or off to school. I push the jar back in the refrigerator behind
their chocolate pudding and several open cans of Diet Coke.

What I can't push as successfully out of sight are my own immigrant   5
childhood fears of having a *gringa* stepmother with foreign tastes in our
house. Except now, I am the foreign stepmother in a gringa household.
I've wondered what my husband's two daughters think of this stranger in
their family. It must be doubly strange for them that I am from another
culture.

Of course, there are mitigating circumstances—my husband's two   6
daughters were teen-agers when we married, older, more mature, able to
understand differences. They had also traveled when they were children
with their father, an eye doctor, who worked on short-term international
projects with various eye foundations. But still, it's one thing to visit a
foreign country, another altogether to find it brought home—a real bear
plopped down in a Goldilocks house.

Sometimes, a whole extended family of bears. My warm, loud Latino 7
family came up for the wedding: my *tia* from Santo Domingo; three
dramatic, enthusiastic sisters and their families; my papi, with a thick accent
I could tell the girls found it hard to understand; and my mami, who had
her eye trained on my soon-to-be stepdaughters for any sign that they were
about to make my life impossible. "How are they behaving themselves?"
she asked me, as if they were 7 and 3, not 19 and 16. "They're wonderful
girls," I replied, already feeling protective of them.

I looked around for the girls in the meadow in front of the house we 8
were building, where we were holding the outdoor wedding ceremony and
party. The oldest hung out with a group of her own friends. The younger
one whizzed in briefly for the ceremony, then left again before the
congratulations started up. There was not much mixing with me and mine.
What was there for them to celebrate on a day so full of confusion and
effort?

On my side, being the newcomer in someone else's territory is a role 9
I'm used to. I can tap into that struggling English speaker, that skinny,
dark-haired, olive-skinned girl in a sixth grade of mostly blond and
blue-eyed giants. Those tall, freckled boys would push me around in the
playground. "Go back to where you came from!" "*No comprendo!*" I'd
reply, though of course there was no misunderstanding the fierce looks on
their faces.

Even now, my first response to a scowl is that old pulling away. (My 10
husband calls it "checking out.") I remember times early on in the marriage
when the girls would be with us, and I'd get out of school and drive around
doing errands, killing time, until my husband, their father, would be leaving
work. I am not proud of my fears, but I understand—as the lingo goes—
where they come from.

And I understand, more than I'd like to sometimes, my stepdaughters' 11
pain. But with me, they need never fear that I'll usurp a mother's place.
No one has ever come up and held their faces and then addressed me,
"They look just like you." If anything, strangers to the remarriage are
probably playing Mr. Potato Head in their minds, trying to figure out how
my foreign features and my husband's fair Nebraskan features got put
together into these two tall, blond girls. "My husband's daughters," I kept
introducing them.

Once, when one of them visited my class and I introduced her as such, 12
two students asked me why. "I'd be so hurt if my stepmom introduced me
that way," the young man said. That night I told my stepdaughter what my
students had said. She scowled at me and agreed. "It's so weird how you

call me Papa's daughter. Like you don't want to be related to me or something."

"I didn't want to presume," I explained. "So it's O.K. if I call you my stepdaughter?" 13

"That's what I am," she said. Relieved, I took it for a teensy inch of acceptance. The takings are small in this stepworld, I've discovered. Sort of like being a minority. It feels as if all the goodies have gone somewhere else. 14

Day to day, I guess I follow my papi's advice. When we first came, he would talk to his children about how to make it in our new country. "Just do your work and put in your heart, and they will accept you!" In this age of remaining true to your roots, of keeping your Spanish, of fighting from inside your culture, that assimilationist approach is highly suspect. My Latino students—who don't want to be called Hispanics anymore—would ditch me as faculty adviser if I came up with that play-nice message. 15

But in a stepfamily where everyone is starting a new life together, it isn't bad advice. Like a potluck supper, an American concept my mami never took to. ("Why invite people to your house and then ask them to bring the food?") You put what you've got together with what everyone else brought and see what comes out of the pot. The luck part is if everyone brings something you like. No potato salad, no deviled eggs, no little party sandwiches with you know what in them. 16

❁ ❁ ❁

AFTER YOU READ

THINK about how Julia Alvarez felt not only as a new stepmother but as a stepmother to children of a different culture. Describe her feelings toward her new stepdaughters. During the story, how do these feelings change and why?

EXAMINE the phrase "my husband's daughters" that Alvarez uses to introduce her stepdaughters. What does this phrase show about her feelings about herself as well as those about her stepdaughters? What prompts her to change the way she introduces her stepdaughters, and how does this simple change improve her relationship with her stepdaughters?

WRITE an essay in which you first identify one or more problems of adjustment that are common to step-families such as Alvarez's family. Then propose a solution for the problem(s) that you have identified.

Wanted—A Mother

ORVILLE RAWLINS

Born on the island of Puerto Rico, Orville Rawlins grew up on the British West Indian island of St. Kitts, which is the setting for the following essay. A journalism and French major, Rawlins first published this essay in the 1993 edition of Write-On, *an annual anthology of essays written in freshman English classes at East Texas State University.*

BEFORE YOU READ

THINK about the title of the essay: "Wanted—A Mother." Since you discover in the first paragraph that Rawlins does indeed have a mother, what do you think he means by this title?

EXAMINE Rawlins's use of the word *bastard* in paragraphs 1 and 4. What does he mean by the word in each case? How do these meanings differ? In your opinion, is the shock value of the word effective? **EXAMINE** also Rawlins's comment about an English assignment designed to increase his vocabulary. Is the vocabulary he uses in his essay more sophisticated than that of the average freshman student? If you find three or four words that you do not know, first try to determine their meanings in context and then look the words up in a dictionary. For example, you will discover that the "maelstrom of emotions" (paragraph 5) that Rawlins felt when he discovered his mother could not read was a "great confusion" of emotions. Literally, a *maelstrom* is a whirlpool.

WRITE a journal entry explaining how a child must feel to "want" a mother or a father. Are a child's major "wants" for a parent physical, emotional, or psychological? Explain.

AS YOU READ

Notice how Rawlins's attitude toward his mother changes. What causes this change, and how and when does he express his new attitude?

I was born the bastard child of a cop and a maid—born in a foreign land 1
called Puerto Rico to illegals who had no green card. We were always on the run. Eventually we ran out of Puerto Rico. They named me Orville Ira Rawlins and I hated them both.

I grew up on a small Caribbean island called St. Kitts where poor 2
niggers lived with rich black folk and stoned-out expatriates afraid to confront their national demons. My mother did her best by me. I can never say like other folks that my life was a struggle; in comparison I had a cruise. She worked at Mr. Blake's plantation house for $30.00 a week, and we all thought that she had one of the plum jobs. Breakfast, lunch, and dinner were always prepared for me but still that hatred inside festered. I could not find cause or escape for it.

Everyone thought that Violet, that's my mom, had a nice child. 3
Everybody said so.

"Laud he look so good," they said in that Caribbean dialect. They 4
always tried to touch me. I hated that, being touched, fondled, and kissed, especially by these toothless crones. I didn't give a damn that my clothes were sometimes hand-me-downs from their kids. I just wanted to be left alone. When I was ten years old, my father left us. No! He left my mother. I never needed him. However, I still hated him for doing that because Violet became a simpering sycophant. Kept telling me how I was the only thing in her world that made sense. I found that scary, because to me, I didn't make sense. She made me angry by her dependance on other people for her happiness. I felt that that was a dangerous weakness. It seems that I was an intelligent child. Everybody said so. I was always at the top of my class. I wanted it that way—not just to be the best that I could be; just better than all the rest. I was a selfish, arrogant bastard who was trying to prove himself better than everyone else.

November 25 came. It was a rainy day. Storm clouds and equally foul 5
winds were the order of the day. That year I was about fourteen years old. I had an assignment for English about increasing your vocabulary. I took it home to Violet to get her help. When I gave her the book she said nothing, did nothing; an opaque film seemed to come across her eyes. I looked at her and then I looked at the book. It was upside down. Then it hit me. My

mother could not read. She could NOT READ. Up to this day it's impossible to totally explain my feelings, to come to grips with the maelstrom of emotions that I felt. Shame, shock, anger, pain, disgust—they all flashed through my mind, heart, and soul; each one more powerful than the last. God, it hurt. I looked at her and in that one moment, it all came together; I felt nothing but an insane, powerful disgust at this woman who could NOT READ.

From that day onward, our roles changed in that household. I became 6 a virtual lord. Never again would I eat boiled rice and chicken. I decided the menu. She would ask me daily what I wanted for dinner and I would order only what I liked, and she would cook it. My excesses were a painful price for her to pay, but my pain and shame were excessive. If someone were to ask me what I was doing to Violet, I wouldn't have a coherent clue of a reason fitting my actions. I thought I was making her pay for being dumb and illiterate, but I was paying more. I was becoming a scary specter, not only to Violet, but to myself.

At nights, I would lie down and think about my thoughts. Yes, I would 7 actually ponder a certain situation, my reaction to it, and then wonder why. Why did I want to hurt her so? She never resisted my demands, never refused me anything. She loved me, I knew. God knows I couldn't feel that soulful connection; our lives just never meshed. I hated her. This relationship continued for about three years. During this time, I was becoming something of a farce. Amongst friends, I was friendly toward her, but at home all my disappointments and frustrations imploded. My anger, like an all-consuming bile, flew outward, and in front of it all, covered my mother. So I gained strength, like a demon sucking the will out of a living, breathing soul. Yes, that's what I was, a damned demon. I half-heartedly tried to exorcise these thoughts, but I failed; the truth was, I was enjoying it.

At age seventeen, graduating from high school, she was there, she was 8 proud, she was crying. I was just hoping that she wouldn't say anything stupid to embarrass me. "If you ain't got anything to say, don't say it," on that we were in total agreement. Man that was a great day, top of my class and valedictorian. I felt good. She gave me a watch that day. My name was inscribed on the back. I'm sure it must have cost her a pretty penny, but she bought it. It's what I had asked for. At that time she must have been hitting forty but still looking all right.

My grandfather came visiting one day. He came down from Nevis for 9 a wedding and was going to stay with us for a couple of days. Violet slept on the couch. He used her bed. It was a beautiful night, the night of his visit.

The next day dawned beautiful. I swear to God it was the most 10
beautiful day that I had ever seen. The flowers were in full bloom. Their
scents filled the Caribbean air. Obviously I wasn't the only one to appreciate
the blue sky and bungainvillea-perfumed air. People were out changing
curtains and taking advantage of the good weather to paint roofs and get
rid of old bric-a-brac accumulated in their houses over the years. I was
supposed to accompany my grandfather up to our family plot in the
mountains. This was the spot where we used to grow our vegetables and
animal feed. He wanted to touch base with his youth I guess; anyway, I
went along.

The path was long and winding, but the views were magnificent. At 11
some points you could see the beautiful Atlantic in the distance, the coral
reef becalming the inner waters. It was so beautiful. I had seen it before,
of course, but this day seemed to have made nature look down upon herself
and improve on her countenance. We were pretty silent up to that point,
content just to take in the vistas. That's when it happened.

A female monkey ran across our path followed by a wild dog foaming 12
at the mouth. Minutes later we heard a shriek of pain and instantly knew
the outcome of the chase. We kept on walking. A few yards into the woods,
crouched on a rock, was a baby monkey, eyes wide open, trembling with
fear. I remember scooping it up and holding it against my chest to comfort
it. It relaxed considerably. Grandfather began talking then.

He spoke a lot about when he was rearing his kids. How he could 13
barely feed them all. He recalled the times when mackerel and dumplings
constituted dinner for months on end. He told me that he used to beat the
hell out of his kids for refusing to eat the same fare. He taught them to be
satisfied with what they had by literally beating it into them. As he spoke,
tears came to his eyes. He told me of times when there was nothing to eat
save for the fruits which grew in the yard: guavas, pineapples, mangoes
and the like. His voice broke when he told me how ashamed he was that
he couldn't provide for his family which numbered fourteen. Then, with
phlegm running from his nose, tears from his eyes, he looked at me and
for the next hour told me the story of my life. This story became my
linchpin for the future.

"You know," he said, "that monkey reminds me a lot of Violet.   14

"She was my first child. I always wanted a boy for my first, but she 15
came—God's will, I guess. She was a very quiet baby, never complained,
yet her eyes always seemed to be laughing at you. Parson said he never saw
such a child.

"He said that she was going to be a strong child, long-suffering, and 16
Lawd, that she was. After her I had eleven sons, yes, a whole bunch of them.

Everybody said how it was killing my wife young, but back then
"frenchies"* weren't around. Every time we did it, a child came along, just
like damn guinea pigs.

"When they got to school age that's when the nightmare started. There 17
was no way in God's world that I could feed them, clothe them, and send
them all to school. Somebody had to be left out. Somebody had to help
with the cattle and sheep and "work the ground."† For days, months even,
I pondered my choices; how could a father in good conscience keep some
of his children out of school, some half-clothed, and all fed? Who among
them should I deny? Believe me, Orville, I loved them all equally.

"One night Violet came to me. She must have been thirteen years old 18
at the time. I tell you, her eyes were wise; she looked as if she knew exactly
what I was holding on my chest, what questions were going through my
mind. And she said quite clearly, 'Daddy, I'm going to drop out of school
and look for a job. You know I don't like school no how.'

"And me, coward that I was, I agreed without pause. And so she got a 19
job at the police cafeteria. That's where she met your father, I suppose. She
started selling the eggs from our chickens in the yard. She was very
industrious. They paid her well, and the money put her brothers through
school. She was the reason they stayed in school. My word, look at them
now—two doctors, a cop, a teacher, a minister, Godwin's a lieutenant-
colonel in the U.S. Army, one's a lab technician, three of them are registered
contractors with their own business, and Bal's an interpreter at Foreign
Affairs. Never in my wildest dreams would I have thought such success
possible."

I wondered if he ever thought about the eleventh child, the success she 20
had. She was, after all, a successful waitress.

He picked up on his story. "That monkey gave up her life to distract 21
the dog from her young. She gave her child a chance to survive. Your mother
gave your uncles that chance, and I'm proud of her for it. I will never be
able to repay her; all I can do is love her for who she is."

I fought myself to deflate the pinpricks of pride that I felt then for my 22
mother. I'm not going to say that I rushed home instantly to beg her
forgiveness. That would be a gross misrepresentation of the truth. We
walked home slowly, silently, our minds on distant oases of times gone by.
When I got home I asked mommy to cook boiled rice and chicken. For me,
it was a start. I got rid of most of my animosities by starting two gardens:

---

*frenchies: french letters, condoms.
†work the ground: engage in land cultivation.

a vegetable garden in the back yard and a flower garden in front. I loved the flower garden more, and I think mommy did too because she used to cut the flowers every day for the vases inside.

August 3, 1989. This day began very ordinarily. I woke up and 23 showered. I walked out into the dining room, and she was there, preparing breakfast as usual. I walked up behind her and held her around the waist. Her body visibly trembled, then sagged as if it had lost some of it's strength. I said, "I hope you have a good day, Mom." And then the tears started. . . .

⚜ ⚜ ⚜

AFTER YOU READ

THINK about Rawlins's shame and resentment of his mother for being illiterate. Is this reaction cruel? Is it realistic? How does it exhibit a kind of emotional abuse more often associated with a parent's actions toward a child? How does Rawlins's description of himself in paragraphs 1–4 prepare you for his reaction?

EXAMINE the passage in paragraph 4 in which Rawlins writes, "When I was ten years old, my father left us. No! He left my mother. I never needed him." How does Rawlins's reaction to his father differ from his reaction to his mother? Do you think that his feelings toward his father and his father's absence have affected Rawlins's feelings and actions toward his mother? If so, how?

EXAMINE also paragraph 12, in which the monkey sacrifices her life for her child. How, according to Violet's father, was Violet like the female monkey?

WRITE an essay in which you discuss some of the problems that may occur in a single-parent family, such as the one described by Rawlins. What causes these problems, and how might they be solved?

The Family Values Debate

JAMES Q. WILSON

Sociologist Ian Robertson has described the family as "the most basic and ancient of all institutions" and "the fundamental social unit in every society."* Yet people disagree widely on the function of the family and on the values that it represents or develops in its members. In the following essay, James Q. Wilson analyzes the "family values debate" as found among public policymakers as well as ordinary citizens.

Wilson began his career as a political science professor and is now a nationally recognized expert in the field of criminology; he is frequently interviewed by news magazines such as Time *and* Newsweek. *Currently the Collins Professor of Management and Public Policy at the University of California at Los Angeles, he is the author of many books including* Crime and Human Nature, On Character, *and* The Moral Sense.

BEFORE YOU READ

THINK about the phrase "family values debate." What does it mean? How—and how often—have you heard this term used in recent years? How does it have political as well as social significance?

EXAMINE the first sentence of the reading, which contrasts the views of "the public" and the "policy elites." Policy elites are those educated and influential members of government, education, and the media who interpret and set policies that the public is encouraged or required to follow. Do you agree or disagree with Wilson that the public and the policy elites hold different views about the contemporary American family—about its

---

*Robertson, Ian. *Sociology,* 3rd ed. (New York: Worth, 1987), p. 137.

definition and about the values it represents? What are these views? Is it possible for these "elites" to set policy about family values? Why or why not?

WRITE a journal entry about the "family values debate" as you have observed it in the media and in your experience. What contrasting views about family do the "debaters" of family values hold? What is your view?

AS YOU READ

Keep a list, underline, or make marginal annotations of the main ideas that you find in the reading. Look especially for the major opposing views in the family values debate as discussed by Wilson and for Wilson's own view.

There are two views about the contemporary American family, one held 1 by the public and the other by policy elites.

The public's view is this: the family is the place in which the most basic 2 values are instilled in children. In recent years, however, these values have become less secure, in part because the family has become weaker and in part because rivals for its influence—notably television and movies—have gotten stronger. One way the family has become weaker is that more and more children are being raised in one-parent families, and often that one parent is a teenage girl. Another way is that parents, whether in one- or two-parent families, are spending less time with their children and are providing poorer discipline. Because family values are so important, political candidates should talk about them, though it is not clear that the government can do much about them. Overwhelmingly, Americans think that it is better for children if one parent stays home and does not work, even if that means having less money.*

No such consensus is found among scholars or policymakers. That in 3 itself is revealing. Beliefs about families that most people regard as virtually self-evident are hotly disputed among people whose job it is to study or support families.

A good example of the elite argument began last fall on the front page 4 of the *Washington Post,* where a reporter quoted certain social scientists as saying that the conventional two-parent family was not as important for the healthy development of children as was once supposed. This prompted David Popenoe, a professor at Rutgers who has written extensively on family issues, to publish in *The New York Times* an op-ed piece challenging the scholars cited in the *Post.* Popenoe asserted that "dozens" of studies had come to the opposite conclusion, and that the weight of the evidence "decisively" supported the view that two-parent families are better than single-parent families.

Decisively to him, perhaps, but not to others. Judith Stacey, another 5 professor of sociology, responded in a letter to the *Times* that the value of a two-parent family was merely a "widely shared prejudice" not confirmed by empirical studies; Popenoe, she said, was trying to convert "misguided nostalgia for 'Ozzie-and-Harriet'-land into social-scientific truth." Arlene and Jerome Skolnick, two more professors, acknowledged that although Popenoe might be correct, saying so publicly would "needlessly stigmatize children raised in families that don't meet the 'Ozzie-and-Harriet' model." After all, the Skolnicks observed, a man raised outside that model had just been elected President of the United States.

The views of Stacey and the Skolnicks are by no means unrepresentative 6 of academic thinking on this subject. Barbara Dafoe Whitehead recently surveyed the most prominent textbooks on marriage and the family. Here is my paraphrase of her summary of what she found:

> The life course is full of exciting options. These include living in a commune, 7
> having a group marriage, being a single parent, or living together. Marriage is
> one life-style choice, but before choosing it people weigh its costs and benefits
> against other options. Divorce is a part of the normal family cycle and is neither
> deviant nor tragic. Rather, it can serve as a foundation for individual renewal
> and new beginnings. Marriage itself should not be regarded as a special,
> privileged institution; on the contrary, it must catch up with the diverse,
> pluralistic society in which we live. For example, same-sex marriages often
> involve more sharing and equality than do heterosexual relationships. But even
> in the conventional family, the relationships between husband and wife need
> to be defined after carefully negotiating agreements that protect each person's
> separate interests and rights.[†]

Many politicians and reporters echo these sentiments and carry the 8 argument one step further. Not only do poor Ozzie and Harriet (surely the most maligned figures in the history of television) stand for nostalgic prejudice and stigmatizing error, they represent a kind of family that in fact

---

[*]Evidence for these beliefs can be found in the poll data gathered in the *American Enterprise*, September–October 1992, pp. 85–86.

[†]Paraphrased from Barbara Dafoe Whitehead; *The Expert's Story of Marriage*, Institute for American Values, Publication No. WP14 (August 1992), pp. 11–12. Whitehead supplies references to the texts she summarizes. She does not endorse—just the opposite!—the views she has compiled.

scarcely exists. Congresswoman Pat Schroeder has been quoted as saying that only about 7 percent of all American families fit the Ozzie-and-Harriet model. Our daily newspapers frequently assert that most children will not grow up in a two-parent family. The message is clear: not only is the two-parent family not especially good for children, but fortunately it is also fast disappearing.

Yet whether or not the two-parent family is good for children, it is 9 plainly false that this kind of family has become a historical relic. For while there has been a dramatic increase in the proportion of children, especially black children, who will spend some or even most of their youth in single-parent families, the vast majority of children—nationally, about 73 percent—live in a home with married parents. Today, the mothers in those families are more likely to work than once was the case, though most do not work full time. (I am old enough to remember that even Harriet worked, at least in real life. She was a singer.)

The proponents of the relic theory fail to use statistics accurately. The 10 way they arrive at the discovery that only 7 percent of all families fit the Ozzie-and-Harriet model is by calculating what proportion of all families consists *exactly* of a father, mother, and two (not three or four) children and in which the mother never works, not even for two weeks during the year helping out with the Christmas rush at the post office.

THE CHANGING CULTURE

Both teenage pregnancies and single-parent families have increased dra- 11 matically since the 1950s. Changes in the economy and in the provision of welfare benefits explain some of this growth but not all or even most of it. There are no doubt some features peculiar to American society that explain some of it, but since the decline of the family—that is, in lasting marriages and legitimate births—has happened in many nations, it cannot be entirely the result of American policies or peculiarities.

We are witnessing a profound, worldwide, long-term change in the 12 family that is likely to continue for a long time. The causes of that change are not entirely understood, but probably involve two main forces: a shift in the family's economic function and a shift in the culture in which it is embedded. The family no longer is the unit that manages economic production, as it was when agriculture was the dominant form of produc- tion, nor is it any longer the principal provider of support for the elderly or education for the young.

At the same time, the family no longer exercises as much control over 13 its members as it once did, and broader kinship groupings (clans, tribes, and extended families) no longer exercise as much control over nuclear families. Since the Enlightenment, the dominant tendency in legal and philosophical thought has been to emancipate the individual from all forms of tutelage—the state, revealed religion, ancient custom—including the tutelage of kin. This emancipation has proceeded episodically and unevenly, but relentlessly. Liberal political theory has celebrated the individual and constrained the state, but it has been silent about the family.

What is remarkable is how well the family has survived this process.   14
Were the family the mere social convention that some scholars imagine, it would long since have gone the way of cottage industries and the owner-occupied farm, the inevitable victim of the individualizing and rationalizing tendencies of modern life. But, of course, the family is not a human contrivance invented to accomplish some goal and capable of being reinvented or reformulated to achieve different goals.

Family—and kinship generally—are the fundamental organizing facts   15
of all human societies, primitive or advanced, and have been such for tens of thousands of years. The family is the product of evolutionary processes that have selected against people who are inclined to abandon their offspring and for people who are prepared to care for them, and to provide this caring within kinship systems defined primarily along genetic lines. If kinship were a cultural artifact, we could as easily define it on the basis of height, athletic skill, or political status, and children would be raised in all manner of collectives, ranging from state-run orphanages to market-supplied foster homes. Orphanages and foster homes do of course exist, but only as matters of last resort designed (with great public anxiety) to provide care when the biological family does not exist or cannot function.

If the family were merely a convenience and if it responded entirely to   16
economic circumstances, the current debate over family policy would be far less rancorous than it is. Liberals would urge that we professionalize child-rearing through day care; conservatives would urge that we subsidize it through earned-income tax credits. Liberals would define the welfare problem as entirely a matter of poverty and recommend more generous benefits as the solution; conservatives would define it as entirely a matter of dependency and recommend slashing benefits as the solution. Liberals would assume that the problem is that families have too little money, conservatives that families get such money as they have from the state. There would still be a battle, but in the end it would come down to some negotiated compromise involving tradeoffs among benefit levels, eligibility rules, and the public-private mix of child-care providers.

But once one conceives of the family problem as involving to a   17
significant degree the conflict between a universal feature of human society

and a profound cultural challenge to the power of that institution, the issue takes on a different character. To the extent that one believes in the cultural challenge—that is, in individual emancipation and individual choice—one tends to question the legitimacy and influence of the family. To the extent that one believes in the family, one is led to question some or all parts of the cultural challenge.

That is why the debate over "family values" has been so strident. On 18 both sides people feel that it is the central battle in the culture war that now grips Americans (or at least American elites). They are absolutely right. To many liberals, family values means a reassertion of male authority, a reduction in the hard-earned rights of women, and a license for abusive or neglectful parents to mistreat their children free of prompt and decisive social intervention. For some liberals, family values means something even more troubling: that human nature is less malleable than is implied by the doctrine of environmental determinism and cultural relativism—that it is to some significant degree fixed, immutable. To many conservatives, family values is the main line of resistance against homosexual marriages, bureaucratized child care, and compulsory sex education in the schools. For some conservatives, the family means a defense against the very idea of a planned society.

Now, reasonable people—say, the typical mother or father—will take a less 19 stark view of the alternatives. They will agree with conservatives that the family is the central institution of society, incapable of being replaced or even much modified without disastrous consequences. They will be troubled by same-sex marriages, upset by teenage girls becoming mothers, angered by public subsidies for illegitimate births, and outraged by the distribution of condoms and explicit sex-education manuals to elementary-school children. But they will agree with many liberals that we ought not to confine women to domestic roles or make them subservient to male power and that we ought to recognize and cope with the financial hardships that young couples have today when they try to live on one income in a big city.

On one issue most parents will squarely identify with the conservative 20 side, and it is, in my view, the central issue. They will want our leaders, the media, television programs, and motion pictures to take their side in the war over what the family is. It is not one of several alternative life-styles; it is not an arena in which rights are negotiated; it is not an old-fashioned and reactionary barrier to a promiscuous sex life; it is not a set of cost-benefit calculations. *It is a commitment.*

It is a commitment required for child-rearing and thus for any realistic 21
prospect of human happiness. It is a commitment that may be entered into
after romantic experimentation and with some misgivings about lost
freedoms, but once entered into it is a commitment that persists for richer
or for poorer, in sickness and in health, for better or for worse. It is a
commitment for which there is no feasible substitute, and hence no child
ought lightly to be brought into a world where that commitment—from
both parents—is absent. It is a commitment that often is joyfully enlivened
by mutual love and deepening friendship, but it is a commitment even when
these things are absent.

There is no way to prepare for the commitment other than to make it. 22
The idea that a man and a woman can live together without a commitment
in order to see if they would like each other after they make the commitment is preposterous. Living together may inform you as to whether your
partner snores or is an alcoholic or sleeps late; it may be fun and exciting;
it may even be the best you can manage in an imperfect world. But it is not
a way of finding out how married life will be, because married life is shaped
by the fact that the couple has made a solemn vow before their family and
friends that this is for keeps and that any children will be their joint and
permanent responsibility. It changes everything.

Despite high divorce rates and a good deal of sleeping around, most 23
people understand this. Certainly women understand it, since one of their
most common complaints about the men they know is that they will not
make a commitment. You bet they won't, not if they can get sex, cooking,
and companionship on a trial basis, all the while keeping their eyes peeled
for a better opportunity elsewhere. Marriage is in large measure a device
for reining in the predatory sexuality of males. It works quite imperfectly,
as is evident from the fact that men are more likely than women to have
extramarital affairs and to abandon their spouses because a younger or
more exciting possibility has presented herself. But it works better than
anything else mankind has been able to invent.

Because most people understand this, the pressures, economic and 24
cultural, on the modern family have not destroyed it. And this is remarkable, considering the spread of no-fault divorce laws. The legal system has,
in effect, said, "Marriage is not a commitment; it is a convenience. If you
feel yours is inconvenient, we will make it easy for you to get out of it."
This radical transformation of family law occurred, as Mary Ann Glendon
of the Harvard Law School has shown, in many industrialized countries at
about the same time. It may or may not have caused the rise in the divorce
rate, but it certainly did nothing to slow it down.

The legal system has also altered child-custody rules so that, instead of 25
being automatically assigned to the father (as was the case in the 19th
century, when the father was thought to "own" all the family's property
including the child), the child is now assigned by the judge on the basis of
its "best interests." In the vast majority of cases, that means with the mother.
I sometimes wonder what would happen to family stability if every father
knew for certain that, should the marriage end, he would have to take
custody of the children. My guess is: more committed fathers.

These cultural and legal changes, all aimed at individualizing and 26
empowering family members, have had an effect. In 1951, 51 percent of
all Americans agreed with the statement that "parents who don't get along
should not stay together because there are children in the family." By 1985,
86 percent agreed.* Still, these changes have not devastated modern
families. The shopping malls, baseball stadiums, and movie theaters are
filled with them doing what families have always done. That fact is a
measure of the innate power of the family bond.

❀   ❀   ❀

AFTER YOU READ

THINK about Wilson's statement that "the debate over 'family values' . . .
is the central battle in the culture war that now grips Americans" (p. 132,
para. 18). As Wilson sees it, the debaters are the public (primarily conservative) and the "policy elites" (primarily liberal). Notice that Wilson
provides arguments for both sides of the debate. With which side does he
agree? What are your own views, and why do you feel as you do?

EXAMINE Wilson's statement that "we are witnessing a profound, worldwide, long-term change in the family that is likely to continue for a long
time" (p. 130, para. 12). Do you agree with this statement? If so, what is
the change and what is causing it? What additional changes do you think
will occur within the family within the next twenty years? What will remain
the same about the family?

WRITE in your own words Wilson's thesis. Then write a double list of some
of the most important liberal and conservative ideas about family values
described in the essay. Use these lists to help you write a summary of the
selection. (Hint: You will need to reread the essay at least once, but your
underlining and marginal notes should be helpful.)

---

*David Popenoe, "The Family Condition of America," paper prepared for a Brookings
Institution seminar on values and public policy (March 1992), citing a study by Norval Glenn.

Unit Two: Critical Thinking and Writing Assignments

❀ ❀ ❀

EXPLORING IDEAS TOGETHER

1. You were asked to write "family stories" in response to Connie May Fowler's essay. Read your stories aloud in a group composed of four or five of your classmates.

2. The poem by Walter McDonald and the essays by Tan, King, and Rawlins describe the difficulty that parents and children—especially teenage children—often have in communicating with one another. Working with a group of your classmates, write a list of guidelines to aid both parents and children in communicating more effectively with one another.

3. James Q. Wilson discusses divorce in his essay, and Julia Alvarez discusses a step-family that has resulted from a divorce. With a group of your classmates, discuss the effects of divorce on a child. As a group, write an open letter to divorced parents suggesting ways that they can help their children adjust to the divorce.

4. One aspect of the family values debate at discussed by James Q. Wilson is whether a child is as well-off in a single-parent family as in a two-parent family. Select at least one reading from this chapter representing a two-parent family (Tan, Cosby, King, Klagsbrun, etc.) and one reading representing a one-parent family (Anaya or Rawlins) to use in debating this issue.

WRITING ESSAYS

1. The essays by Joyce Maynard and Connie May Fowler both focus on family heritage—on searching for or maintaining connections with previous generations as a way of understanding oneself and passing on the family heritage to future generations. Write an essay about your own family heritage. Do you have a special "inheritance" of some sort (emotional, vocational, and so on) from a particular family member? Do you have physical evidence of this heritage, or was this knowledge transmitted orally? If you do not have such a heritage, discuss why this heritage is missing in your life and what you have lost or gained as a result.

2. The readings by Amy Tan, Larry King, and Orville Rawlins focus on a child's rebellion against a parent. In general, does the kind of rebellion described by these writers ultimately have a positive or negative effect on the child? Write an essay in which you argue your position.

3. Francine Klagsbrun describes the intense competition that she felt with her brother, and Amy Tan suggests that the competition that she felt with her cousin Waverly resembled the competition between sisters. Write an essay discussing competition between siblings or other close family members. What causes such competition? What are the effects? Can this competition have positive as well as negative effects?

4. Write an essay on *one* particular family relationship: mother-daughter, mother-son, father-daughter, father-son, grandmother-granddaughter, grandfather-grandson, and so forth. Using support from your own experiences, observations, and reading, show how this relationship is similar to or different from other family relationships.

5. Write an essay for social workers arguing for or against the practice of open adoption. One form of open adoption allows the birth parent(s) and the adoptive parent(s) to meet and exchange family information at the time of the adoption; another form of open adoption encourages continued interaction between the birth parent(s) and the adoptive family, including the child. In arguing your position, be sure to consider and refute arguments for the opposing position.

6. The reading selections by Rudolfo Anaya and Julia Alvarez describe multicultural families. Write an essay in which you discuss *either* the cultural richness gained by members of such families or the problems encountered in such families. Feel free to include support from your own observations and experiences as well as from the readings.

7. In "Exploring Ideas Together," you were asked to debate the family values issue of one-parent versus two-parent families. Write an essay in which you argue whether or not a one-parent family can be as successful as a two-parent family. You may use examples from your reading, but draw more heavily on your own experience and observations.

Self with Friends and Mates

Although your family relationships may be largely predetermined by biology and circumstances, you reach beyond your family to choose your friends and your mate. Friends are a major influence in your life. At work or in class, you often define yourself in terms of your friends. You may even, consciously or unconsciously, choose friends that match your concept of yourself or of the self you want to develop. Or you may choose friends with qualities different from yours—friends of different ages, backgrounds, or interests—to complement your own qualities.

Throughout your lifetime, you will have a great many friends. Unlike your family ties, which remain basically the same, your friendships will change. That is, your friends in college may be different than those you had as a child, or your relationship with a particular friend may change. A friend may move away, or even die. Sometimes a relationship that starts as a friendship may develop into a romantic attachment.

Perhaps the most important "friend" that you will choose is the one that you will select as a mate. Your decision to share your life with a particular person, whether you choose carefully and deliberately or hastily and impulsively, tells more about you and how you perceive yourself than almost any other decision you make. It is, therefore, not surprising that most people spend a great deal of time and energy thinking about, planning for, and selecting their partners.

Individuals usually have many different friends in life, and choosing a mate typically involves dating a variety of potential partners and then deciding, on the basis of these experiences, which one is "right." Ideally this choice results in a long and happy life together—a life in which the two people love and support each other, share an intimate emotional and physical relationship, have children and cooperate in rearing them, and grow old together.

In reality, however, choosing a mate is seldom as tidy and uncomplicated as this description suggests. Finding a partner often involves luck and circumstances as much as or more than love and wisdom. In spite of all the time and energy you devote to the process of selecting a mate, your decision will probably be influenced by where you are and whom you know. And although the romantic ideal in our society continues to be that two people meet, fall in love, get married, and live happily ever after, that ideal is often not realized. You will be joining an increasingly small minority if you spend your entire life happily married to one person. It is possible, perhaps even likely, that you will have a series of partners, each of whom will play a significant role in your life. Often, people in our society may live with someone or with a sequence of someones before deciding to marry. They may divorce and remarry one or more times or may outlive one mate and choose another. In addition, many individuals choose to remain single— sometimes by chance but often by choice—and many other individuals select mates of the same sex.

Relationships with both friends and mates involve companionship, shared activities, and shared interests. In his essay "What Are Friends For," the third selection in this unit, Phillip Lopate not only defines and analyzes friendship but also makes some interesting comparisons between friendship and love. Other essays focus on friends of different ages and backgrounds and on the loss of friends through death or just "drifting away." Reading selections on mates include accounts of both successful and unsuccessful relationships and explore such issues as choosing a mate and communicating with a mate.

As you read, your own experiences will affect your responses to what you read. You will understand the writers' words in light of what you have known and the experiences you have had. This personal response is an inevitable and immensely satisfying part of reading. You enjoy reading if you can relate what you read to your own experiences, but also be aware of the new information that is available to you and of the possibility of gaining different viewpoints.

Liked for Myself

MAYA ANGELOU

Maya Angelou is a successful African-American singer, dancer, and author. You might remember that she read her poem "On the Pulse of Morning" at the inauguration of President Bill Clinton in January 1993. In this excerpt from her autobiographical account I Know Why the Caged Bird Sings, *she vividly describes the beginning of a special friendship between her childhood self (Marguerite) and an older woman. After her parents' divorce in the early 1930s, Marguerite had lived alternately with her grandmother (Momma) and her mother, until she was raped by one of her mother's boyfriends. After this traumatic experience, she and her brother Bailey were sent back to Stamps, Arkansas, to live with their Momma, an enterprising woman who owned the General Merchandise Store in her community. As Angelou's account shows, however, Marguerite has trouble reestablishing a normal life until she is befriended by an older woman.*

BEFORE YOU READ

THINK about an older person who has been a special friend. What do you remember most about this person? How did this person look and act? Why was this person important to you? Did you learn something important from this friendship?

EXAMINE Angelou's use of details and images about food in the selection and especially in the sentences below. These are concrete, or sensory, details because they appeal vividly to the reader's senses. To what sense or senses does each image appeal most strongly?

> For nearly a year, I *sopped* around the house, the Store, the school and the church, *like an old biscuit, dirty and inedible.*

Her skin was a *rich black* that would have *peeled like a plum if snagged.*
. . .

One summer afternoon, *sweet-milk fresh* in my memory, she stopped at
the Store to buy provisions.

They were *flat round wafers, slightly browned on the edges* and *butter-
yellow in the center.*

What do these images suggest to you about Marguerite's background—
about when, where, and how she lived?

WRITE in your journal about people several years older or younger than
you whom you consider to be your friends. Do these friendships differ in
some way from friendships with people nearer your own age? If so, how?
Discuss your responses with a small group of your classmates.

AS YOU READ

Try to determine why this was an especially important experience for
Marguerite at this time in her life, and why Bertha Flowers has remained
for her "the measure of what a human being can be."

For nearly a year, I sopped around the house, the Store, the school and   1
the church, like an old biscuit, dirty and inedible. Then I met, or rather
got to know, the lady who threw me my first life line.

Mrs. Bertha Flowers was the aristocrat of Black Stamps. She had the   2
grace of control to appear warm in the coldest weather, and on the Arkansas
summer days it seemed she had a private breeze which swirled around,
cooling her. She was thin without the taut look of wiry people, and her
printed voile dresses and flowered hats were as right for her as denim
overalls for a farmer. She was our side's answer to the richest white woman
in town.

Her skin was a rich black that would have peeled like a plum if snagged,   3
but then no one would have thought of getting close enough to Mrs.
Flowers to ruffle her dress, let alone snag her skin. She didn't encourage
familiarity. She wore gloves too.

I don't think I ever saw Mrs. Flowers laugh, but she smiled often. A   4
slow widening of her thin black lips to show even, small white teeth, then
the slow effortless closing. When she chose to smile on me, I always wanted
to thank her. The action was so graceful and inclusively benign.

She was one of the few gentlewomen I have ever known, and has   5
remained throughout my life the measure of what a human being can
be. . . .

One summer afternoon, sweet-milk fresh in my memory, she stopped   6
at the Store to buy provisions. Another Negro woman of her health and
age would have been expected to carry the paper sacks home in one hand,
but Momma said, "Sister Flowers, I'll send Bailey up to your house with
these things."

She smiled that slow dragging smile, "Thank you, Mrs. Henderson. I'd   7
prefer Marguerite, though." My name was beautiful when she said it. "I've
been meaning to talk to her, anyway." They gave each other age-group
looks. . . .

There was a little path beside the rocky road, and Mrs. Flowers walked   8
in front swinging her arms and picking her way over the stones.

She said, without turning her head, to me, "I hear you're doing very   9
good school work, Marguerite, but that it's all written. The teachers report
that they have trouble getting you to talk in class." We passed the triangular
farm on our left and the path widened to allow us to walk together. I hung
back in the separate unasked and unanswerable questions.

"Come and walk along with me, Marguerite." I couldn't have refused   10
even if I wanted to. She pronounced my name so nicely. Or more correctly,
she spoke each word with such clarity that I was certain a foreigner who
didn't understand English could have understood her.

"Now no one is going to make you talk—possibly no one can. But bear   11
in mind, language is man's way of communicating with his fellow man and
it is language alone which separates him from the lower animals." That
was a totally new idea to me, and I would need time to think about it.

"Your grandmother says you read a lot. Every chance you get. That's   12
good, but not good enough. Words mean more than what is set down on
paper. It takes the human voice to infuse them with the shades of deeper
meaning."

I memorized the part about the human voice infusing words. It seemed   13
so valid and poetic.

She said she was going to give me some books and that I not only must   14
read them, I must read them aloud. She suggested that I try to make a
sentence sound in as many different ways as possible.

"I'll accept no excuse if you return a book to me that has been badly   15
handled." My imagination boggled at the punishment I would deserve if
in fact I did abuse a book of Mrs. Flowers'. Death would be too kind and
brief.

The odors in the house surprised me. Somehow I had never connected 16
Mrs. Flowers with food or eating or any other common experience of
common people. There must have been an outhouse, too, but my mind
never recorded it.

The sweet scent of vanilla had met us as she opened the door.   17

"I made tea cookies this morning. You see, I had planned to invite you 18
for cookies and lemonade so we could have this little chat. The lemonade
is in the icebox."

It followed that Mrs. Flowers would have ice on an ordinary day, when 19
most families in our town bought ice late on Saturdays only a few times
during the summer to be used in the wooden ice-cream freezers.

She took the bags from me and disappeared through the kitchen door. 20
I looked around the room that I had never in my wildest fantasies imagined
I would see. Browned photographs leered or threatened from the walls and
the white, freshly done curtains pushed against themselves and against the
wind. I wanted to gobble up the room entire and take it to Bailey, who
would help me analyze and enjoy it.

"Have a seat, Marguerite. Over there by the table." She carried a platter 21
covered with a tea towel. Although she warned that she hadn't tried her
hand at baking sweets for some time, I was certain that like everything else
about her the cookies would be perfect.

They were flat round wafers, slightly browned on the edges and 22
butter-yellow in the center. With the cold lemonade they were sufficient
for childhood's lifelong diet. Remembering my manners, I took nice little
lady-like bites off the edges. She said she had made them expressly for me
and that she had a few in the kitchen that I could take home to my brother.
So I jammed one whole cake in my mouth and the rough crumbs scratched
the insides of my jaws, and if I hadn't had to swallow, it would have been
a dream come true.

As I ate she began the first of what we later called "my lessons in living." 23
She said that I must always be intolerant of ignorance but understanding
of illiteracy. That some people, unable to go to school, were more educated
and even more intelligent than college professors. She encouraged me to
listen carefully to what country people called mother wit. That in those
homely sayings was couched the collective wisdom of generations.

When I finished the cookies she brushed off the table and brought a 24
thick, small book from the bookcase. I had read *A Tale of Two Cities* and
found it up to my standards as a romantic novel. She opened the first page
and I heard poetry for the first time in my life.

"It was the best of times and the worst of times . . ." Her voice slid in 25
and curved down through and over the words. She was nearly singing. I

wanted to look at the pages. Were they the same that I had read? Or were there notes, music, lined on the pages, as in a hymn book? Her sounds began cascading gently. I knew from listening to a thousand preachers that she was nearing the end of her reading, and I hadn't really heard, heard to understand, a single word.

"How do you like that?"   26

It occurred to me that she expected a response. The sweet vanilla flavor   27 was still on my tongue and her reading was a wonder in my ears. I had to speak.

I said, "Yes, ma'am." It was the least I could do, but it was the most   28 also.

"There's one more thing. Take this book of poems and memorize one   29 for me. Next time you pay me a visit, I want you to recite."

I have tried often to search behind the sophistication of years for the   30 enchantment I so easily found in those gifts. The essence escapes but its aura remains. To be allowed, no, invited, into the private lives of strangers, and to share their joys and fears, was a chance to exchange the Southern bitter wormwood for a cup of mead with Beowulf or a hot cup of tea and milk with Oliver Twist. When I said aloud, "It is a far, far better thing that I do, than I have ever done . . ." tears of love filled my eyes at my selfishness.

On that first day, I ran down the hill and into the road (few cars ever   31 came along it) and had the good sense to stop running before I reached the Store.

I was liked, and what a difference it made. I was respected not as Mrs.   32 Henderson's grandchild or Bailey's sister but for just being Marguerite Johnson.

Childhood's logic never asks to be proved (all conclusions are abso-   33 lute). I didn't question why Mrs. Flowers had singled me out for attention, nor did it occur to me that Momma might have asked her to give me a little talking to. All I cared about was that she had made tea cookies for *me* and read to *me* from her favorite book. It was enough to prove that she liked me.

❀   ❀   ❀

AFTER YOU READ

THINK about the title "Liked for Myself." Why was it so important to Marguerite to be liked for herself? How did Bertha Flowers show Marguerite how she felt about her? Do you think Marguerite's experience with

Mrs. Flowers will have an important effect on her future development? Explain your response.

EXAMINE paragraphs 2–3, which provide a direct description of Bertha Flowers. What concrete or sensory details does Angelou use to describe Mrs. Flowers? How do these details suggest her character as shown in her later actions?

WRITE an essay about a friendship with a much older or a much younger person. Base your essay on one of these questions: (1) How does your friend look and act? (2) What is at least one memorable experience that you have shared? (3) How has this friendship affected you? (How is your life today different than it might have been if you had not known this person?)

Oil and Water

VALERIE OWEN

Valerie Owen, born and raised in Oklahoma, writes about a friend who has positively affected her life and helped shape the person she is today. She examines the radical personality differences between her friend and herself, relating how these differences actually brought two people together and helped seal a lifelong friendship. In this essay, written in her freshman English course, Owen illustrates that even the most unlikely people can end up being the best of friends.

BEFORE YOU READ

THINK about the title "Oil and Water." What happens when you pour oil and water together? How might two friends be like oil and water?

EXAMINE the first paragraph of the essay. How does this paragraph capture your interest? How does it introduce the subject of the essay?

WRITE a journal entry about your best friend. Are you and your best friend more alike each other or more different?

AS YOU READ

Look for the connection between the title "Oil and Water" and the subject of the essay. Does the friendship between Valerie and Gayla seem at first to be as unlikely a combination as oil and water?

Even though we are separated by 265 miles of long, desolate highway, 1
I know exactly what she's doing right now. She's punching the snooze
button for the third time in a row and muttering a few choice words. Her
name is Gayla Holcomb, and she's my best friend.

We met in junior high school, and it was hate at first sight. I was not 2
able to pinpoint her most annoying habit, because she had so many. While
I had been brought up to be quiet and reserved, she enjoyed burping at will
and often felt compelled to whistle at the boys. Indeed, her backwoods
mannerisms were as shocking to me as a slap in the face.

If I could have, I would have avoided her. This proved to be impossible, 3
for when we compared our class schedules, I realized that they were
identical. Even so, had it not been for a certain incident in our chemistry
class, Gayla and I might have never looked past our differences long enough
to form a friendship of any kind.

Our chemistry class was conducting experiments in the laboratory, and 4
I had the honor of being Gayla's lab partner. She was horsing around as
usual and accidentally started a fire. The entire student body had to
evacuate the building, and the fire department was called. Gayla and I were
the only ones who found any humor in the whole situation. Apparently,
we found too much humor in it, because our teacher called our parents,
and we were both grounded. From that day forward, every time I saw
Gayla, I would think of the "Bunsen Burner Mishap," and I would have to
laugh. It was the beginning of a beautiful friendship.

I began to enjoy spending time with Gayla and even sat next to her 5
during the lunch hour on purpose. In no time at all, we were walking home
from school together on the weekdays and tying up our parents' phone
lines on the weekends. I caught myself admiring the same outspoken
personality that had caused me to shudder just a few short weeks earlier.
As time went on, I even chose to adopt some of her footloose ways.

My poor parents didn't know what to think. I went from a quiet, 6
reserved honor student who spent her spare time playing the violin and
writing poetry to a full-blown adolescent girl who was painting her room
purple and dragging on Main Street until the wee hours of the morning
with some awful girl who liked to burp in public. Fortunately, they also
noticed that I seemed to be happier and decided not to interfere with my
newfound friendship.

As the school days lapsed into summer, our friendship grew. We spent 7
many afternoons in the shade under the old pear tree in my backyard. There
we shared many secrets that had never before been told. I now knew that
John Denver made her weak in the knees, and she knew that I thought my

father was demented. We trusted one another with our secrets, confident that neither one of us would ever breathe a word to another living soul, because we believed we would never, ever fight.

To our surprise, we found that even the best of friends fight. Not only 8 did we fight, but we fought hard and often over stupid things like boys. We also found that even while we were spitting mad at one another, we wouldn't break the trust that we held so dearly. Secrets remained secrets, and we always found the road back to our friendship.

After graduation we both went our own ways. I moved to Kansas and 9 started a family. Gayla moved to Edmond, Oklahoma, and started a family of her own. Although marriage, miles, and years have slowly pulled us apart, we are as close as we have ever been.

While we were once too different to be friends, it was our differences 10 that drew us together and built the memories that have kept us together through all of these years. I find the time to phone Gayla once or twice a month, and from time to time she finds her way into my dreams.

❀ ❀ ❀

AFTER YOU READ

THINK about the "Bunsen Burner Mishap" that Owen describes in her essay. Do you think she and Gayla would have become friends if it had not been for this accident? How did this incident bring them together? Have you ever had a similar experience in forming a friendship?

EXAMINE carefully the language of the essay, pointing out how Owen's vivid word choice makes the friends and their friendship seem real to you. Examples of her effective language include her comparison of Gayla's "backwoods mannerisms" to "a slap in the face" (paragraph 2) and her description of herself as "a full-blown adolescent girl who was painting her room purple and dragging on Main Street until the wee hours of the morning" (paragraph 6). What other effective uses of language do you find in the essay?

WRITE in your own words the thesis, or main idea, of the essay. Before you write this thesis, reread Owen's conclusion. Or **WRITE** an essay about one of your friends who is very different from you. How has this difference affected your friendship?

What Friends Are For

PHILLIP LOPATE

Although New Yorker Phillip Lopate thinks of himself as a creative writer—poet and novelist—he has received high praise for nonfiction writing like the selection that follows. His nonfiction works include Being with Children *(1975), a description of his work as a visiting writer and teacher in the New York City school system;* Bachelorhood: Tales of the Metropolis *(1981), a collection of personal essays about the perspective of bachelorhood; and* Against Joie de Vivre, *a collection of essays that includes "What Friends Are For." As illustrated in this work, Lopate has developed a special interest in the literary tradition of the personal essay.*

BEFORE YOU READ

THINK about the people you count as your friends; make a list of three or four who are most important to you. Why did you select these people as friends? Do you and your friends have interests and opinions in common, or are you—like Valerie Owen and Gayla Holcomb in the previous essay—very different? Do you see a pattern in these friendships?

EXAMINE Lopate's statement, "I clung to the romance of the Best Friend all through high school, college, and beyond, until my circle of university friends began to disperse" (p. 150; paragraph 6). In your opinion, do most adults (college age or beyond) have a single best friend? Or do they have a diversity of friends?

WRITE a journal entry about your "best friend" from childhood. Is this person still your best friend? If so, what has maintained this relationship? If not, what happened to change the friendship?

Notice that Lopate's discussion of friends progresses from a comparison of friendship and love to a discussion of friendships in family and youth to a discussion and analysis of adult friendships. Underline the qualities that Lopate believes are necessary to develop and maintain adult friendships.

F riendship has been called "love without wings." On the other hand, the 1
Stoic definition of love ("Love is the attempt to form a friendship inspired by beauty") seems to suggest that friendship came first. Certainly a case can be made that the buildup of affection and the yearning for more intimacy, without the release of sexual activity, keeps friends in a state of sweet-sorrowful itchiness that has the romantic quality of a love affair. We know that a falling-out between two old friends can leave a deeper and more perplexing hurt than the ending of a love affair, perhaps because we are more pessimistic about the affair's endurance from the start.

Our first attempted friendships are within the family. It is here we 2
practice the techniques of listening sympathetically and proving that we can be trusted, and learn the sort of kindness we can expect in return.

There is something tainted about these family friendships, however. 3
My sister, in her insecure adolescent phase, told me, "You love me because I'm related to you, but if you were to meet me for the first time at a party, you'd think I was a jerk and not worth being your friend." She had me in a bind: I had no way of testing her hypothesis. I should have argued that even if our bond was not freely chosen, our decision to work on it had been. Still, we are quick to dismiss the partiality of our family members when they tell us we are talented, cute, or lovable; we must go out into the world and seduce others.

It is just a few short years from the promiscuity of the sandbox to the 4
tormented, possessive feelings of a fifth grader who has just learned that his best and only friend is playing at another classmate's house after school. There may be worse betrayals in store, but probably none is more influential than the sudden fickleness of an elementary school friend who has dropped us for someone more popular after all our careful, patient wooing. Often we lose no time inflicting the same betrayal on someone else, just to ensure that we have got the victimization dynamic right.

What makes friendships in childhood and adolescence so poignant is 5
that we need the chosen comrade to be everything in order to rescue us from the gothic inwardness of family life. Even if we are lucky enough to have several companions, there must be a Best Friend.

I clung to the romance of the Best Friend all through high school, 6
college, and beyond, until my circle of university friends began to disperse.
At that point, in my mid-20s, I also acted out the dark, competitive side of
friendship that can exist between two young men fighting for a place in life
and love by doing the one unforgivable thing: sleeping with my best friend's
girl. I was baffled at first that there was no way to repair the damage. I lost
this friendship forever, and came away from that debacle much more aware
of the amount of injury that friendship can and cannot sustain. Perhaps I
needed to prove to myself that friendship was not an all-permissive resilient
bond, like a mother's love, but something quite fragile. Precisely because
best friendship promotes such a merging of identities, such seeming
boundarylessness, the first major transgression of trust can cause the injured
party to feel he is fighting for his violated soul against his darkest enemy.
There is not much room to maneuver in a best friendship between
unlimited intimacy and unlimited mistrust.

Still, it was not until the age of thirty that I reluctantly abandoned the 7
best friend expectation and took up a more pluralistic model. At present,
I cherish a dozen friends for their unique personalities, without asking that
any one be my soul-twin. Whether this alteration constitutes a movement
toward maturity or toward cowardly pragmatism is not for me to say. It
may be that, in refusing to depend so much on any one friend, I am opting
for self-protection over intimacy. Or it may be that, as we advance into
middle age, the life problem becomes less that of establishing a tight dyadic
bond and more one of making our way in a broader world, "society."
Indeed, since Americans have so indistinct a notion of society, we often try
to put a network of friendships in its place.

If a certain intensity is lost in the pluralistic model of friendship, there 8
is also the gain of being able to experience all of one's potential, half-buried
selves, through witnessing all the spectacle of the multiple fates of our
friends. As it happens, the harem of friends, so tantalizing a notion, often
translates into feeling pulled in a dozen different directions, with the guilty
sense of having disappointed everyone a little. It is also a risky, contrived
enterprise to try to make one's friends behave in a friendly manner toward
each other. If the effort fails, one feels obliged to mediate; if it succeeds
too well, one is jealous.

Whether friendship is intrinsically singular and exclusive or plural and 9
democratic is a question that has vexed many commentators. Aristotle
distinguished three types of friendship: "friendship based on utility," such
as businessmen cultivating each other for benefit; "friendship based on
pleasure," like young people interested in partying; and "perfect friendship." The first two categories Aristotle calls "qualified and superficial

friendships," because they are founded on circumstances that could easily change. The last, which is based on admiration for another's good character, is more permanent, but also rarer, because good men "are few." Cicero, who wrote perhaps the best treatise on friendship, also insisted that what brings true friends together is "a mutual belief in each other's goodness." This insistence on virtue as a precondition for true friendship may strike us as impossibly demanding: Who, after all, feels himself good nowadays? And yet, if I am honest, I must admit that the friendships of mine that have lasted longest have been with those whose integrity, or humanity, or strength to bear their troubles I continue to admire. Conversely, when I lost respect for someone, however winning he or she otherwise remained, the friendship petered away almost immediately. "Remove respect from friendship," said Cicero, "and you have taken away the most splendid ornament it possesses."

Friendship is a long conversation. I suppose I could imagine a nonver- 10 bal friendship revolving around shared physical work or sport, but for me, good talk is the point of the thing. Indeed, the ability to generate conversation by the hour is the most promising indication, during the uncertain early stages, that a possible friendship will take hold. In the first few conversations there may be an exaggeration of agreement, as both parties angle for adhesive surfaces. But later on, trust builds through the courage to assert disagreement, through the tactful acceptance that differences of opinion will have to remain.

Some view like-mindedness as both the precondition and the product 11 of friendship. Myself, I distrust it. I have one friend who keeps assuming that we see the world eye-to-eye. She is intent on enrolling us in a flattering aristocracy of taste, on the short "we" list against the ignorant "they." Sometimes I do not have the strength to fight her need for consensus with my own stubborn disbelief in the existence of any such inner circle of privileged, cultivated sensibility. Perhaps I have too much invested in a view of myself as idiosyncratic to be eager to join any coterie, even a coterie of two. What attracts me to friends' conversation is the give and take, not necessarily that we come out at the same point.

"Our tastes and aims and views were identical—and that is where the 12 essence of a friendship must always lie," wrote Cicero. To some extent, perhaps, but then the convergence must be natural, not, as Emerson put it, "a mush of concession. Better be a nettle in the side of your friend than his echo."

Friendship is a school for character, allowing us the chance to study, 13 in great detail and over time, temperaments very different from our own. These charming quirks, these contradictions, these nobilities, these blind

spots of our friends we track not out of disinterested curiosity: We must
have this information before knowing how far we may relax our guard,
how much we may rely on them in crises. The learning curve of friendship
involves, to no small extent, filling out this picture of the other's limitations
and making peace with the results. Each time I hit up against a friend's
inflexibility I am relieved as well as disappointed: I can begin to predict,
and arm myself in advance against repeated bruises. I have one friend who
is always late, so I bring a book along when I am to meet her. I give her a
manuscript to read and she promises to look at it over the weekend. I
prepare for a month-long wait.

Though it is often said that with a true friend there is no need to hold   14
anything back ("A friend is a person with whom I may be sincere. Before
him I may think aloud," wrote Emerson), I have never found this to be
entirely the case. Certain words may be too cruel if they are spoken at the
wrong moment—or may fall on deaf ears, for any number of reasons. I also
find with all my friends, as they must with me, that some initial resistance,
restlessness, some psychic weather must be overcome before that tender
ideal attentiveness may be called forth.

I have a good friend, Charlie, who is often very distracted whenever   15
we first get together. If we are sitting in a café he will look around constantly
for the waiter, or be distracted by a pretty woman or the restaurant's cat.
It would be foolish for me to broach an important subject at such moments,
so I resign myself to waiting the half hour or however long it takes until
his jumpiness subsides. Or else I draw this pattern grumpily to his attention.
Once he has settled down, however, I can tell Charlie virtually anything,
and he me. But the candor cannot be rushed. It must be built up to with
the verbal equivalent of limbering exercises.

The friendship scene—a flow of shared confidences, recognitions,   16
humor, advice, speculation, even wisdom—is one of the key elements of
modern friendships. Compared to the rest of life, this ability to lavish one's
best energies on an activity utterly divorced from the profit motive and free
from the routines of domination and inequality that affect most relations
(including, perhaps, the selfsame friendship at other times) seems idyllic.
The friendship scene is by its nature not an everyday occurrence. It
represents the pinnacle, the fruit of the friendship, potentially ever present
but not always arrived at. Both friends' dim yet self-conscious awareness
that they are wandering conversationally toward a goal that they have
previously accomplished but that may elude them this time around creates
a tension, an obligation to communicate as sincerely as possible, like actors

in an improvisation exercise struggling to shape their baggy material into some climactic form. This very pressure to achieve "quality" communication may induce a sort of inauthentic epiphany, not unlike what sometimes happens in the last ten minutes of a psychotherapy session. But a truly achieved friendship scene can be among the best experiences life has to offer.

Contemporary urban life, with its tight schedules and crowded appointment books, has helped to shape modern friendship into something requiring a good deal of intentionality and pursuit. You phone a friend and make a date a week or more in advance; then you set aside an evening, as if for a tryst, during which to squeeze in all your news and advice, confession and opinion. Such intimate compression may add a romantic note to modern friendships, but it also places a strain on the meeting to yield a high quality of meaning and satisfaction, closer to art than life. If I see busy or out-of-town friends only once every six months, we must not only catch up on our lives but also convince ourselves within the allotted two hours together that we still share a special affinity, an inner track to each other's psyches, or the next meeting may be put off for years. Surely there must be another, saner rhythm of friendship in rural areas—or maybe not? I think about "the good old days" when friends would go on walking tours through England together, when Edith Wharton would bundle poor Henry James into her motorcar and they'd drive to the south of France for a month. I'm not sure my friendships could sustain the strain of travel for weeks at a time, and the truth of the matter is that I've gotten used to this urban arrangement of serial friendship "dates," where the pleasure of the rendezvous is enhanced by the knowledge that it will only last, at most, six hours. If the two of us don't happen to mesh that day (always a possibility)—well, it's only a few hours. And if it should go beautifully, one needs an escape hatch from exaltation as well as disenchantment. I am capable of only so much intense, exciting communication before I start to fade: I come to these encounters equipped with a six-hour oxygen tank. Is this an evolutionary pattern of modern friendship, or just a personal limitation?

Perhaps because I conceive of the modern friendship scene as a somewhat theatrical enterprise, a one-act play, I tend to be very much affected by the "set." A restaurant, a museum, a walk in the park through the zoo, even accompanying a friend on shopping errands—I prefer public turf where the stimulation of the city can play a backdrop to our dialogue, feeding it with details when inspiration flags.

I have a number of *chez moi* friends who always invite me to come to their homes while evading offers to visit me. What they view as hospitality

I see as a need to control the mise-en-scène of friendship. I am expected to fit in where they are most comfortable, while they play lord of the manor, distracted by the props of decor, the pool, the unexpected phone call, the swirl of children, animals, and neighbors. Indeed, *chez moi* friends often tend to keep a sort of open house, so that in going over to see them—for a tête-à-tête, I had assumed—I will suddenly find their other friends and neighbors, whom they have also invited, dropping in all afternoon. There are only so many Sundays I care to spend hanging out with a friend's entourage before I become impatient for a private audience.

Married friends who own their own homes are apt to try to draw me 20 into their domestic fold, whereas single people are often more sensitive about establishing a discreet space for the friendship to occur. Perhaps the married assume that a bachelor like me is desperate for home cooking and a little family life. I have noticed that it is not an easy matter to pry a married friend away from mate and milieu. For married people, especially those with children, the home often becomes the wellspring of all their nurturing feelings, and the single friend is invited to partake in the general flow. Maybe there is also a certain tendency on their part to kill two birds with one stone: They don't see enough of their spouse and kids, and they figure they can visit with you at the same time.

From my standpoint, friendship is a jealous goddess. Whenever a friend 21 of mine marries, I have to fight to overcome the feeling that I am being "replaced" by the spouse. I don't mind sharing a friend with his or her family milieu—in fact I like it, up to a point—but eventually I must get the friend alone, or else, as a bachelor at a distinct power disadvantage, I risk becoming a mere spectator of familial rituals instead of a key player in the drama of friendship.

A person who lives alone usually has more energy to give to friendship. 22 The danger is investing too much emotional energy in one's friends. When a single person is going through a romantic dry spell, he or she often tries to extract the missing passion from a circle of friends. This works only up to a point: the frayed nerves of protracted celibacy can lead to hypersensitive imaginings of slights and rejections, and one's platonic friends seem to come particularly into the line of fire.

Today, with the partial decline of the nuclear family and the search for 23 alternatives to it, we also see attempts to substitute the friendship web for intergenerational family life. Since psychoanalysis has alerted us to regard the family as a mine field of unrequited love, manipulation, and ambivalence, it is only natural that people may look to friendship as a more supportive ground for relation. But in our longing for an unequivocally positive bond, we should beware of sentimentalizing friendship, as saccharine "buddy" movies and certain feminist novels do, and of neutering its problematic aspects. Besides, friendship can never substitute for the true meaning of family: if nothing else, it will never be able to duplicate the family's wild capacity for concentrating neurosis.

In short, friends can't be your family, they can't be your lovers, they 24 can't be your psychiatrists. But they can be your friends, which is plenty.

When I think about the qualities that characterize the best friendships 25 I've known, I can identify five: rapport, affection, need, habit, and forgiveness. Rapport and affection can take you only so far; they may leave you at the formal, outer gate of goodwill, which is still not friendship. A persistent need for the other's company, for the person's interest, approval, opinion, will get you inside the gates, especially when it is reciprocated. In the end, however, there are no substitutes for habit and forgiveness. A friendship may travel for years on cozy habit. But it is a melancholy fact that unless you are a saint you are bound to offend every friend deeply at least once in the course of time. The friends I have kept the longest are those who forgave me time and again for wronging them unintentionally, intentionally, or by the plain catastrophe of my personality. There can be no friendship without forgiveness.

AFTER YOU READ

THINK about some of the qualities that Lopate believes are necessary to maintain friendship, including respect, good conversation, independent thought, character, sincerity, and forgiveness. In your opinion, which of these qualities are the most important? Why?

EXAMINE Lopate's reference to Aristotle's classification of friends into the following three categories: those whose friendship is based on utility, those whose friendship is based on pleasure, and those who are perfect friends based on admiration. Do you agree that this categorization is logical and realistic? Can you think of friends whom you would place in each category?

EXAMINE also Lopate's statement that "the friendship scene—a flow of shared confidences, recognitions, humor, advice, speculation, even wisdom—is one of the key elements of modern friendships" (152). How does Lopate further describe "the friendship scene"? According to Lopate, what are some of the best places for such a friendship scene to occur? What are some of the worst places? What is a memorable "friendship scene" that you have experienced?

WRITE an essay in which you classify friends or friendships according to type. You may use Aristotle's method of classification(see paragraph 9), or you may develop your own system.

Death of a Friend: The Delicacy and Strength of Lace

LESLIE MARMON SILKO
AND
JAMES WRIGHT

Although Leslie Silko and James (Jim) Wright met only twice, their friendship had what Jim's wife Annie called the "delicacy and strength of lace." Silko, a Laguna Indian poet and fiction writer, and Wright, a college professor and Pulitzer Prize–winning poet, first met in 1975 at a Michigan writers' conference. They did not meet again until January 1980 when Leslie visited Jim in the hospital where he was being treated for terminal cancer. Their friendship had begun when Jim wrote Leslie a brief complimentary note after reading her novel Ceremony. *Before Jim's death, they had developed the close friendship that is recorded in the letters Silko and Annie Wright published in* The Delicacy and Strength of Lace *(1986).*

BEFORE YOU READ

THINK about a time in which a friend of yours experienced a major personal difficulty. Is it easy to help a friend in a difficult situation such as serious illness or the death of a loved one? How did you try to console your friend? Were you able to help your friend? How did you feel at the time?

EXAMINE the dates of the letters written by Silko and the Wrights. How long did Jim Wright's illness last? How do you suppose Leslie Silko and Annie Wright felt during the time immediately following Jim's death? How long do you suppose it took for them to become emotionally ready to collect, edit, and publish the letters in *The Delicacy and Strength of Lace*?

WRITE a journal entry about a friend who helped you through a difficult time, such as an illness or the death of a loved one. Or WRITE about how you supported a friend during such a time.

AS YOU READ

Notice the natural and easy way in which Jim Wright and Leslie Silko express their feelings in these letters. Would it have been as easy to express these feelings in person or over the telephone? (*Note:* The italicized statements between the letters are editorial comments added by Annie Wright.)

New York, NY
December 18, 1979

Dear Leslie,

I'm afraid this will be a short note for the moment—I'll write at greater 1 length later on. I have some bad news about myself which I nevertheless want to tell you.

I have learned that I have cancer. It is very serious, but it is not hopeless. 2 My doctor is a good man and a highly skilled specialist, and he has assured me and Annie that the operation—radical surgery in the throat—will save my life. I will emerge from the surgery with diminished capacity to speak, and this will create a problem, since I make a living by speaking. But there is a good chance that I will be able to continue teaching all right. The operation is supposed to take place early in the month of January. I will be recuperating here at home most of the time. Because the operation will be serious and debilitating, I have arranged to take off the spring semester from teaching.

It is a shock, of course, perhaps the most cruel shock that a middle-aged 3 person can face. But I have found that I have a number of considerable powers to help me. I have always been happy with my marriage to Annie, for example, but I suddenly have a deeper and clearer understanding of how very strong this marriage is. Furthermore, in determining whom to tell, I have considered that I want to share the worst of this news with a very few people whom I admire and value the most, and it is interesting to me that you stand very high in my mind among those—the people, I mean, who strike me as embodying in their own lives and work something—some value, some spirit—that I absolutely care about and believe in. Of course, my dear friend, over little more than a year we have become excellent friends, and I would hope always to send you happy news. But the tragic news belongs to you too. Please don't despair over my troubles. I will find my way through this difficulty somehow, and one of the best things I have is my knowledge that you exist and that you are going on living and working. I'll be in touch again soon (by the way, if you're in N.Y.C. on February 5th please *do* call us.)

Love,
Jim

Tucson, Arizona
January 3, 1980

Dear Jim,

Your letter was waiting when I returned from Christmas in Gallup. I wanted to wait a few days to digest it in case my feelings changed, but they have not and I trust them. I feel a great deal of distress about your speaking voice because I imagine how you must be feeling about it; but myself, I have always felt that the words and the feeling they were spoken with matter most, and I sense that this is your deepest understanding too, otherwise your letter would not have been so calm. When I was a girl my grandpa on my mother's side had just the same operation. In those days they didn't have the electronic mechanisms they have now. But all my memories of him are of his expressiveness, which I did not perceive before, although I was younger before, and maybe this is the reason. He smiled and gestured a lot and like always, he would cry when he was very happy—he was often overcome with feelings, and my mother is the same, and I am too. We can be in an airport or train depot not even seeing anyone off and when they call the train or plane, we cry. I don't know what or whom we cry for, but we do. Grandpa was always that way, but after the operation it always seemed to me much more a way of speaking than simply some overflow of feeling. I suppose it is because of this and because the operation was successful for him that I read your letter calmly. Perhaps I am seeing your crisis too much like a child, and perhaps this confidence that you will be here for quite some time is my way of protecting myself from pain, but I think not. I know such things immediately; the feeling hits me and I'm never able to think fast enough to create a rationalization. I feel you will be all right, that your health will be restored. You will manage the part about your voice because voice never was sound alone. Which doesn't mean that you won't feel angry sometimes—Grandpa did, but then he learned his own new language. . . .

[To encourage Jim, Leslie tells a rather long story about an old man named Hugh who unexpectedly survives tuberculosis, a terrible automobile accident, a liver disease, and a gunshot wound—living longer than many people who had long before predicted his death.]

You are a dear, dear friend, Jim. In so many ways it was you who helped 5 me through those difficult times last year. At times like these I often wish I had more to say, but somehow it comes out in a story. I hope all this does not strike you as too strange. I seem not to react like most people do at times like these. I think I sense your calm and your deep faith. I know it has to do with your wonderful writing and, more important, with the visions that emerge from it.

                    Love,
                    Leslie

James Wright was hospitalized in mid-January 1980 with cancer of the 6 *tongue, diagnosed upon hospital entry as terminal. He was able to read Leslie's letter of January 3rd before he was too ill to remain in his home.*

   Leslie came to speak at the Manhattan Theatre Club in New York 7 *on February 5th. On the following day I arrived at the hospital after work to find Leslie sitting by James's bedside. Although unable to speak, James did respond to Leslie's conversation by writing on a yellow-lined legal pad.*

   He wrote this about the people who cared for him: "People are lovely 8 *to me here. Mr. Edwards and Mrs. Holmes are amazing, understanding, companions. They are skilled and I trust them."*

   Later that evening, after Leslie had gone, James wrote me a note about 9 *her visit. "I have the sense of a very fine, great person—a true beautiful artist. And I'm glad we've all made friends."*

In March James and I wrote a post card to Leslie together. It was the   10
only thing he wrote while in the hospital.
    This is the message we wrote together from the hospital.   11

Dear Leslie,

    I can't write much of a message. Please write to me.   12

                        Love,
                        Jim

    We loved seeing you last month. James is moving to a fine new hospital   13
on Friday.
    We miss hearing from you. How is the roadrunner?   14

                        Love,
                        Annie

[Leslie's last letter to James, dated March 24th, arrived after his death.]   15

                        Tucson, Arizona
                        March 24, 1980

Dear Jim,

    I have been trusting another sort of communication between you and   16
me—a sort of message from the heart—sent by thinking of you and feeling
great love for you and knowing strongly that you think of me, that you are
sending thoughts and feelings to me; and you and I, Jim, we *trust* in these
messages that move between us.
    I cannot account for this except that perhaps it is a gift of the poetry,   17
or perhaps it should be called "grace"—a special sort of grace. I am never
far from you, Jim, and this feeling I have knows that we will never be far
from each other, you and I. Aunt Susie has taught me this much and my
Grandpa Hank and Great-Grandma have too—that knowing and loving

someone has no end, and that we are together always, over at the Cliff House or walking along the lake edge not far from the home Catullus keeps.

It is not easy to avoid confusion. What I wanted to do was stay in New York, move in with Annie, and sit with you and talk with you. But that would have been confusing one present time with another present time. 18

Anyway, I know you understand, Jim, and I know Annie does too. 19

In one present time, you and I can count the times we've met and the minutes we've actually spent together. I think I was very shy in Michigan when we were introduced, and think I just told you how much I liked your reading. You had been sick and you were careful to rest a lot then. And then in New York this February with you in the hospital, I sat and talked and could already feel that there is another present time where you and I have been together for a long long time and here we continue together. In this place, in a sense, there never has been a time when you and I were not together. I cannot explain this. Maybe it is the continuing or on-going of the telling, the telling in poetry and stories. 20

Since the rains have come, the roadrunner is busy in other places, although he still roosts on the northwest side of the house, up on the roof. 21

After sundown the other night I was sitting on the road with Denny, and a great owl with eight-foot wings landed on a tall saguaro close to us. Jim, this owl was so big that, after he folded his wings, his size matched the diameter of the saguaro and he became part of the cactus top. It was only with the most careful concentration that I could see the owl swivel his head and thus believe that there was an owl sitting there. I thought about you then, Jim, as I always will when I am visited by the owls. He is probably the owl who carries off the cats the coyotes don't bother to catch, and after that night I was ready to believe this owl carries off whatever he damn well pleases. 22

It is so overwhelming to see your writing on the post card and to feel how much I miss your letters. There is no getting around this present time and place even when I feel you and I share this other present time and place. 23

Anyway, I treasure the words you write—your name most of all. But no matter if written words are seldom because we know, Jim, we know. 24

My love to you always,
Leslie

New York, NY
March 25, 1980

[To Leslie Silko:]
  The best days are the first to go. The best of men has gone too.   25

Love,
Annie

❀ ❀ ❀

AFTER YOU READ

THINK about how Leslie responded to Jim's tragic news about his terminal illness. Study her January 3 letter. How did she try to console and encourage him? What is the tone of her letter? Is it positive or negative?

EXAMINE the statement that Jim makes in the note he writes to his wife Annie after Leslie's visit. What are some thoughts he might have had as he wrote "and I'm glad we've all made friends"? In this series of letters, what clues do you find about a second developing friendship—the one between Leslie and Annie. Have you ever made a special friend through the efforts of another friend?

WRITE a letter to a friend—perhaps a friend you haven't seen for a while or one who is in need of encouragement. Your friend may be experiencing a severe illness or the death of someone close. Or your friend may be experiencing problems with college, marriage, or family. Even though most of us have abandoned writing letters to family and friends in favor of personal visits or telephone calls, do you see some important advantages in friends writing letters to one another? What are these advantages?

Where's Dietz?

MIKE TAIBBI

A reporter with the WCBS television news in New York, Mike Taibbi published the following essay in the "About Men" column of The New York Times Magazine *on December 19, 1993. In this essay, Taibbi not only responds to the loss of a friend, as Leslie Marmon Silko does in the previous selection, but also explores the reluctance that male friends often have to express their feelings about friendship.*

BEFORE YOU READ

THINK about friendships between men. How do male friendships differ from female friendships? Are men more reluctant to express their feelings toward each other? Why or why not?

EXAMINE the title and the first paragraph of the essay. Who is asking the question, "Where's Dietz?" What answers do you think you will find in the essay?

WRITE a journal entry in which you explore, from your experience or observations, friendships between men. Do men friends spend more time talking with one another or pursuing activities such as sports?

AS YOU READ

Look for answers to the title question, "Where's Dietz?" What is the first answer that you encounter? What is the final answer given in the reading?

D inner would have just ended, coffee would be on its way, in his 1 apartment or mine or in a restaurant, when suddenly someone at the table would notice that Dietz was gone. With the conversation motoring along, he just wouldn't be there. Guests who had never experienced Dietz's odd habit were surprised the first time; but those who knew him learned to schedule dinners earlier than usual.

Dietz explained his abrupt departures to me this way: his full days 2 started well before daybreak, and when it was time to sleep he just moved for the bedroom. He used to say good night, he explained, but too many people thought he meant it was time to wrap things up. That's not what Dietz meant, so he just stopped saying anything.

More than two years after his death, a wrenching feeling will suddenly 3 grab me. In the first weeks the pain was constant, startling in its newness. A friend had died, along with his mother and the woman he'd told me he would likely marry, all drowned after the crash of his own plane. Dietz was 52, fit and eager for life, his girlfriend younger and equally alive, his mother still sturdy. The engine had failed on takeoff, and though he had managed to clear a tree line and skillfully set the craft down in a lagoon, the three could not get out when the plane sank. Death by drowning. None suffered crash-related injuries.

Any accidental or sudden death is a hammer blow to the victim's family 4 and friends, there being no time to prepare for it. Dietz's death was agonizing, and still is, because we never talked about our still-evolving friendship.

It only occurred to me in the days after the crash that for more than a 5 year Dietz and I had talked to each other several times a week—sometimes several times a day. Perhaps this closeness was an outgrowth of the years when we lived in the same building and, each of us being early risers, walked our dogs together at the crack of dawn. But out conversations in the last year or so had been more than punctuation to our respective lives. In person, by phone or by fax, we explored our respective histories and dilemmas, our anxieties and curiosities, our fears.

We were dissimilar in enough ways that close friendship would have 6 seemed unlikely. I played tennis and basketball, liked pool halls and golf—sociable and competitive sports; he worked out alone in a Spartan gym, just fighting off the years. I'm a television reporter and writer of minor celebrity; he was in sales, happily anonymous, he once said. I had a kid, he had none and had little patience for them. We had no long-shared history. We didn't watch each other's families grow up.

Yet, in my mind, unpredictably, we became good friends. I valued his 7
judgments and good opinion of me, sought his advice, admired his intelligence and curiosity, depended on his brusque honesty, longed to share with
him all that I learned and experienced. He was the best listener I knew, and
though I was the writer, he was the one who never, ever wasted words.

I never told him any of that, though, and if Dietz had any thoughts 8
about our friendship, he chose, as I had chosen, not to express them. At
the time I thought it didn't matter, but now I wish that there had been the
right moment and that I'd told him then what our friendship meant to me.

We all present ourselves to the world through the surfaces we build 9
around ourselves, walls of our own making. Men particularly, and particularly men who, like Dietz—and to some extent myself—take risks, whose
nature doesn't lend itself to easy summation, seem prone to make their
walls of glass. They can see and be seen, but they decide when to touch or
be touched. Those men have a peculiar kind of narcissism, dependent as it
is on the opposing needs to seduce and keep away.

It turns out I never did know as much about Dietz, or of him, as I 10
thought I had. There were women, relationships, he never discussed with
me. There was despair, a relative of his told me, so pronounced that in one
letter to her he wrote openly of suicide. What I knew of him was some of
his history—how he learned as a boy in Germany to despise the Nazis,
because his father did, and how as a young man he left for America and
chose to stay, passionately embracing life in a free society. I knew his
personal characteristics, of course; his puckish delight at life's daily ironies,
his genuine anger at injustices large and small, his nearly obsessive pursuit
of his chosen interests, his gentleness and reserve. And, also, some of his
cruelties and deceptions.

I have other old friendships, friendships I treasure: a girlfriend from 11
when I was fifteen; a guy I worked with and played basketball with just
before we headed off to college; my best friend, a news colleague, whose
life has been entwined with mine for more than two decades; my 23-year-
old son.

But my friendship with Dietz sneaked up on me, beginning and 12
evolving at a time when we'd each thoroughly become the men we were
going to be.

The autumn before the accident, Dietz sold me his sailboat, a double- 13
ended cutter named Peace that was designed for the dream he knew then
he'd never achieve: sailing for the oceans and landfalls of his choosing.
He'd taken up flying instead, had quickly become instrument-rated and
had seen much of the country. He was going through a divorce and had

career problems; Peace was languishing and had to go, and so it went to a friend.

Two months after his death I was sailing Peace up the Connecticut River 14 to Essex, to host a memorial service at a meadow where Dietz and some friends had formed a small private boat club years before. Suddenly I saw a sloop veer toward us on its way down river. Someone who knew the boat, I guessed: Peace is distinctive in design, and only one cutter like this, the one I was steering, called the Connecticut River home. Now the oncoming boat was almost abeam of us. Its skipper, seeing me at the helm, cupped his hand and hollered, "Where's Dietz?" For seconds I was wild with grief and anger and confusion, and he was past me when I shouted to him, into the wind, the only words that came to mind that could concisely tell the truth.

"He's dead!" And I bawled uncontrollably, my convulsions as painful 15 and searing as they are sometimes still.

❀   ❀   ❀

AFTER YOU READ

THINK about how Taibbi must have felt when he first heard the news of Dietz's death. What did he wish he had said or done? Are his feelings just as strong two months after Dietz's death as at the time of the tragedy? How do you know? Have you had an experience similar to Taibbi's in which a friend died before you had an opportunity to tell your friend something you wished him or her to know?

EXAMINE the essay to find the qualities that Taibbi admired in Dietz—the qualities that drew the two men together as friends.

EXAMINE the essay to find passages in which Taibbi expresses the emotion for Dietz that he had neglected to express before his friend's death.

WRITE an essay in which you argue for or against the idea that men are more reluctant to express their friendship for one another than women are. Support your argument with both logical reasons and specific examples from your experience and observation.

Drifting Away

DIANE COLE

The death of a friend, as in the losses suffered by Silko and Taibbi, is not the only way a friendship can end. In the following article from MS. Magazine, *Diane Cole explains that just "drifting away" can also end a friendship. A contributing editor to* Savvy *magazine and* Psychology Today, *Cole has also published the nonfiction self-help books* Hunting the Headhunters: A Woman's Guide *(1988) and* After Great Pain: A New Life *(1990). The latter book, in which she focuses on the phenomenon of loss and grief and the healing process, is similar in theme to this essay.*

BEFORE YOU READ

THINK about the most meaningful gift you ever received from a friend. What was this gift? What made this gift special? Was it expensive? Was it unusual? Was it symbolic in some way? Have you ever received a thoughtless gift that hurt your feelings in some way? What was this gift, and why did it make you feel as it did?

EXAMINE the title. How does "drifting away" differ from other ways of ending a friendship? For example, the friendships in the previous two selections (see pp. 157–167) were ended by death. In your opinion, what is the most difficult way to end a friendship?

WRITE a journal entry in which you tell how one of your friends has "drifted away" from you, or how you have "drifted away" from your friend. What caused the separation? What, if anything, could either of you have done to preserve the friendship? Why didn't you both work harder to keep the friendship?

AS YOU READ

Determine why Diane sent the crystal bowl to Jean as a wedding present. Notice also how the bowl comes to symbolize, or represent, their friendship and its demise.

Whenever I shop for a wedding present, I look for a crystal bowl—one 1 that is round and perfect, like the shape of the world, if the world were so.

Gifts are symbolic. They reflect the giver, the receiver, and the rela- 2 tionship between the two. And so did the perfect crystal bowl that I recently sent one of my oldest friends, who, in another symbolic gesture, had not invited me to her wedding. In a sense, I suppose, we were sparring, gesture for gesture. For a guest list is symbolic, too. Being invited means you hold a place in the happy couple's universe. Not being invited means you do not.

My friend (I'll call her Jean) and I had grown up together, periodically 3 losing then finding each other again as we moved into adulthood. In retrospect, that we managed to keep on seeking and finding each other at all is remarkable: we were always moving to different cities—for a new school, a new job, a new husband—each of us choosing such outwardly similar but inwardly different paths that, increasingly along the way, there had been quarrels, misunderstandings, silences.

But even in silence there was always the pull of the old friendship: we 4 had *always* been friends; how could we not be now? There were all the adventures we had shared of being moonstruck adolescents together, discovering books and movies and crushes on boys. There were the countless, endless late-night tête-à-têtes, heightened by lack of sleep and Tab, in which we would reveal our innermost thoughts. Most of all, there were the hundred million tiny details about each other's lives that we knew and would always know in a way that no one else outside our families would ever know as well—the sweet-peppery scents of our mothers' kitchens, the tense and teasing sound of our brothers' banter, and all the secret hopes our parents carried for us.

Paying tribute to that past, hoping to find some way to weave it into 5 the present, now and then we would write or send a message through a friend, and try to renew that ancient spirit of camaraderie. But once the rhythm of a friendship has been lost, it's hard to regain.

Jean and I were no different from any number of other women I know 6
who have felt the loss, hurt, and anger of a once warm friendship that has
faltered. There was no specific incident or argument, no single conflict
either of us could name. Seldom is there a single "reason," but psychologists
offer both some solace and some explanation. They say we identify our
women friends with our mothers. And as a result we often end up having
to unravel the same tangled and conflicting needs in both relationships: the
desire to be like them and "connect" with them, yet also be independent
and different; and to be mature enough to understand those differences,
yet not feel betrayed by them.

I suppose Jean and I had been going through our own version of this 7
dance for years: my marriage had come just before her sudden split with a
longtime boyfriend; sometime later, her professional preoccupation with
settling into a new career coincided with my two wrenching miscarriages.
In these instances, as in so many smaller ones, not just the beat, but the
very music we heard was different. The friendship, like distant music,
simply faded, perhaps never to be heard, or shared, the same way again.

And so when I learned that Jean was getting married, I expected no 8
invitation. But inwardly, it was as if a final connection had been broken,
and the slight still hurt. The little girl who had first been friends with her
so many years ago cried out: after going through so many paces together,
how could Jean not allow me to dance at her wedding? Didn't she know
that I still cared what happened to her, wanted to celebrate her happiness
with her, loved her in the way that only an old friend can? Should I let her
know? *How* could I let her know? I thought about writing, but didn't.
Instead, I sent her the crystal bowl.

Jean's thank-you note arrived some weeks later. It was as tentative and 9
strained as my gesture had been bold. Neither tone accurately reflected the
friendship I recalled and in some sense had wanted to call back: one that
had once been by turns fun and serious, earnest, jaunty, and perfect, in its
way.

"Dear Diane," she wrote in the loop-filled scrawl still so familiar that 10
I did not need to glance at her signature to recognize it. "Thank you for
the lovely crystal bowl. When we made our wedding plans, I thought about
whether this could be the opportunity for us to renew our friendship, but
I decided this idea was an impractical dream. . . ."

Jean's message was clear—as if it hadn't been before. But in sending 11
that crystal bowl, what kind of a response had I expected, and, in my own
impractically dreamy way, wanted?

"Well, I don't know what you expected, but what you did really wasn't 12 very nice," my husband said quietly, after I read him Jean's words. "You didn't send her a gift, you *threw* it at her. You were angry that she ignored you, and so you sent her something that demanded that she notice you. Even if it was a beautiful gift, even if you *thought* you were doing something special, it wasn't very nice."

My cheeks flushed red, perhaps because words sting so much only 13 when they are true—even when they represent only one part of a more complex truth. Although I had not allowed myself to even glimpse it at the time, I had to admit that part of me had been saying, "I'll show you! See how generous I am, in spite of your snub, to wish you happiness with something so perfect and beautiful as this! If only you had invited me, we *could* have mended the friendship, after all!"

But anger and love are the closest of kin, and on the day that I sent 14 this present, I had persuaded myself that it was only love. The bowl somehow had come to stand for the best part of our friendship. True, it was perfect in a way that no friendship, no relationship between any two people, can ever be. But when I watched the light play off the diamond-patterned glass, all I could think of were the many brilliant, ephemeral glimmers of insight we had seen flash before us in all those late-night conversations when, night after night, we would recount our hurts, weave zany schemes, tell our dreams, imagine our future, and share all the joy and anguish that is known as growing up. And so I sent that bowl, as a memento, a token, an acknowledgment that whether we liked it or not, we were somehow wrapped up in each other's lives.

Only later as I read Jean's letter once again, did I remember another 15 bowl, the gilded crystal at the center of Henry James's novel *The Golden Bowl*. As the novel progresses, the nearly invisible yet irreparable crack beneath the bowl's glittering surface comes to stand for all the unseen faults that mar human relations.

The bowl I had sent was merely glass, but for Jean and me, the crack 16 in our friendship had grown too deep. And, like James's gilded bowl, our friendship could not be repaired. It had cast as intricate a pattern through our lives as a burst of light on a lovely crystal bowl. But now, I realized, it was time to let it rest at last. Let it be remembered fondly and in all its complexity. But let it go.

❀ ❀ ❀

AFTER YOU READ

THINK again about Diane's motivation in sending the crystal bowl to Jean. What were her reasons for sending a gift at all? Why do you think she chose the crystal bowl rather than another present? How is the crystal bowl like their friendship?

EXAMINE the sentence "But once the rhythm of a friendship has been lost, it's hard to regain." Describe how the rhythm of Diane and Jean's friendship was lost. Do you think Diane and Jean were equally responsible for the disintegration of the friendship, or do you believe that one person was more responsible than the other? Why do you feel as you do? How might the friendship have been restored?

WRITE a list of the reasons that friends drift apart. Then discuss your list with a group of your classmates, supporting each reason with specific examples from your own experiences or observations.

Finding a Wife

GARY SOTO

Gary Soto is a writer and university professor from Fresno, California, who is perhaps best known for his poetry. He received the 1976 United States Award of the International Poetry Forum for his book-length poem The Elements of San Joaquin, *and his more recent collection* Black Hair *(1985) has also been highly praised. Soto is also becoming increasingly well known for his collections of autobiographical essays, including* Small Faces *(1986) and* Baseball in April *(1990). In the following essay, Soto argues that it is easy to find a wife, recounting his own experience to prove the point. Yet he also suggests that fortune, or circumstance, plays a rather significant role in the process and implies that people may find mates more easily if they are open-minded and willing to establish relationships with people who are unlike themselves in some way: Soto, who is a Mexican-American, fell in love with his Japanese-American neighbor.*

BEFORE YOU READ

THINK about your own image of an ideal mate. Is this image clear and specific? Do you know exactly the kind of person you want to marry? Are you willing to change this ideal if reality presents you with another kind of person? If you are married, think about the image of a mate you held before you met your husband or wife. Does your spouse conform to the ideal mate you envisioned? If not, do the differences matter, or do you think the real person you married is more suited to you than your ideal mate would have been?

EXAMINE the first two sentences of the essay, in which Soto states simply and directly, "It's easy to find a wife. . . . Pick anybody. . . ." Do you think he means exactly what he says? Or is he being ironic, saying one thing when he means something else entirely?

WRITE in your journal a list of the physical characteristics that appeal to you in a mate. Then list other qualities you would like your mate to have. Finally, reread your list and put a check by those characteristics and features you consider most important.

AS YOU READ

Try to answer this question: Why was the author attracted to the young Japanese-American woman whom he married? Write brief notes in the margins to help you answer this question.

It's easy to find a wife, I told my students. Pick anybody, I said, and they chuckled and fidgeted in their chairs. I laughed a delayed laugh, feeling hearty and foolish as a pup among these young men who were in my house to talk poetry and books. We talked, occasionally making sense, and drank cup after cup of coffee until we were so wired we had to stand up and walk around the block to shake out our nerves. 1

When they left I tried to write a letter, grade papers, and finally nap on the couch. My mind kept turning to how simple it is to find a wife; that we can easily say after a brief two- or three-week courtship, "I want to marry you." 2

When I was twenty, in college and living on a street that was a row of broken apartment buildings, my brother and I returned to our apartment from a game of racquetball to sit in the living room and argue whether we should buy a quart of beer. We were college poor, living off the cheap blessings of rice, raisins, and eggs that I took from our mom's refrigerator when Rick called her into the backyard about a missing sock from his laundry—a ploy from the start. 3

"Rick, I only got a dollar," I told him. He slapped his thigh and told me to wake up. It was almost the end of the month. And he was right. In two days our paychecks from Zak's Car Wash would burn like good report cards in our pockets. So I gave in. I took the fifteen cents—a dime and five pennies—he had plucked from the ashtray of loose change in his bedroom, and went downstairs, across the street and the two blocks to Scott's Liquor. While I was returning home, swinging the quart of beer like a lantern, I saw the Japanese woman who was my neighbor, cracking walnuts on her 4 front porch. I walked slowly so that she looked up, smiling. I smiled, said hello, and continued walking to the rhythm of her hammer rising and falling.

In the apartment I opened the beer and raised it like a chalice before we measured it in glasses, each of us suspicious that the other would get more. I rattled sunflower seeds onto a plate, and we pinched fingersful, the beer in our hands cutting loose a curtain of bubbles. We were at a party with no music, no host, no girls. Our cat, Mensa, dawdled in, blinking from the dull smoke of a sleepy afternoon. She looked at us, and we looked at her. Rick flicked a seed at her and said, "That's what we need—a woman!"

I didn't say anything. I closed my eyes, legs shot out in a V from the couch, and thought of that girl on the porch, the rise and fall of her hammer, and the walnuts cracking open like hearts.

I got up and peeked from our two-story window that looked out onto a lawn and her apartment. No one. A wicker chair, potted plants, and a pile of old newspapers. I looked until she came out with a broom to clean up the shells. "Ah, my little witch," I thought, and raced my heart downstairs, but stopped short of her house because I didn't know what to say or do. I stayed behind the hedge that separated our yards and listened to her broom swish across the porch, then start up the walk to the curb. It was then that I started to walk casually from behind the hedge and, when she looked at me with a quick grin, I said a hearty hello and walked past her without stopping to talk. I made my way to the end of the block where I stood behind another hedge, feeling foolish. I should have said something. "Do you like walnuts," I could have said, or maybe, "Nice day to sweep, isn't it?"—anything that would have my mouth going.

I waited behind that hedge, troubled by my indecision. I started back up the street and found her bending over a potted geranium, a jar of cloudy water in her hand. Lucky guy, I thought, to be fed by her.

I smiled as I passed, and she smiled back. I returned to the apartment and my bedroom where I stared at my homework and occasionally looked out the window to see if she was busy on the porch. But she wasn't there. Only the wicker chair, the plants, the pile of newspapers.

The days passed, white as clouds. I passed her house so often that we began to talk, sit together on the porch, and eventually snack on sandwiches that were thick as Bibles, with tumblers of milk to wash down her baked sweet bread flecked with tiny crushed walnuts.

After the first time I ate at her house, I hurried to the apartment to brag about my lunch to my brother who was in the kitchen sprinkling raisins on his rice. Sandwiches, I screamed, milk, cold cuts, chocolate ice cream! I spoke about her cupboards, creaking like ships weighed down with a cargo of rich food, and about her, that woman who came up to my shoulder. I was in love and didn't know where to go from there.

As the weeks passed, still white as clouds, we saw more of each other. 12 Then it happened. On another Saturday, after browsing at a thrift shop among gooseneck lamps and couches as jolly as fat men, we went to the west side of Fresno for Mexican food—menudo for me and burritos for her, with two beers clunked down on our table. When we finished eating and were ready to go, I wiped my mouth and plucked my sole five-dollar bill from my wallet as I walked to the cashier. It was all the big money I had. I paid and left the restaurant as if it were nothing, as if I spent such money every day. But inside I was thinking, "What am I going to do?"

Scared as I was, I took Carolyn's hand into mine as we walked to the 13 car. I released it to open the door for her. We drove and drove, past thrift shops she longed to browse through, but I didn't want to stop because I was scared I would want to hold her hand again. After turning corners aimlessly, I drove back to her house where we sat together on the front porch, not touching. I was shivering, almost noticeably. But after a while, I did take her hand into mine and that space between us closed. We held hands, little tents opening and closing, and soon I nuzzled my face into her neck to find a place to kiss.

I married this one Carolyn Oda, a woman I found cracking walnuts on 14 an afternoon. It was a chance meeting: I was walking past when she looked up to smile. It could have been somebody else, a girl drying persimmons on a line, or one hosing down her car, and I might have married another and been unhappy. But it was Carolyn, daughter of hard workers, whom I found cracking walnuts. She stirred them into dough that she shaped into loaves, baked in the oven, and set before me so that my mouth would keep talking in its search of the words to make me stay.

❀ ❀ ❀

AFTER YOU READ

THINK about the opening sentences of the essay again. Do you now have a different interpretation of the author's meaning when he says that "it's easy to find a wife"? What was involved in the author's finding a wife? Would it be possible for a woman to find a husband in the same way?

EXAMINE the frequent descriptions of food in this essay. Why do you think these references are included? Why might the author have been particularly interested in food at the time that he was a young student? What kinds of associations do we have with food and with people who feed us or with whom we share food?

WRITE a list of suggestions telling a specific audience how to find a mate. For example, you could advise women who are tall or men who are shy or people who smoke, work nights, or can't afford to date.

The Right to Marry

JOANNE JACOBS

The author of this reading selection, Joanne Jacobs, is a syndicated columnist for the San Jose, California, Mercury News. *In this column she argues that homosexuals should be allowed to form relationships that are legally recognized in the same way marriage is recognized by our society. Her argument is not viewed favorably by everyone; thus she attempts in this essay to* persuade *readers of the validity of her position.*

BEFORE YOU READ

THINK about your own position on this issue. Do you think marriage should be restricted to heterosexual couples? Why or why not?

EXAMINE the words *homosexual* and *heterosexual.* The prefix *homo* means "same, or like" while the prefix *hetero* means "other, or different." Thus, a homosexual mates with a person of the same sex while a heterosexual mates with a person of the opposite sex. What connotations have these words acquired in our society? What stereotypes are associated with each?

WRITE a journal entry supporting your view on the issue of whether homosexuals should have the right to marry.

AS YOU READ

Whether you agree with Jacobs or not, try to evaluate fairly the arguments and evidence she presents.

"It is better to marry than to burn," said the Dear Abby of the first century, St. Paul (1 Corinthians 7:9), but what's going down in flames these days is our traditional ideas of marriage.

The traditional story—boy meets girl, boy gets girl, girl gets pregnant—no longer ends with boy and girl getting married.

When boy meets boy, or girl meets girl, things get complicated.

In Los Angeles, a woman won the right to sue for joint custody of her former female lover's daughter, born during their relationship.

In effect, the ex-lover is seeking the same parental rights as an infertile husband whose wife bears a child through artificial insemination.

In San Francisco, they're about to sanction a sort of non-marriage marriage for gay and heterosexual "domestic partners."

The bill by gay Supervisor Harry Britt allows unmarried couples, gay or straight, who live together and share basic expenses to register as domestic partners at City Hall or in front of a notary and witnesses.

Domestic partners would not accumulate community property, and could "divorce" at will.

City policies would be revised to end discrimination against unmarried couples, which could include legal standing in real estate and rental contracts, and hospital and jail visitation rights.

A task force would develop a plan to extend health benefits to the domestic partners of city employees.

Like dependents of married workers, domestic partners would pay for the coverage.

While the bill primarily affects city employees, the Chamber of Commerce announced a study of how business can extend benefits to employees in non-marital relationships.

"Society is evolving and government has not been keeping up with it," said Matt Coles, an American Civil Liberties Union attorney who helped draft the ordinance.

"People live in relationships without getting married. If government doesn't take account of this, we'll have all sorts of problems."

If heterosexuals want social sanction for their relationship, they should get married. If homosexuals want social sanction for their relationship, they should get married.

St. Paul was right: It's better to marry than to burn. And it's better for society when people form long-term, loving commitments with whomever it is that they love. Let them have all the joys of marriage, all the rights and all the hassles.

"The church is fundamentally opposed to any tinkering with the concept of marriage as a religious sacrament exchanged between a male and female," said Norman J. Phillips, a spokesman for the Archdiocese of San Francisco.

That's the traditional view, but is it sensible?   18

"More things belong to marriage than four bare legs in a bed," as John   19
Heywood wrote in 1546; it's also more than a procreative contract.

If an eighty-year-old man and an eighty-year-old woman wish to marry,   20
nobody would deny them that right on grounds they can't have children.

Why deny a pair of thirty-year-old men who want recognition of their   21
commitment to each other?

With the link between promiscuity and AIDS, society has an interest   22
in encouraging marriage, which encourages monogamy.

For gay men, AIDS has made issues like health benefits, hospital   23
visitation, sick leave and bereavement leave more critical.

When a dying man's lover can't visit intensive care because he's not a   24
"relative," or seeks unemployment benefits after quitting his job to care for
a sick lover, the question arises: What's family?

I once worked with a gay woman who had a love affair with a foreign   25
student. When the other woman completed her degree, her visa ran out,
and there was no chance to change her immigration status through
marriage. She had to go home.

Their relationship was as worthy of respect as that of any two people   26
in love. They would have married gladly. Why deny that human right?

California's marriage law didn't mention gender until 1977, when the   27
legislature added language making it clear that it takes two sexes to tango,
matrimonially.

I say: If marriage is good for straights, it's equally good for gays.   28
Anybody who can form a lasting, loving bond with another human being
deserves society's respect and support and a fondue pot.

❀ ❀ ❀

AFTER YOU READ

THINK about the arguments you listed for your own position on this issue.
Has reading the essay changed your position in any way? If so, how?

EXAMINE the arguments Jacobs presents. What are her main arguments,
and how does she support them? Are her arguments persuasive? What is
her strongest argument? Her weakest?

WRITE a summary of Jacobs's arguments and then state your own position,
explaining why you do or do not agree with the arguments she presents.

The Lies That Bind

PAUL THALER

The following essay was originally published on June 9, 1991, in the "About Men" column of The New York Times Magazine. *In this essay, Paul Thaler, who is director of journalism at Mercy College in Dobbs Ferry, New York, questions the wisdom of always telling the complete truth to one's mate.*

BEFORE YOU READ

THINK about the question of truth and falsehood. Is it always bad to tell a lie? Is it always good to tell the truth?

EXAMINE the title "The Lies That Bind." We usually think of a lie as separating rather than binding people in a relationship. Can lies "bind" a relationship? How? (Note also the play on the phrase "the ties that bind"—referring to marriage.)

WRITE a journal entry in which you tell about a lie that you once told to a wife or husband, girlfriend or boyfriend, or close friend. What was this lie, or mistruth, and why did you tell it? Did you make the right decision, or should you have told the complete truth in this particular instance? Explain.

AS YOU READ

Identify and underline Thaler's thesis statement. What specific supporting examples does he give for this statement?

The other day I lied to Amy. It wasn't a big lie, but it was big enough to 1
assuage her doubts. Asked how I had spent the previous evening, I
explained that work at the college had kept me late into the night. At
another time, with perhaps a different person, another answer—a more
truthful one—would have been offered. But not for Amy. Knowing that
the evening was shared with a former girlfriend—albeit eating an innocent
dinner at a very public restaurant—would have opened an old wound that
has never fully healed. It all seems like a contradiction: our ties are forged
by a strong symbiosis, and yet I realize I have continually lied to keep it so.
The "truth," as I have discovered, often hurts and is less a prerequisite for
a meaningful relationship than we may think.

This realization, a recent one, has come as quite a surprise for me. I 2
once thought that love meant abandoning the lies of your life, those fences
built to quarantine your real self from the everyday world. Falling in love
meant the building of trust, honesty, and openness—the coming together
of two hearts, two minds. Love letters espoused such thoughts; marriage
vows codified them. Certainly this was a delightful myth, sustained by
advertisers, Dr. Ruth, pulp novels, *Cosmopolitan* magazine, and B movies.
Love, explained Erich Segal in his novel *Love Story*, meant never having
to say you're sorry. The translation was clear: love meant complete
acceptance of wrongdoings, disappointments, hurts, character flaws, and
selfishness. And, for the most part, we have bought the script.

But the romantic language of love never included the vocabulary of 3
the lie. Unspoken was the thought that love could also be tied to concealing
the painful truths that trample sensitivities and whittle away at self-esteem.

In our attempt to idealize the notion of romance, we have lost a sense 4
of our own vulnerability. And vulnerable we are, coping with a rapidly
changing and confusing culture. In trying to understand our roles as men
and women, a connection lost in the sweep of societal gender chaos, we
are in danger of being overloaded. A lie can help keep the circuits intact.

Of course, lovers lie all the time, although they may fervently deny it. 5
A close friend insists that honesty is paramount in his relationship with his
wife—well, except for those small "white lies." Indeed, his are small lies
about matters having to do with personal habits and predilections. The lies
protect the vulnerable shell of his relationship and forestall confrontations.
The lie has given him a retreat for doubts and indecisions.

Another friend wags a finger at me, complaining that I should have 6
told Amy about my date with the former girlfriend. Even if it was hard to
swallow, she said, Amy was entitled to a knowledge of "the real world."

Would my friend consider telling her husband about an old affair that 7
had gone sour?

"Of course not," she replied. "It would destroy him and our marriage." 8

And that, of course, is the point. Some truths chip away at relation- 9
ships, others chop them down whole. It is a matter of drawing lines, and
we all draw different ones when it comes to the truth.

Most lies that I spin are inconsequential, simply intent on maintaining 10
the day-to-day stability of my relationship. I have applauded Amy for her
cooking, her new dress, her latest diet. Neither the cooking (overdone
chicken with a peculiar white sauce), her dress (an obtuse floral pattern),
or her weight loss (which effectively cut the appealing lines of her body)
elicited much excitement. Or the truth. In each case, a lie served as a salve,
not a sword.

There are also bigger lies about more important things. Amy has asked 11
me on more than one occasion, "Do you love me?" If ranked, this inquiry
would probably top the universal list. If I were always truthful, and
sometimes I am not, I would confide to Amy the fluctuating tide of my
emotions, a response that might stab into the heart of our relationship. But
at those times I search for a more positive answer. And why not? When we
talk about love, what do we say and what does it mean? Language is often
too neutered to express complex feelings.

And yet, once such hard "truths" are out in the air, it's impossible to 12
push them aside. Misspent words continue to haunt long after that particular emotion has changed into something else. So when Amy asks whether
I love her, I always do, even if, at times, I don't. The lie is a support system
that is part of the ritual of intimacy. It may not be truthful, but it is
confirming. It is a paradox, indeed, that in writing this article, I have
revealed my lies.

I should note that Amy herself is not a great believer of the lie. Amy is 13
especially quick to point out when I try to lie to myself. She fails to
understand that at times self-deception also plays a vital role in a healthy
relationship.

I usually dabbled in self-deception each time the subject of marriage 14
was broached. Ever since we met six years ago, Amy had wanted to marry;
I opted for the status quo. As a single person, I had long valued the
independence and freedom that a marriage might limit. But Amy as-
tutely noted that if bachelorhood were a guiding principle, why then had
I chosen a rather conventional, monogamous relationship with her during these years? She was right, of course, and the contradiction between

my words and life style was evident. But this longstanding lie gave me time to wear the skin of our relationship to see how it fit and felt. Had I been forced to confront my "true" feelings before, our relationship might not have survived, much less flourished. Finally I did reach a decision. Just recently, Amy and I were married, and our lives have never been more secure.

As intimacy deepens, the need for lying deepens also. The more that's 15 exposed, the more there's a need to guard those unflattering secrets. A reflexive action to confide in people outside a relationship—a friend or professional counselor—comes from our emotional wellsprings, our need to protect and not harm the people we love. So we exchange confidences with friends that we could not share with a lover. We find the need to estrange ourselves from an intimate relationship in order to discover the problems that may exist within it. The reason is apparent: often a partner is least capable to help, caught herself (or himself) in the entanglements of intimacy and unable to provide perspective or detachment. In my case, I talk to my brother. I tell him of my fears, insecurities, and doubts; the problems with commitment, monogamy, and sex, the confusion that stems from loving too little or too much.

Within the confines of intimacy, however, such truths can hurt, and 16 often needlessly. The problem of being truthful often centers on what in fact is truth. I have found that it is an entity in constant flux. Yesterday's truth may be less than truthful tomorrow. So perhaps a lie gives us the chance to be introspective about love in a way that truth can't. Perhaps, in a real way, it is a truer reflection of love. The lie allows us to question silently, letting us withhold judgment, at least for the time being. It may not necessarily make intimacy more valuable or answer deep-seeded problems. But perhaps it does.

❀ ❀ ❀

AFTER YOU READ

THINK about the reasons that Thaler gives for lying to his wife, Amy. What are these reasons? Are they good reasons or bad reasons? Explain.

EXAMINE the specific lies that Thaler tells to Amy. Which do you think were the most justified? The least justified? Could Thaler have presented the truth in a way that Amy would have understood and not been hurt? In each case, what do you think would have been the result if Thaler had told the complete truth? Do you think that such small lies as these are an end in themselves, or can they lay the groundwork for a larger dishonesty in a relationship?

WRITE an essay in which you argue for or against Thaler's basic point that in order to maintain a relationship it is sometimes necessary to lie to one's mate.

Distance

RAYMOND CARVER

Raymond Carver is the author of several collections of poems and short stories, many of which are set in his native Pacific Northwest and focus on blue-collar characters with whom he worked, fished, and hunted while he was establishing himself as a writer. In 1957, when Carver was nineteen years old, he married his sixteen-year-old sweetheart Maryann Burk, and their daughter Christine was born during their first year of marriage. Twenty-six years later, after a long struggle with alcoholism and several trial separations, Carver and his wife divorced. After Carver separated from his wife, he met and began a relationship with poet Tess Gallagher, whom he married in June of 1988, the same month that he died of lung cancer. As in the story "Distance," which was published in Fires: Essays, Poems, Stories, 1966–1982 (1984), *much of Carver's fiction focuses on love and marriage, especially on their failure.*

BEFORE YOU READ

THINK about the phrase "crazy in love," which the narrator uses at the beginning of the "story-within-a-story" to describe the feelings shared by the recently married eighteen-year-old boy and his seventeen-year-old wife. What does this phrase suggest to you? Do you associate it with the idea of "romantic love"? Does romantic love, or being "crazy in love," usually last for a lifetime? Why or why not?

EXAMINE the first and last sections of the story, which are set off from the rest of the story by additional space. The events in these sections, which serve as a kind of "frame" for the story, take place twenty years after the events in the central part. These sections focus on a different relationship than the one in the middle section. Skim the introductory section to determine who the characters are and what their relationship is to each other.

WRITE in your journal your prediction of what will happen to the young couple in the story who are "crazy in love." Will they be "crazy in love" twenty years later? Explain why you believe as you do.

AS YOU READ

Identify the two "stories" or relationships in "Distance." You might even want to begin your reading with the central section, which takes place twenty years before the beginning and ending sections. As you read the outer sections, keep in mind that the man—the father—tells the main story between the time "he comes back from the kitchen with drinks, settles into his chair, [and] begins" at the end of the first section and the time "he gets up from his chair and refills their glasses" at the beginning of the last section.

She's in Milan for Christmas and wants to know what it was like when 1
she was a kid. Always that on the rare occasions when he sees her.

Tell me, she says. Tell me what it was like then. She sips Strega, waits, 2
eyes him closely.

She is a cool, slim, attractive girl, a survivor from top to bottom. 3

That was a long time ago. That was twenty years ago, he says. They're 4
in his apartment on the Via Fabroni near the Cascina Gardens.

You can remember, she says. Go on, tell me. 5

What do you want to hear? he asks. What can I tell you? I could tell 6
you about something that happened when you were a baby. It involves you,
he says. But only in a minor way.

Tell me, she says. But first get us another drink, so you won't have to 7
interrupt half way through.

He comes back from the kitchen with drinks, settles into his chair, 8
begins.

They were kids themselves, but they were crazy in love, this eighteen-year- 9
old boy and his seventeen-year-old girlfriend when they married. Not all
that long afterwards they had a daughter.

The baby came along in late November during a severe cold spell that 10
just happened to coincide with the peak of the waterfowl season in that
part of the country. The boy loved to hunt, you see, that's part of it.

The boy and girl, husband and wife now, father and mother, lived in 11
a three-room apartment under a dentist's office. Each night they cleaned
the upstairs office in exchange for their rent and utilities. In the summer
they were expected to maintain the lawn and the flowers, and in winter
the boy shoveled snow from the walks and spread rock salt on the
pavement. The two kids, I'm telling you, were very much in love. On top
of this they had great ambitions and they were wild dreamers. They were
always talking about the things they were going to do and the places they
were going to go.

He gets up from his chair and looks out the window for a minute over 12
the tile rooftops at the snow that falls steadily through the late afternoon
light.

Tell the story, she says.   13

The boy and girl slept in the bedroom, and the baby slept in a crib in 14
the living room. You see, the baby was about three weeks old at this time
and had only just begun to sleep through the night.

One Saturday night, after finishing his work upstairs, the boy went into 15
the dentist's private office, put his feet up on the desk, and called Carl
Sutherland, an old hunting and fishing friend of his father's.

Carl, he said when the man picked up the receiver. I'm a father. We 16
had a baby girl.

Congratulations, boy, Carl said. How is the wife?   17

She's fine, Carl. The baby's fine, too, the boy said. Everybody's fine. 18

That's good, Carl said. I'm glad to hear it. Well, you give my regards 19
to the wife. If you called about going hunting, I'll tell you something. The
geese are flying down there to beat the band. I don't think I've ever seen
so many of them and I've been going for years. I shot five today. Two this
morning and three this afternoon. I'm going back in the morning and you
come along if you want to.

I want to, the boy said. That's why I called.   20

You be here at five-thirty sharp then and we'll go, Carl said. Bring lots 21
of shells. We'll get some shooting in all right. I'll see you in the morning.

The boy liked Carl Sutherland. He'd been a friend of the boy's father, 22
who was dead now. After the father's death, maybe trying to replace a loss
they both felt, the boy and Sutherland had started hunting together.
Sutherland was a heavy-set, balding man who lived alone and was not given

to casual talk. Once in a while, when they were together, the boy felt uncomfortable, wondered if he had said or done something wrong because he was not used to being around people who kept still for long periods of time. But when he did talk the older man was often opinionated, and frequently the boy didn't agree with the opinions. Yet the man had a toughness and woods-savvy about him that the boy liked and admired.

The boy hung up the telephone and went downstairs to tell the girl. 23 She watched while he laid out his things. Hunting coat, shell bag, boots, socks, hunting cap, long underwear, pump gun.

What time will you be back? the girl asked.   24

Probably around noon, he said. But maybe not until after five or six 25 o'clock. Is that too late?

It's fine, she said. We'll get along just fine. You go and have some fun. 26 You deserve it. Maybe tomorrow evening we'll dress Catherine up and go visit Sally.

Sure, that sounds like a good idea, he said. Let's plan on that.   27

Sally was the girl's sister. She was ten years older. The boy was a little 28 in love with her, just as he was a little in love with Betsy, who was another sister the girl had. He'd said to the girl, If we weren't married I could go for Sally.

What about Betsy? the girl said. I hate to admit it but I truly feel she's 29 better looking than Sally or me. What about her?

Betsy too, the boy said and laughed. But not in the same way I could 30 go for Sally. There's something about Sally you could fall for. No, I believe I'd prefer Sally over Betsy, if I had to make a choice.

But who do you really love? the girl asked. Who do you love most in 31 all the world? Who's your wife?

You're my wife, the boy said.   32

And will we always love each other? the girl asked, enormously 33 enjoying this conversation he could tell.

Always, the boy said. And we'll always be together. We're like the 34 Canada geese, he said, taking the first comparison that came to mind, for they were often on his mind in those days. They only marry once. They choose a mate early in life, and they stay together always. If one of them dies or something, the other one will never remarry. It will live off by itself somewhere, or even continue to live with the flock, but it will stay single and alone amongst all the other geese.

That's sad, the girl said. It's sadder for it to live that way, I think, alone 35 but with all the others, than just to live off by itself somewhere.

It is sad, the boy said. But it's Nature.   36

Have you ever killed one of those marriages? she asked. You know   37
what I mean.

He nodded. He said, Two or three times I've shot a goose, then a minute   38
or two later I'd see another goose turn back from the rest and begin to
circle and call over the goose that lay on the ground.

Did you shoot it too? she asked with concern.   39

If I could, he answered. Sometimes I missed.   40

And it didn't bother you? she said.   41

Never, he said. You can't think about it when you're doing it. You see,   42
I love everything there is about geese. I love to just watch them even when
I'm not hunting them. But there are all kinds of contradictions in life. You
can't think about the contradictions.

After dinner he turned up the furnace and helped her bathe the baby.   43
He marveled again at the infant who had half his features, the eyes and
mouth, and half the girl's, the chin and the nose. He powdered the tiny
body and then powdered in between the fingers and toes. He watched the
girl put the baby into its diaper and pajamas.

He emptied the bath into the shower basin and then he went upstairs.   44
It was cold and overcast outside. His breath streamed in the air. The grass,
what there was of it, looked like canvas, stiff and gray under the street light.
Snow lay in piles beside the walk. A car went by and he heard sand grinding
under the tires. He let himself imagine what it might be like tomorrow,
geese milling in the air over his head, the gun plunging against his shoulder.

Then he locked the door and went downstairs.   45

In bed they tried to read but both of them fell asleep, she first, letting   46
the magazine sink to the quilt. His eyes closed, but he roused himself,
checked the alarm, and turned off the lamp.

He woke to the baby's cries. The light was on out in the living room.   47
He could see the girl standing beside the crib rocking the baby in her arms.
In a minute she put the baby down, turned out the light and came back to
bed.

It was two o'clock in the morning and the boy fell asleep once more.   48

The baby's cries woke him again. This time the girl continued to sleep.   49
The baby cried fitfully for a few minutes and stopped. The boy listened,
then began to doze.

He opened his eyes. The living room light was burning. He sat up and   50
turned on the lamp.

I don't know what's wrong, the girl said, walking back and forth with   51
the baby. I've changed her and given her something more to eat. But she

keeps crying. She won't stop crying. I'm so tired I'm afraid I might drop her.

You come back to bed, the boy said. I'll hold her for a while. 52

He got up and took the baby while the girl went to lie down. 53

Just rock her for a few minutes, the girl said from the bathroom. Maybe 54 she'll go back to sleep.

The boy sat on the sofa and held the baby. He jiggled it in his lap until 55 its eyes closed. His own eyes were near closing. He rose carefully and put the baby back in the crib.

It was fifteen minutes to four and he still had forty-five minutes that 56 he could sleep. He crawled into bed.

But a few minutes later the baby began to cry once more. This time 57 they both got up, and the boy swore.

For God's sake what's the matter with you? the girl said to him. Maybe 58 she's sick or something. Maybe we shouldn't have given her the bath.

The boy picked up the baby. The baby kicked its feet and was quiet. 59 Look, the boy said, I really don't think there's anything wrong with her.

How do you know that? the girl said. Here, let me have her. I know 60 that I ought to give her something, but I don't know what I should give her.

After a few minutes had passed and the baby had not cried, the girl put 61 the baby down again. The boy and girl looked at the baby, and then they looked at each other as the baby opened its eyes and began to cry.

The girl took the baby. Baby, baby, she said with tears in her eyes. 62

Probably it's something on her stomach, the boy said. 63

The girl didn't answer. She went on rocking the baby in her arms, 64 paying no attention now to the boy.

The boy waited a minute longer then went to the kitchen and put on 65 water for coffee. He drew on his woolen underwear and buttoned up. Then he got into his clothes.

What are you doing? the girl said to him. 66

Going hunting, he said. 67

I don't think you should, she said. Maybe you could go later on in the 68 day if the baby is all right then. But I don't think you should go hunting this morning. I don't want to be left alone with the baby crying like this.

Carl's planning on me going, the boy said. We've planned it. 69

I don't give a damn about what you and Carl have planned, she said. 70 And I don't give a damn about Carl, either. I don't even know the man. I don't want you to go is all. I don't think you should even consider wanting to go under the circumstances.

You've met Carl before, you know him, the boy said. What do you 71 mean you don't know him?

That's not the point and you know it, the girl said. The point is I don't 72 intend to be left alone with a sick baby.

Wait a minute, the boy said. You don't understand. 73

No, you don't understand, she said. I'm your wife. This is your baby. 74 She's sick or something. Look at her. Why is she crying? You can't leave us to go hunting.

Don't get hysterical, he said. 75

I'm saying you can go hunting any time, she said. Something's wrong 76 with this baby and you want to leave us to go hunting.

She began to cry. She put the baby back in the crib, but the baby started 77 up again. The girl dried her eyes hastily on the sleeve of her nightgown and picked the baby up once more.

The boy laced his boots slowly, put on his shirt, sweater, and his coat. 78 The kettle whistled on the stove in the kitchen.

You're going to have to choose, the girl said. Carl or us. I mean it, 79 you've got to choose.

What do you mean? the boy said. 80

You heard what I said, the girl answered. If you want a family you're 81 going to have to choose.

They stared at each other. Then the boy took his hunting gear and went 82 upstairs. He started the car, went around to the windows and, making a job of it, scraped away the ice.

The temperature had dropped during the night, but the weather had 83 cleared so that the stars had come out. The stars gleamed in the sky over his head. Driving, the boy looked out at the stars and was moved when he considered their distance.

Carl's porchlight was on, his station wagon parked in the drive with 84 the motor idling. Carl came outside as the boy pulled to the curb. The boy had decided.

You might want to park off the street, Carl said as the boy came up the 85 walk. I'm ready, just let me hit the lights. I feel like hell, I really do, he went on. I thought maybe you had overslept so I just this minute called your place. Your wife said you had left. I feel like hell.

It's okay, the boy said, trying to pick his words. He leaned his weight 86 on one leg and turned up his collar. He put his hands in his coat pockets. She was already up, Carl. We've both been up for a while. I guess there's something wrong with the baby. I don't know. The baby keeps crying, I mean. The thing is, I guess I can't go this time, Carl.

You should have just stepped to the phone and called me, boy, Carl 87
said. It's okay. You know you didn't have to come over here to tell me.
What the hell, this hunting business you can take it or leave it. It's not
important. You want a cup of coffee?

I'd better get back, the boy said. 88

Well, I expect I'll go ahead then, Carl said. He looked at the boy. 89

The boy kept standing on the porch, not saying anything. 90

It's cleared up, Carl said. I don't look for much action this morning. 91
Probably you won't have missed anything anyway.

The boy nodded. I'll see you, Carl, he said. 92

So long, Carl said. Hey, don't let anybody ever tell you otherwise, Carl 93
said. You're a lucky boy and I mean that.

The boy started his car and waited. He watched Carl go through the 94
house and turn off all the lights. Then the boy put the car in gear and pulled
away from the curb.

The living room light was on, but the girl was asleep on the bed and 95
the baby was asleep beside her.

The boy took off his boots, pants and shirt. He was quiet about it. In 96
his socks and woolen underwear, he sat on the sofa and read the morning
paper.

Soon it began to turn light outside. The girl and the baby slept on. 97
After a while the boy went to the kitchen and began to fry bacon.

The girl came out in her robe a few minutes later and put her arms 98
around him without saying anything.

Hey, don't catch your robe on fire, the boy said. She was leaning against 99
him but touching the stove, too.

I'm sorry about earlier, she said. I don't know what got into me. I don't 100
know why I said those things.

It's all right, he said. Here, let me get this bacon. 101

I didn't mean to snap like that, she said. It was awful. 102

It was my fault, he said. How's Catherine? 103

She's fine now. I don't know what was the matter with her earlier. I 104
changed her again after you left, and then she was fine. She was just fine
and she went right off to sleep. I don't know what it was. Don't be mad
with us.

The boy laughed. I'm not mad with you. Don't be silly, he said. Here, 105
let me do something with this pan.

You sit down, the girl said. I'll fix this breakfast. How does a waffle 106
sound with this bacon?

Sounds great, he said. I'm starved. 107

She took the bacon out of the pan and then she made waffle batter. 108
He sat at the table, relaxed now, and watched her move around the
kitchen.

She left to close their bedroom door. In the living room she put on a 109
record that they both liked.

We don't want to wake that one up again, the girl said. 110

That's for sure, the boy said and laughed. 111

She put a plate in front of him with bacon, a fried egg, and a waffle. 112
She put another plate on the table for herself. It's ready, she said.

It looks swell, he said. He spread butter and poured syrup over the 113
waffle. But as he started to cut into the waffle, he turned the plate into his
lap.

I don't believe it, he said, jumping up from the table. 114

The girl looked at him and then at the expression on his face. She began 115
to laugh.

If you could see yourself in the mirror, she said. She kept laughing. 116

He looked down at the syrup that covered the front of his woolen 117
underwear, at the pieces of waffle, bacon, and egg that clung to the syrup.
He began to laugh.

I was starved, he said, shaking his head. 118

You were starved, she said, laughing. 119

He peeled off the woolen underwear and threw it at the bathroom 120
door. Then he opened his arms and she moved into them.

We won't fight any more, she said. It's not worth it, is it? 121

That's right, he said. 122

We won't fight any more, she said. 123

The boy said, We won't. Then he kissed her. 124

He gets up from his chair and refills their glasses. 125

That's it, he says. End of story. I admit it's not much of one. 126

I was interested, she says. It was very interesting if you want to know. 127
But what happened? she says. I mean later.

He shrugs and carries his drink over to the window. It's dark now but 128
still snowing.

Things change, he says. I don't know how they do. But they do without 129
your realizing it or wanting them to.

Yes, that's true, only—but she does not finish what she started. 130

She drops the subject then. In the window's reflection he sees her study 131
her nails. Then she raises her head. Speaking brightly, she asks if he is going
to show her the city, after all.

He says, Put your boots on and let's go. 132

But he stays by the window, remembering that life. They had laughed. 133
They had leaned on each other and laughed until the tears had come, while
everything else—the cold and where he'd go in it—was outside, for a while
anyway.

❀   ❀   ❀

AFTER YOU READ

THINK about how marriage changes a person's life by bringing new
responsibilities, especially when a baby is born. Is either the husband or the
wife as free to go out with friends as before the marriage? In Carver's story,
how does the girl feel about her husband going hunting with Carl? Why
does she feel this way? How does the husband feel? Why does he feel as
he does? How do the couple's feelings and the husband's decision cause
tension in the marriage? How is this tension resolved?

EXAMINE more carefully the framing sections of the story for clues not
only to the relationship between the father and daughter but also to what
has happened to the parents' marriage in the twenty years following the
original events. Why does the father see his daughter only on "rare
occasions"? How is this "cool, slim, attractive girl" a "survivor from top
to bottom"? What does their meeting in "his apartment on the Via Fabroni
near the Cascina Gardens" suggest about the father's marital situation?

At the end of the story, what does the daughter want to know when
she asks "But what happened? . . . I mean later"? How does the father
respond to her question? Why, then, does the daughter first "study her
nails," and then speak up "brightly"? Finally, what feelings do you think
the father has as he stands by the window at the end of the story?

WRITE an essay in which you first define "romantic love" as originally felt
by the young couple in the story and then evaluate such love as the basis
for a successful relationship. Or WRITE an essay in which you discuss the
effect of a failed marriage on the children involved.

The Good Marriage

JUDITH S. WALLERSTEIN
AND
SANDRA BLAKESLEE

Judith S. Wallerstein and Sandra Blakeslee have co-authored Second Chances: Men, Women, and Children a Decade after Divorce *and* The Good Marriage: How and Why Love Lasts, *from which this reading selection was taken. Also the coauthor of* Surviving the Breakup: How Children and Parents Cope with Divorce, *Wallerstein is a senior lecturer at the School of Social Welfare at the University of California at Berkeley and the founder and executive director of the Center for the Family in Transition. Blakeslee is an award-winning science writer for* The New York Times. *In* The Good Marriage, *Wallerstein and Blakeslee use interviews with fifty couples and draw on their own experiences (Wallerstein has been happily married for forty-eight years) to try to answer the question "How and why does love last?"*

BEFORE YOU READ

THINK about the title of the selection. What, in your opinion, makes a "good marriage"? What makes a "bad marriage"? Can all marriages be classified as either good or bad?

EXAMINE the second paragraph, in which twenty-one-year-old Randolph Johnson describes the kind of marriage he wants. How is his idea of the ideal marriage similar to yours? How is it different?

WRITE a journal entry in which you describe "the good marriage," perhaps the kind of marriage you would like to have. Do you, or does anyone you know, have such a marriage?

AS YOU READ

Underline the qualities that Wallerstein and Blakeslee associate with "the good marriage."

We have been so preoccupied with divorce and crisis in the American 1
family that we have failed to notice the good marriages that are all around us and from which we can learn. In today's world it's easy to become overwhelmed by problems that seem to have no solution. But we *can* shape our lives at home, including our relationships with our children and marriage itself. The home is the one place where we have the potential to create a world that is to our own liking; it is the last place where we should feel despair. As never before in history, men and women today are free to design the kind of marriage they want, with their own rules and expectations.

Fortunately, many young people have not yet become cynical and are 2 still able to speak directly from the heart. After spending some wonderful hours talking to college students about their views of marriage, I received the next day a letter from Randolph Johnson, a twenty-one-year-old senior at the University of California in Santa Cruz. He wrote: "What I want in a wife is someone whom I know so well that she is a part of who I am and I of her. Someone to fill all that I am not but aspire to be. My wife is someone not just to share a life with but to build a life with. This is what marriage is to me, the sharing of two lives to complete each other. It is true that people change, but if people can change together then they need not grow apart."

Randolph speaks for a new generation that is still capable of optimism 3 about love and marriage and "the sharing of two lives to complete each other." He also speaks for a society that is tired to death of the war on marriage, escalating divorce rates, and the search for new partners in middle age. All of us want a different world for our children. When we're honest, we want it for ourselves.

It is absurd, in fact, to suggest that the need for enduring love and 4 intimacy in marriage is passé. The men and women I've seen in twenty-five years of studying divorce begin actively searching for a new relationship even before the divorce is final. In every study in which Americans are asked what they value most in assessing the quality of their lives, marriage comes first—ahead of friends, jobs, and money. In our fast-paced world men and women need each other more, not less. We want and need erotic love, sympathetic love, passionate love, tender, nurturing love all of our adult lives. We desire friendship, compassion, encouragement, a sense of being understood and appreciated, not only for what we do but for what we try to do and fail at. We want a relationship in which we can test our half-baked ideas without shame or pretense and give voice to our deepest fears. We want a partner who sees us as unique and irreplaceable.

In the past twenty years, marriage in America has undergone a pro- 5 found, irrevocable transformation, driven by changes in women's roles and the heightened expectations of both men and women. Without realizing it, we have crossed a marital Rubicon. For the first time in our history, the decision to stay married is purely voluntary. Anyone can choose to leave at any time—and everyone knows it, including the children. There used to be only two legal routes out of marriage—adultery and abandonment. Today one partner simply has to say, for whatever reason, "I want out." Divorce is as simple as a trip to the nearest courthouse.

Each year two million adults and a million children in this country are 6 newly affected by divorce. One in two American marriages ends in divorce, and one in three children can expect to experience their parents' divorce. This situation has powerful ripple effects that touch us all. The sense that relationships are unstable affects the family next door, the people down the block, the other children in the classroom. Feelings of intense anxiety about marriage permeate the consciousness of all young men and women on the threshold of adulthood. At every wedding the guests wonder, privately, will this marriage last? The bride and groom themselves may question why they should marry, since it's likely to break up.

To understand how our social fabric has been transformed, think of 7 marriage as an institution acted upon by centripetal forces pulling inward and centrifugal forces pulling outward. In times past the centripetal forces—law, tradition, religion, parental influence—exceeded those that could pull a marriage apart, such as infidelity, abuse, financial disaster, failed expectations, or the lure of the frontier. Nowadays the balance has changed. The weakened centripetal forces no longer exceed those that tug marriages apart.

In today's marriages, in which people work long hours, travel exten- 8 sively, and juggle careers with family, more forces tug at the relationship than ever before. Modern marriages are battered by the demands of her workplace as well as his, by changing community values, by anxiety about making ends meet each month, by geographical moves, by unemployment and recession, by the vicissitudes of child care, and by a host of other issues.

Marriage counselors like to tell their clients that there are at least six 9
people in every marital bed—the couple and both sets of parents. I'm here
to say that a crazy quilt of conflicting personal values and shifting social
attitudes is also in that bed. The confusion over roles and the indifference
of the community to long-term conjugal relationships are there, as are the
legacies of a self-absorbed, me-first, feminist-do-or-die, male-backlash
society. The ease of divorce and changing attitudes about the permanence
of marriage have themselves become centrifugal forces.

Our great unacknowledged fear is that these potent outside forces will 10
overwhelm the human commitment that marriage demands and that
marriage as a lasting institution will cease for most people. We are left with
a crushing anxiety about the future of marriage and about the men and
women within it.

My study of divorce has inevitably led me to think deeply about marriage. 11
Just as people who work with the dying worry about death, those of us
who work with troubled marriages are constantly forced to look at our
own relationships. So I have carefully taken note of my marriage and those
of my three grown children. As our fiftieth wedding anniversary approaches, I have thought long and hard about what my husband and I have
done to protect our marriage. Why have we been able to love each other
for so many years? Did we begin differently from those who divorced? Did
we handle crises differently? Or were we just lucky? What have I learned
that I can pass on to my children and my grandchildren?

I certainly have not been happy all through each year of my marriage. 12
There have been good times and bad, angry and joyful moments, times of
ecstasy and times of quiet contentment. But I would never trade my
husband, Robert, for another man. I would not swap my marriage for any
other. This does not mean that I find other men unattractive, but there is
all the difference in the world between a passing fancy and a life plan. For
me, there has always been only one life plan, the one I have lived with my
husband. But why is this so? What makes some marriages work while others
fail?

An acquaintance of mine—a highly regarded psychologist who has 13
done extensive marriage counseling—called me when she became engaged.
She said, "I want to spend several hours with you, drawing on your
experience. My fiancé is several years older than I am and has been through
one divorce. He's afraid of another failure. I'm thirty-eight years old and
have for many years been frightened of marriage. What wisdom do you
have for me based on your own marriage, which has always looked so ideal

to me, and also based on your many years of work with divorce? Help me anticipate what lies ahead for Jim and me, so I can be prepared." Her request intrigued me. What wisdom did she seek? She did not want shortcuts or hints but a realistic vision that could guide their efforts in building a successful marriage.

Not long after her call I decided to design a qualitative study of fifty   14 couples who had built lasting, happy marriages, couples who had confronted the same obstacles, crises, and temptations as everyone else and had overcome them. As I began setting up the study, I drew up a list of questions that would guide my inquiry. Are the people in good marriages different from the men and women whose marriages fall apart? Are there common ideas, ways of dealing with the inevitable crises? What can we learn about selecting a partner, about sex, the stresses of the workplace, infidelity, the arrival of a baby or of adolescence, coping with midlife, aging, and retirement? What is happy in a marriage when people are in their twenties, thirties, forties, or fifties, or when they reach retirement? What are the central themes at each life stage? What makes men happy? What makes women happy? What does each spouse value in one another? What do they regard as the glue of the marriage?

A good marriage is a process of continual change as it reflects new issues,   15 deals with problems that arise, and uses the resources available at each stage of life. All long-lasting marriages change, if simply because we all change as we grow older. People's needs, expectations, and wishes change during the life cycle; biological aging is intertwined with psychological change in every domain, including work, health, sex, parenting, and friends. The social milieu and external circumstances change as well. Thus the individuals change, the marriage changes, and the world outside changes—and not necessarily in sync with one another. As one woman said, "John and I have had at least six different marriages."

Many men and women are still becoming adults as they work on the   16 first chapter of their lives together—getting to know each other sexually, emotionally, and psychologically. This time of absorbing exploration is critically important for defining the couple's core relationship. Sadly, many couples find they cannot navigate this difficult first leg of the course. But if they do succeed, they will have a sturdy foundation for the structure of their marriage.

The birth of a child entirely revamps the internal landscape of mar-   17 riage. Becoming a father or mother is a major step in the life course, a step that requires inner psychological growth as well as changes in every part of the marital relationship and in the extended family. It is also usually a time when one or both partners have made career commitments; the tough road of the workplace stretches ahead, and its stresses are high.

For many people the years when the children are growing up is the 18 busiest time of their lives. A central issue is balancing the demands of work and of home. Children's needs for parental time and attention multiply along with the continuing demands of the workplace and often of school. Many couples cannot find enough time to be together even to exchange greetings, let alone make love.

The course of marriage changes again when children become adoles- 19 cents, when parents dealing with midlife issues and presentiments of aging are suddenly faced with sexually active youngsters. The growing dependency, illness, or death of the spouses' own aging parents adds further turbulence to this period. When the children leave home, the couple must find each other again and rebuild their relationship. This new stage provides an opportunity to re-create the marriage in a different mold, perhaps with time to travel and play together. If a husband and wife have not succeeded in building a good marriage by now, they may find themselves merely sharing a household.

A later part of the journey is retirement, when issues of dependency 20 and illness, as well as the opportunity to pursue new hobbies and interests and the continuing need for sexuality, take center stage. Once again the marriage is redefined, as the couple face life's final chapters and inevitably consider the loss of the partner and their own deaths.

All through adulthood our internal lives change as we create new 21 images of ourselves and call up old images from the past. At each stage we draw on different memories and wishes, pulling them out like cards from a deck held close to the heart. The birth of a child draws on the memories and unconscious images of each parent's own infancy and childhood. That child's adolescence evokes the memories and conflicts of one's own teen years. Parents, watching their teenagers assert their independence, remember their own risk-taking behavior and realize that they were often saved from disaster by the skin of their teeth. And as old age approaches, every person draws on the experiences of prior losses in the family.

We have for many years told our children that marriage requires hard and 22 continuing work, but since we could not tell them where or how to begin this work, we soon lost their attention. How could we tell them what we did not know?

What then are the secrets? How do a man and a woman who meet as 23 strangers create a relationship that will satisfy them both throughout their lives?

First, the answer to the question I started with—what do people define 24 as happy in their marriage?—turned out to be straightforward. For everyone, happiness in marriage meant feeling respected and cherished. Without exception, these couples mentioned the importance of liking and respecting each other and the pleasure and comfort they took in each other's company. Some spoke of the passionate love that began their relationship, but for a surprising number love grew in the rich soil of the marriage, nourished by emotional and physical intimacy, appreciation, and fond memories. Some spoke of feeling well cared for, others of feeling safe, and still others of friendship and trust. Many talked about the family they had created together. But all felt that they were central to their partner's world and believed that creating the marriage and the family was the major commitment of their adult life. For most, marriage and children were the achievements in which they took the greatest pride.

For these couples, respect was based on integrity; a partner was 25 admired and loved for his or her honesty, compassion, generosity of spirit, decency, loyalty to the family, and fairness. An important aspect of respect was admiration of the partner as a sensitive, conscientious parent. The value these couples placed on the partner's moral qualities was an unexpected finding. It helps explain why many divorcing people speak so vehemently of losing respect for their former partner. The love that people feel in a good marriage goes with the conviction that the person is worthy of being loved.

These people were realists. No one denied that there were serious 26 differences—conflict, anger, even some infidelity—along the way. No one envisioned marriage as a rose garden, but all viewed its satisfactions as far outweighing the frustrations over the long haul. Most regarded frustrations, big and small, as an inevitable aspect of life that would follow them no matter whom they married. Everyone had occasional fantasies about the roads not taken, but their commitment to the marriage withstood the impulse to break out.

Above all, they shared the view that their partner was special in some 27 important regard and that the marriage enhanced each of them as individuals. They felt that the fit between their own needs and their partner's responses was unique and probably irreplaceable. In this they considered themselves very lucky, not entitled.

Their marriages had benefited from the new emphasis in our society 28 on equality in relationships between men and women. However they divided up the chores of the household and of raising the children, the couples agreed that men and women had equal rights and responsibilities within the family. Women have taken many casualties in the long fight to achieve equality, and many good men have felt beleaguered, confused, and angry about this contest. But important goals have been achieved: marriages today allow for greater flexibility and greater choice. Relationships are more mature on both sides and more mutually respectful. A couple's sex life can be freer and more pleasurable. Today's men and women meet on a playing field that is more level than ever before.

Unlike many unhappy families, these couples provided no evidence for the popular notion that there is a "his" marriage and a "her" marriage. On the contrary, the men and women were very much in accord. I did not see significant differences between husbands and wives in their goals for the marriage, in their capacity for love and friendship, in their interest in sex, in their desire to have children, or in their love and commitment to the children. They fully shared the credit for the success of the marriage and the family. Both men and women said, "Everything we have we did together." 29

Although some men were inhibited in their expression of feelings at the beginning of the marriage, as compared with their wives, I did not find much difference between the sexes in their ability to express emotions over the course of their relationship. Both spoke easily of their love for their partner. In response to my questioning, both men and women cried when they contemplated losing the other. 30

The children were central, both as individuals and as symbols of a shared vision, giving pleasure and sometimes unexpected meaning to the parents' lives and to the marriage. As the couples reported to me in detail, the children reflected their love and pride. And this powerful bond did not diminish when the children left home. 31

As I compared the happily married couples with the thousands of divorcing couples I have seen in the past twenty-five years, it was clear that these men and women had early on created a firm basis for their relationship and had continued to build it together. Many of the couples that divorced failed to lay such a foundation and did not understand the need to reinforce it over the years. Many marriages broke because the structure was too weak to hold in the face of life's vicissitudes. The happy couples regarded their marriage as a work in progress that needed continued attention lest it fall into disrepair. Even in retirement they did not take each other for granted. Far too many divorcing couples fail to understand that a marriage does not just spring into being after the ceremony. Neither the legal nor the religious ceremony makes the marriage. *People* do, throughout their lives. 32

As I write these final paragraphs, my thoughts turn to my grandmother and 33
to Nikki, my youngest grandchild. My grandmother, who brought her three
young children to the new land in the hold of a ship and raised them by
herself, knew exactly what she wanted for me. When I was growing up,
she used to sing Yiddish folk songs about love and marriage, about
mysterious suitors from distant lands. Whom will you marry? the songs
asked. Her hopes for me were built on her own tears. My future happy
marriage and my unborn healthy children made her sacrifice worthwhile.

Nikki has just turned four. She has recently demoted her twenty or so 34
stuffed bears, puppies, kittens, even her beloved tiger, to the foot of her
bed. They who were her special joy hardly have her attention now. She has
entered a new phase. I am to address her as "Princess" when I call. (The
great advantage of grandmothers, I have discovered, is that they follow
instructions, whereas mothers issue instructions.) She is Princess Jasmine,
and she awaits Aladdin. She is practicing at being a grown-up young lady,
preparing for the future with all the energy and devotion that she brought
to caring for her animals. No one works harder or with greater purpose
than a child at play.

What do I want for Nikki? The roads that were so clear to my 35
grandmother have become harder to follow. They fork often and sometimes lead to a dead end. Some directions, however, are still visible. I, too,
want my granddaughter to be strong and brave and virtuous. I want her to
love and be loved passionately and gently and proudly by a man worth
loving. I want her to experience the joys and terrors of raising children.
But far beyond what my grandmother envisioned for me, I want Nikki to
have the choices in life that I and many others had to fight for, real choices
that the community will respect and support. And I want her to know how
to choose wisely and understand how to make it all work. I hope that Nikki
finds the Aladdin that she has started to look for. If he comes flying into
her life on a magic carpet, so much the better.

AFTER YOU READ

THINK about the statement in the sixth paragraph that "each year two
million adults and a million children in this country are newly affected by
divorce. One in two American marriages ends in divorce, and one in three
children can expect to experience their parents' divorce." What are some

of the causes of divorce? What are some of the effects of divorce on the individuals involved—the wife, the husband, and the children?

EXAMINE the passage ". . . think of marriage as an institution acted upon by centripetal forces pulling inward and centrifugal forces pulling outward" (paragraph 7). How does the context define the terms *centripetal* and *centrifugal*? What centripetal forces have traditionally held marriages—bad ones as well as good ones—together? What centrifugal forces are more and more frequently pulling married couples apart today?

WRITE an essay arguing for or against the idea that most marriages can be classified as "good" or "bad." Do most marriages have both good and bad elements? Support your position with specific examples from one or more marriages. Or WRITE an essay in which you compare a good marriage for a couple in their twenties with a good marriage for a couple in their forties or fifties. How are these marriages alike? How are they different? (*Note:* Before writing your essay, you might want to review paragraphs 15–21, in which Wallerstein and Blakeslee discuss the "process of continual change" in successful marriages, but be sure to include your own ideas and examples as well. You might even interview a happily married couple in their twenties and another one in their forties or fifties.)

On Death and Love

JANET CAMPBELL HALE

This poem was written by Janet Campbell Hale, a Native American poet. Unlike some poets whose verses are difficult to read, Hale uses images and language with which most readers are familiar. The poem is written in free verse, a poetic form with few fixed conventions.

BEFORE YOU READ

THINK about the title of the poem. What do love and death have in common? Why would a poet choose to write about the two together?

EXAMINE the form of the poem. Notice especially the short lines (some consisting of only a single word), the absence of any rhyme scheme, the patterns of indention, and the types of punctuation used. What effect do you think these features of the poem's form will have on you as a reader?

WRITE a journal entry about the connection between love and death. Does being in love make you think of life or death or both? Can love make you forget the possibility of death or remind you that everything, including your love, must someday die? Your entry can be based on your own experience, a book you have read, or a movie or television show you have watched.

AS YOU READ

Try to determine why the person in the poem is thinking of death at this particular time.

He lies
Beside me,
Sleeping,
While outside,
  The wind blows,   5
  Rain falls,
  A dog barks,
We touch, slightly,
Keeping each other
warm. . . .   10
I stare into the darkness,
Thinking of: Dying,
  Of my aged and infirm mother
  Of my father
  Lying in his   15

  cold, dark
  grave,
And I remember,
That I found
My first white hair   20
That morning.
I turn
to my love,
And snuggle nearer
Until I can feel   25
his breath.
Still sleeping,
He
Opens his arms
To me.   30
I lay
My head
Against his chest
And listen
To his heart   35
beat.

❀ ❀ ❀

AFTER YOU READ

THINK about the simple story told in this poem. It is easy to read because of its vocabulary and style, but the narrative form of the poem is another reason that it is easy for you to understand.

EXAMINE first the images in the poem that are related to death and then those related to love. Make one list of the images you associate with death and another of the images you associate with love. What connection do you see between these two lists?

WRITE a single sentence in which you state the thesis of this poem. Your sentence should explain the relationship between love and death as expressed in the poem.

Unit Three: Critical Thinking and Writing Assignments

❀ ❀ ❀

EXPLORING IDEAS TOGETHER

1. Meet with a group of your classmates to discuss and define the term *friend*. Write a group definition of friendship. Then compare your group's definition with definitions composed by other groups in the class. What qualities do all definitions have in common? What qualities are unique to certain groups? Keep notes from this discussion for possible use in writing an essay on this subject.

2. As a class, divide into three groups, with each group discussing one of these types of friendships: friendships between men, friendships between women, and friendships between a man and a woman. What makes each type of friendship unique? What makes each type different from the other types? When your group finishes its discussion, write a collaborative essay on the type of friendship your group has chosen to discuss.

3. Reread paragraph 14 of "The Good Marriage" (page 200). Then, working in groups of three of four, discuss several of the questions posed by Wallerstein and Blakeslee. (Each group should select a different question.) Then give group reports to the rest of the class.

4. Although European and American cultures consider romantic love important, other cultures base marriage on other factors. Using the readings in this unit as well as your own experiences and observations, discuss whether you think romantic love is the most sound foundation for choosing a mate. What other foundations can there be for a long-lasting love?

WRITING ESSAYS

1. Write an essay defining the word *friend* or *friendship*. Before you begin your essay, review your notes from Question 1, Exploring Ideas Together (above) as well as from the Lopate essay (pages 148–156). You may want to include a formal definition in your introduction ("A friend is someone who . . ."), but expand your definition with examples, comparisons, and so on.

2. In this unit, Mike Taibbi describes a friendship between men, and Diane Cole describes a friendship between women. Write an essay in

which you use your own experiences and observations as well as information from class discussions to compare types of friendships—those between men and those between women.

3. The essay by Diane Cole and the short story by Raymond Carver focus on the way an individual's marriage, or a romantic relationship, can change his or her relationship with friends. Write an essay in which you advise newly married couples how to sustain previous friendships after marriage.

4. Write an essay in which you argue whether good friendships (or romantic relationships) are based on similarities or differences between the people involved. Consider ages, careers, interests, and so on.

5. As several of the essays in this unit suggest, successful communication is essential between friends or mates. Write an essay giving suggestions for successful communication in either type of relationship.

6. Interview someone who is considerably older or younger than you about the process of mate selection that existed when this person was selecting a mate. Write an essay in which you compare the process as you know it with the process this person experienced. Write your essay for an audience unfamiliar with either your experience or that of the person you interview.

7. Reread the essay by Joanne Jacobs, "The Right to Marry," and write an essay for a particular audience in which you argue that homosexual partners should or should not be allowed to marry. For example, you may address your essay to college students, gay rights advocates or opponents, or lawmakers.

8. Write an essay in which you argue why you do or do not think married life is better than single life. Note that Phillip Lopate, author of "What Friends Are For," pp. 148–155, shows his contentment with a single life.

9. Wallerstein and Blakeslee write that marriage is in the "process of continual change." Write an essay in which you discuss the changes, or stages, that usually occur in a marriage.

Self with Work

People are often defined by the work they do. Individuals are identified as teachers or lawyers or accountants in the same way they are identified by their names. In fact, once we have asked a person's name, we next want to know what he or she does. Even before children become adolescents, they are asked what they want to do or be when they grow up. In our society it is assumed that everyone, or almost everyone, will work.

However, the nature of work has changed. Relatively few people in this country now engage in work that requires hard physical labor. In contrast, our ancestors often worked long hours at tasks that required great physical strength and endurance. Both men and women (and often children as well) accepted physical labor as a fact of life. Although some people in our society still work in jobs that are physically demanding, most heavy labor has been taken over by machines. Today when we talk about work, we often mean working with our minds and/or our hands. Even though many people still have jobs that require them to work long hours or to be on their feet all day, most of us spend more time operating a machine or thinking or talking than working physically. But we still call what we do work.

Not only is work less physically demanding than it once was, but it is also less defined in terms of gender differences. Fifty years ago, some types of work were typically performed by males while other types were performed by females. Nurses and secretaries were nearly always females, while doctors, construction workers, and mail carriers were almost inevitably males. Today most of those distinctions have been erased. In fact, it is difficult to think of any job that is associated exclusively with either males or females. Women pilot airplanes while men serve snacks to the passengers; men take care of small children while women serve as presidents of universities. Both men and women are lawyers, doctors, senators, professors, and truck drivers. It is only a matter of time, surely, until a woman becomes president of the United States.

Even though the kind of work we do has changed, working has not become less important. Work is still how we define ourselves and how we spend most of our time. When technology began to make work less physically demanding and production faster, many people predicted that Americans would work fewer hours—but this has not happened. Most people still work eight hours a day, and many people work far more—bringing work home or holding two jobs instead of one. Couples often come home from their jobs to face child rearing and housekeeping responsibilities. Instead of becoming a society in which people work less, we have become a society in which people work more.

We continue to redefine what it means to work: more people work at home as well as at offices and factories; technology plays an increasingly important role in work; and people share jobs. But the importance of work will not change. Children will continue to pretend they are working; young people will continue to worry about what career to pursue; and adults will continue to focus on their jobs as a major feature of their lives. Perhaps most important, people will continue to define themselves in terms of their work.

The reading selections in this unit describe the effect of work on individuals, explore the difference between work and play, analyze how the role of work is changing in our society, and predict what jobs and careers will be available in the future. You will be asked to think about your attitude toward work and your choice of a career, to consider the place of work in our culture, and to reflect on why work is so important to us as a society and as individuals.

American Dreams: Stanley Cygan, 90

STUDS TERKEL

Studs Terkel grew up in Chicago just before the Great Depression and graduated from the University of Chicago Law School in 1934. Rather than practicing law, however, he pursued various careers, including being an actor in radio soap operas, a disc jockey, a sports commentator, and a television host. But he is most famous for the on-the-spot interviews he conducted and recorded. These interviews, many of which were with working people, capture the struggles and triumphs of working-class Americans.

BEFORE YOU READ

THINK about the American dream of success through hard work. Does hard work always result in success? Is this dream the same today as it was in the past? Are people today still willing to work hard in order to succeed?

EXAMINE the format of this reading selection. Except for the first paragraph, which sets the scene, it is essentially a monologue, or extended speech. Rather than being a formal speech, however, it is simply the record of what the speaker, Stanley Cygan, said when Terkel asked him about his life.

WRITE in your journal about a time when you did hard physical labor. What effect did this work have on you? Were these effects positive or negative?

AS YOU READ

Notice the speaker's references to working hard.

We're in the first-floor apartment of a neat two-flat building, reflective 1
of this Slavic community in Chicago. It is a Sunday afternoon. He is
seated in a deep easy chair; he had been casually following the pro football
game on TV. He is a small man, slender, soft and gentle in manner. Wistfully,
he apologizes for his difficulty in remembering details.

My father was a farmer in Poland. It was a hard life. So he came to 2
America in 1893. He landed in McKeesport, Pennsylvania, worked in a
steel mill. Three years later, he saved up enough money to send for my
mother, my sister, and me. I was six. I remember the trip because I was sick
all the way. (Laughs)

There were not many Poles in McKeesport. There were mostly German 3
and Irish. The jobs we had were the lowest paid. (Laughs) The Poles began
to come to us from our part of the country. They stayed with us until they
got resettled. Then we had a Polish community. Our school, parochial, was
up in the hills. Eight grades in two rooms. Besides the Polish reader, we
had an English reader.

I used to take my father's dinner pail to work. That's how I knew what 4
he was doing. All sweated up with his little cap on. He died when I was ten
years old. Mother couldn't afford to keep us, so I was sent to a boys'
orphanage in Polonia, Wisconsin. Polonia was like a farm village, mostly
German Poles. We called them Kaszubik. I remember it was the Fourth of
July when we were sent there. In bed, watching the fireworks from the
window, I was cryin'. I spent a year there. They only kept you until you
were eleven. They said: "You're old enough to earn your daily bread."
(Laughs)

My mother remarried and I came back to McKeesport. My stepfather 5
was ailing. He worked in one of them steel mills, hard job. Doctors told
him if he wants to live, he better go on a farm. He couldn't afford to go
on a farm here. He had some land in the Old Country, only about an acre
or two. So they decided to go back to Poland. I was then close to thirteen.
I refused to go. I was always told, when I didn't want to eat something, in
Poland, you'd pick the crumbs off the floor. (Laughs) So, of course, they
scared me. Here, you don't do that. They left me with an aunt.

I went in the steel mills when I was sixteen. I'm sorry I ever did.   6

The boys coming from Poland, my age, they all worked hard. My salary 7
was three and a half dollars a week. Ten-hour days, twelve-hour nights, six
days a week. The lowest paid job in the steel mill. All the better-paid jobs
were either Irish or German. I got a better job there because they ran short
of Englishmen and Irish and Germans. (Laughs) My mother said the Poles
were downgraded in McKeesport. "Go to Chicago." I came to East

Chicago. That was 1909, hard times, no work. Finally, I got a job in a rolling mill. The boss would come out and pick the people he wanted. There were always twenty-five of us out there, waiting to get hired. He'd pick 'em out like that. I had an uncle that had pretty good standing with this foreman. That's why he picked me.

I did some hard work. During the day, they had two men working on 8
it. In the evening, I was there alone. I couldn't keep up with the mill. I lost favor with the superintendent.

In 1913, '14, I went to this stove-repair company. I started for ten and 9
a half dollars a week. I started out sweeping floors and ended up being in charge of the pattern department. Maybe half a million patterns. You wouldn't believe there were so many different stoves in the world.

I worked with them until they closed down the place. Forty-two years. 10
The Dan Ryan Expressway was goin' through. They got half a million dollars for the place. We had to go. They gave me three months' wages. (*Laughs*) I was lucky. I doubt if others really got that much. They got what they wanted: our muscle.

When I came to America, I wanted to have a real job. I wanted to be 11
smart. I enrolled in school when I was twenty-nine. After a season, I got my eighth-grade papers. I enrolled in high school, a couple of hours a night. I had three children already, but I wanted to be smart.

I used to attend lectures at Hull House. The things that bothered me 12
were so many things I couldn't understand. I figured after I get through school, I'll know more about things. I don't know. I guess I got too old.

I dreamt I was gonna be a chemist. I talked to a professor about it who 13
was giving lectures. He told me it would take at least six years. He told me out of half a dozen of his schoolmates, there are only two that make a good living. I figured six years is too much.

There was a professor from the university lecturing on relativity. 14
Einstein. You read about it, it just makes you curious. I'd spend an hour and a half there, listening to him. But the worst of it was I didn't understand half the words he used. I never did understand relativity. There's a lot of things I don't understand, that if I had more schooling I would.

❀   ❀   ❀

AFTER YOU READ

THINK about Cygan's desire "to be smart." Did he want to be smart in order to be more successful financially or in order to be more educated and informed?

EXAMINE the first paragraph, in which Terkel describes Cygan and the place where he lives. What do you learn about Cygan from this description?

WRITE a descriptive essay about someone you know who has worked hard physically all his or her life. If possible, base your essay or report on an interview with the person.

Work and Play

ROBERT MURRAY DAVIS

A professor of literature at the University of Oklahoma, Robert M. Davis is also a prolific writer and scholar. In addition to his scholarly work, Davis has published poetry, personal essays, and two books about his own childhood and education. In this essay, taken from a book he wrote about growing up in a small town in Missouri, he explores the relationship between work and play and recounts what his father taught him about both.

BEFORE YOU READ

THINK about the difference between work and play. Are work and play always opposites? Why do young children often play by pretending to work? Can play be like work or work like play?

EXAMINE the first paragraph in which Davis sets the scene for his essay. What information does he provide in this paragraph? How does this first paragraph compare in purpose and content to the first paragraph of the previous selection by Studs Terkel?

WRITE a journal entry in which you tell about a person who taught you something about work.

AS YOU READ

Pay particular attention to the relationship between Davis and his father.

Late in the afternoon on a hot August day in 1957, I had come home ₁
after a summer of working on my master's thesis before leaving to study
for a doctorate. The thick walls of the house and the high ceiling of the
living room shut out most of the heat, and I sat in an easy chair, a notepad
on one arm, a bourbon and water over ice on the other, a book in my lap.

My father entered the front door and came through the hall into the ₂
living room. He was hot. He may have remembered his father reading
novels instead of tending to any business at all. He was moving, and I was
sitting down. He slowed, but didn't stop, and said, "When you going to
get off your ass and do some work?"

Nearly twenty-three, I was used to carrying on a conversation with a ₃
moving target. "I *am* working, Dad. This is what I do when I work."

"Bullshit!" And he disappeared through the door to the dining room ₄
on his way to the kitchen.

Ten years later, a not-so-young assistant professor trying to publish ₅
enough to make a name for myself, I stopped at the door of the department's senior professor and most distinguished scholar to say hello. With
the kind of diffidence that comes from complete confidence, he said, "I
hope you won't think I'm impertinent, but some of us are concerned that
you are working so hard that you will injure your health."

I thanked him for his concern, assured him that I felt fine, and added, ₆
"I can't wait to tell my father that, but I'm not going to tell him over the
phone. I want to see his face." With Dad, you had to be able to read faint
signs. He almost never laughed, and he rarely smiled. But when I told him
the story, his lip twitched just a little. Perhaps he didn't remember what
Grandpa Murray said on hearing him praised for being hard-working:
"Well, it's no wonder. He got enough rest when he was young."

More than ten years later, several days into my annual visit, Dad and ₇
I were looking out over his lawn. I noticed that the large lilac bush by the
fence between lawn and pasture was full of volunteer maple trees, and I
went over and pulled up some of the smaller ones. Soon I had a trimming
saw and tree-trimming tool and had moved out of the lilac bush to take
care of the fencerow. Dad finally got his electric saw and took care of the
thickest trunks. After a while, we were dusty, scratched a little here and
there, and wet through with sweat. But the lilac bush and fence were a lot
cleaner. Still, the pasture side of the fence was littered with debris from our
work, and I suggested that we get the tractor and trailer, load up the trash,
and take it down to the hollow to retard erosion.

"No," Dad said, "let's leave it for a while." A pause. Then, almost ₈
plaintively, "You worked me too hard."

I raised my eyes to heaven and said, only part mockingly, "Thank you, 9 God!" I had become an adult.

Dad wasn't always as grim as he might sound or as serious as he may 10 have felt he had to be to set the right example. In fact, I began to suspect that he regarded life not just as a test but a series of contests. He had done a lot of things, and it was always a dilemma what to put down in the blanks after "father's occupation." "Trader" seemed to connote the South Seas. "Dealer" was OK until the current connotation got locked in. What he actually did, or did best, was buy and sell things: cars, cattle, farm machinery, almost anything that wasn't nailed down and some things that were. When I was a boy it seemed that Dad made play seem like work. And work was deadly serious. When I got old enough to tease him—about age thirty-five—I told him that his motto ought to be, "If it feels good, you must be doing it wrong." When concentrating on a physical or mechanical job, he would stick his tongue between his teeth at one edge of his mouth and frown in concentration. My major contribution to repair jobs was holding the flashlight while mysterious stuff went on in the bowels of whatever it was. Every job was a test with no make-up. The worst beating I ever got—bad enough that it was the last—was because, even though I had not been told to, I had not fed the pigs on my own initiative. (At least that was the only reason I was ever given. Having since been a parent myself, I wonder if something else might not have been going on.)

Looking back, I can see that Dad was more intense than anything else. 11 It was always surprising to find that he could play. For Christmas (of 1941, I think) he got me a full electric train set, the better for being used because the tracks were already mounted on big boards, which he set up in the basement of the duplex on Fourth Street and played with for hours to wind down after a run on the Katy. Later he would sometimes stop by the basketball goal he had installed under the walnut trees, call for the ball, and throw it up, while moving, the kind of two-handed underhand shot popular in his high school days. I remember his playing catch with me only once, when he demonstrated how to throw a curveball. For several days afterward he moved his right arm carefully, and as with various other situations, I sympathize more now than I did then. But the only time he really surprised me was at his wholesale fruit and vegetable business. We were unloading a truckload of watermelons, and Dad promised that if one got broken, we could take it home. We had almost finished, with no damage, and I was starting to worry. Dad looked over the few remaining, hefted the most promising knee-high, looked at me, grinned slightly, lowered the melon to shin level, and dropped it. It may not have been the best-tasting melon I ever had, but it was the most satisfying.

My father taught me almost everything about work—finally, even, that 12
it could be more fun than nominal play—except how to do what he did, and that was because, knowing I was incompetent, I didn't even try to learn. In fact, the fathers of my contemporaries did not pass on this kind of knowledge. Of the boys I can trace from my crowd, only one, a farmer, does anything like what his father did. Or where he did it. The fathers weren't holding out on us; they wanted us to live different lives and finally, I think, my father was pleased that I did. If he never understood what I do when I work, he was glad to have a son clever enough to get away with doing whatever it was and energetic enough to do a lot of it. If it was a bluff, it was a bluff a good card player could respect.

Because he went to bed about 9:00 P.M., I never managed to get up in 13
the morning before he did. But I get up a lot earlier and more voluntarily than I used to, I go to work a lot more willingly, and I enjoy doing it a lot more than I do most forms of play. He didn't necessarily want me to go out and clear that last fencerow, but I suspect that despite his exhaustion he was pleased that I hadn't forgotten how to do a job that wasn't mine without having to be told and how to insist on carrying it through to the end.

Later I told the story to his oldest surviving friend and added, "Working 14
for Dad makes every job I've had since look easy." Dad snorted, and I don't know whether or not he believed me. He should have. And it should have pleased him.

※   ※   ※

AFTER YOU READ

THINK about which is more important in a person's life—work or play.

EXAMINE the reversal of roles that takes place between Davis and his father. Identify specific incidents in the essay that suggest this role reversal.

WRITE an essay in which you analyze the effect that the relationship between Davis and his father had on his attitude toward work. Be sure that your essay has a clear thesis and that you support it with specific information from Davis's essay.

My Mother Enters the Workforce

RITA DOVE

Presently the poet laureate of the United States, Rita Dove is the Pulitzer Prize–winning author of a novel, a play, and five books of verse. The poem that follows, which is based on Dove's mother's life, tells of her mother's struggle to support her family by working first as a seamstress and later as a secretary.

BEFORE YOU READ

THINK about who is making your education possible. Are you putting yourself through school, or is someone helping you? Why do parents typically help their children get an education? Should children expect their parents' financial support while they attend college?

EXAMINE the term *seamstress,* usually defined as a woman who is expert at sewing, especially one who makes her living by sewing. The word comes from a Middle English word that referred to both males and females who sewed. Now we usually call a man who sews a tailor. What connotations do the words *seamstress* and *tailor* have? Which is more prestigious?

WRITE a journal entry in which you first describe your image of a seamstress, then your image of a secretary. Analyze why both now seem rather old-fashioned even though people still do these types of work.

AS YOU READ

Think about what it would be like to try to earn a living by sewing clothes for other people.

The path to ABC Business School
was paid for by a lucky sign:
Alterations, Qualified Seamstress Inquire Within.
Tested on Sleeves, hers
never puckered—puffed or sleek,   5
Leg o' Mutton or Raglan—
they barely needed the
damp cloth
to steam them
perfect.   10

Those were the
afternoons.
Evenings
she took in
piecework,   15
the treadle
machine
with its
locomotive whir
traveling the lit path   20
of the needle
through quicksand taffeta
or velvet deep as a forest.
And now and now sang the treadle,
I know, I know . . .   25

And then it was dry again, all morning
at the office machines, their clack and chatter
another journey—rougher,
that would go on forever
until she could break a hundred words   30
with no errors—ah, and then
no more postponed groceries,
and that blue pair of shoes!

AFTER YOU READ

THINK about what happens in the poem and then identify the poet's thesis. Because Dove does not articulate her thesis explicitly, you will need to infer it from the poem and state it in your own words. Cite evidence from the poem that supports the thesis you identify.

EXAMINE the final phrase in the poem, "that blue pair of shoes." Whom are the shoes for? Why is it significant that they are blue?

WRITE an essay in which you argue for or against the idea that education is the best means of improving a person's status.

The Case Against Chores

JANE SMILEY

This essay by Jane Smiley first appeared in Harper's Magazine, *although it was originally part of a longer essay that appeared in the* Hungry Mind Review. *In this selection Smiley, who is best known as a novelist, argues that children should not be given chores. Smiley's most recent novel is entitled* Moo, *and her 1992 novel,* A Thousand Acres, *won the Pulitzer Prize.*

BEFORE YOU READ

THINK about the types of chores you were asked to do as a child. Do you think doing these chores improved you in any way?

EXAMINE your own attitudes about chores. Do you think children should be given routine chores? Why or why not?

WRITE a journal entry in which you describe in detail a chore you were given as a child, and tell what you learned from performing this chore.

AS YOU READ

Underline Smiley's arguments against giving children chores, and put a check mark by the arguments that you think are most convincing.

I've lived in the upper Midwest for twenty-one years now, and I'm here   1
to tell you that the pressure to put your children to work is unrelenting.
So far I've squirmed out from under it, and my daughters have led a life of
almost tropical idleness, much to their benefit. My son, however, may not
be so lucky. His father was himself raised in Iowa and put to work at an
early age, and you never know when, in spite of all my husband's best
intentions, that early training might kick in.

Although "chores" are so sacred in my neck of the woods that almost   2
no one ever discusses their purpose, I have over the years gleaned some of
the reasons parents give for assigning them. I'm not impressed. Mostly the
reasons have to do with developing good work habits or, in the absence of
good work habits, at least habits of working. No such thing as a free lunch,
any job worth doing is worth doing right, work before play, all of that.
According to this reasoning, the world is full of jobs that no one wants to
do. If we divide them up and get them over with, then we can go on to
pastimes we like. If we do them "right," then we won't have to do them
again. Lots of times, though, in a family, that *we* doesn't operate. The
operative word is *you*. The practical result of almost every child-labor
scheme that I've witnessed is the child doing the dirty work and the parent
getting the fun: Mom cooks and Sis does the dishes; the parents plan and
plant the garden, the kids weed it. To me, what this teaches the child is the
lesson of alienated labor: not to love the work but to get it over with; not
to feel pride in one's contribution but to feel resentment at the waste of
one's time.

Another goal of chores: the child contributes to the work of maintain-   3
ing the family. According to this rationale, the child comes to understand
what it takes to have a family, and to feel that he or she is an important,
even indispensable member of it. But come on. Would you really want to
feel loved primarily because you're the one who gets the floors mopped?
Wouldn't you rather feel that your family's love simply exists all around
you, no matter what your contribution? And don't the parents love their
children anyway, whether the children vacuum or not? Why lie about it
just to get the housework done? Let's be frank about the other half of the
equation too. In this day and age, it doesn't take much work at all to manage
a household, at least in the middle class—maybe four hours a week to clean
the house and another four to throw the laundry into the washing machine,
move it to the dryer, and fold it. Is it really a good idea to set the sort of
example my former neighbors used to set, of mopping the floor every two
days, cleaning the toilets every week, vacuuming every day, dusting,
dusting, dusting? Didn't they have anything better to do than serve their
house?

Let me confess that I wasn't expected to lift a finger when I was growing 4
up. Even when my mother had a full-time job, she cleaned up after me, as
did my grandmother. Later there was a housekeeper. I would leave my
room in a mess when I headed off for school and find it miraculously neat
when I returned. Once in a while I vacuumed, just because I liked the
pattern the Hoover made on the carpet. I did learn to run water in my
cereal bowl before setting it in the sink.

Where I discovered work was at the stable, and, in fact, there is no 5
housework like horsework. You've got to clean the horses' stalls, feed them,
groom them, tack them up, wrap their legs, exercise them, turn them out,
and catch them. You've got to clip them and shave them. You have to sweep
the aisle, clean your tack and your boots, carry bales of hay and buckets of
water. Minimal horsekeeping, rising just to the level of humaneness,
requires many more hours than making a few beds, and horsework turned
out to be a good preparation for the real work of adulthood, which is
rearing children. It was a good preparation not only because it was similar
in many ways but also because my desire to do it, and to do a good job of
it, grew out of my love of and interest in my horse. I can't say that cleaning
out her bucket when she manured in it was an actual joy, but I knew she
wasn't going to do it herself. I saw the purpose of my labor, and I wasn't
alienated from it.

Probably to the surprise of some of those who knew me as a child, I 6
have turned out to be gainfully employed. I remember when I was in
seventh grade, one of my teachers said to me, strongly disapproving, "The
trouble with you is you do only what you want to do!" That continues to
be the trouble with me, except that over the years I have wanted to do more
and more.

My husband worked hard as a child, out-Iowa-ing the Iowans, if such 7
a thing is possible. His dad had him mixing cement with a stick when he
was five, pushing wheelbarrows not long after. It's a long sad tale on the
order of two miles to school and both ways uphill. The result is, he's a great
worker, much better than I am, but all the while he's doing it he wishes he
weren't. He thinks of it as work; he's torn between doing a good job and
longing not to be doing it at all. Later, when he's out on the golf course,
where he really wants to be, he feels a little guilty, knowing there's work
that should have been done before he gave in and took advantage of the
beautiful day.

Good work is not the work we assign children but the work they want 8
to do, whether it's reading in bed (where would I be today if my parents
had rousted me out and put me to scrubbing floors?) or cleaning their

rooms or practicing the flute or making roasted potatoes with rosemary and Parmesan for the family dinner. It's good for a teenager to suddenly decide that the bathtub is so disgusting she'd better clean it herself. I admit that for the parent, this can involve years of waiting. But if she doesn't want to wait, she can always spend her time dusting.

❀   ❀   ❀

AFTER YOU READ

THINK about Smiley's argument against chores. First, review her arguments by reading the sections you underlined as you read the essay. How many of her arguments are based on her own experience? Can you refute these arguments by using your own experiences, or do you agree with Smiley?

EXAMINE Smiley's definition of good work for children is "the work they want to do." Do you agree with this definition? Why or why not?

WRITE a "case for chores" in which you refute Smiley's arguments. You may use your own experiences or the experiences of others as evidence, but you may also want to use the essay by Robert Murray Davis as a source.

Initiation

REBECCA MAY

*This story, written by Rebecca May for a freshman com-
position assignment, tells of her experience as a volunteer
in a large urban hospital's emergency room. The experience she recounts, in which a patient dies, served as a harsh
initiation to the practice of medicine and almost changed
her mind about becoming a doctor.*

BEFORE YOU READ

THINK about what it would be like to work in an emergency room in a
large urban hospital. What would you see, hear, and smell? What would
the atmosphere of such a place be—calm, quiet, and orderly? Or hectic,
noisy, and busy?

EXAMINE the word *gurney*, which occurs in the following context in the
essay:

> ". . . I saw two EMTs wheeling a bloodied man in on a gurney. One EMT
> was holding the bottle of saline for his IV, and the other was trying to
> awaken the seemingly unconscious man."

Can you figure out from the way this word is used what a gurney is?

WRITE a journal entry in which you describe a situation when you felt
inadequate.

AS YOU READ

Think about what it would be like to watch someone die.

As the scent of sterilized air filled my lungs, I donned the flimsy, red 1
cotton jacket, just pulled from my backpack. Hastily rolling up the
sleeves, I tossed my backpack on the table by the guard, and attempted to
brush down the crumpled volunteer jacket. I was late. The guard and I
exchanged a brief hello, and I briskly walked into the emergency room.

It was 7:15 A.M., and I was regretting my trip to Fenway Park the night 2
before. My head throbbed with the pressure of a flattened penny on the
rails of the T,* and I prayed that the ibuprofin would remove the constant
drumming.

I was greeted with a chirping hello from the RN at the desk and was 3
once again bombarded with new faces that only name badges gave away.
Doctors and nurses worked different rotations, so I never encountered the
same people; it was frustrating. Volunteering at the New England Medical
Center in Boston had so far been a blur of terminology, directions, door
codes, bedpans, and homeless drug addicts. My only comfort was Julie, a
nursing intern from Northeastern University, who was there with me on
alternating weeks.

She was a short girl, with an amicable demeanor and bedside manner, 4
but Julie appeared harsh at a glance. Maybe it was her rugged, makeupless
features or perhaps her slight resemblance to Roseanne Barr that could
persuade the most obstinate patients to get into their wheelchairs, to take
their medication, or just to lie still while she was trying to take an EKG
reading. Julie was going to be an excellent addition to any hospital staff
when she finished training in two months.

Today her blonde hair was pulled back and her eyes were bloodshot. 5

"Long night?" I inquired, as I moved to the bandage cart, pulling up 6
the inventory chart, beginning to count.

"Wenta see Bim Skala Bim at Avalon, and didn' get home tull foa this 7
mahnin'," she replied in an accent like that of a female Cliff Clavin.

"What's been going on this morning?" I inquired, looking across the 8
bandage cart at the board with a listing of all the patients who had been
brought in, their conditions, and what room they were in. I walked toward
the storage closet to retrieve more bandages, and . . .

"Let me out! LET ME OUT!" shouted the man in Room 12, one of 9
the psychiatric rooms. Cautiously, I peered in the thick plastic window and
a scream that made me jump back resounded in the small white cubicle. I

---

*"The T" is the public transit system serving the Boston area. It operates subways, streetcars, trains, and buses.

immediately looked to make sure no one had seen this man scare me, while taking another retreating step. Seeing me, he examined my sloppy jacket and squinted his eyes, surely sensing my heart knocking against my chest.

"GET ME SOME WATER! Damn it! I'm going to DIE in here if I don't 10 get some water! YOU!" He pointed accusatorially, as if he was holding me personally responsible. I scurried to find a nurse from whom I needed approval to give this man the water; but at the same time, I saw two EMTs wheeling a bloodied man in on a gurney. One EMT was holding the bottle of saline for his IV, and the other was trying to awaken the seemingly unconscious man.

His bloody shirt was ripped open, his shoes were removed, and his 11 face, which seemed inhuman at the time, was covered in clotted and drying blood. They moved him into the immediate care room, Room 1, and I heard a nurse shout for equipment. One of the two doctors attending to the man glanced around and called for me to get the EKG from the other room. Dazed, I took a moment to respond to him; then I ran into the next room to fetch the instrument.

Pulling the EKG closer to the table, I was overcome with the sickening 12 odors of fresh blood and iodine that assailed my senses. I felt helpless, watching Julie assist the doctors in a composed, prompt manner. Horrified and with shaking hands, I took the smooth film off the back of the EKG's round stickers and placed five of them on the man's chest. As I moved aside, Julie swiftly put on the rest of the stickers. She smiled slightly, kind of a rugged Annie Oakley smile, trying to reassure me that everything would be all right. I stared as two stone-faced nurses applied pressure to the still bleeding wounds of his motionless body, hoping his wounds would cauterize.

Drifting, as though watching a movie, I kept hoping to hear the music 13 that would inevitably lead to the credits. Becoming more aware, I saw the man's black, hairy chest covered by EKG monitoring patches, and I watched an oxygen mask being held to his mouth and nose. One doctor was setting the charge and quickly rubbed the two pads of the defibrillator together.

THUD! The first jolt was given.   14

"No response," said the nurse blandly, as she looked at her watch.   15

THUD! The man's body was yanked from the table as if it was my old 16 Raggedy Andy doll, and I felt the knot in my stomach, clamping upon the pit of anxiety, causing me to shiver. I felt compelled to pray, thinking all the while about my friends and family, but I didn't cry—I couldn't. I felt pathetic for wanting to pass out, even though becoming a surgeon had been my dream. Was I cut out for this?

They kept thudding the poor man; voices and commands became more 17 strained. He was beginning to look more human as they removed some of the blood from his face and body. The area was littered with dirty gauze, towels, instruments, and people standing around. The man wasn't moving and finally the doctors just stopped. After that, everything seemed to stop.

I heard the man in Room 12 shouting again, and I wanted to tell him 18 to shut up. A man had just died. Where was his family? Where was a priest or a pastor or a rabbi? I didn't stay any longer than to see the body covered with the thin, sanitized, blue paper blanket. Then I was gone.

I went home, grabbed a Dr. Pepper from the fridge, cursed my 19 headache, downed a few Advil and went into my roommate's room to watch football. I wanted to tell everyone; I wanted to tell no one. I was angry with myself for feeling weak, sick, and repulsed. Later, I called Julie, and we talked.

I went back to the hospital the next week, with the smell of blood and 20 iodine still within my wrinkled jacket. I grabbed another jacket from the back closet and balled mine up in the corner, making a mental note to wash it. It'd be all right, and so would I.

❀ ❀ ❀

AFTER YOU READ

THINK about the contrast between the way the writer felt when she entered the emergency room and the way she felt when she left for the day. What details does May include to make this contrast more vivid?

EXAMINE the medical terminology used in this essay: *RN, intern, EKG, EMT, saline, cauterize, defibrillator,* and so on. Working with a small group of your classmates, try to determine the meaning of the terms by using the context in which each term occurs in the essay and your own knowledge of what goes on in a hospital.

WRITE an essay in which you tell of an initiation you have experienced—a time when you learned something important or became part of a group by going through an ordeal or challenge of some type.

Spokesperson

JANE ARMSTRONG

Jane Armstrong, who teaches English at Northern Arizona University, wrote this essay for a creative writing course while she was a student at the University of Southern Mississippi. The essay, which was first published in Product, *tells of her experience as director of a family planning clinic.*

BEFORE YOU READ

THINK about what it would be like to work in a place like an abortion clinic. How would the controversy or even the threat of physical violence affect you?

EXAMINE the term *spokesperson*. This term, which means literally one who does the speaking, is a relatively new word. In the past, the word was *spokesman*. In recent years, however, most people have avoided using words that refer to males, even though both males and females are intended. Given the history of this term, why would it be an appropriate title for an essay that tells about a woman who worked in a family planning clinic?

WRITE a journal entry about a time when you were identified by what you did rather than by who you were.

AS YOU READ

Notice the type of training and the advice given to Armstrong to prepare her for her role as a spokesperson.

For three years, I was the director of a family planning clinic. My clinic, 1
part of a large, private, non-profit agency, provided contraceptive care,
vasectomy, STD treatment and education, AIDS testing, counseling, and,
once a week, abortion. The only abortion provider in a two-hundred-mile
radius, we were the focus of the area's antiabortion protesters. Every
Thursday morning, patients and staff crossed picket lines, endured threats
and curses. Scuffles were common. The police were called so often that
they knew me by my first name, offered me an escort to work. At times the
local media showed up and instead of being inside assisting the surgeon,
I'd be out on the sidewalk, keeping the cameras off the patients and making
statements to some TV reporter.

As one of the three people in the agency authorized to speak to the 2
press, I'd been trained as a media spokesperson. Once a year, I was sent to
an intensive media workshop where I and several other advocates of
various social causes were taught to perform for print, broadcast, and radio.
We learned never to wear black on television, never to speak off the record,
not to worry about answering questions—to make our one or two key
points over and over. That was style training. For substance, I spent a
weekend with political consultants who taught me, if confronted in a public
forum by antichoice slander, to firmly state, "That's a lie and you know
it!" I learned how to seize the issue, frame the agenda.

In addition to Thursday mornings, I had opportunities to use my 3
spokesperson skills speaking to various groups—sororities, college classes,
the Soroptimists, the Democratic Women's Club. Once, when the agency's
directors were overbooked, it fell to me to travel to an ultraconservative
neighboring town to debate a former president of National Right to Life.

The day before the debate, the agency's director of public affairs called 4
me with some pre-debate tips. She told me to wear pearls and a pink
dress—Laura Ashley if I had one—and to demurely correct the moderator
if he called me "Ms." I laughed and told her that surely the audience would
see right through this. But when the time came and the moderator
introduced me, I smiled sweetly, fingered my pearls and softly but audibly
said, "Excuse me, please. I prefer *Mrs.*" Hearts melted. My opponent was
a dowdy Phyllis Schlafly emulator who kept taking off her glasses and
wiping the lenses with her thumb. It was my show.

I concluded the debate with a rehearsed speech about the value of a 5
woman's life. I held my little hand over my heart, threw in a few strategic
voice quavers. Afterward, a woman from the audience, tears in her eyes,
told me she hadn't felt as good about being a woman since the seventies. I

suddenly felt tall and tough, a rousing orator standing at the forefront of a burning social issue.

A few months after the debate, my clinic was made the first target in 6 the state for an attack by the aggressive antiabortion group Operation Rescue. Eighty-nine protesters, a notable effort for our town's small band of true believers, blocked our clinic doors; twenty-seven were arrested. The event received statewide coverage. While driving home that evening, I heard my own voice on the radio, a little girl's voice, speaking of choice and individual freedom and denouncing neighborhood bullies. At home, I saw myself on the six o'clock news, standing in my oversized green scrubs before a bank of protesters, warning them that they had five minutes to leave the premises before they'd be forcibly removed.

The following week, the local newspaper ran a front page feature on 7 me. The cutline under my photo called me the town's "face of pro-choice." The article, a what-sort-of-person-would-do-this-awful-work piece, described my hair, my laugh, the Gumby collection in my office, and mentioned my Master's in English. But when the letters and calls started coming to the clinic, they were, of course, about abortion. One note was from a woman who'd had an illegal abortion; she thanked me for my courage. One man who called told me I deserved to die.

In my small town I was often recognized in shops and restaurants, 8 usually, excruciatingly, by people who'd loudly beseech me to "stop the killing." The local feminist faction adopted me as their frontline darling and whenever I chanced to meet one of the rank and file, I was expected to hold forth with war dispatches and political platitudes. When I met someone new, I began to dread the inevitable questions, "What do you do? Where do you work?" My answers erased me from the conversation. In my place stood The Issue.

I'd always thought I wanted my life to stand for something. I'd been 9 taught to admire those whose lives stand for something—the way Martin Luther King Jr. stands for the fight for racial equality, Katharine Hepburn for beauty, intelligence, a woman's strength, or Vita Sackville-West for the fine English garden.

In my small community, I'd come to stand for abortion rights and I 10 hated it. I had real enemies. Not what I thought enemies were, snippy gossips or the girl in high school who tried to steal my boyfriend, but people in my town who had threatened me with bodily harm and eternal damnation, who'd actually tried to hit me.

At all times, I carried with me the political burden of the unwanted 11 pregnancies of my community. I couldn't go to a party, to church, to lunch with friends without being drawn into an abortion discussion. Even my hairdresser chatted incessantly about picketers while rolling my perm rods. I longed to gab about *Vanity Fair*'s celeb of the month, Friday night's *MacNeil/Lehrer*, the local symphony, stirrup pants with ankle boots, anything. But I was denied small talk. I was denied real conversation. Instead, everyone I met felt compelled to make a statement, pro or con, and wait for my reaction. Most often, I fell back on programmed lines.

And after a while, the lines felt phony. So many who'd spoken to me,   12
told me their stories and pledged their support, were sincere. I'm even certain that some of my enemies genuinely believed their brutality was justified. They were all hemorrhaging with emotion. I tried to care, but after three years of being a professional wind-up doll, I'd lost my empathy.

After three years, I came to realize that of all the things for which I'd   13
like my life to stand, abortion rights was close to the bottom of the list. What my life, or anyone's life, really stands for is a complex tangle of silly, sad, sometimes conflicting details, feelings difficult to articulate. Not at all like my prepackaged, well-groomed advocacy, these things are simple, unglamorous, without heat, and too dear for public display.

❀   ❀   ❀

AFTER YOU READ

THINK about the process of disillusionment that Armstrong experienced. How did she feel when she began her job? How did she feel later? What influenced her feelings about herself and her job as a spokesperson? Was her disillusionment primarily the result of her being a spokesperson or being associated with an abortion clinic?

EXAMINE the sentence "In my place stood The Issue." Analyze what Armstrong means by this statement.

WRITE an essay in which you identify the ideas or goals or values you want your life to stand for. Be sure to explain your choice clearly to your readers.

The Family Farm

DAVID MAS MASUMOTO

David Mas Masumoto, like his father before him, lives and works on the family farm, but he is also a farm activist and writer. This essay, taken from his book, Epitaph for a Peach: Four Seasons on My Family Farm, *focuses on his growing realization that his father created for the family a home as well as a farm and explains his decision to continue that effort.*

236

I grew up knowing my father's work. He was a peach and grape farmer, and I saw him at work daily, sometimes working alongside him. As a young child I knew some of the crises he faced. I cringed at the sight of worms attacking ripe fruit. I too could feel the searing heat of the summer sun as it blistered exposed fruit.

Now I farm the California land that my father and mother farmed, the land where my grandparents labored as farm workers. My children will know the work of their father, too. But where my father rarely showed emotion, I show it all. My daughter has seen me yell at the sky as September rain clouds approach my raisins or curse about lousy fruit prices when no one wants my peaches. It is a family farm—my parents, wife and children spend time in the fields—and our family is bound to the land. Our farm survives as both a home and a workplace.

When I was in college, I asked friends about their parents' work. I thought my questions would be a safe way of getting to know someone. But most of my friends never ventured beyond one-line answers: "My dad is an engineer" or "He works for a bank" or "He handles sheet metal for an air-conditioning company."

I would respond, "What kind of engineer?" or "Why'd he choose banking?" or "How's the sheet-metal business?" Such questions alienated some of my friends: family seemed to be a painful subject. After I told them my dad was a farmer, rarely did they ask a second question. I stopped interpreting their initial response, "Oh, really?" as one of positive surprise.

Returning home after college, I felt uncomfortable telling others, "I farm." I translated blank looks as disdain mixed with condescension. I could see images flashing through their minds of Old MacDonald and hayseeds who spend weekends watching corn grow. As my peers were securing their corporate jobs and advancing as professionals in law or medicine, I spent long hours talking with my dad, getting to know fifty acres of vines and twenty acres of peach trees, preparing to take over the farm.

I'd listened for hours before I noticed that Dad's stories of growing up on the farm seemed to revolve around the pronoun *they*. "They" meant my grandparents and the entire family of four sons and two daughters. I had to adjust my thinking. My image of work was singular in nature, one man in one job, not a family's combined effort to make a living. I learned the significance of work that is inseparable from home, when work is also the place you live and play and sleep.

Dad tells the story of hot, summer nights when he was a boy and the wooden platform that *Jiichan* (grandfather) built. Fresno's one-hundred-degree heat would beat down on the place where they lived, a shack with a tin roof that required hours to cool after sunset. They didn't have a cooler or fan (out in the country there was no electricity), but it didn't matter.

Jiichan made a low wooden platform from old barn wood. It rose about   8 two feet off the ground with a flat area big enough for the whole family. In the evenings everyone would lie on the platform, side by side, almost touching.

After a long day together in the fields, and following a simple dinner   9 and refreshing *ofuro* (Japanese bath), the family would gather and begin an evening ritual of talking, resting, and gazing upward at the night sky, waiting until their shack home had cooled down. The dirt yard was beneath them, the closest vineyards a few feet away. If a little breeze came they could hear the grape leaves shifting and rustling, creating an illusion of coolness. It seemed to make everyone feel better.

Years later, my brother and I passed hot summer nights together,   10 sometimes camping out in the fields. During a break between the summer fruits and the family packing-shed work, we pitched a tent made from an old bed sheet and tree rope. You would think after working all day with the peaches and grapes, we'd be weary of them. But we wanted to sleep "in the wilderness" and drew no lines between our fields of play and the fields of work. This wasn't just a farm, it was our home.

When I tell these stories to friends, their eyes widen and they smile.   11 They tell me how fine it must be to raise children on a farm. I now realize that my college friends' reluctance to talk about family arose from a youthful notion that one could get away from them. We hoped to journey beyond that horizon; what we didn't know was that some of us were actually seeking what was right in front of us.

It's been a struggle to keep the farm, but I know now that I am not just   12 competing with nature—I am creating, as my father did, something called home.

❀   ❀   ❀

AFTER YOU READ

THINK about the stereotypes that the author describes of the farmer as "Old MacDonald" or "hayseeds who spend weekends watching corn grow." What image do you have of farmers? Has the general perception of farmers changed in recent years? If so, how and why?

EXAMINE Masumoto's explanation of why his college friends reacted as they did when he asked them what their fathers did. He says he now realizes that their reluctance to talk about their family "arose from a youthful notion that one could get away from them [their families]." Do you think most young people want to get away from their families? Why or why not?

WRITE an essay in which you tell why you would or would not like to assume your family's business or pursue a career like that of one of your parents. In your essay compare the advantages and disadvantages of following in your parents' footsteps.

The Workman's Compensation

REG THERIAULT

This essay, which appeared in Harper's Magazine, *is from a book entitled* How to Tell When You're Tired: A Brief Examination of Work. *The author, Reg Theriault, should know about work because for the last thirty years he has worked as a longshoreman in San Francisco. In this essay, Theriault defends the practice of "taking it easy" on the job. He argues that workers, especially if their jobs are physically or mentally demanding, need to work "on and off" rather than continuously.*

BEFORE YOU READ

THINK about your own work experiences. Do you take it easy occasionally even though you are being paid for working?

EXAMINE the term *workman's compensation.* Compensation, in terms of working, can simply be wages or money paid to an employee who is injured on the job. However, Theriault uses the term in his title to mean another kind of compensation that he believes workers deserve.

WRITE a journal entry in which you tell of a time when you "took it easy" while you were being paid to work.

AS YOU READ

Identify the form of compensation that Theriault refers to in his title.

How can someone, hour after hour, day after day, year in and year out, tighten approximately the same nut to the same bolt and not go mad? That most working people do not, in fact, go mad is due in large measure to a phenomenon so common that it is found wherever people labor in industry: taking it easy. It would take some kind of real mental case to do all the work one could all day long. No one expects it. Taking it easy on the job while someone else covers your work, or "working on and off," as it is usually called in America, is an established part of the working life.

Working on and off, however, has its limits. The rules are infinitely varied, subtle, and flexible, and, of course, they are always changing. Management, up to a certain level at least, is aware of the practice, and in some industries employs entire cadres of people to curtail or put an end to it. Simultaneously, the workers are subtly doing their best to keep it going, and to extend it wherever possible.

Every worker has a highly developed sense of how much work is expected of him. When he feels that the expectation is excessive, he tries to do something about it. This instinct has to do with the political nature of work itself, something every modern worker understands. The bosses want more from the worker than they are willing to give in return. The workers give work, and the bosses give money. The exchange is never quite equal, and the discrepancy is called profit. Since the bosses cannot do without profit, workers have an edge. A good worker in a key spot could, so long as he kept up production, take all the coffee breaks he wanted, and the bosses would very likely look the other way. He could also choose to cut down on the coffee breaks, apply himself, and increase production, and then ask for and get more money. But that would be self-defeating, and he knows it. It would also place him in competition with other workers, which would be playing into the bosses' hands. What he would rather do is create some slack for himself and enjoy his job more.

At present on the West Coast, when a gang of longshoremen working on cargo starts a shift, they often divide themselves into two equal groups and flip a coin. One group goes into the far reaches of the ship's hold and sits around. The other group starts loading cargo, usually working with a vengeance, since each one of them is doing the work of two men. An hour later, the groups change places. In other words, although my fellow longshoremen and I are getting paid for eight hours, on occasion we work only four. If someone reading this feels a swelling sense of moral outrage because we are sitting down on the job, I am sorry.

If you *are* that reader, I would recommend that you abandon your outrage and begin thinking about doing something similar for yourself. You probably already have, even if you won't admit it. White-collar office workers, too, have come under criticism recently for robbing their bosses of their full-time services. Too much time is being spent around the Mr. Coffee machine, and some people (would you believe it?) have even been having personal conversations on company time. In fact, one office-system expert recently said that he had yet to encounter a business workplace that was functioning at more than about 60 percent efficiency.

Management often strives to set up a situation where work is done in series: 6 a worker receives an article of manufacture, does something to it, and passes it on to another worker, who does something else to it and then passes it on to the next guy, and so on. The assembly line is a perfect example of this. Managers like this type of manufacture because it is more efficient—that is, it achieves more production. They also like it for another reason, even if they will not admit it: it makes it very difficult for the worker to do anything other than work.

Frederick W. Taylor, the efficiency expert who early in this century 7 conducted the time-and-motion studies that led to the assembly-line process, tried to reduce workers to robots, all in the name of greater production. His staff of experts, each armed with clipboard and stopwatch, studied individual workers with a view toward eliminating unnecessary movement. Even ditchdigging could be made more efficient, they bragged, as if they had discovered something new in the world. Grasp the shovel, sink it into the earth with the arch of your boot for a good bite, and heave out the dirt. Then repeat the steps. Don't lean on that shovel between times! That's an unnecessary movement! The Taylorites soon found a great deal of opposition from some very tired workers. They discovered that the best shovelers were mentally retarded young men, who accepted directions readily and were less bored by repetitious acts. They got some pretty healthy shoveling done, but even they tended to goof off when a staff member wandered away.

Most people not directly engaged in daily work express disapproval 8 when they hear of people working on and off. A studied campaign with carefully chosen language—"featherbedding," "a full day's work for a full day's pay," "taking a free ride"—has been pushed by certain employers to discredit the practice, and their success is such that I rarely discuss it except with other workers. My response is personal, and I feel no need to defend it: If I am getting a free ride, how come I am so tired when I go home at the end of a shift?

❀   ❀   ❀

AFTER YOU READ

THINK about the issue of workers taking time off while on the job from an employer's or manager's point of view. Are there reasons for employers and managers to support this form of workman's compensation? Why or why not?

EXAMINE Theriault's arguments for "working on and off" rather than working every minute for which you are being paid. Are his arguments sensible, fair, convincing?

WRITE an essay in which you summarize Theriault's arguments and then argue for or against his position.

Out of College, Out of Work

STEPHEN SHERRILL

Stephen Sherrill is a free-lance writer who lives in New York City. In this essay he describes a time when he was unemployed and went to the unemployment office. He also reflects on the difference between his generation's experience with work and that of earlier generations.

BEFORE YOU READ

THINK about what it would be like to be out of work. Have you ever lost a job or known someone who did? How did you or that person feel?

EXAMINE the title of this essay. Notice that Sherrill uses the same word, *out,* for different effects. What are the connotations of the term "out of college," as opposed to the term "out of work"?

WRITE a journal entry in which you explain what you would like to do in terms of a career when you are "out of college."

AS YOU READ

Notice that Sherrill weaves into the story of his visit to the unemployment office comments about the job market in general. He also compares the problems his generation faces with those faced by generations before him.

One of the things my classmates and I were not told at our college
graduation four years ago was what papers we would need for a visit
to the unemployment office. Luckily, however, in addition to being told
that we were the future, etc., we were told always to be prepared. Thus,
when I made my first visit a few months ago, all of my papers were in order.
I had suspected that getting "processed" would be time-consuming, and I
was right. But that was OK; I wanted it that way. Like graduation
ceremonies and funeral services, applying for unemployment insurance is
one of those lengthy rituals whose duration almost seems designed to make
one sit and think. It's a valuable time to take stock.

What I was not prepared for was the TV crew facing me as I walked
in. The "MacNeil/Lehrer" news team was doing a story on white-collar
unemployment, and they had come to the right place. I had expected the
office to be like a great mixing pool, like the Department of Motor Vehicles.
But the people in the endless line ahead of me—with their trenchcoats and
folded newspapers—looked like the same ones I used to fight with for a
seat on the Wall Street–bound subway train every morning when we all had
jobs. Like them, I did my indicted-mobster-leaving-the-courthouse imitation, evading the cameras as I inched ahead in line. After finally reaching
the front, and giving the clerk evidence of the life and impending death of
Wigwag magazine, where I was a writer, I was told to sit down in the next
room and wait.

The next room looked exactly like a college classroom (when I
squeezed into a seat I realized I'd forgotten how uncomfortable school
desks are). Looking around me, I was struck by the number of people in
the room who were, like me, twenty-something—not the middle-aged
crowd I'd expected. But after giving it some thought, it made more sense.
I knew that, along with seemingly every other industry, Wall Street and the
big law firms were trimming down after the fat years of the eighties: last
hired, first fired, sit down in the next room and wait. So here we were,
members of the generation accused by our older siblings of being merce-
nary and venal, back in the classroom again, only this time having to raise
our hands with questions like, "I didn't get the little pink form in my
information booklet." Who among us would have guessed it in the heady
days of 1986?

In truth, I was never that proud of my generation. I too had been
scornful of those who happily graduated to fast, easy money. And although
I had rejected that route myself, that suddenly seemed irrelevant. At this
perverse reunion I found myself feeling a kinship with my new daylong
classmates, squirming in their desks around me, who had embraced the

eighties. Most of these wunderkinder were now counting themselves lucky to have found their little pink forms.

Like most of them, my notions of college and post-college life were ₅ formed by watching the sixties generation. To be young, energetic, and full of conviction seemed important and exciting. The world had listened to them and we looked forward to our turn. There were many of us who would have liked to help stop a war, disrupt political conventions, take over deans' offices, or volunteer in the South for civil rights. We would have welcomed the chance for a few years of world-changing before settling down to more responsible (i.e., lucrative) activities, as so many of the thirty-something crowd, now with kids and mortgages, had done.

But we had graduated into a different world—one so harsh and ₆ competitive that a Republican president would soon declare the need for something "kinder and gentler." AIDS, skyrocketing tuition, disappearing federal grants, the lack of so easy a common cause as peace and love (or hating hatred), and a dazzling job market offering salaries that, when offered to people so young with four years of loan indebtedness, left virtually no other choices. We weren't in the sixties anymore—we never had been. Those who hadn't realized this by graduation quickly found out that student-loan officials don't grant deferments for time spent "finding" oneself.

When comparing themselves to us, members of the sixties generation, ₇ while using their own college years to rationalize their recent, less than idealistic choices, imply that we younger "careerists" didn't pay our dues before joining them in their twentieth-story offices. Ironically, though, depending on the severity of the recession, my generation may ultimately come to resemble our grandparents' generation more than the one we always wanted to be a part of. When I talk to my friends about job prospects and we compare our experiences at various unemployment offices (one ex-coworker had *two* camera crews to dodge), I wonder if we, like our grandparents in the thirties, will be permanently shaped by these few years. Will we one day say, "Son, when I was your age, in the Great White-Collar Depression, we didn't fool around after college. We took whatever office-temp or bicycle messenger work we could get, and we were *grateful.*"

My name was soon called and, along with several others, I filed into ₈ another classroom for a ninety-minute lecture on how unemployment insurance works—sort of a "Principles of Bureaucracy 101." The last item on my day's agenda was figuring out how to leave while avoiding the only people in the room with jobs: the camera crew. (I began to wonder if their eagerness was due to spending the day with a bunch of former jobholders.)

When we all finally left the office, most of us had been there for about three hours. But we were not the irritated, impatient New York crowd one would expect—we had lots of time on our hands, and we were learning how to deal with having even more. We were at last getting the long-awaited "year off," albeit a crueler and less gentler version. Although we can't be quite as free and easy as our counterparts were twenty years ago—we have to mail in our coupons every week, and we've promised to look for work—this may be the only chance for a coming of age my generation will get.

❀   ❀   ❀

AFTER YOU READ

THINK about Sherrill's comparison of the unemployment office to the college classroom. Why is this an appropriate comparison for him to make? What similarities and differences does he notice between these two places?

THINK also about the comparison Sherrill makes between his generation and the generation of the 1960s. In his opinion, how are these generations similar and how are they different?

EXAMINE the phrase "Great White-Collar Depression," which includes two allusions. First, it alludes to the Great Depression of the 1930s, when banks failed, the stock market plunged, and many people lost their fortunes and jobs. Second, it alludes to the white shirts that most men who worked in offices wore in the past. Referring to someone as a white-collar worker is a way of indicating status because men who did manual labor usually wore blue shirts. Today such distinctions are largely meaningless (women as well as men hold jobs at all levels, and everyone wears clothing of different colors), but the terms *blue-collar* and *white-collar* continue to be used as a way of distinguishing unskilled, manual laborers from those who are employed in positions that require more education and involve less manual labor.

WRITE an essay in which you identify and analyze a problem faced by the members of your generation as they attempt to find jobs and establish careers.

20 Hot Job Tracks

This report, prepared by U.S. News and World Report, *identifies the twenty professions that seem to promise the brightest career for the future. The purpose of a report such as this is to provide readers with information. You may want to read this report selectively, focusing on those sections that describe careers in which you are interested.*

BEFORE YOU READ

THINK about your own career goals and whether they are realistic in view of present and future job markets.

EXAMINE the headings of this report, which indicate clearly the twenty professions referred to in the title. Which tracks are closest to your own interests and goals?

EXAMINE also the subheadings, which indicate the type of information provided about each profession. Can you think of other information that might have been included?

WRITE in your journal a projection of what changes you expect to occur in the next fifty years in the career in which you are interested.

AS YOU READ

Notice especially the training and education required for the careers that interest you.

ACCOUNTING

International Accountant

As fast as the economies in Eastern Europe, Latin America, and China have opened up, U.S. companies have rushed in to capitalize: exporting, buying firms, building plants, planning joint ventures. The North American Free Trade Agreement provided $20 billion in new trade with Mexico alone in 1994. To make the deals happen, companies need accountants who know international financial-reporting standards, merger-and-acquisition protocol, and foreign business customs. The number of international accountants at the accounting firm Deloitte & Touche has increased more than fourfold in the past five years and is expected to double again in the next five.

Hot Track Salaries (Average)

ENTRY LEVEL: $28,000–$32,250; **MANAGER:** $43,000–$62,500; **PARTNER:** $55,000–$84,500.

Training

An accounting or business degree and another language. Overseas experience helps.

Runner-up Hot Track

Forensic accountant. Companies and law firms hire them to check financial reports for signs of fraud or evidence of criminal conduct.

WHAT ACCOUNTING JOBS PAY

Accounting Clerk	$19,500–$24,500
Internal Auditor*	$24,000–$30,000
Assistant Credit Manager	$24,500–$42,000
Senior Budget and Cost Analyst	$38,000–$46,500
Manager, Public Accounting Firm	$42,000–$62,500
Corporate Tax Manager†	$67,000–$105,000

Note: Average salaries for 1995. *Entry level. †At companies with more than $250 million in volume

ARCHITECTURE
Design/Build Specialist

Traditionally, an architect handles the design and a contractor is hired to execute it—and both, plus the owner, frequently end up mad. Now many architectural firms are offering clients designer and builder as a package deal. Instead of becoming an observer when the blueprints are complete, the design/build architect works closely with the contractor to execute the design and make modifications where necessary. About 28 percent of new nonresidential buildings are now put up through the design/build process, up from about 10 percent in 1989. By 2005, that share could reach nearly 50 percent.

Hot Track Salaries (Average)

ENTRY LEVEL: $30,300; **MIDLEVEL:** $44,900; **TOP:** $61,500 and up.

Training

A bachelor's degree in architecture and passage of the architect registration examination. People with coursework in construction-related fields and business have an edge.

Runner-up Hot Track

High-tech home office specialist. These pros ensure that the home offices of telecommuters and entrepreneurs are designed to handle the equipment to get the job done.

WHAT ARCHITECTURE JOBS PAY

Drafter	$24,600
Landscape Architect	$35,600
Architect	
3–6 Years' Experience	$30,300
6–8 Years' Experience	$34,400
8–10 Years' Experience	$39,000
Manager in a Firm	$44,900
Principal/Partner	$61,500

Note: Average salaries for 1993 (latest available)

CONSULTING

Human Resources Pro

The army of re-engineers charged with routing corporate fat has often taken an early whack at the human resources department. Experts say the "outsourcing" of HR duties to independent contractors now represents about a quarter of the $20 billion yearly consulting revenue in the United States; that $5 billion is expected to grow about 10 percent in the next two to three years. Human resources specialists might be hired to install an automated system so employees can monitor their retirement plans, say, or to recruit a top executive. Or they could get extended duty: Benefits specialists might be retained to evaluate health plans, handle enrollment, and field employee questions.

Hot Track Salaries (Median)

ENTRY LEVEL: $40,200; **MIDLEVEL:** $43,700; **TOP:** $62,000.

Training

A bachelor's degree in business, math, or accounting; an M.B.A. or master's in labor relations is a plus.

Runner-up Hot Track

Management consultant. The explosion of global trade has created a need for advisers with language skills and knowledge of emerging Eastern European and Asian markets.

WHAT CONSULTING JOBS PAY

Consultant (Entry)	$46,900
Strategic Planner (Entry)	$50,000
Management Consultant	$67,000
Strategic-Planning Consultant	$78,700
Senior Consultant	$92,100
Senior Strategic Planner	$118,400

Note: Median earnings, including bonus, for 1994

EDUCATION

Specialist in English as a Second Language

Half the student population of Fairfax County, Va., has a native language other than English; some 100 languages are spoken in the school system. All told, the population of U.S. students who are designated as "limited English proficient" has jumped 22 percent in just two years. Teachers of English as a Second Language (ESL) take students in small groups for a period each day to instruct them in basic English or team-teach in the classroom to help students understand the work. They rarely use the students' languages to get their messages across, unlike bilingual programs. Bilingual education has created a ranging controversy over whether teaching kids in their native tongues does them a disservice in the long run.

Hot Track Salaries (Average)

ENTRY LEVEL: $21,900; MIDLEVEL: $25,200; TOP: $40,500.

Training

A degree in education with emphasis on foreign language is typically required; however, fluency in another language is not mandatory. Some states also require ESL certification, which may mean two years of study in multicultural education and linguistics.

Runner-up Hot Track

Special-education teacher. Estimates show schools are short 30,000 or so special-ed teachers, who work with learning-disabled and emotionally disturbed kids in small-group settings.

WHAT EDUCATION JOBS PAY

Beginning Teacher	$24,400
Teacher (16 Years' Experience)	$37,300
Principal	$68,000
Superintendent	$90,000
Associate Professor	$47,000
Professor	$63,500
Dean (Undergraduate)	$57,740
University President	$103,301

Note: Average salaries for 1994–95

ENGINEERING

Software Engineer

It shouldn't come as a revelation that software is hot—or that the engineers who feed the hunger have become a precious commodity. Sales in the United States have been up 27 percent yearly, on average, since 1982; last year's $35.6 billion in revenue from packaged software is expected to more than double by the year 2000. As rapidly as computers and networks become more sophisticated, so do consumer expectations; thus, programming must constantly be upgraded to do a better, quicker, or fancier job. Carnegie Mellon University reports that recruitment of its software engineering students is up this year by more than 20 percent.

Hot Track Salaries (Median)

ENTRY LEVEL: $30,000; **MIDLEVEL:** $45,000; **SENIOR:** $60,000.

Training

A computer science degree is the most common preparation, but some schools offer computer engineering programs. Programming experience is helpful.

Runner-up Hot Track

Environmental engineer. Legislation that would cut cleanup programs could come to a vote in the next few weeks. Assuming the president vetoes such a bill as promised, engineers who guide the work will be in great demand for years to come.

WHAT ENGINEERING JOBS PAY

Industrial	$39,200–$138,800
Aerospace	$40,200–$104,000
Environmental	$40,200–$108,000
Agricultural	$41,500–$101,400
Electrical	$42,000–$103,000
Chemical	$48,500–$130,500
Petroleum	$51,600–$165,200

Note: Average salaries for 1995

ENTERTAINMENT

Computer Animator

Anyone who has experienced the roaring dinosaurs of *Jurassic Park* or Jim Carrey's facial contortions in *The Mask* will understand why computer animation is a sizzling medium. Filmmakers, television show creators, video game producers, and advertisers are rushing to add dazzling computer effects; Industrial Light & Magic in San Rafael, Calif., one of the top computer effects shops, has seen its computer graphics staff grow from two in 1985 to more than 295 today. Much of the demand will be at smaller firms focused on television and video game animation, which are springing up rapidly as equipment prices plummet. (One complete top-of-the-line package of animation hardware and software has gone from as much as $100,000 in price three years ago to less than $20,000.)

Hot Track Salaries (Average)

ENTRY LEVEL: $27,000–$40,000; **MIDLEVEL:** $40,000–$80,000; **TOP:** $80,000 and up.

Training

A two- or four-year degree from a computer animation or graphics program. Two years of experience is desirable at top firms.

Runner-up Hot Track

Entertainment lawyer. Changing technology has made copyright and trade issues devilishly complex. Entertainment companies need lawyers with the know-how to protect their products.

WHAT ENTERTAINMENT JOBS PAY

Dancer/Choreographer	$24,200
Art Director	$33,800
Staff Video Editor	$45,430
Chief Video Engineer	$47,300
Staff Director (Commercials)	$57,250
Vice President (Entertainment Company)	$86,100

Note: Average salaries for 1994; dancer/choreographer salary is for 1992–93

ENVIRONMENT

Computer Mapper

When a city-planning agency is debating the best location for a new waste dump, or a manufacturer the site of a new plant, the decision makers are apt to first commission a computer-created geographic map of current sites; many are hiring folks who do the job in-house. Geographic information systems software allows a visual understanding of a project's impact on surrounding areas; GIS specialists are the technical pros who create the maps and help analyze the results. Last year, sales of GIS software reached $760 million worldwide, up 15 percent over 1993; sales are expected to keep growing by 12 percent a year through 1999.

Hot Track Salaries (Average)

ENTRY LEVEL: $26,000–$35,000; **MIDLEVEL:** $45,000–$50,000; **TOP:** $75,000 and up.

Training

A bachelor's or master's degree in geography or computer science is preferred. Familiarity with the software is helpful.

Runner-up Hot Track

Environmental technician. Manufacturers used to hire techs with master's degrees to collect water, soil, and air samples; they now realize those with two-year degrees can do the job at a fraction of the former cost.

WHAT ENVIRONMENTAL JOBS PAY

Waste Site Facility Foreman	$32,000–$42,000
Chemist	$25,000–$35,000
Environmental Auditor	$33,000–$48,000
Air Quality Specialist	$40,000–$55,000
Risk Assessment Specialist	$40,000–$50,000
Project Manager	$45,000–$55,000

Note: Average salaries for 1995; five years' experience

FINANCE

Investment Manager

Lending money isn't such a hot way to make money anymore: Banks have seen their profit margins from loans eaten away by a third in the past four years because of competition and a glut of capital. *Managing* money, however, offers real potential. Hungry for fee-generating business, financial institutions have rapidly expanded their mutual fund and pension fund operations—and they need pros to manage the investments. All told, banks now hold some 13.5 percent of the industry's $2.6 trillion in assets. J. P. Morgan Investment Management, for example, hired more than 100 professionals this year and expects to add even more than that in '96.

Hot Track Salaries (Average)

ANALYST: $40,000–$55,000; **PORTFOLIO MANAGER:** $110,000–$160,000; **CHIEF INVESTMENT OFFICER:** $175,000–$325,000.

Training

A B.S. degree in economics or business; an M.B.A. is a plus.

Runner-up Hot Track

Derivatives consultant. Companies using these complex instruments need help assessing the risks and monitoring the investments.

WHAT FINANCE JOBS PAY

Foreign-Exchange Clerk	$28,000–$40,000
Vice President (Consumer Lending)	$60,000–$95,000
Settlements Manager (Brokerage)	$75,000–$95,000
Vice President (International Bank)	$85,000–$165,000
Senior Derivatives Trader	$95,000–$135,000
Manager of Trading (Brokerage)	$125,000–$175,000

Note: Average salaries for 1995

HEALTH CARE
Information Specialist

Any hospital, clinic, health maintenance organization, or medical practice that wants to work cheaper and faster—all health care providers, in other words—either has scrapped or soon will scrap paper medical records in favor of digital data. Advantages: Electronic data can be updated and retrieved quickly; specialists can tap into a patient's records and consult on a case long distance; and research can be conducted more easily. According to one estimate, the need for staffers conversant with medical information and computer databases is expected to outstrip supply by 54 percent by the year 2000.

Hot Track Salaries (Average)
ENTRY LEVEL: $27,500; MIDLEVEL: 47,500; TOP: $82,500.

Training

A two- or four-year health information management degree is required, as is passage of a national certification exam.

Runner-up Hot Track

Physical therapist. According to the American Hospital Association, there's a 15 percent vacancy rate—at least—in the field.

WHAT HEALTH CARE JOBS PAY

Medical Technician	$19,000–$20,000
Medical Technologist	$23,000–$24,000
Dietitian	$27,924
Staff Nurse, RN	$35,464
Speech Therapist	$36,036
Pharmacist	$49,608
Physician Assistant	$50,000–$55,000
Nurse Practitioner, RN	$50,000–$55,000

Note: Median salaries for 1994

HOSPITALITY
Food Service Manager

A study by the National Restaurant Association found that when a woman works outside the home, she and her family are more apt to dine out or order in than to have a home-cooked supper. Little wonder the food service industry now takes about 44 cents of every dollar spent on food. The Bureau of Labor Statistics predicts that by 2005, jobs in food service management will jump by 44 percent; besides restaurants, hotels, hospitals, and contract food service companies will be recruiting. Food service managers purchase food and supplies, hire, plan menus, and oversee operations.

Hot Track Salaries (Median)

ENTRY LEVEL: $30,000; MIDLEVEL: $37,000; TOP: $48,000.

Training

More than 60 percent of restaurant owners and managers began as dishwashers, servers, and cooks, so experience is important. A degree in hotel or restaurant management may mean faster advancement.

Runner-up Hot Track

Hotel general manager. The travel industry is booming—by year's end, there will be 40 percent more hotel jobs than there were in 1992. Managers oversee all hotel employees, operations, and sales and marketing.

WHAT HOSPITALITY JOBS PAY

Flight Attendant (Entry)	$13,700
Travel Agent (3–5 Years' Experience)	$19,500
General Manager (Fast-Food Restaurant)	$27,000
Executive Chef	$37,000
Hotel General Manager	$56,000
Hotel Chief Financial Officer	$95,000

Note: Median salaries for 1994–95

HUMAN SERVICES

Residential Counselor

Group homes for the developmentally disabled have grown in number by 29 percent in the past two years, as governments continue to close mental institutions. For troubled or drug-abusing teens and former prisoners, too, residential services have become a favored way to deliver therapy and ease the transition to a normal life. Counselors supervise residents in house-keeping tasks, provide emotional support and counseling, and lead recreational activities. They also analyze each client's needs by reviewing records, talking with families, and conferring with medical personnel.

Hot Track Salaries (Average)

ENTRY LEVEL: $15,000–$23,000; **MIDLEVEL:** $18,000–$27,000; **TOP:** $25,000–$35,000.

Training

A degree in human services, with coursework in crisis intervention, drug and alcohol counseling, and mental health. Many two-year colleges offer degrees in human services.

Runner-up Hot Track

Life skills instructor. Developmentally disabled clients learn from these pros to handle tasks such as cooking, using public transportation, and mixing with people.

WHAT HUMAN SERVICES JOBS PAY

Life Skills Instructor	$15,000–$23,000
Home Health/Hospice Aid	$15,000–$23,000
Case Manager	$19,000–$27,000
Residential Manager	$19,000–$27,000
Group Home Director	$30,000–$45,000
Social Science Administrator	$40,000–$50,000

Note: Average salaries for 1994–95

INFORMATION SERVICES

Web Master

The cyberpros who design and maintain a company's World Wide Web site on the Internet are a new species; headhunters say the job title is only about a year old. A home page is becoming *de rigueur* as a way to create awareness of a company and advertise its products; Yahoo, the largest guide to Web sites, reports the list is growing by 10 to 15 percent monthly. Responsibilities include the graphics and editorial content of the home page, the public relations and marketing message, and overseeing technical decisions—the choice of software and hardware, for example.

Hot Track Salaries (Average)

ENTRY LEVEL: $50,000; **MIDLEVEL:** $75,000; **SENIOR:** $100,000 and up.

Training

A Web master might have a background in computer science, marketing, or English. What's key: online experience, knowledge of computer technology, and writing skills.

Runner-up Hot Track

Online-service developer. Corporations in virtually every industry are developing moneymaking online ventures—BellSouth's electronic phone directories, for example.

WHAT INFORMATION JOBS PAY

Programmer	$26,000–$37,500
Systems Analyst	$36,000–$55,000
PC Network Specialist	$45,000–$61,000
Systems Manager	$46,000–$76,000
Database Analyst (Large Firm)	$46,000–$58,000
Database Manager (Large Firm)	$63,500–$79,000
Software Product Manager	$62,500–$90,000

Note: Median salaries for 1995

LAW

Employment Lawyer

In 1994, the Equal Employment Opportunity Commission received 14,420 complaints regarding sexual harassment, up from 5,623 a mere five years earlier. Since 1992, when the EEOC began enforcing the Americans with Disabilities Act, some 50,000 claims of discrimination against disabled workers have been counted. The evolution of workplace law, plus the greater willingness of workers to come forward, means more jobs for lawyers on both sides of the courtroom. The choice, high-paying jobs tend to be at large firms, which usually consult with and defend corporate clients. One New York legal recruiter, Ann Israel & Associates, has seen the number of requests for employment lawyers jump 200 percent in the past year alone.

Hot Track Salaries (Average)

PARALEGAL: $43,262; **ASSOCIATE:** $63,001–$77,131; **PARTNER:** $173,774–$191,300.

Training

Besides a J.D., firms want their hires to have an interest in litigation and employment issues.

Runner-up Hot Track

Corporate securities lawyer. Mergers are in vogue; these lawyers are needed to verify financial statements and draw up the forms required to get sales approved by the SEC and others.

WHAT LEGAL JOBS PAY

Paralegal (Business Law)	$43,414
FBI Attorney/Adviser, GS-14	$64,000
Associate (Real Estate)	$81,560
Trial Court Judge	$85,699
U.S. Bankruptcy Court Judge	$122,912
U.S. Supreme Court Justice (Associate)	$164,100
Partner in Firm (Litigation)	$189,462
Partner (Tax)	$207,700

Note: Average salaries for 1995

MEDIA

Online Content Developer

Electronic newspapers now number around 500, up from virtually zero a few years ago; media watchers expect that number to triple or quadruple in the next two years. Magazines and newsletters, too, are creating online editions—and new slots for pros who can infuse text with visual and audio life. Online content developers produce stories, commission others to write for the publication, and repackage previously published material (all articles on O. J. Simpson, say, might be made accessible). They also might host chat sessions with readers and update news throughout the day. Further, they might help the company produce other electronic products, such as CD-ROMs.

Hot Track Salaries (Average)

ENTRY LEVEL: $25,000–$35,000; **MIDLEVEL:** $50,000; **TOP:** $80,000.

Training

A bachelor's degree in communications or journalism; experience in publishing, graphic design, or multimedia programming is also helpful.

Runner-up Hot Track

Online marketer. All those new online publications require sales pros to sell ads and subscriptions.

WHAT MEDIA JOBS PAY

Magazine Ad Sales Manager	$44,300
Magazine Senior Editor	$44,500
Magazine Editor-in-Chief	$67,100
Newspaper Reporter (Entry)	$19,700
Newspaper Editor	$67,600
Radio News Announcer	$27,900
Radio Program Director	$53,900
TV News Director	$60,000

Note: Median salaries for 1995 (for magazines, averages; for newspaper reporter, average for 1994)

MEDICINE

Internist in Infectious Diseases

Specialists in infectious diseases don't face quite the level of crisis that Dustin Hoffman did in *Outbreak*. But the medical profession is very worried that the rise of antibiotic-resistant "superbugs" could mean a serious increase looms in dangerous—even deadly—diseases. Since 1989, the incidence of drug-resistant infection in hospitals has increased a whopping 34-fold. Last month, the Centers for Disease Control and Prevention strongly warned doctors to use germ-fighting drugs more sparingly. The spread of hepatitis, gonorrhea, tuberculosis, and HIV is contributing to demand for the doctors who treat—and when possible, prevent—contagious diseases.

Hot Track Salaries (Average)

ENTRY LEVEL: $117,048; **MIDLEVEL:** $145,300; **TOP:** $214,637.

Training

College, medical school, a residency in pediatrics or internal medicine, and a period of specialization in infectious diseases.

Runner-up Hot Track

Geriatrician. The explanation is in the numbers: It won't be *that* long until the baby boomers are senior citizens.

WHAT MEDICAL JOBS PAY

Family Practitioner	$122,000
Pediatrician	$126,401
Psychiatrist	$132,929
Internist	$133,581
General Surgeon	$200,211
Pathologist	$208,694
Ob-Gyn	$210,703
Anesthesiologist	$244,600
Radiologist	$264,446
Orthopedic Surgeon	$292,000

Note: Median salaries for 1994 for doctors in group practice

SALES

Wireless Salesperson

The Federal Communications Commission raked in more than $7 billion earlier this year when it auctioned off 99 licenses for broadband personal communications services (PCS). The new services will push state-of-the-art wireless technology—mobile cordless phones, for example—and challenge cellular firms; the number of wireless providers per market should rise from two to as many as eight. Salespeople will be needed to market not only the new phones but mobile fax machines and pagers, too. The best-paid sales jobs tend to be with manufacturers who sell to retailers and other companies.

Hot Track Salaries (Average)

ENTRY LEVEL: $41,000; **MIDLEVEL:** $50,000–$60,000; **TOP:** $70,000.

Training

A degree in engineering or a strong sales background is helpful, but many companies will train staffers in the new technologies.

Runner-up Hot Track

Computer equipment salesperson. Pros are needed who can sell rapidly changing technology—from computer monitors to fax machines to virtual-office products.

WHAT SALES JOBS PAY

Entry-Level Sales Rep	$27,600
Senior Sales Rep	$47,000
Major Account Rep	$49,300
District Sales Manager	$54,800
National Account Rep	$57,600
Regional Sales Manager	$58,600
National Account Manager	$62,800
Top Sales Executive	$81,000

Note: Average salaries for 1995 for average performers, including bonuses

SCIENCE RESEARCH
Genetic Researcher

The scientists who are mapping human chromosomes are well along toward their goal: Nearly half of the body's 80,000 genes have been located so far. Every new discovery spells possibility for the pharmaceutical industry, which has used the information to seek new treatments for diseases like diabetes, schizophrenia, and cancer. Some $15 billion will be spent on drug development this year, nearly double 1990's investment; much of that will fund genetic research at university laboratories and in-house. There should be plenty of work for such researchers well beyond 2002—when the mapping is likely to be complete.

Hot Track Salaries (Average)

ENTRY LEVEL: $47,000; **MIDLEVEL:** $60,000; **TOP:** $80,000.

Training

A B.S. in biology or chemistry; increasingly, a Ph.D. in molecular or human genetics is needed. Postdoctorate work in genetics can also be important.

Runner-up Hot Track

Computer-trained biologist. Computers often supply answers faster than test tubes do. Scientists who know how to ask a computer to process and analyze data are needed.

WHAT RESEARCH JOBS PAY

Biologist (B.S.)	$29,000
with Ph.D.	$53,100
Medical Scientist	$36,296
Physicist (B.S.)	$37,566
with Ph.D.	$54,750
Geologist (B.S.)	$54,100
with Ph.D.	$70,600
Chemist (B.S.)	$29,625
with Ph.D.	$60,000

Note: Median salaries for 1994

SOCIAL WORK

Geriatric Case Manager

Two trends account for the emergence of this new professional: the distances that often separate the elderly from their children and the swelling ranks of the "oldest old." The number of people age 85 and up—now 3.5 million—will more than double by 2025, the year the whole baby boom bulge will pass 65. Case managers assess the physical and mental health of elderly clients and make sure they get care; advise on living arrangements; point to sources of financial and legal aid; and counsel the families. Many case managers are entrepreneurs; larger firms are also becoming common. Nursing homes have slots, too.

Hot Track Salaries (Average)

ENTRY LEVEL: $30,000; **MIDLEVEL:** $36,000; **TOP:** $45,000.

Training

A master's degree in social work, with a certificate in gerontology or experience with the elderly.

Runner-up Hot Track

Employee assistance counselor. Some 90 percent of *Fortune* 500 companies have employee assistance programs in place to provide counseling to workers with emotional, job-related, or substance abuse problems.

WHAT SOCIAL WORK JOBS PAY

Public Welfare Caseworker	$30,000
Court Social Worker	$32,000
School Social Worker	$32,500
HMO Social Worker	$36,000
Member, Private Practice	$40,000
Employee Assistance Counselor	$43,000
Solo Private Practitioner	$50,000

Note: Average salaries for 1993 (latest available)

SPORTS MANAGEMENT
Corporate Sales Representative

It costs $3,500 to be top sponsor of the Hoopla Aurora Youth Basketball Tournament in Colorado; $200,000 buys the honors for college football's Peach Bowl. At all levels of play, sporting events, teams, and the arenas they compete in are aggressively selling sponsorships as a way to make money: Companies in North America will spend a stunning $3.05 billion as sponsors this year, up 44 percent since 1992. The sales force cuts the deals, which generally give a company logo rights (San Francisco's Candlestick Park is now 3Com Park after the computer maker, for example), TV advertising during an event, and free tickets.

Hot Track Salaries (Average)

ENTRY LEVEL: $18,000; **MIDLEVEL:** $60,000; **TOP:** $80,000 and up.

Training

A business degree with an emphasis in marketing is helpful but not necessary. A background in sales or media plus knowledge of the sports industry should open doors.

Runner-up Hot Track

Sports marketer. These pros battle for spectators by devising the right PR and advertising message. The number of sports-marketing firms has grown from 110 in 1980 to about 800 today.

WHAT SPORTS MANAGEMENT JOBS PAY

Public Relations Staffer (Entry)	$19,000
Assistant Athletic Director (College)	$45,710
General Manager (Minor League)	$60,280
Ticket Sales Director	$75,000
Chief Financial Officer (Pro Team)	$90,000
Executive Vice President (Arena)	$191,670

Note: Average salaries for 1993–94 (latest available)

TELECOMMUNICATIONS

Computer Security Expert

The rapid move by corporate America to computer networks, plus the explosive surge in Internet traffic, has created real opportunity for high-tech snoops and cyberthieves. The annual loss to U.S. businesses is estimated at $6.5 billion to $9 billion and is expected to swell by 25 percent in 1996. Result: Companies want computer security pros to design and monitor protections for computer-stored trade secrets, employee data, etc. They might install software that mandates password changes every so often, say, or develop an encryption technique that converts all sensitive information into code.

Hot Track Salaries (Average)

ENTRY LEVEL: $30,000–$40,000; **MIDLEVEL:** $65,000–$78,000; **TOP:** $90,000 and up.

Training

A degree in computer science, engineering, or telecommunications, plus an understanding of networking and communication systems, is required. To reach the top, security experience is key.

Runner-up Hot Track

Wireless specialist. Desire for ever smaller, more sophisticated cellular phones and pagers drives demand for these designers and technicians.

WHAT TELECOMMUNICATIONS JOBS PAY

Sales Rep (Entry Level)	$22,000
Junior Technician	$25,500
Midlevel Technician	$29,400
Entry-Level Engineer	$40,600
Sales/Marketing Executive	$53,100
Top-Level Engineer	$59,100
Online Content Project Manager	$80,000

Note: Average salaries for 1995

❁   ❁   ❁

AFTER YOU READ

THINK about the life span of different professions. Although some professions have been around for a very long time, others have come and gone. For example, blacksmiths, telephone operators, and seamstresses are relatively rare these days. Can you think of other types of jobs that have become obsolete? Can you think of new jobs that have been created in recent years?

EXAMINE the salaries that are projected for the twenty professions. Which are expected to bring the highest salaries? Is salary the most important factor in choosing a job? If not, what other factors are more important and why?

WRITE a brief report in which you summarize the information included in this report. Organize your report into different sections and include headings to identify these sections, but do not use the same ones included in the original report.

The Work Ahead

This chart, which was called a forecast, appeared in Harper's Magazine. *As the introductory note makes clear, the chart is taken from a bulletin called* The American Work Force: 1992–2005. *The chart is divided into two parts: Positive Job Growth and Negative Job Growth. By studying this chart, you will be able to identify which jobs are likely to increase in number and which are likely to decrease in number.*

BEFORE YOU READ

THINK about the factors that influence your decision about a career. Is availability of jobs one of these factors? Should it be?

EXAMINE the introductory note at the top of the chart. It provides a context for the chart, identifies the information found in the chart, and explains how the chart is organized.

WRITE a journal entry in which you list the factors that have influenced you as you decide on a career.

AS YOU READ

Locate on the chart those jobs in which you are interested.

F rom *The American Work Force: 1992–2005,* a bulletin of employment projections issued last year by the U.S. Department of Labor. The study found that nearly half of the jobs that the economy will gain over the next decade will be in three service industries—retail trade, health services, and educational services—and that most of the jobs lost will be in agriculture and manufacturing. The list on the left shows the professions that will experience the greatest growth over the next decade and the projected number of new jobs; the list on the right shows the professions that will experience the greatest decline and the projected number of jobs that will be lost.

POSITIVE JOB GROWTH		NEGATIVE JOB GROWTH	
Occupation	*Increase (No. of jobs)*	*Occupation*	*Decrease (No. of jobs)*
Retail salespersons	786,000	Farmers	−231,000
Registered nurses	765,000	Sewing-machine operators	−162,000
Cashiers	670,000	Cleaners/servants (domestic)	−157,000
General office clerks	654,000	Farmworkers	−133,000
Truck drivers	648,000	Typists and word processors	−125,000
Waiters and waitresses	637,000	Childcare workers (domestic)	−123,000
Nursing aids and orderlies	594,000	Computer operators	−104,000
Janitors and cleaners	548,000	Packaging machine operators	−71,000
Food-preparation workers	524,000	Precision inspectors	−65,000
Systems analysts	501,000	Switchboard operators	−51,000
Home health aides	479,000	Telephone and cable-TV line installers and repairers	−40,000
Secondary-school teachers	462,000	Textile-machine operators	−35,000
Childcare workers (institutional)	450,000	Bartenders	−32,000
Security guards	408,000	Forming-machine operators	−32,000
Marketing/sales supervisors	407,000	Butchers and meat cutters	−31,000
Teacher aides	381,000	Bookkeeping-machine operators	−28,000
Top executives and managers	380,000	Central communications-equipment installers and repairers	−25,000
General maintenance and repair workers	319,000	Telephone operators	−24,000
Elementary-school teachers	311,000	Bank tellers	−24,000
Gardeners and groundskeepers	311,000		
Fast-food counter workers	308,000		

❀ ❀ ❀

AFTER YOU READ

THINK about how the information in this chart affects your decision about a career. If you really want to be a farmer, for example, will you change your mind about pursuing that career because this chart indicates a decline of 231,000 farming jobs between 1992 and 2005?

THINK also about how this same information might have been presented in an article or essay rather than as a chart. Which format is more useful and accessible? Why?

EXAMINE the generalization found in the introductory note that "nearly half of the jobs that the economy will gain over the next decade will be in three service industries—retail trade, health services, and educational services—and that most of the jobs lost will be in agriculture and manufacturing." What other generalizations can you make on the basis of the information included in the chart?

WRITE a brief report in which you summarize the information in the chart.

Unit Four: Critical Thinking and Writing Assignments

❀ ❀ ❀

EXPLORING IDEAS TOGETHER

1. Many of the authors included in this unit write about hard work—times when they or someone they knew worked long hours doing something that required significant physical labor. Most often this type of hard work is associated with previous generations rather than present ones. With a group of your classmates, discuss whether people of your generation work as hard as people did in the past. Consider also whether work that does not require physical labor can be "hard work" and what effects working hard has on people. You may want to refer to the reading selections by Terkel, Davis, Dove, and Theriault.

2. Role models often influence a person's choice of career. Review the reading selections by Davis, Dove, May, and Masumoto and determine who their role models were and how they were influenced by them.

3. A person's entry into the work force is sometimes viewed as an initiation into real life or adulthood. Review the reading selections by May and Armstrong, and discuss how the work experiences they write about served as initiation rites. Identify what each of them learned from these experiences.

4. Discuss the current job market for college graduates, and review the information given in the reading selection by Sherrill, the report in *U.S. News and World Report,* and the chart from *Harper's Magazine.* Then write at least three suggestions that you think would help college students as they prepare for this job market.

WRITING ESSAYS

1. Research the career in which you are interested by searching for information in your library and/or by interviewing someone in that field. Then write an essay in which you share the information you have collected with other college students who are interested in the same career.

2. Write an essay in which you explore the effects of work and/or a career on a person's life. Consider such issues as the effects of working too hard or too much versus the effects of not finding a job, the stereotypi-cal way people define those who work in certain professions, or the

role of work in establishing a healthy self-concept. The reading selections by Terkel, Davis, Smiley, Masumoto, and Sherrill will provide you with useful information for your essay.

3. The type of work Americans do has changed dramatically in the last fifty years. Choose one type of work or career and write an essay in which you describe the changes that have occurred; identify the factors responsible for these changes. You will find the information in the reading selections taken from *Harper's Magazine* and *U.S. News and World Report* useful as your sources.

4. Write an essay in which you tell how the roles that males and females assume in the work force have changed in recent years.

5. Write an essay in which you compare and contrast the problems your generation faces in establishing careers with those faced by another generation. The reading selections by Davis, Dove, and Sherrill as well as the reports from *Harper's Magazine* and *U.S. News and World Report* will supplement the information derived from your own experiences.

6. Summarize the information in the report from *U.S. News and World Report* and the chart from *Harper's Magazine* and include this summary in a brief report on the current job market. Your report should be appropriate for college students.

7. Write an essay in which you compare work and play and the roles they play in a person's life. You may want to reread the selections by Davis, Smiley, and Masumoto before beginning your essay.

Self with Society

Interactions with individuals can be complicated and at times even difficult, but your relationship with society—all the diverse people who exist in this country under one government—is even more complex. Our society is made up of many different selves, so each self must find a way to coexist with many other selves. As a member of such a diverse society, you are called upon to make decisions about people who are very different from you, people who live in different parts of the country, who have different religious and ethnic backgrounds and different social and economic conditions. While such diversity is clearly a strength, giving the American culture a texture and energy and variety that it would otherwise lack, it can also create problems. How can a society with such diversity function effectively? How can laws be enacted that are fair to all members of such a diverse society? How can this large, pluralistic, often antagonistic, society solve the problems of both the rich and the poor, the young and the old, the healthy and the sick?

This unit focuses on some of the problems that exist in our complex society—problems that make some people's lives less productive and secure. Information about these problems will enable you to understand the responsibilities you face as a member of a society that is blessed with great resources and immense potential yet weakened by serious problems.

The problems discussed in this unit range from those that affect children and teenagers to those that affect older people. Several reading selections focus on education—its failure as well as its success, its costs as well as its rewards. Some writers not only explore problems of racial and ethnic prejudice and tension in our schools and universities but also reassess the success of racial integration. Other writers report on the increasing problems of crime, violence, and drugs on our campuses, in our streets, and in our neighborhoods. One essay focuses on the hopeless situation of the homeless while a companion essay tells the story of a successful career woman who escaped the trap of welfare. Finally, the last two essays examine the process of aging and the way aging and old people are viewed by society in general and by youth in particular. All of the readings in this unit focus on people with problems that will not be solved easily or quickly but that deserve the concern of an informed and caring society.

Before you begin this unit, think about the rights and privileges of citizenship in this country. What rights should every member of society have? Is economic security one of these rights? What about education? Medical care? Food? Housing? Freedom of religion? Freedom from fear? Can a society choose to grant certain rights to one group and not to others? Which groups in our society enjoy the greatest privileges? Which groups suffer most?

Next think about the responsibilities that every member of society should have. Should belonging to a certain group, having an education, or being wealthy exempt people from these responsibilities? Should one individual or group have any responsibilities toward other individuals or groups? Does the person living on a farm in Alabama have a responsibility toward the homeless man on the streets of Chicago? Does the professor at Purdue need to be concerned about the high-school dropout in Phoenix? Should the retiree in Florida care if the young people in Los Angeles are rioting, or should the teenager in Detroit care if the nursing homes in Dallas are a disgrace? In other words, to what extent can we be individuals rather than members of society?

As you read the selections in this unit, keep in mind that our society consists of a collection of people—different groups with different interests, contributions, and problems—who combine to form a single society. Can a society such as ours endure if all groups do not have a voice? Can problems be solved if we do not understand the people who have the problems?

The Scholarship Jacket

MARTA SALINAS

Marta Salinas has published stories in California Living *and the* Los Angeles Herald Examiner. *In "The Scholarship Jacket," which was originally published in* Growing Up Chicana/o: An Anthology, *Salinas writes about her experience as a Chicana student in a public school in south Texas.*

BEFORE YOU READ

THINK about some award or recognition that you wanted very much or worked very hard to achieve. Why was this goal so important to you? Did you achieve it? Why or why not?

EXAMINE the title, "The Scholarship Jacket," as well as the first paragraph, in which Salinas describes the jacket and its significance. In Salinas's story, earning this jacket becomes not only a personal goal but also a symbol of achievement for her family and for her people.

WRITE a journal entry about a situation in which you feel you were treated unfairly because of your social situation—because you were too poor or too rich; because of your parents or family; or because of your race, nationality, or religion.

AS YOU READ

Try to determine the motivations of the characters in the story.

The small Texas school that I attended carried out a tradition every year 1
during the eighth grade graduation: a beautiful gold and green jacket,
the school colors, was awarded to the class valedictorian, the student who
had maintained the highest grades for eight years. The scholarship jacket
had a big gold S on the left front side, and the winner's name was written
in gold letters on the pocket.

My oldest sister Rosie had won the jacket a few years back, and I fully 2
expected to win also. I was fourteen and in the eighth grade. I had been a
straight A student since the first grade, and the last year I had looked
forward to owning that jacket. My father was a farm laborer who couldn't
earn enough money to feed eight children, so when I was six I was given
to my grandparents to raise. We couldn't participate in sports at school
because there were registration fees, uniform costs, and trips out of town;
so even though we were quite agile and athletic, there would never be a
sports school jacket for us. This one, the scholarship jacket, was our only
chance.

In May, close to graduation, spring fever struck, and no one paid any 3
attention in class; instead we stared out the windows and at each other,
wanting to speed up the last few weeks of school. I despaired every time I
looked in the mirror. Pencil thin, not a curve anywhere, I was called
"Beanpole" and "String Bean," and I knew that's what I looked like. A flat
chest, no hips, and a brain, that's what I had. That really isn't much for a
fourteen-year-old to work with, I thought, as I absentmindedly wandered
from my history class to the gym. Another hour of sweating in basketball
and displaying my toothpick legs was coming up. Then I remembered my
P.E. shorts were still in a bag under my desk where I'd forgotten them. I
had to walk all the way back and get them. Coach Thompson was a real
bear if anyone wasn't dressed for P.E. She had said I was a good forward
and once she even tried to talk Grandma into letting me join the team.
Grandma, of course, said no.

I was almost back at my classroom door when I heard angry voices and 4
arguing. I stopped. I didn't mean to eavesdrop; I just hesitated, not knowing
what to do. I needed those shorts and I was going to be late, but I didn't
want to interrupt an argument between my teachers. I recognized the
voices: Mr. Schmidt, my history teacher, and Mr. Boone, my math teacher.
They seemed to be arguing about me. I couldn't believe it. I still remember
the shock that rooted me flat against the wall as if I were trying to blend
in with the graffiti written there.

"I refuse to do it! I don't care who her father is, her grades don't even 5
begin to compare to Martha's. I won't lie or falsify records. Martha has a

straight A plus average and you know it." That was Mr. Schmidt and he sounded very angry. Mr. Boone's voice sounded calm and quiet.

"Look, Joann's father is not only on the Board, he owns the only store 6 in town; we could say it was a close tie and—"

The pounding in my ears drowned out the rest of the words, only a 7 word here and there filtered through. ". . . Martha is Mexican. . . . resign. . . . won't do it. . . ." Mr. Schmidt came rushing out, and luckily for me went down the opposite way toward the auditorium, so he didn't see me. Shaking, I waited a few minutes and then went in and grabbed my bag and fled from the room. Mr. Boone looked up when I came in but didn't say anything. To this day I don't remember if I got in trouble in P.E. for being late or how I made it through the rest of the afternoon. I went home very sad and cried into my pillow that night so Grandmother wouldn't hear me. It seemed a cruel coincidence that I had overheard that conversation.

The next day when the principal called me into his office, I knew what 8 it would be about. He looked uncomfortable and unhappy. I decided I wasn't going to make it any easier for him so I looked him straight in the eye. He looked away and fidgeted with the papers on his desk.

"Martha," he said, "there's been a change in policy this year regarding 9 the scholarship jacket. As you know, it has always been free." He cleared his throat and continued. "This year the Board decided to charge fifteen dollars—which still won't cover the complete cost of the jacket."

I stared at him in shock and a small sound of dismay escaped my throat. 10 I hadn't expected this. He still avoided looking in my eyes.

"So if you are unable to pay the fifteen dollars for the jacket, it will be 11 given to the next one in line."

Standing with all the dignity I could muster, I said, "I'll speak to my 12 grandfather about it, sir, and let you know tomorrow." I cried on the walk home from the bus stop. The dirt road was a quarter of a mile from the highway, so by the time I got home, my eyes were red and puffy.

"Where's Grandpa?" I asked Grandma, looking down at the floor so 13 she wouldn't ask me why I'd been crying. She was sewing on a quilt and didn't look up.

"I think he's out back working in the bean field." 14

I went outside and looked out at the fields. There he was. I could see 15 him walking between the rows, his body bent over the little plants, hoe in hand. I walked slowly out to him, trying to think how I could best ask him for the money. There was a cool breeze blowing and a sweet smell of mesquite in the air, but I didn't appreciate it. I kicked at a dirt clod. I wanted that jacket so much. It was more than just being a valedictorian and giving a little thank you speech for the jacket on graduation night. It represented eight years of hard work and expectation. I knew I had to be honest with Grandpa; it was my only chance. He saw me and looked up.

He waited for me to speak. I cleared my throat nervously and clasped 16 my hands behind my back so he wouldn't see them shaking. "Grandpa, I have a big favor to ask you," I said in Spanish, the only language he knew. He still waited silently. I tried again. "Grandpa, this year the principal said the scholarship jacket is not going to be free. It's going to cost fifteen dollars and I have to take the money in tomorrow, otherwise it'll be given to someone else." The last words came out in an eager rush. Grandpa straightened up tiredly and leaned his chin on the hoe handle. He looked out over the field that was filled with the tiny green bean plants. I waited, desperately hoping he'd say I could have the money.

He turned to me and asked quietly, "What does a scholarship jacket 17 mean?"

I answered quickly; maybe there was a chance. "It means you've earned 18 it by having the highest grades for eight years and that's why they're giving it to you." Too late I realized the significance of my words. Grandpa knew that I understood it was not a matter of money. It wasn't that. He went back to hoeing the weeds that sprang up between the delicate little bean plants. It was a time-consuming job; sometimes the small shoots were right next to each other. Finally he spoke again.

"Then if you pay for it, Marta, it's not a scholarship jacket, is it? Tell 19 your principal I will not pay the fifteen dollars."

I walked back to the house and locked myself in the bathroom for a 20 long time. I was angry with Grandfather even though I knew he was right, and I was angry with the Board, whoever they were. Why did they have to change the rules just when it was my turn to win the jacket?

It was a very sad and withdrawn girl who dragged into the principal's 21 office the next day. This time he did look me in the eyes.

"What did your grandfather say?"   22

I sat very straight in my chair.   23

"He said to tell you he won't pay the fifteen dollars."   24

The principal muttered something I couldn't understand under his 25 breath, and walked over to the window. He stood looking out at something outside. He looked bigger than usual when he stood up; he was a tall gaunt man with gray hair, and I watched the back of his head while I waited for him to speak.

"Why?" he finally asked. "Your grandfather has the money. Doesn't he 26 own a small bean farm?"

I looked at him, forcing my eyes to stay dry. "He said if I had to pay 27
for it, then it wouldn't be a scholarship jacket," I said and stood up to leave.
"I guess you'll just have to give it to Joann." I hadn't meant to say that; it
had just slipped out. I was almost to the door when he stopped me.

"Martha—wait." 28

I turned and looked at him, waiting. What did he want now? I could 29
feel my heart pounding. Something bitter and vile tasting was coming up
in my mouth; I was afraid I was going to be sick. I didn't need any sympathy
speeches. He sighed loudly and went back to his big desk. He looked at
me, biting his lip, as if thinking.

"Okay, damn it. We'll make an exception in your case. I'll tell the 30
Board, you'll get your jacket."

I could hardly believe it. I spoke in a trembling rush. "Oh, thank you, 31
sir!" Suddenly I felt great. I didn't know about adrenaline in those days,
but I knew something was pumping through me, making me feel as tall as
the sky. I wanted to yell, jump, run the mile, do something. I ran out so I
could cry in the hall where there was no one to see me. At the end of the
day, Mr. Schmidt winked at me and said, "I hear you're getting a scholarship
jacket this year."

His face looked as happy and innocent as a baby's, but I knew better. 32
Without answering I gave him a quick hug and ran to the bus. I cried on
the walk home again, but this time because I was so happy. I couldn't wait
to tell Grandpa and ran straight to the field. I joined him in the row where
he was working and without saying anything I crouched down and started
pulling up the weeds with my hands. Grandpa worked alongside me for a
few minutes, but he didn't ask what had happened. After I had a little pile
of weeds between the rows, I stood up and faced him.

"The principal said he's making an exception for me, Grandpa, and 33
I'm getting the jacket after all. That's after I told him what you said."

Grandpa didn't say anything, he just gave me a pat on the shoulder 34
and a smile. He pulled out the crumpled red handkerchief that he always
carried in his back pocket and wiped the sweat off his forehead.

"Better go see if your grandmother needs any help with supper." 35

I gave him a big grin. He didn't fool me. I skipped and ran back to the 36
house whistling some silly tune.

❀ ❀ ❀

AFTER YOU READ

THINK again about the motivations of the people in the story. Why does Martha want to win the scholarship jacket? Why does Mr. Boone make the proposal that he makes? Why does the grandfather refuse to pay the money for the jacket even though he can afford it? And why does the principal make an exception to the new rule in Martha's case?

EXAMINE the conversation between Mr. Schmidt and Mr. Boone in paragraphs 5–7. What does this conversation reveal about racial and economic prejudice? In your opinion, is such prejudice found today in educational and social institutions—even among people in authority such as teachers and administrators?

WRITE an essay in which you use your own experience and observations to identify and analyze a school or college policy that you believe discriminates against some group, such as handicapped students, students who smoke, or students of a particular ethnic or religious background. In your analysis, explain why this policy is unfair, and give specific supporting examples.

In Praise of the F Word

MARY SHERRY

In recent years our public educational system has been the target of much criticism. Many parents feel that public schools are increasingly ineffective. In this guest editorial for Newsweek, *a mother and teacher of adult-literacy courses suggests that schools would be more effective if teachers and administrators were not reluctant to fail students. She argues in favor of flunking students, citing her own son's experience in a high school English class to support her argument. Mary Sherry, who lives near Minneapolis, Minnesota, believes that "flunking as a regular policy has just as much merit today as it did two generations ago."*

BEFORE YOU READ

THINK about what it means to flunk. Why is the word so ominous and ugly? (It even sounds ugly.) What do we associate with flunking?

EXAMINE the first sentence of this article: "Tens of thousands of 18-year-olds will graduate this year and be handed meaningless diplomas." Do you agree or disagree with this statement? What makes a diploma meaningless or valuable? How valuable is your diploma?

WRITE a journal entry about how it feels to fail or fear failing a particular assignment or course or grade in school.

AS YOU READ

Evaluate Sherry's arguments in favor of flunking as a school policy. What is her evidence? How sound is her reasoning? How convincing is her example of her son's experience?

Tens of thousands of 18-year-olds will graduate this year and be handed 1
meaningless diplomas. These diplomas won't look any different from
those awarded their luckier classmates. Their validity will be questioned
only when their employers discover that these graduates are semiliterate.

Eventually a fortunate few will find their way into educational-repair 2
shops—adult-literacy programs, such as the one where I teach basic
grammar and writing. There, high school graduates and high school
dropouts pursuing graduate-equivalency certificates will learn the skills
they should have learned in school. They will also discover they have been
cheated by our educational system.

As I teach, I learn a lot about our schools. Early in each session I ask 3
my students to write about an unpleasant experience they had in
school. No writers' block here! "I wish someone would have made
me stop doing drugs and made me study." "I liked to party and no one
seemed to care." "I was a good kid and didn't cause any trouble, so they
just passed me along even though I didn't read well and couldn't write."
And so on.

I am your basic do-gooder, and prior to teaching this class I blamed 4
the poor academic skills our kids have today on drugs, divorce, and other
impediments to concentration necessary for doing well in school. But, as I
rediscover each time I walk into the classroom, before a teacher can expect
students to concentrate, he has to get their attention, no matter what
distractions may be at hand. There are many ways to do this, and they have
much to do with teaching style. However, if style alone won't do it, there
is another way to show who holds the winning hand in the classroom. That
is to reveal the trump card of failure.

I will never forget a teacher who played that card to get the attention 5
of one of my children. Our youngest, a world-class charmer, did little to
develop his intellectual talents but always got by. Until Mrs. Stifter.

Our son was a high school senior when he had her for English. "He 6
sits in the back of the room talking to his friends," she told me. "Why don't
you move him to the front row?" I urged, believing the embarrassment
would get him to settle down. Mrs. Stifter looked at me steely-eyed over
her glasses. "I don't move seniors," she said. "I flunk them." I was flustered.
Our son's academic life flashed before my eyes. No teacher had ever
threatened him with that before. I regained my composure and managed
to say that I thought she was right. By the time I got home, I was feeling
pretty good about this. It was a radical approach for these times, but, well,
why not? "She's going to flunk you," I told my son. I did not discuss it any
further. Suddenly English became a priority in his life. He finished out the
semester with an A.

I know one example doesn't make a case, but at night I see a parade 7
of students who are angry and resentful for having been passed along until
they could no longer even pretend to keep up. Of average intelligence or
better, they eventually quit school, concluding they were too dumb to
finish. "I should have been held back," is a comment I hear frequently. Even
sadder are those students who are high school graduates who say to me
after a few weeks of class, "I don't know how I ever got a high school
diploma."

Passing students who have not mastered the work cheats them and the 8
employers who expect graduates to have basic skills. We excuse this
dishonest behavior by saying kids can't learn if they come from terrible
environments. No one seems to stop to think that—no matter what
environments they come from—most kids don't put school first on their
list unless they perceive something is at stake. They'd rather be sailing.

Many students I see at night could give expert testimony on unemploy- 9
ment, chemical dependency, abusive relationships. In spite of these difficulties, they have decided to make education a priority. They are motivated
by the desire for a better job or the need to hang on to the one they've got.
They have a healthy fear of failure.

People of all ages can rise above their problems, but they need to have 10
a reason to do so. Young people generally don't have the maturity to value
education in the same way my adult students value it. But fear of failure,
whether economic or academic, can motivate both.

Flunking as a regular policy has just as much merit today as it did two 11
generations ago. We must review the threat of flunking and see it as it really
is—a positive teaching tool. It is an expression of confidence by both
teachers and parents that the students have the ability to learn the material
presented to them. However, making it work again would take a dedicated,
caring conspiracy between teachers and parents. It would mean facing the
tough reality that passing kids who haven't learned the material—while it
might save them grief for the short term—dooms them to long-term
illiteracy. It would mean that teachers would have to follow through on
their threats, and parents would have to stand behind them, knowing their
children's best interests are indeed at stake. This means no more doing
Scott's assignments for him because he might fail. No more passing Jodi
because she's such a nice kid.

This is a policy that worked in the past and can work today. A wise 12
teacher, with the support of his parents, gave our son the opportunity to
succeed—or fail. It's time we return this choice to all students.

❀ ❀ ❀

AFTER YOU READ

THINK about how Sherry's own experiences as a mother and teacher shaped her conviction that flunking is a useful pedagogical tool. Would she have felt the same way had her son actually flunked the English class rather than making an A? Was her son's fear of flunking the only factor in his success?

EXAMINE your own convictions about the policy of flunking students. What experiences shaped your convictions on this subject? Did this article change your convictions? Why or why not? Do you agree with Sherry that our schools would be more effective if students knew they would fail if they did not meet the school's academic standards?

WRITE a letter to your local school board arguing for or against the policy of flunking students who do not meet the standards in a course.

The Big Squeeze

DAVID SAMUELS

In "The Big Squeeze," which was originally published in Rolling Stone *magazine in October 1995, David Samuels reports on the escalating costs of a college education. In this essay, Samuels combines quotations from experts, statistics, and specific examples of students to portray what he views as the "bleak" outlook for educational opportunity in America today.*

BEFORE YOU READ

THINK about your own college expenses. How much do you pay each year for tuition? For books? For travel to and from college and work? For living expenses?

EXAMINE the first three paragraphs, which provide information about how much college costs have risen between the 1950s and the 1990s. How much more must a student at the Stevens Institute of Technology pay today than in the 1950s? How much longer must Rochal Sykes work today than Richard Reeves worked in the 1950s to pay for a college education?

WRITE a journal entry about how you are paying your college expenses. Are you getting help from your family or from a government program? If you are paying your own expenses, are you working part-time or full-time? Are you using savings, or are you taking out loans?

AS YOU READ

Try to answer this question: Why are college costs rising so rapidly? Underline passages and write notes in the margins to answer this question.

T his was America's deal with me," writes syndicated columnist Richard 1
Reeves. "If I kept my nose clean and paid attention in school, I could
go to college, even if I had to work in the summers and part-time during
the school year." To pay for his tuition—$800 a year in the late 1950s—
Reeves worked "as a lifeguard at the Jersey shore and teaching swimming
at camps."

Like Reeves, Rochal Sykes, a University of Virginia undergrad, works 2
part-time during the school year, putting in 20 hours a week as a manager
at the box office for campus events. But these days that's not enough. Sykes
is taking this semester off; she's working full-time, trying to raise money
to return for the spring semester. She will also be applying for a government
loan, "as big as I can get," to pay for books, electricity, telephone, and food.
She counts herself lucky. "I know a lot of people who are really stressed
out about loans," she says. "My roommate took out loans for all four years,
and she also worked two jobs. She worked from 7 to 12, went to class, and
then worked again from 9 to 12 at night. When I was getting up in the
morning, she was already going out to work."

If a college degree is still a ticket to the American dream, the cost of 3
that ticket continues to rise at more than twice the rate of inflation. Today's
college students work harder for their degrees than their parents did.
According to the U.S. Bureau of Labor Statistics, the average full-time
college student works 25 hours a week to pay for tuition, room, and board,
which, at Reeves's alma mater, the Stevens Institute of Technology, now
exceeds $22,000 a year. Working a $7-an-hour work-study job 25 hours a
week during the school year and a full-time job during the summer, it would
take a young, aspiring Richard Reeves more than 10 years to pay for his
B.A. alone.

And that's only the beginning of the bad news for college students and 4
their parents this year: The loans that students are taking out in record
numbers to pay for college are getting harder and harder to pay back as
the real incomes of college graduates decline. The new direct-student-loan
program, which introduced a welcome flexibility to the loan-repayment
process, may not survive renewed attacks by right-wing Republican parti-
sans in Congress this fall. And if all this bad news seems like a good reason
to forget about college altogether, think again: The incomes of high school
graduates are falling even faster.

No wonder then that students are taking out loans like high-stakes 5
gamblers on a losing streak that never seems to end. Last year's freshman
class will, on average, leave college $13,600 in debt, 30 percent higher than

the graduating seniors they replaced. According to a recent study by Fred
J. Galloway and Terry Hartle of the American Council on Education, last
year's rise in student borrowing was even more dramatic than reporters,
administrators and politicians had recognized. "Increases in student borrowing reported over the past year are far greater than any previous year's
increases," Galloway and Hartle report, pointing to rates of growth ranging
from 10 percent in the popular Stafford Loans to upward of 40 percent in
smaller loan programs. As loan burdens increase, the ability of students to
pay back their borrowed dollars has declined: In the last five years alone
the real income of college graduates had shrunk by 2.6 percent.

The rise in student indebtedness may be having effects beyond the 6
pocketbooks of students and their parents. Behind the increasingly money-
conscious career choices of college graduates since the '70s, Illinois senator
Paul Simon believes, are the stacks of IOUs that students are handing over
to their bankers. "You don't have to have great imagination to understand
that if you become a lawyer, you're going to be able to pay that loan back
much more rapidly," says Simon. "We need teachers, we need social
workers, we need people who are not just looking at how they can get into
a profession that allows them to pay back their loans." For Simon and other
skills-training advocates like Labor Secretary Robert Reich, helping students pay for higher education is a direct investment in the future strength
of the American economy; the dollars spent on students today will show
up in the balance sheets of American companies tomorrow.

American companies—and their conservative Republican tribunes in 7
Congress—take a less generous view of the matter. Paying for college, they
believe, is the responsibility of the individual—not the government. "I was
talking to a group recently at a college," says Rep. William Goodling, R-Pa.,
"and a little girl said, 'Well, don't they realize we're going to be the doctors
and the lawyers of the future?' And I said, 'Well, put yourself in their shoes.
If they're making seven bucks an hour, are they really thinking a great deal
about whether you're going to become a doctor or a lawyer . . . ?'" As for
the soaring tuition bills that are rapidly putting the cost of college well
beyond the means of many working families, Goodling—like many of his
Republican colleagues—wonders whether federal loan dollars are not at
the root of the problem: "I can't imagine some of the colleges and
universities in my district charging $25,000 a year—that's utterly ridicu-
lous. And I worry that the more federal money you put out there, the more
opportunity they will have to charge more and more." Others—like
Secretary of Education Richard Riley—see such explanations as simplistic

at best. "There are a lot of things that cause tuition to go up," says Riley, "but you can't just do away with a method that allows working families to send their kids to college."

The current debate over the government's role in funding higher 8 education may mark the end of an extraordinary half-century during which more Americans were educated at a higher level than ever before in our history. Before World War II, only 1 in 10 Americans could afford college. Those who did go, says Columbia University historian Alan Brinkley, were "mostly members of elites—people who went to private schools, whose parents had also been to college." Today, more than half of all Americans receive some form of higher education. The 1 million bachelor's degrees that American colleges and universities grant each year are in part the legacy of the Serviceman's Readjustment Act of 1944—the GI Bill—whose 50th anniversary last year was overlooked in the more public commemorations of D-Day and Woodstock. Sen. Joel B. Clark, introducing the GI Bill in the Senate, pronounced it "one of the most important measures that has ever come before the Congress" and predicted that "we will have a better country to live in than the world has yet seen." Clark was right. The GI Bill paid returning veterans an allowance of $50 a month plus up to $500 a year for tuition and books: At a cost of $5.5 billion, the program educated 450,000 engineers, 238,000 teachers, 67,000 doctors and hundreds of thousands of others who would man the engines of the economic boom that made postwar America the envy of the world.

Among those educated through the GI Bill was Sen. Claiborne Pell. "It 9 was really a tremendous step forward," Pell says in his slow Rhode Island drawl, "and I think it accounted for the wealth and the strength of our nation in the years that followed World War II." Pell's experience with the GI Bill made him a lifelong supporter of higher education and led him to sponsor the 1973 legislation that created the federal grant program for lower-income families that now bears his name: the Pell Grant. "I saw what the GI Bill had done for our country," says Pell, "and I saw that those things still needed to be done. To have an educated citizenry is to have a stronger country, and so it is to our own benefit as a nation to have all of our citizens with their high school and college behind them." Yet in the years since the Pell Grants were established, their average value has slid by more than 30 percent; more than half that decrease came in the 1980s. A GI Bill scholarship in constant dollars would be worth $9,400—six times the average Pell Grant today. While President Clinton has proposed expanding the Pell Grant program and beefing up grants made to students, Congressional Republicans are talking about narrowing eligibility, a move that may eliminate assistance to 200,000 poor and working-class families.

The biggest threat to educational opportunity in America may not 10 come from Congress, however, but from the colleges and universities themselves. In the '80s, the sticker price of a year of college rose at an annual rate of close to 9 percent, or more than twice the rate of inflation. As the flow of federal dollars to higher education has narrowed, state governments have been cutting back on their subsidies to their own colleges and universities, causing huge increases in tuitions. At Massachusetts state universities, tuitions rose by 110 percent in the last five years. In California, state tuitions rose by 75 percent in the last two years alone. Those who aspire to the loftier heights of private higher education—at a current price tag of $30,000 a year—can expect to pay even more for the privilege in the future: According to Kalman Chaney, author of the ever-popular *Student Access Guide to Paying for College,* a child born today will pay $360,000 for an Ivy League degree.

Where does all the money go? "Universities make a profit on people 11 who pay full tuition," says Brinkley. "People who can afford to pay full tuition are subsidizing those who can't." The wholesale movement of professors out of the classroom and into research laboratories, Brinkley says, is also responsible for much of the rise in tuitions. When college cost only $500 a year, professors taught an average of five classes a semester; today's professors teach two or three classes at most. Yet if teaching loads are down, professors of engineering, chemistry, and medicine are working harder than ever before, using their laboratories to churn out basic and applied research for American corporations. This means that students' tuition dollars—and the federal loan programs that often supply them— are, in effect, subsidizing laboratories and researchers that corporations would otherwise have to pay for themselves. "The real costs," Brinkley says, "come from supporting scientific and medical research, and a lot of that is being covered by the universities."

If the corporations get subsidized research, students take for granted 12 a dizzying variety of services that have transformed American universities from small-town assemblies of classrooms, libraries, and dorms to vast, sprawling cities. Universities now provide their inhabitants with food, security, psychiatric and health care, sports facilities, and entertainment. "The only way out," Columbia University emeritus professor Jacques Barzun recently told the *New York Times,* "is to strip these institutions down to their basics—students, teachers, and blackboards."

In search of a way to control their costs, some colleges are doing just 13 that. Syracuse University recently trimmed nearly 100 faculty members from its payroll, and Bennington College fired 25 faculty members and ended on-campus instruction in foreign languages. Another obvious target is the bloated administrative staffs at many schools: In 1950, public universities spent 27 cents on administration for every dollar they spent on instruction; by 1988 they were spending 45 cents.

There is also evidence that prices may come down—or at least stop 14 rising—under the sheer weight of two decades' worth of tuition increases. At the University of Rochester, which charges $25,000 for tuition, room, and board, 70 percent of the students were on some form of financial aid. Because only 30 percent of Rochester students could afford full tuition, administrators calculated, the university was taking in less money than it would if its tuition were lower. When Rochester cut its tuition, applications jumped. "I'm sure a lot of colleges and universities are watching to see what their experience will be," said Mary Jo Mayhew, treasurer of Mount Holyoke College, when the price cuts were announced. "We certainly are."

With fewer students able to pay full price, guidance counselors regu- 15 larly advise students to shop around, compare, and bargain, as if they were in the market for a new home or car: More than half the students at private colleges in New York state, according to one recent survey, pay less than list price. NYU Law School gives free tuition to students who forswear the lucrative world of corporate law for low-paying public-service jobs; Harvard, Tulane, and UCLA law schools offer similar, if less generous, programs. And if you look hard enough, it's even possible to go to college free of charge. The 1,500 undergraduates at the College of the Ozarks, in Missouri, one of the top liberal-arts colleges in the Midwest according to *US News and World Report,* pay nothing at all in exchange for working on campus 15 hours a week and 40 hours a week during the summer.

If there are points of light in the university firmament, the outlook for 16 educational opportunity in America is still bleak. Today, perhaps more than at any time since the end of World War II, your chances of going to college depend on how much money your parents make. Those whose family earnings are in the bottom 25 percent are only one-tenth as likely to attain a B.A. by the age of 24 as their well-born peers in the top 25 percent. A recent UCLA study, reported the *Washington Monthly,* found that the median parental income of college freshmen rose more than twice as fast in the 1980s as the median income of all families with children, "a clear sign," the *Monthly* commented, "that students from less-affluent families were again getting shut out of higher education." With college graduates earning almost twice the income of those with only high school degrees, we are fast retreating from the American ideal of educational opportunity toward a system that would have made our forefathers wince: The rich are getting richer, and the children of poor and working-class families are being denied an equal shot at the middle-class comforts so many Americans once took for granted.

❀   ❀   ❀

AFTER YOU READ

THINK about why college costs are rising so much and so rapidly. What reasons does Samuels give? In your own opinion, who or what is most responsible for these rising costs?

EXAMINE the title of the essay. What does Samuels mean by the phrase "the big squeeze"? If you aren't sure, reread the third paragraph.

EXAMINE also paragraphs 13–15 to identify some ways that college costs can be reduced or at least contained. What other solutions can you suggest?

WRITE an essay in which you take a position on "the current debate over the government's role in funding higher education" for its citizens (paragraph 8). Argue for or against governmental support for students. You might focus your argument on a particular support program such as the GI Bill or Pell Grants. Use specific support from Samuels's essay—from the experts he quotes as well as his own comments.

The Resegregation of a
Southern School

DOUGLAS A. BLACKMON

This essay first appeared in the Perspective section of the
Atlanta Journal-Constitution *and was later reprinted in*
Harper's Magazine. *The author, who is a reporter for the*
Atlanta Journal-Constitution, *grew up in Leland, Missis-*
sippi, which is located in the fertile, flat, northwestern part
of the state known as the Delta. In this essay he tells of the
changes that have taken place in Leland in the ten years
since he graduated from the high school there.

BEFORE YOU READ

THINK about the racial makeup of your college. How do the different races
get along? Is there much social interaction? If not, why? Are different races
represented on the faculty as well as among the student body?

EXAMINE the title of the essay. What does it mean to resegregate? Why
would anyone want to resegregate? What connotations are associated in
your mind with the word *segregation*? Do you associate these same
connotations with the word *resegregate*? Why or why not?

WRITE a journal entry about a significant personal experience you have
had with a member of a race different from your own. What did you learn
from this experience?

AS YOU READ

Compare the author's racial experiences in high school with your own.

Another long hot summer has ended in the Mississippi Delta, and the 1
students in my hometown are coming back to Leland High School.
Seventy-five seniors are expected to graduate this year, sixty-one of them
black and fourteen white. I entered the first grade in the Leland school
system in 1970—Leland's first year of fully integrated classes. That spring,
sixty white faces peered out from the Leland senior-class portrait. In 1982,
when my class was the first to graduate after twelve full years of black and
white children studying together, only two dozen whites remained in a class
of just under ninety.

Despite the fact that the number of white graduates diminished slowly 2
during the time I was there, the class of 1982's graduation symbolized the
culmination of the struggle to integrate public education in a state long
defined by racial hatred. Our rite of passage was Mississippi's rite of
passage, and when my classmates ventured into the world, Mississippians
who believed in the ideal of integration hoped they had sown the seeds of
a more equal and tolerant society.

But now, ten years later, hardly anyone, black or white, even remem- 3
bers that dream. Integration here in Leland and across much of Mississippi
has largely failed. The Delta school system is almost as segregated today as
it was in 1968, although now it is characterized by mostly black public
schools and all-white private institutions. In many towns, there are virtually
no whites left in the public school system.

At Leland High, extracurricular activities are fading as community 4
support for them diminishes among whites. The school newspaper, started
in the 1970s by my oldest brother, vanished several years ago. Academic
clubs are struggling. When a newspaper story recently reported that Leland
High might no longer be able to afford a yearbook, most townsfolk just
rolled their eyes.

What is most noticeably absent in Leland's schools today is the biracial 5
community spirit that initially made them some of the most integrated in
the Delta—an achievement that was supposed to be a dramatic first step
toward integrating all of society. While desegregation succeeded in easing
overt racial hostility and opening up Leland's restaurants, motels, and
libraries, black and white children today face one another across the same
awkward divide that we did twenty years ago. And they leave high school
on opposite sides of an economic gulf almost as wide as before. Yet Leland
has become a place where few blacks or whites find it objectionable—or
even odd—that there are racially divided schools. And almost no one
believes it will ever change. Integration, born amid outcries of both hope
and excoriation, has withered in virtual silence.

Leland is a rather typical Mississippi Delta town of 6,000 residents, 6
mostly merchants, planters, and laborers. The population is—and has been
for as long as anyone recalls—about 60 percent black. My family moved
there in 1967, into an old, rambling yellow house in a white middle-class
neighborhood. Like the rest of Mississippi, Leland inched its way toward
integration only at the steady prod of the federal government. The tide
turned on October 29, 1969, when the Supreme Court issued a sweeping
ruling that required almost immediate integration in Leland and twenty-
nine other Mississippi school districts. I began the first grade the following
fall.

After the Court's ruling, a flood of hysterical white Mississippi fami- 7
lies fled to newly created private segregationist academies—schools with
Confederate-colonel mascots and rebel-flag logos. But in Leland, a biracial
coalition of school leaders and parents, my own included, began a campaign to encourage whites to stay with the public schools. They handed
out stickers at school board meetings that read, "Think Positive," and
published a full-page ad in the local paper with the names of more than
200 white parents who promised that their children would remain in the
public-school system. In that first year, Leland retained about half of its
white students—a remarkable achievement for a Delta town.

Those were curious times of racial exploration for me. I was completely 8
unaware of the turmoil that had preceded my first day of school, and, as
best I recall, it was a topic that our teachers never encouraged us to discuss.
My parents didn't talk about it either, but they somehow drilled into me
the notion that there was one evil perhaps greater than any other, this thing
called "prejudice."

I wasn't exactly sure what it meant. I just knew I was supposed to avoid 9
it, and that my friends from church who went to "the academy" were
somehow tainted by it. The word was so ominous and omnipresent that it
terrified me. Occasionally a black classmate would suddenly ask me, "Are
you prejudiced?" "Of course not," I would quickly respond, while thinking,
"It's the private-school people who are prejudiced."

But I was receiving other signals that were confusing. I became fast 10
friends with a black classmate, Donald Richardson, and at some point in
the fourth grade we began talking about visiting each other's homes to
combine our GI Joe collections. His parents were schoolteachers, just like
my mother, and his grandfather was a retired school principal.

Donald and I never did visit each other, though. He's a band director 11
at Leland High now, and recently I asked him why he thought we never
spent time at each other's homes—or, for that matter, why black and white

classmates almost never visited each other's homes. He remembers that time the same way I do—no specific recollection of which teacher or parent or classmate had conveyed it, but the sense of getting a clear message: visiting each other was "not a good idea."

By the time I was in junior high school, segregation was evident in 12 almost every facet of my life except the classroom. I earned merit badges in an all-white Boy Scout troop and played Little League baseball on an all-white team, the Planters. My friends and I spent our summers at segregated swimming pools, and our families had picnics in segregated parks. Blacks and whites even played on opposite sides of Lake Monocnoc on the edge of town.

At school, racial tension characterized the daily dynamic. Fistfights on 13 the playground between blacks and whites were routine, and being harassed by blacks as I walked home through their neighborhood after school was so common that I was later amazed to learn that anyone else had grown up differently. The school stopped sponsoring senior proms, student banquets, senior trips, and other social gatherings long before I was old enough to know what they were.

Some of the reluctance to integrate children outside of the classroom 14 came, ironically, from desegregation supporters. Many of these parents believed that the immediate goal was simply to integrate the schools. They feared that sanctioning socializing between black and white students might cause anxious white parents to pull their children out of the schools altogether. But much of the hesitation about social integration was triggered by far more extreme sentiments. Blacks were seething with the anger of decades of humiliation and years of white obstructionism, even after segregation was illegal. Whites were gripped by misgivings about integration: everything from the innocuous "decline in quality education" to more bizarre concerns that whites would no longer be able to compete athletically, or that lecherous black boys would attack innocent white girls.

The anger and fear I witnessed daily, I now realize, reflected a complex 15 set of emotions being vented at dinner tables in every part of town. During the first years of integration, dedicated black and white adults worked within the institutions of church, jobs, and city hall to resolve the fear and anger. But over the long haul, they left it to their children, for the most part, to fight it out around the swing sets.

Despite the racial tension, we whites were well served by the integrated 16 public schools. We gained from the rough-and-tumble mix of cultures and, I think, were strengthened by the confrontations it sparked. Most of the whites in the class of 1982—generally from wealthier, more educated families than the blacks—finished college and never returned to Leland. My black classmates did not fare as well. A few went to college and then to cities in the North or West; several others went into the military. But the basic threshold of "success" for blacks in the Delta is leaving it, and most of my classmates never did.

Recently, I went back to Leland to see what had become of my 17 classmates who stayed behind during the decade since we graduated. I found that being black in the Delta typically still means a lifetime of barely scraping by in a place where factory jobs are few and the only big industry, farming, is controlled by an old-fashioned white elite. Brandon Taylor, who broke my undefeated spelling-bee record when he entered our class in the sixth grade, briefly played professional basketball in Europe. Now he's back in the Delta struggling to make a living. Elaine and Eloise Chillis, one of two sets of fraternal twins in my class, have worked since graduation for Delta Pride, a catfish company in Indianola, notorious for its oppressive working conditions. With experience and good performance, they told me they can look forward to eventually making top pay at the plant: $5.30 an hour. By Delta standards they are fairly successful, each with steady work and one beautiful boy. They don't particularly want to leave.

Elaine and Eloise were precisely the kind of children—smart, but 18 deprived of opportunity—that integration was supposed to help. No one spelled out exactly what integration was meant to accomplish at the time it was ordered, but there was an overwhelming sense that it was going to bring genuine change for the Elaines and Eloises of this country.

Instead, integration became a game of numbers that fell far short of 19 any real effort to secure civil—and human—rights. In the tremendous and exhausting struggle to prove on paper that public schools no longer discriminated, the larger question of how truly to unite a divided society was forgotten. "We didn't have a really specific vision," my father told me recently. "We thought we were in the midst of some very profound changes. In retrospect, it may have been an overexpectation."

Naive or not, the goals of school integration were doomed when the 20 community leadership that had worked so hard to sustain the public schools slowly melted away: the newspaper editor who had weathered scorn for his pro-integration positions moved to another town; the white school superintendent and the top black school administrator who had worked tirelessly behind the scenes to promote understanding retired; the white school-board members, who despite their political conservatism believed that good public schools were essential to a small town, resigned after years of frustration.

But why didn't others come forward to replace them? Why are there no 21
present-day counterparts to the white leaders who supported school
integration twenty years ago? Part of the reason, perhaps, is that the moral
urgency of the late 1960s—the sense of rapid social change that compelled
people to take strong stands—is gone.

For white Mississippians who considered themselves enlightened, the 22
idea of sending their children to all-white private schools twenty-five years
ago was taboo. The academies held the torch in those days for all of the
old Southern evils against which America was railing. But today, those
crude segregationist trappings have largely fallen away. Most of the small-
est, most retrograde academies have closed, and their students have been
consolidated into larger, better schools. Supporters of these schools extol
their "quality" educational environment in nonracial terms, and the student
body may well include the children of one or two black professionals.

Personal convenience has prevailed over community good. The moral 23
conviction that integrated my school has given way to an indifference and
numbness—the same numbness that allowed me (and most white Deltans)
to accept abject black poverty just a stone's throw away from our own
homes. Today, many of the children of the early white graduates of Leland's
integrated public schools are attending private academies.

In the black community too, almost no one is complaining about the 24
resegregation of Leland's schools. In recent months, black activists have
been more focused on keeping alive the traditions of the old all-black high
school, which now houses grades four, five, and six. Last fall, the building's
white principal wanted to replace some athletic trophies from the days
before integration in a display case with the work of current students. The
black community was outraged.

This acute nostalgia reflects a growing sense among some blacks that 25
the cost of giving up schools that they controlled may have been greater
than the benefits of integration. Before desegregation, black children
learned in institutions that, despite all the adversity these schools faced,
succeeded entirely because of the efforts and talents of many respected
black adults. The schools were woven into the fabric of the community and
were a sanctuary from the racial denigration that marked life outside.
Integration changed all that, removing blacks from top policy-making
positions in the schools and raising racial questions about every faculty
promotion and every student disciplinary action.

Perhaps the lesson to be drawn from a place like Leland is that destroying 26
the formal institutions of racism has little effect on integrating people's
day-to-day personal lives—or on advancing economic equality. The eco-

nomic situation for blacks in the Delta today has changed little despite the
good intentions of the people who pushed for diverse schools in Leland.

Maybe that was inevitable. Maybe it's impossible to effect dramatic 27
change in only a quarter of a century. Maybe desegregation was doomed
from its first day. But I can't help thinking that these are little more than
excuses. The preachers and teachers and aldermen and grocers and research
scientists and high-minded farmers of today's Leland could re-create the
coalition that first integrated my school. They could talk boldly not just
about schools, but about the broader issues of race and poverty and
opportunity. I don't know whether such an effort would assure Elaine's
and Eloise's baby boys of something more than the catfish plant, but it's
the only thing that might.

❀   ❀   ❀

AFTER YOU READ

THINK about Blackmon's assertion that both blacks and whites are allowing schools to become resegregated. Do you agree or disagree with this
assertion? Why? Do you think that public schools are becoming resegregated all across the nation or just in the South?

EXAMINE Blackmon's statement that "destroying the formal institutions of
racism has little effect on integrating people's day-to-day personal lives—or
on advancing economic equality." Do you agree with this statement, or do
you find it pessimistic and even cynical?

WRITE an essay or journal entry responding to this essay. You may focus
on the author's main idea or on some specific statement that he makes. Or
WRITE a personal essay about your own experiences with resegregation,
using Blackmon's essay as a point of departure.

The Recoloring of
Campus Life

SHELBY STEELE

Shelby Steele, a black writer and professor at San Jose State University in California, has called himself a "classic liberal" who focuses on "freedom, on the sacredness of the individual, [and] the power to be found in the individual" (Time, *August 12, 1991*). *However, his conservative views on civil rights and affirmative action have drawn sharp criticism from black leaders such as Jesse Jackson. Steele has articulated his ideas in a collection of essays entitled* The Content of Our Character; *the following selection is part of his essay "The Recoloring of Campus Life."*

BEFORE YOU READ

THINK about the racial harmony or disharmony that exists on your own campus. Do you agree or disagree with Steele's assertion that "racial tension on campus is more the result of racial equality than inequality" (paragraph 1)? Why do you feel as you do?

EXAMINE the sentences below to be sure that you understand the meanings of the italicized words.

1. The word *paradox,* which occurs in the following two sentences in the reading, is central to Steele's main point.

   "But there is a *paradox* here: on a campus where members of all races are gathered, mixed together in the classroom as well as socially, differences are more exposed than ever" (paragraph 2).

   "But there is another, related *paradox,* stemming from the notion of—and practice of—affirmative action. . . . What has emerged on campus in recent years—as a result of the new equality and of affirmative action and, in a sense, as a result of progress—is a *politics of difference,* a troubling, volatile politics in which each group justifies itself, its sense of worth, and its pursuit of power, through difference alone" (paragraph 3).

As illustrated in these two sentences, a *paradox* is a statement that seems contradictory but is nevertheless true. Another word in the second sentence that you may not know is *volatile,* which means "explosive" or "violent" in this context.

2. "For members of each race—young adults coming into their own, often away from home for the first time—bring to this site of freedom, exploration, and (now, today) equality, very deep fears, anxieties, *inchoate* feelings of racial shame, anger, and guilt" (paragraph 2).

    Feelings that are *inchoate* are immature and/or at an early stage, just beginning.

3. "The politics of difference leads each group to pick at the *vulnerabilities* of the other" (paragraph 4).

    A *vulnerability* is a weak spot; to be *vulnerable* is to be defenseless and unprotected.

4. "Universities can never be free of guilt until they truly help black students, which means leading and challenging them rather than negotiating and capitulating. It means inspiring them to achieve academic *parity,* nothing less, and helping them to see their own weaknesses as their greatest challenge" (paragraph 8).

    Academic *parity* is academic equality. You should also know that to *capitulate* means "to relent" or "to give in."

WRITE a journal entry in which you agree or disagree with Steele's statement that living "with racial difference has been America's profound social problem" (paragraph 2).

AS YOU READ

Evaluate the support that Steele gives for his thesis that racial tension on campus is born from a setting that promotes both "interaction and equality" and a "politics of difference" between races.

I have long believed that the trouble between the races is seldom what it appears to be. It was not hard to see after my first talks with students that racial tension on campus is a problem that misrepresents itself. It has the same look, the archetypal pattern, of America's timeless racial conflict—white racism and black protest. And I think part of our concern over it comes from the fact that it has the feel of a relapse, illness gone and come again. But if we are seeing the same symptoms, I don't believe we are dealing with the same illness. For one thing, I think racial tension on campus is more the result of racial equality than inequality.

How to live with racial difference has been America's profound social 2 problem. For the first hundred years or so following emancipation it was controlled by a legally sanctioned inequality that kept the races from each other. No longer is this the case. On campuses today, as throughout society, blacks enjoy equality under the law—a profound social advancement. No student may be kept out of a class or a dormitory or an extracurricular activity because of his or her race. But there is a paradox here: on a campus where members of all races are gathered, mixed together in the classroom as well as socially, differences are more exposed than ever. And this is where the trouble starts. For members of each race—young adults coming into their own, often away from home for the first time—bring to this site of freedom, exploration, and (now, today) equality, very deep fears, anxieties, inchoate feelings of racial shame, anger, and guilt. These feelings could lie dormant in the home, in familiar neighborhoods, in simpler days of childhood. But the college campus, with its structures of interaction and adult-level competition—the big exam, the dorm, the mixer—is another matter. I think campus racism is born of the rub between racial difference and a setting, the campus itself, devoted to interaction and equality. On our campuses, such concentrated micro-societies, all that remains unresolved between blacks and whites, all the old wounds and shames that have never been addressed, present themselves for attention—and present our youth with pressures they cannot always handle.

I have mentioned one paradox: racial fears and anxieties among blacks 3 and whites, bubbling up in an era of racial equality under the law, in settings that are among the freest and fairest in society. But there is another, related paradox, stemming from the notion of—and practice of—affirmative action. Under the provisions of the Equal Employment Opportunity Act of 1972, all state governments and institutions (including universities) were forced to initiate plans to increase the proportion of minority and women employees and, in the case of universities, of students too. Affirmative action plans that establish racial quotas were ruled unconstitutional more than ten years ago in *University of California* v. *Bakke,* but such plans are still thought by some to secretly exist, and lawsuits having to do with alleged quotas are still very much with us. But quotas are only the most controversial aspect of affirmative action; the principal of affirmative action is reflected in various university programs aimed at redressing and overcoming past patterns of discrimination. Of course, to be conscious of past patterns of discriminations—the fact, say, that public schools in the black inner cities are more crowded and employ fewer top-notch teachers than a white suburban public school, and that this is a factor in student performance—is only reasonable. But in doing this we also call attention quite obviously to difference: in the case of blacks and whites, racial difference. What has emerged on campus in recent years—as a result of the new equality and of affirmative action and, in a sense, as a result of progress—is a *politics of difference*, a troubling, volatile politics in which each group justifies itself, its sense of worth, and its pursuit of power, through difference alone. . . .

The politics of difference sets up a struggle for innocence among all 4 groups. When difference is the currency of power, each group must fight for the innocence that entitles it to power. To gain this innocence, blacks sting whites with guilt, remind them of their racial past, accuse them of new and more subtle forms of racism. One way whites retrieve their innocence is to discredit blacks and deny their difficulties, for in this denial is the denial of their own guilt. To blacks this denial looks like racism, a racism that feeds black innocence and encourages them to throw more guilt at whites. And so the cycle continues. The politics of difference leads each group to pick at the vulnerabilities of the other.

Men and women who run universities—whites, mostly—participate in 5 the politics of difference because they handle their guilt differently than do many of their students. They don't deny it, but still they don't want to *feel* it. And to avoid this feeling of guilt they have tended to go along with whatever blacks put on the table rather than work with them to assess their real needs. University administrators have too often been afraid of guilt and have relied on negotiation and capitulation more to appease their own guilt than to help blacks and other minorities. Administrators would never give white students a racial theme dorm where they could be "more comfortable with people of their own kind," yet more and more universities are doing this for black students, thus fostering a kind of voluntary segregation. To avoid the anxieties of integrated situations, blacks ask for theme dorms; to avoid guilt, white administrators give theme dorms.

When everyone is on the run from their anxieties about race, race 6 relations on campus can be reduced to the negotiation of avoidances. A pattern of demand and concession develops in which both sides use the other to escape themselves. Black studies departments, black deans of student affairs, black counseling programs, Afro houses, black theme dorms, black homecoming dances and graduation ceremonies—black students and white administrators have slowly engineered a machinery of separatism that, in the name of sacred difference, redraws the ugly lines of segregation.

Black students have not sufficiently helped themselves, and universi- 7 ties, despite all their concessions, have not really done much for blacks. If both faced their anxieties, I think they would see the same thing: academic parity with all other groups should be the overriding mission of black students, and it should also be the first goal that universities have for their black students. Blacks can only *know* they are as good as others when they are, in fact, as good—when their grades are higher and their dropout rate lower. Nothing under the sun will substitute for this, and no amount of concessions will bring it about.

Universities can never be free of guilt until they truly help black 8 students, which means leading and challenging them rather than negotiating and capitulating. It means inspiring them to achieve academic parity, nothing less, and helping them to see their own weaknesses as their greatest challenge. It also means dismantling the machinery of separatism, breaking the link between difference and power, and skewing the formula for entitlement away from race and gender and back to constitutional rights.

As for the young white students who have rediscovered swastikas and 9 the word "nigger," I think that they suffer from an exaggerated sense of their own innocence, as if they were incapable of evil and beyond the reach of guilt. But it is also true that the politics of difference creates an environment that threatens their innocence and makes them defensive. White students are not invited to the negotiating table from which they see blacks and others walk away with concessions. The presumption is that they do not deserve to be there because they are white. So they can only be defensive, and the less mature among them will be aggressive. Guerrilla activity will ensue. Of course this is wrong, but it is also a reflection of an environment where difference carries power and where whites have the wrong "difference."

I think universities should emphasize commonality as a higher value 10 than "diversity" and "pluralism"—buzzwords for the politics of difference. Difference that does not rest on a clearly delineated foundation of commonality is not only inaccessible to those who are not part of the ethnic or racial group, but also antagonistic to them. Difference can enrich only the common ground.

Integration has become an abstract term today, having to do with little 11 more than numbers and racial balances. But it once stood for a high and admirable set of values. It made difference second to commonality, and it asked members of all races to face whatever fears they inspired in each other. I doubt the word will have a new vogue, but the values, under whatever name, are worth working for.

AFTER YOU READ

THINK about the racial situation on your own college campus. Do the students and administrators pursue a "politics of difference" or the goal of "commonality" in regard to race, ethnicity, and gender? How, specifically, does your institution pursue either goal? With which objective do you agree? Why do you feel as you do?

EXAMINE paragraph 3, in which Steele discusses the practice of affirmative action on campus. How, according to Steele, is affirmative action applied on most campuses? What does he believe are the results of the policy? Do you agree or disagree with Steele? Why do you feel as you do?

WRITE a letter to your college newspaper in which you argue that official policy at your institution should either follow a politics of difference or aim for commonality in racial, ethnic, and gender questions. Make specific suggestions about campus courses, programs, and policies.

What Is Behind the Growth of Violence on College Campuses?

DOROTHY SIEGEL

Growing public concern over the growth of violence on college campuses has resulted in national recognition of the problem and in growing efforts to solve it. According to an article in The New York Times Magazine *(March 7, 1993), Congress has passed three important pieces of relevant legislation: the Campus Sexual Assault Victims' Bill of Rights, which allows victims of sexual assault to call off-campus investigators; clarification of the Buckley Privacy Amendment, which allows victims on campus to access the criminal records of students who have committed violence; and the National Higher Education Security Act, which requires colleges to publish university crime statistics. As vice president for student services at Towson State University in Maryland, Dorothy Siegel has been in a unique position to study the growth of violence on college campuses—its causes and its effects. The following report of her findings was published in the May 1994 issue of* USA Today.

BEFORE YOU READ

THINK about crime on college and university campuses. Do you consider "crime on campus" to be a major problem or a minor problem in America today? What kinds of crimes are committed on your own campus? Who commits these crimes? Try to visualize the typical "criminal" on campus today. Do you see a masked hood creeping onto the campus and into dorm rooms? Or do you see one of your fellow students?

307

EXAMINE the first paragraph of the essay to see who, according to Siegel, is "responsible for 80 percent of campus crime" today. Does Siegel's finding surprise you? Why or why not?

EXAMINE also the sentence "Universities formerly had acted *in loco paren- tis*" (paragraph 16). This phrase means "standing in the place of one's parents" or "guarding the student's physical safety and moral actions." After the "national age of majority was lowered to 18" (paragraph 16), except for drinking, Siegal reports, universities have not served in this capacity. However, the new legislation nevertheless increases a university's responsibility to both students and parents. Do you agree or disagree with the principle of *in loco parentis* for protecting students from crime? For student activities in general?

WRITE a journal entry about a campus crime that you have experienced, observed, or read about on your own campus or on another campus.

AS YOU READ

Identify the major causes of campus crime discussed by Siegel.

America's college campuses are not the war zones newspaper and magazine articles would lead the public to believe. Those crimes committed against students get major attention from the media probably because campuses are expected to be serene and safe. What is perhaps most troubling about campus crime is that the majority of the incidents, exclud- ing theft, but including rape and other sexual assaults, are impulsive acts committed by students themselves, according to nationwide studies con- ducted by Towson State University's Campus Violence Prevention Center. Students are responsible for 80 percent of campus crime, although rarely with weapons.

It is an uphill battle to ensure student safety. Schools provide es- cort services, tamper-proof windows, and continually upgraded state-of- the-art exterior lighting and electronic alarm systems. These institutional efforts frequently are undone by the immortal feelings of college-age men and women. That "it-can't-happen-to-me" attitude leads to lax security behaviors that literally leave the door open for an outside threat. Univer- sities are challenged to help students develop and keep that awareness, except for the two weeks following an on-campus assault, when caution prevailed.

The same students who sponsor night walks to check the lighting and grounds to increase safety will hold the door open for a stranger entering their residence hall. Despite frequent warnings, students—and even faculty, administrators, and other campus personnel—act less judiciously than they would elsewhere.

The mind-set of the students and probably of most of us is that crime is going to happen at night. Following a daylight abduction at one school, students demanded better lighting and evening patrols. They are loathe to follow the cautions about garages and out-of-the-way places during the day. They have trouble acknowledging, as we all probably do, that current criminal acts require new precautions, more appropriate to what is happening now.

Today, as part of the orientation programs at campuses across the nation, most administrators welcome students with information about crime on campus and ways they better can ensure their own safety. Because The Higher Education Security Act requires schools to report their previous year's crime statistics to the campus [community], colleges greet many new students and their parents with the previous year's count of violations and wise warnings. They are united in their efforts to command students' attention and enlist them as active partners in prevention. They use theater, video, discussions, posters, and circulars to inform students. Police statistics and reports are disseminated widely.

Despite this, if a stranger is seen entering a building, it is unlikely that any observers will notify the police, even if the potential assailant is dressed strangely and/or behaving oddly. If that stranger attacks someone the community will demand more protection. A series of seminars will produce good ideas and vigilant behavior for about two weeks, after which much of the more casual behavior about safety reappears.

When students discuss safety, it always is about dangers from outside the campus. Students are both the perpetrators and victims of most campus crime, yet it still is protection from trespassers that motivates most safety programs and is most in demand. It is an arduous and mostly unsuccessful process to convince students that they are more likely to be a victim of crime perpetrated by a member of their class or athletic team than by a stranger. It appears unthinkable that they themselves may become assailants. Although this message is included in many orientation programs for new students, it is nearly impossible to alert them to the potential danger from people they trust simply because they are members of the same community. Yet, eight percent of students report that they have been perpetrators and approximately 12 percent say they have been victims of assault.

Visitors to a campus during the day will see a reasonably civil society. Students will congregate in various common areas and study, talk, laugh, or even sleep. The homeless may gather on the campus benches while a non-student stands and shouts what he or she maintains is God's will. Literally thousands of people will pass without incident. If campus police are writing citations, it is likely to be for parking violations. 8

Yet, on any night from Thursday to Saturday on the same campus, the majority of students will be drinking, some excessively, and fights will erupt over seemingly trivial issues—who can have the bedroom, the keys, the boyfriend or girlfriend, the Nintendo. Small differences may escalate into brawls when combined with drug and alcohol abuse. Student assistants in residence halls may write up hundreds of classmates for violation of the campus alcohol policy. These reports are forwarded for administrative action. Few, if any, students will be arrested. Other drunk students will be returning from town where similar incidents may have occurred. Police rarely are called for fear of endangering the bar's liquor license. Still other students are on their way to parties, where recreational drinking is the featured attraction. 9

My first experience with campus violence came after I had spent two years in my current position as vice president for student services at Towson State University. One Friday evening, a drunk student trying to enter a residence hall to visit a friend beat the student worker who denied him access. The employee was hospitalized overnight. Although the student was criminally charged, the university immediately had to create procedures for an on-campus hearing to determine how the institution should respond. He was the first student suspended from the university because of assault charges stemming from a campus incident. 10

In the late 1970s, some students on campuses around the country reported being victims of assaults by fellow students. Residence directors observed increases in vandalism. Personnel at different schools thought they were experiencing situations unique to their own campuses. Rural and urban, large and small schools noted the existence of violent incidents, quantified in Towson State's surveys of over 1,000 colleges. Those studies became the nation's first national data on student-perpetrated violence. It documented that students were both victims and perpetrators of rape, other sexual violence, and physical assault. 11

UNITED STATES OF VIOLENCE

When sexual assaults and rapes are reported, an interviewer most fre- 12
quently will learn that the two students have known each other, sometimes
meeting at a party earlier that evening. Typically, they both will have been
drinking. One may have accepted the other's invitation to share a room
because a roommate was entertaining someone. He may make advances.
She says she only will accept the offer of the room (or extend the offer) if
it is a non-sexual relationship. He accepts the terms, but believes her
accompanying him means she is willing. She thinks she has communicated
effectively. He thinks he has understood. Such misunderstanding makes
one appreciate the clear consent to sex that Antioch College demands of
its students as set forth in its most recent handbook.

One percent of students reported more physically brutal rapes. Four 13
percent of female students stated that they had been raped, predominantly
by other students. Researchers report that 74 percent of sexually related
crimes were committed by fellow students. More than 30 percent of these
sexual crimes were committed by fraternity members, while 14 percent
were committed by athletes, some by friends of friends.

The majority of perpetrators indicated that they were drunk, high, or 14
in need of drugs when the crimes were committed. Substance abuse is a
direct correlate of violent campus behavior. Researchers from Towson
State's Campus Violence Prevention Center reported in a study of responses from 1,800 college students nationwide that abuse of alcohol was
heavier among victims and perpetrators than the rest of the campus
population. A later study of more than 13,000 students corroborated those
results, adding that students who used drugs were likely to be among the
perpetrators and the victims. Perpetrators reported using intoxicants more
often than did victims. In turn, the victims reported heavier drinking habits
than those who were neither victims nor assailants. Whether drunk or not,
a substantial majority of victims and perpetrators said that, on the day of
the crime, they had been drinking and/or using drugs. It is a logical
conclusion that students usually will not become victims or perpetrators in
student-to-student violence if they do not use drugs or abuse alcohol.

In spite of all the messages of abstinence that are drilled into the 15
nation's youth from elementary school years on, many students come to
higher education with histories of excessive drinking. Against the backdrop
of violence that exists in American society, the loss of control heightened
by substance abuse, including alcohol, often is accompanied by violent
outbursts. The various preventive efforts such as mediation and conflict

resolution offered by some schools are not effective techniques for preventing the acts fueled by the presence of alcohol.

Universities formerly had acted *in loco parentis*. When the national age 16 of majority was lowered to 18, college administrators had to alter their relationship with students because institutions no longer could behave as substitute parents for youths who now could vote, drink, and go to war. While it is not documented how effective such supervision of students was, it is clear that those who wished to violate the rules had to work harder to do so. The current relationship is adult-to-adult, even though the institutions recognize that many students are not fully mature. That poses a continuing dilemma for campus personnel in helping students to develop control over their behavior, thus assuring their own safety and that of their peers.

Although the legal drinking age has been raised to 21 in each state, the 17 national community of 18- to 20-year-olds simply does not accept this constraint. Some estimates are that as many as 80 percent of underage students carry fake proof-of-age identification. Drinking has become a standard pastime, and binge drinking—five or more drinks at a sitting—is condoned by 85 percent of college freshmen. The number of students who report excessive drinking is less in the sophomore year and decreases in each of the subsequent years. It has not been determined if the excessive drinkers have dropped out or changed their ways. It probably is some of both. The people who have been most responsive to the substance abuse education programs are the casual users who reportedly are abstaining totally now. The laws are not effective despite substantial efforts. No way has been found to govern a population by laws they do not accept.

SEEKING UNDERSTANDING

College students are among the nation's brightest and most successful 18 people. In general, they come from higher socioeconomic backgrounds than the non-college-attending members of their age group. Although there has been no formal study of their behavior after university attendance, it is unlikely that perpetrators of college incidents will commit other violent crimes later. Most do not repeat offenses on campus. A contributing factor may be that many schools require those responsible to attend substance abuse intervention programs as a condition of returning to or continuing to attend the university.

Administrators are at a loss to understand why such an increase in 19
student violence has emerged in the past two decades. They have tried to
study the problem from several approaches, but the only factor that
remains the same in the majority of cases is alcohol abuse. It is not known
if as many students in the past drank as much as current ones do. Research
shows, though, that almost 50 percent of freshmen had been drunk within
two weeks preceding the study.

Behaviors that lead to violence usually are tolerated by students. 20
Resident students are reluctant to complain, even in cases where their rights
and their living space are violated by the conduct of others. They may ask
for alternate housing, but are not apt to make a formal complaint. Only
victims report crimes. Most actions that lead to assaultive behaviors are
tolerated by the student community. Students who dislike the rowdiness
are more apt to move away than to assert their rights to a more appropriate
living environment.

On more and more campuses, housing options available to students 21
include alcohol-free residence halls. Those who choose them have quieter
and less disruptive lives. Such an option is not successful when someone
other than the students themselves make those choices.

It is easy to prevent violence if each student is kept under lock and key. 22
It is a more challenging problem in a society that values freedom. The
message to students is that a safe community requires their participation.
The role of police is to facilitate safety, not assure it. It is a challenge to
have an environment appropriate for growth and learning and safe in
today's society.

Student society evolves and changes. For instance, women increasingly 23
are the assaulters. Though still in the single-digit numbers and not nearly
as high as the amount of incidents with male perpetrators, the total is going
up. More students are participating in communal efforts to help others,
which may indicate that they are assuming more membership in the campus
community. They increasingly are riding the escort vans that for so long
were available, but appeared inconvenient. More are working actively for
a civil environment Although they continue to prop open doors for the
pizza man, we are seeing some effort to make the school safer. More are
complaining about the amount of drinking on campus, but they still are
not willing to say that a roommate drinks too much. Many student
governments, fraternities, and sororities have supported the efforts, but
continue alcohol-dominated parties. Students at many colleges no longer
sponsor dances because of the enforcement of alcohol laws by the institu-

tions. More students are walking with others at night. Nevertheless, the struggle remains to help students pursue safer ways.

In our community of 10,000 full-time students, we held administrative 24 hearings for 11 cases of physical assault in 1992. No sexual assaults were reported. Other years, the number of assaults was as high as 35, and the highest number of sexual assaults in any year was six. When colleges were required by the 1992 National Higher Education Security Act to inform their faculty, staff, and students about crime statistics on campuses, several reporters were sure that the colleges were hiding numbers. However, the amount of crimes on campuses never has been large. Still, even a single violent act requires that everyone become more discerning.

AFTER YOU READ

THINK about the attitude toward crime on your campus. Are you and your fellow students more afraid of "criminals" from outside the campus or of classmates, dormmates, and dates on your own campus? According to Siegel, which should you fear most? Do you agree or disagree with Siegel's findings? What support can you give for your opinion?

EXAMINE paragraphs 13 and 14 of the essay. What statistics does Siegel give about the types of crime committed on campus? What statistical information does she give about who commits campus crime? According to Siegel, what behavior, associated with either the victim or the perpetrator, is directly correlated with most campus crime? Do you agree with Siegel about the relationship between campus crime and drugs or alcohol? Why or why not?

WRITE a letter to your campus newspaper in which you identify a problem on campus that has lead, or could lead, to violence or crime. Then suggest (to students, faculty, or administration) a solution for that problem.

Kids Who Kill

GORDON WITKIN

This article about the increasing use of guns among young people was first published in U.S. News & World Report. *The author, Gordon Witkin, points out that "disputes once settled with fists are now settled with guns" and cites some grim statistics to support his claim. For example, firearm murders committed by offenders under age eighteen increased from 444 in 1984 to 952 in 1989. Do you think this number has continued to increase in the 1990s?*

BEFORE YOU READ

THINK about someone you know or have heard about who has been killed or injured by a young person with a firearm. Why was this person shot? Was the reason for the shooting serious or trivial?

EXAMINE the word *ethos* in the following sentence: "This is the stone-hearted *ethos* of an astonishingly large segment of the teenage population." *Ethos* (pronounced ee-thos) is from the Greek language and refers to the disposition, character, or values of a person or group. Thus a person with a "stone-hearted ethos" is an unfeeling, unmerciful person.

WRITE a journal entry in which you attempt to explain why the number of young people who use guns is increasing.

AS YOU READ

Mark in the text the reasons the author gives for the increasing use of guns by young people.

*K*evin's mother was a drug addict, his father a dope dealer. After being 1
taken from them by social workers in his native Massachusetts, Kevin*
went to live with his grandparents in Texas. His grandfather, a security guard,
let him shoot a .22, and "firing it made me feel like I was on top." By his
early teens, he was firing a gun out windows at a nearby day-care center to
show off and he had joined a gang. He began carrying a .38-caliber revolver
at 14 and obtained guns by burglarizing nearby homes. "I wanted to carry
a weapon because I wasn't going to tolerate anything. I was scared and I
was mad." At 15, Kevin began working for a Jamaican drug trafficking posse
and eventually became an enforcer who did his work by shooting people in
the arm.

One day, $2,000 of the Jamaicans' money was lost, and though Kevin 2
says he was innocent, the blame fell on him. Panicking, he confronted an
acquaintance whom he suspected of the theft. "I figured if I shot him, the
Jamaicans wouldn't think I'd taken the money," he says. "He begged for his
life five times. I shot him in the face at point-blank range and killed him
instantly. Blood was everywhere, and some parts of his head were laying in
the doorway. I didn't have to kill him. If I'd just pulled the gun, I could have
gotten my money. But still I shot him. The man lost his life over nothing."

This is the stone-hearted ethos of an astonishingly large segment of the 3
teenage population. It saturates not only the gang-ridden environment of
the cities but the supposedly more benign suburban world as well. Everyday
quarrels that used to result in flailing fists and bloody noses—over a bump
on the shoulder, a misinterpreted glance, romantic complications or flashy
clothes—now end, with epidemic frequency, in gunshots.

The reasons why are clear. Today's kids are desensitized to violence as 4
never before, surrounded by gunfire and stuffed with media images of
Rambos who kill at will. For many inner-city youngsters, poverty and
hopelessness yield a "what the hell" attitude that provides the backdrop
for gunplay. Family breakdowns further fuel the crisis; a survey of Baltimore public-school students showed that 59 percent of the males who came
from one-parent or no-parent homes have carried a handgun. But by far
the biggest difference in today's atmosphere is that the no-problem availability of guns in every nook of the nation has turned record numbers of
everyday encounters into deadly ones.

The datelines change daily, but the stories are chillingly similar. In 5
Washington, D.C., 15-year-old Jermaine Daniel is shot to death by his best

*Names with an asterisk are pseudonyms, required in some cases by legal restrictions.

friend. In New Haven, Conn., Markiest Alexander, 14, is killed in a
drive-by shooting. In St. Louis, Leo Wilson, 16, is robbed of his tennis shoes
and Raiders jacket and then shot dead. In New York, a 14-year-old boy
opens up with a semiautomatic pistol in a Bronx schoolyard, wounding
one youngster and narrowly missing another, apparently in a dispute over
a girl.

Those outside the city are no less vulnerable. Within the past fortnight, 6
in an exclusive neighborhood of Pasadena, Calif., police say two teenage
boys passed a shotgun between them to shoot three young women to death
at close range. Asked why, the suspects reportedly told police they'd had
angry words with the victims but couldn't remember what the fight was
about. In middle-class Lumberton, N.J., outside Philadelphia, a 14-year-old
boy took a revolver from his father's gun cabinet in late February and fatally
shot a basketball teammate in the back of the head.

These tales from the streets were punctuated last month by some 7
knee-weakening numbers from the government's National Center for
Health Statistics, which analyzed youth firearm death rates from 1979 to
1988. The study showed that gun homicides felled 1,022 teens ages 15 to
19 in 1984; the number spiked to 1,641 in 1988. The picture was especially
bleak for young black males 15 to 19, for whom firearm homicides climbed
from 418 in 1984 to 955 in 1988. Their homicide rate in 1988 was more
than 11 times the rate for their white counterparts. And research by James
Alan Fox of Northeastern University shows that the number of black
teenage gunmen who have killed has risen sharply, from 181 in 1984 to a
record 555 in 1989.

"During every 100 hours on our streets we lose more young men than 8
were killed in 100 hours of ground war in the Persian Gulf," lamented
Louis Sullivan, secretary of the Department of Health and Human Services.
"Where are the yellow ribbons of hope and remembrance for our youth
dying in the streets?"

Amid the carnage, much of the political discussion seems sterile and 9
off the point. . . . When Ronald Reagan endorsed the Brady bill, a modest
measure that would require a seven-day waiting period to buy a gun, it was
heralded by gun-control advocates. In fact, almost all teens who kill with
guns *already* get them illegally, and nothing in the bill . . . will address the
existing system that places more and more guns with greater and greater
firepower in the hands of kids.

Some communities are taking small steps to halt the tragic cycle of 10
teenage gun violence. But psychologist Charles Patrick Ewing, author of
When Children Kill, argues that the confluence of several trends is forebod-

ing. Among them: the continuing proliferation of guns, increases in numbers of abused and neglected children, hefty juvenile poverty rates and a
projected 7.7 percent increase in the population of 5-to-17-year-olds.
Ewing predicts this will be "the bloodiest decade of juvenile violence we've
ever seen."

❀   ❀   ❀

AFTER YOU READ

THINK about the prediction by psychologist Charles Patrick Ewing that the
1990s will be "the bloodiest decade of juvenile violence we've ever seen"
(paragraph 10). Do you agree or disagree with this prediction? What are
the results so far?

EXAMINE the kinds of evidence that Witkin uses in his essay. Notice that
he begins with a single illustrative example of Kevin's experience (paragraphs 1–2). Then he includes several shorter examples of deadly shootings
by young people (paragraphs 5–6). Finally, he includes specific statistics
about young people killed by guns (paragraphs 7–8). In your opinion,
which kind of evidence is most effective? Would the essay have been more
or less effective if Witkin had begun with the statistics instead of the story
about Kevin? Explain.

WRITE an essay in which you summarize the causes of gun-related violence
among young people today as enumerated by Witkin (see paragraphs 3, 4,
and 10), identify the cause you think is most serious, and explain why you
feel as you do.

in the inner city

LUCILLE CLIFTON

A prolific and versatile writer, Lucille Clifton is best known for her poetry and her fiction books for children, although she has also written nonfiction and criticism. Her most popular children's books are Some of the Days of Everett Anderson *(1970) and its sequels, which focus on the life of a young black child. Clifton's African-American heritage and urban lifestyle are essential themes in most of her work. The poem "in the inner city" originally appeared in 1969 in her first book of poetry,* Good Times.

BEFORE YOU READ

THINK about the mental associations that you have with the phrase "the inner city." Is your view of the inner city primarily positive or negative? Are your ideas based on media coverage or on personal experience? Would you like—or do you like—to live there? Why or why not?

EXAMINE the title "in the inner city." What is unusual about this title? Clifton often writes without using capital letters. Why do you think she uses this style? What is the effect?

WRITE a journal entry in which you list concrete images of the inner city as you think about it. What sights and sounds do you associate with the inner city?

AS YOU READ

Look for the images that Clifton uses to recreate her view of the inner city.

in the inner city   1
or
like we call it
home
we think a lot about uptown   5
and the silent nights
and the houses straight as
dead men
and the pastel lights
and we hang on to our no place   10
happy to be alive
and in the inner city
or
like we call it
home   15

AFTER YOU READ

THINK about how Clifton's idea of the inner city compares to your own. What positive images does she associate with the inner city? What negative images does she associate with the inner city? For her, what one word represents the inner city, with all its positive and negative connotations?

EXAMINE lines 5–9, in which Clifton describes the place she calls "uptown." In contrast to the poverty of the inner city, the phrase "uptown" suggests a place of wealth and success. However, the images that Clifton uses to describe "uptown" are perhaps even more negative than those she uses to describe the inner city. In particular, what do the phrases "silent nights," "houses straight as/dead men," and "pastel lights" suggest about uptown and the people who live there? What does the contrast between the inner city and uptown suggest about differences in economic and social conditions under which people live?

WRITE a brief poem or a paragraph in which you describe a place that represents a particular social and economic condition: a shopping mall, a housing project, a barrio, a suburb, a country club, and so on. You may choose to represent this place positively or negatively, but be sure that your attitude is represented in concrete images—sights, sounds, smells, tastes, or textures.

Slow Descent into Hell

JON D. HULL

This selection was first published in Time *magazine (February 2, 1987). At the time he wrote the article, Jon Hull was a Los Angeles correspondent for* Time. *To research the article, Hull spent a week in Philadelphia living with the homeless. The essay is neither a short story nor a case study but has elements of both.*

BEFORE YOU READ

THINK about the different forms that urban poverty takes. Although homelessness is perhaps the most visible form, what other forms can poverty in a large urban center assume? With which form of urban poverty are you most familiar? Which form do you think is the most painful? The most humiliating? Why?

EXAMINE each word in the title of this article and consider the implications of each. What does the title suggest about the lives of the people who live on the streets of a large city?

WRITE as many definitions as you can of the word *homeless*. Has the word acquired new meanings recently? What did it once mean to be homeless? What does it mean now?

AS YOU READ

Notice the differences among the men described in the article. Although they are all homeless, they are different in some significant ways. In the margin of your text, identify each man as he is discussed and mark the important characteristics of each.

A smooth bar of soap, wrapped neatly in a white handkerchief and 1
tucked safely in the breast pocket of a faded leather jacket, is all that
keeps George from losing himself to the streets. When he wakes each
morning from his makeshift bed of newspapers in the subway tunnels of
Philadelphia, he heads for the rest room of a nearby bus station or
McDonald's and begins an elaborate ritual of washing off the dirt and
smells of homelessness: first the hands and forearms, then the face and
neck, and finally the fingernails and teeth. Twice a week he takes off his
worn Converse high tops and socks and washes his feet in the sink, ignoring
the cold stares of well-dressed commuters.

George, twenty-eight, is a stocky, round-faced former high school 2
basketball star who once made a living as a construction worker. But after
he lost his job just over a year ago, his wife kicked him out of the house.
For a few weeks he lived on the couches of friends, but the friendships soon
wore thin. Since then he has been on the street, starting from scratch and
looking for a job. "I got to get my life back," George says after rinsing his
face for the fourth time. He begins brushing his teeth with his forefinger.
"If I don't stay clean," he mutters, "the world ain't even going to look me
in the face. I just couldn't take that."

George lives in a world where time is meaningless and it's possible to 3
go months without being touched by anyone but a thug. Lack of sleep,
food, or conversation breeds confusion and depression. He feels himself
slipping but struggles to remember what he once had and to figure out how
to get it back. He rarely drinks alcohol and keeps his light brown corduroy
pants and red-checked shirt meticulously clean. Underneath, he wears two
other shirts to fight off the cold, and he sleeps with his large hands buried
deep within his coat pockets amid old sandwiches and doughnuts from the
soup kitchens and garbage cans.

Last fall he held a job for six weeks at a pizza joint, making $3.65 an 4
hour kneading dough and clearing tables. Before work, he would take off
two of his three shirts and hide them in an alley. It pleases him that no one
knew he was homeless. Says George: "Sure I could have spent that money
on some good drink or food, but you gotta suffer to save. You gotta have
money to get out of here and I gotta get out of here." Some days he was
scolded for eating too much of the food. He often worked without sleep,
and with no alarm clock to wake him from the subways or abandoned
tenements, he missed several days and was finally fired. He observes, "Can't
get no job without a home, and you can't get a home without a job. They
take one and you lose both."

George had sixty-four dollars tucked in his pocket on the evening he 5
was beaten senseless in an alley near the Continental Trailways station.

"Those damn chumps," he says, gritting his teeth, "took every goddam penny. I'm gonna kill 'em." Violence is a constant threat to the homeless. It's only a matter of time before newcomers are beaten, robbed, or raped. The young prey on the old, the big on the small, and groups attack lonely individuals in the back alleys and subway tunnels. After it's over, there is no one to tell about the pain, nothing to do but walk away.

Behind a dumpster sits a man who calls himself Red enjoying the last 6 drops of a bottle of wine called Wild Irish Rose. It's 1 A.M., and the thermometer hovers around 20 degrees with a biting wind. His nickname comes from a golden retriever his family once had back in Memphis, and a sparkle comes to his eyes as he recalls examples of the dog's loyalty. One day he plans to get another dog, and says, "I'm getting to the point where I can't talk to people. They're always telling me to do something or get out of their way. But a dog is different."

At thirty-five, he looks fifty, and his gaunt face carries discolored scars 7 from the falls and fights of three years on the streets. An upper incisor is missing, and his lower teeth jut outward against his lower lip, giving the impression that he can't close his mouth. His baggy pants are about five inches too long and when he walks, their frayed ends drag on the ground. "You know something?" he asks, holding up the bottle. "I wasn't stuck to this stuff until the cold got to me. Now I'll freeze without it. I could go to Florida or someplace, but I know this town and I know who the creeps are. Besides, it's not too bad in the summer."

Finishing the bottle, and not yet drunk enough to sleep out in the cold, 8 he gathers his blanket around his neck and heads for the subways beneath city hall, where hundreds of the homeless seek warmth. Once inside, the game of cat-and-mouse begins with the police, who patrol the maze of tunnels and stairways and insist that everybody remain off the floor and keep moving. Sitting can be an invitation to trouble, and the choice between sleep and warmth becomes agonizing as the night wears on.

For the first hour, Red shuffles through the tunnels, stopping occasion- 9 ally to urinate against the graffiti-covered walls. Then he picks a spot and stands for half an hour, peering out from the large hood of his coat. In the distance, the barking of German shepherds echoes through the tunnels as a canine unit patrols the darker recesses of the underground. Nearby, a young man in a ragged trench coat stands against the wall, slapping his palms against his sides and uttering, "I've got to get some paperwork done. I've just got to get some paperwork done!" Red shakes his head. "Home sweet home," he says. Finally exhausted, he curls up on the littered floor, lying on his side with his hands in his pockets and his hood pulled all the way over his face to keep the rats away. He is asleep instantly.

Whack! A police baton slaps his legs and a voice booms, "Get the hell 10 up, you're outta here. Right now!" Another police officer whacks his nightstick against a metal grating as the twelve men sprawled along the tunnel crawl to their feet. Red pulls himself up and walks slowly up the stairs to the street, never looking back.

Pausing at every pay phone to check the coin-return slots, he makes 11 his way to a long steam grate whose warm hiss bears the acrid smell of a dry cleaner's shop. He searches for newspaper and cardboard to block the moisture but retain the heat. With his makeshift bed made, he curls up again, but the rest is short-lived. "This s.o.b. use to give off more heat," he says, staring with disgust at the grate. He gathers the newspapers and moves down the block, all the while muttering about the differences among grates. "Some are good, some are bad. I remember I was getting a beautiful sleep on this one baby and then all this honking starts. I was laying right in a damn driveway and nearly got run over by a garbage truck."

Stopping at a small circular vent shooting jets of steam, Red shakes his 12 head and curses: "This one is too wet, and it'll go off sometimes, leaving you to freeze." Shaking now with the cold, he walks four more blocks and finds another grate, where he curls up and fishes a half-spent cigarette from his pocket. The grate is warm, but soon the moisture from the steam has soaked his newspapers and begins to gather on his clothes. Too tired to find another grate, he sets down more newspapers, throws his blanket over his head, and sprawls across the grate. By morning he is soaked.

At the St. John's Hospice for Men, close to the red neon marquees of 13 the porno shops near city hall, a crowd begins to gather at 4 P.M. Men and women dressed in ill-fitting clothes stamp their feet to ward off the cold and keep their arms pressed against their sides. Some are drunk; others simply talk aloud to nobody in words that none can understand. Most are loners who stand in silence with the sullen expression of the tired and hungry.

A hospice worker lets in a stream of women and old men. The young 14 men must wait until 5 P.M., and the crowd of more than two hundred are asked to form four rows behind a yellow line and watch their language. It seems an impossible task. A trembling man who goes by the name Carper cries, "What goddam row am I in!" as he pulls his red wool hat down until it covers his eyebrows. Carper has spent five to six years on the streets, and thinks he may be thirty-three. The smell of putrid wine and decaying teeth poisons his breath; the fluid running from his swollen eyes streaks his dirty cheeks before disappearing into his beard. "Am I in a goddam row? Who the hell's running the rows?" he swears. An older man with a thick gray beard informs Carper he is in Row 3 and assures him it is the best of them all. Carper's face softens into a smile; he stuffs his hands under his armpits and begins rocking his shoulders with delight.

Beds at the shelters are scarce, and fill up first with the old, the very [15] young, and women. Young men have little hope of getting a bed, and some have even come to scorn the shelters. Says Michael Brown, twenty-four: "It stinks to high heaven in those places. They're just packed with people and when the lights go out, it's everybody for themselves." Michael, a short, self-described con man, has been living on the streets three years, ever since holding up a convenience store in Little Rock. He fled, fearing capture, but now misses the two young children he left behind. He says he is tired of the streets and plans to turn himself in to serve his time.

Michael refuses to eat at the soup kitchens, preferring to panhandle [16] for a meal: "I don't like to be around those people. It makes you feel like some sort of crazy. Before you know it, you're one of them." He keeps a tear in the left seam of his pants, just below the pocket; when he panhandles among commuters, he tells them that his subway fare fell out of his pants. When that fails, he wanders past fast-food outlets, waiting for a large group eating near the door to get up and leave. Then he snatches the remaining food off the table and heads down the street, smiling all the more if the food is still warm. At night he sleeps in the subway stations, catnapping between police rounds amid the thunder of the trains. "Some of these guys sleep right on the damn floor," he says. "Not me. I always use two newspapers and lay them out neatly. Then I pray the rats don't get me."

It was the last swig of the bottle, and the cheap red wine contained [17] flotsam from the mouths of three men gathered in a vacant lot in northeast Philadelphia. Moments before, a homeless and dying man named Gary had vomited. The stench and nausea were dulled only by exhaustion and the cold. Gary, wheezing noisily, his lips dripping with puke, was the last to drink from the half-gallon jug of Thunderbird before passing it on, but no one seemed to care. There was no way to avoid the honor of downing the last few drops. It was an offer to share extended by those with nothing, and there was no time to think about the sores on the lips of the previous drinkers or the strange things floating in the bottle or the fact that it was daybreak and time for breakfast. It was better to drink and stay warm and forget about everything.

Though he is now dying on the streets, Gary used to be a respectable [18] citizen. His full name is Gary Shaw, forty-eight, and he is a lifelong resident of Philadelphia and a father of three. He once worked as a precision machinist, making metal dies for casting tools. "I could work with my eyes closed," he says. "I was the best there was." But he lost his job and wife to alcohol. Now his home is an old red couch with the springs exposed in a garbage-strewn clearing amid abandoned tenements. Nearby, wood pulled from buildings burns in a fifty-five-gallon metal drum while the Thunder-bird is passed around. When evening falls, Gary has trouble standing, and he believes his liver and kidneys are on the verge of failing. His thighs carry deep burn marks from sleeping on grates, and a severe beating the previous night has left bruises on his lower back and a long scab across his nose. The pain is apparent in his eyes, still brilliant blue, and the handsome features of his face are hidden beneath a layer of grime.

By 3 A.M., Gary's back pains are unbearable, and he begins rocking back 19 and forth while the others try to keep him warm. "Ah, please God help me. I'm f—ing dying, man. I'm dying." Two friends try to wave down a patrol car. After forty-five minutes, a suspicious cop rolls up to the curb and listens impatiently to their plea: "It's not drugs, man, I promise. The guy was beat up bad and he's dying. Come on, man, you've got to take us to the hospital." The cop nods and points his thumb toward the car. As Gary screams, his two friends carefully lift him into the back seat for the ride to St. Mary Hospital.

In the emergency room, half an hour passes before a nurse appears 20 with a clipboard. Address: unknown. No insurance. After an x-ray, Gary is told that a bone in his back may be chipped. He is advised to go home, put some ice on it and get some rest. "I don't have a goddam home!" he cries, his face twisted in pain. "Don't you know what I am? I'm a goddam bum, that's what, and I'm dying!" After an awkward moment, he is told to come back tomorrow and see the radiologist. The hospital pays his cab fare back to the couch.

Gary returns in time to share another bottle of Thunderbird, and the 21 warm rush brings his spirits up. "What the hell are we doing in the city?" asks Ray Kelly, thirty-seven, who was once a merchant seaman. "I know a place in Vermont where the fishing's great and you can build a whole damn house in the woods. There's nobody to bother you and plenty of food." Gary interrupts to recall fishing as a boy, and the memories prior to his six years on the street come back with crystal clarity. "You got it, man, we're all getting out of here tomorrow,"he says with a grin. In the spirit of celebration, King, a thirty-four-year-old from Puerto Rico, removes a tube of glue from his pocket with the care of a sommelier, sniffs it and passes it around.

When the sun rises, Ray and King are fast asleep under a blanket on 22 the couch. Gary is sitting at the other end, staring straight ahead and breathing heavily in the cold air. Curling his numb and swollen fingers around the arm of the couch, he tries to pull himself up but fails. When another try fails, he sits motionless and closes his eyes. Then the pain hits his back again and he starts to cry. He won't be getting out of here today and probably not tomorrow either.

Meanwhile, somewhere across town in the washroom of a McDonald's, George braces for another day of job hunting, washing the streets from his face so that nobody knows where he lives. 23

❀   ❀   ❀

AFTER YOU READ

THINK about the men described in the article. Did you feel sympathy for these men? For which one did you feel the most sympathy? If you were to encounter one of these men on the street, would you feel sympathy or contempt or fear?

EXAMINE Hull's use of chronological order. Although the entire article is not structured by chronological order, each separate segment follows a definite time sequence. How many different segments and characters does Hull include? Which one of the men does he return to in the final paragraph of the article? What effect does this have? Why do you think he chose this particular man for the beginning and ending of his article rather than one of the other men?

WRITE a brief "factual" report on one of the men described in this article. Try to be as objective as possible. Then write a brief description of the same man in which you write from your own point of view. Write the description so that a reader will feel sympathy, disgust, or fear. This time do not worry about being objective.

So How Did I Get Here?

ROSEMARY L. BRAY

A former editor of The Times Book Review, *Rosemary L.
Bray is currently working on a book entitled* Unafraid of
the Dark, *which focuses on African-American identity and
attitudes. In the following essay, originally published in*
The New York Times Magazine, *Bray shows how she
became independent of the welfare system that supported
her and her family when she was a child.*

BEFORE YOU READ

THINK about your own ideas about the welfare system. What is good about
the system? What is bad about it? What changes have occurred to the system
since Bray wrote this article in 1992? Have these changes been positive or
negative?

EXAMINE the first two sentences of the essay, in particular the initials
A.F.D.C. What do these initials represent? How does your reaction to the
official name of the program compare to your reaction to the more
common term, "welfare"? Which name allows more dignity to recipients
of aid?

EXAMINE also the following sentences and italicized words:

1. "In both blunt and coded terms, comfortable Americans more and
   more often bemoan the waste of their tax money on lazy black women
   with a love of *copulation*" (paragraph 2).

   In this context, *copulation* means sexual intercourse. Thus Bray
   suggests that these thoughts of "comfortable Americans" are deroga-
   tory and bigoted.
2. "Mama found an *autonomy* denied her by my father" (paragraph
   8).

   The Greek prefix *auto-* means "self"; to have *autonomy* is to be
   self-governing, to have independence and freedom.

3. "Ours was a best-case phenomenon, based on the *synergy* of church and state, the government and the private sector and the thousand points of light that we called friends and neighbors" (paragraph 18).

   The Greek prefix *syn-* means "together"; the word *synergy* means working together in a way that individuals cannot work alone.

4. "A few have made welfare fraud a *lucrative* career; a great many more have pushed the rules on outside income to their very limits" (paragraph 20).

   A *lucrative* career is profitable, or well-paying.

WRITE a journal entry about your impression of someone who is "on welfare." Is your impression positive or negative? If you personally know someone who is, or has been, on welfare, write about this person. What circumstances caused this person to apply for welfare? Do you think the system was beneficial or harmful for this person? Why do you feel as you do?

AS YOU READ

Answer the question Bray poses in her title. That is, how was Bray able to get off of welfare and become a successful and independent career woman?

Growing up on welfare was a story I had planned to tell a long time   1
from now, when I had children of my own. My childhood on Aid to Families with Dependent Children (A.F.D.C.) was going to be one of those stories I would tell my kids about the bad old days, an urban legend equivalent to Abe Lincoln studying by firelight. But I know now I cannot wait, because in spite of a wealth of evidence about the true nature of welfare and poverty in America, the debate has turned ugly, vicious, and racist. The "welfare question" has become the race question and the woman question in disguise, and so far the answers bode well for no one.

In both blunt and coded terms, comfortable Americans more and more   2
often bemoan the waste of their tax money on lazy black women with a love of copulation, a horror of birth control and a lack of interest in marriage. Were it not for the experiences of half my life, were I not black and female and of a certain age, perhaps I would be like so many people who blindly accept the lies and distortions, half-truths and wrongheaded notions about welfare. But for better or worse, I do know better. I know more than I want to know about being poor. I know that the welfare system

is designed to be inadequate, to leave its constituents on the edge of survival. I know because I've been there.

And finally, I know that perhaps even more dependent on welfare than its recipients are the large number of Americans who would rather accept this patchwork of economic horrors than fully address the real needs of real people. 3

My mother came to Chicago in 1947 with a fourth-grade education, cut short by working in the Mississippi fields. She pressed shirts in a laundry for a while and later waited tables in a restaurant, where she met my father. Mercurial and independent, with a sixth-grade education, my Arkansas-born father worked at whatever came to hand. He owned a lunch wagon for a time and prepared food for hours in our kitchen on the nights before he took the wagon out. Sometimes he hauled junk and sold it in the open-air markets of Maxwell Street on Sunday mornings. Eight years after they met—seven years after they married—I was born. My father made her quit her job; her work, he told her, was taking care of me. By the time I was 4, I had a sister, a brother and another brother on the way. My parents, like most other American couples of the 1950s, had their own American dream—a husband who worked, a wife who stayed home, a family of smiling children. But as was true for so many African-American couples, their American dream was an illusion. 4

The house on the corner of Berkeley Avenue and 45th Street is long gone. The other houses still stand, but today the neighborhood is an emptier, bleaker place. When we moved there, it was a street of old limestones with beveled glass windows, all falling into vague disrepair. Home was a four-room apartment on the first floor, in what must have been the public rooms of a formerly grand house. The rent was $110 a month. All of us kids slept in the big front room. Because I was the oldest, I had a bed of my own, near a big plate-glass window. 5

My mother and father had been married for several years before she realized he was a gambler who would never stay away from the track. By the time we moved to Berkeley Avenue, Daddy was spending more time gambling, and bringing home less and less money and more and more anger. Mama's simplest requests were met with rage. They fought once for hours when she asked for money to buy a tube of lipstick. It didn't help that I always seemed to need a doctor. I had allergies and bronchitis so severe that I nearly died one Sunday after church when I was about 3. 6

It was around this time that my mother decided to sign up for A.F.D.C. She explained to the caseworker that Daddy wasn't home much, and when 7 he was he didn't have any money. Daddy was furious; Mama was adamant. "There were times when we hardly had a loaf of bread in here," she told me years later. "It was close. I wasn't going to let you all go hungry."

Going on welfare closed a door between my parents that never 8 reopened. She joined the ranks of unskilled women who were forced to turn to the state for the security their men could not provide. In the sterile relationship between herself and the State of Illinois, Mama found an autonomy denied her by my father. It was she who could decide, at last, some part of her own fate and ours. A.F.D.C. relegated marginally productive men like my father to the ranks of failed patriarchs who no longer controlled the destiny of their families. Like so many of his peers, he could no longer afford the luxury of a woman who did as she was told because her economic life depended on it. Daddy became one of the shadow men who walked out back doors as caseworkers came in through the front. Why did he acquiesce? For all his anger, for all his frightening brutality, he loved us, so much that he swallowed his pride and periodically ceased to exist so that we might survive.

In 1960, the year my mother went on public aid, the poverty threshold for 9 a family of five in the United States was $3,560 and the monthly payment to a family of five from the State of Illinois was $182.56, a total of $2,190.72 a year. Once the $110 rent was paid, Mama was left with $72.56 a month to take care of all the other expenses. By any standard, we were poor. All our lives were proscribed by the narrow line between not quite and just enough.

What did it take to live?   10

It took the kindness of friends as well as strangers, the charity of 11 churches, low expectations, deprivation and patience. I can't begin to count the hours spent in long lines, long waits, long walks in pursuit of basic things. A visit to a local clinic (one housing doctors, a dentist and pharmacy in an incredibly crowded series of rooms) invariably took the better part of a day. I never saw the same doctor twice.

It took, as well, a turning of our collective backs on the letter of a law 12 that required reporting even a small and important miracle like a present of $5. All families have their secrets, but I remember the weight of an extra burden. In a world where caseworkers were empowered to probe into every nook and cranny of our lives, silence became defense. Even now, there are things I will not publicly discuss because I cannot shake the fear that we might be hounded by the state, eager to prosecute us for the crime of survival.

All my memories of our years on A.F.D.C. are seasoned with unease. It's 13
painful to remember how much every penny counted, how even a gap of
25 cents could make a difference in any given week. Few people understand
how precarious life is from welfare check to welfare check, how the word
"extra" had no meaning. Late mail, a bureaucratic mix-up . . . and a
carefully planned method of survival lies in tatters.

What made our lives work as well as they did was my mother's genius 14
at making do—worn into her by a childhood of rural poverty—along with
her vivid imagination. She worked at home endlessly, shopped ruthlessly,
bargained, cajoled, charmed. Her food store of choice was the one that
stocked pork and beans, creamed corn, sardines, Vienna sausages and
potted meat all at 10 cents a can. Clothing was the stuff of rummage sales,
trips to Goodwill and bargain basements, where thin cotton and polyester
reigned supreme. Our shoes came from a discount store that sold two pairs
for $5.

It was an uphill climb, but there was no time for reflection; we were 15
too busy with our everyday lives. Yet I remember how much it pained me
to know that Mama, who recruited a neighbor to help her teach me how
to read when I was 3, found herself left behind by her eldest daughter, then
by each of us in turn. Her biggest worry was that we would grow up
uneducated, so Mama enrolled us in parochial school.

When one caseworker angrily questioned how she could afford to send 16
four children to St. Ambrose School, my mother, who emphatically declared "My kids need an education," told her it was none of her business.
(In fact, the school had a volume discount of sorts; the price of tuition
dropped with each child you sent. I still don't know quite how she managed
it.) She organized our lives around church and school, including Mass every
morning at 7:45. My brother was an altar boy; I laid out the vestments each
afternoon for the next day's Mass. She volunteered as a chaperone for every
class trip, sat with us as we did homework she did not understand herself.
She and my father reminded us again and again and again that every book,
every test, every page of homework was in fact a ticket out and away from
the life we lived.

My life on welfare ended on June 4, 1976—a month after my 21st birthday, 17
two weeks after I graduated from Yale. My father, eaten up with cancer
and rage, lived just long enough to know the oldest two of us had graduated
from college and were on our own. Before the decade ended, all of us had
left the welfare rolls. The eldest of my brothers worked at the post office,
assumed support of my mother (who also went to work, as a companion

to an elderly woman) and earned his master's degree at night. My sister married and got a job at a bank. My baby brother parked cars and found a wife. Mama's biggest job was done at last; the investment made in our lives by the State of Illinois had come to fruition. Five people on welfare for 18 years had become five working, taxpaying adults. Three of us went to college, two of us finished; one of us has an advanced degree, all of us can take care of ourselves.

Ours was a best-case phenomenon, based on the synergy of church and state, the government and the private sector and the thousand points of light that we called friends and neighbors. But there was something more: What fueled our dreams and fired our belief that our lives could change for the better was the promise of the civil rights movement and the war on poverty—for millions of African-Americans the defining events of the 1960s. Caught up in the heady atmosphere of imminent change, our world was filled not only with issues and ideas but with amazing images of black people engaged in the struggle for long-denied rights and freedoms. We knew other people lived differently than we did, we knew we didn't have much, but we didn't mind, because we knew it wouldn't be long. My mother borrowed a phrase I had read to her once from Dick Gregory's autobiography. Not poor, just broke. She would repeat it often, as often as she sang hymns in the kitchen. She loved to sing a spiritual Mahalia Jackson had made famous: "Move On Up a Little Higher." Like so many others, Mama was singing about earth as well as heaven. 18

These are the things I remember every time I read another article outlining America's welfare crisis. The rage I feel about the welfare debate comes from listening to a host of lies, distortions and exaggerations—and taking them personally. 19

I am no fool. I know of few women—on welfare or off—with my mother's grace and courage and stamina. I know not all women on welfare are cut from the same cloth. Some are lazy; some are ground down. Some are too young; many are without husbands. A few have made welfare fraud a lucrative career; a great many more have pushed the rules on outside income to their very limits. 20

I also know that none of these things justify our making welfare a test of character and worthiness, rather than an acknowledgment of need. Near-sainthood should not be a requirement for financial and medical assistance. 21

But all manner of sociologists and policy gurus continue to equate issues that simply aren't equivalent—welfare, race, rates of poverty, crime, marriage and childbirth—and to reach conclusions that serve to demonize 22 the poor. More than one social arbiter would have us believe that we have all been mistaken for the last 30 years—that the efforts to relieve the most severe effects of poverty have not only failed but have served instead to increase and expand the ranks of the poor. In keeping women, children and men from starvation, we are told, we have also kept them from self-sufficiency. In our zeal to do good, we have undermined the work ethic, the family and thus, by association, the country itself.

So how did I get here?   23

❀   ❀   ❀

AFTER YOU READ

THINK about Bray's description of the relationship between her mother and her father both before and after her mother applied for welfare. Why was it necessary for her mother to ask for help? What change did this decision make in her marriage? How and why did Bray's father become a "shadow man" (paragraph 8)? What changes did the mother's decision make in her family's welfare as a whole? Would you have made the same decision?

EXAMINE the essay to see how Bray uses narrative examples about her family's experience to support her point that the welfare system has helped her and many other proud, hardworking individuals to get a start in life that eventually allowed them to become financial and personal successes. Examine especially paragraphs 14–16, in which she declares that "What made our lives work as well as they did was my mother's genius at making do . . . along with her vivid imagination" (paragraph 14). What examples of her mother's "making do" and using her imagination does Bray give? Have you and your family ever had to "make do"?

WRITE an essay arguing for or against the welfare system as it is currently applied in your state. If you think that the system works as it is, give reasons to support your opinion. If you believe the system needs reforming, give suggestions for change. Or WRITE an answer to the question: "How did Rosemary L. Bray get off welfare?"

Nobody Ever Died of Old Age

SHARON R. CURTIN

In her book Nobody Ever Died of Old Age, *Sharon R. Curtin describes the lives of her own aging grandparents before their deaths, analyzes the causes and effects of aging, reports on society's attitude toward the aged, and suggests some alternative ways of treating them. In this selection from the book, part of which was reprinted in* The Atlantic *under the title "Aging in the Land of the Young," Curtin discusses the aging process itself as well as the attitude that society—especially younger people—have toward the aged.*

BEFORE YOU READ

THINK about the position elderly people have in our society. What problems do they have? How are the elderly depicted in movies? On television? In advertisements? How are they treated by their employees? By their own families? What are some of their economic problems or health problems?

EXAMINE the title. Is it an accurate statement? Why or why not? What does the author mean by it? What do you believe are the primary causes of death in older people?

WRITE a journal entry in which you "report" on how American society treats old people. Include in your journal specific examples of three old people that you have read about, that you have observed on television, or that you know personally.

AS YOU READ

Underline the problems of older people that Curtin identifies.

Like conspirators the old walk all bent over, as if hiding some precious ₁
secret, filled with self-protection. The body seems to gather itself
around those vital parts, folding shoulders, arms, pelvis like a fading rose.
Watch and you see how fragile old people come to think they are made.

Aging paints every action gray, lies heavy on every movement, impris- ₂
ons every thought. It governs each decision with a ruthless and single-
minded perversity. To age is to learn the feeling of no longer growing, of
struggling to do old tasks, to remember familiar actions. The cells of the
brain are destroyed with thousands of unfelt tiny strokes, little pockets of
clotted blood wiping out memories and abilities without warning. The
body seems to slowly give up, randomly stopping, starting again as if to
torture and tease with the memory of lost strength. Hands become clumsy,
frail transparencies, held together with knotted blue veins, fluttering in
front of your eyes and reminding you of growing infirmity.

Sometimes it seems as if the distance between your feet and the floor ₃
is constantly changing, as if you walk on shifting and not quite solid ground.
One foot down, slowly, carefully, force the other foot forward. Sometimes
you are a shuffler, not daring to lift your feet from the uncertain earth but
forced to slide hesitantly forward in little whispering movements. Sometimes you are able to really "step out" but this effort—in fact the pure
exhilaration of easy movement—soon exhausts you.

The world becomes narrower as friends and family die or move away. ₄
To climb stairs, to ride in a car, to walk to the corner, to talk on the
telephone; each action seems to take energy needed to stay alive. Everything is limited by the strength you hoard greedily. Your needs decrease,
you require less food, less sleep, and finally less human contact; yet this
little bit becomes more and more difficult. You fear that one day you will
be reduced to the simple acts of breathing and taking nourishment. This is
the ultimate stage you dread, the period of helplessness and hopelessness,
when any further independence will be over.

There is nothing to prepare you for the experience of growing old. ₅
Living is a process, an irreversible progression toward old age and eventual
death. You see men of eighty still vital and tall and straight as oaks; you see
men of fifty reduced to gray shadows in the human landscapes. The cellular
clock differs for each one of us, and is profoundly affected by our own life
experiences, our heredity, and perhaps most importantly, by the concepts
of aging encountered in society and in oneself.

Nobody ever died of old age.   ₆

Accidents kill, cancer kills, bullets kill, coronary occlusions kill; but no ₇
one ever died just because of age. Today in the United States there are

twenty million persons over sixty-five. Modern medicine has enabled man to survive the diseases of early and middle age and live to a "ripe old age" hitherto unknown except in Biblical lore. Most families have members who are in their late eighties. Hearts beating to a rhythm set by quinidine and digitalis, they are kept free of the killer pneumonia by antibiotics, kept walking with cortisone and aspirin for crippling arthritis.

The aged live with enforced leisure, on fixed incomes, subject to many ₈ chronic illnesses, and most of their money goes to keep a roof over their heads. But that profile leaves one thing out. . . .

Attitudes. That used to be what my teachers told me I had plenty of. ₉ All wrong. But the kind of culturally, socially enforced attitude I want to talk about makes me bigoted against old people; it makes me think young is best; it makes me treat old people like outcasts.

> *Hate that gray? Wash it away!*
> *Wrinkle cream.*
> *Monkey glands.*
> *Face lifting.*
> *Look like a bride again.*
> *Old is ugly.*
> *Don't trust anyone over thirty.*
> *I fear growing old.*
> *Feel Young Again!*
> *Old is ugly.*

I am afraid to grow old—we're all afraid. In fact, the fear of growing ₁₀ old is so great that every aged person is an insult and a threat to the society. They remind us of our own death—that our body won't always remain smooth and responsive, but will someday betray us by aging, wrinkling, faltering, failing. The ideal way to age would be to grow slowly invisible, gradually disappearing, without causing worry or discomfort to the young. In some ways that does happen. Sitting in a small park across from a nursing home one day, I noticed that the young mothers and their children gathered on one side, and the old people from the home on the other. Whenever a youngster would run over to the "wrong" side, chasing a ball or just trying to cover all the available space, the old people would lean forward and smile. But before any communication could be established, the mother would come over, murmuring embarrassed apologies, and take her child back to the "young" side.

Now, it seemed to me that the children didn't feel any particular fear, 11
and the old people didn't seem to be threatened by the children. The
division of space was drawn by the mothers. And the mothers never looked
at the old people who lined the old side of the park like so many pigeons
perched on the benches. These well-dressed young matrons had a way of
sliding their eyes over, around, through, the old people; they never looked
at them directly. The old people might as well have been invisible; they had
no reality for the youngsters, who were not permitted to speak to them,
and they offended the aesthetic eye of the mothers.

My early experiences were somewhat different; since I grew up in a 12
small town, my childhood had more of a nineteenth-century flavor. I knew
a lot of old people, and considered some of them friends. There was no
culturally defined way for me to "relate" to old people, except the rules of
courtesy which applied to all adults. My grandparents were an integral and
important part of the family and of the community. I sometimes have a
dreadful fear that mine will be the last generation to know old people as
friends, to have a sense of what growing old means, to respect and
understand man's mortality and his courage in the face of death. Mine may
be the last generation to have a sense of living history, of stories passed
from generation to generation, of identity established by family history.

❀ ❀ ❀

AFTER YOU READ

THINK about the effects of aging described in paragraphs 1–4. Notice
especially Curtin's observation that "the cells of the brain are destroyed
with thousands of unfelt tiny strokes, little pockets of clotted blood wiping
out memories and abilities without warning. The body seems to slowly give
up, randomly stopping, starting again as if to torture and tease with the
memory of lost strength" (paragraph 2). The mental deterioration described here may result in one of several forms of senile dementia, including
Alzheimer's disease. In your opinion, which is the more devastating for
older people—the loss of their mental faculties or their physical abilities?
Which loss is more devasting for family members? Why do you feel as you
do?

EXAMINE paragraph 9 and the italicized sentences that follow it. What do
these lines suggest about the attitude toward youth and aging in our culture
today? How is the fascination with youth that is held by many people

reflected in our society? How does this attitude affect young people? How does it affect old people?

EXAMINE also paragraph 10, which describes the way a group of mothers and their children react to older people in a park. Do you agree with Curtin's explanation for the reaction of these younger people? Why or why not? Is this scene typical of the way young people in our society react to older people?

WRITE an essay in which you identify and analyze one major problem faced by older people. You may want to focus on how older people function with regard to family, friends, health, economics, work, or any other aspect of our society. Describe the problem, identify its causes, and propose a solution.

We Don't Want to Grow Old

KARLA COLE

A native of southern Louisiana, Karla Cole is an education major who plans to teach art. The mother of three children, one of whom is about to start college, Cole wrote this essay in a freshman English class at the University of Southern Mississippi. Cole reports that she based the essay on her observation of her peers—fellow "baby-boomers"—at various high school reunions. Written from the point of view of a generation that still considers itself young, this essay complements Curtin's essay on aging.

BEFORE YOU READ

THINK about how younger people today—those of the "baby-boomer" generation as well as younger generations—view older people in our society. Has the attitude toward older people changed in the last twenty or thirty years? If so, how has it changed and why has it changed?

EXAMINE the first two paragraphs of Cole's essay. What does she suggest about the relationship between growing up and growing old? How, in her opinion, do younger generations feel about both processes? In your opinion, do young people equate growing up with growing old, or do they see the processes as completely different?

WRITE a journal entry in which you explain why you do or do not want to grow old.

AS YOU READ

Identify Cole's attitudes toward "growing up" and "growing old." Do you share her attitudes? Are these attitudes shared by most young people today?

S omething has happened in my own generation that hasn't happened in 1
my parents', or in any generation that I know of before that. It appears
we forgot to grow up. Baby-boomers are the ones I'm referring to, a group
that I identify strongly with, because I am one.

For those of you too young to understand, baby-boomers are those 2
people born between 1946 and 1964, during the population explosion
after World War II. This growth had far-reaching effects upon education,
politics, culture, and economics. Nothing was left unchallenged or un-
changed. There was one change to be avoided at all costs though: aging.
And no amount of time, money, or effort was too great a sacrifice to delay
the appearance of getting older.

Have you ever looked at pictures of your grandparents when they were 3
in their thirties? Didn't they look middle aged? It seems they didn't even
try to look otherwise, as if they aspired to old age. Now look at today's
thirty-somethings. The difference is alarming.

Older generations lived through some very difficult times: world wars, 4
economic depression, lack of luxury items that we call necessities, such as
televisions and VCRs. Life was hard, and people earned their maturity at
a young age. My grandmother, who was born at the turn of the century,
says people identified with their elders. "We knew we were getting older,
and it never occurred to us to try to hide it."

But trying to hide it is what baby-boomers excel at. As a group we are 5
now at least thirty years old with the oldest being dangerously close to fifty.
With the ever increasing life expectancy, thanks to the miracles of modern
medicine, we are still quite young. And don't we look it? Compare us to
the way we looked ten or fifteen years ago, and don't be surprised if we
look younger now. A look at our past contains some clues as to why the
sudden shift in attitudes toward aging.

Ours was a generation set apart from the rest of society—from nursery 6
school all the way through college. Prior to the fifties, families had the most
influence in shaping the values and behavior of children. There seemed to
be nothing wrong with that until the experts, like Dr. Benjamin Spock,
taught parents to relax and replace firmness and discipline with freedom.
And so we were emancipated to associate mainly with each other.

But the biggest influence on our generation was the media, namely 7
television. Baby-boomers were the first to grow up with it. Our values were
largely determined by advertisers who told us what we wanted and our
parents gladly supplied as much as they could. It was a prosperous time
compared to our parents' childhood, and they made sure we would not
suffer the hardships they had endured. So it was our collective buying

power that made fads overnight, and entire industries were built to meet our wants and needs. Parents and society focused on us and we focused on ourselves. Life was easy.

For that reason, no one was prepared for what happened in the sixties 8 and seventies. A counterculture emerged, and it seems we rebelled against everything. We were held together by a "don't trust anyone over thirty" mentality. Our government lied to us, materialism proved shallow and unfulfilling, and our televisions brought to us all the world's problems and none of the solutions. It's no wonder we "tuned in, turned on, and dropped out." Our innocence had been taken from us, and our parents were often more naive about the world we lived in than we were. So maybe we started growing up too fast and missed something important in our growing up years that we continually try to recapture. If we're still growing up, how could we possibly be growing old?

Whatever the reasons, we think younger, we act younger, and many of 9 us look younger. And with a little help from our friends in the fitness, cosmetics, and plastic surgery industries, maybe we can postpone the aging process indefinitely. Maybe we don't have to grow old.

AFTER YOU READ

THINK about the way modern science has improved health, increased life expectancy, and lengthened lives for many people (see paragraph 5). What are the direct and indirect effects of this scientific advance on the lives of older people and their families? What are the effects on the government and on society as a whole?

EXAMINE paragraph 7, in which Cole discusses the influence of the media on society's attitudes toward aging. Do you agree or disagree with Cole about the media's role in establishing these attitudes? What specific movies, television shows, and advertisements can you think of that promote this attitude?

WRITE an essay in which you argue whether it is wise or unwise to keep looking, feeling, and acting "young" even at an advanced physical age.

Unit Five: Critical Thinking and Writing Assignments

❀   ❀   ❀

EXPLORING IDEAS TOGETHER

1. Discuss with a group of your classmates the different social problems addressed in this unit. Make a list of these problems, then rank the problems you listed from most to least serious.

2. Educational success and educational failure are illustrated in the essays by Salinas and Sherry. Working with a group of your classmates, make one list of factors that contribute to educational success and another list of those that contribute to educational failure.

3. Blackmon and Steele both discuss the racial phenomenon of "resegregation" or the "politics of difference" in our schools and universities and, by implication, in our society as a whole. Although these authors describe a similar social phenomenon, their explanations for this situation differ greatly. Compare and contrast their explanations as well as their attitudes.

4. Work with a group of your classmates to identify the most serious crime on your campus. Then formulate a set of guidelines for students to follow in order to reduce or prevent this crime on campus.

WRITING ESSAYS

1. Review the reading selections by Salinas, Sherry, Samuels, Blackmon, Steele, and Siegel that pertain, directly or indirectly, to education. Make a list of problems that are identified in these articles, and add to your list other problems that you think our educational system faces today. From your list, select the problem that you believe to be the most serious for education today, and write an essay in which you describe the problem, analyze its causes, and propose a solution.

2. Write an essay in which you discuss whether you think our diversity strengthens or weakens our society. To prepare to write your essay, list the problems that result from having a diverse population and the strengths that result from this diversity. Support your thesis with specific examples from your reading, observation, and experience.

3. Write an essay giving incoming college freshmen advice about how to finance their college education. Include ways to get money to use for college and ways to save money as a college student.

4. Dorothy Siegel's article reports on crime on several campuses, including her own. Write an essay about crime on your campus. What is the most serious crime on your campus, what causes it, and what can be done to reduce or prevent it?

5. Gordon Witkin discusses the problem of gun-related violence among young people. Argue for or against gun-control legislation as a way to reduce crime and violence by young people in our neighborhoods and on our campuses.

6. Clifton, Hull, and Bray all focus on poverty in our country—especially in our cities. Write an essay in which you identify a particular problem associated with poverty or homelessness in your community or town, and propose possible solutions for this problem.

7. Two of the essays in this unit focus on aging and the elderly. Many older people spend their last years in institutions commonly known as "nursing homes." Write an essay in which you either support the use of nursing homes or argue for an alternative solution for caring for the aged.

8. Write a letter to the editor of your campus newspaper arguing that the federal government should or should not assume responsibility for one of the social problems included in this unit. For example, should the government provide homes for the homeless, provide a free college education for its citizens, enforce integration even if segregation is voluntary, legislate gun control, clean up urban slums, or provide care for the aged?

Self with Environment

Your environment extends from your immediate surroundings—your home, college, or workplace—to the entire world. The focus of the readings in this unit, however, is not on the environment in general but on your natural surroundings. You will read about how human beings interact with nature and how they have changed, and are changing, their environments in visible and invisible ways. You will read about some natural environments that seem friendly to humans and about others that seem hostile to humans. You will read about the problems of pollution and of vanishing natural resources. Finally you will read about some predictions of major ecological changes that may threaten life as we know it.

To prepare yourself to read the selections in this unit more effectively, you can write about your own attitude toward and knowledge about your environment. Use one of the following sets of questions as the basis for a freewriting or journal entry:

1. What kind of personal environment do you enjoy? Do you like to be outside in nature or inside in an artificially cooled or heated environment? What natural surroundings do you prefer? Do you like a climate that is cool or warm? Moist or dry?

2. In what ways do you interact with your natural environment?

3. How do you dispose of your trash when you are at home? In a public place? In your car? How does your community or town dispose of its trash?

4. How many throw-away products do you use in your home? For example, do you regularly use packaged or prepared foods or frozen dinners in throw-away trays? Do you drink soft drinks from cans or bottles? Do you use aerosol cans? If you are a parent, do you use (or have you used) disposable diapers with your baby? Have you thought of possible long-range effects of using so many throw-away products—especially paper and styrofoam products?

5. Can you name three endangered species? Can you explain why one species is endangered and what can be done to revive the species? When the protection of an endangered species conflicts with economic or human values, such as job security or health, which is more important?

6. Should private landowners be able to do whatever they want with their land regardless of environmental consequences? Should public land be protected as natural environments or devoted to the economic survival of those who live in the area?

After you have written your response to one of these questions, meet with other classmates who chose the same question, discuss your responses, and then report briefly to the class. Do not be concerned if you have problems answering some of the questions because you do not have enough information at this time. Write out questions that give you trouble and, as you discuss these questions in your groups and in class, jot down other questions about the environment that you have. Keep these questions in mind as you read the selections in this unit. As you read, write in the margins your own comments and reactions, related information, and new questions that occur as you read.

Weather Reports

KATHLEEN NORRIS

About twenty years ago, poet Kathleen Norris returned to live in a house built by her grandparents in a small town on the border between North and South Dakota. Here she explored not only the isolated, elemental landscape of the region but also the values and customs of this land from which her family had come. The result was a book she entitled Dakota: A Spiritual Geography. *Interspersed between the chapters of the book are short pieces called "Weather Reports." Read in sequence, these reports form a poetic narrative of the year she spent in this small North Dakota town.*

BEFORE YOU READ

THINK about the information we get from weather reports. What do weather reports tell us about a region and the people who inhabit it?

EXAMINE the dates of these reports. At what intervals were they written, and what period of time do they span?

WRITE in your journal an objective description of the weather you are currently experiencing.

AS YOU READ

Notice the narrative of events in the author's life that are revealed in these weather reports.

WEATHER REPORT: JANUARY 17

Encircled. The sea that stretched out before me in Maili, on the Waianae 1
coast of Oahu, as this month began, has been transformed into the
plains of North Dakota. I am riding a Greyhound bus to the small town
where I'll be teaching writing to schoolchildren for the next two weeks.
Snow in the fields has crusted over; wind-lines, restless as waves, flash like
the ocean in sunlight.

"Never turn your back on the sea," is Hawaii's wisdom. "Or the sky," 2
we Plains folk might add. Like sailors, we learn to read cloud banks coming
from the west. We watch for sundogs and count rings around the moon.

I have turned with the circle: away from gentle air and birdsong, the 3
Waianae Range unfolding like a fan in mist, toward a wind gritty with spent
soil burning my tongue, a freezing rain that stings my hands and face.

In the schoolyard, a snow angel's wings are torn, caught in grass 4
exposed by the sudden thaw. In the stuffy classroom, a little girl, restless
and distracted, probably a bad student, becomes White Buffalo Calf
Woman, speaking of a world in which all people are warm in winter and
have enough to eat.

"They sing, 'the rain is new,'" she writes, "'the rain is always new.'" 5

WEATHER REPORT: FEBRUARY 10

I walk downtown, wearing a good many of the clothes I own, keeping my 6
head down and breathing through several thicknesses of a wool scarf. A
day so cold it hurts to breathe; dry enough to freeze spit. Kids crack it on
the sidewalk.

Walking with care, snow barely covering the patches of ice, I begin to 7
recall a canticle or a psalm—I can't remember which—and my body keeps
time:

Cold and chill, bless the Lord
Dew and rain, bless the Lord
Frost and chill, bless the Lord
Ice and snow, bless the Lord
Nights and days, bless the Lord
Light and darkness, bless the Lord.

Another line comes to mind: "at the breath of God's mouth the waters 8
flow." Spring seems far off, impossible, but it is coming. Already there is
dusk instead of darkness at five in the afternoon; already hope is stirring
at the edges of the day.

WEATHER REPORT: MARCH 25

Mud and new grass push up through melting snow. Lilacs in bud by my 9
front door, bent low by last week's ice storm, begin to rise again in today's
cold rain. Thin clouds scatter in a loud wind.

Suddenly, fir trees seem like tired old women stooped under winter 10
coats. I want to be light, to cast off impediments, and push like a tulip
through a muddy smear of snow. I want to take the rain to heart, let it move
like possibility, the idea of change.

WEATHER REPORT: JUNE 30

I get started early, before six. It promises to be a good laundry day: a steady 11
wind but not too strong. I come by my love of laundry honestly: my earliest
memory is of my mother pulling clothes in from the sky on a line that ran
out our apartment window in Washington, D.C.

Hanging up wet clothes while it is still cool, I think of her. Though 12
she's lived in Honolulu for more than thirty years, she's a plainswoman at
heart; her backyard clothesline is a dead giveaway. The challenge of drying
clothes in a tropical valley agrees with her; mountain rains sweep down at
least once a day, and she must be vigilant.

Here no rain is likely, unless, as so often happens, our most beautiful 13
summer days turn dark and violent in late afternoon, thunderstorms pelting
us with rain or hail. I think of a friend who was dying, who had saved up
all her laundry for my visit. "I can't trust my husband with it," she
whispered conspiratorially. "Men don't understand that clothes must be
hung on a line."

She was right. Hanging up wet clothes gives me time alone under the 14
sky to think, to grieve, and gathering the clean clothes in, smelling the
sunlight on them, is victory.

WEATHER REPORT: JULY 3

Rains came late in June and haying was delayed. But today it was 65 degrees 15
by six A.M., and that means a hot day, 100 degrees or more; it means haying
can't wait.

It's one of the miracles of nature that this empty-looking land can be 16
of such great use, that cattle can convert its grasses to milk and meat.

I know that the brome and wheatgrass will lose its value as feed if it 17
isn't hayed soon, but ever since I moved to Dakota I've felt a kind of grief
at haying time. I hate to see the high grass fall.

Alfalfa and clover still stand tall by the road, smelling sweet and clean, 18
like a milkfed infant's breath. In a few days these vigorous plants will be
coffin-size heaps in the ditch.

WEATHER REPORT: OCTOBER 2

"When my third snail died," the little girl writes, sitting halfway in, halfway 19
out of her desk, one leg swinging in air, "I said, 'I'm through with snails.'"
She sits up to let me pass down the aisle, the visiting poet working with the
third grade: in this dying school, this dying town, we are writing about our
lives. I'm hungry, looking forward to the lefse I bought for lunch at the
Norwegian Food Festival sponsored by the Senior Citizen Center, one of
the few busy places on Main Street. That and the post office, the café, the
grocery. The other buildings are empty.

The teacher's writing too. Yesterday she told me that when I asked the 20
kids to make silence and the room was suddenly quiet, she thought of her
mother. "She's been dead for years," she said, adding almost apologetically,
"I don't know why I thought of her. But then I just had to write." She told
me about the smells, how this time of year the lingering scent of pickling
spices in the house would gradually give way to cinnamon, peppermint,
cloves, the smells of Christmas baking. "It was the candy I loved most,"
she wrote, "nut fudge, caramels, divinity."

The sunsets here have been extraordinary, blazing up like distant fire 21
in the window of the old boarding house where the school has put me. Last
night I was reading when the light changed: I looked up and gasped at the
intensity of color, a slash of gold and scarlet on the long scribble of horizon.

I was reading one of the old ones who said, "One who keeps death 22
before his eyes conquers despair." The little girl calls me, holding up her
paper for me to read:

When my third snail died, I said,
"I'm through with snails."
But I didn't mean it.

WEATHER REPORT: NOVEMBER 2

Wind prowled the monastery grounds, giving night silence an increased air 23
of watchfulness. Glass shook in the window frames and sleep was slow in
coming.

We had prayed at vespers for the deceased members of the community, 24
from Isidore who died in 1898 to Michael who died last year. We sang of
"the narrow stream of death," as if the distance were not so far. I woke to
find the ground dusted with snow, the Killdeer Mountains looming white
on the horizon, a distance of forty-five miles.

All Souls', blustery and chill. I hear them before I see them, six lines 25
scribbling across the white sky. I look up at the tiny crosses beating above
me. The pain is new each year, and I'm surprised, even though I expect it:
the sudden cold, the geese passing over.

❀　❀　❀

AFTER YOU READ

THINK about how the author changed and what she learned during the
year she describes in these reports.

EXAMINE the events recorded in the final weather report (November 2).
Next describe the tone of this report. Finally identify the weather images
the author includes in this report. How do these images reinforce the tone?

WRITE a weather report similar to those included in this reading selection.
Describe current weather conditions but include subjective as well as
objective details. In your report use vivid images that appeal to your
reader's sense of touch and hearing as well as sight. Begin or end your
report with an account of a single event that is related in some way to the
weather conditions you describe.

Wild Geese

MARY OLIVER

Mary Oliver's book American Primitive *won the Pulitzer Prize for poetry in 1984, and in 1992 her* New and Selected Poems *won the National Book Award. In this poem, from her book entitled* Dream Work, *Oliver expresses her belief that animals, humans, and the land are all part of what she calls the "family of things."*

BEFORE YOU READ

THINK about a time when you felt at one with nature—part of the "family of things." Be specific about when this feeling happened and where you were at the time.

EXAMINE lines 2 and 3 of the poem. What image does this sentence evoke? Have you heard or read of people performing acts of penance such as this? What is the purpose of such acts?

WRITE a journal entry describing something in nature that you find particularly beautiful or meaningful.

AS YOU READ

Notice the vivid images the poet includes. After you have read the poem through several times, read it again, underlining each image and noting whether it appeals to your sense of sight, hearing, or touch.

You do not have to be good.   1
You do not have to walk on your knees
for a hundred miles through the desert, repenting.
You only have to let the soft animal of your body
        love what it loves.   5
Tell me about despair, yours, and I will tell you mine.
Meanwhile the world goes on.
Meanwhile the sun and the clear pebbles of the rain
are moving across the landscapes,
over the prairies and deep trees,   10
the mountains and the rivers.
Meanwhile the wild geese, high in the clean blue air,
are heading home again.
Whoever you are, no matter how lonely,
the world offers itself to your imagination,   15
calls to you like the wild geese, harsh and exciting—
over and over announcing your place
in the family of things.

AFTER YOU READ

THINK about wild geese and what they represent to the poet. Have you ever seen wild geese in flight? How did you respond? Compare Oliver's description of wild geese to that included in the final weather report (November 2) in the previous selection by Kathleen Norris. Which do you find more realistic? Which do you find more meaningful?

EXAMINE the three parts of this poem: lines 1–6; lines 7–13; and lines 14–18. How does seeing the poem in terms of this three-part structure help you understand what the poet is trying to communicate?

WRITE a paraphrase of the poem. Using your own words, rewrite each sentence, trying to reflect as accurately as possible the poet's meaning.

Song of the Sky Loom

NATIVE AMERICAN (TEWA)

For centuries the Tewas have lived in New Mexico and northeastern Arizona, residing in the pueblos of Nambe, San Ildefonso, San Juan, Santa Clara, Tesuque, and Hano. As shown by their earthen dwellings and simple agricultural practices, the Tewas try to live in harmony with nature. The following poem is a Tewa chant about the "sky loom," a light desert rain that—as reflected by the late afternoon sun—hangs from the sky like a loom.*

BEFORE YOU READ

THINK about the idea of the earth as a mother and the sky as a father. What do the earth and sky give their children? How is the relationship between the earth and sky and their "children" similar to the relationship you share with your own parents or children? How are these relationships different?

EXAMINE the words *warp* and *weft*. In the art of weaving, the threads that run lengthwise (vertical) up and down the fabric are called the warp; the threads that run crosswise (horizontal) are called the weft or the woof. As a fabric is woven, both the warp and weft are held in place by means of a loom.

WRITE a journal entry in which you explore the relationship between earth and the people who inhabit it.

AS YOU READ

Try to visualize the "garment of brightness" described by the poet.

---

*From Herbert J. Spinden, *Songs of the Tewa*, p. 94.

O our Mother the Earth, O our Father the Sky,   1
Your children are we, and with tired backs
We bring you the gifts you love.
Then weave for us a garment of brightness;
May the warp be the white light of morning,   5
May the weft be the red light of evening,
May the fringes be the falling rain,
May the border be the standing rainbow.
Thus weave for us a garment of brightness,
That we may walk fittingly where birds sing,   10
That we may walk fittingly where grass is green,
O our Mother the Earth, O our Father the Sky.

AFTER YOU READ

THINK about the phrase "We bring you the gifts you love." What kinds of gifts could we give to the earth and the sky?

EXAMINE the structure and imagery of the poem. Notice that the lines are tied together by repetition rather than rhyme. For example, four parallel lines begin with *May,* and two parallel lines begin with *That.* Locate these parallel lines. How does this parallelism emphasize meaning in the poem? Also, notice that the last line of the poem is the same as the first line. What does this circular structure suggest about the meaning of the poem?

EXAMINE also the phrase "garment of brightness" developed in lines 4–9. What is the garment of brightness described in the poem? Notice that lines 5–8 include four different comparisons that develop this metaphor of the sky as a garment of brightness woven by Mother Earth and Father Sky. What are these specific comparisons? Can you visualize this garment as a work of art—perhaps as a rug or a tapestry?

WRITE an essay in which you discuss "Song of the Sky Loom" as a pro-environment argument.

The Gift

LOUIS DOLLARHIDE

*A professor of English at the University of Mississippi,
Louis Dollarhide has written short stories, plays, and
poetry as well as articles and books about literature. In the
following short story from the anthology* Mississippi Writers, *he describes a lone woman's encounter with the
Mississippi River swollen by flood waters.*

BEFORE YOU READ

THINK about a time when you were in a storm or some kind of severe
weather such as high water, extreme cold, or dangerously high winds. What
did you do? How did you feel? Were you alone or with other people? If
you were alone, do you think you were more frightened than you would
have been if others had been with you? Why or why not?

EXAMINE the first paragraph of the story. How does Dollarhide personify
(give human characteristics to) the rising river?

WRITE a journal entry about a time that you felt threatened by your
environment. For example, has heavy rain ever made it hard for you to
walk or drive from one place to another, or has the electricity or gas at your
house or apartment ever been cut off on a cold winter day? How did you
feel? What did you do to survive in the situation?

AS YOU READ

Look for the conflicts experienced by the woman in the story. What are
the primary external conflicts? What internal conflict does the woman
experience? How are these conflicts resolved?

How many days, she wondered, had she sat like this, watching the cold   1
brown water inch up the dissolving bluff. She could just faintly
remember the beginning of the rain, driving in across the swamp from the
south and beating against the shell of her house. Then the river itself started
rising, slowly at first until at last it paused as if to turn back. From hour to
hour it slithered up creeks and ditches and poured over low places. In the
night, while she slept, it claimed the road and surrounded her so that she
sat alone, her boat gone, the house like a piece of drift lodged on its bluff.
Now even against the tarred planks of the supports the waters touched.
And still they rose.

As far as she could see, to the treetops where the opposite banks had   2
been, the swamp was an empty sea, awash with sheets of rain, the river lost
somewhere in its vastness. Her house with its boat bottom had been built
to ride just such a flood, if one ever came, but now it was old. Maybe the
boards underneath were partly rotted away. Maybe the cable mooring the
house to the great live oak would snap loose and let her go turning
downstream, the way her boat had gone.

No one could come now. She could cry out but it would be no use, no   3
one would hear. Down the length and breadth of the swamp others were
fighting to save what little they could, maybe even their lives. She had seen
a whole house go floating by, so quiet she was reminded of sitting at a
funeral. She thought when she saw it she knew whose house it was. It had
been bad seeing it drift by, but the owners must have escaped to higher
ground. Later, with the rain and darkness pressing in, she had heard a
panther scream upriver.

Now the house seemed to shudder around her like something alive.   4
She reached out to catch a lamp as it tilted off the table by her bed and put
it between her feet to hold it steady. Then creaking and groaning with effort
the house struggled up from the clay, floated free, bobbing like a cork, and
swung out slowly with the pull of the river. She gripped the edge of the
bed. Swaying from side to side, the house moved to the length of its
mooring. There was a jolt and a complaining of old timbers and then a
pause. Slowly the current released it and let it swing back, rasping across
its resting place. She caught her breath and sat for a long time feeling the
slow pendulous sweeps. The dark sifted down through the incessant rain,
and, head on arm, she slept holding on to the bed.

Sometime in the night the cry awoke her, a sound so anguished she   5
was on her feet before she was awake. In the dark she stumbled against the
bed. It came from out there, from the river. She could hear something

moving, something large that made a dredging, sweeping sound. It could be another house. Then it hit, not head on but glancing and sliding down the length of her house. It was a tree. She listened as the branches and leaves cleared themselves and went on downstream, leaving only the rain and the lappings of the flood, sounds so constant now that they seemed a part of the silence. Huddled on the bed, she was almost asleep again when another cry sounded, this time so close it could have been in the room. Staring into the dark, she eased back on the bed until her hand caught the cold shape of the rifle. Then crouched on the pillow, she cradled the gun across her knees. "Who's there?" she called.

The answer was a repeated cry, but less shrill, tired sounding, then the   6 empty silence closing in. She drew back against the bed. Whatever was there she could hear it moving about on the porch. Planks creaked and she could distinguish the sounds of objects being knocked over. There was a scratching on the wall as if it would tear its way in. She knew now what it was, a big cat, deposited by the uprooted tree that had passed her. It had come with the flood, a gift.

Unconsciously she pressed her hand against her face and along her   7 tightened throat. The rifle rocked across her knees. She had never seen a panther in her life. She had heard about them from others and had heard their cries, like suffering, in the distance. The cat was scratching on the wall again, rattling the window by the door. As long as she guarded the window and kept the cat hemmed in by the wall and water, caged, she would be all right. Outside, the animal paused to rake his claws across the rusted outer screen. Now and then, it whined and growled.

When the light filtered down through the rain at last, coming like   8 another kind of dark, she was still sitting on the bed, stiff and cold. Her arms, used to rowing on the river, ached from the stillness of holding the rifle. She had hardly allowed herself to move for fear any sound might give strength to the cat. Rigid, she swayed with the movement of the house. The rain still fell as if it would never stop. Through the gray light, finally, she could see the rainpitted flood and far away the cloudy shape of drowned treetops. The cat was not moving now. Maybe he had gone away. Laying the gun aside she slipped off the bed and moved without a sound to the window. It was still there, crouched at the edge of the porch, staring up at the live oak, the mooring of her house, as if gauging its chances of leaping to an overhanging branch. It did not seem so frightening now that she could see it, its coarse fur napped into twigs, its sides pinched and ribs showing. It would be easy to shoot it where it sat, its long tail whipping back and forth. She was moving back to get the gun when it turned around. With no warning, no crouch or tensing of muscles, it sprang at the window, shattering a pane of glass. She fell back, stifling a scream, and taking up the rifle, she fired through the window. She could not see the panther now, but she had missed. It began to pace again. She could glimpse its head and the arch of its back as it passed the window.

Shivering, she pulled back on the bed and lay down. The lulling 9 constant sound of the river and the rain, the penetrating chill, drained away her purpose. She watched the window and kept the gun ready. After waiting a long while she moved again to look. The panther had fallen asleep, its head on its paws, like a housecat. For the first time since the rains began she wanted to cry, for herself, for all the people, for everything in the flood. Sliding down on the bed, she pulled the quilt around her shoulders. She should have got out when she could, while the roads were still open or before her boat was washed away. As she rocked back and forth with the sway of the house a deep ache in her stomach reminded her she hadn't eaten. She couldn't remember for how long. Like the cat, she was starving. Easing into the kitchen, she made a fire with the few remaining sticks of wood. If the flood lasted she would have to burn the chair, maybe even the table itself. Taking down the remains of a smoked ham from the ceiling, she cut thick slices of the brownish red meat and placed them in a skillet. The smell of the frying meat made her dizzy. There were stale biscuits from the last time she had cooked and she could make some coffee. There was plenty of water.

While she was cooking her food, she almost forgot about the cat until 10 it whined. It was hungry too. "Let me eat," she called to it, "and then I'll see to *you*." And she laughed under her breath. As she hung the rest of the ham back on its nail the cat growled a deep throaty rumble that made her hand shake.

After she had eaten, she went to the bed again and took up the rifle. 11 The house had risen so high now it no longer scraped across the bluff when it swung back from the river. The food had warmed her. She could get rid of the cat while light still hung in the rain. She crept slowly to the window. It was still there, mewing, beginning again to move about the porch. She stared at it a long time, unafraid. Then without thinking what she was doing, she laid the gun aside and started around the edge of the bed to the kitchen. Behind her the cat was moving, fretting. She took down what was left of the ham and making her way back across the swaying floor to the window she shoved it through the broken pane. On the other side there was a hungry snarl and something like a shock passed from the animal to her. Stunned by what she had done, she drew back to the bed. She heard the sounds of the panther tearing at the meat. The house rocked around her.

The next time she awoke she knew at once that everything had   12
changed. The rain had stopped. She felt for the movement of the house but it no longer swayed on the flood. Drawing her door open, she saw through the torn screen a different world. The house was resting on the bluff where it always had. A few feet down, the river still raced on in a torrent, but it no longer covered the few feet between the house and the live oak. And the cat was gone. Leading from the porch to the live oak and doubtless on into the swamp were tracks, indistinct and already disappearing in the soft mud. And there on the porch, gnawed to whiteness, was what was left of the ham.

❀   ❀   ❀

AFTER YOU READ

THINK about the title of the story. What literal, or actual, gift does the woman give the panther? How does this gift bring with it another very important gift—the gift of life? Why does the woman give this gift to an animal that could be a threat to her own life? Do you think she feels some sense of identification with the animal? How are their situations similar? Do you think the panther understands the gift?

EXAMINE the story (especially paragraph 4) for examples of personification. What nonhuman objects or animals does Dollarhide personify? What specific words personify these objects?

WRITE an essay about the conflicts experienced by the woman in the story and about the resolution of those conflicts. What primary external conflicts does she experience? What internal conflict does she feel? Or WRITE a persuasive essay arguing that animals do or do not understand human behavior.

A Fable for Tomorrow

RACHEL CARSON

Rachel Carson was a well-known biologist who wrote about the land and sea that she loved. Perhaps her most controversial and influential book was Silent Spring *(1962), a frightening description of the harmful effects that pesticides can have on the natural environment. In fact, the book caused such a furor that President John F. Kennedy ordered a federal investigation that confirmed Carson's concern and resulted in tighter controls on the use of pesticides. In the following selection, the introductory chapter from* Silent Spring, *Carson fantasizes about a future that human beings could bring upon themselves if they do not respect and protect their environment.*

BEFORE YOU READ

THINK about the title of this selection. What fables have you read? You might recall some of Aesop's fables, such as the stories of the boy who cried wolf, the fox and the crow, or the fox and the grapes. Do you expect a fable to be fact or fiction? Do you expect a fable to teach a lesson? How might a fable apply to tomorrow?

EXAMINE the first paragraph. What is the subject of this paragraph? Is the tone positive or negative? From this paragraph, what content and tone do you expect to find in the remainder of the selection? Preview the entire reading by examining the first sentence of each paragraph. At what point are your expectations reversed?

EXAMINE also the following words from the selection. Notice that the context—or surrounding text—helps to define each of these words.

Blight: "Then a strange *blight* crept over the area and everything began to change."

The next sentence states that "mysterious maladies" have attacked the chickens and that other animals have "sickened and died." Thus the context helps to define a *blight* as "a disease, sickness, or pestilence."

Maladies: "Some evil spell had settled on the community: mysterious *maladies* swept the flocks of chickens; the cattle and sheep sickened and died."

Again, the context provides clear clues to the meaning of this word. Not only *blight* but also the phrase *sickened and died* suggests that *maladies* are illnesses, sicknesses, diseases, or afflictions.

Moribund: "The few birds seen anywhere were *moribund;* they trembled violently and could not fly."

The description of the birds' violent trembling and inability to fly implies that *moribund* means "dying, deteriorating, or ailing." It is also helpful to know that the root *mor* or *mort* means "death," as in *morgue, mortuary,* and *mortician.*

Specter: "A grim *specter* has crept upon us almost unnoticed, and this imagined tragedy may easily become a stark reality we all shall know."

The reference to an "evil spell" in the previous sentence leads logically to the image of a specter as a ghost, a phantom, or an apparition.

WRITE in your journal a focused freewriting entry about the title *Silent Spring.* What images do the words *spring* and *springtime* bring to your mind? Are these images silent? What would a silent spring be like?

AS YOU READ

Try to guess who or what has caused the strange silence described in this "fable for tomorrow." Before you finish the reading, also try to determine Carson's purpose in writing this fable.

There was once a town in the heart of America where all life seemed to   1
live in harmony with its surroundings. The town lay in the midst of a checkerboard of prosperous farms, with fields of grain and hillsides of orchards where, in spring, white clouds of bloom drifted above the green fields. In autumn, oak and maple and birch set up a blaze of color that flamed and flickered across a backdrop of pines. Then foxes barked in the hills and deer silently crossed the fields, half hidden in the mists of the fall mornings.

Along the roads, laurel, viburnum and alder, great ferns and wildflow- 2
ers delighted the traveler's eye through much of the year. Even in winter
the roadsides were places of beauty, where countless birds came to feed on
the berries and on the seed heads of the dried weeds rising above the snow.
The countryside was, in fact, famous for the abundance and variety of its
bird life, and when the flood of migrants was pouring through in spring
and fall people traveled from great distances to observe them. Others came
to fish the streams, which flowed clear and cold out of the hills and
contained shady pools where trout lay. So it had been from the days many
years ago when the first settlers raised their houses, sank their wells, and
built their barns.

Then a strange blight crept over the area and everything began to 3
change. Some evil spell had settled on the community: mysterious maladies
swept the flocks of chickens; the cattle and sheep sickened and died.
Everywhere was a shadow of death. The farmers spoke of much illness
among their families. In the town the doctors had become more and more
puzzled by new kinds of sickness appearing among their patients. There
had been several sudden and unexplained deaths, not only among adults
but even among children, who would be stricken suddenly while at play
and die within a few hours.

There was a strange stillness. The birds, for example—where had they 4
gone? Many people spoke of them, puzzled and disturbed. The feeding
stations in the backyards were deserted. The few birds seen anywhere were
moribund; they trembled violently and could not fly. It was a spring without
voices. On the mornings that had once throbbed with the dawn chorus of
robins, catbirds, doves, jays, wrens, and scores of other bird voices there
was now no sound; only silence lay over the fields and woods and marsh.

On the farms the hens brooded, but no chicks hatched. The farmers 5
complained that they were unable to raise any pigs—the litters were small
and the young survived only a few days. The apple trees were coming into
bloom but no bees droned among the blossoms, so there was no pollination
and there would be no fruit.

The roadsides, once so attractive, were now lined with browned and 6
withered vegetation as though swept by fire. These, too, were silent,
deserted by all living things. Even the streams were now lifeless. Anglers
no longer visited them, for all the fish had died.

In the gutters under the eaves and between the shingles of the roofs, a 7
white granular powder still showed a few patches; some weeks before it
had fallen like snow upon the roofs and the lawns, the fields and streams.

No witchcraft, no enemy action had silenced the rebirth of new life in 8
this stricken world. The people had done it themselves.

This town does not actually exist, but it might easily have a thousand 9
counterparts in America or elsewhere in the world. I know of no community that has experienced all the misfortunes I describe. Yet every one of
these disasters has actually happened somewhere, and many real communities have already suffered a substantial number of them. A grim specter
has crept upon us almost unnoticed, and this imagined tragedy may easily
become a stark reality we all shall know.

❀ ❀ ❀

AFTER YOU READ

THINK about the fate of the birds, fish, and other animals in Carson's fable.
Have you ever used a pesticide to kill roaches or other insects? What is the
effect? Have you ever seen a stream that has been polluted by pesticides or
other toxic substances? What has happened to the fish and vegetation?

EXAMINE the last two paragraphs of the reading. Notice that Carson
concludes her fable—her mythical story—in the next-to-the-last paragraph. How does the last paragraph differ from the rest of the selection?
Is it fact or fiction? How does this paragraph serve as an explanation of
the preceding fable? What thesis does Carson state or imply in this
paragraph?

WRITE an essay in which you describe what your home town might be like
if it suffered the same fate Carson describes.

Down with the Forests

CHARLES KURALT

For over thirty years, Charles Kuralt has been a news correspondent, searching for offbeat human interest stories. This article originally appeared in Dateline America, *a collection of seemingly light—but sometimes serious— reports that Kuralt made for his CBS radio and television series "On the Road." The specific topic that Kuralt addresses in this article is the problem of our vanishing forests.*

BEFORE YOU READ

THINK about how much paper you use in a single day at home, at school, at work, at restaurants, and in other places. Where does all this paper come from? Do you need to use as much paper as you do?

EXAMINE the words *clear-cut* and *clear-cutting*. One meaning of *clear-cut* is "distinctly and sharply defined or outlined; plain; evident." But Kuralt uses a different meaning. As you read the article, write in the margin a definition of *clear-cutting* as Kuralt uses it.

WRITE in your journal a three- or four-column list of the different paper products you use. List paper products you use at home in the first column, those you use at school in the second column, those you use at restaurants and other places in the third column, and—if you have a job—those you use at work in the last column.

AS YOU READ

Think about why Kuralt combines a description of eating breakfast in a restaurant with a discussion of clear-cutting in our national forests.

Baltimore, Maryland. I was waiting for breakfast in a coffee shop the 1
other morning and reading the paper. The paper had sixty-six pages.
The waitress brought a paper place mat and a paper napkin and took my
order, and I paged through the paper.

The headline said, "House Panel Studies a Bill Allowing Clear-Cutting 2
in U.S. Forests."

I put the paper napkin in my lap, spread the paper out on the paper 3
place mat, and read on: "The House Agriculture Committee," it said, "is
looking over legislation that would once again open national forests to the
clear-cutting of trees by private companies under government permits."

The waitress brought the coffee. I opened a paper sugar envelope and 4
tore open a little paper cup of cream and went on reading the paper: "The
Senate voted without dissent yesterday to allow clear-cutting," the paper
said. "Critics have said clear-cutting in the national forests can lead to
erosion and destruction of wildlife habitats. Forest Service and industry
spokesmen said a flat ban on clear-cutting would bring paralysis to the
lumber industry." And to the paper industry, I thought. Clear-cutting a
forest is one way to get a lot of paper, and we sure seem to need a lot of
paper.

The waitress brought the toast. I looked for the butter. It came on a 5
little paper tray with a covering of paper. I opened a paper package of
marmalade and read on: "Senator Jennings Randolph, Democrat of West
Virginia, urged his colleagues to take a more restrictive view and permit
clear-cutting only under specific guidelines for certain types of forest. But
neither he nor anyone else voted against the bill, which was sent to the
House on a 90 to 0 vote."

The eggs came, with little paper packages of salt and pepper. I finished 6
breakfast, put the paper under my arm, and left the table with its used and
useless paper napkin, paper place mat, paper salt and pepper packages,
paper butter and marmalade wrappings, paper sugar envelope, and paper
cream holder, and I walked out into the morning wondering how our
national forests can ever survive our breakfasts.

❀　❀　❀

AFTER YOU READ

THINK about Kuralt's purpose and tone. What is his purpose? How would
you describe his tone? Would another tone have been as effective in helping
him achieve his purpose? Why or why not?

EXAMINE the use of the words *clear-cutting* and *paper* in the report. What does *clear-cutting* mean in the context of this selection? How many times can you find the word *paper*? What does this repetition of the word *paper* suggest about Kuralt's purpose? How important are these two words to Kuralt's thesis, or main idea?

WRITE a draft of a plan for conserving paper products in a particular setting such as your home, classroom, or workplace. Decide on a specific audience for this plan (students, fellow workers, or the general public). Then rewrite your plan in the form of a letter or memorandum to communicate to your chosen audience.

Dice or Doves?

CINDY CAMBURN

This essay by Cindy Camburn was one of several she included in the portfolio she submitted for her freshman composition course. Having lived on the Gulf Coast all her life, Camburn had mixed emotions when offshore gambling became legal a few years ago. This essay focuses on one of the changes that resulted from the coming of the gambling casinos to that area. As you read, notice how Camburn supplements her observations and experiences with other sources.

BEFORE YOU READ

THINK about the environmental cost of progress. Identify several examples that illustrate this cost. Is progress always harmful to the environment? If the choice is between protecting the environment and providing a community or region with economic security (new jobs, more money for schools, increased incomes, and so on), which would you choose? Are there other options?

EXAMINE the following sentence from the second paragraph:

> Even so, I am aware of a beam of light that washes across the backyard, penetrates the closed blinds, and bounces off my mirror every thirty seconds.

Notice how Camburn's choice of strong verbs (*washes, penetrates,* and *bounces*) and her use of parallelism combine to make this an effective sentence.

WRITE a journal entry in which you tell about a change that has occurred in a place you know well.

368

AS YOU READ

Notice how Camburn combines her own experiences with information from other sources to lead her readers to her point of view.

O ne of my earliest memories of growing up on the Mississippi Gulf   1
Coast is waking every morning to the sounds of birds in the trees around the feeder. The types of birds varied with the season, but the most common visitors were a pair of doves with distinctive markings. Some mornings the doves would not be there, but they always eventually reappeared. I would watch them walk slowly around the deck, one bird pecking at the seeds which had fallen from the feeder while the other stayed alert for danger. At breakfast on these mornings, my mother would always say, "My doves are back." I was constantly surprised that the birds were hers because I felt they had returned for me.

Now when I go home for a visit, I always close the blinds before I go   2
to bed. Even so, I am aware of a beam of light that washes across the backyard, penetrates the closed blinds, and bounces off my mirror every thirty seconds. That beam comes from the laser show at Palace Casino, ten miles across the bay from my home. The Palace is one of fifteen casinos which have opened on the twenty-six mile stretch of coast in the last two years, creating an economic boom for the area. "Things couldn't be better," according to George Lammons, editor of the *Coast Business Journal.* The Coast, he explains is "enjoying robust economic growth. The biggest reason for our turnaround and one of the biggest reasons for the expectation of a good, long-term outlook is probably our newest industry—casino gambling." Lammons adds that the casinos have "put smiles on the faces of coastians."

If Lammons were to look a little more closely, he would find that many   3
coastians are not smiling. They feel that their quality of life has been destroyed. These casinos have turned the coast highway into a perpetual construction project and traffic jam. Their employees dump trash and waste water into the Mississippi River sound. Their six-story parking garages have replaced the palm trees and shrimp fleets and blocked the views of the beach. The casinos have changed the entire face of the Coast. In particular, they have changed the habitat of one of the coast's greatest attractions, its flocks of birds.

According to Becky Gillette in the *Coast Business Journal,* the Wildlife   4
and Nature Preservation Society Center is already citing a large increase in

orphaned and injured wildlife due to habitat destruction caused by the rapid growth that has accompanied the new casino industry. In "Silence of the Songbirds" in the June 1993 issue of *National Geographic,* Les Line puts the problem in a larger perspective. "Thirty years ago," he says, "when Rachel Carson wrote of 'a spring without voices' and the silence of the dawn without the chorus of robins, catbirds, doves, jays, and wrens, we thought the culprit was TOXINS. Now," he adds, "we know that habitat destruction is an even greater threat" (79–80). He explains

> Each spring, from mid-March to mid-May, [the birds] come north across the Gulf of Mexico in great waves, riding flows of warm humid air on a flight launched shortly after sunset from staging areas like the Yucatán Peninsula. Under the best conditions the . . . larger, faster fliers . . . will reach the coast by mid-morning after a 600-mile journey; smaller birds . . . lag behind. The travelers' goal is to make a rest stop in the first line of extensive forest on the mainland, perhaps 30 miles inland. But if they are buffeted by head winds or storms en route, they will drop exhausted into remnant scrub woodlands along the coast. . . . (72)

When the rest and recovery areas of forests and shrubs have been 5 replaced by buildings and concrete parking areas, many exhausted birds die. The survivors, who would have rested on the coast, cannot reproduce. In the early 60s, "Thirty thousand [migrating birds] would cross a given mile of coast . . . every hour for five hours" (Line, 73) every day during the peak season in April. Today, however, those numbers have already been reduced by more than forty percent (Line, 74).

In addition to losing their natural resting and nesting areas, birds 6 arriving on the Mississippi Gulf Coast face another hazard, the casinos' laser lights. The Palace Casino's lights are considered to be hazardous within 2,000 feet because they cause "temporary flash blindness and/or permanent retina damage" (Gillette). Local wildlife specialists feel that the threat to birds is even greater. Judith Toups, a local ornithologist, says any strong beam of light is a major hazard for migrating birds, especially in foggy or stormy weather, because birds get disoriented and head toward the light (Gillette). Janet Miller, president of the Mississippi Gulf Coast Audubon Society, adds, "We end up with migrating birds being attracted to the bright lights of the casinos and then having their eyesight damaged by the laser shows" (Gillette).

Of course, casino officials are quick to defend their lasers. "The laser 7 show draws people," explains the chief executive of Palace Casino. "The lights can be seen as far as fifty miles away. We receive lots of compliments and have had very few complaints" (Gillette).

I am complaining. The laser shows and the economic boom the casinos 8
represent do not put a smile on my face. If the unrestrained development
continues, the Mississippi Gulf Coast will have to depend on the lasers to
produce holographs of birds. Then the casino officials can receive compliments on how real the holographic birds look. I do not want the laser
versions. I want my (and my mother's) doves to keep reappearing.

Works Cited

Gillette, Becky. "Will It Harm Birds? Will It Harm Planes?" *Coast Business Journal,* 1 August 1994, 1, 31+.

Lammons, George. "State of the Coast: Taking off after Tough Times." *Coast Business Journal,* 15 February 1993, 4.

Line, Les. "Silence of the Songbirds." *National Geographic,* June 1993, 68–92.

❀   ❀   ❀

AFTER YOU READ

THINK about the relationship between change and progress. People often
resist change, especially changes that transform a familiar scene from
childhood into something new and strange. Does Camburn's description
of the changes that she has witnessed on the Gulf Coast seem to be simple
resistance to change, or does she convince you that these changes have
altered not only the birds' quality of life but also that of the residents of
that area? How does she make her own experience one that readers can
understand?

THINK also about Camburn's concession that the gambling casinos have
brought economic prosperity to the Gulf Coast. Does this concession
weaken her argument? Why or why not?

EXAMINE Camburn's system of documentation—the way she identifies
and gives credit to her sources.

EXAMINE also the different methods of development that Camburn uses
in her essay.

WRITE an essay in which you identify an environmental problem with
which you are familiar and suggest a reasonable, fair solution.

Waste

WENDELL BERRY

Although Wendell Berry has written two novels, he is known primarily as a poet and essayist. Berry currently lives on the Kentucky farm that was also the home of his parents, grandparents, and great-grandparents. As a writer and an organic farmer, he is deeply concerned about the environment, and his goal is to live in harmony with nature. In the following selection from What Are People For? *(1990), one of his most recent books of essays, Berry describes the contamination of our countryside with trash and explores the relationship between the waste of physical items and what he views as the related decline in human potential and achievement.*

BEFORE YOU READ

THINK about the amount of waste or trash that you produce each day. How much of this trash is organic—vegetable peelings, leftover food, and so on? How much is inorganic—paper, metal, plastic? Do you throw away cans, bottles, styrofoam containers, old toasters or radios, or other appliances? How do you dispose of this trash? Do you ever think about what happens to the trash that you throw away?

EXAMINE the following words from this selection and the sentences in which they occur.

Ubiquitous, perpetrators: "The truth is that we Americans, all of us, have become a kind of human trash, living our lives in the midst of a *ubiquitous* damned mess of which we are at once the victims and the *perpetrators.*"

The sentence provides context clues to the meanings of both of these words. The mess is *ubiquitous;* that is, trash is widespread, everywhere. *Perpetrators* are those who commit, or carry out, an act, such as creating the mess of trash with which we live.

Symbiosis: "But our waste problem is . . . the fault of an economy that is wasteful from top to bottom—a *symbiosis* of an unlimited greed at the top and a lazy, passive, and self-indulgent consumptiveness at the bottom— and all of us are involved in it."

Word analysis provides helpful clues to the meaning of this word. Because you know that *biology* is the study of life, you already know that *bio* means "life." Since *sym* means "together," *symbiosis* is the practice of two or more organisms—or, in this case, two or more ideas—existing together.

Ecological: "The *ecological* damage of centralization and waste is thus inextricably involved with human damage."

The word *ecological* means "related to *ecology.*" *Ecology,* which is a central concept in this unit, is the study of relationships between organisms and their environment. In this reading, you are studying about the relationship between human beings and their environment, about the way humans clutter and damage their environment—and themselves—with their wasteful practices.

WRITE a journal entry in which you list or draw a map (see pp. 6–7) of all the items that you throw away (or have seen thrown away) in a particular day. Subdivide your list or map into organic and inorganic materials. If possible, further subdivide these groups. For example, you probably can subdivide inorganic materials into three groups—paper products, metal products, and plastic products.

AS YOU READ

Think about what *you* can do to reduce the problem of waste disposal.

As a country person, I often feel that I am on the bottom end of the waste problem. I live on the Kentucky River about ten miles from its entrance into the Ohio. The Kentucky, in many ways a lovely river, receives an abundance of pollution from the Eastern Kentucky coal mines and the central Kentucky cities. When the river rises, it carries a continuous raft of cans, bottles, plastic jugs, chunks of styrofoam, and other imperishable trash. After the floods subside, I, like many other farmers, must pick up the trash before I can use my bottomland fields. I have seen the Ohio, whose name (*Oyo* in Iroquois) means "beautiful river," so choked with this manufactured filth than an ant could crawl dry-footed from Kentucky to

Indiana. The air of both river valleys is seriously polluted. Our roadsides and roadside fields lie under a constant precipitation of cans, bottles, the plastic-ware of fast food joints, soiled plastic diapers, and sometimes whole bags of garbage. In our county we now have a "sanitary landfill" which daily receives, in addition to our local production, fifty to sixty large truckloads of garbage from Pennsylvania, New Jersey, and New York.

Moreover, a close inspection of our countryside would reveal, strewn   2 over it from one end to the other, thousands of derelict and worthless automobiles, house trailers, refrigerators, stoves, freezers, washing machines, and dryers; as well as thousands of unregulated dumps in hollows and sink holes, on streambanks and roadsides, filled not only with "disposable" containers but also with broken toasters, television sets, toys of all kinds, furniture, lamps, stereos, radios, scales, coffeemakers, mixers, blenders, corn poppers, hair dryers, and microwave ovens. Much of our waste problem is to be accounted for by the intentional flimsiness and unrepairability of the labor-savers and gadgets that we have become addicted to.

Of course, my sometime impression that I live on the receiving end of   3 this problem is false, for country people contribute their full share. The truth is that we Americans, all of us, have become a kind of human trash, living our lives in the midst of a ubiquitous damned mess of which we are at once the victims and the perpetrators. We are all unwilling victims, perhaps; and some of us even are unwilling perpetrators, but we must count ourselves among the guilty nonetheless. In my household we produce much of our own food and try to do without as many frivolous "necessities" as possible—and yet, like everyone else, we must shop, and when we shop we must bring home a load of plastic, aluminum, and glass containers designed to be thrown away, and "appliances" designed to wear out quickly and be thrown away.

I confess that I am angry at the manufacturers who make these things.   4 There are days when I would be delighted if certain corporation executives could somehow be obliged to eat their products. I know of no good reason why these containers and all other forms of manufactured "waste"—solid, liquid, toxic, or whatever—should not be outlawed. There is no sense and no sanity in objecting to the desecration of the flag while tolerating and justifying and encouraging as a daily business the desecration of the country for which it stands.

But our waste problem is not the fault only of producers. It is the fault   5 of an economy that is wasteful from top to bottom—a symbiosis of an unlimited greed at the top and a lazy, passive, and self-indulgent consumptiveness at the bottom—and all of us are involved in it. If we wish to correct this economy, we must be careful to understand and to demonstrate how much waste of human life is involved in our waste of the material goods of Creation. For example, much of the litter that now defaces our country is fairly directly caused by the massive secession or exclusion of most of our people from active participation in the food economy. We have made a social ideal of minimal involvement in the growing and cooking of food. This is one of the dearest "liberations" of our affluence. Nevertheless, the more dependent we become on the *industries* of eating and drinking, the more waste we are going to produce. The mess that surrounds us, then, must be understood not just as a problem in itself but as a symptom of a greater and graver problem: the centralization of our economy, the gathering of the productive property and power into fewer and fewer hands, and the consequent destruction, everywhere, of the local economies of household, neighborhood, and community. This is the source of our unemployment problem, and I am not talking just about the unemployment of eligible members of the "labor force." I mean also the unemployment of children and old people, who, in viable household and local economies, would have work to do by which they would be useful to themselves and to others. The ecological damage of centralization and waste is thus inextricably involved with human damage. For we have, as a result, not only a desecrated, ugly, and dangerous country in which to live until we are in some manner poisoned by it, and a constant and now generally accepted problem of unemployed or unemployable workers, but also classrooms full of children who lack the experience and discipline of fundamental human tasks, and various institutions full of still capable old people who are useless and lonely.

I think that we must learn to see the trash on our streets and roadsides, in our rivers, and in our woods and fields, not as the side effects of "more jobs" as its manufacturers invariably insist that it is, but as evidence of good work *not* done by people able to do it. 6

❀ ❀ ❀

AFTER YOU READ

THINK again about the waste in our society. Do you agree or disagree with Berry that we are perpetrators as well as victims of the waste, that we cause as well as suffer from waste? Berry declares that our society is "wasteful from top to bottom . . . and all of us are involved in it," and he suggests further that our throw-away society also pays a price in a "waste of human life." Do you agree or disagree with Berry? Discuss your reasons for feeling as you do.

EXAMINE the analogy "There is no sense and no sanity in objecting to the desecration of the flag while tolerating and justifying and encouraging as a daily business the desecration of the country for which it stands" (paragraph 4). An *analogy* is a balanced comparison that suggests that if two things are alike in some ways they must be alike in others. In this analogy, Berry implies that disrespectful abuse of the country is senseless and insane just as disrespectful abuse of the flag is senseless and insane.

EXAMINE also Berry's statement that "we must learn to see the trash on our streets and roadsides, in our rivers, and in our woods and fields, not as the side effects of 'more jobs' as its manufacturers invariably insist that it is, but as evidence of good work *not* done by people able to do it" (paragraph 6). Can you think of examples of how trash represents work *not* done? For example, what good work is *not* done when a family uses disposable diapers, plastic plates, styrofoam cups, or frozen packaged dinners?

WRITE an essay in which you identify and describe a waste disposal problem with which you are personally familiar. Conclude your essay by proposing a reasonable, practical solution to this problem.

America's "Garbage Crisis":
A Toxic Myth

PATRICIA POORE

This essay appeared in a 1994 issue of Harper's Magazine.
*It was adapted from an earlier essay by Patricia Poore that
was published in a 1993 issue of* Garbage: The Practical
Journal for the Environment, *a magazine Poore founded
in 1989.*

BEFORE YOU READ

THINK about what you have heard or read about predictions of impending
environmental disasters related to the garbage crisis, acid rain, urban smog,
and so on. How seriously do you take these predictions? What, if anything,
have you done to help prevent them?

EXAMINE the "Toxic Myth" part of the title. We are accustomed to phrases
such as *toxic waste, toxic runoff,* and *toxic dumps* to which this title alludes.
To what does the term *toxic myth* refer? Can you think of more than one
meaning?

WRITE a journal entry about the threat to the environment that concerns
you most.

AS YOU READ

Identify the author's thesis statement and her main supporting arguments.

Let us recall, for a moment, the *Mobro*—the infamous garbage barge 1
that, in 1987, laden with an increasingly ripe pile of waste, wandered
from port to port in search of a home. The *Mobro,* which was carrying
plain old municipal solid waste—household garbage—occasioned head-
lines about the nation's looming "garbage crisis": we were throwing away
too much, our landfills were running out of space, and soon the seas would
be full of *Mobros,* all looking for a place to dump our trash. And yet here
we are, seven years later, and our landfills are not overflowing; our
waterways are not crowded with wandering barges. What happened to the
garbage crisis?

The environmental movement continues to focus its attention on 2
garbage and recycling, as if household garbage were the single most
important issue we face and recycling the only solution. Of course, garbage
does have an environmental impact; so does almost everything, from
prairie-grass fires to the breath you just took. But, contrary to the rhetoric
of some environmentalists, garbage is not a serious environmental hazard.
True hazards are ones that threaten human lives and health. There are
plenty of these, including toxic waste (which is quite distinct from household garbage), groundwater pollution, and urban smog. Compared with
these real crises, the problems of municipal garbage disposal pale. There
are times and places when household garbage *can* cause environmental
problems—like when toxic runoff leaches into drinking water—but these
are increasingly rare. Newer landfills are double-lined, piped, vented,
leachate-tested, and eventually capped. These new standards have made
current American waste management safer by far than ever before.

Some critics argue that we shouldn't downplay the threat of garbage 3
because of its symbolic value to the environmentalist agenda. Environmental organizations are well aware of the emotional power of garbage:
nothing can trigger a bounteous direct-mail response or inspire a powerful
grass-roots campaign like the threat of a new landfill or incineration plant.
But when symbols like the *Mobro* barge are used to divert attention and
money from more pressing environmental and social problems, the symbol
itself becomes a threat.

If there is a garbage crisis, it is that we are treating garbage as an 4
environmental threat and not as what it is: a manageable—though admit-
tedly complex—civic issue. Although many old urban landfills are reaching
their capacity, the reality is that there is—and always will be—plenty of
room in this country for safe landfill. We've chosen to look at garbage not
as a management issue, however, but as a moral crisis. The result is that

recycling is now seen as an irreproachable virtue, beyond the scrutiny of cost-benefit analysis. But in the real world, the money municipalities spend on recycling is money that can't be spent on schools, libraries, health clinics, and police. In the real world, the sort of gigantic recycling programs that many cities and towns have embarked upon may not be the best use of scarce government funds.

These programs were often sold to local taxpayers as money-saving 5 ventures. In fact, the costs associated with consumer education, separate pickup (often in newly purchased trucks), hand- and machine-sorting, transfer stations, trucking, cleaning, and reprocessing are considerably higher than initial estimates, far higher than receipts from buyers of recyclables, and, in many areas, higher than disposal costs.

Putting aside financial concerns, let's consider other justifications for 6 the recycling-above-all-else movement. Do we need recycling to extend the life of landfills? No. Landfill sites, in fact, are not scarce, and incineration remains a reasonable and safe option. The most ambitious collection programs still leave well over half of municipal waste to be disposed of, so recycling cannot completely replace disposal facilities, even if we needed it to.

Do we need recycling to save resources? No, not in the real world. The 7 reason recycling is unprofitable is that most of the materials being recycled are either renewable (paper from tree farms) or cheap and plentiful (glass from silica). Aluminum is profitable to recycle—and private concerns were already recycling it before the legislated mandates.

Recycling is beginning to lose its halo as its costs become apparent and 8 its effect on the volume of waste is found to be smaller than anticipated. Quotas and fines may force people to separate their trash, but they can't create industrial markets for the waste we recycle. Recycling can work, very effectively, on a region-by-region and commodity-by-commodity basis. But recycling as a government-mandated garbage-management option has largely failed.

Although the special attention we pay to garbage, to the exclusion of 9 more serious environmental threats, may be irrational, it does make a certain emotional sense. We as individuals are intimate with our trash, which makes it a more tangible issue than, say, groundwater contamination. Nobody particularly likes garbage; nobody likes taking it out or paying to have it hauled away. We feel we should be able to control it. Furthermore, controlling it—whether by banning plastics or sorting materials neatly at curbside—alleviates consumer guilt. "There," we say, tossing our bundled newspapers on the curb, "I've done my part for the environment."

But for all the psychological benefit that approach may confer, it is   10
distracting us from much more pressing national problems. Trash-handling
issues should be debated and decided regionally, and those decisions have
to be based, at least in part, on economics. That can't happen when one
option—recycling—is elevated by environmentalist rhetoric into a national
moral imperative. We have real environmental problems to worry about:
We have to protect the water supply. We must improve the quality of the
air we breathe. We need a better plan for energy management. And we have
to monitor toxic waste more effectively. In that context, it is foolish and
extremely wasteful to expend so much effort wringing our hands (and
spending our money) on garbage.

❀   ❀   ❀

AFTER YOU READ

THINK about the author's argument that the threat of a nation overwhelmed by garbage has "symbolic value to the environmentalist agenda."
Do you agree that this issue has been used as a symbol to generate support
for environmental causes? Can you think of other symbols that have been
used as persuasive tools in different types of arguments?

EXAMINE the credibility of the author. As the editor of a magazine entitled
Garbage, would you expect Poore to argue for or against the idea that
garbage disposal is a threat to the environment? Does her position as the
editor of this journal make her more or less credible on this issue? Why?

WRITE a summary of Poore's argument and then respond to her argument
by supporting it or arguing against it. Or WRITE an essay in which you
compare and contrast Poore's argument with the argument Wendell Berry
makes in "Waste."

What's Best for the West?

DAVID DIAMOND

This article provides an overview of the problem of land use in the West—that is, whether the wilderness land that still exists in the West should be "left to wildlife and hikers" or "devoted to economic survival."

BEFORE YOU READ

THINK about what you know about the wilderness areas of the West. Do you think these areas should be protected by the government or open to economic development? Why or why not?

EXAMINE a map that shows the wilderness land remaining in the West.

WRITE a journal entry in which you state your position on this issue.

AS YOU READ

Underline information or arguments that might lead you to revise your initial position on this issue.

It's just another sunny weekend in beautiful, war-torn southern Utah. 1
Long a source of solace and awe, the region's majestic cliffs and rugged
red canyons have become a battleground over the future of the nation's
fastest-growing region. This new war for the West is over wilderness itself:
how much should be left to wildlife and hikers, how much should be
devoted to economic survival.

Listen to His Honor Phil Bimstein, 47, a new wave composer who 2
serves as mayor of Springdale, Utah (population 350). At the moment, he
is scrambling up a salmon-colored cliff, pointing out land he says could be
flooded by a dam if Congress approves a growth bill backed by the Utah
delegation. "There are people who complain they can't sustain an economy
and the wilderness. But wilderness offers abundant economic benefits to
those who are willing to embrace and preserve it," says the Chicago native.

Some 100 miles east, a 77-year-old cowboy named Obie Shakespeare 3
is causing a traffic jam: running a herd of cattle down the center of scenic
state Highway 12, delaying visitors to Bryce Canyon National Park. "They
could make it zero acres of wilderness as far as I'm concerned," he says,
looking down from a black quarterhorse. "We want to make a living. We
don't want wilderness. They already got the parks. That ought to be
enough."

In Utah, where almost overnight the techies have outnumbered the 4
cowboys, the battle lines are clearly drawn. The outcome may redefine how
people live in the West, and how we as a nation view a region Americans
love to romanticize.

At stake: 22 million acres administered by the federal Bureau of Land 5
Management. Environmentalists want 5.7 million acres set aside as wilderness; the Utah congressional delegation has introduced legislation desig-
nating 1.8 million acres as wilderness, with the rest available for uses such
as mining, oil drilling, road construction and water development. (Mining
already is a $2 billion-a-year industry in Utah.) "There's got to be some
kind of boom" if more land is designated for development, says Paul Smith,
press secretary for Sen. Orrin Hatch, R-Utah. "But we don't know yet what
it will be."

The legislation . . . had the backing of mining, development, lumbering 6
and livestock interests; opponents included environmental organizations
such as the Wilderness Society. Passions are inflamed on both sides, and
words like "rape," "tyranny," and "pillage" are flying.

No wonder: "It's about the most beautiful chunk of real estate in the 7
world," says novelist Tony Hillerman, whose mysteries are often set in the

region. . . . "I've got a love affair with it." But because of air pollution, "you look across the Grand Canyon now, and it makes your heart sick."

The battle over Utah's wilderness—the largest remaining wild area in the   8 continental USA—could set a precedent for other states deciding the fate of expanses of undeveloped lands, including Pennsylvania, Missouri, Alaska, Minnesota, Tennessee, the Carolinas and Georgia.

"Particularly for rural counties that provide natural resources . . . the   9 designation of wilderness delays their ability to have a thriving economy and support the people who live there," argues William Perry Pendley of the Mountain States Legal Foundation, a non-profit conservative public interest law firm. Pendley is author of the . . . book *War on the West: Government Tyranny on America's Great Frontier.*

But Tom Dougherty of the National Wildlife Federation, the nation's   10 largest conservation organization, doesn't think that's what we should worry about. "To not designate truly unique areas as wilderness would terminate our ability to leave the only true gift that we still have for our children and our grandchildren. Pendley has demonstrated the typical mentality of former U.S. Secretary of the Interior James Watt, which mandates our need to rape and pillage every square inch of this country . . . to justify our existence. We don't have to exhaust every last resource on Earth."

The issue is particularly controversial in the Rocky Mountain states,   11 where a 10-year population boom has altered the landscape by planting rows of tract houses and outlet shopping centers up against mesas and buttes. The people responsible for that boom—families fleeing the tough crime and economy of Los Angeles, retirees escaping Buffalo winters, and computer-networking employees downsized out of jobs in Silicon Valley—expect the deserts and forests to show no evidence of human existence.

One need only fly into Las Vegas, drive into St. George, Utah, or spend a   12 few nights in the settlement of Springdale, at the gate of Zion National Park, to experience the profound changes taking place in the West. Las Vegas is making itself over as America's next great city, a family-friendly fantasyland built on infusions of money and water and air conditioning that seem unending. Take to the freeway on a sunbaked afternoon and you're reminded of Los Angeles in the blue-sky '50s: It feels as if the entire population of 1 million-plus is on the road at the same time.

The once quiet town of St. George is becoming a southern California 13
spinoff, too, complete with new ranch-style homes, new homeless people,
disaffected minimum-wage earners and Canadian real estate investors
checking out the potential along neon-bleached St. George Boulevard.

Then there is Springdale, a piece of paradise with a strip of well-land- 14
scaped motels, art galleries and its own Cinemax theater. To get breakfast
you can wait in line for a table with a retired couple who credit the Lord
for their marital success, or buy a quick muffin from a Deadhead who
knows the best hiking trails. (The Grateful Dead played Vegas last May.)
Springdale reflects the fusion that is occurring, with greater frequency than
ever, in every available and willing outpost. "What we have," mayor
Bimstein explains, "is a mix of latter-day hippies and Latter-day Saints
[Mormons]."

But while newcomers are drawn to places like Provo, Utah—headquar- 15
ters of the high-tech computer firm Novell—for its access to recreation,
open spaces and relatively fresh air, communities surrounding undeveloped
acreage now managed by the Bureau of Land Management have unemployment rates as high as 18 percent in the winter.

Growth isn't the problem in southern Utah's 4,020-population Gar- 16
field County: 92 percent of the land is owned by the U.S. government, and
6 percent is owned by the state. The county wants to open up as much land
as possible for development, particularly because it sits on deposits of coal,
uranium and claimable tar sands. "It's hard to swallow wanting to take the
land just for the hikers," says Louise Liston, 62, chairwoman of the county
commission. "It's a selfish position."

It sometimes seems only the Church of Jesus Christ of Latter-day 17
Saints, whose 1.4 million members in Utah represent most of the state's
1.9 million population, isn't taking sides. "We don't like to be perceived as
throwing our weight around," says church spokesman Clayton Newell.
Besides, he says, church members are split over the issue.

As is just about everyone. "It seems like the people in the cities want 18
to protect [wilderness] for themselves and their generation," says Kent
Alexander, 33, of Glendale, Utah, who sometimes works as a lumberman
and believes the Hatch bill would provide more work for him. But Ken
Rait of the Southern Utah Wilderness Alliance says proponents of
development are "looking at the future through a rear-view mirror." Only
2 percent of the state's total earnings, he says, now come from mining and
livestock grazing.

Novelist Hillerman confesses to mixed emotions. He wants mining 19
laws changed because "a lot of the most beautiful country and best streams
in the West are sold off to private owners through that system, barring us

plain folks from access." But he detects "Ivy League elitism" in environ-mentalists who champion vast, roadless tracts of wilderness: Hillerman suspects that their real fear is of "unwashed working-class people" and their "snotty-nosed kids" overrunning their treasured turf.

In Utah, it seems, the only terrain that's in short supply is common 20 ground.

❀ ❀ ❀

AFTER YOU READ

THINK about the arguments that are presented by people on both sides of this issue. Which do you find more convincing and why? Is it possible to take a position on this issue that is neither pro nor con? Is it ever a good idea to see an issue in terms of only two sides or a problem in terms of only a single solution?

EXAMINE the comments by Phil Bimstein, Obie Shakespeare, Paul Smith, Tony Hillerman, William Perry Pendley, Tom Dougherty, Louise Liston, Clayton Newell, Kent Alexander, and Ken Rait that are included in Diamond's article. Diamond identifies these people briefly, mainly by stating what they do and/or where they live. Review who they are and what position they are taking. List each on a sheet of paper as either for or against using wilderness areas for economic development. How convincing do you find their comments? Which of these people do you find most persuasive? Why?

WRITE an essay in which you take a stand on this issue and argue for a specific solution.

Is a Lab Rat's Fate More Poignant Than a Child's?

JANE McCABE

We Must Find Alternatives to Animals in Research

ROGER CARAS

These two articles, which present opposing viewpoints about using animals in research, appeared together in Newsweek. Jane McCabe, who lives with her husband and daughter Claire in northern California, writes from personal experience. In contrast, Roger Caras writes from a more scientific point of view. The author of over forty books for adults and children on nature and wildlife, Caras has been a guest or a host on numerous talk shows, such as "Tonight," and has appeared on "Today," "World News Tonight," "Good Morning, America," "20/20," and "Nightline." Currently, he reports on the environment and on animals for ABC-TV News.

BEFORE YOU READ

THINK about your own view on the use of animals in medical research. Do you think animals should be used in research for cures for human diseases such as cancer, heart disease, cystic fibrosis, Alzheimer's, and AIDS? Do you consider human rights more important than animal rights? Do you think scientists should strive for alternative methods of research?

EXAMINE the titles of these two articles. Do the titles suggest that these articles will be informative or persuasive? What approach and appeal do you think McCabe will make in her article? What approach and appeal do you think Caras will make? Will the methods of persuasion be similar or different?

WRITE a list of reasons for continuing animal research. Then write another list of reasons for discontinuing animal research or seeking alternate methods.

AS YOU READ

Decide which article appeals more to your emotions and which appeals more to your sense of reason. Then decide which appeal is more effective.

IS A LAB RAT'S FATE MORE POIGNANT
THAN A CHILD'S?

I see the debate about using animals in medical research in stark terms. 1
If you had to choose between saving a very cute dog or my equally cute, blond, brown-eyed daughter, whose life would you choose? It's not a difficult choice, is it? My daughter has cystic fibrosis. Her only hope for a normal life is that researchers, some of them using animals, will find a cure. Don't misunderstand. It's not that I don't love animals, it's just that I love Claire more.

Nine years ago I had no idea that I would be joining the fraternity of 2 those who have a vital interest in seeing that medical research continues. I was a very pregnant woman in labor; with my husband beside me I gave birth to a 7-pound 1-ounce daughter. It all seemed so easy. But for the next four months she could not gain weight. She was a textbook case of failure to thrive. Finally a hospital test of the salt content in her sweat led to the diagnosis of cystic fibrosis.

The doctor gave us a little reason for hope. "Your daughter will not 3 have a long life, but for most of the time, it will be a good life. Her life expectancy is about 13 years, though it could be longer or shorter. As research continues, we're keeping them alive longer."

"As research continues." It's not a lot to rely on but what's our 4 alternative? We haven't waited passively. We learned how to take care of our little girl; her medical problems affect her digestion and lungs. We protected her from colds, learned about supplemental vitamins and antibiotics. We moved to California where the winters aren't so harsh and the cold and flu season isn't so severe. Our new doctor told us that the children at his center were surviving, on the average, to age 21. So far, our daughter is doing well. She is a fast runner and plays a mean first base. She loves her friends and is, in general, a happy little girl. All things considered, I feel very lucky.

How has research using animals helped those with CF? Three times a 5 day my daughter uses enzymes from the pancreas of pigs to digest her food. She takes antibiotics tested on rats before they are tried on humans. As an adult, she will probably develop diabetes and need insulin—a drug developed by research on dogs and rabbits. If she ever needs a heart-lung transplant, one might be possible because of the cows that surgeons practiced on. There is no animal model to help CF research, but once the CF gene is located, new gene-splicing techniques may create a family of mice afflicted with the disease. Researchers would first learn to cure the mice with drugs, then cautiously try with humans.

There are only about 10,000 people with CF in the United States. But 6 the number of people dependent on research is much larger. Walk with me through Children's Hospital at Stanford University: here are the youngsters fighting cancer, rare genetic illnesses, immunological diseases. Amid their laughter and desperate attempts to retain a semblance of childhood, there is suffering.

I think the motivation of animal-rights activists is to cut down on the 7 suffering in this world, but I have yet to hear them acknowledge that people—young and old—suffer, too. Why is a laboratory rat's fate more poignant than that of an incurably ill child?

There are advocates for animals who only seek to cut down on 8 "unnecessary research." They don't specify how to decide what is unnecessary, but they do create an atmosphere in which doing medical research is seen as distasteful work. I think that's wrong. Researchers should be thanked, not hassled.

Every time I see a bumper sticker that says "Lab animals never have a 9 nice day," a fantasy plays in my brain. I get out of my car, tap on the driver's window and ask to talk. In my fantasy, the other driver gets out, we find a coffee shop and I show her photos of my kids. I ask her if she has ever visited Children's Hospital. I am so eloquent that her eyes fill with tears and she promises to think of the children who are wasting away as she considers the whole complicated issue of suffering.

I have other fantasies, too, that a cure is found for what ails my 10 daughter, that she marries and gives us some grandchildren, and does great work in her chosen profession, which at this moment appears to be cartooning or computer programming. We can still hope—as long as the research continues.

WE MUST FIND ALTERNATIVES TO
ANIMALS IN RESEARCH

I believe that animals have rights which, although different from our own, 1 are just as inalienable. I believe animals have the right not to have pain, fear or physical deprivation inflicted upon them by us. Even if they are on the way to the slaughterhouse, animals have the right to food and water and shelter if it is needed. They have the right not to be brutalized in any way as food resources, for entertainment or any other purpose.

Since animals must be classified as property if we are to have the power 2 of life and death over them (and we must, even over our pets), there is a vast philosophical/legal rift to be negotiated. No other property has rights, yet animals must. It is going to take some fine legal minds to work out the details so that we can get across that gulch.

One of the most difficult problems is our unrelenting use of animals 3 in biomedical research. Until recently the arguments between biomedical researchers and the humane movement centered on the conditions under which laboratory animals are maintained. Lately, in keeping with our "age of activism," it has become a raging name-calling contest over whether one species, ours, has the right to use other species to solve our own health problems. If tens of millions of people elect to smoke and expose themselves to the risks of cancer and heart disease, do we have the right to subject animals that would never smoke to those same cancers and heart diseases?

A great many researchers I have met would love to have alternatives. 4 They are against vivisection in spirit but believe that today's research protocols require—and grant money goes to—research involving animals. Often they are right. What's more, the use of animals in research is not limited to the good of humans. Vaccines used on animals were developed using animals. Animal-rights advocates who decry using animals for research on human diseases have not made it clear what models should have been used for canine distemper, parvovirus or feline leukemia.

Animal-rights activists say that far too little effort has gone into seeking 5 substitute methods such as cell culture and computer modeling. They are right. Finding a substitute for animals in research has only recently become an imperative in the scientific community. And that change has coincided with a change in the techniques employed by the militant animal-rights movement. When leaflets and picket signs were replaced by night raiders and bombers, science sat up and paid attention. Personally, I decry terrorism as the solution to any problem.

Many laboratories provide too little in the way of creature comforts 6 (no pun intended) for laboratory animals. That has to change and in many places it is. Jane Goodall has fought to upgrade the psychological environment provided for chimpanzees. For an animal as bright as a chimp (its genetic package varies from our own by no more than 1 percent, most researchers agree), boredom and lack of social interaction is nothing less than cruelty, according to Goodall.

Much of the research done on chimps involves their immune systems, 7 current work on AIDS being an obvious example. Since scientists know that stress alters any animal's power to respond to invading organisms, why do they stress chimps by confining them in isolation when the research protocol doesn't demand it?

What has happened is analogous to current geopolitical problems. 8 Everybody is so angry at everybody else nobody is really listening. The animal-rights groups are at odds with each other. That could be because they are all looking for the same membership dollars, the same bequests. Then, of course, there are the antivivisectionists vs. the provivisectionists. They are so busy shrieking at each other no one can be heard.

One day animals will not be used in the laboratory. How soon that day 9 comes depends on how soon people stop screaming and make the search for alternatives a major research imperative. As long as conferences on the subject sound like feeding time in the monkey house, monkeys along with millions of other animals are going to stay right where they are now—in the laboratory.

AFTER YOU READ

THINK about the difference in purpose in the two articles. How does each author suit his or her primary method of appeal to his or her purpose? Would a logical appeal have been as effective for McCabe's article as her emotional appeal? Would an emotional appeal have been as effective for Caras's article? Why or why not?

EXAMINE the details and examples that each writer uses. How do these details differ? Identify several of the most effective supporting details used by each author. Which details and examples are most convincing to you? Does either essay contain examples of weak or illogical reasoning?

WRITE a persuasive letter on the subject of animal research. You might write to the editor of *Newsweek,* the magazine in which these readings appeared. Or you might write to McCabe to try to convince her to support alternate methods of research or to Caras to try to convince him to support the use of animals in research. If possible, use your own personal knowledge and experiences as well as the knowledge you have gained from reading these articles.

Unit Six: Critical Thinking and Writing Assignments

❀   ❀   ❀

EXPLORING IDEAS TOGETHER

1. Discuss with a group of your classmates the significance of environment in establishing a healthy, productive life.

2. Based on the readings in this unit, make one list of reasons people give for believing that environmentalism has gone too far; then make a second list of reasons people give for believing that environmentalism hasn't gone far enough. What is your position? What is the position of the other members of your group?

3. With a small group of your classmates, discuss one of the controversial issues you have read about in this unit. For example, you could discuss whether farmers should be allowed to use pesticides to increase crop yield or whether the environment should be considered more or less important than the economic and health needs of human beings. Your class might even select one of these issues to debate, with the class divided into two teams.

WRITING ESSAYS

1. The Tewa chant at the beginning of this unit describes an environment friendly to humankind; the story by Louis Dollarhide, on the other hand, describes an environment that is hostile to humankind. Think about the different environments that you have experienced. In an essay, compare and contrast an environment that seems friendly to you with an environment that seems hostile to you. You could choose to compare two different places, or you could compare the same place under different conditions.

2. Write your own "fable for tomorrow" in which you envision a world that has solved all of its environmental problems. What would life be like in this world? How would this world differ from the world as you know it? From the world as described in Rachel Carson's fable?

3. The article by Wendell Berry focuses on what writer Alvin Toffler has called our society's "throwaway" mentality. Write an essay analyzing the causes of this throwaway mentality.

4. Write a brief narrative essay set in a world that has been overwhelmed by one of these environmental hazards: the greenhouse effect, acid

rain, or nuclear winter. Before you begin your narrative, brainstorm about your characters and major events. Who is the major character? With whom or what is this character in conflict? What is the high point, or climax, of your narrative? What is its main point, or theme?

5. Identify a local environmental issue that you can investigate or that you already know something about. Then write an informative or persuasive essay on this topic.

6. Write an essay in which you respond to one of the reading selections in this unit. You may agree or disagree with the author's position. Begin your essay by summarizing briefly the essay to which you are responding. Be sure you identify the title and author's name in your summary.

Self with Technology

This unit focuses on your relationship to something that is not living—to the machines and gadgets that you use each day and perhaps take for granted. Your days and nights are filled with machines that make your life easier and more pleasant. An alarm clock or radio wakes you each morning, a coffeemaker brews your coffee, a dishwasher washes the mug, a hair dryer styles your hair, a car or bus or truck transports you to school or work, a radio or stereo keeps you company during the day, computers perform many of the routine tasks that you once did manually, a washing machine launders your clothes, a microwave or at least a stove cooks your dinner, a television entertains you in the evening, and a VCR may even record shows for you while you sleep.

Technology affects not only how you live your life but how you relate to other people. As a teenager, you probably spent countless hours with your friends riding around in a car or talking about cars. You maintain long-distance relationships by talking on the telephone or sending messages by e-mail or fax machines. And if your family is typical, you gather around a television set in the evenings. In fact, the television set has become the focal point of many homes, replacing the fireplace and kitchen table that once served this purpose.

In addition to the role that technology assumes in your relationships with other people, you may also establish relationships with certain ma-

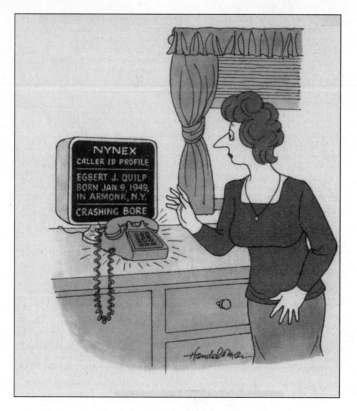

Drawing by Handelsman, © 1994 The New Yorker Magazine, Inc.

chines. You may not have thought of machines as something with which you could have a relationship, and certainly you do not relate to machines in the same way that you do to people, yet there are similarities. Although many of the machines you use may evoke little emotional response from you, some you may love or hate. For example, do you remember your first bicycle or car or stereo and how you loved it? Or your excitement when you first had a telephone of your own? Perhaps you are one of millions of Americans who depend on the television to keep you company. Or you may have caught yourself actually talking to your computer.

But all of your relationships with machines may not be love relationships. You may also hate certain machines—the computer that has a mind of its own, the car that won't start, the toaster that always burns your toast, the vending machine that robs you of your money. Although machines are usually designed to make your life easier, they may also, on occasion, make your life frustrating if not miserable. Machines certainly contribute to much that is bad in our lives: Guns contribute to the high crime rate; automobiles increase air pollution and cause accidents; computers reduce human interaction to blips on a screen; and machines in general often put people out of work. Yet no one is eager to do without machines. Having become used to them, to the convenience and entertainment and stimulation they provide, people cannot imagine a life in which machines do not play a major role.

So it is likely that you will continue your love/hate relationship with technology—occasionally even loving and hating the same form of technology at different times. This unit explores those relationships. Some of the reading selections focus on the close, almost intimate relationships some people establish with the machines that are important to them. Others tell of negative feelings that machines and technology in general evoke in people at times. And still others explain the effects, both positive and negative, that technology has on our society.

As you prepare to read the selections in this unit, think about your own attitude toward machines. Is there a particular machine or form of technology that you love? Do you think males relate better to technology than do females? If you could keep only one machine, which one would it be? In general, are you a gadget-lover or a gadget-hater? To answer this last question, do the following exercise: On a blank piece of paper, write your name in the center and draw a circle around it. Now write on the paper, around your name, all of the gadgets and machines that you use routinely. Circle those that you view positively and draw a box around those that you view negatively. Now determine whether your relationship with technology is generally positive or negative.

As you read the selections in this unit, your attitude toward technology may change. You should begin to understand more clearly the force that technology represents in your life and how it shapes your life.

At the Electronic Frontier

MIGUEL ALGARIN

Born in Puerto Rico in 1941, Miguel Algarin has had a varied career as not only a poet but also a playwright, director, editor, and teacher. In this poem, Algarin describes what it means to be a "child of the Electronic Frontier."

BEFORE YOU READ

THINK about what it means to be living in an age in which electronic products are increasingly sophisticated and commonplace. Everyone thinks at times about how different life would be if electricity had not been invented. But think also about how electronic marvels have shaped the kind of person you are.

EXAMINE the word *frontier.* What connotations do you have with this word? Are they positive or negative? What image is evoked by the term *electronic frontier*?

WRITE a journal entry in which you describe in detail how a specific machine or electronic product defines your generation.

AS YOU READ

Notice the specific details and images the poet includes in his description.

I search the chemistry of specific emotions,   1
a combination of earth and air
that evokes the vital detail,
the phrase that heats the frying pan,
the look that smiles,   5
offering signals that localize,
where I am, and clarify what I see.
I'm child of the Electronic Frontier.
I learn off the radio waves
of 98.7 Kiss F.M. salsa/disco jams,   10
that come from a Sony,
bought even though I need a coat,
even though I'm behind on my payments
for the Trinitron Remote Control Color T.V.
that I picked up at Crazy Eddie's last month.   15
I'm child of the Columbia Space Shuttle,
and I need to know all the electronic gimmicks
invented yesterday
that are already primitive cousins
to those developed today   20
from eight to five P.M. in Japan.

❀ ❀ ❀

AFTER YOU READ

THINK about the *electronic frontier,* and compare and contrast it to other frontiers (e.g., the Western frontier of the past or the frontier of outer space).

EXAMINE the four sentences that make up this poem. Which one is the shortest? Why do you think this sentence is unlike the other three?

WRITE a poem that begins "I'm a child of the ."

Living with My VCR

NORA EPHRON

*Nora Ephron has written novels, screenplays, and news-
paper columns. Her writing is often about humorous
situations or about common daily experiences in which
she finds humor. Ephron is not afraid to include herself in
her work. In this essay, which first appeared in the* New
York Times, *she describes her love/hate relationship with
her videocassette recorder (VCR).*

BEFORE YOU READ

THINK about the popularity of VCRs and the effect they have on our
society. How have they affected the way people spend their time and
money? How have they affected the television and movie industries? How
have they affected your life?

EXAMINE the words used in this essay that are part of the growing video
vocabulary: *VCR, videocassette, Home Box Office, Cinemax, Video Review,
Video Village, heads, videotape, time record, channel selector,* and so forth.
How many of these terms do you recognize?

WRITE in your journal about a machine that you both love and hate. List
the reasons that the machine evokes both emotions in you.

AS YOU READ

Try to determine why Ephron both loves and hates her VCR. Which
emotion is stronger? How do you think her affair with her VCR will end?

W hen all this started, two Christmases ago, I did not have a video- 1 cassette recorder. What I had was a position on video-cassette recorders. I was against them. It seemed to me that the fundamental idea of the VCR—which is that if you go out and miss what's on television, you can always watch it later—flew in the face of almost the only thing I truly believed—which is that the whole point of going out is to miss what's on television. Let's face it: Part of being a grown-up is that every day you have to choose between going out at night or staying home, and it is one of life's unhappy truths that there is not enough time to do both.

Finally, though, I broke down, but not entirely. I did not buy a 2 video-cassette recorder. I rented one. And I didn't rent one for myself—I myself intended to stand firm and hold to my only principle. I rented one for my children. For $29 a month, I would tape "The Wizard of Oz" and "Mary Poppins" and "Born Free," and my children would be able to watch them from time to time. In six months, when my rental contract expired, I would re-evaluate.

For quite a while, I taped for my children. Of course I had to subscribe 3 to Home Box Office and Cinemax in addition to my normal cable service, for $19 more a month—but for the children. I taped "Oliver" and "Annie" and "My Fair Lady" for the children. And then I stopped taping for the children—who don't watch much television, in any case—and started to tape for myself.

I now tape for myself all the time. I tape when I am out, I tape when 4 I am at home and doing other things, and I tape when I am asleep. At this very moment, as I am typing, I am taping. The entire length of my bedroom bookshelf has been turned over to video cassettes, mostly of movies; they are numbered and indexed and stacked in order in a household where absolutely nothing else is. Occasionally I find myself browsing through publications like *Video Review* and worrying whether I shouldn't switch to chrome-based videotape or have my heads cleaned or upgrade to a machine that does six or seven things at once and can be set to tape six or seven months in advance. No doubt I will find myself shopping at some Video Village for racks and storage systems especially made for what is known as "the serious collector."

How this happened, how I became a compulsive videotaper, is a 5 mystery to me, because my position on video-cassette recorders is very much the same as the one I started with. I am still against them. Now, though, I am against them for different reasons: Now I hate them out of knowledge rather than ignorance. The other technological break-throughs that have made their way into my life after my initial pigheaded opposition to them—like the electric typewriter and the Cuisinart—have all settled peacefully into my home. I never think about them except when I'm using them, and when I'm using them I take them for granted. They do exactly what I want them to do. I put the slicing disk into the Cuisinart, and damned if the thing doesn't slice things up just the way it's supposed to. But there's no taking a VCR for granted. It squats there, next to the television, ready to rebuke any fool who expects something of it.

A child can operate a VCR, of course. Only a few maneuvers are 6 required to tape something, and only a few more are required to tape something while you are out. You must set the time to the correct time you wish the recording to begin and end. You must punch the channel selector. You must insert a videotape. And, on my set, you must switch the "on" button to "time record." Theoretically, you can then go out and have a high old time, knowing that even if you waste the evening, your video-cassette recorder will not.

Sometimes things work out. Sometimes I return home, rewind the tape, 7 and discover that the machine has recorded exactly what I'd hoped it would. But more often than not, what is on the tape is not at all what I'd intended; in fact, the moments leading up to the revelation of what is actually on my video-cassettes are without doubt the most suspenseful of my humdrum existence. As I rewind the tape, I have no idea of what, if anything, will be on it; as I press the "play" button, I have not a clue as to what in particular has gone wrong. All I ever know for certain is that something has.

Usually it's my fault. I admit it. I have misset the timer or channel 8 selector or misread the newspaper listing. I have knelt at the foot of my machine and methodically, carefully, painstakingly set it—and set it wrong. This is extremely upsetting to me—I am normally quite competent when it comes to machines—but I can live with it. What is far more disturbing are the times when what has gone wrong is not my fault at all but the fault of outside forces over which I have no control whatsoever. The program listing in the newspaper lists the channel incorrectly. The cable guide inaccurately lists the length of the movie, lopping off the last 10 minutes. The evening's schedule of television programming is thrown off by an athletic event. The educational station is having a fund-raiser.

You would be amazed at how often outside forces affect a video- 9 cassette recorder, and I think I am safe in saying that video-cassette recorders are the only household appliances that outside forces are even relevant to. As a result, my video-cassette library is a raggedy collection of near misses: "The Thin Man" without the opening; "King Kong" without the ending; a football game instead of "Murder, She Wrote"; dozens of PBS auctions and fundraisers instead of dozens of episodes of "Masterpiece Theater." All told, my success rate at videotaping is even lower than my success rate at buying clothes I turn out to like as much as I did in the store; the machine provides more opportunities per week to make mistakes than anything else in my life.

Every summer and at Christmastime, I re-evaluate my six-month rental 10 contract. I have three options: I can buy the video-cassette recorder, which I would never do because I hate it so much; I can cancel the contract and turn in the machine, which I would never do because I am so addicted to videotaping; or I can go on renting. I go on renting. In two years I have spent enough money renting to buy two video-cassette recorders at the discount electronics place in the neighborhood, but I don't care. Renting is my way of deluding myself that I have some power over my VCR; it's my way of believing that I can still some day reject the machine in an ultimate way (by sending it back)—or else forgive it (by buying it)—for all the times it has rejected me.

In the meantime, I have my pathetic but ever-expanding collection of 11 cassettes. "Why don't you just rent the movies?" a friend said to me recently, after I finished complaining about the fact that my tape of "The Maltese Falcon" now has a segment of "Little House on the Prairie" in the middle of it. Rent them? What a bizarre suggestion. Then I would have to watch them. And I don't watch my videotapes. I don't have time. I would virtually have to watch my videotapes for the next two years just to catch up with what my VCR has recorded so far; and in any event, even if I did have time, the VCR would be taping and would therefore be unavailable for use in viewing.

So I merely accumulate video-cassettes. I haven't accumulated any- 12 thing this mindlessly since my days in college, when I was obsessed with filling my bookshelf, it didn't matter with what; what mattered was that I believed that if I had a lot of books, it would say something about my intelligence and taste. On some level, I suppose I believe that if I have a lot of video-cassettes, it will say something—not about my intelligence or taste, but about my intentions. I intend to live long enough to have time to watch my videotapes. Any way you look at it, that means forever.

❀ ❀ ❀

AFTER YOU READ

THINK about your own reaction to VCRs. Do you see them as a mere convenience about which you have no strong feelings? Or can you sympathize with Ephron's "addiction"? Are there other machines to which you, like Ephron, have become addicted?

EXAMINE the titles of movies and television programs that Ephron includes in her essay. Are you familiar with these titles, most of which are now considered classics? Would the essay make as much sense if you did not know something about them? What does her inclusion of these particular titles tell you about the author? Would your attitude toward the author be different if she had included titles of movies and programs that you knew nothing about or that were clearly Grade B slasher movies, X-rated films, or inane, tasteless comedies?

WRITE a summary of the reasons Ephron both loves and hates her VCR. You might begin with a short introductory paragraph stating the author, the title of the essay, and the author's thesis. Then continue with a paragraph summarizing Ephron's reasons for *loving* her VCR and another paragraph summarizing her reasons for *hating* it. Conclude with a paragraph in which you state your own response to the essay or to VCRs.

Television Addiction

MARIE WINN

We hear a great deal these days about different forms of addiction, but we don't usually think of our television viewing habits as a form of addiction. However, Marie Winn, who was born in Czechoslovakia and educated at Radcliffe, suggests just that in her book Television: The Plug-in Drug. *This reading selection, in which Winn defines television addiction, was taken from that book.*

BEFORE YOU READ

THINK about your own television viewing habits. How many hours a day do you typically spend in front of a television set? How would you react if you suddenly had to give up watching television? Would you describe yourself as television dependent or television addicted?

EXAMINE the words *passive* and *enervated,* which Winn uses to describe certain types of television viewers. A *passive* person is not involved or not active, and to be *enervated* means to be physically weakened. Do these words have negative connotations? That is, do they suggest negative rather than positive qualities?

WRITE in your journal a brief description of a person who is addicted to television. How does this person (yourself or someone you know) think, look, and act? How does this person react to others?

AS YOU READ

Focus on Winn's comparison of television addiction to other types of addiction. Mark the text as you read to highlight her definition of television addiction.

The word "addiction" is often used loosely and wryly in conversation. 1
People will refer to themselves as "mystery book addicts" or "cookie addicts." E. B. White writes of his annual surge of interest in gardening: "We are hooked and are making an attempt to kick the habit." Yet nobody really believes that reading mysteries or ordering seeds by catalogue is serious enough to be compared with addictions to heroin or alcohol. The word "addiction" is here used jokingly to denote a tendency to overindulge in some pleasurable activity.

People often refer to being "hooked on TV." Does this, too, fall into 2 the lighthearted category of cookie eating and other pleasures that people pursue with unusual intensity, or is there a kind of television viewing that falls into the more serious category of destructive addiction?

When we think about addiction to drugs or alcohol, we frequently 3 focus on negative aspects, ignoring the pleasures that accompany drinking or drug-taking. And yet the essence of any serious addiction is a pursuit of pleasure, a search for a "high" that normal life does not supply. It is only the inability to function without the addictive substance that is dismaying, the dependence of the organism upon a certain experience and an increasing inability to function normally without it. Thus a person will take two or three drinks at the end of the day not merely for the pleasure drinking provides, but also because he "doesn't feel normal" without them.

Real addicts do not merely pursue a pleasurable experience one time 4 in order to function normally. They need to *repeat* it again and again. Something about that particular experience makes life without it less than complete. Other potentially pleasurable experiences are no longer possible, for under the spell of the addictive experience, their lives are peculiarly distorted. The addict craves an experience and yet is never really satisfied. The organism may be temporarily sated, but soon it begins to crave again.

Finally a serious addiction is distinguished from a harmless pursuit of 5 pleasure by its distinctly destructive elements. Heroin addicts, for instance, lead damaged lives: their increasing need for heroin in increasing doses prevents them from working, from maintaining relationships, from developing in human ways. Similarly alcoholics' lives are narrowed and dehumanized by their dependence on alcohol.

Let us consider television viewing in the light of the conditions that 6 define serious addictions.

Not unlike drugs or alcohol, the television experience allows the 7 participant to blot out the real world and enter into a pleasurable and passive mental state. The worries and anxieties of reality are as effectively deferred by becoming absorbed in a television program as by going on a "trip" induced by drugs or alcohol. And just as alcoholics are only vaguely aware of their addiction, feeling that they control their drinking more than they really do ("I can cut it out any time I want—I just like to have three or four drinks before dinner"), people similarly overestimate their control over television watching. Even as they put off other activities to spend hour after hour watching television, they feel they could easily resume living in a different, less passive style. But somehow or other while the television set is present in their homes, the click doesn't sound. With television pleasures available, those other experiences seem less attractive, more difficult somehow.

A heavy viewer (a college English instructor) observes: "I find televi- 8 sion almost irresistible. When the set is on, I cannot ignore it. I can't turn it off. I feel sapped, will-less, enervated. As I reach out to turn off the set, the strength goes out of my arms. So I sit there for hours and hours."

Self-confessed television addicts often feel they "ought" to do other 9 things—but the fact that they don't read and don't plant their garden or sew or crochet or play games or have conversations means that those activities are no longer as desirable as television viewing. In a way the lives of heavy viewers are as imbalanced by their television "habit" as a drug addict's or an alcoholic's. They are living in a holding pattern, as it were, passing up the activities that lead to growth or development or a sense of accomplishment. This is one reason people talk about their television viewing so ruefully, so apologetically. They are aware that it is an unproductive experience, that almost any other endeavor is more worthwhile by any human measure.

Finally it is the adverse effect of television viewing on the lives of so 10 many people that defines it as a serious addiction. The television habit distorts the sense of time. It renders other experiences vague and curiously unreal while taking on a greater reality for itself. It weakens relationships by reducing and sometimes eliminating normal opportunities for talking, for communicating.

And yet television does not satisfy, else why would the viewer continue 11 to watch hour after hour, day after day? "The measure of health," writes Lawrence Kubie, "is flexibility . . . and especially the freedom to cease when sated."* But heavy television viewers can never be sated with their television experiences—these do not provide the true nourishment that satiation requires—and thus they find that they cannot stop watching.

---

*Lawrence Kubie, *Neurotic Distortion and the Creative Process* (Lawrence: University of Kansas Press, 1958).

AFTER YOU READ

THINK about television viewing as a form of addiction. How is it like other addictions? How is it different? In what ways is it more harmful than other addictions? In what ways is it less harmful?

EXAMINE Winn's assertion that "the essence of any serious addiction is a pursuit of pleasure, a search for a 'high' that normal life does not supply." What other forms of addiction can be viewed as "pursuits of pleasure"? According to Winn, when does an innocent pursuit of pleasure become a destructive addiction?

WRITE an argument *against* Winn's thesis that extensive and habitual television viewing is a form of addiction.

Technology and the Hearing Impaired

TAMMY HOLM

The semester Tammy Holm wrote the following essay, she was enrolled in both a composition course and an audiology course. She was able to use the information she had learned in the audiology course to write an essay for her composition course. Her essay explains how technology has both hurt and helped people with hearing impairments.

BEFORE YOU READ

THINK about the noise pollution created by different forms of technology. What effects can result from noise pollution?

EXAMINE the way in which Holm defines technical terms in the context of her essay. For example, in the second paragraph she includes the following sentence:

> Located in the middle ear is the eardrum and a number of tiny bones which convey the vibrations of the noise to the cochlea.

In the next sentence, she defines the term *cochlea:*

> The cochlea is a spinal canal in the inner ear that is lined with thousands of cells with microscopic hairs.

Does her definition help you understand the process she is describing?

WRITE a journal entry in which you identify a particular form of technology (for example, automobiles, telephones, computers) and explain how it both helps and hurts people.

AS YOU READ

Notice that Holm defines the technical terms she uses.

In 1989, 22 million Americans had lost some or all of their hearing. Some   1
of this hearing loss is due to genetic defects, damage to the developing
fetus, infections, physical problems, and the natural process of aging, but
more and more cases of hearing loss are due to the loud noises Americans'
ears are exposed to daily.

Diesel trucks, loud music, and factory machinery are all examples of   2
noises we hear daily that cause damage to our hearing. The noises travel
to the middle ear via the ear canal. Located in the middle ear is the eardrum
and a number of tiny bones which convey the vibrations of the noise to the
cochlea. The cochlea is a spinal canal in the inner ear that is lined with
thousands of cells with microscopic hairs. The response of the cells to the
noise causes the hairs to vibrate. These hairs are the stimulant of the
auditory nerves. When the nerves are stimulated, they send the message to
the areas of the brain that are responsible for sound perception. The loud
noises we expose our ears to damage the tiny hairs. When these hairs are
damaged, the high frequencies are not sensed and the auditory nerve is not
stimulated. This lack of stimulation stops the message of high frequencies
from arriving at the brain. The damage may be immediate or it may develop
slowly. It may also be temporary or permanent. Repeated exposure to loud
noises may enhance the hearing loss associated with age.

Even though technological advances indirectly cause some hearing   3
loss, they can also be the cure or a source of improvement for hearing loss.
Technological advances have been used to develop a more advanced
hearing aid called the Phoenix. New improvements in technology have also
led to the development of a cochlear transplant. Other advancements
include the use of computers to help hearing impaired people learn to speak
and make phone calls and the development of closed caption for television
viewing purposes.

First, the Phoenix hearing aid helps a person hear higher frequencies   4
such as some consonants in speech. With hearing aids developed before the
Phoenix, a person would hear lower frequencies such as an air conditioner
and the quiet conversation of other patrons in a restaurant over the spoken
words of the person's companion. The difference between the Phoenix and
other hearing aids is that the Phoenix has a computer circuitry which
analyzes the incoming sounds to determine their frequency, rhythms, and

loudness. Then it suppresses background noise and enhances speech by using the results from the analysis. Even though the Phoenix costs more and is bulkier, it works better than regular hearing aids.

If a person's hearing loss is so great that a digital hearing aid such as 5 the Phoenix does not improve hearing, the person may want to consider a cochlear transplant. A cochlear transplant is an electronic prosthesis that acts as a substitute for hair cells that have been damaged by loud noises or other causes. When a person has a cochlear transplant, a microphone is worn behind the ear. The microphone transmits sounds to a computer, which then transforms the sound into an electronic signal. The signal is sent to a device located behind the ear and then to one or more of the twenty-two electrodes implanted in the cochlea. The electrodes function like hairs, protruding out of the cells and stimulating the auditory nerves. The stimulation causes the sounds to be perceived. The sounds may be distorted, but people report that there is improvement in the sounds they hear.

With the help of the cochlear transplant, people who lost their hearing 6 after they learned to speak may be able to learn to speak again by the use of sensors and computers. Hearing impaired people are fitted with sensors that are placed on their nose and inside their mouth. A speech pathologist is fitted with these same types of sensors. The sensors are hooked to a computer that generates an image on a video screen which illustrates the vibration of the speech pathologist's nose, the tongue position within the mouth, and the intensity of the speech pathologist's voice when he or she speaks sounds or words. The hearing impaired person then tries to duplicate the items on the video screen.

Once hearing impaired people learn to speak, they can communicate 7 via telephone with the use of a keyboard that allows messages to be sent over the telephone lines to a small videoscreen or a printer. In addition, they need a telecommunication device for the deaf (T.D.D.). At one time, both people communicating had to have the T.D.D., but now an operator acts as a go-between for someone using the T.D.D. and someone with a normal phone. The hearing impaired person types a message into the T.D.D., and this message appears on the operator's computer. The operator then reads the message to the other person, who types a response back to the hearing impaired person's T.D.D.

Another technological advancement is closed caption, the process of 8 displaying dialogue on a television screen. A digital code, activated by a computer chip, prints the words of the television show on the screen. Closed caption has become more available in the past ten years due to the

Television Decoder Circuitry Act, passed by Congress in 1990. The act states that any television set with a screen larger than 33 centimeters (13 inches) must have a built-in closed caption decoder by July 1, 1993. After this time, any production without the decoder will be declared illegal.

By reducing the noises we hear to under ninety decibels or by taking 9 simple precautions such as wearing ear plugs when working around loud equipment, we can prevent damage to our hearing. The inconveniences of hearing loss far outweigh the inconveniences of prevention. The sense of hearing is important for survival and should be taken care of just as we take care of our lives. More and more advances are being developed every year to improve hearing problems that could have been prevented, but they are expensive and do not always cure the problem. Prevention is the only one hundred percent cure for hearing impairments.

❁   ❁   ❁

AFTER YOU READ

THINK about both the positive and negative effects of technology on not just the hearing impaired but everyone in our society. Do the positive effects outweigh the negative ones? Why or why not?

EXAMINE the causes of hearing loss that Holm identifies in paragraph 2. Which of these noises have you experienced? Can you identify other noises that could lead to hearing loss?

WRITE an essay in which you argue that some form of technology has been detrimental to our society in general or to some segment of society. In your introduction, explain its benefits to society and then in the body of your essay argue that it has also had harmful effects.

Lonely Hearts, Classy Dreams, Empty Wallets

AMY WALDMAN

This article was first published in The Washington Monthly. *In the article the author, Amy Waldman, describes how home shopping channels prey on people's hunger for companionship. Although she does not state an argument, she clearly suggests that there is something unethical about the way these programs take advantage of people who are lonely.*

BEFORE YOU READ

THINK about why people buy products offered for sale on home shopping networks. EXAMINE one of these programs or infomercials, analyzing the appeals it uses to convince people to buy.

WRITE a journal entry in which you speculate about who is most likely to buy a product in this way.

AS YOU READ

Underline the sentences that tell you how much money people spend on products sold by home shopping channels.

After a man died several months ago at the Virginian Retirement 1
Community in Fairfax, his family went to collect his worldly goods.
They found more than they bargained for: His home was crammed, floor
to ceiling, with possessions they never knew he had. There were kitchen
gadgets, costume jewelry, bed linens, and cleansers, all by the dozens.

He had bought it all from the world's most accessible stores: the home 2
shopping networks that came through his television into his living room
24 hours a day, seven days a week. This man, whose name the retirement
home withheld for privacy, ordered a package from QVC or Home
Shopping Network (HSN), the two leading home shopping channels,
almost every day. Some of what came he gave away. Most of it simply piled
up, unused.

What had brought him to line his walls with the fruits of home 3
shopping? In a word, companionship. Home shopping hosts didn't just sell
to him—they spoke to him. An employee at the Virginian recalls that the
man spent a lot of time by himself. He did not make friends easily and he
spoke of being lonely. But when he bought, he said he could keep operators
chatting to him for half an hour. He had found a way to fill his days and
sleepless nights.

He was not alone in his discovery. As the hours cycle past on home 4
shopping channels, the disembodied voices of buyers, calling in to offer
"testimonials" on their purchases, float above the sparkling descriptions of
cubic zirconium jewelry. Most are female—Dorothy from Daytona, Betty
from Fresno, Helen from Mexico City, Indiana. Many of the voices are
beginning to crack with age. And their extraordinary enthusiasm for the
products—and the hosts, and the show itself—masks something else: a
deep, abiding need for human contact. "I live alone," says a woman named
Erma who calls in on a Monday morning. "All I've got to do is watch QVC."

To Erma, the man from Virginia, and many others like them, home 5
shopping channels sold more than $3 billion of goods last year. QVC, which
stands for Quality Value Control, alone sold $1.4 billion worth of goods
in 1994, logging 55 million phone calls. The channel is the world's largest
purveyor of gold jewelry. It once sold $1.4 million worth of Kodak products
in 70 minutes and $1.9 million of Mighty Morphin Power Rangers
paraphernalia in two hours. In a record day, it took $18 million in orders.
The second-place Home Shopping Network, or "Club" (as it's known on
the air), nearly matches that pace.

That the two channels, and a host of smaller rivals, could do so well 6
runs counter to conventional wisdom, for in an age of ironic, sophisticated
advertising, the home shopping pitch seems amateurish. The camera zooms

in on an item, which rocks back and forth, back and forth on a pedestal; the hosts, in living-room sets, praise each bauble in a frenzy of superlatives. A clock counts down to whip up a sense of urgency as the number sold mounts on the screen. The suggested retail price hovers above the low, low home shopping price.

Many of the goods—imitation jewelry, collectibles, gadgets, polyester 7 pantsuits—are junk, often selling at more-than-junk prices. And while "convenience" is a favorite home shopping buzzword, the description could not be less apt: It might take hours, even days, of home shopping viewing to come upon something you need.

Spend some time in front of the television, though, and you sense that 8 while the pitch is predictable, it is anything but amateurish. As low-tech as they are, the home shopping networks understand that the real work of advertising is not to publicize bargains—it is to appeal to deeper needs. They turn their constant, mesmerizing presence and viewer participation into a mock community, a "universe," as QVC calls it, that seems to break the isolation television perpetuates. And even for those who are not lonely, home shopping promises something else: the lives of the rich, the famous, the glamorous—on the cheap, and just a phone call away.

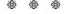

AFTER YOU READ

THINK about the ethical issue involved in selling products to people who buy not because they need what is being sold but because they need someone to talk to.

EXAMINE the sentences you underlined that include information about the amount of money involved in this type of merchandising. Are the people running the home shopping networks likely to change their strategies when the results are so profitable? Should there be some restrictions on these programs, or would restrictions be a form of censorship?

WRITE an essay in which you argue that home shopping networks should be (1) abolished, (2) allowed to continue but restricted, (3) allowed to continue as they are, or (4) commended because they are giving lonely people some form of companionship, even if it is at a price.

ERROR ERROR ERROR

DAVE BARRY

Dave Barry is a Pulitzer Prize–winning columnist. His humorous syndicated columns appear in newspapers across the country. Barry often focuses on the frustrations of daily life, as in this essay in which he describes his experience with computers. His description is obviously exaggerated to achieve a humorous effect, but the frustration he describes is real to anyone who has used a computer.

BEFORE YOU READ

THINK about how often you hear the expressions "computer error" or "the computer is down." How many different situations can you think of in which these reasons have been given to you to explain a delay or a problem involving computers?

EXAMINE the way in which Barry uses quotation marks not only to indicate what he says to the computer but also to indicate what the computer responds. Notice that marks of punctuation are placed within quotation marks.

WRITE a journal entry in which you describe and analyze your own attitude toward computers. For example, you might describe your reaction to operating a computer or to your name being on a computerized list. Or you might describe how it feels to be told that "the computer is down" when you are trying to make a hotel or airline reservation or to pay a bill. Then you might analyze why you react as you do in such situations. Does using a computer give you a sense of power or frustrate you? Do you enjoy and feel comfortable with computers, or do they frighten and/or intimidate you?

AS YOU READ

Notice the ways in which Barry personifies the computer—that is, the ways in which he makes it seem like a person.

W ithout question the most important invention in human history, next 1
to frozen yogurt, is the computer. Without computers, it would be virtually impossible for us to accomploiwur xow;gkc,mf(&(

Hold it, there seems to be a keyboard problem here. Let me just try 2 plugging this cable into . . .

ERROR ERROR ERROR ALL FILES HAVE BEEN DESTROYED 3 YOU STUPID BAZOOTYHEAD

Ha ha! Considering what a wonderful invention computers are, they 4 certainly have a way of making you sometimes feel like pouring coffee into their private parts and listening to them scream. Of course you should not do this. The first rule of data processing is: "Never pour hot beverages into a computer, unless it belongs to somebody else, such as your employer."

For many of us, the first "hands-on" experience with computers occurs 5 in the workplace. This was certainly true in the newspaper business. One day we reporters came to work and discovered that our old, slow, horse-drawn typewriters had been replaced by sleek, efficient computers with keys that said mysterious scary things like "BREAK" and "NUM LOCK." Fortunately we were trained by highly skilled professional computer personnel who spoke no English. "Before you macro your ASCII, you have to format your RAM," they would advise us, in a tone of voice clearly suggesting that any member of the vegetable family should know this instinctively.

So we reporters were wary at first, but after just 175 weeks of training, 6 we discovered that, instead of writing on clumsy, old-fashioned paper, we could create lengthy stories entirely on the computer screen, and then, simply by pushing a button, send them to the Planet Zembar. Or maybe even farther. We definitely couldn't find them anywhere in the building.

"WHERE THE HELL IS MY STORY??" we would say, shaking the 7 computer personnel by their necks. But the lost stories always turned out to be our own fault. We had invariably committed some basic bonehead data-processing error such as—you are going to laugh when I tell you this—failing to modem our ROM BIOS VGA megahertz cache.

But gradually we got the hang of it, and today we journalists routinely 8 use highly sophisticated, multimillion-dollar computer systems to perform a function that is vital to the survival of a free society, namely, sending personal messages to each other. Walk into a newspaper, and you'll see serious-looking journalists clattering away on their keyboards; it looks as though they're writing important stories about the plight of the Kurds, but in fact they're sending each other the joke about what the male giraffe said to the female giraffe in the bar. In the old days, journalists had to transmit jokes manually.

Also computers now have "spell-checkers," which enable us to catch 9 and correct common misspellings such as "bazootiehead."

Of course there are some problems. You have probably read about 10 computer "viruses," which computers get when they're left uncovered in drafty rooms. This is bad, because if you're working on an infected computer, it will periodically emit electronic sneezes, which unfortunately are not detectable by the naked eye—the word "ACHOO" appears on the screen for less than a millionth of a second—and you'll be showered with billions of tiny invisible pieces of electronic phlegm, called "bytes," which penetrate into your brain and gradually make you stupid.

This is definitely happening to me. I'll sit down at my home computer 11 to write a thoughtful column about, say, foreign policy, and I'll type: "In view of the recent dramatic changes in the world geopolitical situation, it's time to play some solitaire." My computer has a solitaire-playing program on it, probably invented by the Japanese in an effort to sabotage the American economy. I used to think solitaire was boring, but now that my brain is clogged with computer boogers I find it more fascinating than, say, the Sistine Chapel. I spend hours moving the little electronic cards around, staring at the screen with the same facial expression as a mullet, while the computer sneezes on me. None of this was possible just 15 years ago.

The computer is also a great teaching tool for young people. For 12 example, my home computer has an educational program that enables you to control an entire simulated planet—its ecology, its technology, its weather, etc. My 10-year-old son and his friends use this program a lot, and we've all learned some important ecological lessons, the main one being: Never, ever put 10-year-old boys in charge of a planet ("Let's see what happens when you have volcanoes AND nuclear war!").

So if you don't already have a home computer, I strongly recommend 13 that you get one. Of course before you buy, you'll want to know the answers to some pertinent questions, especially: What DID the male giraffe say to the female giraffe in the bar? The answer—this'll kill you—is: "The higpowoifj &kjfkjO,dmjd ERROR ERROR ERROR"

❀   ❀   ❀

AFTER YOU READ

THINK about the personality that the author gives the computer. What kind of "person" is the computer? Does Barry make the computer seem superior to humans? Is this attitude one that you frequently see reflected in our technological society? In spite of our tendency to think of computers as human, are they also responsible for depersonalizing humans, making them feel less human?

THINK also about what this essay suggests about human beings. Do we adjust to change easily? How important is human interaction to us—even if the interaction takes place through a machine such as a computer?

EXAMINE the computer expressions included in the essay—terms such as *data processing, macro, megahertz, format, and files.* Are these terms familiar to you, or can you figure out what they mean by their context? What other computer terminology have you acquired in recent years?

WRITE a mock dialogue between you and a computer, observing the standard conventions of punctuation.

Getting a Degree by E-mail

MARY LORD

In this article, which appeared in U.S. News & World Report, *the author, Mary Lord, describes how some students are pursuing degrees by enrolling in "online courses"—that is, college courses that can be accessed via the Internet. Lord not only describes how to get a degree by using e-mail but also offers advice to students who choose to pursue a college degree in this way.*

BEFORE YOU READ

THINK about what it would be like to take an "online course." How would such a course be like a course taken at a college or university? How would it be different?

EXAMINE the terms *online* and *on-campus*. What connotations does each term have for you? That is, what are your emotional reactions to these two terms?

WRITE a journal entry in which you argue for or against the idea of online courses.

AS YOU·READ

Underline any information or argument that influences your attitude toward this new form of education.

To advance in the Air Force, Lt. Jay Jones needs an advanced degree—no 1
small obstacle given his frequent stints underground in a nuclear
missile silo in Wyoming. So three years ago he launched into an MBA
program at Colorado State University that allows him to "attend" class by
VCR and file homework anytime he wants.

For Patti Shank, head of patient education at a small health mainte- 2
nance organization in Columbia, Md., the challenge was to "stay ahead of
the curve" in the rapidly evolving managed-care field while working
60-hour weeks and raising two children. Her solution: an online master's
degree in educational technology leadership from George Washington
University. She reads the same texts as her campus peers, watches lectures
on satellite TV, sends papers through an electronic bulletin board and
"talks" with professors and classmates during the wee hours via E-mail. At
$574, online courses cost less than half the traditional program's.

The old correspondence course has stormed into the high-tech age— 3
and it's proving to be a big hit. As many as 4 million Americans are now
buffing their professional credentials by padding over to their PCs and
plugging into "distance learning." Need to get over your fear of public
speaking? Front Range Community College near Denver will teach you
the techniques over the Internet. (Note: There's no escaping four live on-
campus presentations.) How about accounting? Great Britain's Open
University, with nearly 150,000 students worldwide, offers a highly regarded curriculum. The University of Massachusetts at Dartmouth recently
started an online course in writing for the World Wide Web.

All told, some 75 universities and colleges offer online degree pro- 4
grams, according to a tally on CompuServe's Education Forum. "We're
beginning to see a revolution in higher education," says Milton Blood,
director of accreditation at the American Assembly of Collegiate Schools
of Business. He calls the explosion of electronic courses "mind-boggling."

As has long been true with by-mail courses, which date back to 1890, 5
the quality of online programs varies from superb to subpar. And students
have little help distinguishing the one from the other. No certification
system exists for online programs, though the American Council on
Education hopes to announce good-practice guidelines soon. (The Distance Education and Training Council, which accredits home-study
courses, can lead you to programs that pass muster—some of which include
online courses.) Some courses consist solely of long-winded lectures transmitted over the wires or videos, with scant opportunity for interaction with
a professor. The top-notch choices are as academically rigorous as their
on-campus counterparts. "This is probably the best education I've gotten,

but you have to be extremely self-motivated," says Shank, who read 30 books to research a recent paper on workplace technology.

Good programs use the medium itself to enhance the learning experi- 6 ence. For its cybercourse on the Holocaust, for instance, the University of Massachusetts at Dartmouth is connecting a geographically dispersed group of online students with a Nazi death camp survivor living in Israel—an experience the students would never have otherwise. In worthwhile programs, students can debate with professors on the school bulletin board and through E-mail. And they can electronically brainstorm with their peers.

Such discourse is an especially important feature of distance business 7 programs like that of Britain's Henley Management College—which counts a fishing captain off the Falkland Islands among its 7,000 MBA students. While much of Henley's courseware consists of mailed packs of videotaped lectures and case-study readings, far-flung students can work in groups by conferring via E-mail. Such teamwork is a hallmark of the best on-campus MBA programs. Online, the collaboration has the advantage of mimicking the way employees at muscular multinationals increasingly find themselves working: in "virtual teams" with colleagues around the globe.

To harried professionals, distance learning's greatest attribute may be 8 that the student decides when to hear a lecture, do a paper, graduate. "What other class can you go to in your pajamas and red fuzzy slippers?" asks Janice Norman, a sight-impaired student at Montgomery College in Rockville, Md., who welcomes the lack of prejudice online—and of intimidating class loudmouths. Instructors also benefit by having more time to ruminate over a response to a student's performance. "I'm more persnickety with my online students," says Montgomery College computer Prof. Ben Acton.

For now, the surest way to find the fussy professors and quality 9 programs is to stick with those schools whose classroom courses are accredited. "We are applying the technology to proven theories and existing courses, not developing a curriculum to fit the technology," says Bruce Heasley, associate director for student services at Pennsylvania State University, which has one of the nation's largest distance learning programs, with nearly 18,000 students. "Anyone can throw an accounting course together, but do you have enough to put four or five courses together for a certificate or degree? It has to add up and mean something."

A worthy institution also will treat credits earned on campus and at a 10 distance as interchangeable. If missile officer Jones wanted to, he would have the flexibility to attend class at Colorado State or transfer to another school. Henley managers who are assigned to jobs that lack Internet access have the option of coming to campus. Their diplomas don't distinguish between distance degrees and the on-campus kind.

Finally, for online courses, you'll want strong technical support. Along 11 with keeping the school's electronic bulletin board humming, Montgomery College's Acton fields regular calls from students with the computer-era equivalent complaint of "the dog ate my homework." Colorado State has a 24-hour hot line, while Henley includes software help in its courseware.

Remote courses won't ever shut down campus. But even people who 12 prefer the familiar ways of learning are apt to get a taste of distance education. Businesses, which currently spend $30 billion a year on formal training, are among the biggest proponents of cost-saving CD-ROM instruction, for example. Denver-based Re/Max International beams recertification courses over the company's own satellite-TV system to 25,000 real-estate brokers in North America. The U.S. Postal Service uses teleconferencing to bring far-flung mail workers up to speed on new equipment.

Even such bastions of tradition as the Harvard Business School are 13 bowing to the inevitable. Instead of wasting their first weeks plugging gaps in such fundamentals as accounting or basic computer skills, future MBAs will take an assessment test—and receive refresher exercises—over the World Wide Web.

❀ ❀ ❀

AFTER YOU READ

THINK about whether you would like to take an online course. What are the advantages of online courses? What are the disadvantages of such courses? Is the technology involved in such courses a positive feature for you or an obstacle to overcome?

EXAMINE the term *distance learning,* which can apply to online courses or televised courses. Compare online courses and televised courses. Which has more potential for learning? Why? How does each compare to a course in which you are actually present in the same room with your instructor and classmates?

WRITE an essay in which you describe a time in the future when schools as we know them will not exist. Or **WRITE** an essay arguing that online courses are or are not the best way to ensure that everyone receives a college education. In your essay you may focus on the effectiveness of online courses, the cost of such courses, their accessibility to students, and so on.

Gender Gap in Cyberspace

DEBORAH TANNEN

Deborah Tannen is a university professor and author of
You Just Don't Understand: Women and Men in Conversation, *which explores the differences between male and
female communication patterns. This article, which first
appeared in* Newsweek, *reflects Tannen's continued interest in gender differences in communication. It focuses on
how males and females differ in their perception and use
of a new type of electronic conversation known as e-mail.*

BEFORE YOU READ

THINK about the idea that males and females tend to differ in the way they
communicate. Do you agree with this observation? If so, identify several
differences.

EXAMINE the word *novice,* which appears in the first sentence of this
article. A novice is a beginner, someone who is new to a field or activity. It
comes from the Latin *novus,* which means "new." Thus when Tannen states
that she is "still something of a novice" as a computer user, she means that
she is still a beginner when it comes to some aspects of computer use.

EXAMINE also the word *paradox,* which is in the second sentence ("That
paradox is telling."). A paradox is a seemingly contradictory statement that
is actually true. The paradox Tannen refers to appears in the first sentence
when Tannen claims she is both a "computer pioneer" and "something of
a novice." In the article that follows, Tannen explains how both of these
claims are true.

WRITE a journal entry in which you contrast the way males and females
communicate.

AS YOU READ

Think about how technology has changed the ways in which people communicate with one another.

I was a computer pioneer, but I'm still something of a novice. That paradox is telling.

I was the second person on my block to get a computer. The first was my colleague Ralph. It was 1980. Ralph got a Radio Shack TRS-80; I got a used Apple II+. He helped me get started and went on to become a maven, reading computer magazines, hungering for the new technology he read about, and buying and mastering it as quickly as he could afford. I hung on to old equipment far too long because I dislike giving up what I'm used to, fear making the wrong decision about what to buy and resent the time it takes to install and learn a new system.

My first Apple came with videogames: I gave them away. Playing games on the computer didn't interest me. If I had free time I'd spend it talking on the telephone to friends.

Ralph got hooked. His wife was often annoyed by the hours he spent at his computer and the money he spent upgrading it. My marriage had no such strains—until I discovered e-mail. Then I got hooked. E-mail draws me the same way the phone does: it's a souped-up conversation.

E-mail deepened my friendship with Ralph. Though his office was next to mine, we rarely had extended conversations because he is shy. Face to face he mumbled so, I could barely tell he was speaking. But when we both got on e-mail, I started receiving long, self-revealing messages; we poured our hearts out to each other. A friend discovered that e-mail opened up that kind of communication with her father. He would never talk much on the phone (as her mother would), but they have become close since they both got online.

Why, I wondered, would some men find it easier to open up on e-mail? It's a combination of the technology (which they enjoy) and the obliqueness of the written word, just as many men will reveal feelings in dribs and drabs while riding in the car or doing something, which they'd never talk about sitting face to face. It's too intense, too bearing-down on them, and once you start you have to keep going. With a computer in between, it's safer.

It was on e-mail, in fact, that I described to Ralph how boys in groups often struggle to get the upper hand whereas girls tend to maintain an appearance of cooperation. And he pointed out that this explained why boys are more likely to be captivated by computers than girls are. Boys are

typically motivated by a social structure that says if you don't dominate
you will be dominated. Computers, by their nature, balk: you type a
perfectly appropriate command and it refuses to do what it should. Many
boys and men are incited by this defiance: "I'm going to whip this into line
and teach it who's boss! I'll get it to do what I say!" (and if they work hard
enough, they always can). Girls and women are more likely to respond,
"This thing won't cooperate. Get it away from me!"

Although no one wants to think of herself as "typical"—how much 8
nicer to be sui generis—my relationship to my computer is—gulp—fairly
typical for a woman. Most women (with plenty of exceptions) aren't
excited by tinkering with the technology, grappling with the challenge of
eliminating bugs or getting the biggest and best computer. These dynamics
appeal to many men's interest in making sure they're on the top side of the
inevitable who's-up-who's-down struggle that life is for them. E-mail
appeals to my view of life as a contest for connections to others. When I
see that I have 15 messages I feel loved.

I once posted a technical question on a computer network for linguists 9
and was flooded with long dispositions, some pages long, I was staggered
by the generosity and the expertise, but wondered where these guys found
the time—and why all the answers I got were from men.

Like coed classrooms and meetings, discussions on e-mail networks 10
tend to be dominated by male voices, unless they're specifically women-
only, like single-sex schools. On line, women don't have to worry about
getting the floor (you just send a message when you feel like it), but,
according to linguists Susan Herring and Laurel Sutton, who have studied
this, they have the usual problems of having their messages ignored or
attacked. The anonymity of public networks frees a small number of men
to send long, vituperative, sarcastic messages that many other men either
can tolerate or actually enjoy, but turn most women off.

The anonymity of networks leads to another sad part of the e-mail 11
story: there are men who deluge women with questions about their
appearance and invitations to sex. On college campuses, as soon as women
students log on, they are bombarded by references to sex, like going to
work and finding pornographic posters adorning the walls.

TAKING TIME

Most women want one thing from a computer—to work. This is significant 12
counterevidence to the claim that men want to focus on information while

women are interested in rapport. That claim I found was often true in casual conversation, in which there is no particular information to be conveyed. But with computers, it is often women who are more focused on information, because they don't respond to the challenge of getting equipment to submit.

Once I had learned the basics, my interest in computers waned. I use 13
it to write books (though I never mastered having it do bibliographies or tables of contents) and write checks (but not balance my checkbook). Much as I'd like to use it to do more, I begrudge the time it would take to learn.

Ralph's computer expertise costs him a lot of time. Chivalry requires 14
that he rescue novices in need, and he is called upon by damsel novices far more often than knaves. More men would rather study the instruction booklet than ask directions, as it were, from another person. "When I do help men," Ralph wrote (on e-mail, of course), "they want to be more involved. I once installed a hard drive for a guy, and he wanted to be there with me, wielding the screwdriver and giving his own advice where he could." Women, he finds, usually are not interested in what he's doing; they just want him to get the computer to the point where they can do what they want.

Which pretty much explains how I managed to be a pioneer without 15
becoming an expert.

❀ ❀ ❀

AFTER YOU READ

THINK about why some men view computer conversations as safer than real, face-to-face conversations. What could be frightening about a real conversation? Do you agree with Tannen's generalization that men are reluctant to engage in real conversations?

EXAMINE the generalization that Tannen makes when she states that "boys in groups often struggle to get the upper hand whereas girls tend to maintain an appearance of cooperation." Do you agree with this generalization? What evidence do you have to support your position? What evidence does Tannen present to justify her generalization?

EXAMINE also the words and phrases Tannen uses to qualify many of her claims. For example, when she states that "most women . . . aren't excited by tinkering with the technology," she qualifies this claim by adding in parentheses "with plenty of exceptions" (see paragraph 8). Can you find other instances in which Tannen uses words such as *typically, some, most, tend,* and so on to qualify her assertions?

WRITE an essay in which you summarize Tannen's main assertions about male/female responses to computers in general and e-mail in particular. Then respond to her assertions by arguing for or against them.

The Beep Goes On

CAROL ORLOCK

Carol Orlock is a novelist whose first novel, The Goddess Letters, *won the Pacific Northwest Bookseller's Award. This essay appeared in a 1989 issue of* Lear's, *a magazine intended primarily for women. In the essay Orlock expresses reservations about how beneficial machines are to our society. Most of the other authors in this unit take a position on machines based on their individual experiences with them; however, Orlock is expressing her concern about the effect that machines can have on our society as a whole. In fact, Orlock suggests that machines can even affect the future of the world.*

BEFORE YOU READ

THINK about how many machines you use in a single day. How many of these machines make your life easier or more pleasant? How many make your life more tedious or frustrating?

EXAMINE the following words, which appear in the essay and may be unfamiliar to you:

Terra incognita: "The *terra incognita* at our fingertips is made up of buttons and dials, registers that dance with prickles of electricity, diodes that blip, and switches smooth and effortless as sleep."

This Latin phrase means "unknown land" but is used by Orlock metaphorically, not literally. That is, she is not referring to a geographical place, to real land, but to the unknown territory created by modern technology. Notice that the word *territory* comes from the Latin word *terra*.

Elliptical: "Creatures from this land breed among themselves and speak a language only they can comprehend—CD-ROM, fully buffered RAM, Ethernet . . . phrases brief and *elliptical* as an electron's leap toward the future."

When writers want to indicate that material has been omitted from a text, they use ellipses—three spaced periods. Thus the word *elliptical* means "containing or characterized by ellipsis." But it can also be used to refer to a writing style that is characterized by economy or obscurity of expression. Which of these definitions applies to the word as it is used by Orlock?

Inaudible: "This device emits an *inaudible* sound. . . ."

If something is audible, it can be heard. Thus an *inaudible* sound is one that cannot be heard.

Unfathomable: "Then there are *unfathomable* miracles—like the machines that can keep me alive."

A fathom is a unit of length equal to six feet. It is used primarily to measure the depth of water. However, as a verb, fathom means not only "to determine the depth of" but also "to get to the bottom of and understand." Thus *unfathomable* means "not capable of being understood." Notice that the prefixes *in* (as in *inaudible*) and *un* (as in *unfathomable*) can both mean "not."

Proliferation: "I have seen the *proliferation* of electronic transmissions. . . ."

The word *proliferation* means "rapid growth," but it applies to all types of rapid expansion, not just the growth of living things. Thus *prolific* means "rapidly growing," and *proliferate* means "to grow rapidly."

WRITE a list of the machines you typically use each day. Make your list as accurate and complete as possible.

AS YOU READ

Keep two lists—one that includes the machines Orlock is positive toward and one that includes the machines she thinks are useless or silly.

They gleam—cool aluminum servants more agile than their masters. 1 They flash reflections, fractionalizing our lives in segmented lines on black plastic and chrome. They are tech toys and tech tools, born at the rate of some 60 electronic patents each day. If these inventions are exhilarating, they are also eerie. Occasionally they are downright silly.

The terra incognita at our fingertips is made up of buttons and dials, 2 registers that dance with prickles of electricity, diodes that blip, and switches smooth and effortless as sleep. Creatures from this land breed

among themselves and speak a language only they can comprehend—
CD-ROM, fully buffered RAM, Ethernet . . . phrases brief and elliptical as
an electron's leap toward the future. As these creatures enter our world
with accelerating velocity, we perform quick sleights of mind to absorb the
latest miracle.

A few of these miracles strike absurd notes. It is possible, for example, 3
to purchase a battery-powered ultrasonic canine flea collar. This device
emits an inaudible sound field around the at-risk pet, giving perimeter
protection against midair insects hopping in its direction. Lacking the dog,
I still crave the device, with a lust I inherited from my ancestors who tamed
wolves. They too must have craved the new; in their case it was probably
sharper flint.

Equally absurd, but no less desirable, is the latest hand-held language 4
translator. With this polyglot computer, and a Eurailpass, I can manage
pleasantries in five languages. My hostess may doze off while I input FIND
WORD: GOOD NIGHT AND THANKS FOR THE STRUDEL, but I will have been polite as
well as postmodern.

Alongside the absurdities, there are useful miracles. Ever since my son, 5
who is in sales, installed the cellular phone in his car, I no longer pay for
groceries to be delivered. I call his number, and he stops between appointments to pick up what we need. There are drawbacks, of course. If my son
is out of his car, I must dictate my list to a real, live mobile-intercept
operator, who is notoriously poor at distinguishing the word *cases* from
cans. But we like stewed tomatoes and expect to use them up before next
autumn.

Likewise, I appreciate bar-code pricing in supermarkets. At least I think 6
I do. But if I ever see short black stripes worked into the mottling on a
zucchini, I will immediately flee the market screaming.

I definitely like cash machines. I like the snap of a plastic card slipping 7
like a tongue into a dark mouth of a machine, and I like to imagine chips
pondering my secret code and thoughtfully checking my balance. I like
when the money comes out. I like that best. I have hoodwinked my
creditors, gotten ahead of the signatory on my paycheck, and possibly
mortgaged my future, but for a brief electronic instant no one knew. It is
a secret between the machine and me, and when it asks whether I want a
report on my balance, I always punch *No*.

Then there are unfathomable miracles—like the machines that can 8
keep me alive. I walk past a hospital and see through porthole windows
the shining surfaces and serpentine wiring of these medical wonders. Or I
can hear a screaming siren and believe a life is about to be saved. The value

of that life cannot be calculated, yet the miracle of saving it is played out in numbers: starting with the digits *911,* transmitted as an address and an estimated time of arrival, figured as a pulse rate and a blood pressure, calibrated for tomography and sonography, measured into millimeters, minute dosages, and statistics regarding recovery. I will never understand all this but I'm reassured knowing it is there.

I have seen men walking on the moon via live television. I have watched 9 a brain cell actually grow threads as it was stimulated toward a new memory trace. I have seen the banded pattern from a DNA test display the unique secretions of a rapist. I have seen the proliferation of electronic transmissions and have felt, on some days, as though it were all aimed at me.

We covet the new technology because, like an unclimbed mountain, it 10 is there. We fear it because, as in toxic-waste dumps and acid rain, it is here.

The everyday can become terrifying: I see myself standing in a grocery 11 line while the bar-code reader goes *peep-peep-peep.* The checker angles his wrist, sliding my purchases past a red pencil of light, and the register prints out exactly what I bought and exactly when, right down to the date, the hour, and the minute. Will I ever have to prove I was buying figs at precisely 10:02 the morning of the 24th? I save receipts. The blue vein on the checker's wrist passes over the red light, reminding me that we can now read genetic codes from blood samples. These codes are not yet legible to the masses, but they will be one day. What will happen to us when a single drop of blood reveals our ancestry? Divulges our diet? Predicts our appeal to certain viruses?

Meanwhile, the new science of molecular psychology studies brain 12 chemistry to explain mood and behavior. When the chemical formula for the experience of pure terror is understood, surely some dictator will want to purchase the ingredients. The day may come when defense systems will have to guard our hearts and minds on the molecular level.

On better days I persuade myself I will actually be protected by laser 13 weapons in space. If I open my arms wide and throw my head back to drink in a blue September afternoon, the machinery is too distant to imagine. On such days the approaching clouds are shaped like Sunday school cutouts. Will they reconfigure to dark, slouching beasts when I know that a silicon-and-steel "miracle" is actually out there, watching over me? I feel unable to prepare, except to think up better uses for the new technology. If we can all talk to one another—instantly—and if we can all understand one another—anthropologically, linguistically, genetically—let's all get on the wire together one fine day. Let's talk peace.

❀ ❀ ❀

AFTER YOU READ

THINK about Orlock's statement that "we covet the new technology because, like an unclimbed mountain, it is there. We fear it because, as in toxic-waste dumps and acid rain, it is here." What do you think she means by this statement?

EXAMINE the machines that Orlock thinks are silly or useless. What are they?

EXAMINE also the machines that she likes or describes positively. What are they? What do these "good" machines have in common? Why does she like them?

WRITE a summary of this essay. Begin by stating what you think Orlock's thesis is. Include in your summary only the main points that she makes to support her thesis; then argue for or against her thesis.

Unit Seven: Critical Thinking and Writing Assignments

❦   ❦   ❦

EXPLORING IDEAS TOGETHER

1. Technology has affected not only modern life but also modern language. Our vocabulary is full of words that are associated with commonly used machines. Working as a group, select a particular type of technology (such as the airplane or the computer) and brainstorm on the words that this technology has added to our vocabulary.

2. Discuss with your group the effects of technology on individuals as opposed to its effects on society as a whole. That is, is it possible that a certain technology or machine may benefit an individual yet harm society? For example, cars make life easier on individuals but create problems (pollution, dependency on oil-producing nations, deteriorating highways, and so on) for our society. Make a list of different technologies and machines, and decide whether each benefits both individuals and society or just individuals.

3. Working with the members of your group, write a brief technical definition of a simple machine, identifying its function, describing it, and telling how it differs from machines with similar functions. Be as factual and objective as possible in this definition.

4. Writers often *personify* the machines about which they are writing. That is, they give the machines the attributes and characteristics of a human. Work with a group of your classmates to write a brief narrative or description of a common machine (such as a computer, a car, a vending machine, an alarm clock, or a microwave oven), personifying it by giving it a name and other human characteristics. Exaggerate your narrative for humorous effect.

WRITING ESSAYS

1. Imagine that all of the machines on which you depend were suddenly destroyed or inoperative. Write an imaginative narrative describing what a typical day in your life would be like if this were to happen.

2. Write a humorous essay about a time when you were frustrated by a certain machine (for example, when your car wouldn't start, a vending machine wouldn't give you your selection or return your money, your smoke alarm kept going off, or your microwave burned your dinner).

3. Write an essay in which you argue for or against the idea that men are more fascinated by machines and technology than are women. Before you write, decide whether you are writing for an audience of males, females, or both. Be sure to include both causes and effects in your essay.

4. Write an essay in which you inform readers about both the positive and negative effects of some form of technology.

5. Write an essay in which you argue that Americans have a love/hate relationship with technology or with a particular machine such as computers, guns, televisions, cars, or pickup trucks. Use selections from this unit such as Dave Barry's "ERROR ERROR ERROR" and Nora Ephron's "Living with My VCR" to support your argument.

6. Write an essay in which you tell of a time when you skillfully operated a machine and felt a sense of unity with the machine, or at least a sense of mastery because you had manipulated the machine successfully.

7. Write an essay in which you analyze the role of television in our society. Use the selections from this unit that focus on television as well as your own experiences and observations to support your analysis.

8. Using the selections in this unit as sources, write an essay in which you argue for or against the assertion that technology has improved our lives.

Self with Heroes

We all have heroes—people whom we admire because they have done something we consider noble, brave, or generous. Traditionally, heroes were male figures who performed remarkable feats of bravery. These traditional heroes slew dragons, fought in battles, and embarked on exciting adventures or went on long, difficult quests. Today we still have heroes, but these heroes have changed. They are often female as well as male. Quiet and unassuming, their courage is frequently moral rather than physical. Their adventures sometimes take place not on earth but in space. And occasionally they are not heroes so much as role models or even antiheroes.

But the roles heroes assume in our lives have not changed. Heroes still inspire us to be better and challenge us to look beyond ourselves to the needs of others. They shape the people we become and influence our beliefs and our goals, showing us the potential for goodness that lies within us all. Ultimately, heroes teach us as much about who we are as about who they are.

In this unit you will read about male and female heroes, about heroes and role models, about traditional heroes and nontraditional heroes. You will consider how society's view of its heroes is affected by the media, and you will discover that heroes can be ordinary as well as extraordinary. Finally, you will turn your focus back to yourself, considering yourself in the context of the heroes and heroic acts that you have read about.

Before reading the selections in this unit, consider the following questions. You may want to respond to one or more of these questions in the form of a journal entry or freewriting. Or you may want to discuss one or more of them with a group of your classmates.

1. How do you define a hero? What qualities do you associate with a hero? Is a hero the same as a role model or something quite different?

2. Do you define male and female heroes in the same way? Are the terms *female hero* and *heroine* interchangeable? How would you react to the terms *heroes* and *sheroes*?

3. Does our society have more male heroes than female heroes? Why? Does this situation reflect the basic heroism of men and women or the beliefs and traditions of our society?

4. How do the media portray heroes? Do the media confuse heroes and celebrities?

5. Are heroes "born" or "made"? In other words, is character a qualification for heroes, or is the act of heroism the issue?

6. Have you ever witnessed a heroic act? What was this act and why was it heroic?

7. What characteristics do heroic acts have in common?

8. Who is your favorite hero? Why did you select this person?

9. Are heroes perfect or imperfect? Have you ever been disappointed with or disillusioned by someone you considered a hero? How?

10. Have you ever been a hero? Do you think you could be? Why or why not?

As you read the following selections, remember to *interact* with your reading by underlining passages, writing questions and comments in the margins, and relating what you read to your own personal life.

Note: Although individual usage and preferences differ, we use the word *heroes* to refer to both male and female heroes.

Larger Than Life

PHIL SUDO

You have probably read about famous legendary heroes such as King Arthur, Joan of Arc, and Odysseus. You have also seen fictional television shows and movies about popular culture heroes such as Wonder Woman, Batman, and Dick Tracy. But real heroes also exist in history and in contemporary life. In fact, every society has its heroes— individuals who represent the best their society can offer. A society's heroes can tell us much about the values of that society. In the following article, published in November 1990 just after Nelson Mandela visited the United States, Phil Sudo defines the word hero *and comments on its meaning.*

BEFORE YOU READ

THINK about your own heroes. That is, think about the men and women you look up to as heroes. Do you look up to these people because they are attractive, famous, or wealthy? Or do you look up to them because they have performed some great good, not for themselves but for humanity?

EXAMINE the title "Larger Than Life." What does this title suggest about Sudo's view of heroes? Examine also the headings that Sudo uses. What do these headings suggest about Sudo's definition of a hero?

WRITE a journal entry listing some living men and women whom you consider to be heroes.

AS YOU READ

Underline Sudo's definitions of *hero*.

When Nelson Mandela visited the United States in June [1990], 1
cheering throngs of Americans hailed him as a hero. His decades-
long struggle against South Africa's system of racial separation, unwavering
through years of imprisonment, was inspiring not only to South Africans,
but to freedom-loving people in this country as well.

Imagine if Iraqi leader Saddam Hussein were to visit the United States. 2
The crowds would still turn out—only they'd be hostile. Many here view
him as a murderous, ruthless dictator. And yet, in his own part of the world,
Hussein is as big a hero as Mandela is in South Africa.

How can Mandela and Hussein—one admired in this country, the 3
other despised—*both* be heroes? . . .

COURAGE AND LOYALTY

The word "hero" comes from the Greek word *heros,* meaning to protect 4
or to serve. Originally, the term applied only to mythical figures—gods or
semidivine beings, such as Hercules and Perseus, who excelled in battle and
embodied such values as courage and loyalty. The ancient Greeks developed an entire tradition of literature around such heroes; in classic epics
like the *Iliad* and the *Odyssey,* Homer spun tales of the brave Odysseus and
other warriors, whose adventures were first passed down orally, then later
through the written word.

The notion of heroes was not unique to the West. Other early societies, 5
such as China and India, developed similar traditions, around heroes such
as Kuan Ti and epics like the *Mahabharata.*

Over time, historians began to look upon real people as heroes—Simón 6
Bolívar, Sun Yat-sen, George Washington—larger-than-life individuals who
founded countries or dedicated their lives to liberation. These were the
rare men and women who embodied, as one historian wrote, "the perfect
expression of the ideal of a group, in whom all human virtues unite."

Learning the tales of these greats helps forge values and a cultural 7
identity. When you read the story of George Washington cutting down a
cherry tree and saying, "I cannot tell a lie," you learn the value of honesty
in American society. In Japan, when schoolchildren read the tale of the
47 Ronin, a band of samurai who stick together through years of hardship
to avenge their master's death, they learn the value of loyalty and group
togetherness. . . .

In this country, some educators believe our heroes are too one-sided. 8
U.S. history books, they say, are filled with the accomplishments of white
European males to the exclusion of women and minorities.

In fact, many Americans today are beginning to question the very 9
definition of a "hero." These days, we bestow the honor mainly on sports
figures, movie stars, musicians, and comedians. "The word 'hero' is a
debased word," says Michael Lesy, a professor at Hampshire College in
Amherst, Mass., and author of the . . . book *Rescues.* It has become confused
with "celebrity," "role model," and "idol," he says. . . .

WHAT MAKES A HERO?

But if there is argument over what constitutes a "hero," few among us fail 10
to admire heroic acts. Thwarting a robbery, rescuing a drowning man,
pulling a child from a burning house—these are all unquestionable acts of
heroism. And while the brave souls who perform them may never become
famous or reap rewards, they are certainly heroes.

In fact, the one trait of heroes that transcends all cultural boundaries, 11
Lesy says, is the willingness to risk one's life for the good of others. "It's
not an American trait, it's not Japanese, it's not Iraqi, it's the bottom-line
of the human species," he says.

Consider the words of Nelson Mandela: "I have cherished the idea of 12
a democratic and free society. It is an ideal which I hope to live for and to
achieve. But if needs be, it is an ideal for which I am prepared to die."

And these words from slain civil rights leader Martin Luther King, Jr.: 13
"If a man hasn't found something he will die for, he isn't fit to live."

POTENTIAL WITHIN US ALL

We hail these men as heroes because their courage gives us strength, their 14
ideals give us vision, and their spirit enlarges our own. But keep in mind
that, extraordinary as these heroes may seem, they are still human beings
like you and me. And as such, they demonstrate that within all of us, there
is the potential to become heroes ourselves.

Look around you, at your friends, your family, your school. Is there 15
someone among them that you'd call a hero? Probably so.

Now take a look in the mirror. What do you see? 16

What do you *want* to see? 17

❀ ❀ ❀

AFTER YOU READ

THINK about the question that Sudo asks in the third paragraph: "How can Mandela and Hussein—one admired in this country, the other despised—*both* be heroes?" How would you answer this question?

EXAMINE this statement: "In this country, some educators believe our heroes are too one-sided. U.S. history books, they say, are filled with the accomplishments of white European males to the exclusion of women and minorities" (paragraph 8). Do you agree or disagree with educators who hold this belief? Why do you feel as you do?

WRITE a paragraph giving your own definition of *hero*. That is, answer Sudo's question, "What makes a hero?" Before you write your definition, review the list of heroes that you wrote before reading the selection. What qualities do these people have in common? How is your definition similar to or different from Sudo's definition? (*Note:* If you quote from Sudo's article, be sure to include his words within quotation marks.)

I Have a Dream

MARTIN LUTHER KING, JR.

Martin Luther King Jr.

GWENDOLYN BROOKS

Phil Sudo's definition of a hero as a "larger-than-life" individual who is willing to risk his life "for the good of others" certainly applies to African-American civil rights leader Martin Luther King, Jr. Throughout his all-too-brief career, King worked with the Southern Christian Leadership Conference to gain for African-Americans the freedom and justice promised all Americans in the Constitution but denied for many years to its nonwhite citizens. King was assassinated in Memphis in 1968, but he left a rich heritage of courage and faith for his followers. This reading selection combines King's most influential speech with a poetic tribute to him written by Pulitzer Prize–winning poet Gwendolyn Brooks.

BEFORE YOU READ

THINK about what life was like for African-Americans in 1963 when this speech was made. What kind of dreams did King and other civil rights leaders have at this time? How has our society changed today? Do you think some of the improvements in civil rights were directly influenced by King? Has our society changed enough?

EXAMINE the first two paragraphs of King's speech. In his first paragraph, he states the purpose of the rally and of his speech. What is this purpose?

Notice that King begins his second paragraph with the phrase "Five score years ago." This phrase recalls Abraham Lincoln's famous Gettysburg Address, which begins "Four score and seven years ago, our fathers brought forth on this continent a new nation, conceived in liberty, and dedicated to the proposition that all men are created equal." By using a phrase similar to the one Lincoln used, King reminds his hearers and readers of the promises—or at least assumptions—in Lincoln's speech that all people are equal and that liberty and justice belong to all humankind.

WRITE a journal entry about your own personal dream for the future of America. If you could have only one dream for this country, what would it be?

AS YOU READ

Think about the line "A man went forth with gifts," the first line of a poem by Gwendolyn Brooks entitled "Martin Luther King Jr." The word *gifts* can suggest positive qualities that an individual has as well as "presents" that he or she gives to others. What personal gifts does King display in his speech? Is one of his gifts an effective use of language? What gifts does he try to help other African-Americans realize?

I am happy to join with you today in what will go down in history as the   1
greatest demonstration for freedom in the history of our nation.

Five score years ago, a great American, in whose symbolic shadow we   2
stand today, signed the Emancipation Proclamation. This momentous decree came as a great beacon light of hope to millions of Negro slaves who had been seared in the flames of withering injustice. It came as a joyous daybreak to end the long night of their captivity.

But one hundred years later, the Negro still is not free; one hundred   3
years later, the life of the Negro is still sadly crippled by the manacles of segregation and the chains of discrimination; one hundred years later, the Negro lives on a lonely island of poverty in the midst of a vast ocean of material prosperity; one hundred years later, the Negro is still languished in the corners of American society and finds himself in exile in his own land.

So we've come here today to dramatize a shameful condition. In a sense   4
we've come to our nation's capital to cash a check. When the architects of

our republic wrote the magnificent words of the Constitution and the Declaration of Independence, they were signing a promissory note to which every American was to fall heir. This note was the promise that all men, yes, black men as well as white men, would be guaranteed the unalienable rights of life, liberty, and the pursuit of happiness.

It is obvious today that America has defaulted on this promissory note 5 in so far as her citizens of color are concerned. Instead of honoring this sacred obligation, America has given the Negro people a bad check; a check which has come back marked "insufficient funds." But we refuse to believe that the bank of justice is bankrupt. We refuse to believe that there are insufficient funds in the great vaults of opportunity of this nation. And so we've come to cash this check, a check that will give us upon demand the riches of freedom and the security of justice.

We have also come to this hallowed spot to remind America of the 6 fierce urgency of now. This is no time to engage in the luxury of cooling off or to take the tranquilizing drug of gradualism. Now is the time to make real the promises of democracy; now is the time to rise from the dark and desolate valley of segregation to the sunlit path of racial justice; now is the time to lift our nation from the quicksands of racial injustice to the solid rock of brotherhood; now is the time to make justice a reality for all of God's children. It would be fatal for the nation to overlook the urgency of the moment. This sweltering summer of the Negro's legitimate discontent will not pass until there is an invigorating autumn of freedom and equality.

Nineteen sixty-three is not an end, but a beginning. And those who 7 hope that the Negro needed to blow off steam and will now be content, will have a rude awakening if the nation returns to business as usual. There will be neither rest nor tranquility in America until the Negro is granted his citizenship rights. The whirlwinds of revolt will continue to shake the foundations of our nation until the bright day of justice emerges.

But there is something that I must say to my people, who stand on the 8 worn threshold which leads into the palace of justice. In the process of gaining our rightful place, we must not be guilty of wrongful deeds. Let us not seek to satisfy our thirst for freedom by drinking from the cup of bitterness and hatred. We must forever conduct our struggle on the high plain of dignity and discipline. We must not allow our creative protests to degenerate into physical violence. Again and again we must rise to the majestic heights of meeting physical force with soul force. The marvelous new militancy, which has engulfed the Negro community, must not lead us to a distrust of all white people. For many of our white brothers, as evidenced by their presence here today, have come to realize that their destiny is tied up with our destiny. And they have come to realize that their freedom is inextricably bound to our freedom. We cannot walk alone. And as we walk, we must make the pledge that we shall always march ahead. We cannot turn back.

There are those who are asking the devotees of Civil Rights, "When 9 will you be satisfied?" We can never be satisfied as long as the Negro is the victim of the unspeakable horrors of police brutality; we can never be satisfied as long as our bodies, heavy with the fatigue of travel, cannot gain lodging in the motels of the highways and the hotels of the cities; we cannot be satisfied as long as the Negro's basic mobility is from a smaller ghetto to a larger one; we can never be satisfied as long as our children are stripped of their selfhood and robbed of their dignity by signs stating "For Whites Only"; we cannot be satisfied as long as the Negro in Mississippi cannot vote and a Negro in New York believes he has nothing for which to vote. No! No, we are not satisfied, and we will not be satisfied until "justice rolls down like waters and righteousness like a mighty stream."

I am not unmindful that some of you have come here out of great trials 10 and tribulations. Some of you have come fresh from narrow jail cells. Some of you have come from areas where your quest for freedom left you battered by the storms of persecution and staggered by the winds of police brutality. You have been the veterans of creative suffering. Continue to work with the faith that unearned suffering is redemptive. Go back to Mississippi. Go back to Alabama. Go back to South Carolina. Go back to Georgia. Go back to Louisiana. Go back to the slums and ghettos of our Northern cities, knowing that somehow this situation can and will be changed. Let us not wallow in the valley of despair.

I say to you today, my friends, so even though we face the difficulties 11 of today and tomorrow, I still have a dream. It is a dream deeply rooted in the American dream. I have a dream that one day this nation will rise up and live out the true meaning of its creed, "We hold these truths to be self-evident, that all men are created equal." I have a dream that one day on the red hills of Georgia, sons of former slaves and the sons of former slave owners will be able to sit down together at the table of brotherhood. I have a dream that one day even the state of Mississippi, a state sweltering with the heat of injustice, sweltering with the heat of oppression, will be transformed into an oasis of freedom and justice. I have a dream that my four little children will one day live in a nation where they will not be judged by the color of their skin, but by the content of their character.

I HAVE A DREAM TODAY!   12

I have a dream that one day down in Alabama—with its vicious racists,   13
with its Governor having his lips dripping with the words of interposition
and nullification—one day right there in Alabama, little black boys and
black girls will be able to join hands with little white boys and white girls
as sisters and brothers.

I HAVE A DREAM TODAY!   14

I have a dream that one day every valley shall be exalted, every hill   15
and mountain shall be made low. The rough places will be plain and the
crooked places will be made straight, "and the glory of the Lord shall be
revealed, and all flesh shall see it together."

This is our hope. This is the faith that I go back to the South with. With   16
this faith we will be able to hew out of the mountain of despair, a stone of
hope. With this faith we will be able to transform the jangling discords of
our nation into a beautiful symphony of brotherhood. With this faith we
will be able to work together, to pray together, to struggle together, to go
to jail together, to stand up for freedom together, knowing that we will be
free one day. And this will be the day. This will be the day when all of God's
children will be able to sing with new meaning, "My country 'tis of thee,
sweet land of liberty, of thee I sing. Land where my father died, land of the
pilgrim's pride, from every mountain side, let freedom ring." And if
America is to be a great nation, this must become true.

So let freedom ring from the prodigious hilltops of New Hampshire;   17
let freedom ring from the mighty mountains of New York; let freedom ring
from the heightening Alleghenies of Pennsylvania; let freedom ring from
the snow-capped Rockies of Colorado; let freedom ring from the curva-
ceous slopes of California. But not only that. Let freedom ring from Stone
Mountain of Georgia; let freedom ring from Lookout Mountain of Tennessee; let freedom ring from every hill and mole hill of Mississippi. "From
every mountainside, let freedom ring."

And when this happens, and when we allow freedom to ring, when we   18
let it ring from every village and every hamlet, from every state and every
city, we will be able to speed up that day when all of God's children, black
men and white men, Jews and Gentiles, Protestants and Catholics, will be
able to join hands and sing in the words of the old Negro spiritual: "Free
at last. Free at last. Thank God Almighty, we are free at last."

❀ ❀ ❀

AFTER YOU READ

THINK about the words and ideas that King repeats in his speech. What word does King use most often? What other words are repeated frequently? What effect does this repetition of key words have on the reader or listener?

EXAMINE King's use of parallel structure to emphasize important points. For example, in his third paragraph, King repeats four times the introductory phrase "one hundred years later, the Negro is. . . ." King follows each repeated phrase with a different point, but the drumlike—almost poetic—repetition of the similar statements emphasizes the fact that the life of African-Americans had not changed appreciably between the time of Emancipation and the time in which King was speaking. Reread King's essay carefully, looking for other places where he effectively uses repeated structures to emphasize a point.

EXAMINE also the following poem, in which Gwendolyn Brooks memorializes and describes King:

Martin Luther King Jr.

A man went forth with gifts.

He was a prose poem.
He was a tragic grace.
He was a warm music.

He tried to heal the vivid volcanoes.   5
His ashes are
    reading the world.

His Dream still wishes to anoint
    the barricades of faith and of control.

His word still burns the center of the sun,   10
    above the thousands and the
    hundred thousands.

The word was Justice. It was spoken.

So it shall be spoken.
So it shall be done.   15

What gifts, or positive qualities, does Brooks attribute to King? Are these qualities similar to those you identified as you were reading King's speech?

If not, can you find connections between the qualities mentioned in Brooks's poem and King's speech? What specific word does Brooks associate with King? Circle this word (or variations on it) in King's speech.

WRITE your own "prose poem" describing Martin Luther King. Begin by thinking of three words that you associate with King—words that describe him or his ideal. Then use these words as the basis of a series of brief sentences about King.

Extraordinary People

HERBERT BUCHSBAUM

Heroes are not limited to a single country or to a particular historical period. Each culture has its own different heroes, and yet these heroes often have important qualities in common. As stated in Phil Sudo's essay "Larger Than Life," a cultural hero is "the perfect expression of the ideal of a group, in whom all human virtues unite." Just as Martin Luther King is an American hero, so Rigoberta Menchú of Guatemala, Tenzin Gyasto of Tibet, and Aung San Suu Kyi of Myanmar are heroes of their own cultures. In the following essay, originally published in Scholastic Update, *Herbert Buchsbaum writes about these three extraordinary individuals.*

BEFORE YOU READ

THINK about the word *extraordinary* in the title. The Latin prefix *extra-* means "above" or "beyond." Literally, then, this word describes someone or something that is "above" or "beyond the ordinary." How is this word a fitting description for a hero?

EXAMINE the three-paragraph introduction and the structure of the essay. What prize have all three of the subjects of this essay been awarded? What struggle—or goal—do they have in common?

WRITE a journal entry in which you describe the qualities that you think a winner of the Nobel Peace Prize should possess.

AS YOU READ

In the stories about each of the three extraordinary individuals described by Buchsbaum, look for the qualities that you associate with a Nobel Peace Prize winner.

450

When the Dalai Lama, the religious and political leader of Tibet, 1 emerged from his hotel room for an interview with *UPDATE*, he introduced himself, then suddenly stopped short, and burst into a deep, resonant laugh. "One moment, please," he said, holding a finger in the air. The Dalai Lama, a world religious leader and winner of the Nobel Peace Prize, had forgotten to tie his shoes.

The incident reminded us that the heroes in the struggle for human 2 rights, even though they have become international symbols, are still just people. Too often. the human rights debate turns into an abstract discussion of philosophy, or a list of crimes and abuses. It's easy to forget that human rights is really about people.

What follows are the stories of three people, all winners of the Nobel 3 Peace Prize, who in many ways are very ordinary. But all three have been thrust into extraordinary circumstances by events beyond their control. None of them have any power in their own lands, where they are considered enemies by the ruling governments. Their only power lies in their voices, which won't let us forget what people can do to people.

RIGOBERTA MENCHÚ

Rigoberta Menchú, a 34-year-old Quiché Maya Indian from the highlands 4 of northern Guatemala, learned about injustice the hard way.

In September 1979, when she was 19, her younger brother was 5 kidnapped by the Guatemalan army and accused of trying to help peasants win the right to own land. They cut off his fingernails, then his fingers, then the skin on his face, then the soles of his feet. Then he was marched to a village square where, in front of his family, he was doused with gasoline and set aflame.

A few months later, Menchú's father, who had also been arrested and 6 tortured, led a peaceful protest to call attention to their grievances. The state security forces set fire to the building he was in, and he too was burned to death.

A few weeks after that, the army arrested, tortured, and killed her 7 mother, then left her body hanging from a tree to be eaten by dogs.

Menchú fled to Mexico, but vowed to continue the struggle where her 8 parents left off. That was the first step on an extraordinary journey that would take an illiterate farm worker from a small village in Guatemala to the honor of the 1992 Nobel Peace Prize.

The oppression of Guatemala's native Maya peoples dates from 1524, 9 when the tiny Central American country was conquered by Spain. Ever since, the Indian majority has been ruled by the Spanish-speaking minority, the *Ladinos,* most of whom are descended from the Spanish colonists. For centuries, the Indians have accepted their fate with little resistance. They have kept mostly to themselves, maintaining their 2,000-year-old traditions in their own villages.

Starting in 1954, when the army overthrew Guatemala's elected 10 government, the military has waged a brutal war against the Indians. In the 40 years since, 150,000 Indians have been killed, 1 million displaced, and 50,000 made to "disappear."

In the late 1970s, as the repression grew especially severe, some Indians 11 began to resist. Menchú's family was among them. Like many Indians, Menchú had become a farm laborer as a small child, moving south when she was 8 to work on coffee, cotton, and sugar plantations. There, she lived with other Indians in crowded, open sheds with no toilets.

As a teenager, Menchú began to teach herself to read and write Spanish, 12 which would one day allow her to tell the story of her people to the outside world. Meanwhile, the Ladino landowners, who had been taking land from peasants over the years, came one day to seize her home village. When her father tried to resist, he was arrested and tortured. The whole family was branded troublemakers, and the arrests began.

"The important thing is that what happened to me has happened to 13 many other people too," Menchú writes in her autobiography. "My story is the story of all poor Guatemalans. My personal experience is the reality of a whole people."

While her suffering was typical, her resistance was not. In Mexico, 14 where she lived in a slum with other refugees, Menchú continued to fight. She worked with international human rights groups and became a frequent visitor to the United Nations. There she was often seen walking the halls in her colorful native dress and bare feet, telling her story to the world.

Still, she remains a controversial figure in Guatemala, where govern- 15 ment officials criticized her selection, in 1992, for the Nobel Prize. They accused her of supporting the country's leftist guerrillas and harming Guatemala's image abroad. Despite death threats if she returned, Menchú flew to the capital. Thousands of supporters—Indians who had long kept quietly to themselves—lined the streets from the airport, cheering and shouting, "Viva Rigoberta!"

"I am overcome with emotion," she said. "I only wish that my parents 16 could have been present."

In awarding the prize, the Nobel committee wanted to draw attention 17 to the plight of Guatemala's Indians in the hope that it would lead to improved conditions. Recently Guatemalans have found cause for that hope. In June, Ramiro de Leon Carpio, a human rights leader, was elected president. The nation is cautiously optimistic.

THE DALAI LAMA

Tenzin Gyasto is a leader without a country.　　　　　　　　　　18

As a child at age 4, Gyasto was chosen as the Dalai Lama of Tibet, a 19 snowy, mountainous land on China's southern border. To some 14 million followers, that made him a god; in the Tibetan Buddhist religion, the Dalai Lama is the Lord of Compassion, as well as the country's religious and political ruler.

But in 1950, when the Dalai Lama was 15, Chinese troops invaded his 20 land and seized power. The "Land of the Snows" has been under Chinese military rule ever since.

At age 24, after a failed rebellion by Tibetans, the Dalai Lama fled, 21 riding a mule through the treacherous Himalaya mountains to India, where he lives today. Now 58, the Dalai Lama has become a one-man campaign for a free Tibet.

"Sometimes I really feel desperate," he told *UPDATE* reporter Denise 22 Willi in an exclusive interview. "The Tibetan nation, with its unique cultural heritage, is now facing a real danger of extinction."

Since the Chinese invasion, 1.2 million Tibetans—about 20 percent of 23 the population—have been killed, many by the Chinese army and national security forces. Others have starved to death in massive famines because of China's policy of shipping Tibetan grain to China.

According to human rights monitors, Chinese troops and police offi- 24 cers routinely torture and imprison any Tibetan who speaks of inde-pendence or mentions the Dalai Lama. Thousands of political opponents have been jailed and tortured. Labeling Buddhism "a disease," the govern-ment has destroyed some 6,000 Buddhist monasteries, the centers of Tibetan culture and scholastic life.

China is not just intent on eliminating Tibetan culture, but the Tibetans 25 themselves. Tibetan women are subject to forced sterilization and abortion. The government has begun a massive population transfer, offering Chinese men financial bonuses if they settle in Tibet and marry Tibetan women. "Because of Chinese policy, our people are becoming a minority in their own homeland," the Dalai Lama says. "If this carries on, soon we will be nothing more than a curiosity, a tourist attraction."

Despite these atrocities, the Dalai Lama has consistently rejected calls 26 for violence. "Violence is essentially against human nature," he says. "It may solve one problem, but it often creates another." There's also a practical reason: There are 6 million Tibetans and 1 billion Chinese, who have several hundred thousand troops in Tibet. Instead of war, the Dalai Lama's idea of struggle is to travel the world, drawing attention to his cause and trying to persuade world leaders to exert pressure on China.

"We need to raise world awareness about Tibet, to tell the truth about 27 what is really happening," he says. "An ancient nation with a precious culture is almost dying."

AUNG SAN SUU KYI

Sometimes what a person symbolizes can be more powerful than the person 28 herself. Aung San Suu Kyi, a 49-year-old writer, has not been seen or heard in public since she was arrested on July 20, 1989. Yet she represents the hope of all those who oppose the brutal government of Myanmar, where she is being held prisoner.

Suu Kyi (pronounced *soo chee*) became the hero of Myanmar's struggle 29 for democracy partly by chance and partly by fate. She is the daughter of Aung San, a legendary general who helped lead Myanmar (then known as Burma) to independence from British colonial rule in the 1940s. In 1946, when Suu Kyi was 2 years old, the general was gunned down by a rival faction.

In 1962, a military dictatorship seized power, declaring war against 30 the country's ethnic minorities. In attempts to "purify" the nation, the army looted and burned some 850 rural villages, raped several thousand women, killed and tortured thousands, enslaved hundreds of young boys, and forced more than a million refugees to flee their homes, according to a United Nations report.

But as Myanmar plunged into poverty and civil war, Suu Kyi was living 31 comfortably in England with her British husband and their two sons. In 1988, she received news from Yangon, the nation's capital, that her mother was gravely ill. She immediately packed a suitcase and flew home. As she slept by her mother's side, a protest movement among the nation's students began to pick up steam.

At first Suu Kyi stayed out of the fray. But after a massacre that August, 32 in which thousands of protesters were killed, she could no longer keep silent. "This was not a time when anyone who cares can stay out," she said then. "As my father's daughter, I felt I had a duty to get involved." When she spoke, half a million people came to listen. The speech, which advocated a nonviolent "revolution of the spirit," electrified the nation and established her as leader of the struggle for democracy and human rights.

As she began to campaign around the country, the army fought back 33 with bullets. Once, in April 1989, she was walking down the street with a group of supporters when a squad of soldiers jumped from a jeep, knelt, and prepared to fire. Suu Kyi motioned her companions away and marched straight up to the riflemen. "It seemed so much simpler to provide them with a single target than to bring everyone else in," she said later. The soldiers withdrew.

In July 1989, she was placed under "house arrest," forbidden to leave 34 her home or have any contact with the outside world, including her family in England. Her house was surrounded by tanks and barbed wire. Soldiers with bayonets were stationed outside. She has not been allowed out since.

But her imprisonment did not stop her party from winning a landslide 35 election in 1990, making her the nation's legally elected leader. And it didn't keep her from winning the Nobel Peace Prize in 1991. The army, which had ignored the election results, offered her the chance to travel to Norway to accept the prize if she promised never to return. She refused.

Her father, until he was killed, had always said he expected to make 36 whatever sacrifice his struggle required. "My only concern," said Suu Kyi, "is that I prove worthy of him."

❀   ❀   ❀

AFTER YOU READ

THINK about the ages of the heroes described in this article. At the time the article was written, how old was Rigoberta Menchú? How old was the Dalai Lama, Tenzin Gyasto? How old was Aung San Suu Kyi? Is the age of each of these individuals relevant or irrelevant to his or her heroic act? Why or why not? Think also about the gender of these individuals. Who is male? Who is female? Has being a man or a woman affected the heroism of these extraordinary individuals? Why do you feel as you do?

EXAMINE the maps on page 456, which show the locations of Guatemala, Tibet, and Myanmar (formerly Burma).

From these maps, these countries—and therefore their heroes—seem very far away. Why, in spite of this distance, are these stories and the people they represent relevant to you in the United States today?

WRITE a summary of the heroic accomplishments of each of the individuals described in this article. Include in your summary a thesis statement that explains what the lives of all three have in common. Or **WRITE** a letter nominating a prominent individual for the Nobel Peace Prize. You may choose a person from the United States or from another country.

On Heroes and the Media

JEAN PICKER FIRSTENBERG

World events are filtered into our minds through the media—newspapers, magazines, radio, and, most frequently, television. Truth and fiction become increasingly harder to separate when both are aired on the same medium. Thus a fictional hero such as Matlock, Columbo, or Jessica Fletcher may seem more real to us than the police officers who give their lives trying to arrest criminals or rescue hostages. After all, a television hero intrudes upon our consciousness for an hour every week, whereas the death of a police officer receives only thirty seconds on the ten o'clock news. And the rescue of victims of earthquakes or airplane crashes may seem like little more than an entertaining show with unknown actors. In this editorial, "On Heroes and the Media," Firstenberg comments on the role the media play in creating on-the-spot heroes and in confusing the public about the nature and value of heroism.

BEFORE YOU READ

THINK about the influence of television and movies on your life and values. More specifically, how do these media influence your ideas of heroes and heroism?

EXAMINE the word *antihero*. The word begins with the Greek prefix *anti-*, meaning "opposite" or "against." Using this information, think about how you would define an antihero. Then read paragraph 6 carefully to see how Firstenberg defines an antihero. How does her definition compare to your own observation of antiheroes in the media?

WRITE in your journal a list of heroes who you believe have been created by the media. Then write another list of antiheroes who you believe have been created by the media. Discuss your lists with at least one other class member.

AS YOU READ

Keep in mind Firstenberg's thesis that "film and television have had enormous impact on the evolution of the modern hero" (paragraph 1). Underline the effects that Firstenberg identifies.

Storytellers, bards, and dramatists have always shared with us the legends 1 of our heroes. And in this era of the moving image, filmmakers have become the prime chroniclers of the twentieth-century experience. As a result, the images of film and television have had enormous impact on the evolution of the modern hero.

Our earliest heroes were god figures from mythology, later half-divine 2 and half-man (or half-animal); then heroes became men, which is to say "persons"—like you and me. Or perhaps not quite like you and me, because, as the great scholar Joseph Campbell tells us in his book *The Hero With a Thousand Faces,* in every incarnation, and age, certain recurrent characteristics have defined the hero and set him apart from ordinary men.

"The hero ventures forth from the world of common day," Campbell 3 says, "into a region of supernatural wonder; fabulous forces are there encountered and a decisive victory is won; the hero comes back from this mysterious journey with the power to bestow boons on his fellow man."

With minor variations, this classic heroic adventure has been related 4 in myths, folk legends, and fairy tales for thousands of years. It is only in the last two hundred years that we've modified the formula to downplay its "supernatural" and "fabulous" elements and recast our heroes to reflect the changes that modernization has wrought. Clearly, the nature of a hero changes with, and mirrors, the values of the times.

In the forties and fifties, Americans still embraced heroes who were 5 "larger than life." John Wayne, Gary Cooper, Jimmy Stewart, and Henry Fonda obeyed most of the traditional heroic rules: overcoming "evil"— rustlers, venal politicians, and other forms of corruption—in order to create a new order, as Campbell would have it.

But by the midfifties, and for the next fifteen to twenty years, huge 6 advances in technology and increased sophistication in the audiences

shouldered these supermen aside in favor of what has been called the
"antihero"—an ordinary man with recognizable frailties. Dustin Hoffman
in *The Graduate,* Paul Newman in *Hud* and *Cool Hand Luke,* Alan Arkin
in *Catch-22,* Al Pacino in *Dog Day Afternoon,* and Woody Allen in all his
films personified a modern hero whose biggest victory was frequently the
mere fact of this survival in a mechanized world that often seemed
unhealthy for children and other living things.

By the late seventies, the war in Vietnam and the Watergate affair had 7
taken their toll on the American spirit, leaving a need for the old-school
heroes again—larger-than-life types like Rocky and even those with supernatural qualities like Luke Skywalker and Superman.

Recently, however, the immediacy and intimacy of the media have 8
somehow confused the issue of heroism, blurring the traditional criteria by
which we measure our heroes and allowing mere exposure—that is,
"fame"—to precede, and occasionally preempt, "worthiness" as a qualification for heroism.

It was also during the late seventies that television-news coverage, 9
assisted by the new satellite technology, began to bring "instant news" into
our living rooms. Before that, Walter Cronkite, with his thoughtful objectivity and measured delivery, had been the most trusted man in America—
Dante's Virgil guiding us through the confusion and chaos of the day's
events. Now we often find ourselves abandoned, watching the news along
with the commentator as it unfolds. The laurels for broadcast journalism
often seem to be going to the first, as opposed to the "best," coverage.

And paralleling the trend in movies and fictional television, the 10
emphasis in news began to shift away from analysis and toward action: We
could watch a hostage crisis unfold right on the runway, see crash victims
hoisted from an icy river, watch firemen spray water on a burning hotel.
News began to resemble drama, except that with drama, the hero is readily
identified, and in reality, he often is not.

Have we in fact begun to create heroes in order to make reality more 11
dramatic? . . . Debates over Sen. Gary Hart, Jim and Tammy Bakker, and
Lt. Col. Oliver North should have made abundantly clear to us that we
need to take a long, hard look at the role the media has begun to play in
creating/evaluating/rejecting/destroying contemporary heroes.

Are we now confusing fiction with fact and imbuing people who simply 12
have wide media exposure with the heroic ideals that fictional figures
represent? Against what criteria are we measuring their "victories" and
what "boons have they bestowed on [their] fellow men"? These are

disturbing thoughts, but ones that we should all begin to consider. If we don't know where reality ends and fiction begins, I think we need to be concerned with our visual literacy.

❀   ❀   ❀

AFTER YOU READ

THINK about your own favorite heroes, both men and women. Who are your heroes? How many became your heroes through the influence of television or movies?

EXAMINE the reading selection carefully to identify the categories into which Firstenberg groups heroes. Her first category is based on Joseph Campbell's definition of a godlike figure who "ventures forth from the world of common day into a region of supernatural wonder," encounters "fabulous forces" and wins a victory, and then "comes back from this mysterious journey with the power to bestow boons [gifts] on his fellow man." Firstenberg's later categories, however, are often associated with certain historical periods, dating through the late 1980s, when this essay was first published.

WRITE a description of "the hero" as created by the media in the 1990s, being sure to give specific examples. How does this hero differ from those in previous periods described by Firstenberg? What qualities does this hero have in common with other periods? Does the hero of the 1990s have more in common with the traditional hero or the antihero?

Lenny Skutnik—Accidental Hero

RICHARD SHEREIKIS

Originally published in a collection of readings devoted to The Hero in Transition, *this article by Richard Shereikis focuses on a heroic rescue that occurred during the Air Florida crash in Washington, D.C., in the winter of 1982. In his essay, Shereikis, like Firstenberg in the previous reading, explores the relationship between fame and heroism.*

BEFORE YOU READ

THINK about what you would do if you saw someone—perhaps a stranger—in great danger and were in a position to help. Do you think you would have the strength and courage to act quickly and decisively?

EXAMINE the title of this article. You might be interested to know that the complete original title of this essay was "Heroes Don't Need Zip Codes: Lenny Skutnik—Accidental Hero." What questions does this title suggest?

EXAMINE also the following words from the selection:

Lionized: "He's been toasted by governors, *lionized* by legislators and proclaimed a savior by our President."

The surrounding context should help you realize that to *lionize* a person is to treat that person as if he or she were a famous and important person, a celebrity. This word derives from the use of the word *lion* to mean a "celebrity or an important person," a meaning that probably derived from the idea of the lion as the king of the beasts.

Subliminal: "If the name sounds familiar, it's because, like one of those *subliminal* messages that hidden persuaders can put into movies, Lenny blipped his way into the national consciousness for one brief shining moment on a dismal day in January 1982."

461

Word structure provides you with a clue to the meaning of this word. From such words as *subway* and *submerge,* you probably know that the prefix *sub* means "under." You may not, however, know the Latin root *limin,* which means "threshold." These word parts suggest that a *subliminal* message is one that is below the level or "under the threshold" of consciousness.

Specious: "He's justly proud of his heroism, but he recognizes mere celebrity for the *specious* and fleeting thing it is."

You probably cannot define this word from the context, but *specious* refers to something that is not what it appears to be, to something that only seems to be fair or true.

Quasi-illusion: "In this life of illusion and *quasi-illusion,* the person with solid virtues who can be admired for something more substantial than his well-knownness often proves to be the unsung hero . . ."

The Latin root *quasi* means "almost," and thus a *quasi-illusion* is a near-illusion. Remember that, in contrast to *allusion* (which means "a reference to literature or history"), an *illusion* is a fantasy or a dream—even a delusion.

WRITE in your journal several reasons why, as suggested in the original title, "Heroes Don't Need Zip Codes."

AS YOU READ

Try to determine how Lenny Skutnik became a hero and how this heroism was accidental.

Lenny Skutnik. It's a name you think you remember. Maybe a utility 1 infielder for the Cubs or Phillies back in the '50s. Scrappy little guy. Got his uniform dirty a lot. Batted maybe .230 lifetime in a short career. Or maybe a guy from your old high school. Kind of an average student. Wrestled at one of the lighter weight divisions and worked hard to keep in shape. Even when people hear the name for the first time, they furrow brows and rummage in their memories. "Lenny Skutnik. Lenny Skutnik. I'm sure I know the guy, but I just can't place him." It's that kind of name.

But however unromantic the name may sound, Martin Leonard Skut- 2 nik III is an American hero. He's been toasted by governors, lionized by legislators and proclaimed a savior by our President. Millions have seen him on television, short and sturdy with dark brown hair that is cut most unromantically. For a hero, he's quiet and modest and really very shy, which makes his appearances before large and distinguished groups a bit of a trial for him. "In school," he remembers, "I'd go up to do an oral report and hide behind the paper and just start reading it without any punctuation. And the teacher would tell me to sit down because I was making a fool of myself." But recently he's talked to huge audiences that have included politicians and other public figures. "Sometimes I'll say to myself afterwards, 'How am I doing this? I just talked to 800 people. How am I doing this?'" But the audiences, big and important, hang on his few and simple words, and Lenny has grown easier in the mantle of fame which has been thrust upon him willy-nilly.

If the name sounds familiar, it's because, like one of those subliminal 3 messages that hidden persuaders can put into movies, Lenny blipped his way into the national consciousness for one brief shining moment on a dismal day in January 1982. On Wednesday, January 13, Lenny was the one who leaped into the freezing Potomac River to save a sinking victim of the crash of Air Florida Flight 90. The 737 had gone down soon after take-off at 4:00 p.m. from Washington's National Airport, ripping into the 14th Street bridge and crashing into the Potomac. Seventy-four passengers and four people on the bridge were killed in the disaster, and Priscilla Tirado, 23, would have been among them had it not been for Lenny's quick and decisive act.

Along with other commuters who were snarled in the traffic caused by 4 the crash and the swirling snowstorm that hit Washington that day, Lenny and the others in his carpool had gone down to the shore to see what the problem was. Lenny and the others had watched as a U.S. Park Police helicopter had first lowered a ring to Priscilla and another man who were somehow, miraculously, afloat on the ice. They had watched as Priscilla had let go soon after the lift, her frozen hands unable to hold on. She had fallen back to the ice while the helicopter had dropped the man safely ashore. The copter tried again, and again Priscilla had grabbed, but this time, too, she had slipped off, now splashing into the freezing water about 20 feet from shore.

Lenny didn't think about what he ought to do, about the cold or about 5 his lack of lifesaving skills. He kicked off his boots, shed his jacket, and dived in, swimming surely as he'd learned to do in his youth in Upper Michigan, where his father, an army man, had been stationed for a while. "I just did what I had to do," Lenny says quietly, as is his way. "I got out behind her and then I kinda pushed and stroked, pushed and stroked, until we got to shore. Her eyes were rolling back in her head, and she looked real bad." When they got Priscilla to the hospital, her body temperature was 81 degrees, Lenny recalls. If he had hesitated even slightly, she might have perished with her husband, Jose, 23, and her two-month-old son Jason, both of whom were lost in the crash.

It was a noble and courageous act. Lenny had risked his life to save a   6 life. He had responded like a hero. A hero, as opposed to the mere celebrity, as outlined by Daniel Boorstin, is "a human figure—real or imaginary or both—who has shown greatness in some achievement. He is a man or woman of great deeds."*

But Lenny's deed alone, as selfless as it was, would not have been   7 enough to change his life as it has been changed since that awful winter afternoon. There was another force involved, and that was what pushed Lenny so vigorously into the spotlight of celebrity he endured in the months following his heroic act. There was a television camera on shore that day, and Lenny's deed was beamed across the country. That made all the difference. "The hero created himself," says Boorstin. "The celebrity is created by the media" (p. 61).

As Lenny himself says, these kinds of things are not rare. "You hear of   8 firemen who go into burning buildings and come out with a kid under each arm. It happens daily. It's just that the cameras aren't there all the time. It was just that that day, that place, everything was so dramatic and unexpected, it was a big deal."

But that day, because it was in the nation's capital and the cameras were   9 there, Lenny Skutnik, 28, a $14,000-a-year service assistant at the Congressional Budget Office, a family man and a former painter and supermarket porter and Burger Chef cook and worker in a meat packing plant and furniture factory, became a national figure. Because the cameras were there, Lenny Skutnik the hero, also became Lenny Skutnik the celebrity—a "person who is known for his well-knownness," as Boorstin expresses it. On that bleak and tragic day, Lenny had seized the moment, given the country something to cheer about, something to admire; but because the cameras were there, he was also threatened by the danger of celebrity.

He got nearly 1600 pieces of mail in the first few weeks, some of it   10 addressed to "Lenny Skutnik, Hero of the Potomac." Heroes don't need zip codes. The letters came from everywhere, according to Skutnik, mostly "short, real personal notes, telling how it made them feel. How they were

---

*Daniel Boorstin, *The Image: or What Happened to the American Dream* (New York: Atheneum, 1974), 49. Subsequent references to this work will be made parenthetically in the body of the text.

watching TV and saw the girl and started screaming, 'Somebody save that girl!' They came from young, old, elementary school kids, classrooms, from all walks of life. Anybody and everybody."

Other, more public tributes came quickly over those same weeks. The 11 state of Mississippi, where Lenny was born, celebrated "Lenny Skutnik Day" on February 10, and Lenny was flown there in the governor's private plane. Columbia, Mississippi, the home town of Lenny's mother, had used February 9 to celebrate another "Lenny Skutnik Day." He was honored by the Virginia legislature and had lunch with Governor Charles Robb. . . . The walls of his living room in Lorton, Virginia, are lined with over 20 handsome plaques and framed testimonials and citations. . . . He's had other honors and gifts, too. An anonymous check for $7000 came from somewhere in Virginia, telling Lenny to pay his rent or buy a car or whatever he wanted with the money. A Washington, D.C., auto dealer offered him the use of a car for a year. . . . But most prominent and suggestive in his collection of awards and tributes is a picture that hangs in the middle of the living room wall above his television set. It's a large framed color photograph of Lenny and his wife Linda, standing with Nancy Reagan during the President's State of the Union message. During the speech on national television, the President had paid special tribute to Lenny, who had stood to acknowledge the generous applause which the distinguished audience had given him. . . .

But with Lenny Skutnik we should also remind ourselves of another 12 kind of heroism, which may be more precious and more rare than the courage he showed in the Potomac. It isn't really embodied in the act of saving another human life, as important as that act was. Lenny's real heroism lies in how he's handled the mantle of celebrity that was flung at him so unexpectedly. It lies, too, in his ability to realize the real significance of his act. It lies in his ability to maintain his sense of basic human decency even while those around him, starting with the journalists, are losing theirs.

A few days after the crash, for example, he was called by CBS News 13 and asked if he would be interested in meeting Priscilla's father, Beirne Keefer, of Clearwater, Florida. The man had just lost his grandson and son-in-law, and Lenny had misgivings about the appropriateness of such a meeting. "I had a weird feeling about that," Lenny recalls. "I thought, 'Well this is too soon.' But I finally said, 'Well, if it's all right with him, OK.'"

Ike Pappas, the CBS newsman, warned Lenny not to tell any other 14 reporters about the meeting, or else he'd have a hundred of them invading his house, as they had on another occasion, a day or two earlier. Lenny didn't want any more disruptions of his life or his living room, so he agreed, and only the CBS camera crew waited outside his town house, preparing to capture the meeting between the hero and the father of the person he saved. Later, Lenny learned that Mr. Keefer had not expected any cameras there, that he was expecting only a simple, personal meeting arranged by Pappas, who was an acquaintance of his from their days in the service. In any case, Lenny knew it was all wrong as soon as he saw Mr. Keefer. "The minute I laid eyes on him, I could tell he was in no condition, that he shouldn't even be there," Lenny says.

And then, after they were all seated, and the cameras were rolling, 15 Pappas asked the time-honored tasteless question: "Mr. Skutnik, how do you feel about meeting Priscilla's father?"

Lenny recalls his shock at the banality of the question. "Here's the 16 man, his eyes all swelled up, he's all emotional. How can you answer something stupid like that? What can you say? And I told him [Pappas], I said, 'What kind of question is that?' I said that. And I just gave him short snappy answers to the rest of the questions he asked." That act alone should make Lenny a hero, a defender of some little nook of privacy against the ravages of the media.

There's something heroic and very telling, too, about Lenny's criteria 17 for accepting the trips and vacations he's been offered over the months which followed his deed. "If there's family there, I'll go," he says quite simply. "If there isn't, I won't." Hence his acceptance of those trips to Mississippi, to Chicago, and Philadelphia, and his rejection of the ones to Hawaii, Germany and Canada, where he wouldn't feel comfortable because he wouldn't know anyone. The heroic restraint seems refreshing, in these times when "Where's mine?" has become all but a national motto.

Finally, there's his heroically sensible and modest perspective on the 18 act he performed and the subsequent handling of it by the press and other media. "They embarrassed me," he says, "because what they were doing is they were bragging on me, which I never did and don't do. I just did what I had to do. And they're trying to make a macho man out of me." They tried to turn a hero into a mere celebrity, in other words, and Lenny has been Olympian in his resistance. . . .

He pauses, sorting through his thoughts and feelings about all the fuss 19 and attention. "It's a big deal to me personally that I saved someone's life. That's important," he says softly. "Other than that, all this that's come about is mostly . . ." and his voice trails off before he can say anything too negative or nasty, which would be against his nature. He's justly proud of his heroism, but he recognizes mere celebrity for the specious and fleeting thing it is.

Other words of Boorstin's come to mind. "In our world of big names,   20
curiously, our true heroes tend to be anonymous. In this life of illusion and
quasi-illusion, the person with solid virtues who can be admired for
something more substantial than his well-knownness often proves to be the
unsung hero" (p. 76).

So it is with Lenny Skutnik, now that the blinding light of his celebrity   21
has dimmed, and we can see his virtues clear.

❀   ❀   ❀

AFTER YOU READ

THINK about how Lenny Skutnik reacted to the crisis in the Potomac and
then about how he reacted to his fame. Which reaction was more heroic
and why?

EXAMINE the actions of the newspeople as described in the selection. How
do you view these actions? Were they necessary and appropriate? Were they
sensitive or insensitive? How would you have reacted if you had been
Lenny or the father?

WRITE a persuasive essay about the origin of heroism. In your opinion,
does a person become a hero because of qualities that he or she possesses
or because of specific circumstances? What was the source of Lenny
Skutnik's heroism? What other examples support your point of view?

The Man in the Water

ROGER ROSENBLATT

This essay, which was first published in Time, *focuses on the same air tragedy that was the subject of the previous essay by Richard Shereikis. Indeed, Shereikis provides an excellent introduction to this related article when he quotes Daniel Boorstin's statement that "in our world of big names, curiously, our true heroes tend to be anonymous"*. Although Shereikis's essay focuses on an originally anonymous hero whose identity later becomes well known, the hero of Rosenblatt's essay remains anonymous. Rosenblatt is himself a resident of Washington, D.C., the site of the crash.*

BEFORE YOU READ

THINK about how the title of this selection differs from the title of the previous selection. The two readings focus on specific—but different—heroes of the 1982 Air Florida crash in Washington, D.C. At least one important piece of information that is available in the title "Lenny Skutnik—Accidental Hero," however, is absent in the title "The Man in the Water." What is this information?

EXAMINE the first paragraph of the selection. Notice that the first sentence states that "as disasters go, this one was terrible, but not unique, certainly not among the worst on the roster of U.S. air crashes." And yet Rosenblatt goes on to list several details that help to make this crash different. Notice that Rosenblatt concludes this paragraph with a question that increases our interest in the remainder of the article.

EXAMINE also the following words from the selection:

---

*Daniel Boorstin, *The Image: or What Happened to the American Dream* (New York: Atheneum, 1974), 76.

Emblemized: "The jets from Washington National Airport . . . are, for the moment, *emblemized* by the one that fell. . . ."

As you probably know, an emblem is an object or symbol that represents a particular idea, concept, company, country, and so on. For example, the American flag is an emblem of America. To *emblemize,* then, would be to use such an object to represent the idea associated with it.

Anonymity: "His selflessness was one reason the story held national attention; his *anonymity* another."

Anonymity is literally the state of being without a name or identity (*a* = "without," *onym* = "name"). In this sentence, Rosenblatt introduces one of his major points in the essay, for he continues by saying that "the fact that he went unidentified invested him with a universal character."

Implacable: "The man in the water pitted himself against an *implacable,* impersonal enemy; he fought it with charity; and he held it to a standoff."

You may have heard the word *placate* (pronounced PLAY′ kate), which means "to calm or to appease." Someone who is *placable* (pronounced PLAK′ able) can be easily calmed or appeased, but an *implacable* enemy is not easily appeased, will not yield or give up.

WRITE in your journal, based on your preview of the first paragraph and the vocabulary sentences, your prediction of why this crash was different from most other air crashes.

AS YOU READ

Try to answer the question at the end of the introductory paragraph: "Why, then, the shock here [in this crash]?" In searching for the answer to this question, look also for the meaning of the title "The Man in the Water."

As disasters go, this one was terrible, but not unique, certainly not among   1
the worst on the roster of U.S. air crashes. There was the unusual element of the bridge, of course, and the fact that the plane clipped it at a moment of high traffic, one routine thus intersecting another and disrupting both. Then, too, there was the location of the event. Washington, the city of form and regulations, turned chaotic, deregulated, by a blast of real winter and a single slap of metal on metal. The jets from Washington National Airport that normally swoop around the presidential monuments like famished gulls are, for the moment, emblemized by the one that fell;

so there is that detail. And there was the aesthetic clash as well—blue-and-green Air Florida, the name a flying garden, sunk down among gray chunks in a black river. All that was worth noticing, to be sure. Still, there was nothing very special in any of it, except death, which, while always special, does not necessarily bring millions to tears or to attention. Why, then, the shock here?

Perhaps because the nation saw in this disaster something more than a 2 mechanical failure. Perhaps because people saw in it no failure at all, but rather something successful about their makeup. Here, after all, were two forms of nature in collision: the elements and human character. Last Wednesday, the elements, indifferent as ever, brought down Flight 90. And on that same afternoon, human nature—groping and flailing in mysteries of its own—rose to the occasion.

Of the four acknowledged heroes of the event, three are able to account 3 for their behavior. Donald Usher and Eugene Windsor, a park police helicopter team, risked their lives every time they dipped the skids into the water to pick up survivors. On television, side by side in bright blue jumpsuits, they described their courage as all in the line of duty. Lenny Skutnik, a 28-year-old employee of the Congressional Budget Office, said: "It's something I never thought I would do"—referring to his jumping into the water to drag an injured woman to shore. Skutnik added that "somebody had to go in the water," delivering every hero's line that is no less admirable for its repetitions. In fact, nobody had to go into the water. That somebody actually did so is part of the reason this particular tragedy sticks in the mind.

But the person most responsible for the emotional impact of the 4 disaster is the one known at first simply as "the man in the water." (Balding, probably in his 50s, an extravagant mustache.) He was seen clinging with five other survivors to the tail section of the airplane. This man was described by Usher and Windsor as appearing alert and in control. Every time they lowered a lifeline and flotation ring to him, he passed it on to another of the passengers. "In a mass casualty, you'll find people like him," said Windsor. "But I've never seen one with that commitment." When the helicopter came back for him, the man had gone under. His selflessness was one reason the story held national attention; his anonymity another. The fact that he went unidentified invested him with a universal character. For a while he was Everyman, and thus proof (as if one needed it) that no man is ordinary.

Still, he could never have imagined such a capacity in himself. Only 5 minutes before his character was tested, he was sitting in the ordinary plane among the ordinary passengers, dutifully listening to the stewardess telling him to fasten his seat belt and saying something about the "no smoking sign." So our man relaxed with the others, some of whom would owe their lives to him. Perhaps he started to read, or to doze, or to regret some harsh remark made in the office that morning. Then suddenly he knew that the trip would not be ordinary. Like every other person on that flight, he was desperate to live, which makes his final act so stunning.

For at some moment in the water he must have realized that he would 6 not live if he continued to hand over the rope and ring to others. He *had* to know it, no matter how gradual the effect of the cold. In his judgment he had no choice. When the helicopter took off with what was to be the last survivor, he watched everything in the world move away from him, and he deliberately let it happen.

Yet there was something else about our man that kept our thoughts on 7 him, and which keeps our thoughts on him still. He was *there,* in the essential, classic circumstance. Man in nature. The man in the water. For its part, nature cared nothing about the five passengers. Our man, on the other hand, cared totally. So the timeless battle commenced in the Potomac. For as long as that man could last, they went at each other, nature and man; the one making no distinctions of good and evil, acting on no principles, offering no lifelines; the other acting wholly on distinctions, principles and, one supposes, on faith.

Since it was he who lost the fight, we ought to come again to the 8 conclusion that people are powerless in the world. In reality, we believe the reverse, and it takes the act of the man in the water to remind us of our true feelings in this matter. It is not to say that everyone would have acted as he did, or as Usher, Windsor and Skutnik. Yet whatever moved these men to challenge death on behalf of their fellows is not peculiar to them. Everyone feels the possibility in himself. That is the abiding wonder of the story. That is why we would not let go of it. If the man in the water gave a lifeline to the people gasping for survival, he was likewise giving a lifeline to those who observed him.

The odd thing is that we do not even really believe that the man in the 9 water lost his fight. "Everything in Nature contains all the powers of Nature," said Emerson. Exactly. So the man in the water had his own natural powers. He could not make ice storms, or freeze the water until it froze the blood. But he could hand life over to a stranger, and that is a power of nature too. The man in the water pitted himself against an implacable, impersonal enemy; he fought it with charity; and he held it to a standoff. He was the best we can do.

❀   ❀   ❀

AFTER YOU READ

THINK about what "the man in the water" comes to symbolize to those who observe his actions. How is he an "Everyman hero"? Why is such a hero especially important to society? Would the man's heroism have been as effective if his identity had been known? Why or why not?

EXAMINE the conflict between nature and "the man in the water," especially as shown in paragraphs 2, 7, and 9. What strengths does nature have? What strengths does "the man in the water" have? Who, or what, is victorious?

WRITE in your own words the point of Rosenblatt's essay. That is, what is his thesis? Compare your version of the thesis with those of your classmates.

Fall of the Legends

MIKE LUPICA

When individuals act heroically in crisis situations such as plane crashes, earthquakes, and bombings, the media faithfully reports and even embellishes the story. But reports of such individual heroic acts take only a fraction of the time and space spent by the media on sports "superstars." Americans—especially young people—idolize the stars of football, basketball, baseball, and other major sports. But, as Mike Lupica reports in the following essay from the November 1994 issue of Esquire, *many sports stars have recently fallen from the pedestals on which fans have placed them. Lupica is a syndicated columnist for the* New York Daily News *and* Esquire.

BEFORE YOU READ

THINK about your own sports heroes. What sports figures do you admire most, and why do you admire them? Do you admire the same figures that you admired five years ago? Ten years ago? If not, why has your opinion changed?

EXAMINE the title and the first five sentences of the third paragraph. A *legend* may be defined as a "romanticized or popularized myth" or as "a person who achieves legendary fame." How, according to Lupica, are the legendary heroes of sports different from "real heroes"? Do you agree or disagree with Lupica that "the idea of the sports hero in this country is dead"?

WRITE a journal entry in which you not only identify two or three sports heroes that have fallen from legendary status but also explain why (in your opinion) they fell.

AS YOU READ

Notice that Lupica's purpose in this essay is not only to describe and give examples of the fall of the sports legends but also to analyze the causes of this fall. Identify and underline the causes that Lupica discusses. (*Note:* Mickey Mantle, the subject of paragraphs 4–14 and 19–22, died of cancer in August of 1995, not quite a year after Lupica's article was published.)

O nce it was common—the most normal thing in the world—to put the 1 stars of sports up on pedestals. Now the national pastime seems to be watching them fall one after another.

The memorable pictures in sports no longer catch Emmitt Smith 2 running for a touchdown or Barry Bonds at the plate, another baseball on its way out of the park. They show O.J. Simpson's mug shot or Mike Tyson in handcuffs or Magic Johnson announcing his retirement from basketball because he has contracted the AIDS virus after years of promiscuity. You can put Michael Jordan, the most famous athlete in the world, on that list, too: Jordan in sunglasses on national television, addressing allegations of million-dollar gambling losses; Jordan on the golf course, wagering a thousand dollars per hole; Jordan on ESPN's SportsCenter almost every night of the summer, striking out as a Double-A baseball player struggling to hit .200.

We are not talking about real heroes here, policemen or firemen or 3 soldiers fighting for something important. The great heroes of sports are more like those of movies or fiction. They are larger than life. In a way, Babe Ruth was no more real than Beowulf. But now, forty years after Ruth's death, even the idea of the sports hero in this country is dead, as dead as the Game of the Week in baseball or the Friday Night Fights, dead as the Polo Grounds or Ebbets Field. The list of casualties is long and storied, from blue-collar champion Pete Rose to Hall of Fame ace Steve Carlton. In 1994 alone, Dwight Gooden, the most luminous baseball pitcher since Sandy Koufax, tested positive for drugs (his second offense); Darryl Strawberry, one of Gooden's closest friends, checked himself into rehab (his second visit); Scottie Pippen refused to take the court in an NBA playoff game; Jack Nicklaus served up a few uncensored thoughts on race and golf; Tonya Harding, one of America's darling figure skaters, looked the other way while her husband planned an assault on her closest rival; and John Daly, a golfer who came out of nowhere to win the PGA a few years ago, capturing the imagination of everyone who follows sports, updated his troubled history of alcohol abuse and domestic disputes to include a parking-lot scuffle with an elderly man.

Legends are not made by game footage or file tape. They are born in 4 memory and imagination and by word of mouth. Mickey Mantle is a legend. In his playing days and beyond, he was the kind of mythical star Ruth had been. He played the second half of his career on ruined knees, but he always seemed larger than life. Now the Mantle of legend, the Mantle of memory, has been replaced by Mantle the recovering alcoholic, a February graduate of the Betty Ford Clinic.

Looking frail and human, more so than he was ever supposed to look, 5 Mantle admitted this year that he had a drinking problem. After he returned from rehab, I sent a note to his New York hotel, wishing him luck, telling him I was rooting harder for him now than I ever did as a kid. At the bottom of the note, I asked Mantle to give me a call. I thought I might write a column about his experience.

Later that night, I was watching the Yankees on television when the 6 phone rang.

"Mike?"   7

I smiled. "Hey, Mickey, thanks for calling."   8

There was a pause at the other end of the line, and then in a quiet voice 9 Mantle said, "How'd you know it was me?"

If you grew up in Upstate New York in the fifties and sixties—as I 10 did—you rooted for the Yankees, listened to them on the radio, and watched them on television. Mel Allen and Red Barber and Phil Rizzuto brought you the games. Mantle was the sports hero. I tried to explain that to him. "If I don't know your voice by now . . ." I said, letting the thought drift away, back toward the time when Mantle hit those balls out of sight, the ones Mel Allen described as going . . . going . . . gone.

There was another pause. "Thanks for the note," Mantle said.   11

I told him I meant it.   12

"I get a lot of notes just like it these days," he said. "My mail's so 13 different now you wouldn't believe it. You can't even call it fan mail anymore. It's more like letters from close friends. It's so unbelievable it touches my heart. It makes me cry."

Cheers never did that.   14

There is no one thing that killed the American sports hero. Some got sick 15 and some were arrested. Some got drunk and some got high. Some of them beat up women. And some blew it all on gambling. The only real culprit, it seems, is time. In a different age, Magic Johnson would have been able to . . . face no physical consequences. In another era of sports and life, Desiree Washington might not have had the courage to charge Mike Tyson with rape. Still, it's hard to imagine Roberto Clemente charging fifteen bucks for an autograph or Y. A. Tittle skipping camp to up his paycheck.

If the athletes have changed, it's because the landscape has changed. 16 Today's players come to the big time with their wallets full and some preconceived idea of what a sports hero should be, how they should play things, and how they should be marketed. They are handed $60 million contracts when they leave college. You have to wonder how many of the heroes of the past could have taken that kind of hit and had the same careers. Would it have gone as well for Willie Mays if he had been rich beyond imagination at the age of twenty? Or Jack Kramer? Or even Jack Nicklaus?

There is more to this than money, though. The fan has changed as well. 17 He wants to know too much. And those of us in the media are only too willing to give him what he wants. With each passing year, it seems the fan gets closer to the field. He gets into the action, then all the way into the locker room. And soon he discovers what I found out a long time ago: A seat in the stands is still the best seat in sports. The athletes may look small from high up in the stadium, but you can still make them out to be big. It's safe to assume, though, that Willie Mays's public relations would have been no better today than those of his godson Barry Bonds, who is known to be prickly himself. . . . And I do not believe Joe DiMaggio, one of the few enduring sports heroes, would have stood up to the day-to-day scrutiny that modern ballplayers face. He would not enjoy being staked out by autograph hunters in a hotel lobby; he would not like hiding from the reporters and talk-show producers who stalk today's stars.

It's true. Sports heroes have destroyed themselves, but we have helped 18 them off the pedestal. We love their skills but hate the money they make. We demand that they reveal themselves, and then when we see them as they really are, we blame *them* for letting us down. That is why most fans react with such viciousness when one of their heroes turns out to be a drunk or an addict. We don't ever want to hear how sick these guys are. After all, they are rich and talented and, by God, they should know better.

The best chance an athlete has is to be someone from the past. Mantle, 19 who comes from a time when sports heroes were still gods, was greeted as warmly as ever when he showed himself to the world as just another aging, beat-up ex-drunk. He was celebrated for his recovery from alcoholism at the very time that Gooden was vilified by the angry children of sports journalism for having the nerve to act like an addict.

When Mantle and I spoke on the telephone, I told him that he might 20 hear the biggest cheer of his life when he returned to Yankee Stadium for Oldtimer's Day.

"If that is true," Mantle said, "it would have to be some cheer, wouldn't 21 it?"

As it turned out, the reception he got was not the greatest of his life. 22 Just another one. They cheered Mickey Mantle at Yankee Stadium because he is still around. In a time when the sports hero is dead, he is a survivor.

❀   ❀   ❀

AFTER YOU READ

THINK about the image (introduced by Lupica in the first paragraph and extended throughout the essay) of putting a sports star "on a pedestal." What does a pedestal look like? Why would it be particularly hard to stay secure on a pedestal? Why is this image an effective one to describe the lives of sports stars today?

EXAMINE the essay to determine, according to Lupica, which sports stars of the past and the present have "fallen" from their pedestal and which have remained on it. Then make two lists, one for each group. Do you know all of the sports stars that Lupica mentions? Try to identify through class discussion or outside research those you do not recognize. Then decide whether you agree with Lupica's estimation of these individuals.

EXAMINE also the sections that focus on the example of Mickey Mantle, paragraphs 4–14 and 19–22. (You might recall that Mantle died of cancer in August of 1995, just a few months after Lupica's essay was published.) Does Lupica believe that Mantle fell off the pedestal or stayed on it? Why does he feel as he does?

WRITE an essay about a sports hero who, in your opinion, has remained "on the pedestal" as an admirable human being as well as a famous sports star. What qualities have allowed this individual to avoid the pitfalls that, according to Lupica, have destroyed so many sports stars?

Heroines and Role Models

MAXINE F. SINGER

In the following essay, which was presented as a commencement address at Barnard College in New York City on May 14, 1991, Maxine F. Singer distinguishes between heroines and role models. Singer is the President of Carnegie Institution of Washington in Washington, D.C.

BEFORE YOU READ

THINK about the terms *heroine* and *role model*. How would you define a heroine? How would you define a role model? How are a heroine and a role model similar? How are they different?

EXAMINE the following words from the selection and the definitions that follow them:

Emulate: "And none of us would want to *emulate* her disregard for the known dangers of radiation, a disregard that ended in the destruction of her life."

To *emulate* is to copy, follow, or imitate. Thus Singer says that we would not want to imitate Curie's disregard for danger but implies that we may want to model some of her other qualities.

Exemplars: "Still, these heroines are more worthy *exemplars* than contemporary women occupying the roles to which young American women aspire."

As suggested by the context of this sentence, an *exemplar* is an ideal example or a model worthy of being imitated.

Proximal: "For one thing, a heroine is distant while a role model's *proximal* reality encourages too close scrutiny. . . ."

The context of this sentence suggests that *proximal* means the opposite of "distant." Thus *proximal* means "near or nearest." *Proximal* is an adjective form of *proximity*, which means "the state of being near; closeness."

WRITE in your journal a list of women whom you consider heroines. Then write another list of women whom you consider role models. Discuss your lists, comparing them with those of your classmates.

AS YOU READ

Look for Singer's definitions of *heroine* and *role model*. How are her definitions similar to or different from your own?

The label "role model" is well intended, and the concept is useful. Yet, the term is bothersome. Why?

Young women in the 1930s and '40s, when I grew up, had real heroines. Isadora Duncan and Martha Graham were among them. Their extraordinary talents made dance into an original art form. They initiated schools, had followers, were leaders; their unconventional personal lives were romantic. Heroines, yes, but role models? Most American women of my generation could not have imagined an unconventional personal life, and most lacked the talents of Duncan and Graham, not to mention their courage.

Marie Curie was another heroine of ours. The biography of Curie, written by her daughter Eve, inspired scientifically inclined young women in an age when heroism still mattered and not many women were scientists. Through the book, and the famous movie based on it, we were touched by the image of Marie and Pierre Curie stirring great vats of pitchblend in their dark shed of a laboratory. Nor could anyone forget that this hard physical work led to two Nobel prizes: one in physics in 1903, shared by Marie and Pierre Curie with Antoine Bequerel, and another in 1911, for Marie alone in chemistry for the discovery of radium.

The description in Eve Curie's book is of a heroine, not a role model. No young American woman could imagine the sacrifice of the lonely years Marie Curie spent in Poland as a governess, sending money to her sister who was studying medicine in Paris, saving what was left for her own eventual opportunity to study. And none of us would want to emulate her disregard for the known dangers of radiation, a disregard that ended in the destruction of her life.

Still, these heroines are more worthy exemplars than contemporary women occupying the roles to which young American women aspire. For one thing, a heroine is distant while a role model's proximal reality encourages too close scrutiny and a destructive mimicry of both public and private behavior. More importantly a heroine is, by definition, known for courage and nobility of purpose, thereby uplifting our own ambitions out of narrow, self-centered concerns.

Why then do young women now speak so often of role models and so 6 rarely of heroines? Why are heroines and even heroes so out of fashion? Nobility of purpose is not currently admired; our society is afraid that following such a leader will extract too high a cost from us as individuals or as a nation. Rather, we deny greatness and seek instead a false image of equality. In our compulsive effort to make everyone ordinary we assume license to delve into personal matters, from the trivial to the profound; unsurprisingly, the glorious images are tarnished. And for those who are truly great, where the effort to make them ordinary cannot succeed, we strive to make them evil. Not even the giants of our world can escape. Consider the sad efforts to tarnish Martin Luther King's image, as if that could undermine his greatness.

Technology makes this program easier. Television is unforgiving in its 7 ability to reveal the personal flaws of everyone from athletic stars to scientists. Modern high-speed journalism sometimes seems to make the whole world into a soap opera.

People have always known that heroines and heroes are imperfect. But 8 they chose to ignore the warts so that the greatness could inspire new achievement. We are all diminished by the disappearance of heroism. Role models will be for naught if there are no heroines and heroes from whom to learn about courage, about noble purpose, about how to reach within and beyond ourselves to find greatness.

Young women now have more freedom to shape themselves than 9 young women anywhere or at anytime in history. That freedom is a lonely and difficult burden, but it is also a blessing. The burden cannot be conquered nor the blessing realized by standing in anyone's shadow. But both can be achieved by standing on the shoulders of the great heroines.

❀   ❀   ❀

AFTER YOU READ

THINK about the distinctions that Singer makes between heroines and role models. With a group of your classmates, make one list of the qualities that she associates with heroines and another list of the qualities that she associates with role models. In Singer's opinion, who are the more vital to a society—heroines or role models?

EXAMINE the questions that Singer asks at the beginning of paragraph 6: "Why then do young women now speak so often of role models and so rarely of heroines? Why are heroines and even heroes so out of fashion?" How does Singer answer these questions? How would you answer them? Do you agree or disagree with Singer?

WRITE an essay comparing a contemporary heroine with a contemporary female role model. You may want to begin with definitions of a heroine and a role model. For these definitions, use your own ideas as well as the list of qualities you made in the "THINK about" assignment above.

Mother Teresa and Her Endless Fight

ELLEN GOODMAN

A Pulitzer Prize–winning journalist, Ellen Goodman is chiefly known for her syndicated newspaper columns. Some of these columns have been collected in her books Close to Home *(1979),* At Large *(1981), and* Keeping in Touch *(1985). Goodman wrote the following tribute to Mother Teresa in October 1979 just after Mother Teresa had been awarded the Nobel Peace Prize.*

BEFORE YOU READ

THINK about the kind of person who can devote his or her life completely to taking care of the poor and sick of this world. Born in 1910 to wealthy Yugoslavian parents, Agnes Gonxha Bojaxhiu first became Sister Teresa and began her work with the poor in India in 1928. In 1950, she became Mother Teresa and received Vatican approval for her Missionaries of Charity order. In 1965, with the approval of the Catholic Church, she sent her missionaries outside of India, even moving into New York City in the 1970s.

EXAMINE the word *emaciated,* which occurs in the first paragraph. An emaciated person is extremely thin, due to starvation or illness.

EXAMINE also the title. Why is the fight against poverty and illness in India and other places "endless"? What, if anything, could bring such a fight to a successful conclusion?

WRITE a journal entry in which you list actions that individuals and national governments could take to reduce world poverty.

AS YOU READ

Notice that Goodman begins her article with a reference to a photograph of Mother Teresa and then continues by creating a portrait of her in words through visual images and Mother Teresa's own words.

In the photograph, she is holding an emaciated child. There have been, 1 surely, enough of them, a ready supply of emaciated children in Mother Teresa's life. She has lived in a sea of sick, a Black Hole of Calcutta's poor.

Even now, if she were to distribute every dollar of her $192,000 Nobel 2 Peace Prize, one by one, she would run out of money long before she ran out of poor in that one teeming city.

The portrait of this woman is absolutely awesome. She is no statesman 3 who makes a treaty in an air-conditioned chamber and then goes home to a ticker-tape parade. Here is a woman who gets up every morning of her life to tend endless streams of victims of life's longest war of attrition. Without an expectation of victory.

Most of us in her place could not have stood a week or a two-year tour 4 of duty before being overwhelmed by pain and a sense of futility. There are times we all look at good work and good workers as if they were shoveling sand into the wind. But here is a woman who always sees people.

So, the awarding of the Nobel Prize for Peace to Mother Teresa is a 5 pinch at our consciences—that unpopular and obsolete part of our ethical anatomy. People today don't talk about their consciences and how to appease them; they talk about guilt-trips and how to avoid them.

But Mother Teresa reminds us how often we think of the poor of the 6 world as sand. Most of us live according to self-interest. The truly selfless are as rare as Nobel Prize winners.

But it is a question of how wide our definition of self-interest is and 7 how much it rules our lives.

It is hard, at a time when many Americans feel desperate about their 8 heating bills or their ability to buy a home of their own, to think about the emaciated child. It's hard when we haven't eliminated poverty in America to think about Calcutta. I don't fault this. It just is.

We can't measure one person's pain against another's. But it isn't hard 9 to measure one person's standard of living against another. The anxiety of the couple worried about a 12 percent mortgage and the anxiety of a couple worried about food is utterly different.

When the Nobel committee awarded its peace prize to Mother Teresa 10 (and I do not forget that they also awarded one to Henry Kissinger), they did so because "poverty and hunger and distress also constitute a threat to peace."

The gap between the rich and the poor of the world makes this country 11 look like an egalitarian utopia. The gap between the rich and the poor of the world is a true source of insecurity and hostility. We are the rich and it is harder and harder to get away from it.

It's odd to quote Fidel Castro and Pope John Paul II in one breath. But 12 in their back-to-back visits to this country, they both gave the same message: "Some countries possess abundant resources while others have nothing."

However dubious Castro's credentials or motivations, his words ring 13 true and we know it. "I have come to warn that, if we do not eliminate our present injustices and inequalities peacefully and wisely, the future will be apocalyptic. Bombs may kill the hungry, the sick and the ignorant, but they cannot kill hunger, disease and ignorance. Nor can they kill the righteous rebellion of the people; and in the holocaust, the rich who are the ones who have the most to lose in this world will also die."

Mother Teresa said that, "The great thing about the poor is that they 14 are not discontented. They don't hate us despite their immense suffering. It is a mystery we cannot understand."

Perhaps she is right. Perhaps they are too tired or too concerned with 15 survival for hatred. But I doubt it. When "have nots" see the "haves," they want to know why.

The Nobel Prize award and the words of two visitors from two 16 different worlds suggest that each year we need a broader definition of self-interest: one that sees the world as our neighborhood, one that sees our conscience as a guide, not as a guilt-trip.

"I have been told I spoil the poor by my work," says Mother Teresa. 17 "Well at least one congregation is spoiling the poor, because everyone else is spoiling the rich."

Few of us are or can be as selfless or dedicated as this woman. But 18 perhaps, for a few minutes, she helped us wipe the sand from our eyes, so we could see the people.

❀   ❀   ❀

AFTER YOU READ

THINK about the distinction between heroines (female heroes) and role models made by Maxine F. Singer (see pp. 478–481). If you made a list of the qualities of heroines and role models as suggested in the "THINK about" assignment on page 480, review this list. If not, make such a list now.

EXAMINE the statement that "poverty and hunger and distress also constitute a threat to peace" (paragraph 10). Do you agree or disagree with this statement that served as the basis for the decision of the Nobel Peace Prize committee to award the prize to Mother Teresa? Support your opinion with specific references to historical and current events.

WRITE a paragraph in which you classify Mother Teresa as a heroine or a role model. Before writing your essay, review your lists of the qualities of both heroines and role models. Be sure to include details, examples, and quotations from Goodman's essay to support your opinion.

Having Our Say

SARAH AND
A. ELIZABETH DELANY

In her introduction to the Delanys' memoir Having Our
Say, *which has also been adapted for the Broadway stage,
Amy Hill Hearth writes, "Both more than one hundred
years old, Sarah (Sadie) Delany and her sister, Annie
Elizabeth (Bessie) Delany, are among the oldest living
witnesses to American history. They are also the oldest
surviving members of one of the nation's preeminent black
families which rose to prominence just one generation after
the Civil War." In alternating chapters, Sadie and Bessie
record their personal lives and the history through which
they lived. In the following essay, Dr. Bessie Delany describes her struggle to succeed in dental school in 1919.
Dr. Delany died in September of 1995 at the age of 104.*

BEFORE YOU READ

THINK about what pressures must have been like for dental students at
Columbia University in 1919. Then think about how much greater these
pressures must have been for Bessie Delany as the only black woman in her
class.

EXAMINE the title, "Having Our Say." Do you think that Bessie Delany's
being 101 years old when she wrote this essay causes her to be more or less
direct in "having her say" about her experiences? Why do you feel as you
do?

WRITE a journal entry in which you "have your say" about an experience
that you felt was unfair or demeaning.

AS YOU READ

Look for instances of prejudice and discrimination that Bessie experienced and the way she handled these instances.

I had always dreamed I would become a medical doctor, but I ran out of 1 time and money. I was in my late twenties already and I would have needed a few more credits to get into medical school. I was worried that by the time I earned the money and took those classes, I'd be too old.

So I picked up some science courses at Shaw University in Raleigh with 2 the intention of being ready to enroll in a dental degree program in New York. My brother Harry was a dentist, and he was going to see if I could enroll at New York University, where he had graduated. But this was in 1918, and New York University would not take women in its dentistry program.

Instead, I enrolled at Columbia University. This was in the fall of 1919. 3 There were eleven women out of a class of about 170. There were about six colored men. And then there was me. I was the only colored woman!

Columbia was intimidating, but so was everything else. The city was 4 exciting and terrifying at the same time. I couldn't understand why the high-rise buildings didn't fall down, and the subway, well, that about worried me to death! A classmate of mine at Columbia said, "Let's try that old subway." And I said, "I don't think so." And he said, "What, are you afraid?" And I said, "Of course not! If you're willing to try it, so will I!" So we went and everything worked out OK, though once we were on it, I remember whispering to him, "You sure you know how we can get off this thing?"

Most of the students at the dental school were self-assured city folk, 5 and their families were paying their tuition. I never had the luxury of focusing completely on my studies. I always had money on my mind. I needed more, honey! I had saved money from my teaching years in the South, but it wasn't enough. I remember that I always wore an old brown sweater to my classes, because I couldn't even afford a coat. One day, my brother Harry surprised me. He bought me a beautiful coat, with a small fur collar! When I put that coat on, honey, I looked sensational. I looked as good as Mrs. Astor's pet mule. And the first time I wore it to class, the students stood up and applauded. In a way, it was mean, because they were sort of making fun of me. It was like, "Oh, that Bessie Delany finally has something decent to wear." But I didn't care, no, sir!

My brothers were having the same difficulty with money, so they all 6
worked their way through college as Pullman porters, which was one of
the few jobs a Negro man could get. Hubert used to joke that he had earned
an MBC degree—"master's of baggage carrying."

It was always harder for a Negro to get work than a white person. Even 7
the street merchants in Harlem, in those days, were mostly white. There
were certain companies that were nicer to colored people than others. For
instance, everybody knew that Nestlé's would hire Negroes, but Hershey's
wouldn't. Once I had encountered that, I used to walk through Harlem
and scold any Negro eating a Hershey bar. Usually, they would stop eating
it but sometimes they thought I was crazy. Well, honey, I do not allow
Hershey candy in my home to this day.

As a woman, you couldn't be a Pullman porter, and I refused to work 8
as a maid for white folks. So in the summer, I would go with my little sister
Julia, who had come up from Raleigh to study at Juilliard, to look for
factory jobs. And you know what? They would want to hire Julia, because
she was lighter than me. But we made it clear it was both of us or neither
of us, and sometimes we'd get the job.

Once, we had an assembly-line job where they made sewing needles, 9
and our job was to package them in these little batches, so they were ready
for sale. Then for a while, we worked as ushers at a movie house. The pay
was $12 a week, and we saw all these wonderful movies. My favorite movie
star was Bing Crosby. Lord, we had fun. But I was always treated worse
than Julia, and it was made clear that it was because I was darker-skinned.
Julia was quite light—more like Sadie—and I guess she might even have
passed for white if she had tried.

One time, we were waiting on line to get factory work and this white 10
man tried to give me a break. It was always a white guy who was in charge,
of course. He said, "Oh, I see. You are Spanish." This was supposed to be
my cue to nod my head, since they'd hire you if you were Spanish. But this
made me furious. I said, "No, I am not Spanish. I am an *American Negro!*"
I turned and walked out of there and Julia followed me.

Today I know they have this thing called Affirmative Action. I can see 11
why they need it. There are some places where colored folks would *never,*
not in a thousand years, get a job. But you know what? I really am
philosophically against it. I say: "Let the best person get the job, period."
Everybody's better off in the long run.

It was probably a good thing that I was a little older, mature, and so 12
determined or I never would have made it through dental school. I had a

few girlfriends, but I never told any of them that I was about ten years older. I never talked about where I came from, my teaching years, or any of that. I was always a big talker, but at dental school I was a private person. There was one girl in particular who used to bug me. She would say, "Bessie, how old are you?" or "Bessie, were you a teacher before you came to dental school?" But I didn't tell her anything.

The reason I was so secretive is that I wanted to be taken seriously. 13 Most of the women were not taken seriously. Truth is, it was just after World War I and a lot of men were still overseas, or killed, so those girls were just looking for husbands. But not me. The boys, well, I stayed away from them. The white boys looked down on me and the colored boys were too busy trying to goose my behind! I had no interest in their shenanigans. I was a good-looking gal, and that always got me in trouble. But I was there to learn!

Before I enrolled in dental school I had a long talk with my Mama. 14 She said, "You must decide whether you want to get married someday, or have a career. Don't go putting all that time and effort into your education and career if you think you want to get married."

It didn't occur to anyone that you could be married *and* have a career. 15 Well, I set my sights on the career. I thought, what does any man really have to offer me? I've already raised half the world, so I don't feel the desire to have babies! And why would I want to give up my freedom and independence to take care of some man? In those days, a man expected you to be in charge of a perfect household, to look after his every need. Honey, I wasn't interested! I wasn't going to be bossed around by some man! So the men at college learned to leave me alone, after a while. There was no foolin' with me! In my yearbook, under the picture, they wrote: "Bessie Delany, the Perfect Lady." And that was the truth.

I studied very hard in dentistry school. My brother Harry—he was 16 called "Hap" once he moved to New York—helped me out. He was a sweet brother. He loaned me some dental instruments, which were very expensive—things like that.

I remember like yesterday the first time our class had to do dissections. 17 This was at the morgue at Bellevue Hospital in New York. The first two years of dental school at that time were identical to medical school, and we all had to do them. Sometimes there weren't enough corpses to go around and the dental students would fight for a head because, well, what we really wanted to examine were the teeth and jaw. And some dental students got stuck with body parts that weren't exactly relevant.

Well, that first day all the girls in the class were just a-squealing and 18
a-screaming and a-carrying on. And I strode in there like I was born to do
it. They all said, "Look at that Bessie Delany, why, she sure isn't scared."
Truth is, I was a wreck. I had never touched a dead body before!

When we were children, the Webb family, who were farmers at Saint 19
Aug's, had a baby that died, and this little girl at the school named Maggie
dared Sadie to touch that baby. People weren't propped up in funeral homes
the way they are today. You were wrapped in a shroud and laid out in your
own parlor, and that's where this baby was. Afterward, I said to Sadie,
"Well, what was it like?" And Sadie said, "Oooh, it was just like touching
a piece of marble, hard and cold."

Well, I kept thinking about that poor, marble-like baby while I dissected 20
my first cadaver. We had to fish around and look for these veins and arteries
and nerves and things. Yes, it was pretty disgusting but I was a great actress.
I was determined to be the best dentist there ever was, and I knew I had to
get through this!

I'd dissect a cadaver any day, rather than have to deal with some of 21
those old white professors. Yes, sir! To be fair—oh, it's so hard to be fair—I
have to admit that some of them treated me just fine, especially the dean
of students. He was an old white man, yet he was particularly supportive
of me. But one instructor really had it out for me. There was an assignment
where he failed me, yet I knew my work was good. One of my white girl
friends said, "Bessie, let me turn in your work as if it was mine, and see
what grade he gives it."

I'll tell you what happened, honey. She passed with my failed work! 22
That was the kind of thing that could make you crazy, as a Negro. It's no
wonder some of us have stopped trying altogether. But as my Papa used to
say, "Don't ever give up. Remember, they can segregate you, but they can't
control your mind. Your mind's still yours." Ain't it the truth.

Another thing that happened to me at Columbia was that I was accused 23
of stealing. Me, Bessie Delany! Honey, I had never stolen nothin' in my
life. This is what happened: There was a white girl who was taking
expensive dental instruments. Even my things started disappearing, one by
one. It was puzzling. They cost a lot of money, and some of mine belonged
to Hap, and I took great pains not to lose them. So none of us could
understand where this stuff was going off to.

This girl was a dental student, and we learned later that her boyfriend, 24
also a dental student, had talked her into stealing these tools. He was
selling them somewhere in New York. Well, it got to the point where they

brought in police detectives. And we were summoned in the hallway where our lockers were, and the police asked me to open my locker and they searched it.

We were all gathered around, and I saw that this girl—her name was 25 Rose—was standing closest to my locker. When it was opened, behind her back she sort of casually tossed a dental instrument in there. No one saw it but me and I said in a loud voice, "Rose, what did you toss into my locker?" And the detective and everyone else realized what she had done, and she was caught. She was trying to frame me! And she knew she'd have gotten away with it because it would be easy for everyone to believe that this little darkey was a thief. Now, that just kills me.

Would you believe that Rose and her boyfriend were allowed to finish 26 dental school? They graduated! Honey, if it had been me, I would have been expelled. I would have gone to jail.

I'll tell you something else that annoyed me. When they opened my 27 locker, everybody was surprised at how neat it was. They thought Negroes were dirty, sloppy people, but my locker was perfectly clean and neat, and my one uniform—the only one I could afford—was scrubbed, starched, and ironed. The other girls' lockers were pigsties. And the dean said, "Look at Miss Delany's locker! It is an example to you all."

You see, when you are colored, everyone is always looking for your 28 faults. If you are going to make it, you have to be entirely honest, clean, brilliant, and so on. Because if you slip up once, the white folks say to each other, "See, what'd I tell you." So you don't have to be as good as white people, you have to be *better or the best*. When Negroes are average, *they fail*, unless they are very, very lucky. Now, if you're average and *white*, honey, you can go far. Just look at Dan Quayle. If that boy was colored he'd be washing dishes somewhere.

There are plenty of white folks who say, "Why haven't Negroes gotten 29 further than they have?" They say about Negroes, "What's wrong with them?" To those white people, I have this to say: *Are you kidding?*

Let me tell you something. Even on my graduation day at Columbia, 30 I ran into prejudice. It was the sixth of June, 1923. There I was, getting my Doctor of Dental Surgery Degree, and I was on top of the world. But you know what? The class selected me as the marshall, and I thought it was an honor. And then I found out—I heard them talking—it was because no one wanted to march beside me in front of their parents. It was a way to get rid of me. The class marshall carried the flag and marched out front, alone.

I suppose I should be grateful to Columbia, that at that time they let 31 in colored people. Well, I'm not. They let me in but they beat me down for being there! I don't know how I got through that place, except when I was young nothing could hold me back. No, sir! I thought I could change the world. It took me a hundred years to figure out I *can't* change the world. I can only change Bessie. And, honey, that ain't easy, either.

❀   ❀   ❀

AFTER YOU READ

THINK about what you would have done in Dr. Delany's place if you had been accused of stealing dental instruments and had seen someone trying to frame you. Would you have had the courage to act as Bessie did? What chance did she take?

EXAMINE the advice that Bessie Delany's mother gave her before she enrolled in dental school: "You must decide whether you want to get married someday, or have a career. Don't go putting all that time and effort into your education and career if you think you want to get married." Was this good advice for her? Why or why not? Would it be good advice today?

EXAMINE also the last paragraph in the essay in which Delany writes, "I thought I could change the world. It took me a hundred years to figure out I *can't* change the world. I can only change Bessie. And, honey, that ain't easy, either." From your reading of the essay, how did she change herself? Notice also the oral style of the selection. The Delany sisters told these stories orally to Amy Hill Hearth, who recorded them.

WRITE an essay in which you argue whether Bessie Delany is a hero or a role model. Before you write your essay, review the definitions by Maxine F. Singer.

Selena: Dreaming of You

ILAN STAVANS

When Tejana superstar Selena Quintanilla Perez was shot by the founder of her fan club, thousands of her admirers reacted with shock and grief. As many as 50,000 people from as far away as Guatemala and Canada met in Corpus Christi, Texas, to honor the twenty-three-year-old Grammy winner who specialized in Tejana music, a lively blend of American pop tunes, Spanish lyrics, Tex-Mex rhythms, and polka rhythms incorporated into the music of Northern Mexico. In the following article from The New Republic, *Ilan Stavans explores the powerful and complex feelings that Selena's followers had—and still have—for her.*

BEFORE YOU READ

THINK about the distinctions among heroes, role models, and celebrities that Phil Sudo, Jean Picker Firstenberg, Richard Shereikis, and Maxine F. Singer have made in previous reading selections. From what you have heard about Selena in the media, would you consider her a hero, a role model, a celebrity, some combination of these types, or something different altogether?

EXAMINE the first paragraph of the reading selection. How does the view of Selena reported here differ from the traditional view of a hero? Does she take on a religious or spiritual dimension? How is this dimension reflective of the culture she represents?

EXAMINE also the following Spanish words used in the essay. English translations and definitions have been provided for you.

la frontera (paragraphs 2, 4, 8, and 9)—the frontier, the border between Mexico and the United States.

gabacha (paragraph 3)—a term for a female Spaniard, usually deroga-
tory.

descamisados (paragraph 3)—translates as "without a shirt" but is used
to mean "poor, humble people."

conjunto (paragraph 4)—literally means "a group of people who play
music," but in the Southwest it means "a certain type of music from
northern Mexico."

una de nosotros (paragraph 7)—literally means "one of us"; suggests
that Selena is accessible to her Mexican and Mexican-American fans.

sabor (paragraph 7)—flavor.

WRITE a journal entry in which you discuss your view of an entertainer,
perhaps a singer like Selena, whom you particularly admire. What does this
person represent to you?

AS YOU READ

Underline words and phrases that Stavans uses to describe the way Selena
is viewed by her Mexican-American admirers.

During a recent trip to South Texas, I talked to a respectable old man   1
who told me Selena died because heaven was desperate for another
cherub. Selena was a "celestial beauty," he signed, "whose time on earth
was spent helping the poor and unattended." In San Antonio, a mother of
four has constructed an altar at home, with the dead singer's photograph
surrounded by candles and flowers, just below the image of the Virgen de
Guadalupe, Selena's holy predecessor among Mex-Americans. Amalia
Gonzalez, a Spanish-language radio host, told a journalist that Selena had
visited us "to unite all creeds and races." And a young lady from Corpus
Christi, one of Selena's passionate fans, who spends a good portion of her
days singing "selenatas," swears she has repeatedly seen Selena's ghost at
night on her TV screen—once her set has been turned off.

Welcome to *la frontera,* a land of kitsch and missed opportunities   2
where bizarre dreams and hard-working lives intertwine. Made up of
12 million people, its capital is Tijuana, where *el día de los muertos,* the
Day of the Dead, remains the most popular holiday, an occasion for the
living to spend a long night of food and joy at the cemetery, at the side of
their beloved deceased. *La frontera* is where NAFTA and Kafka cohabit,
where English isn't spoken but broken, and where *yo* becomes I, and I turns

into *Ay, carajo*—a free zone, autonomous and self-referential, perceived by Mexicans as *el fin del mundo,* the end of the world, and by Anglos as a galaxy of *rascuachismo,* i.e., low taste.

Elvis, John Lennon, Kurt Cobain and Jerry Garcia . . . roll over: Selena 3 is here to grant voice to the silenced and oppressed. Née Selena Quintanilla Perez, a Jehovah's Witness with a perpetually bare midriff and an electric voice, she's the uncontested queen of hybrid pop culture, part wetback and part *gabacha.* Her life might have been short and tragic, but death has granted her an imposing stature. At 1:05 p.m. on Friday, March 31, 1995, she became immortal: short of her 24th birthday, she ceased to be the tejana singer she had grown up to be, with modest means and high ambitions, ready to cross over to the mainstream market, and became not only a fearsome competitor to Madonna (her album *Dreaming of You,* with a handful of songs in English, including one by David Byrne, sold 175,000 copies in a single day) but a cult figure, a Hispanic Marilyn Monroe—an object of relentless adoration and adulation. Magically, she has joined Evita Perón in the contemporary pantheon of mystical and magical *hispanas,* a patron saint of the *descamisados.*

How many of us far from *la frontera* had heard from her before her 4 fatal end? Not many, really. But even if we had, her music is *cursi*—melodramatic, cheesy, overemotional, not too far from Juan Gabriel and a relative of Julio Iglesias. In the end it doesn't matter: her *conjunto* pieces, as well as the mental unbalance of Yolanda Saldivar, the woman convicted of the singer's murder last week and sentenced to life in prison, are only props in a theatrical act that presents Selena as a superstar regardless of her talents. Selena was a symbol, not a genius.

A life quilted by sheer coincidence, when studied in retrospect, takes 5 the shape of a perfectly designed odyssey. By a strange luck, Selena's killing took place on César Chávez's birthday. In an already legendary scene Saldivar comes out of Room 158 in Corpus Christi's Days Inn on Navigation Boulevard with a .38-caliber revolver. Blood, tears, desperation. Selena is ahead of her, wounded, crying for help. She names her assassin and then dies a close-up death. Commercial cut: *Vea El Show de Cristina.* The next scene takes place minutes later, as Saldivar seals herself in a pickup truck with a pistol to her temple and, à la O.J., keeps the police at bay for nine and a half hours. Saldivar had been a fan, then a good friend, then a business partner in charge of Selena, Inc., the company comprised of the singer's boutiques and beauty salons in Corpus Christi and San Antonio. She had been embezzling funds, and Selena had come to confront her. But what really went wrong between the two women? Stay tuned and catch the answer in our next episode, in the form of a Hollywood movie by director Gregory Nava, who brought you *El Note,* about the plight of poor Guatemalan immigrants in *el otro lado.*

Selena's father, a singer and Tex-Mex restauranteur named Abraham 6
Quintanilla Jr., whose family has been in South Texas for at least 100 years, forced her to learn *español* in order to further her career; English was her first language, but he thought she could more easily find a following singing in Spanish. Her debut, at age 5, was in her father's group, *Los Dinos.* Less than two decades later, married but with a sexy public persona built around a halter top and tight pants, she was a Grammy winner worth more than $5 million. She was lucky, then, to die just as her crossover dreams were beginning to materialize.

For those mourning her, she was a brave, astonishingly courageous 7
chicana, ambivalent about but never ashamed of her background. Selena drove her Porsche to the Wal-Mart. "You'd see her shopping at the mall," people in South Texas told me. "And you'd see her working at home. A real sweetheart." They like to recall how accessible she was—*una de nosotros:* Selena performed in Mexican variety shows and soap operas, from the long-running *Siempre en Domingo* to the melodrama *Dos mujeres, un camino.* Small parts, no doubt, but the real *sabor:* corny and sentimental. Had Selena been visited by the angel of death only a few years later, a very different story would have been told. She would have been an American Star, and her misfortune would not be useful today to highlight the reticence with which *la frontera* in particular, and Latino culture in general, is taken in by the rest of the country.

Now Selena is a pantheistic deity in *la frontera*—everywhere you look, 8
there she is: on TV screens and CDs, on book covers and calendars, on velvet slippers, T-shirts, lithographs, baseball hats, stickers, plastic bracelets, shampoos and *piñatas.* In Texas, more than 600 baby girls have been named after Selena in the months since her death. "Thanks to her, tejanos are being heard," a disk jockey from Houston told me. "She put us in the news—and on the front page of *The New York Times.*" George W. Bush, the governor of Texas, whose knowledge of tejano culture, according to most Mex-Americans, is nothing but null, declared April 16, 1995, Selena's birthday and Easter Sunday, *El día de Selena.* There's a move to issue a postage stamp in her honor and to build a plaza with her statue in its center in Corpus Christi.

Meanwhile, many people north and south of the Rio Grande have been 9
engaging in active prayer to Vírgen Selena, their own Madonna, so that

heaven above might send some miracles to *la frontera:* more *dólares* descending once the media craze is over, for instance; or a less condescending attitude toward its idols while they are alive. Otherwise Mex-American youngsters might get the wrong message, thinking they will only be heard by Anglo ears after they are dead and buried.

❀ ❀ ❀

AFTER YOU READ

THINK about the effect that Selena's death had not only on the Hispanic community but also on their view of Selena herself. How has she been transformed into a "cult figure" (paragraph 3), a "symbol" (paragraph 4) of her culture? Is a symbol the same as a hero? Why or why not?

EXAMINE the phrase *la frontera,* which means "the frontier" or "the border" and which is used in several different contexts in the article. In paragraph 2 *la frontera* literally means "the border area between Mexico and the United States"—the fascinating but poor and sometimes dangerous region described in this paragraph. In paragraph 7, however, Stavans uses the term to mean a "musical frontier," to suggest that Selena was becoming a "crossover" star, moving from the relatively limited Tejano audience into mainstream pop culture. Has her tragic death made this crossover more complete? How can this crossover promote greater understanding and respect of Mexican and Mexican-American culture? What examples of this greater respect does Stavans give in the article?

WRITE an essay in which you compare and contrast the *real* Selena as she is described by Stavans with the idealized view of her held by many of her followers. Or **WRITE** an essay in which you use outside research to compare and contrast Selena with another Hispanic hero such as Evita Perón or César Chávez, both of whom are mentioned in the essay.

A Hero's Journey:
Neil Armstrong's Walk on
the Moon

THOMAS TALLEY

Thomas Talley has, in many ways, lived the life of an adventurer himself. He served as a photojournalist in Vietnam in 1965–1966, has worked with high-pressure natural gas wells and steam drilling, and enjoys mountain climbing and white-water canoeing. Therefore, he made an immediate personal connection with the concept of the hero's adventure when he read about it in Joseph Campbell's The Hero with a Thousand Faces,* a book that was required reading for an interdisciplinary class on the hero that Talley took at East Texas State University. According to Campbell:*

> The standard path of the mythological adventure of the hero is a magnification of the formula represented in the rites of passage: *separation—initiation—return:* which might be named the nuclear unit of the monomyth.
>
> *A hero ventures forth from the world of common day into a region of supernatural wonder: fabulous forces are there encountered and a decisive victory is won: the hero comes back from this mysterious adventure with the power to bestow boons on his fellow man.* (30)

Talley believes, however, that his greatest adventure has been to return to college in mid-life as a full-time student

---

*Campbell, Joseph. *The Hero with a Thousand Faces,* 1949. Princeton, N.J.: Princeton University Press, 1968.

*majoring in English and history. In the following essay,
Talley responds to his reading by applying Campbell's
description of the hero's quest to Neil Armstrong's walk
on the moon.*

BEFORE YOU READ

THINK about how Neil Armstrong must have felt as he became the first
human being to stand on the moon and look back at the earth. How would
you have felt? Can you think of any comparable experiences that other
human beings have experienced, or could experience in the future?

EXAMINE the title of Talley's essay. How was Armstrong a hero? How did
his experience fit Campbell's description of the hero adventure?

WRITE a journal entry in which you describe an experience that you believe
is—or could be—comparable to Neil Armstrong's walk on the moon.

AS YOU READ

Identify the valuable knowledge or gifts that Armstrong, in Talley's opinion, brought back to humanity from his adventure. Also, notice how Talley
uses quotations from Campbell in his essay.

What Neil Armstrong found when he went on the greatest heroic   1
adventure in the history of the world was not the moon. When
Armstrong stood in the moon dust and looked back, he discovered the
Earth. Mankind had seen the moon forever; now through the marvel of
television, he could see the most beautiful object in the heavens, his own
home. Having had this unique experience, Armstrong placed humanity
precisely in the cosmos, much like a "you are here" map in a universal mall.
The sight was powerful in terms of changing perspective.

As I read Joseph Campbell's description of a hero, I felt Neil Armstrong   2
fit the model perfectly, especially the ritual heroic journey, the initiation,
and finally the returning with knowledge. Campbell explains that the
purpose of a ritual adventure is ". . . to conduct people across those difficult
thresholds of transformation that demand a change in the patterns not only
of conscious but also of unconscious life" (10). The idea of a man on the
moon and the sight of a small earth satisfy these mythical requirements.

Campbell explains the goal of a hero's journey: 3

> The two—the hero and his ultimate god, the seeker and the found—are thus
> understood as the outside and inside of a single, self-mirrored mystery, which
> is identical with the mystery of the manifest world. The great deed of the
> supreme hero is to come to the knowledge of this unity in multiplicity and
> then to make it known. (40)

There can be no question that, through the power of television, on that   4
July night in 1969, Neil Armstrong became the "great" hero to every
culture on Earth, something no one god or hero had ever done before. His
courageous quest united humankind for the first time in a shared experience. There was loud applause in Russia and Red China; the aborigines in
Australia prayed for him. He transcended the crude political ambitions that
may have placed him there. He was a man who became Everyman. A human
like the rest of us, he was standing on the face of the moon. Neil Armstrong
was actually looking back from a place of great peril. Homer never dreamed
of placing the hero Odysseus in such distant danger.

Campbell says, the hero must obtain some knowledge or boon, and   5
"the hero must make this knowledge known" (40). One of the world's
greatest heroes should bring back an equally great message—and Armstrong did. He brought back the power to change humanity's belief about
itself. Armstrong cracked open a door, "the secret opening through which
the inexhaustible energies of the cosmos pour into human cultural mani-
festations" (3). Intellectual chains fell from minds all over the world. If we
can go to the moon, then nothing, not even world peace, is impossible.
Armstrong gave us a new cosmic view of ourselves and thus a new
appreciation of the Earth and our capabilities.

You and I are the ones making this new myth. When Armstrong   6
returned, he splashed down in the Pacific Ocean and into the world's
subconscious. Since that time, the inward journey of meaning in Armstrong's outward heroic journey has been bouncing from Chinese poets to
African dancers, from European painters to American cowboys, from you
to me. Daily we struggle to comprehend our invasion of realms once
reserved for the gods. In contemplation of humanity's first cosmic foot-
prints, we all are shaping the shared myth. For as Franz Boas said, ". . . in
the main the mental characteristics of man are the same all over the world"
(18).

Can a new myth be born—where man should love his neighbor for the   7
benefit of all? Or is it as Campbell says, "that the perilous journey was a
labor not of attainment but of reattainment, not discovery but rediscovery"

(39). The rediscovery is that humans must find a way to live with respect, not only for each other but for all life. A world hero has appeared, perhaps just in time, to show us how tiny and frail our Earth is—and how beautiful.

❀   ❀   ❀

AFTER YOU READ

THINK about the "boon"—the knowledge that Armstrong brought back to humanity. How does Talley describe this boon? Do you agree with Talley, or do you believe that Armstrong brought back something different?

EXAMINE Talley's use of quotations throughout his essay. Notice that he puts quotation marks around short quotations of only two or three lines but that he intended one long passage to show that it was quoted. When a passage is set off and indented in this way, it does not require quotation marks. Notice also that Talley included the page number of each quotation in parentheses following the quotation. Look closely at the inset quotation on p. 500, especially the phrase, "The great deed of the supreme hero is to come to the knowledge of . . . unity in multiplicity and then to make it known." How does Talley use Armstrong's experience to illustrate this point in paragraph 4?

EXAMINE also Talley's use of the word *myth*. You may have thought of a myth as something that is false or untrue, but as Campbell and Talley use the word, it means a set of values or beliefs.

WRITE a reaction to the phrase "Armstrong gave us a new cosmic view of ourselves and thus a new appreciation of the Earth and our capabilities." Do you agree or disagree with Talley? If you agree, what is this "new cosmic view" and "new appreciation of the Earth and our capabilities"? Is this appreciation as great today as it was in 1969? Why or why not?

Christa McAuliffe:
An Ordinary Hero

MIKE PRIDE

As Thomas Talley discusses in his essay, Neil Armstrong was able to complete the "hero's journey" in space by leaving the earth, walking on the moon, and then returning home successfully. Along with the other Challenger astronauts, however, Christa McAuliffe had her own hero's journey cut tragically short as the shuttle exploded immediately after take-off from Cape Canaveral, Florida, in January of 1986. Just as Armstrong was the first man to walk on the moon, McAuliffe was to have been the first teacher (and one of the first women) in space. In the following essay, Mike Pride, the editor of McAuliffe's hometown newspaper, The Concord Monitor, *remembers McAuliffe and comments about her heroism.*

BEFORE YOU READ

THINK about the idea of women as heroes. In his essay "Larger Than Life," Phil Sudo calls attention to the small number of women treated as heroes in American history. In your opinion, why do we have so few female heroes? Are women more likely to be viewed as role models than as heroes? How does a female hero differ from a female role model? From what you know about Christa McAuliffe, would you consider her a hero? Why or why not?

EXAMINE the use of the word *odyssey* in the second paragraph: "From before that July day until the moment she disappeared in a pink-white puff on the newsroom television screen, we helped her neighbors follow her *odyssey*." The word *odyssey* can be traced back to Odysseus, a mythical Greek hero. Because of Odysseus's epic quest for his homeland, the word *odyssey* now means a personal journey or search.

502

WRITE a journal entry explaining why our society has so few female heroes.

AS YOU READ

Determine whether Christa McAuliffe was a hero or a role model.

In the journal I keep, the entry for July 20, 1985, begins: "Yesterday was   1
an incredible day to be editor of the local paper." The day before at the
White House, Christa McAuliffe, from my hometown, Concord, N.H., had
been named the teacher in space. Near the end of my journal entry is this
quotation from her: "I think the students will say that an ordinary person
is contributing to history, and if they can make that connection, they are
going to get excited about history and about the future."

Christa made the future—space—an area we covered in the small   2
newspaper I edit. From before that July day until the moment she disappeared in a pink-white puff on the newsroom television screen, we helped
her neighbors follow her odyssey. Last week we had a different job. There
had been a death in the family, and we groped, with our readers, for what
it meant.

Christa made Concord proud. The people in our city saw in her the   3
best that we have to offer. Concord is a family town, and it cares about
education. A mother, a wife, and a teacher, Christa spoke out for her
profession. She was robust and confident; she played volleyball and loved
the outdoors. She was a volunteer in a city that seems at times to be run
by volunteers. She also taught what Roman Catholics used to call a
catechism class. She let no one forget that when she was growing up,
teaching was one of the few fields open to women. She was a role model,
bringing home the message again and again: if I can do this, think what
you can do.

And she became a media darling. In front of a semicircle of TV cameras,   4
she would describe deadpan how the shuttle's toilet worked. The people
of Concord, of course, knew that Christa was not performing for the media.
The camera didn't lie, and Christa didn't act. This was the real *her*. Whether
she was waving Paul Giles's baton to conduct Nevers' Band—it dates back
to the Civil War—or chatting with her son's hockey teammates at the
Everett Arena, she was the same vibrant, positive person the rest of America
saw on TV.

CRAZY ABOUT CHRISTA

It is assumed in our society that people who capture the nation, as Christa ₅
had, go on to fame and fortune. Those who knew her best knew that Christa
had no such intention. She would have used her celebrity to advocate causes
she believed in, but she could hardly wait to get back to her classroom at
Concord High. She had chosen the profession and chosen Concord, and
her selection as teacher in space had done nothing but affirm those choices.

If Christa liked Concord, Concord was crazy about Christa. It made ₆
her the grand marshal in a parade. It gave her a day. Her high school sent
her off to Houston with a banner that read "Good luck from the Class of
'86 . . . Mrs. McAuliffe . . . Have a blast!" A committee made big plans for
her homecoming. New Year's Eve, the city featured ice sculptures of rocket
ships and stars on the New Hampshire State House lawn.

Bob Hohler, our paper's columnist, became Christa's shadow, sending ₇
back dispatches from Washington, Houston, and finally, Cape Canaveral.
Her beaming face graced our front page countless times, floating weightless
during training, dwarfed by *Challenger* before an earlier launch, grinning
with her husband, Steve. Her story always seemed too good to be true, and
too American. No one is really the girl next door. No one rides in a parade
down Main Street on a bright, sunny Saturday afternoon. No one equates
a modern venture with the pioneers crossing the plains in Conestoga
wagons.

In the journal I keep, the entry for Jan. 28, 1986, begins: "What a ₈
tragic day for Concord." Tears have flowed in my city for days—long,
wearying days. Words have flowed, too, in verse, in letters to the editor,
on radio talk shows.

INTENSE AND PERSONAL

All the media people who have interviewed me and others at the newspaper ₉
want to know how it feels here. Our pain is more intense and personal, I
tell them, but we know we are not alone; nearly everyone I know was
consoled by a call from someone. Ordinary people, the kind McAuliffe's
mission had intended to reach, have called from out of the blue. One man
from Alberta, Canada, told me that his family felt terrible and needed to
speak with someone here because if they felt that bad, he said, we must feel
much worse.

I thought at first that Christa's death would be hardest on the children. ₁₀
They had learned all about the shuttle, and in an age without heroes, they

had found one in her. Most had witnessed the dreadful moment. Yet times like these remind us that children are resilient. Age robs us of the instinct to go forward without a backward glance. I even suspect now that we have tried too hard to make our children feel what we want them to feel. It is the adults in Concord who still have swollen eyes and stricken looks. They comprehend what was lost, and what was lost was a part of them. It is not a myth to say that everyone in town knew Christa. She was easy to meet, easy to talk to. Even those who never had the chance felt as though they had.

Since we picked up Christa McAuliffe's trail, our town has traversed 11 from the green, fertile days of midsummer to the cold heart of winter. The subtle daily changes of nature have played tricks on us; sometimes, at this time of year, it can seem as if summer might never come again.

Many people have compared Christa's death with the assassination of 12 John F. Kennedy, the inspiration of her youth. There are differences, but for the people of Concord—even for the nation as a whole—the comparison is valid. She stood for what was best in us at a time when we wanted to believe that the American spirit was reborn. That makes her death hard.

❀ ❀ ❀

AFTER YOU READ

THINK about the statement that Pride makes in paragraph 10 that "in an age without heroes, they [the children] had found one in her [McAuliffe]." Do you agree with Pride that we live in an age without heroes? Explain your response.

EXAMINE the title "Christa McAuliffe: An Ordinary Hero." How many times does Pride use the word *ordinary* in his essay? What does he mean by the phrase "an ordinary hero"? How was McAuliffe an ordinary hero? How was she an extraordinary hero?

WRITE a paragraph arguing whether Christa McAuliffe was *primarily* a hero or a role model. Begin your paragraph with a definition of the category into which you place McAuliffe. Then develop your paragraph by discussing how McAuliffe fits your definition.

Those Winter Sundays

ROBERT HAYDEN

African-American poet Robert Hayden learned only after he was grown to appreciate the foster father who took him into his home, adopted him, and took care of him even though arguments with his wife filled their house with "chronic angers." In the following poem, Hayden pays tribute to this father's heroic selflessness—to the quiet kind of courage that often goes unrecognized.

BEFORE YOU READ

THINK about some of the acts of daily heroism that your mother, father, or another special person in your life has performed for you.

EXAMINE the question posed in the last two lines of the poem: "What did I know, what did I know/of love's austere and lonely offices?" In this context, *austere* means "harsh" or "severe," and *offices* means "favors" or "duties" performed for another.

WRITE in your journal a list of services that parents perform for their children, often with little or no thanks in return.

AS YOU READ

Look for the *offices,* the favors or duties, that the father performs for his family and especially for the son who is the speaker.

Sundays too my father got up early
and put his clothes on in the blueblack cold,
then with cracked hands that ached
from labor in the weekday weather made
banked fires blaze. No one ever thanked him.   5

I'd wake and hear the cold splintering, breaking.
When the rooms were warm, he'd call,
and slowly I would rise and dress,
fearing the chronic angers of that house.

Speaking indifferently to him,   10
who had driven out the cold
and polished my good shoes as well.
What did I know, what did I know
of love's austere and lonely offices?

❀ ❀ ❀

AFTER YOU READ

THINK about what it would be like to get up every winter morning in a cold climate in an unheated house. If you lived in these conditions, would you be willing to get up first and get the house warm for your family?

EXAMINE the language of the poem. What words and images suggest the cold most effectively?

EXAMINE also the reaction of the son to the father. How would you describe this reaction? How do you suppose this reaction made the father feel? Why did the father continue to get up early on Sundays as well as on weekdays to perform his "austere and lonely offices"?

WRITE a character sketch describing someone who has performed, or who performs, "love's austere and lonely offices" for you.

A Song of Greatness

(from the Chippewa)

MARY AUSTIN

In 1888, when she was twenty years old, Mary Austin moved to Southern California to homestead with her mother. Austin not only grew to love the Southwestern landscape, but she also developed great sympathy and understanding for Native American cultures. By retelling many stories and chants from various tribes, she helped to preserve these vanishing cultures. "A Song of Greatness" comes from the Chippewa, or Ojibway, tribe of the far Northeast, which was also Austin's home for a while. This Native American chant connects the theme of heroes with the theme of self, and thus completes the circle of investigation that you began in the first chapter of Interactions.

BEFORE YOU READ

THINK about how the idea of heroism relates to *you*. Do you consider—or have you ever considered—yourself a hero? Why or why not? What would it take for you to become a hero in your own eyes?

EXAMINE the title of the chant. Does the title suggest a positive or a negative view of life?

WRITE a journal entry in which you define greatness.

AS YOU READ

Think about the effect the stories told by the elders of this tribe have on the speaker.

When I hear the old men   1
Telling of heroes,
Telling of great deeds
Of ancient days,
When I hear that telling   5
Then I think within me
I too am one of these.

When I hear the people
Praising great ones,
Then I know that I too   10
Shall be esteemed,
I too when my time comes
Shall do mightily.

❀ ❀ ❀

AFTER YOU READ

THINK about the speaker's growing self-confidence—to "be esteemed"
and to "do mightily." What causes the speaker to become more confident?

EXAMINE the last line of the first stanza: "I too am one of these." Notice
that this line suggests the growing feeling of community, of oneness, that
the speaker feels. How does such a feeling of community contribute to an
individual's self-confidence and belief in his or her potential?

WRITE about yourself as a hero or a heroine. Do you consider yourself or
some aspect of your life to be heroic? If so, how? If not, how might you
become heroic? Or **WRITE** your own "song of greatness."

Unit Eight: Critical Thinking and Writing Assignments

❀ ❀ ❀

EXPLORING IDEAS TOGETHER

1. With a group of your classmates, make a list of all the heroes—male and female—that you have read about in this unit. Then categorize, or group, these heroes. What categories do you have? Which qualities distinguish the heroes of each category? Into which category, or categories, do most heroes fit?

2. The main characters of many recent movies are what Jean Picker Firstenberg calls antiheroes—people who do not exhibit the traditional strength and courage of heroes. For example, Clark Kent is the antihero who corresponds to the traditional hero Superman. With a group of your classmates, brainstorm about the main characters of movies you have recently seen. How many of these characters are true hero figures? How many are antiheroes? Which type of hero do you prefer? Why?

3. With a group of your classmates, try to answer the question: "Can a celebrity be a hero?" In forming your answer, you may want to review the readings by Sudo, Firstenberg, Shereikis, and Singer. After you have discussed this question with a group of your classmates, write a collaborative essay explaining your position.

4. Mike Pride states that we live in "an age without heroes," and Mike Lupica discusses the fallen legends of sports. Discuss with a group of classmates the idea that our society has no real heroes today. Do you agree or disagree with this idea? How could a lack of heroes affect a society?

WRITING ESSAYS

1. Write a letter (or an essay) recommending someone you know for a Medal of Valor. Your purpose is to persuade the committee awarding the medal to select your nominee. Therefore, you should include specific supporting details and examples that will convince your audience.

2. Several of the readings in this unit focus on heroes of particular ethnic groups. Write an essay about a hero who has contributed to a particular

culture. If necessary, do some research on this person before writing your essay.

3. The reading selections by Buchsbaum, Singer, Goodman, the Delanys, Stavans, and Pride all focus on female heroes. What other woman do you consider a hero? Write an essay about this person.

4. Firstenberg, Shereikis, and Rosenblatt focus on the influence of the media on our perception of heroes. Write an essay in which you argue that this influence is negative or positive. Be sure to use specific supporting details.

5. Write an essay in which you argue for or against the idea that a sports figure or an entertainer can be a true hero. Remember to use specific support.

6. Write an essay in which you compare the heroic actions of Lenny Skutnik and "the man in the water." In your conclusion, state who—in your opinion—was the more heroic and why.

7. Several readings in this unit—notably those by Shereikis, the Delanys, Pride, and Hayden—focus on the concept of the "ordinary hero." Write an essay about an ordinary person whom you consider a hero.

8. In his essay on Christa McAuliffe, Mike Pride uses the phrase "an age without heroes," and Mike Lupica discusses the fallen legends in sports. Write an essay agreeing or disagreeing with the idea that we have no real heroes in our society. Support your essay with examples.

Acknowledgments

Text Credits

"My Name" from *The House on Mango Street* by Sandra Cisneros. Copyright © 1984, 1988 by Sandra Cisneros. All rights and inquiries: Sandra Cisneros, c/o Susan Bergholz Literary Service, 340 W. 72nd St., NYC 10023. Page 17.

From *The Woman Warrior* by Maxine Hong Kingston. Copyright © 1975, 1976 by Maxine Hong Kingston. Reprinted by permission of Alfred A. Knopf Inc. Page 20.

From *Lives on the Boundary: The Struggles and Achievements of America's Under-prepared* by Mike Rose. Copyright © by Mike Rose. Reprinted with the permission of The Free Press, a division of Simon and Schuster. Page 25.

Copyright © 1976 by the New York Times Co. Reprinted by permission. Page 33.

Copyright © 1987 by The New York Times Co. Reprinted by permission. Page 37.

From *Newsweek,* March 7, 1994. All rights reserved. Reprinted by permission. Page 41.

"The Wedding Dress: What Do Women Want?" from *Real Property* by Sara Davidson. Copyright © 1980 by Sara Davidson. Used by permission of Doubleday, a division of Bantam Doubleday Dell Publishing Group, Inc. Page 45.

From *Iron John* by Robert Bly, pp. 1–4. Copyright © 1990 by Robert Bly. Reprinted by permission of Addison-Wesley Longman Publishing Company, Inc. Page 50.

"Getting Started" and "On Death and Love" from *Voices of the Rainbow* by Janet Campbell Hale, Kenneth Rosen, Ed., Viking Penguin. Reprinted by permission of the author. Page 54, 206.

"Generations" by Joyce Maynard. Copyright © 1979 by Joyce Maynard. Reprinted by permission of the author. Page 66.

"No Snapshots in the Attic: A Granddaughter's Search for a Cherokee Past" by Connie May Fowler, *The New York Times Book Review,* Vol. 99, May 22, 1994, pp. 49–50. Reprinted by permission of the author. Page 71.

"Two Kinds" from *The Joy Luck Club* by Amy Tan. Copyright © 1989 by Amy Tan. Reprinted by permission of G. P. Putnam's Sons. Page 80.

From *Fatherhood* by Bill Cosby. Copyright © 1986 by William H. Cosby, Jr. Used by permission of Doubleday, a division of Bantam Doubleday Dell Publishing Group, Inc. Page 92.

From *Nobody Ever Died of Old Age* by Sharon R. Curtin. Copyright © 1972 by Sharon R. Curtin. Reprinted by permission of Little, Brown & Company. Page 335.

"Weather Reports" from *Dakota*. Copyright © 1993 by Kathleen Norris. Reprinted by permission of Ticknor & Field/Houghton Mifflin Co. All rights reserved. Page 347.

From *Dream Work* by Mary Oliver. Copyright © 1986 by Mary Oliver. Used by permission of Grove/Atlantic, Inc. Page 352.

Reprinted courtesy of AMS Press, inc. Page 354.

Copyright © 1969 by The University of Georgia. Reprinted by permission of the *Georgia Review*. Page 356.

"A Fable for Tomorrow" from *Silent Spring*. Copyright © 1962 by Rachel L. Carson. Copyright © renewed 1990 by Roger Christie. Reprinted by permission of Houghton Mifflin Co. All rights reserved. Page 361.

"Down with Forests" from *Dateline America* by Charles Kuralt. Copyright © 1979 by CBS, Inc. Reprinted by permission of Harcourt Brace & company. Page 365.

"Waste" from What Are People For? By Wendell Berry. Copyright © 1990 by Wendell Berry. Reprinted by permission of North point Press, a division of Farrar, Straus & Giroux, Inc. Page 372.

From the December 1993 issue of *Garbage* The independent Environmental Quarterly, 2 Main street, Gloucester, MA 01930. Reprinted with permission. Page 377.

"What's Best for the West?" by David Diamond, *USA Weekend*, November 3–5, 1995. Reprinted by permission of the author. Page 381.

Reprinted by permission of Roger Caras and Roberta Pryor, Inc. Copyright © 1988 by Roger Caras. Page 389.

"At the Electronic Frontier" by Miguel Algarin from *Times Now*. Reprinted by permission of the Susan Bergolz Agency, for the author. Page 398.

Reprinted by permission of International Creative Management, Inc. Copyright © 1985 by Nora Ephron. First appeared in the New York Times magazine. Page 400.

"Television Addiction" from *The Plug-in Drug*, revised edition by Marie Winn. Copyright © 1977, 1985 by Marie Winn Miller. Used by permission of Viking Penguin, a division of Penguin Books USA Inc. Page 405.

Reprinted with permission from *The Washington Monthly*. Copyright © by the Washington Monthly Company, 1611 Connecticut Ave., N.W. Washington, D.C. 20009 (202) 462-0128. Page 413.

Reprinted by permission of the author. Page 416.

Copyright © October 30, 1995, U.S. News & World Report. Page 420.

"Gender Gap in Cyberspace" by Deborah Tannen, *Newsweek*, May 16, 1994, copyright © by Deborah Tannen. Reprinted by permission. Page 424.

"The Beep Goes On" by Barbara Orlock first published in *Lear's* November 1989. Used by permission of the author. Page 429.

From *Scholastic Update,* December 1993. Copyright © 1993 by Scholastic Inc. Reprinted by permission of Scholastic Inc. Page 439.

Reprinted by arrangement with The Heirs to the Estate of Martin Luther King, Jr., c/o Writers House, Inc., as agent for the proprietor. Copyright © 1963 by Martin Luther King, Jr., copyright © renewed 1991 by Coretta Scott King. Page 443.

"Martin Luther King, Jr." By Gwendolyn Brooks, *A Brother's Treasury* edited by Gwendolyn Brooks. Used by permission of Broadside Press. Page 448.

From *Scholastic Update,* November 1990. Copyright © 1990 by Scholastic Inc. Reprinted by permission of Scholastic Inc. Page 450.

Copyright © 1987 American Film. Reprinted by permission of Jean Picker Firstenberg. Page 457.

Extracts from "Heroes Don't Need Zip Codes: Lenny Skutnik—Accidental Hero" by Richard Shereikis. Reprinted from *The Hero in Transition,* Ray B. Browne & Marshall W. Fishwick, eds., by permission of Bowling Green University Popular Press. Page 461.

Copyright © 1982 by Time Inc. Reprinted by permission. Page 468.

Reprinted by permission of International Creative Management, Inc. Copyright © 1994. Page 473.

Reprinted with the permission of Simon & Schuster from *At Large* by Ellen Goodman. Copyright © 1981 by The Washington Post Company. Page 482.

"Having Our Say" by Sarah and A. Elizabeth Delany, from *Having Our Say: The Delany Sister' First 100 Years.* Copyright © 1993. Reprinted by permission of Kodansha America, Inc. Page 486.

Reprinted by permission of The New Republic, copyright © 1995, The New Republic, Inc. Page 493.

Reprinted by permission of the author. Page 502.

"Those Winter Sundays" copyright © 1966 by Robert Hayden, from *Collected Poems of Robert Hayden* by Frederick Glaysher, editor. Reprinted by permission of Liveright Publishing Corporation. Page 506.

"A Song of Greatness" from *The Children Sing in the Far West* by Mary Austin. Copyright © 1928 by Mary Austin, copyright © renewed 1956 by Kenneth M. Chapman and Mary C. Wheelwright. Reprinted by permission of Houghton Mifflin Company. All rights reserved. Page 508.

Index

Algarin, Miguel, 398–399
Alvarez, Julia, 117–120
"American Dreams: Stanley Cygan, 90" (Terkel), 213–216
"America's 'Garbage Crisis': A Toxic Myth" (Poore), 377–380
Anaya, Rudolfo, 111–116
Angelou, Maya, 139–144
Armstrong, Jane, 232–235
"At the Electronic Frontier" (Algarin), 398–399
Austin, Mary, 508–509

"Beep Goes On, The" (Orlock), 429–433
Barry, Dave, 416–419
Berry, Wendell, 372–376
"Big Squeeze, The" (Samuels), 287–293
Blackmon, Douglas A., 294–300
Blakeslee, Sandra, 196–205
Bly, Robert, 50–53
Bray, Rosemary L., 328–334
Brooks, Gwendolyn, 443–444, 448–449
Brown, Margaret R., 41–44
Buchsbaum, Herbert, 450–456

Camburn, Cindy, 368–371
Caras, Robert, 386, 389–391
Carson, Rachel, 361–364
Carver, Raymond, 186–195
"Case Against Chores, The" (Smiley), 224–227
Chippewa tribe, 508–509
"Christa McAuliffe: An Ordinary Hero" (Pride), 502–505
Cisneros, Sandra, 17–19
Clifton, Lucille, 319–320
Cole, Diane, 168–172
Cole, Karla, 340–342
Cosby, Bill, 92–94
Curtin, Sharon R., 335–339

Davidson, Sara, 45–49
Davis, Robert Murray, 217–220

"Death of a Friend: The Delicacy and Strength of Lace" (Silko and Wright), 157–163
Delany, A. Elizabeth, 486–494
Delany, Sarah, 486–494
Diamond, David, 381–387
"Dice or Doves?" (Camburn), 368–371
"Distance" (Carver), 186–195
Dollarhide, Louis, 356–360
Dove, Rita, 217–219
"Down With the Forests" (Kuralt), 365–367
"Drifting Away" (Cole), 168–172

Ephron, Nora, 400–404
"Error, Error, Error" (Barry), 416–419
"Extraordinary People" (Buchsbaum), 450–454

"Fable for Tomorrow, A" (Carson), 361–364
"Fall of the Legends" (Lupica), 473–477
"Family Farm, The" (Masumoto), 236–239
"Family Values Debate, The" (Wilson), 127–134
"Fatherhood" (Cosby), 92–94
"Finding a Wife" (Soto), 173–177
Firstenberg, Jean Picker, 457–460
Fowler, Connie May, 71–79

"Gender Gap in Cyberspace" (Tannen), 424–428
"Generations" (Maynard), 66–70
"Getting a Degree by Email" (Lord), 420–423
"Getting Started" (Hale), 54–56
"Gift, The" (Dollarhide), 356–360
"Good Marriage, The" (Wallerstein and Blakeslee), 196–205
Goodman, Ellen, 482–485

Hale, Janet Campbell, 54–56, 206–208

519

"Having Our Say" (Delany), 486–492
Hayden, Robert, 506–507
"Heroines and Role Models" (Singer), 478–481
"Hero's Journey: Neil Armstrong's Walk on the Moon, A" (Talley), 498–501
"Hold the Mayonnaise" (Alvarez), 117–120
Holm, Tammy, 409–412
Hull, Jon D., 321–327
"I Have a Dream" (King), 443–448
"In Praise of the F Word" (Sherry), 283–286
"in the inner city" (Clifton), 319–320
"Initiation" (May), 228–231
"Is a Lab Rat's Fate More Poignant Than a Child's?" (McCabe), 386–389

Jacobs, Joanne, 178–180

"Kids Who Kill" (Witkin), 315–318
King, Larry, 95–99
King, Martin Luther, Jr., 443–448
Kingston, Maxine Hong, 20–24
Klagsbrun, Francine, 104–110
Kuralt, Charles, 365–367

"Larger than Life" (Sudo), 439–443
"Lenny Skutnik—Accidental Hero" (Shereikis), 461–467
"Letter, The" (Anaya), 111–116
"Lies That Bind, The" (Thaler), 181–185
"Liked for Myself" (Angelou), 139–144
"Lives on the Boundary" (Rose), 25–32
"Living With My VCR" (Ephron), 400–404
"Lonely Hearts, Classy Dreams, Empty Wallets" (Waldman), 413–415
Lopate, Phillip, 148–156
Lord, Mary, 420–423
Lupica, Mike, 473–477

McCabe, Jane, 386–389
McDonald, Walter, 100–103
Machida, Shozo, 57–61
"Man in the Water, The" (Rosenblatt), 468–472
"Martin Luther King Jr." (Brooks), 443–444, 448–449
Masumoto, David Mas, 236–239
May, Rebecca, 228–231
Maynard, Joyce, 66–70

"Misery of Silence, The" (Kingston), 20–24
"Mother Teresa and Her Endless Fight" (Goodman), 482–485
"My Mother Enters the Workforce" (Dove), 221–224
"My Name" (Cisneros), 17–19

Native American (Chippewa), 508–509
Native American (Tewa), 354–355
"Never in My Life" (McDonald), 100–103
"New American Man, The" (Bly), 50–53
"No Snapshots in the Attic: A Grand-daughter's Search for a Cherokee Past" (Fowler), 71–79
"Nobody Ever Died of Old Age" (Curtin), 335–339
Norris, Kathleen, 347–351

"Oil and Water" (Owen), 145–147
"Old at Seventeen" (Vecsey), 37–40
"Old Man, The" (King), 95–99
Oliver, Mary, 352–353
"On Being 17, Bright, and Unable to Read" (Raymond), 33–36
"On Death and Love" (Hale), 206–208
"On Heroes and the Media" (Firstenberg), 457–460
Orlock, Carol, 429–433
"Out of College, Out of Work" (Sherrill), 244–247
Owen, Valerie, 145–147

Poore, Patricia, 377–380
Pride, Mike, 502–505

Rawlins, Orville, 121–126
Raymond, David, 33–36
"Recoloring of Campus Life, The" (Steele), 301–306
"Resegregation of a Southern School, The" (Blackmon), 294–300
"Right to Know, The" (Brown), 41–44
"Right to Marry, The" (Jacobs), 178–180
Rose, Mike, 25–32
Rosenblatt, Roger, 468–472

Salinas, Marta, 277–282
Samuels, David, 287–295
"Scholarship Jacket, The" (Salinas), 277–282

"Selena: Dreaming of You" (Stavans), 493–497

Shereikis, Richard, 461–467

Sherrill, Stephen, 244–247

Sherry, Mary, 283–286

"Sibling Imprints" (Klagsbrun), 104–110

Siegel, Dorothy, 307–314

Silko, Leslie Marmon, 157–163

Singer, Maxine F., 478–481

"Slow Descent into Hell" (Hull), 321–327

Smiley, Jane, 224–227

"So How Did I Get Here?" (Bray), 328–334

"Song of Greatness, A" (from the Chippewa) (Austin), 508–509

"Song of the Sky Loom" (Native American—Tewa), 354–355

Soto, Gary, 173–177

"Spokesperson" (Armstrong), 232–235

"Stars of the Whole Sky, The" (Machida), 57–61

Stavans, Ilan, 493–497

Steele, Shelby, 301–306

Sudo, Phil, 439–442

Taibbi, Mike, 164–167

Talley, Thomas, 498–501

Tan, Amy, 80–91

Tannen, Deborah, 424–428

"Technology and the Hearing Impaired" (Holm), 409–412

"Television Addiction" (Winn), 405–408

Terkel, Studs, 213–216

Tewa tribe, 354–355

Thaler, Paul, 181–185

Theriault, Reg, 240–243

"Those Winter Sundays" (Hayden), 506–507

"20 Hot Job Tracks," 248–269

"Two Kinds" (Tan), 80–91

Vecsey, David, 37–40

Waldman, Amy, 413–415

Wallerstein, Judith S., 196–205

"Wanted—A Mother" (Rawlins), 121–126

"Waste" (Berry), 372–376

"We Don't Want to Grow Old" (Cole), 340–342

"We Must Find Alternatives to Animals in Research" (Caras), 389–391

"Weather Reports" (Norris), 347–351

"What Do Women Want?" (Davidson), 45–49

"What Friends Are For" (Lopate), 148–156

"What Is Behind the Growth of Violence on College Campuses?" (Siegel), 307–314

"What's Best for the West?" (Diamond), 381–387

"Where's Dietz?" (Taibbi), 164–167

"Wild Geese" (Oliver), 352–353

Wilson, James Q., 127–134

Winn, Marie, 405–408

Witkin, Gordon, 315–318

"Work Ahead, The," 270–272

"Work and Play" (Davis), 217–220

"Workman's Compensation, The" (Theriault), 240–243

Wright, James, 157–163

INSTRUCTOR'S RESOURCE MANUAL

Interactions

INSTRUCTOR'S RESOURCE MANUAL

Interactions

A Thematic Reader

THIRD EDITION

Ann Moseley

Texas A & M University-Commerce

Jeanette Harris

University of Southern Mississippi

HOUGHTON MIFFLIN COMPANY   BOSTON   NEW YORK

Sponsoring Editor: Renee Deljon
Senior Associate Editor: Ellen Darion
Editorial Assistants: Christian Zabriskie and Joy Park
Senior Project Editor: Fred Burns
Production/Design Coordinator: Deb Frydman
Manufacturing Manager: Florence Cadran
Marketing Manager: Nancy Lyman

Printed in the U.S.A.

0-395-84071-6

1234565789 CS 00 99 98 97 96

Contents

Genre Table of Contents   vii

Making Connections Among the Units: Alternative
    Thematic Table of Contents   xi

INTRODUCTION   1

UNIT ONE: THE SELF   12
Critical Thinking and Writing Assignments   18

UNIT TWO: SELF WITH FAMILY   19
Critical Thinking and Writing Assignments   27

UNIT THREE: SELF WITH FRIENDS AND MATES   28
Critical Thinking and Writing Assignments   37

UNIT FOUR: SELF WITH WORK   38
Critical Thinking and Writing Assignments   44

UNIT FIVE: SELF WITH SOCIETY   45
Critical Thinking and Writing Assignments   53

UNIT SIX: SELF WITH ENVIRONMENT   54
Critical Thinking and Writing Assignments   60

UNIT SEVEN: SELF WITH TECHNOLOGY   61
Critical Thinking and Writing Assignments   66

UNIT EIGHT: SELF WITH HEROES   67
Critical Thinking and Writing Assignments   78

Genre Table of Contents

Autobiography and Autobiographical Essays

The Misery of Silence, Maxine Hong Kingston (Unit One)
Lives on the Boundary, Mike Rose (Unit One)
On Being 17, Bright, and Unable to Read, David Raymond (Unit One)
Old at Seventeen, David Vecsey (Unit One)
The Stars of the Whole Sky, Shoza Machida (Unit One)

Generations, Joyce Maynard (Unit Two)
No Snapshots in the Attic: A Granddaughter's Search for a Cherokee Past,
    Connie May Fowler (Unit Two)
Fatherhood, Bill Cosby (Unit Two)
The Old Man, Larry King (Unit Two)
Sibling Imprints, Francine Klagsbrun (Unit Two)
Hold the Mayonnaise, Julia Alvarez (Unit Two)
Wanted—A Mother, Orville Rawlins (Unit Two)

Liked for Myself, Maya Angelou (Unit Three)
Oil and Water, Valerie Owen (Unit Three)
Where's Dietz?, Mike Taibbi (Unit Three)
Drifting Away, Diane Cole (Unit Three)
Finding a Wife, Gary Soto (Unit Three)
The Lies That Bind, Paul Thaler (Unit Three)

Work and Play, Robert Murray Davis (Unit Four)
Initiation, Rebecca May (Unit Four)
Spokesperson, Jane Armstrong (Unit Four)
The Family Farm, David Mas Masumoto (Unit Four)
Out of College, Out of Work, Stephen Sherrill (Unit Four)

The Scholarship Jacket, Marta Salinas (Unit Five)
So How Did I Get Here?, Rosemary L. Bray (Unit Five)

Weather Reports, Kathleen Norris (Unit Six)

Living with My VCR, Nora Ephron (Unit Seven)

Having Our Say, Sarah and A. Elizabeth Delany (Unit Eight)

Case Studies

Kids Who Kill (first part), Gordon Witkin (Unit Five)
Slow Descent into Hell, Jon D. Hull (Unit Five)
Extraordinary People, Herbert Buchsbaum (Unit Eight)

Character Sketches

Generations, Joyce Maynard (Unit Two)
The Old Man, Larry King (Unit Two)
Wanted—A Mother, Orville Rawlins (Unit Two)
Liked for Myself, Maya Angelou (Unit Three)
So How Did I Get Here?, Rosemary L. Bray (Unit Five)
Extraordinary People, Herbert Buchsbaum (Unit Eight)
Lenny Skutnik—Accidental Hero, Richard Shereikis (Unit Eight)
Fall of the Legends, Mike Lupica (Unit Eight)
Mother Teresa and Her Endless Fight, Ellen Goodman (Unit Eight)
Selena: Dreaming of You, Ilan Stavans (Unit Eight)
Christa McAuliffe: An Ordinary Hero, Mike Pride (Unit Eight)

Charts

20 Hot Job Tracks, *U.S. News & World Report* (Unit Four)
The Work Ahead, *Harper's Magazine* (Unit Four)

Editorials and Newspaper Columns

The Right to Know, Margaret R. Brown (Unit One)
The Right to Marry, Joanne Jacobs (Unit Three)
In Praise of the F Word, Mary Sherry (Unit Five)
Down with the Forests, Charles Kuralt (Unit Six)
ERROR ERROR ERROR, Dave Barry (Unit Seven)
On Heroes and the Media, Jean Picker Firstenberg (Unit Eight)
Mother Teresa and Her Endless Fight, Ellen Goodman (Unit Eight)
Christa McAuliffe: An Ordinary Hero, Mike Pride (Unit Eight)

Essays and Articles (professional, not primarily autobiographical)

The New American Man, Robert Bly (Unit One)
What Friends Are For, Phillip Lopate (Unit Three)
The Case Against Chores, Jane Smiley (Unit Four)
The Workman's Compensation, Reg Theriault (Unit Four)
The Resegregation of a Southern School, Douglas A. Blackmon (Unit Five)
The Recoloring of Campus Life, Shelby Steele (Unit Five)
Slow Descent into Hell, Jon D. Hull (Unit Five)
Nobody Ever Died of Old Age, Sharon R. Curtin (Unit Five)
Waste, Wendell Berry (Unit Six)

Larger than Life, Phil Sudo (Unit Eight)
Extraordinary People, Herbert Buchsbaum (Unit Eight)
Lenny Skutnik—Accidental Hero, Richard Shereikis (Unit Eight)
The Man in the Water, Roger Rosenblatt (Unit Eight)
Fall of the Legends, Mike Lupica (Unit Eight)
Selena: Dreaming of You, Ilan Stavans (Unit Eight)

Eulogies

Where's Dietz?, Mike Taibbi (Unit Three)
Martin Luther King, Jr., Gwendolyn Brooks (Unit Eight)
The Man in the Water, Roger Rosenblatt (Unit Eight)
Selena: Dreaming of You, Ilan Stavans (Unit Eight)
Christa McAuliffe: An Ordinary Hero, Mike Pride (Unit Eight)

Fiction

Two Kinds, Amy Tan (Unit Two)
The Letter, Rudolfo Anaya (Unit Two)
Distance, Raymond Carver (Unit Three)
The Gift, Louis Dollarhide (Unit Six)

History (written and oral)

No Snapshots in the Attic: A Granddaughter's Search for a Cherokee Past,
    Connie May Fowler (Unit Two)
The Resegregation of a Southern School, Douglas A. Blackmon (Unit Five)
American Dreams: Stanley Cygan, 90, Studs Terkel (Unit Four)
Having Our Say, Sarah and A. Elizabeth Delany (Unit Eight)

Humor

Fatherhood, Bill Cosby (Unit Two)
Living with My VCR, Nora Ephron (Unit Seven)
ERROR ERROR ERROR, Dave Barry (Unit Seven)

Letters

Death of a Friend: The Delicacy and Strength of Lace, Leslie Marmon Silko and
    James Wright (Unit Three)

Poetry

Getting Started, Janet Campbell Hale (Unit One)
Never in My Life, Walter McDonald (Unit Two)
On Death and Love, Janet Campbell Hale (Unit Three)
My Mother Enters the Workforce, Rita Dove (Unit Four)
in the inner city, Lucille Clifton (Unit Five)

Wild Geese, Mary Oliver (Unit Six)
Song of the Sky Loom, Native American (Tewa) (Unit Six)
At the Electronic Frontier, Miguel Algarin (Unit Seven)
Martin Luther King, Jr., Gwendolyn Brooks (Unit Eight)
Those Winter Sundays, Robert Hayden (Unit Eight)
A Song of Greatness (from the Chippewa), Mary Austin (Unit Eight)

Reports or Articles Based on Research or Interviews

Sibling Imprints, Francine Klagsbrun (Unit Two)
The Family Values Debate, James Q. Wilson (Unit Two)
The Good Marriage, Judith S. Wallerstein and Sandra Blakeslee (Unit Three)
20 Hot Job Tracks, *U.S. News & World Report* (Unit Four)
The Big Squeeze, David Samuels (Unit Five)
What Is Behind the Growth of Violence on College Campuses?, Dorothy Siegel
   (Unit Five)
Kids Who Kill, Gordon Witkin (Unit Five)
Slow Descent into Hell, Jon D. Hull (Unit Five)
Nobody Ever Died of Old Age, Sharon R. Curtin (Unit Five)
America's "Garbage Crisis": A Toxic Myth, Patricia Poore (Unit Six)
Television Addiction, Marie Winn (Unit Seven)
Lonely Hearts, Classy Dreams, Empty Wallets, Amy Waldman (Unit Seven)
Gender Gap in Cyberspace, Deborah Tannen (Unit Seven)
Extraordinary People, Herbert Buchsbaum (Unit Eight)

Speeches

I Have a Dream, Martin Luther King, Jr. (Unit Eight)
Heroines and Role Models, Maxine F. Singer (Unit Eight)

Student Essays

On Being 17, Bright, and Unable to Read, David Raymond (Unit One)
The Right to Know, Margaret Brown (Unit One)
The Stars of the Whole Sky, Shozo Machida (Unit One)
Wanted—A Mother, Orville Rawlins (Unit Two)
Oil and Water, Valerie Owen (Unit Three)
Initiation, Rebecca May (Unit Four)
We Don't Want to Grow Old, Karla Cole (Unit Five)
Dice or Doves?, Cindy Camburn (Unit Six)
Technology and the Hearing Impaired, Tammy Holm (Unit Seven)
A Hero's Journey: Neil Armstrong's Walk on the Moon, Thomas Talley
   (Unit Eight)

Making Connections Among the Units: Alternative Thematic Table of Contents

Age and Youth

Old at Seventeen, David Vecsey (Unit One)
Generations, Joyce Maynard (Unit Two)
The Old Man, Larry King (Unit Two)
Liked for Myself, Maya Angelou (Unit Three)
Work and Play, Robert Murray Davis (Unit Four)
Out of College, Out of Work, Stephen Sherrill (Unit Four)
Kids Who Kill, Gordon Witkin (Unit Five)
Nobody Ever Died of Old Age, Sharon R. Curtin (Unit Five)
We Don't Want to Grow Old, Karla Cole (Unit Five)
At the Electronic Frontier, Miguel Algarin (Unit Seven)
Having Our Say, Sarah and A. Elizabeth Delany (Unit Eight)

Alienation and Isolation

My Name, Sandra Cisneros (Unit One)
The Misery of Silence, Maxine Hong Kingston (Unit One)
Lives on the Boundary, Mike Rose (Unit One)
Two Kinds, Amy Tan (Unit Two)
The Old Man, Larry King (Unit Two)
Never in My Life, Walter McDonald (Unit Two)
The Letter, Rudolfo Anaya (Unit Two)
Hold the Mayonnaise, Julia Alvarez (Unit Two)
Wanted—A Mother, Orville Rawlins (Unit Two)
Drifting Away, Diane Cole (Unit Three)
Distance, Raymond Carver (Unit Three)
Slow Descent into Hell, Jon D. Hull (Unit Five)
Nobody Ever Died of Old Age, Sharon R. Curtin (Unit Five)
Lonely Hearts, Classy Dreams, Empty Wallets, Amy Waldman (Unit Seven)
Those Winter Sundays, Robert Hayden (Unit Eight)

American Dream

Lives on the Boundary, Mike Rose (Unit One)
American Dreams: Stanley Cygan, 90, Studs Terkel (Unit Four)

So How Did I Get Here?, Rosemary L. Bray (Unit Five)
I Have a Dream, Martin Luther King, Jr. (Unit Eight)

Communication and Language

The Misery of Silence, Maxine Hong Kingston (Unit One)
On Being 17, Bright, and Unable to Read, David Raymond (Unit One)
Two Kinds, Amy Tan (Unit Two)
Never in My Life, Walter McDonald (Unit Two)
The Letter, Rudolfo Anaya (Unit Two)
Hold the Mayonnaise, Julia Alvarez (Unit Two)
Wanted—A Mother, Orville Rawlins (Unit Two)
Liked for Myself, Maya Angelou (Unit Three)
Death of a Friend: The Delicacy and Strength of Lace, Leslie Marmon Silko
    and James Wright (Unit Three)
Where's Dietz?, Mike Taibbi (Unit Three)
Drifting Away, Diane Cole (Unit Three)
Finding a Wife, Gary Soto (Unit Three)
The Lies That Bind, Paul Thaler (Unit Three)
Distance, Raymond Carver (Unit Three)
Gender Gap in Cyberspace, Deborah Tannen (Unit Seven)
Those Winter Sundays, Robert Hayden (Unit Eight)

Crime and Violence

What Is Behind the Growth of Violence on College Campuses?, (Dorothy
    Siegel (Unit Five)
Kids Who Kill, Gordon Witkin (Unit Five)
Slow Descent into Hell, Jon D. Hull (Unit Five)
Extraordinary People, Herbert Buchsbaum (Unit Eight)

Death and Illness

Generations, Joyce Maynard (Unit Two)
Never in My Life, Walter McDonald (Unit Two)
Death of a Friend: Delicacy and Strength of Lace, Leslie Marmon Silko and
    James Wright (Unit Three)
Where's Dietz?, Mike Taibbi (Unit Three)
On Death and Love, Janet Campbell Hale (Unit Three)
Kids Who Kill, Gordon Witkin (Unit Five)
Slow Descent into Hell, Jon D. Hull (Unit Five)
Technology and the Hearing Impaired, Tammy Holm (Unit Seven)
The Man in the Water, Roger Rosenblatt (Unit Eight)
Fall of the Legends, Mike Lupica (Unit Eight)

Selena: Dreaming of You, Ilan Stavans (Unit Eight)
Christa McAuliffe: An Ordinary Hero, Mike Pride (Unit Eight)

Education and Its Institutions

Lives on the Boundary, Mike Rose (Unit One)
On Being 17, Bright, and Unable to Read, David Raymond (Unit One)
Liked for Myself, Maya Angelou (Unit Three)
The Scholarship Jacket, Marta Salinas (Unit Five)
In Praise of the F Word, Mary Sherry (Unit Five)
The Big Squeeze, David Samuels (Unit Five)
The Resegregation of a Southern School, Douglas A. Blackmon (Unit Five)
The Recoloring of Campus Life, Shelby Steele (Unit Five)
What Is Behind the Growth of Violence on College Campuses?, Dorothy
    Siegel (Unit Five)
So How Did I Get Here?, Rosemary L. Bray (Unit Five)
Getting a Degree by E-mail, Mary Lord (Unit Seven)
Having Our Say, Sarah and A. Elizabeth Delany (Unit Eight)

Ethnic and Racial Identity

My Name, Sandra Cisneros (Unit One)
The Misery of Silence, Maxine Hong Kingston (Unit One)
No Snapshots in the Attic: A Granddaughter's Search for a Cherokee Past,
    Connie May Fowler (Unit Two)
The Letter, Rudolfo Anaya (Unit Two)
Hold the Mayonnaise, Julia Alvarez (Unit Two)
The Scholarship Jacket, Marta Salinas (Unit Five)
Extraordinary People, Herbert Buchsbaum (Unit Eight)
Having Our Say, Sarah and A. Elizabeth Delany (Unit Eight)
Selena: Dreaming of You, Ilan Stavans (Unit Eight)

Family and Home (from units other than Unit Two)

The Right to Know, Margaret R. Brown (Unit One)
The Right to Mary, Joanne Jacobs (Unit Three)
Distance, Raymond Carver (Unit Three)
The Good Marriage, Judith S. Wallerstein and Sandra Blakeslee (Unit Three)
My Mother Enters the Workforce, Rita Dove (Unit Four)
The Family Farm, David Mas Masumoto (Unit Four)
The Scholarship Jacket, Marta Salinas (Unit Five)
in the inner city, Lucille Clifton (Unit Five)
So How Did I Get Here?, Rosemary L. Bray (Unit Five)
Having Our Say, Sarah and A. Elizabeth Delany (Unit Eight)
Those Winter Sundays, Robert Hayden (Unit Eight)

Gender Roles

What Do Women Want?, Sara Davidson (Unit One)
The New American Man, Robert Bly (Unit One)
Sibling Imprints, Francine Klagsbrun (Unit Two)
Where's Dietz?, Mike Taibbi (Unit Three)
The Right to Marry, Joanne Jacobs (Unit Three)
The Good Marriage, Judith S. Wallerstein and Sandra Blakeslee (Unit Three)
Gender Gap in Cyberspace, Deborah Tannen (Unit Seven)
Heroines and Role Models, Maxine F. Singer (Unit Eight)
Having Our Say, Sarah and A. Elizabeth Delany (Unit Eight)

Goals, Dreams, and Expectations: Competition, Success, and Failure

Getting Started, Janet Campbell Hale (Unit One)
The Stars of the Whole Sky, Shozo Machida (Unit One)
Two Kinds, Amy Tan (Unit Two)
Sibling Imprints, Francine Klagsbrun (Unit Two)
Liked for Myself, Maya Angelou (Unit Three)
The Good Marriage, Judith S.Wallerstein and Sandra Blakeslee (Unit Three)
American Dreams: Stanley Cygan, 90, Studs Terkel (Unit Four)
Initiation, Rebecca May (Unit Four)
Spokesperson, Jane Armstrong (Unit Four)
The Family Farm, David Mas Masumoto (Unit Four)
20 Hot Job Tracks, *U.S. News & World Report* (Unit Four)
The Work Ahead, *Harper's Magazine* (Unit Four)
The Scholarship Jacket, Marta Salinas (Unit Five)
In Praise of the F Word, Mary Sherry (Unit Five)
So How Did I Get Here?, Rosemary L. Bray (Unit Five)
I Have a Dream, Martin Luther King, Jr. (Unit Eight)
Extraordinary People, Herbert Buchsbaum (Unit Eight)
Having Our Say, Sarah and A. Elizabeth Delany (Unit Eight)
A Hero's Journey: Neil Armstrong's Walk on the Moon, Thomas Talley
    (Unit Eight)
Christa McAuliffe: An Ordinary Hero, Mike Pride (Unit Eight)
A Song of Greatness (from the Chippewa), Mary Austin (Unit Eight)

Media

Spokesperson, Jane Armstrong (Unit Four)
We Don't Want to Grow Old, Karla Cole (Unit Five)
Television Addiction, Marie Winn (Unit Seven)
Lonely Hearts, Classy Dreams, Empty Wallets, Amy Waldman (Unit Seven)
On Heroes and the Media, Jean Picker Firstenberg (Unit Eight)
Lenny Skutnik—Accidental Hero, Richard Shereikis (Unit Eight)
The Man in the Water, Roger Rosenblatt (Unit Eight)

Fall of the Legends, Mike Lupica (Unit Eight)
Selena: Dreaming of You, Ilan Stavans (Unit Eight)
A Hero's Journey: Neil Armstrong's Walk on the Moon, Thomas Talley
  (Unit Eight)
Christa McAuliffe: An Ordinary Hero, Mike Pride (Unit Eight)

Poverty and Economic Problems

Lives on the Boundary, Mike Rose (Unit One)
Wanted—A Mother, Orville Rawlins (Unit Two)
Finding a Wife, Gary Soto (Unit Three)
American Dreams: Stanley Cygan, 90, Studs Terkel (Unit Four)
My Mother Enters the Workforce, Rita Dove (Unit Four)
Out of College, Out of Work, Stephen Sherrill (Unit Four)
The Scholarship Jacket, Marta Salinas (Unit Five)
The Big Squeeze, David Samuels (Unit Five)
The Resegregation of a Southern School, Douglas A. Blackmon (Unit Five)
Slow Descent into Hell, Jon D. Hull (Unit Five)
So How Did I Get Here?, Rosemary L. Bray (Unit Five)
Mother Teresa and Her Endless Fight, Ellen Goodman (Unit Eight)
Having Our Say, Sarah and A. Elizabeth Delany (Unit Eight)
Those Winter Sundays, Robert Hayden (Unit Eight)

Prejudice and Discrimination

No Snapshots in the Attic: A Granddaughter's Search for a Cherokee Past,
  Connie May Fowler (Unit Two)
The Right to Marry, Joanne Jacobs (Unit Three)
The Scholarship Jacket, Marta Salinas (Unit Five)
The Resegregation of a Southern School, Douglas A. Blackmon (Unit Five)
The Recoloring of Campus Life, Shelby Steele (Unit Five)
So How Did I Get Here?, Rosemary L. Bray (Unit Five)
Nobody Ever Died of Old Age, Sharon R. Curtin (Unit Five)
I Have a Dream, Martin Luther King, Jr. (Unit Eight)
Extraordinary People, Herbert Buchsbaum (Unit Eight)
Having Our Say, Sarah and A. Elizabeth Delany (Unit Eight)
Selena: Dreaming of You, Ilan Stavans (Unit Eight)

Rebellion

The New American Man, Robert Bly (Unit One)
Two Kinds, Amy Tan (Unit Two)
The Old Man, Larry King (Unit Two)
Wanted—A Mother, Orville Rawlins (Unit Two)
I Have a Dream, Martin Luther King, Jr. (Unit Eight)

Rural and Urban Life

Lives on the Boundary, Mike Rose (Unit One)
The Family Farm, David Mas Masumoto (Unit Four)
in the inner city, Lucille Clifton (Unit Five)
Slow Descent into Hell, Jon D. Hull (Unit Five)
Weather Reports, Kathleen Norris (Unit Six)
Waste, Wendell Berry (Unit Six)
What's Best for the West?, David Diamond (Unit Six)

INTRODUCTION

The title of this reader, *Interactions*, reflects its primary purpose as well as the theory on which it is based. The primary purpose of the book is to encourage students to become more aware of their relationships with other people, places, and things. Thus, the book's thematic emphasis on self is really a way of leading students outward from themselves—from their interest in self to an awareness of their interactions with other phenomena in their environment.

Since *Interactions* is based on the theoretical assumption that reading and writing are dynamic, interactive processes, the title also reflects this theoretical emphasis. In this book we attempt to reinforce the natural interactions that occur between a reader and a writer and between a reader and a text. In addition, we encourage students using this text to interact with one another, with you as their teacher, with their classmates, and with us as the authors of the text.

This instructor's resource manual will explain the purposes and theories that inform the text and will provide you with suggestions for teaching the individual units that it includes.

PURPOSES

Anthologies are frequently used in composition courses to supplement writing instruction. These anthologies usually consist of reading selections (primarily essays) that serve as models for student writing. In most instances, therefore, these anthologies are primarily designed to improve student writing. However, because many students, especially developmental students, are inexperienced readers as well as inexperienced writers, *Interactions* is designed to help improve both reading and writing skills.

In general, therefore, *Interactions* is designed to achieve the following purposes.

- To increase students' understanding of themselves not only as individuals but also as interactive beings
- To help students move beyond themselves by becoming aware of their relationships with other individuals, with their society and physical

1

environment, and with the ideas that shape them as individuals as well as the culture in which they exist

- To provide interesting, accessible, diversified reading and writing experiences for students
- To improve students' skills as readers and writers
- To help students understand that reading and writing are dynamic, interactive processes that occur in a rhetorical context

THEMATIC EMPHASIS AND ORGANIZATION

The theme of this book, the interactive self, is particularly appropriate for beginning college students, who are usually interested in learning more about themselves but who also need to increase their awareness of what lies beyond the self. Therefore, each of the eight units in *Interactions* explores the general theme of the interactive self while focusing on a different relationship the self has with other people and phenomena. Beginning with the most basic relationship, the first unit focuses on an individual's relationship to himself or herself. Moving outward, the second unit explores an individual's interactions with family members. The third unit is devoted to interactions with friends and mates—how an individual forms relationships with others and what happens as these relationships develop, change, and—in many instances—end.

Continuing the pattern of moving outward from the self, the fourth unit examines the work that an individual performs and how that work has changed in our society. The fifth and sixth units explore the interactions between an individual and the society and physical environment in which he or she exists. The seventh unit focuses on an individual's relationships with machines and reactions to the increased level of technology in our society. Finally, the eighth unit emphasizes the more abstract interactions between the individual self and his or her heroes, exploring the role that these beings play in the shaping of an individual.

THEORIES AND METHODS

Because we believe that reading and writing skills are best developed in combination with each other in a context that encourages students to interact with the written text and with one another, *Interactions* provides instruction that is thoroughly integrated. That is, we do not distinguish between writing instruction and reading instruction. The instructional matter that accompanies each reading selection encourages students to engage in meaningful reading and writing activities that reinforce each other.

The instruction in this text is also consistently interactive, encouraging students to interact with their own prior experiences and knowledge, with the text and the authors represented in it, with their fellow students, and with you as their instructor. Moreover, students are encouraged to think of reading and writing as interactive processes in which readers and writers attempt to share their experiences and knowledge with one another.

Numerous composition theorists agree that this interactive approach to reading and writing instruction is the most productive. As early as 1977, Mina Shaughnessy realized that "a writing approach to reading" helps the student understand that "the meaning of what he reads or writes resides not in the page nor in the reader but in the encounter between the two" (*Errors and Expectations*, 224). More recently, Lynn Troyka suggested the connection between the text and the student's prior knowledge and experiences when she observed that "Reading . . . is clearly not a passive activity. . . . It is a dynamic process of interaction between what is on the printed page and what the reader brings to the printed page" ("The Writer as Conscious Reader," *A Sourcebook for Basic Writing Teachers*, ed. Theresa Enos. New York: Random, 1987, p. 310). And, finally, Mariolina Salvatori calls attention to the important influence of the reader on the text and of the text on the reader: when a "writer [or reader] . . . actively interacts with the text, she composes [the text] as that text composes her" ("Reading and Writing a Text: Correlations Between Reading and Writing Patterns," *A Sourcebook for Basic Writing Teachers*, ed. Theresa Enos. New York: Random, 1987).

The model of reading and writing that informs the instruction in *Interactions* reflects this interactive process. Rather than being sequential, linear processes, both reading and writing are recursive, interactive processes. A writer creates a physical text that is a reflection of an interior text, a mental image of the text that exists prior to the physical text and serves as both an impetus and a model for it. Likewise, a reader constructs an interior text that is a reflection of his or her understanding of the writer's physical text. But the physical text is never identical to the writer's interior text, and the reader's interior text is never identical to either the physical text or the writer's interior text. The reader's interior text is his or her version of the text—that which continues to exist in some form after the reader has read the text. A reader may forget much of what is read, may even forget that something has been read, but the reading experience in some way alters the reader's knowledge of the world and perception of reality.

Thus, insofar as possible, *Interactions* emphasizes the student's response to what he or she reads. For example, we do not include questions on specific details. Rather than emphasizing literal recall, we encourage students to understand the ideas in the text and to form their own internalized version of what they read—an interior text that is theirs to use in various personal and professional ways rather than a collection of facts that has little meaning to them. Thus, we include no tests but rather focus on main ideas, summaries, personal reactions and responses, argumentative rebuttals, and assignments that require students to synthesize, apply, analyze, and evaluate what they have read.

The reading and writing assignments in this book are in some ways atypical of those usually found in anthologies. Although many of the assignments involve what can be loosely described as essays, we have not focused exclusively on either the personal or the academic essay. Rather, we have included a wide variety of reading and writing assignments that represent the types of reading and writing experiences that students will encounter in other courses and later in their professional and personal lives. Our purpose is to expose students to as many different reading and writing experiences as possible and thus to help them become more experienced readers and writers.

SPECIAL FEATURES OF THIS TEXT

The following features of this text deserve special attention:

Instructional Apparatus

The suggestions for reading and writing that accompany each reading selection are primarily designed to help students become experienced and successful readers and writers. Thus, our main concern is not that students master the content of the reading selections, but rather that they understand and enjoy what they read. One of the ways in which we attempt to achieve this objective is by providing students with information about what they are going to read before they actually begin reading the selection, because reading is always enhanced by prior knowledge. We also attempt to help students by explaining difficult words and concepts in context before they encounter them and by encouraging students to relate what they are reading to their own experiences. The writing assignments are used not only to reinforce these reading objectives but also to give students varied and successful writing experiences. Rather than expecting students to produce discourse that is similar to the selections they are reading, we suggest writing assignments that both enhance the reading experience and provide new writing experiences. The instruction that accompanies each reading selection is structured according to the following pattern:

General Introduction Initially, students are given some general information about the selection. This information may focus on the author or on the reading selection itself (its main idea or the general topic addressed), but it always encourages students to think about what they are going to read.

Before You Read Next, students are asked to work through a series of activities that prepare them more specifically for the reading assignment that follows. This section suggests that students THINK about certain ideas found in the selection and relate these to their own experiences, EXAMINE specific features of the selections, and WRITE a journal entry related to what they are going to read.

As You Read This section consists of a brief suggestion that focuses students' attention on a particular purpose for reading or on specific features of the text. In addition, in this section we often suggest ways in which students may annotate the text as they read. In general, the suggestions relate to the identification of specific information, the evaluation of the author's ideas, and the formulation of subjective responses to the ideas and information the students encounter in the selection.

After You Read This section consists of the same sequence of THINK/ EXAMINE/WRITE activities that are included in the **Before You Read** sections. These activities, however, emphasize the students' response to what they have read as well as their understanding of ideas in the reading selection. Many of these activities encourage students to think critically about what they have read and to synthesize their own ideas with those they have encountered in the reading selection. The THINK activities usually focus on the students' understanding and interpretation of the author's ideas. The EXAMINE activities often encourage students to reread the selection in order to look more closely at specific features. The WRITE activities are slightly more structured and nearly always more extensive than those included in the **Before You Read** section (but less structured and less extensive than those in the **Critical Thinking and Writing Assignments** described below). Here we typically ask students to write a summary, a paragraph, or a brief essay, often instructing them to develop more fully the writing (or thinking) activity they have done earlier.

Critical Thinking and Writing Assignments At the end of each unit, we provide both collaborative activities and individual writing assignments that require students to synthesize and respond to what they have read. These assignments are more challenging and more structured than those that accompany each of the reading selections in the unit. Therefore, we suggest that you usually choose only one or two of each type. Or you may want to allow your students to choose what they want to do, either individually or in groups.

Vocabulary Instruction

We make no attempt to include comprehensive vocabulary instruction. That is, although we assume that students will not know all of the words they encounter in the reading selections, we make no attempt to define all of these new words for them. We also avoid the traditional vocabulary assignments that require students to define words by looking them up in a dictionary. Instead, we call students' attention to some of the words that may be new to them before they begin to read the selection. We are selective in the words we choose to emphasize because we are convinced that students are overwhelmed by long lists of unfamiliar words. We select those words that we think are important to students' understanding of the reading selection, those that we think they need to know as college freshmen, or those that they will be interested in knowing. Rather than instructing them to look these words up for themselves, we give them the sentence or clause in which the word appears in the reading selection, define it as simply as possible, and discuss it briefly, pointing out, for example, something about its derivation, structure, or use, or about the context in which it occurs, that may help students add the word to their reading vocabularies. We believe that this informal, indirect approach works far better than expecting students to define and memorize an extensive list of words.

Journal Entries

Before reading each selection, students are ask to write a journal entry on a topic related to the subject of the reading. These entries prepare students to read by providing writing experiences that encourage them to bring related prior knowledge to the surface of their memories. These entries, along with the other prereading activities that accompany them, also improve reading motivation and comprehension by asking students to make predictions about the reading selection itself.

Reading Level

Because we do not believe that readability formulas accurately measure reading level, we did not use them in choosing the reading selections for this text. Nevertheless, we think you will find that your students will be able to read the selections even though they are not all short or written with simple vocabularies. Students need sustained reading experiences; therefore, we have included some fairly long selections. They also need to be challenged; therefore, some readings include words and concepts with which students will not initially be familiar. All of the selections, however, are accessible to students. We consistently and carefully selected readings that are well written and that are not needlessly complex in either sentence structure or vocabulary. In addition, we have structured the reading assignments so that students are prepared to read even the more difficult selections.

To prepare students for the more challenging reading selections, we have arranged the selections within each unit so that there is usually a general progression from less difficult to more difficult. This progression allows students to become more knowledgeable about the general topic and to recall information and experiences related to this topic before they confront the more challenging assignments. In the instances in which we chose not to arrange the selections according to this progression, it was because we wanted to introduce students to a basic concept earlier in the unit or to present two particular selections in sequence.

In addition, before students read a selection, we provide them with assistance in relating it to their own experiences, in understanding its main idea, and in recognizing some of the difficult words in the selection. Perhaps even more important, we chose readings that we believe are interesting to students because we find that students read best when they are interested in what they are reading and are engaged in the ideas that are being presented.

Variety of Reading Selections

The reading selections in this book vary in a number of important ways. First, they vary in terms of genre (see Genre Table of Contents, page v of this manual); that is, although most of the readings can be classified as non-fiction prose, we also include fiction and poetry. In addition, the nonfiction prose selections vary widely. They include professional essays, student essays, editorials, biographical sketches, case studies, letters, interviews, articles from magazines and newspapers, and technical reports (including charts). Finally, the authors of the selections also vary. We have tried to balance the number of male and female writers and to include writers from different ethnic and geographic backgrounds. We have also attempted to include reading selections that represent a variety of reading purposes—from aesthetic to pragmatic.

Increasing Emphasis on Critical Reading and Thinking

Although basic skills such as determining main ideas, developing effective vocabulary strategies, and recognizing and using familiar patterns of development and organization are addressed in each unit, critical reading skills are also addressed in each assignment. The emphasis on critical reading and thinking—that is, on thinking that is focused on deciding what to believe or do—becomes more pronounced as students progress through each lesson, through each unit, and through the entire book. This progression is designed to take advantage of the fact that once students have information on a subject, they are able to read and write about the subject at increasingly complex levels. Thus, the reading selections in each unit provide students with new information to supplement their own prior knowledge, and in moving from the self outward, each unit prepares students for the units that follow. Because developmental students in particular typically lack information about the subjects on which they are asked to write and thus often resort to writing meager accounts of personal experiences, we believe this feature of the text will result in writing that is more informed and less subjective.

In general, writing assignments and activities in each lesson and each unit progress from informal and unstructured to more formal and more structured. Thus, the first writing activity that we suggest for each lesson is a journal entry, which may also involve listing freewriting, or describing. This type of writing does not involve extensive development and requires little or no revising or editing. The suggestions for writing activities that follow each selection are not only more challenging critically but also more structured. Thus, students may be asked to revise or expand what they have written previously or to write a paragraph, summary, report, or brief essay. The most challenging and structured assignments for critical reading, thinking, and writing are those found at the end of each unit.

Critical Thinking and Writing Assignments

The **Critical Thinking and Writing Assignments** consist of two parts: **Exploring Ideas Together** and **Writing Essays.** Both types of assignments require students to synthesize ideas and information from the various selections and from their own observations and experiences. In **Exploring Ideas Together,** students are often asked to work in groups in order to compare and contrast readings, to brainstorm ideas, and to write collaborative essays. The **Writing Essays** section contains more assignments than you and your students will be able to use, but it provides both you and your students with choices for a variety of backgrounds and purposes. Choices include not only narrative essays but also expository, analytical, and persuasive writing. In addition, these essay assignments require students to consider their purposes and their audiences.

GENERAL SUGGESTIONS FOR TEACHING THIS TEXT

In general, we encourage you and your students to enjoy *Interactions* by using it as a sourcebook that allows students to gain reading and writing experience, helps them to discover new reasons for reading and writing, and enables them to become more effective readers and writers. To achieve these goals, we suggest that you include the following in your course:

1. *Student journals*—Because we think that student journals provide students with effective reinforcement of both reading and writing skills, we strongly urge you to consider asking your students to keep some type of journal. You will discover that each **Before You Read** section in *Interactions* asks students to write a journal entry. These assignments can, of course, be omitted or changed into freewriting, mapping, or brainstorming activities. However, we hope you will use journals as suggested by at least some of these assignments. You may require students to write the journal entry from *Interactions* for each lesson you assign, or you may be more selective in assigning the journal ideas provided. You may even want to expand on our suggestions for journal response by requiring additional entries or by allowing students to write independent entries on topics of their own choosing. Depending on your own purposes and preferences, you may have students write their entries on the computer, on looseleaf paper, or in a bound notebook. You may also want to consider other types of journals, such as a reading journal, in which students routinely record their responses to each reading selection you assign; a process journal, in which students record their impressions of their own reading or writing processes; or a vocabulary journal, in which students record and define unfamiliar words not discussed in the text.

2. *Opportunities for group work*—Allowing students to work in small groups encourages the type of interaction that is the focus of this book. Peer editing groups can be an effective way of teaching students editing and revising skills. But we also encourage you to allow students to work in small groups at other times—to brainstorm on a topic, to discuss a reading selection, or to collaborate on a writing assignment. Finally, in the **Exploring Ideas Together** sections at the end of each unit, we provide specific suggestions for collaborative activities designed to help students synthesize ideas from their reading and experience.

   Many students are reluctant to speak out before an entire class but will express their opinions in a small group. In addition, working in a small group enables students to get to know one another; as a result, they often begin to feel more comfortable in class and more willing to share their ideas in class discussions. Although dividing a class into groups can result in an unproductive, chaotic class period, group work that is carefully structured and monitored can be a rewarding experience for both students and teachers.

3. *Opportunities for discussions*—Ideally, students should spend most of their time in class reading, writing, or talking rather than listening to

lectures. Studies suggest that learning takes place primarily when students are active participants. Talking about their ideas and responding to your ideas and to those of their classmates are effective ways of involving students in active learning. Thus, class discussions are an important feature of a reading/writing course.

4. *Opportunities for informal, ungraded writing*—In addition to journals, we suggest that you provide a variety of other informal writing assignments that will give students writing experience but will not require a formal grading procedure on your part. Although it is always important to *respond* to student writing, it is not always necessary to *evaluate* student writing. Students need to write far more than you have time to grade. Thus, we encourage you to use the ideas suggested in the Introduction to *Interactions*, pages 1–13, to create additional informal writing assignments for students to complete both before and after reading the selections in the text. For example, you can ask students to freewrite or brainstorm about a related topic before reading a selection, or to map or summarize the ideas in a selection after reading it.

5. *Additional vocabulary instruction*—Because we do not attempt to include comprehensive vocabulary instruction, it is important that you supplement our material. We suggest that this supplemental instruction be informal. For example, you can divide students into groups and ask each group to produce from a reading selection a list of five or ten words that are unfamiliar to them. These lists can then be circulated from group to group to see if members of the other groups can define the unfamiliar words. Finally, the entire class can discuss the words, with you providing the definitions of the words that remain undefined.

   It is important that in working with vocabulary, you do not emphasize formal definitions. Students should feel free to make guesses or to contribute any ideas about a word's meaning in a particular context or any associations they may have with the word. In addition to vocabulary exercises and activities, you will certainly want to include in your discussions of all reading selections incidental comments and instruction about words that students do not know. We strongly suggest that you avoid using lists of words for students to define by looking them up in a dictionary. We know of no student who ever really increased his or her vocabulary in this way.

6. *Modes of discourse*—Unlike many reading anthologies, *Interactions* does not focus on the modes of discourse. However, if you like to include instruction on these familiar patterns of development and organization in your reading/writing course, *Interactions* can certainly be used for that purpose, since the reading selections in it can be classified according to a primary mode of discourse (see Rhetorical Table of Contents, text page xvii). We suggest that you encourage students to think of the

different modes as methods of invention and development as well as of organization and that you point out in your discussions that a given piece of discourse usually includes a variety of modes, even though one may be primary.

7. *Student essays*—One new feature in the third edition of *Interactions* is that each unit includes at least one student essay. We have found that including student essays serves at least two important pedagogical purposes: (1) these essays, which are often shorter and simpler than professional essays, are less intimidating to students and thus allow students to feel more comfortable with the text and its assignments; and (2) seeing student essays in print often motivates students to strive harder to achieve what these other student writers have achieved— effectively written essays that communicate to a wide audience. In addition to assigning and discussing with your class the student essays in *Interactions*, we also suggest that you make your own students' essays part of the "reading" of the class.

8. *Computer publication*—Making your students' essays one of the "texts" of the class, as suggested above, is much easier if you and your class have access to a computer classroom or laboratory. Encourage students to write their essays on word processors and to share their essays with each other, through a network or multiple hard copies. Students may work in peer groups to share ideas for revision and editing, but to truly give students the sense of accomplishment of a published writer, be sure that you also discuss their essays as "readings" in the same way that you discuss the student essays in *Interactions*. You might even bind student essays on one or more of the themes represented in *Interactions*, using these booklets as actual classroom texts.

SUGGESTIONS FOR TEACHING THE INTRODUCTION

The Introduction to *Interactions* serves two main purposes: (1) to provide students with an overview of the writing and reading processes and their similarities, and (2) to give students a preview of how *Interactions* works— how it is organized and why. Although students can read the Introduction on their own, we suggest that you also discuss it in class, emphasizing the three-stage process that students will follow in reading each selection. Be sure they understand the importance of each stage—what they do before and after they read as well as what they do while they are actually reading. This is also a good time to emphasize to students the importance of their interacting (physically as well as mentally) with the text as they read. That is, encourage them to annotate their texts freely as they read. Finally, this is a good place to introduce the concepts of purpose and audience.

UNIT ONE
The Self

This unit introduces students to the book and its theme—the interactive self. Thus, it focuses on how an individual understands and relates to himself or herself. Whether they are nineteen or forty-nine years old, students should respond positively to the idea of getting to know themselves better.

My Name   *Sandra Cisneros*

We have placed "My Name" first in this unit because one of our reviewers wisely suggested that it would provide teachers with an opportunity to begin the semester by emphasizing students' names. Therefore, you may want to spend some time letting students get to know one another's names as an introduction to this selection.

Because the selection focuses on a young girl's feelings about her Spanish name, Esperanza, it also provides an opportunity to involve nonnative students in a discussion of what their names mean and what their names are in English. You will want to expand the discussion so that all students talk about their feelings about their names and whether they think their names have affected the kind of people they are.

The Misery of Silence   *Maxine Hong Kingston*

In this selection from her memoirs, Kingston speaks dramatically of being silenced by the confusion that she experienced as a young child growing up in two very different cultures. You may want to discuss with your students the similarities and differences of various immigrant experiences—whether, for example, Chinese immigrants have a more difficult time adjusting to our culture and language than Spanish immigrants. You may also want to discuss whether adjusting should be the goal and whether adjusting should mean adoption of the dominate culture's customs, values, and language. Finally, you will want students to consider how growing up in two cultures affects the process of self-definition.

Students may have some difficult with Kingston's prose, which is often elliptical and fragmented (perhaps a reflection of the feelings about which

she is writing). Encourage your students to see her style as an integral part
of what she is saying—an extension of the incoherence she experienced.
Students may want to discuss why this person who felt so silenced as a child
chose to become a writer. Does her becoming a successful writer negate her
claim that she was reduced to silence by her childhood experiences? Or does
it confirm her claim, since writing is an act of silence or a way of subverting
silence to gain expression?

You may need to explain some of the allusions in the selection. Paragraph 4 mentions the Japanese kids who had been released from the concentration camp. You may need to explain that Japanese-American citizens were
placed in concentration camps during World War II. In addition, you may
want to explain that Sun Yat-sen and Chiang Kai-shek were respected
leaders of the Republic of China. Sun Yat-sen was a Chinese revolutionary
leader and statesman who founded the Republic of China in 1911. Chiang
Kai-shek was the first president of the Republic of China and moved his
government to Taiwan in 1949 when the Communists took over.

If the final suggestion for writing seems too difficult, you can substitute
a less challenging assignment. For example, you can ask your students to
describe an experience in which they felt inadequate to express themselves
orally—a time when they had to speak before a group or to a person who
intimidated them.

Lives on the Boundary   *Mike Rose*

Mike Rose, whom you probably know by his professional reputation as a
basic writing scholar and teacher, writes in this selection from *Lives on the
boundary* about growing up in the 1950s in Los Angeles. Thanks to "L.A.
Law," Rodney King, and countless movies, Los Angeles is a city that everyone knows something about. You might begin your study of this selection
with a discussion of Los Angeles. Even before you assign the reading,
students can discuss the images, connotations, and stories they associate with
this famous city. At the time of this initial discussion, you might introduce
the term *abyss of paradise*, which Rose uses to describe the city. Since Rose
grew up in Los Angeles during the 1950s, you may also want to discuss with
your students how the city and perceptions of it have changed since that
time, especially recently.

Although this selection is rather long and includes details about life in
the 1950s that may be unfamiliar to your students, it should not be difficult
for them to understand the anger and frustration as well as the longing and
dreams that Rose felt as he grew up in this marginal neighborhood of a city
known for its prosperity, beauty, and excitement. You may want to emphasize Rose's Italian-American background, or you may prefer to view his

experiences as typical for anyone growing up in a marginal neighborhood in a large city. But be sure to point out Rose's use of specific details, which makes the setting he describes so vivid, and to discuss the effects that environment may have on shaping who and what a person becomes.

Finally, you can focus on Rose's title and relate it to his own life as well as to his decision to become a teacher of basic writing students.

On Being 17, Bright, and Unable to Read   *David Raymond (student)*

This first-person narrative account by a young high school student who has a learning disability should be easy for your students to read but may be difficult for them to discuss. Because most of them will also have experienced problems with learning at some point in their careers as students, they may identify too closely with the young man in the story and find it awkward or embarrassing to discuss his experiences. Thus, you may want to focus not on subjective responses but rather on an objective consideration of learning disabilities—what they are and how they compare to physical disabilities such as vision or hearing impairments. Then you can perhaps talk about the mistaken perception that people who cannot read, for whatever reason, are dumb. Your discussion could also encompass what can be done to compensate for learning disabilities, how schools (and parents) often fail to deal effectively with learning disabilities, and more general considerations of the importance of literacy in a society such as ours.

The term *dyslexia* is nonspecific and is no longer in general use because it is so vague; however, at the time this story was written, it was frequently used to mean a specific type of reading problem. You may need to explain to your students that any type of learning problem can make it difficult for a person to learn how to read because reading is such a complex mental process.

You may also want to focus the class discussion on the idea that everyone has strengths and weaknesses—both physical and mental. Therefore, a learning disability can be viewed as a weakness, just as an inability to run fast or lift large weights can be considered a weakness. Point out that the author of this selection mentions several of his strengths (he excelled at track and pottery making) and also mentions that his awareness of these strengths made him feel better about himself.

Old at Seventeen   *David Vecsey*

"Old at Seventeen" reinforces several of the ideas that students have encountered in previous selections. For example, you can relate the author's use of narrative to Raymond's. You can also compare the cause-and-effect relationship that Vecsey emphasizes with that which Kingston develops in her essay. As you progress through each unit in *Interactions*, you will find similar points of comparison that students should be encouraged to recognize and develop. Rather than focusing on each selection individually, students should be encouraged to identify similarities and differences in the ideas and methods used by the different authors and to begin to synthesize the ideas they have discovered in their reading with their own ideas.

The Right to Know   *Margaret R. Brown (student)*

This essay was published in *Newsweek Magazine*, but we are considering it a student essay because it was written by the author when she was nineteen years old and a freshman biology major attending St. Edward's University in Austin, Texas. Your students will identify not only with the author's status as a student but also with her struggle to know who she is. As a person created by donor insemination, Brown's need to know her identity is perhaps more dramatic than most, but we all understand what it is like to wonder where we came from.

The main issue in this essay is whether "donor babies" should have the right to know about their biological origins. Help your students appreciate why the author's personal experience with this issue gives her credibility. Point out how skillfully she uses her own experiences as well as information about the process of donor insemination to create a persuasive, thought-provoking essay. You may want to ask your students how someone who did not have Brown's personal experience with this issue might construct an essay that took the same position. Then you can ask them how they might refute Brown's arguments if they were assuming the position that "donor babies" should *not* know about their biological origins.

This essay is the most explicitly persuasive essay the students have encountered in this unit thus far, so you may want to point out how it differs from the other essays they have read. But help them understand also that all writing is at some level persuasive. They can then discuss the "arguments" that are implicit in the other essays from the unit they have read.

What Do Women Want?   *Sara Davidson*

If you assign this selection about women, you will probably want to assign the Bly selection about men as well. The two selections can be taught separately, of course, but they work well together as a dialogue on the subject of gender roles.

Students will enjoy discussing the riddle that Davidson poses—what do women want—and the significance of her answer—sovereignty. You may want to ask them to write their answers to this riddle in a journal entry before they read the selection. Then, after they have read the selection, they can discuss both the author's answer and their own.

Many developmental students do not understand the difference between a story and an essay. In fact, many of them refer to essays as stories. Thus, as you discuss this selection, you may want to focus on its dual nature, for it is both an essay and a narrative. The author not only uses narration and description in the first part of this essay but also includes the separate story of King Arthur in the second part. Although students may initially be confused by this blending, it provides you with an opportunity to point out that narrative is often used to develop texts that we do not consider primarily narrative. You can also discuss the other selections that your students have read in this unit, identifying their narrative elements. Students need to realize that not all discourse is narrative, but they also need to understand that narrative is a basic, pervasive type of discourse that is used in all types of texts.

You may want to conclude your discussion by asking students to identify Davidson's thesis. They need to realize that even though the author relies extensively on narration and does not make an explicit assertion about gender roles, she is nevertheless arguing that women as well as men enjoy power and independence and is asking her readers to ponder the question of whether it is possible for both men and women to have sovereignty.

The New American Man   *Robert Bly*

Although there is no explicit reference to Iron John in the following selection from Bly's book, some of your students may have heard of Bly's "Iron John" concept—the idea that American men have grown soft and need to become stronger and more primitive. Engaging them in a discussion of this issue should not be difficult; most of them will have definite ideas on this subject. Getting them to analyze Bly's essay and the arguments it presents will be more difficult. The following questions may help students define the issue and evaluate Bly's arguments:

1. Have men really changed, or is it simply society that has changed?
2. Which have changed more in the past fifty years—men's or women's roles?
3. How have the ways in which women's roles have changed affected the roles that men assume?
4. Are Bly's arguments primarily rational or emotional?

5. Is Bly's analogy between males who existed in ancient Greece and men who live in today's society relevant? (You may want to compare Bly's use of Greek myths with Davidson's use of Arthurian legend.)

6. Are Bly's direct arguments more or less effective than Davidson's indirect arguments?

Getting Started　　　　　　　　　　　　　　*Janet Campbell Hale*

"Getting Started" is a contemporary poem that students will probably understand even though it includes several words that may be unfamiliar to them. This might be a good time to point out that vocabulary does not necessarily determine the difficulty of a reading selection.

Encourage your students to read through the poem several times to identify the reasons and excuses the speaker gives for not attaining her goals. Having a specific reason to reread the poem helps convince students that rereading is necessary, but you can take this opportunity to persuade them that readers frequently need to read a piece of discourse (especially poetry) more than once to form a clear understanding of it.

Help students relate this poem to a list of goals they generate for themselves. (You might even have students discuss their lists in small groups.) They need to understand the ramifications of setting goals that are too ambitious or of students' feeling bad because they have not attained certain goals.

Finally, you may want to spend some time analyzing the poem's format and discussing with your students why Hale chose to present her ideas in this particular form. It is important that students begin to understand some of the choices that writers make and the effect these choices have on a reader.

The Stars of the Whole Sky　　　　　　　*Shozo Machida (student)*

This second student essay in Unit One was written by a Japanese student. Thus, the language is not consistently idiomatic. However, we decided to edit it only slightly, leaving most of the language exactly as the student wrote it. If your students are distracted by what they perceive as awkward phrasing, you may want to point out that Machida's use of the English language, although not entirely idiomatic, has a certain poetic quality that would be lost if it were changed.

Because most classes include students like Machida, who are not native speakers of English, this essay provides you with an opportunity to point out that even though their English may not be perfect, they can still write strong, engaging essays. Because Machida is also what we call a returning student, one who is not just out of high school, some of your more mature, adult students may identify with him also.

I wish each of you could know Mr. Machida. He was a delight to have in class, enthusiastically sharing his experiences and knowledge of Japanese life and culture with the other students in the class—mostly young people who had spent their lives in rural Mississippi. His essay allows students to see that the quest for self-identity does not end with youth and that people have goals and dreams at all ages.

CRITICAL THINKING AND WRITING ASSIGNMENTS

The assignments at the end of each unit are of two types: collaborative thinking/discussing/writing assignments and individual writing assignments. The collaborative assignments encourage critical thinking by providing students with group projects that require them to think about and discuss an issue and then to reach a conclusion that involves some type of writing.

The individual writing assignments provide students with a number of different essay topics. These assignments provide students with more structured writing experiences, in which they are writing for a definite purpose and audience, and which encourage them to synthesize the ideas in the selections they have read with their own ideas. Select one or two of these assignments on the basis of your own goals for your course and the abilities of your students. (Some assignments are clearly easier than others.) Be sure to discuss each assignment carefully with students so that they understand what you expect of them. These assignments require extensive editing and revising; therefore, students will need some time to complete them. You may want to go on to the next unit and begin the reading assignments in it while your students are still working on writing assignments from the first unit.

UNIT TWO
Self with Family

This unit expands the focus of Unit One, emphasizing the self as it relates to the family. Because so many contemporary families are nontraditional, we have tried to avoid the assumption that all students come from families consisting of a mother, father, and two children living happily together in an idyllic neighborhood. In most college classes, many students will have been reared in families that have been significantly modified by divorce. Additional students may have been reared by grandparents or some family member other than their birth parents. Thus, we have emphasized in this unit the diversity of families in our modern society.

But at the same time we have encouraged students to recognize the universality and importance of family relations. The unit focuses on issues such as how an individual is shaped by his or her family, how a family is defined, and how family relations develop and change during the course of a person's life.

The introduction to this unit provides several questions for student journals or freewriting. You may want to allow your students freedom to select the questions to which they wish to respond. Or you may want to guide student discussion by focusing on a specific question, such as the first question, which asks students to describe the families in which they grew up. Or you may want to have students work in small groups to discuss different questions, perhaps reporting a summary of their findings back to the entire class.

In addition, the introduction to this unit includes a definition of the family taken from a sociology textbook by Ian Robertson. Ask students to find and discuss this definition, which should be a useful point of reference throughout their study of this unit. However, encourage students to write in their journals their own definitions of *family*, definitions that may or may not be similar to Robertson's. Students can work on their definitions in small groups and then share their definitions with students in other groups. This type of interaction should stimulate productive discussion of the family and how it can be defined, as well as prepare students for the readings that follow. As you progress through the unit, ask students periodically to recall these early definitions and, if they wish, to revise them on the basis of new ideas from their readings.

Generations   *Joyce Maynard*

"Generations" is a personal essay about a trip Joyce Maynard made to visit her dying grandmother. Help students to understand that the point of the essay is that the bond between parent and child progresses from generation to generation and that we become more like our parents as we get older, but give them the opportunity to agree or disagree with this thesis.

In preparing to read this essay, the students should begin to think about how they are and are not like their own parents (or some other member of their family who may have reared them). And they should also look for specific details in the Maynard essay to show how each generation in Maynard's family is like those before it. Also ask students to think about the title "Generations" and to look for the number of family generations represented in this narrative (there are four).

After students have read the essay, direct the discussion to the different attitudes that the characters in the story have toward one another. How does the speaker feel about her mother as opposed to her grandmother? What is the attitude of the speaker's mother toward her own mother? Can an awareness of past and present family relationships alter future relationships (such as the relationship between the speaker and her own daughter)? You might also want to initiate a discussion of differences between mother-daughter and father-son relationships.

Be sure that students recognize the difference between the story the author tells and the essay in which it is included. Help them to understand how narratives can be used in different types of discourse to make a point or argue a thesis. For example, you might want to discuss with students what effect this indirect approach to arguing a thesis has on them as readers. Would they prefer a stated thesis, or do they find the author's implicit thesis effective?

For further readings by Maynard on the subject of family, see her 1987 collection of newspaper columns entitled *Domestic Affairs: Enduring the Pleasures of Motherhood and Family Life*. A more recent book is *Where Love Goes* (1995).

No Snapshots in the Attic: A Granddaughter's
Search for a Cherokee Past   *Connie May Fowler*

If your students have read "Generations," you may want to introduce Connie May Fowler's essay by explaining that it also focuses on successive family generations but that it describes a kind of heritage very different from that described by Maynard. Remind students of the specific objects—the lamb coat and the china—that Maynard will eventually inherit from her grandmother and mother. Ask students whether such heirlooms exist in their family, and encourage students to write a journal entry about one or more of these objects. We are aware, however, that many of your students will—like Fowler—have "no snapshots in the attic," no family treasures, however small or monetarily worthless, and we have therefore provided alternative journal assignments. Thus, students can write about a family object, an important ancestor, or the effect of *not* knowing about one's ancestors.

Use the **As You Read** questions to guide your students' reading, asking them to further determine the important substitute Fowler finds for "snapshots in the attic": oral storytelling. After reading the selection, students are asked to write a story about their family, but you may want to vary this assignment by asking them instead to "tell" this story to a group of their classmates. If students do not know a family story, suggest that they interview an older family member if possible.

If you want to pursue the subject of family stories further, see Elizabeth Stone's *Black Sheep and Kissing Cousins* (1988) or her essay "Family Stories," which was reprinted in the second edition of *Interactions*.

Two Kinds   *Amy Tan*

This story by Amy Tan continues the focus on mother-daughter relationships begun in "Generations." Unlike the preceding selections, however, this one focuses on the expectations that Jing-Mei Woo's mother has for her and on Jing-Mei Woo's reactions to those expectations. In the **Before You Read** section, we ask students to think about the expectations their parents had for them; in **After You Read**, we ask students to write an essay on this subject. Thus, students use a process of writing/reading/writing to let this subject incubate before developing it into an essay.

You can ask students to identify unfamiliar words in the reading, or you can discuss with them the meanings of such words as *frenzied* (22), *mesmerizing* (22), *arpeggio* (41), *staccato* (41), and *discordant* (43). In addition, you might ask students to think about the meaning of the title "Two Kinds" (perhaps the mother and daughter, the two cousins, the two piano pieces).

Finally, you can focus on style in the reading by asking students to examine the parallel structures in paragraphs 9 and 41. For example, in paragraph 9, Tan uses the parallel structure of "I was a dainty ballerina . . . ," "I was like the Christ child . . . ," and "I was Cinderella . . ." to emphasize the mental images she had of herself.

Fatherhood   *Bill Cosby*

This selection employs a narrative to help define *fatherhood*. The **Before You Read** WRITE assignment asks students to provide their own journal definitions of the term. To extend this writing assignment, you can have students write definitions of *fatherhood* and *motherhood*, identifying the qualities that are common to both and those that are unique to each.

As students read, remind them to look not only for Cosby's advice to parents but also for what he considers the "hardest truth for a father to learn"—that his child is growing up and that he must "let go." To parallel this parental discovery, you might also ask students to identify the "hardest truth" that children learn about their parents. This discussion can lead naturally to the **After You Read** questions about communication and honesty between parents and children. Students may want to share their advice columns with one another in small groups.

Students might be interested to know not only that *Fatherhood* was Cosby's first book but also that it was an outgrowth of his successful television show. As reported by *Contemporary Authors: New Revision Series*, "The paternal image of Cliff Huxtable led a publisher to ask Cosby for a humorous book" on the subject. *Fatherhood* sold "a record 2.6 million hardcover copies and was quite well-received by critics" (Vol. 42, p. 101).

The Old Man   *Larry King*

Like "Two Kinds," "The Old Man" is a story of rebellion, of the painful differences that often exist between parent and child, in this case a father and son. In fact, critic Foster Hirsch states that the essays in King's book *The Old Man and Lesser Mortals*, from which this essay was taken, exhibit King's "continuing wrestling match" with his heritage (*Contemporary Authors: New Revision Series*, Vol. 42, p. 266).

The vocabulary—the words discussed in the EXAMINE section and other words such as *exhortations* (1), *eschew* (2), and *neophyte* (6)—will be challenging for students, but they should find the narrative easy to follow and the characters recognizable. In addition, King's lively, humorous way of telling a story should engage students and enable them to read comfortably even though they will not know all the words he uses. The story is set in West Texas and has a strong Southwest flavor, so you may need to introduce the students to this part of the country before they read, especially if your students are predominantly urban.

Although King does not state a thesis, there is a strong implied thesis, which students should recognize. Help them to articulate what they think the speaker in the narrative realizes at the bus station. They should go beyond the simple idea that he realizes that he loves his father, to understand his realization of not just his father's mortality but his own and his sudden awareness of the strong bond of kinship between himself and his father.

Because King portrays both the young man and the father so vividly, you might want to ask students to brainstorm about ways in which the two men are alike and ways in which they are different. Then you can ask them to write an essay comparing the two characters. This assignment can be substituted for one of the writing assignments suggested in the text.

Never in My Life   *Walter McDonald*

Like "The Old Man," "Never in My Life" focuses on a father-son relationship and the difficulty that males often seem to have in expressing affection, especially for one another. (The speaker in the poem and his father had never been able to say "I love you" to each other.)

McDonald, who is a Vietnam veteran, makes a point of including in the poem a number of references to war (allusions indicate that the speaker in the poem served in Vietnam and the father in World War II), as if to suggest that even courageous men falter before the ordeal of saying "I love you" to another man, even (or perhaps especially) to their own fathers or sons. Students should be encouraged to explore this issue, discussing first whether they think men *are* reluctant to express feelings and, second, if so, why.

Note McDonald's use of the term *our blood*. ("I touched the blue vein/ of our blood that throbbed / beneath his head's pale skin.") You may want to relate this phrase to King's reference to blood in the final sentence of his narrative. ("In that moment, I think, I first sensed—if I did not understand—something of mortality; of tribes, blood, and inherited rituals.") Students can discuss why blood is frequently used as a symbol of familial relations—what it means to have the "same" blood, to share a bloodline, and so on.

McDonald may not be a poet with whom you are familiar. Although he has published widely, he is primarily a regional poet. He has lived in West Texas most of his life and teaches creative writing at Texas Tech University. He is in many ways a very masculine poet, writing with simplicity yet great power about flying airplanes, farming, hunting, fighting, and the harsh, spare West Texas landscape. Yet he also writes with great tenderness about human relations, especially those among family members.

After students finish the writing assignments, encourage them to read their poems (or paragraphs) beginning "Never in my life . . ." aloud in small groups.

Sibling Imprints   *Francine Klagsbrun*

All students should enjoy the humor and emotion of the introductory narrative, but instructors should remember that students who do not have siblings cannot identify with this scene in the same way as those who do have siblings. However, all students will have felt for someone—siblings, friends, classmates—the emotions of love, hate, rivalry, and reconciliation listed in the title of the book from which this reading was excerpted.

Before and after students read the essay, call their attention to the word *imprints* in the title. Ask students to give examples of how one sibling can "imprint," or influence, the life of another sibling. Ask students what siblings make the largest imprints—older or younger siblings, females or males.

To make the experiences described by Klagsbrun more meaningful to all students, you may want to divide your class into small groups—each of which has both students with and students without siblings—and ask them to share their reactions to the reading and their experiences with (or observing) siblings. This group discussion will help prepare students for the writing assignment at the end of the lesson. If students choose to write the comparative essay, you may want to introduce them to possible organizational formats.

The Letter   *Rudolfo Anaya*

If you have Hispanic students in your class, this reading gives you an excellent opportunity to involve them directly in explaining the vocabulary used in the selection and providing background cultural information. These students could even give you and the rest of the class a pronunciation lesson!

Some of your students may have been adopted, and most of them will have a friend or acquaintance who was adopted. Therefore, you will want to approach this reading with great sensitivity. Your students will probably have opinions, however, about whether or not adopted children should be told about their adoption at a young age. Opinions will vary even more on other issues related to adoption, such as open adoption and interracial adoption. You may want to discuss one or more of these issues in class, or you may want to ask students to write journals about one of these issues and then share their opinions with a small group of their classmates. You could even substitute a more formal persuasive essay assignment on open adoption or interracial adoption for the letter called for in the **After You Read** WRITE assignment.

In addition to being a successful novelist, Anaya is a professor of English at the University of New Mexico in Albuquerque, the setting for this essay and for the novel from which it was excerpted. You might tempt students to read Anaya's *Albuquerque* by telling him that Abrán reacts to the news in the letter by beginning a search for his father and his new identity.

Hold the Mayonnaise   *Julia Alvarez*

Julia Alvarez's essay provides you with two focal points for discussion: (1) the role that culture plays in family and (2) the dynamics of stepfamilies. Alvarez discusses the interplay of two cultures within one family, but you may want to have students freewrite or discuss how a single culture—Anglo, Latino, African-American, Chinese, Vietnamese, rural, urban—influences the food, customs, and values shared by the family.

The writing journal assignment, which asks students to focus specifically on a particular cultural food, should produce a variety of interesting responses. Give students class time to share these responses in small groups. Most students will be familiar with Mexican and Chinese food. However, if your class represents a variety of cultural backgrounds, you and your students may learn something about cultural foods less common in popular restaurants. During your discussion, ask students why a food such as mayonnaise or tacos is such an effective symbol of a family's culture.

Most students in your class will have had indirect, if not direct, experience with stepfamilies. Ask students to consider the difficulties that step-parents as well as stepchildren have in adjusting to this new relationship. Then ask them to evaluate Alvarez's success as a stepmother and to compare her experience with that of other stepmothers or stepfathers they know.

Students might be interested to know that although Alvarez was born in New York City, she lived in the Dominican Republic until she was ten years old. Like this essay, her first novel, *How the Garcia Girls Lost Their Accents*, focuses on the family. The novel "recounts—through interrelated stories—the experience of four sisters and their family" (*Contemporary Authors*, Vol. 147, p. 16). You might encourage students to read this novel or provide them with an excerpt from it.

Wanted—A Mother   *Orville Rawlins (student)*

Written by a freshman in a regular freshman English class, this essay exhibits both strengths and weaknesses. Emphasize to your students that this essay was written by a student, and then encourage them to find and discuss these strengths and weaknesses. For example, students may praise the

interest-catching introduction, the description, and the effective (and symbolic) use of the episode of the mother monkey. Ask students to give specific
examples of effective description (see especially paragraphs 10–12). Students
may react differently to the mixed styles of the essay (both oral and literary).
We made few editorial changes in Rawlins's essay, but the better editors in
your class may find a few changes that they would have made. Ask them to
look for a misspelled word in paragraph 4 (*dependance* for *dependence*) and
an incorrectly used word in paragraph 7 (*imploded* for *exploded*). Also ask
them to read carefully the first sentence of paragraph 8 to see if it is clear,
and help them to find the problems of modification and punctuation in the
sentence. You and your students will also find other ways to clarify or "correct" this essay, but we hope that you will use this essay to help students
realize that writing does not have to be "perfect" to be effective.

A good focus for discussion in this lesson is Rawlins's vocabulary. You
may want to ask what students think about Rawlins's use of slang terms
such as *bastard* and *nigger*. Remind students, however, that Rawlins, who
is a native of the Caribbean islands, is himself black. Point out also the
important connection between Rawlins's rather sophisticated vocabulary,
referred to in the **Before You Read** EXAMINE, and the reaction he had to
his mother's illiteracy in paragraph 5. Base your discussion of the words
identified by students, but be prepared to discuss such words as *sycophant*
(4), *maelstrom* (5), and *exorcise* (7).

Finally, you will want to discuss with students the inner conflict about
his mother and his changing attitude toward her. After students read the
essay, follow up on your initial discussion of the title "Wanted—A Mother."

The Family Values Debate   *James Q. Wilson*

Wilson's essay is undoubtedly the most difficult essay in the unit on family.
However, since it is the last essay in the unit, students should be much more
prepared to read it than they would have been had it occurred earlier.

Call students' attention to the title to make sure that they understand the
general meaning of the family values debate. You may want to simplify the
debate by couching it in terms of liberal and conservative views, described
by Wilson as the views of "scholars and policy elites" versus the public.
You may even want to tell, or remind, students of the Dan Quayle/Murphy
Brown controversy in which Quayle and the television character Murphy
Brown, played by Candace Bergen, disagreed about the effectiveness of
single-parent homes.

Remind students to look for Wilson's own viewpoint as they read, explaining that he presents both the liberal and the conservative viewpoints so

that they must read carefully to discover his own views. His conservative view is perhaps most clearly expressed in paragraphs 2, 15, and 20–24.

This is a good essay to illustrate the use of quotations and statistics to support an argument. You may, however, need to explain to your students some allusions, such as the reference to "the Ozzie-and-Harriet model" (paragraph 8), which refers to the television show "Ozzie and Harriet." Popular in the 1950s and 1960s, this show focused on the "model" family— Ozzie and Harriet Nelson and their two sons, David and Ricky.

CRITICAL THINKING AND WRITING ASSIGNMENTS

The collaborative assignments for **Exploring Ideas Together** give you an opportunity to involve your students in the social and cognitive interaction that is such an important part of the learning style of developmental readers and writers. You may want to assign one of these assignments to your entire class, with different groups working on the same assignment. Or you may want to have different groups select different assignments and then share their findings. Whereas the first and last assignments provide opportunities for oral presentations and debate, the middle two assignments involve students in true collaborative writing.

The assignments for **Writing Essays** encourage students to work independently to synthesize the information and opinions they have gained from the readings with their own prior knowledge and present attitudes about families. More formal and structured than the assignments that accompany each reading selection, these assignments give students experience in communicating clearly and purposefully for an audience. Whatever essay assignment(s) you or your students choose, encourage students to write for a particular audience. For example, an essay written in response to the second assignment, to write a persuasive essay on the positive or negative effects of rebellion on children, could be written to a teenage audience. Or students could direct their essays from assignment 5 to adoption agencies or to parents involved in adoption.

UNIT THREE
Self with Friends and Mates

Although the units and individual selection sin *Interactions* can be taught in whatever order you choose, this unit on friends and mates follows naturally from the unit on family. To introduce this unit, you might ask students to make two lists—one listing three to five qualities of "the ideal friend" and the other listing three to five qualities of "the ideal mate." When students complete their lists, ask them to discuss their lists in small groups. How are the qualities of the ideal friend and the ideal mate similar? How are these qualities different?

You might also ask your students to complete a mapping exercise, creating a map or visual diagram that explores various relationships among friends or types of mates. (Refer students to the introduction for a sample map.) To map the network of their friendships, students can each write their names in the center of a page and then branch out to various types of friends (best friends, childhood friends, school friends, work friends, young friends, older friends, new friends, former friends, and so forth), to individual friends, and to specific experiences with friends. Encourage students to be creative with their maps.

In creating their maps, students will inevitably relate the topic of friends or mates to their own experiences. Thus, this mapping not only becomes an effective prewriting activity for the entire unit but also encourages students to call to mind some prior knowledge of the topic before they begin to read about it. You might also tell students that they can create maps, or diagrams, that identify and show relationships among important ideas (main ideas and details) in a reading selection. Judith Westphal Irwin, among others, suggests using such maps to help students with the "global" or "macro" structures of content-area textbooks and thus increase comprehension (*Teaching Reading Comprehension Processes.* Englewood Cliffs, NJ: Prentice-Hall, 1986, p. 54).

Liked for Myself   *Maya Angelou*

"Liked for Myself" is the first of several autobiographical accounts of friendship in this unit. Although later accounts include some expository analysis, the narrative structure of this essay and of the one that follows

28

("Oil and Water") provides your students with accessible readings early in the unit. In addition, with its emphasis on a friendship between a child and an older person, Angleou's essay recalls the family relationships discussed in Unit Two.

In preparing your students to read this selection, you may want to expand the **Before You Read** EXAMINE section by asking students to look for clues to setting in paragraphs 2–5. Their discoveries about the rural southern setting should help prepare students for the reading. You may also wish to explain the allusions on pages 150–151 to British novelist Charles Dickens's *A Tale of Two Cities* and *Oliver Twist*, and to the Anglo-Saxon epic *Beowulf*. The quotation in paragraph 30 ("It is a far, far better thing that I do, than I have ever done . . .") is from the conclusion of *A Tale of Two Cities*, for example.

As an alternative writing assignment, you could ask students to write a character sketch of Bertha Flowers. Or you can suggest an assignment that focuses on the idea of Mrs. Flowers as a teacher as well as a friend. In preparing students to write this alternative assignment, ask students to reread paragraph 23, which explains Mrs. Flowers's "lessons in living" for Marguerite. Be sure that students understand that good "teachers" can be found in places other than a formal classroom.

Oil and Water   *Valerie Owen (student)*

Students should particularly enjoy this reading selection because it is written by a student like themselves. Because the essay is a simple narrative of personal experience, they should find it easy to read the essay and to identify with the author, but don't let students overlook the very real strengths of the essay—strengths that they should try to emulate.

Ask students to evaluate the essay for interest, organization, development, style, and clarity. This evaluation process provides you with an excellent opportunity to involve your students in (or introduce them to) peer revision groups. In fact, you can use the discussion of a student essay like this one as practice for peer evaluation of their own essays. Using a student essay written by someone who is not in their own class for early peer review is a good idea because, initially at least, students are often reluctant to discuss one another's essays honestly.

In evaluating Owen's essay, students should note how the introductory paragraph captures reader interest, the chronological organization, the use of details and strong images as mentioned in **After You Read** EXAMINE ("backwoods mannerisms were as shocking to me as a slap in the face," paragraph 2), and the clear thesis in the conclusion. After students have written Owen's thesis in their own words, have them compare their thesis statements. In sharing the statements they have written, students will discover that no two are exactly alike, but they should find their statements to be similar in including the idea that individuals with different personalities can be good friends.

One of the final writing assignments in this lesson asks students to write an essay about a friend who is quite different from the writer. An alternate, if somewhat overworked assignment is for the student to write an essay about his or her "best friend."

What Friends Are For   *Phillip Lopate*

This is one of the longest essays, and probably the most difficult reading selection, in this unit. However, we have placed it third in the unit because it provides not only an excellent overview of different qualities and types of friendship but also because it compares feelings of friendship with those of romance—the parallel focus of this unit.

You might use the **Before You Read** EXAMINE questions to introduce this essay, asking students to compare Lopate's more skeptical view of a "best friend" to Valerie Owen's description of her own best friend and their friendship. Especially if a variety of ages is represented in your class, ask students to comment on the respective ages of Lopate and Owen. Most will realize that Lopate is older, more experienced, and—depending on your viewpoint—either wiser or more cynical than Owen.

The comparison/analogy that Lopate makes between friendship and love (he begins by defining *friendship* as "love without wings") is interesting, even fun, but the concept as well as Lopate's whimsical attitude can be difficult for developmental students. Be sure that students understand not only the meaning of *promiscuity* (paragraph 4) but, more important, that they understand the wry irony and humor—and innocence—of Lopate's use of the word. The phrase "promiscuity of the sandbox" simply means that small children are "friends" with everyone, that they switch quickly and easily from one friend to another rather than remaining "loyal" to the child who has just left the playground. The essay as a whole contains several words that may be unfamiliar to your students, words that you may want to have your students circle for class discussion or addition to their vocabulary journals, but this is the only word that could, we think, cause real confusion.

Possibilities for discussion and writing abound with this rich essay. For example, you might have students expand the journal assignment about their best friends into essays, you might ask students to describe or "act out" a friendship "scene," or you may have them write the classification essay assigned on page 164.

Because we combined the units on friends and mates into one unit for this edition, we did not have room for an essay on the single life. However, you may easily adapt this essay for that purpose. Several times throughout the essay, Lopate refers to his life as a single man—a man who has obviously chosen *not* to marry but who has a rich life with many friends. If you want to pursue this topic, you might refer to Lopate's book *Bachelorhood: Tales of the Metropolis* (1981). In the Introduction to this book, Lopate writes, "I wanted to add . . . an unmarried perspective, because, for all that writers and human beings share, it makes a difference—having a mate—in how one sees or 'receives' the world" (*Contemporary Literary Criticism*, Vol. 29, p. 298).

Death of a Friend: The Delicacy and Strength of Lace

Leslie Marmon Silko and James Wright

For its form and its personal intensity, "Death of a Friend: The Delicacy and Strength of Lace" is unique among the readings in *Interactions*. Because it is the only group of letters in the book, you may want to spend some time talking about the letter form and format—perhaps discussing the differences between personal letters such as these and business letters that students might write to make a complaint or apply for a position. Such a discussion is an excellent opportunity to expand your instruction on purpose and audience, because students can readily see in letters the application of these concepts, which so often seem abstract.

After students have examined the dates of the letters and determined that Jim Wright died just three months after he first learned of his cancer, you may want to have them examine some words that may be unfamiliar. You might focus on *radical, emerge, diminished, recuperating, debilitating,* and *embodying* in paragraphs 2 and 3 of Wright's letter; on *rationalization* in Silko's first letter; and on *saguaro* in Silko's last letter.

We believe that personal writing assignments—the journal and the letter—are a fitting response to the personal nature of the reading itself. However, you may want to respect students' privacy and avoid grading—or perhaps even reading—what they produce.

Where's Dietz?

Mike Taibbi

In selecting the readings for this edition of *Interactions*, we debated about including two readings about the death of a friend—this one and the previous collection of letters by Silko and Wright. Ultimately, however, we decided to include both because the friends and friendships are so different in the two readings. The friendship between Wright and Silko is a non-romantic male-female friendship; the friendship between Taibbi and Dietz is one between two men.

In fact, if you have assigned the letters by Silko and Wright, you might introduce this reading selection by asking students to compare these two friendships—not only the types of friends involved but also the kind and quality of friendship. Students will probably note that although Silko and Wright shared a close friendship, it was a long-distance one in which they seldom saw each other in person but rather exchanged letters. The communication shared in these letters is sincere but rather literary. The friendship between Taibbi and Dietz, on the other hand, was a friendship of almost daily communication, conversation, and activities.

In fact, the central focus of the activities that we provide for "Where's Dietz?" is on the idea of communication between male friends rather than on the loss of a friend through death. Taibbi certainly grieves over the loss of his friend, but he also grieves that he had never expressed his friendship for Dietz openly while his friend was alive. Ask students whether they agree or disagree with Taibbi's statement that "Men particularly . . . seem prone to make their walls of glass" (page 174) and thus have difficulty expressing their feelings and emotions, especially feelings of friendship for other men or feelings of grief. If students agree with Taibbi, ask them to explain why they believe this situation exists and whether, in particular, it has anything to do with our society's emphasis on "manly behavior."

Because Taibbi also discusses the differences between him and his friend Dietz, you might teach this essay in conjunction with Owen's "Oil and Water."

Drifting Away   *Diane Cole*

Your students should be able to understand and identify with this reading on a literal level. Most of them will have "drifted away" from a friend from an earlier phase of their lives. You may want to begin discussing this reading on this literal level—assigning the **Before You Read** WRITE journal entry in which they are asked to describe such an experience.

The symbolic level of this story, however, will be much more difficult for your students. After students have read the story, ask them to meet in small groups to discuss the symbolism of the crystal bowl. Tell students to begin by listing actual characteristics of the bowl (round, beautiful, clear, hard or brittle, and cracked). Then ask students to write a sentence or two showing how each of these literal qualities suggests a quality of the friendship between Diane and Jean. Students may see that the round quality implies a perfect and long-lasting relationship, a quality that is ironic at this point in the friendship. Students may also come to understand that the friendship was once clear and pure but is now strained and brittle—open for the crack that will destroy it. You might direct the symbolic meaning of the bowl back to the story by asking students which friend put the biggest crack in the bowl, or friendship.

For writing assignments accompanying this reading, you could follow up on the **Before You Read** THINK question by asking students to analyze the meaning of an important personal gift (given or received). Or you could ask students to use the writing assignments in **Before You Read** (journal about a friend who has "drifted away") and **After You Read** (list of reasons why friends drift apart) as prewriting for an essay analyzing and giving support for reasons why friends drift apart. To further help students prepare to write this essay, allow them to discuss their reasons in small groups, taking notes to use in their own essays.

Finding a Wife   *Gary Soto*

"Finding a Wife" presents a view of courtship and marriage that is rather subjective and romantic. In spite of his blunt, pragmatic title, Soto does not give his readers a step-by-step formula for finding a wife, but rather gives a philosophy for living that makes finding a wife easy. In effect, he seems to argue (indirectly, of course) that if one is open to new people and new experiences, mating is not too difficult. He also seems to suggest that luck plays an important role. Thus, he views mating as a state of mind and a stroke of luck rather than a process that can be analyzed and defined. And yet, as suggested by the **Before You Read** EXAMINE questions, although Soto encounters his future wife by a happy circumstance, he *does* have some difficulty in meeting and "courting" her because he is basically shy. Thus, students may read the essay as completely romantic or as partly ironic.

Audience is an interesting topic for discussion with Soto's essay. Ask students to identify the audience Soto had in mind. Call their attention specifically to the first paragraph of the essay, in which Soto himself identifies the audience to whom he first said, "It's easy to find a wife"—his young college students. Discuss with your students how the audience—actual and hypothetical—may have affected the romantic tone of Soto's essay.

Many of your students may already be married, so they need to be encouraged to reflect on their previous experience rather than to think about future plans of "finding" a wife or a husband. But the essay should strike a responsive chord in nearly all of your students—young and old, married and unmarried—because everyone loves a love story. However, students also need to think beyond the story that Soto relates, to the thesis he is arguing. Although he is not explicit, and your students may not agree on what his main point is, they should be encouraged to view the essay as argumentative as well as narrative.

The Right to Marry   *Joanne Jacobs*

"The Right to Marry" is one of the most controversial selections that we include. It was an editorial that appeared in a California newspaper prior to a vote to determine whether homosexuals should have the legal right to marry. (The proposition was defeated.)

Although students may respond to the selection emotionally at first, you can encourage them to view the editorial objectively. Is it persuasive? What arguments are most effective? Least effective? Help students understand that the issue behind the editorial is not moral but legal. Given the fact that some people in our society choose to live with members of the same sex, should these relationships be protected by law? Are these people entitled to the same legal privileges afforded to people who choose to live with someone of the opposite sex? Encourage students to be objective in analyzing whether a homosexual relationship functions in the same way as a heterosexual relationship.

If you think your students will be uncomfortable with the subject matter of this selection, you may certainly omit it. But the editorial provides you with a good opportunity to teach argument and to present students with a view of marriage that may be new to them.

The Lies That Bind   *Paul Thaler*

As suggested in the **Before You Read** EXAMINE section, the title is a good introductory focus for discussing this essay. Ask students when and how lies can bind, and when and how they can separate. Or, to put the question another way, how is being tactful distinguished from being dishonest? Also, be sure that students recognize the last sentence of the first paragraph as the stated thesis.

We expect that most or all of your students will have had personal experience with this ethical dilemma in a relationship with a mate, date, or friend. Therefore, they will probably have strong opinions about the issue. Give them the opportunity both to share personal experiences (perhaps in small groups) and to react freely to Thaler's essay and to specific statements, such as "Most lies that I spin are inconsequential" (page 191, paragraph 10) or "as intimacy deepens, the need for lying deepens also" (page 192, paragraph 15). Ask students to consider whether any lie is ever "inconsequential" or whether the need for honesty instead of lying increases with intimacy.

This discussion should prepare students for writing the argumentative essay assigned at the end of the lesson.

A more creative assignment is to ask students to put themselves in Amy's position, perhaps even to write a personal response to Thaler. You might even comment on the irony—recognized by Thaler himself—that the publication of this essay reveals to Amy the incidents he lied about in order to, as he says, protect her feelings.

Finally, this essay has a number of challenging vocabulary words, such as *vulnerable* (4), *predilections* (5), and so forth. In most instances, the context will allow students to understand these words well enough to proceed, but you may want to ask them to circle unfamiliar words for class discussion or to add these words to their vocabulary journals.

Distance   *Raymond Carver*

Raymond Carver's "Distance" is a complex but fascinating story about marital and family relationships. Because of the story's complex structure, we have asked students questions (see **Before You Read** EXAMINE) that help them understand the framing device that Carver uses in the story. You may want to have students begin their reading with the "story-within-a-story" of the young lovers and then direct them to go back and read the framing sections. Or you may want to introduce the story by reading the introductory frame, thus setting up the remainder of the narrative for them.

After students have read the entire story, ask them to contrast the tone and content of the central section with those of the framing sections. Lead them to see that the central section presents a more "romantic" view of love as opposed to the more "pessimistic" or "realistic" view shown in the frames.

Carver's title is a masterful example of compressed meaning. Ask students how many kinds of "distance" exist in the story. Possible responses include the distances between the young husband and the young wife after their disagreement, the distance between the older man and his (estranged— separated or divorced?) wife, the distance in time between the two parts of the story, the distance between the father and the daughter, and so forth.

Other possibilities for discussion include the characters of the three principal actors in the story and the use of the Canada geese (paragraphs 34–44) to symbolize the young lovers.

You may also want to comment on Carver's unorthodox presentation of dialogue without quotation marks. Explain that although this is not the "accepted" way to present dialogue, this technique allows Carver to achieve the effect of the father's telling the story rather than the story's actually happening as we read.

The Good Marriage   *Judith S. Wallerstein and Sandra Blakeslee*

Although this is the longest selection in Unit Three, it is relatively easy to read. Because it is so long, however, you may want to break it into sections for reading and discussion. The subsections focus on the following topics: marriages surviving destructive forces (pages 205–207); origin and scope of study (pages 207–208); process of change in and various stages of marriage pages 208–209); "secrets" of good marriages (pages 209–211); personal application to writer's granddaughter (page 212).

You may want to have students read and discuss their journal entries in small groups, comparing their ideas of "the good marriage." You might even create an idea map on a transparency, the chalkboard, or a computer, reflecting the qualities of a good marriage as identified by the class. A parallel assignment is to ask students to list or discuss the qualities of a bad marriage, perhaps qualities that lead to separation or divorce.

If your class is composed of students of varying ages, organize the class into small groups based on stages of marriage, and have each group discuss a good marriage for a particular stage (people in their twenties, forties, sixties, and so forth). Then have each group share their ideas with the rest of the class. This discussion can help prepare students for the last writing assignment, on page 213.

On Death and Love   *Janet Campbell Hale*

"On Death and Love" is essentially a love poem, but it is very different from the love poems most students know. Students will probably find this poem strange and may have difficulty understanding it. Reading it aloud to them initially may help them, and discussing each sentence individually will probably be useful. (Some students will not even recognize the sentences unless you point them out.)

Students may find the coupling of death and love especially strange, even incomprehensible, depending on their ages. Mature students should not have any trouble with this concept, but an eighteen year old may have trouble understanding what death has to do with love. Therefore, this might be a good time to let your older students contribute to the class. For example, you might divide the class into small groups to discuss the poem, making sure that each group includes a mature student.

This poem is a good example of how poetic conventions differ from prose conventions. Students need to realize that poetry, like every other form of discourse, has certain conventions that are purely arbitrary. But they also need to recognize that the format a poet chooses affects the way a reader perceives and understands the poem.

CRITICAL THINKING AND WRITING ASSIGNMENTS

The **Critical Thinking and Writing Assignments** give your students the opportunity to synthesize and analyze information from their reading and their experience. The first two assignments from **Exploring Ideas Together** emphasize collaborative writing, whereas the last two emphasize oral discussion and reports. The final discussion question on romantic love, however, could also be used as the basis for a persuasive essay on the topic.

The **Writing Essays** section provides assignments that vary in purpose, mode, and audience. For example, you or your students may select from assignments that ask students to define, compare and contrast, persuade, or analyze. The sixth essay assignment asks students to gather new information by interviewing an older or younger person about the process of dating. To prepare students for this part of the assignment, you will need to discuss interviewing strategies and courtesies. For example, students need to set up a specific time and place for the interview. Students also need to prepare specific questions before the interview, but they should also be willing to let the person being interviewed talk about what interests him or her. You might encourage students to use a tape recorder (with the interviewee's permission, of course) rather than try to write everything the person says.

Once again, we suggest that you (or your students) select only one or two of the writing assignments provided here. It is far more productive for students to spend time doing one assignment well than to rush through several. Because each assignment requires some form of research or preparation (interviewing, rereading of previous selections, comparing, analyzing, or synthesizing information), as well as time for writing and revision, one assignment per unit is a reasonable expectation.

UNIT FOUR
Self with Work

This unit is new to this edition of *Interactions*. We think you and your students will find the topic a productive one to explore together. Students are nearly always interested in their own career plans, so you may want to begin the unit by focusing on their expectations and hopes for the future. Then you can lead them into consideration of the general concept of work by asking them to compare the two terms *career* and *work*. How is each defined? What connotations does each have? This discussion should lead naturally into a consideration of such issues as the role work plays in our lives and our attitude toward physical labor.

You can then ask students to read the introduction to the unit, which focuses on how the nature of work has changed in our society in recent years. The reading selections in the unit consider a range of work-related issues—from the effect of work on individuals and the difference between work and play to predictions for career opportunities in the future. Before you assign any of these selections, however, you might ask your students to write a journal entry describing an experience they have had with work.

American Dreams: Stanley Cygan, 90   *Studs Terkel*

Students will probably not be familiar with Studs Terkel, but the introduction to this selection explains that he is known for the interviews he has conducted with working-class Americans. This selection is, in fact, a transcript of such an interview. It is the first-person account of Stanley Cygan, a ninety-year old immigrant who worked for many years as a laborer, first in the steel mills and later for a stove-repair company.

In addition to being a vivid description of a way of life that many of your students have not known, this interview provides a glimpse of the dream that Cygan had as a young man. He wanted to get an education, "to be smart," but was unable to realize his dream. Students can discuss the role that education plays in determining not only the type of work people do but also the kinds of lives they live. You may also want to emphasize Cygan's immigrant experience and how this affected his life.

Work and Play   *Robert Murray Davis*

This selection is taken from a memoir entitled *Mid-lands*, which tells of the author's experiences as a young man growing up in a small town in Missouri in the 1940s. Davis focuses in this chapter on what he learned from his father about both work and play and the difference between the two. But he also reveals a great deal about his own attitude toward work and his relationship with his father, and how both of these changed and did not change over the years.

This selection may be rather difficult for some of your students to read, but it is well worth their effort. Because it is based largely on the author's experiences, students should be able to understand it, even though they may struggle with the author's ironic tone and sophisticated point of view. It is one of the most thoughtful and complex readings in the unit, and well worth the effort it may require.

Some of the language is rather direct, so you should probably not assign this selection if you have students who are offended by words like *ass* or *bullshit*. But these terms are used in the context of an informal conversation between two grown males, and most students will recognize that in this type of situation such language is, if not typical, at least common.

My Mother Enters the Workforce   *Rita Dove*

Some of your students may not know that Rita Dove is an African-American, so you may want to give them this information. In addition, because poetry is often difficult for students to understand and appreciate, you may want to read this selection in class rather than assign it for students to read on their own. You can introduce the poet and poem briefly, ask students to read it to themselves, and then read it aloud to them (or ask one of them to read it aloud to the class). Then you can discuss the poem or ask the students to write about it in their journals.

This poem, like the pieces by Terkel and Davis, emphasizes the relationship between education and work. If your class has read all three pieces, you may want to focus on a discussion or writing assignment that requires students to synthesize the information from all three selections. For example, do all three writers suggest that education determines to a great extent the kind of work people are able to do? What other forces influence the kinds of careers people pursue? Is an education more or less essential now than it was in the past? You might also want to encourage students to explore the differences between the types of physical labor that men typically do and those that women typically do. How is this traditional division of work changing?

The Case Against Chores   *Jane Smiley*

This selection by Jane Smiley is a good illustration of an essay that challenges conventional wisdom. Although Smiley is writing specifically about attitudes in the Midwest, most people, regardless of where they live, would probably agree that giving children chores to do teaches them something positive and reinforces the work ethic. Smiley examines this prevailing assumption and argues against it. Her essay provides you with an opportunity to teach your students how to construct an argument. For example, you might point out to them the following strategies that Smiley uses in her essay:

1. She begins with a "myth" or assumption that is generally held to be true; then argues against it.

2. She explains the opposing point of view and refutes each supporting argument.

3. She uses her own experiences to support her own point of view.

4. She compares her own experiences to those of her husband to reinforce her argument.

5. She concludes her essay effectively by arguing that what is really important is not how much work people do but how much they enjoy the work they do.

You may also want to point out to your students that the effectiveness of Smiley's arguments is, to a great extent, the result of who she is as well as what she says. If we did not know that Jane Smiley is a very successful writer, would we find her arguments so compelling? In effect, her success argues for her. Because she was not forced to do chores and yet became a success, all children should be allowed to do only the work they want to do. Your students will enjoy analyzing this implicit argument. They might also enjoy speculating about the effectiveness of this essay had it been written by someone who was completely unknown or who admitted to being a failure.

Initiation   *Rebecca May (student)*

This student essay tells of the author's experience in a large urban hospital's emergency room. Students should find it both easy to read and interesting. Because the author does not include an explicit thesis statement, you may want your students to discuss the essay's thesis. Help them to see that there is a controlling idea that is communicated indirectly by the author's choice of details and concluding comments about her reaction to this experience. You may want to ask students to consider what effect would be created if the author had begun with a traditional introduction and thesis statement.

Be sure they understand the importance of the thesis, whether it is stated explicitly or merely implied.

You may also want to focus on May's skillful use of specific details to help her readers understand her experience. Point out that she uses not only visual details but also details that appeal to a reader's senses of smell, sound, and touch.

Spokesperson   *Jane Armstrong (student)*

This essay, like the preceding one, was written by a student. However, Jane Armstrong was a graduate student who was taking a course in nonfiction prose rather than freshman composition. Armstrong's essay can be paired with the one by May because both tell of experiences the young women had when they began work. May is upset when she assists with a patient who dies, but she decides that she will be "all right"; that is, that she can handle this unpleasant aspect of her job. Armstrong, in contrast, decides that in her case, the price is too high and quits her job as a media spokesperson for a family planning clinic.

Like the May essay, this one does not begin with a thesis statement, but the author concludes by summing up her feelings about the experience she recounts. Both essays are essentially narratives with conclusions that explain how the author reacted to the events she has narrated. Students may find it difficult to understand why Armstrong reacted as she did. Help them understand that it was not so much that her job was difficult or unpleasant but rather that it subsumed her. She felt that she was a spokesperson rather than a person—that her own identity was lost as she became defined by the issue of abortion.

Students may want to discuss the issue of abortion, but make it clear that this essay is not concerned with the abortion issue but with Armstrong's realization that her own identity was more important than her pro-choice sentiments. She is not saying that she changed her mind on the issue of abortion but that she decided she could no longer function as a media spokesperson because her actions and words had become a rote performance rather than an act of conviction.

The Family Farm   *David Mas Masumoto*

This essay is interesting on several levels. First, the author is Japanese-American, the son of farm laborers, and second, the essay argues that family and land, like work, can define us. In the essay, Masumoto explains why he chose to stay and work the family farm rather than seek a new career. He develops his essay primarily by comparing and contrasting, first, his own generation with that of his parents and second, his own attitudes and choices with those of his college friends. The essay provides us with a viewpoint that is often overlooked.

You may want to begin your discussion by asking students how many of them plan to follow in their parents' footsteps when they choose a career or how many of them plan to return home to live after they complete their degrees. You can then discuss the values that determine how we respond to these choices as well as the economic conditions that influence our decisions.

The Workman's Compensation   *Reg Theriault*

Like the essays by Masumoto and Smiley, this one argues for a point of view that is not commonly accepted. Theriault, a longshoreman, argues that "taking it easy" on the job is not only justified but essential. This position may appear unethical to your students. Encourage them to evaluate Theriault's arguments fairly rather than just denouncing him as lazy or unethical.

One of the ways Theriault supports his argument is by contrasting labor's point of view with management's. Students should pay close attention to how fairly he presents both sides of this issue. Because Theriault clearly identifies with labor, he must convince his readers that he is not demonizing or misrepresenting management. Ask students to evaluate whether he does this successfully and, if so, how.

Help your students understand the importance of Theriault's credibility as a laborer himself. This is not merely an academic issue that he is debating. As he clearly states in his conclusion, he has worked as a laborer (in a physically demanding job) and thus is speaking from experience. He is, in effect, an expert on this subject. Students need to appreciate the power of personal experience as a persuasive strategy.

Out of College, Out of Work   *Stephen Sherrill*

This essay focuses on a problem that will be of great interest to most of your students—the increasing difficulty that many college graduates have in finding work. The author, Stephen Sherrill, describes a time after graduating from college when he was unemployed. Point out to your students how Sherrill weaves into his story about a visit to the unemployment office a comparison of his generation's work experiences with those of earlier generations. (You may want to emphasize at this point how many of the essays in this unit include comparison and contrast.) You may need to explain some of the allusions to the events of preceding generations, especially the Great Depression.

Ask students to sum up Sherrill's attitude toward this new phenomenon of being unemployed after graduation from college. Is he bitter, resigned, discouraged, resentful, or accepting? You can point out that in the last paragraph, he compares his unemployment experience to a rite of passage and discuss what this analogy indicates about his attitude.

You may also want to discuss with your students the effects of working too hard as opposed to not being able to work. Which is more demoralizing? How can our society achieve a balance between these two extremes?

20 Hot Job Tracks   *U.S. News & World Report*

Students will be interested in the information this article provides but may need help with how to read this type of text. You may want to begin by discussing the differences between this article and the previous reading selections in this unit. Focus on the purpose of the article (to inform) and its format (designed to make information accessible). This would be a good time to point out to students that we read different texts in different ways and to discuss reading strategies such as skimming and scanning with them. You may also want to spend some time examining the charts included in each section. You can point out how difficult it would be to read this information about salaries if it were included in the text rather than presented in a chart.

Rather than asking all the students to read the entire article, let each student scan the article to find the sections of interest to him or her. You can then engage the students in a general discussion so that they can share the information they gained. Or you can divide the students into groups based on the job tracks they chose and let each group come to some conclusions about their professional futures.

The Work Ahead   *Harper's Magazine*

This reading selection is simply a chart that predicts positive and negative job growth in a number of selected fields. It offers you an opportunity to help your students learn how to read a chart. Do not assume that even a relatively simple, straightforward chart like this will be easy for your students to understand. Explain carefully how the chart is organized and its purpose. Then ask questions that require students to interpret the chart. Once they are comfortable with the chart and know how to read it, you may want to ask your students to reach a conclusion based on the information available in the chart. For example, can they determine which *types* of professions are predicted to show the most growth? the least growth? Can they figure out whether more jobs will be lost than gained in all the areas included on the chart? You can also divide students into groups and give each group a question to answer.

CRITICAL THINKING AND WRITING ASSIGNMENTS

The suggestions for **Exploring Ideas Together** include several activities that require students to work collaboratively to synthesize information from different reading selections in this unit. Because most students find it difficult to synthesize information from different sources, they benefit from the opportunity to collaborate on such an assignment.

The **Writing Essays** assignments offer students a variety of writing experiences, but most of them include suggestions for researching, synthesizing, and summarizing—activities that are essential for writing from sources. Because this is one of the later units in the book, we think that students need to move beyond personal experience essays at this point and begin to write informative and persuasive essays that include elements of research. However, students also need to realize that narrative can be persuasive and that personal experience is a valuable form of evidence. So, if some of your students prefer to include their own experiences in their essays, they should not be discouraged from doing so.

UNIT FIVE
Self with Society

The readings in this unit encourage students to view themselves as members of a society and to explore the issues that are important to that society. The reading selections focus not just on the problems that our society faces, but on the people that make up that society, emphasizing that a society is not just one group of people but a combination of many groups who share common problems and concerns despite their diversity.

Most of the readings in this unit can be connected to one or more other readings to form a subunit, or concentration. For example, several selections focus on young people and education; several, on the reaction to ethnic diversity within our schools and society; some, on violence and crime in our society; others, on the inner city, poverty, and welfare; and still others, on how our society views aging and the aged.

The Scholarship Jacket   *Marta Salinas*

As in Unit Three, this unit begins with what seems to be a simple narrative. However, whereas the Angelou reading focuses on the personal implications of the incident described, Salinas's essay explores both the personal and the societal effects of the narrative. Thus, as the introductory apparatus suggests, Martha's personal goal of winning her school's scholarship jacket symbolizes for her and her family the achievement of the Hispanic people.

Because the journal entry requires students to write about a situation in which they were treated unfairly, it is a "way into" the reading for students, a way of promoting identification with the narrator. Be sure that students understand, however, that the reasons why Mr. Schmidt and the Board wanted to keep Martha from getting the scholarship jacket (see paragraphs 5–7) were societal ("Joann's father is not only on the Board, he owns the only store in town") and ethnic (". . . Martha is Mexican"). Many of your students will themselves have experienced racial, ethnic, or economic prejudice, but perhaps this essay can help those who have not had such an experience understand more clearly the unfairness of such treatment and the personal devastation it causes.

Although this selection is an essay, its narrative form allows students to think of the people in the essay as "characters" in a story. Thus, the **As You**

Read and After You Read questions encourage students to consider the motivations of these characters. You might divide students into groups to consider the motivations of Mr. Schmidt (selfishness, prejudice); Mr. Boone (unselfishness, fairness); and the grandfather (pride in Martha and her achievements, in his family, and in his ethnic heritage).

The After You Read WRITE assignment gives students the opportunity to experience primary research about a particular policy at an educational institution. Encourage your students to interview school or college personnel, as well as other students, about the policy they choose to discuss.

In Praise of the F Word   *Mary Sherry*

In contrast to the previous essay, which focuses on scholarly achievement, this opinion piece from *Newsweek* focuses on the problems of school. Sherry argues in favor of flunking students who do not meet reasonable standards, even giving her own son as an example. She focuses primarily on students who fail to learn or to do the work required of them, but she does not address other problems, such as learning disabilities or racial inequities, which may also contribute to failure. For readings that deal with these issues, see David Raymond's "On Being 17, Bright, and Unable to Read" (Unit One, pages 33–36) and Douglas A. Blackmon's "The resegregation of a Southern School" in this unit (pages 302–308).

Be sure that students recognize that Sherry's argument is based primarily on reasons supported by her own experiences as a mother and a teacher of adult literacy classes, rather than on statistics or other authorities. Explain to your students that Sherry's experience has made her an "expert" on the issue, just as their own experiences with education have qualified them to write about the subject. Remind students, though, that although personal experience is a valid form of evidence, other forms of evidence will strengthen an argument. Thus, in writing their letters to the local school board for or against the policy of failure, students can benefit by obtaining statistics, quotations, or other information from the administrative offices.

The Big Squeeze   *David Samuels*

This essay continues the focus on education but switches the emphasis to the economic aspects of higher education. Because most students are directly involved in paying for their college education, they should identify closely with the problems discussed by Samuels. Give students an opportunity to discuss their own expenses and the relative costs of an education at area colleges and universities. Frustrated with the rising costs of higher education and the increasing difficulty of paying these costs, your students have surely wondered "Why?" Thus, they should be interested not only in comparing their situations with those of the students discussed in the essay, but also in identifying the reasons Samuels gives for the increasing "squeeze" in higher education costs.

In reading the essay, students should be especially motivated to look for ways in which college costs can be reduced or contained (paragraphs 13–15). Depending on their backgrounds as taxpayers or recipients of educational grants, students should also have strong opinions to express in the persuasive essay assignment. Before making this assignment, however, you may want to have your students debate, or at least discuss, the use of government educational programs such as the GI Bill or Pell Grants.

The Resegregation of a Southern School   *Douglas A. Blackmon*

Like the reading selection by Marta Salinas, this essay focuses on the results of racial and ethnic prejudice, and on the ineffectiveness or unfairness of many educational practices. Therefore, you may want to assign the two essays together.

Students, especially those from the South, may be tempted to dismiss this essay because it is about what is happening in Mississippi, a state that has become superficially known for racial conflict not only because of its history but also because it has been the setting for movies about civil rights issues. Thus, you may want to begin your discussion of this selection (even before students read it) by talking about Mississippi's media image and evaluating how accurate that image is. Once students have read the essay, you can then lead the discussion into a consideration of how similar or different the situation in Leland, Mississippi, is from that in their own home towns. Most of your students will have completed high school recently and should know first hand whether their public school system is segregated, desegregated, or resegregated.

Help your students appreciate the powerful combination of personal experience narrative and argument that Blackmon uses in this essay. You may even want to compare it to the earlier selection by Sherry, who uses the same combination, but less effectively because she fails to explore the complexities of the situation she is addressing. Or you may want to share with your students some of the facts and incidents about de facto segregation and racial inequities reported by Jonothan Kozol in his book *Savage Inequalities*.

The Recoloring of Campus Life   *Shelby Steele*

The essays by Blackmon and Steele make an excellent pair of readings for classroom discussion and debate. Whereas Blackmon's essay points out the problems of racial inequalities and resegregation in his home town, Steele argues that "racial tension is more the result of racial equality than inequality." The two readings, therefore, contrast a more liberal viewpoint (Blackmon's) with a more conservative view (Steele's). You r students may be surprised to know that Steele is black whereas Blackmon is white.

Helping students to understand the vocabulary in this reading will help them follow Steele's thoughtful but complex reasoning. Focus on what Steele views as major paradoxes (point out definition of *paradox*) in **Before You Read** EXAMINE: (1) the "melting pot" of the university classroom seems to expose more differences than similarities among the races; and (2) the policy of affirmative action, intended to promote racial progress and equality, has instead produced a "politics of difference." Ask students to give examples of the support that Steele gives for the existence of this "politics of difference" on college campuses. Then ask students to respond to Steele's basic point that such a politics of difference—diversity or plurality—is less desirable on campus than the promotion of the goal of commonality. Many of your students will have strong views on this subject, in particular with regard to affirmative action and educational quotas. Encourage free discussion, but be prepared to moderate.

In their discussions, students will no doubt draw on their own experiences but encourage them to consider not only whether your own college or university campus promotes primarily diversity or commonality but also whether these goals can be compatible rather than incompatible. Such a discussion will help prepare students for the final writing assignment in the lesson, which requires them to write a letter to the editor of their college newspaper about a particular campus policy.

What Is Behind the Growth of
Violence on College Campuses?   *Dorothy Siegel*

In contrast to the essays by Salinas, Sherry, and Blackmon—which are supported mostly by personal experiences—Siegel's article is based primarily on research studies and statistical reports about campus crime. Ask students to identify Siegel's most effective statistical support (see paragraphs 1, 7, 11, 13–14, 17, 19, and 24). You might then ask students to compare Siegel's article with one of these previous essays for purpose, style, and effectiveness.

Ask students if they are surprised by Siegel's findings that most frequent perpetrators of campus crime are students themselves. Then ask students to speculate about why they are surprised by these findings (assuming that they are) and why students in Siegel's studies—and probably your students also—find it so difficult to accept this proven finding.

Students will probably have definite opinions about university personnel acting *in loco parentis*. If you (or any of your students) attended school before 1970, when this practice was more common, make comparisons between campus policies of today and those of this earlier era. In fact, you might suggest that students interview a neighbor or family member who attended college twenty, thirty, or forty years ago and write a report on how various policies and safety measures differed in these earlier times.

When students finish reading the article, ask them to write a list of major causes of campus crime identified by Siegel (students' mind-set that nothing can happen to them, that other students will not harm them, that all crime happens at night; excessive drinking; the use of drugs; misunderstanding signals about willingness to have sex; carelessness in letting strangers into secure areas; and so forth).

The final writing assignment in this lesson gives students practice in problem-solving discourse. Remind students to clearly state both the problem and the solution in their letters to the campus newspaper.

Kids Who Kill   *Gordon Witkin*

Like the previous article, this article from *U.S. News & World Report* focuses on crime and violence in our society. Also like the previous article, this reading selection uses statistics to make its point. In addition, however, this article employs a long illustrative example as well as several briefer examples.

You may be surprised, as we were, to discover that many students have had some type of experience with violence related to firearms. However, we have also found that often these same students oppose gun control. The tension between their experience with guns and their position on gun control should provide you with the basis for a lively discussion of this issue.

Be sure that your students identify the main reasons that Witkin gives for the increasing use of guns among young people:

1. They have been desensitized to violence.
2. They are victims of poverty and hopelessness.
3. Families have become less strong.
4. Guns are more available.

Once they identify Witkin's reasons, students can evaluate and debate each one. Be sure also that they recognize the author's use of statistics to support his arguments. They should understand that his reasons plus his use of statistics serve as evidence to support his thesis. Then, in groups or as a class, students can consider which of Witkin's reasons are valid and which can be considered a solution to this problem.

The final writing assignment in the lesson provides students with a clear essay structure. The first part of the essay gives students practice in the important reading/study skill strategy of summarizing, whereas the last two parts of the essay require them to think and write critically—identifying the cause that they think is most serious and supporting their opinion.

in the inner city   *Lucille Clifton*

To provide a more well rounded picture of the city, you may want to assign together this poem and the essay on homelessness in the inner city that follows. Clifton's poem is superficially rather simple but actually quite complex in its implications.

Introduce this poem by asking students to think about its title and the images they have of the inner city—positive or negative. Ask students how the term *inner city* differs from the simpler term *city*. To most, the term *inner city* will call up images of poverty and ghetto living. When they actually read the poem, students may be surprised that the people living in Clifton's "inner city" are "happy to be alive / and in the inner city," which is "home" to them. Use the EXAMINE questions in **Before You Read** and **After You Read** to discuss the style and content of the poem—its lack of capitalization and its contrast of the "home" of the inner city with the "silent nights" and "straight" houses of "uptown" and the "pastel lights," perhaps of downtown. In discussing *Good Times*, the poetry collection in which this poem first appeared, one of Clifton's critics wrote that although the "portraits of human devastation [in the book] reflect the trying circumstances of life in the ghetto . . . the writer also records some joy in her world, however strained and limited that joy might be" (*Contemporary Authors: New Revision Series*, Vol. 42, p. 87). This poem is an example of that "strained" joy.

Depending on their backgrounds, students will react differently to Clifton's poem, but they can all use her effective poetic style as a model for writing their own poems (or paragraphs) about the city, the country, or a specific space at or between either of these extremes.

Slow Descent into Hell   *John D. Hull*

"Slow Descent into Hell" focuses on homelessness, the experiences of people who live on the streets, in this case the streets of Philadelphia. If your students come primarily from small towns or rural areas, they may need an introduction to the conditions that indigents experience in large cities.

However, most of them will have at least visited large cities, and there are presently few, if any, cities in this country that do not have homeless people on their streets. So it is likely that some of your students will have seen evidence of homelessness and be able to describe what they have seen to their classmates.

This selection relies primarily on narration and description to make its point. It is a combination of case study and story, but the author varies the chronological order. The entire article is not structured chronologically, but each separate segment is told in chronological order. This article focuses on a number of different subjects. You may want to discuss with your students how these multiple brief case studies suggest the pervasiveness of the problem of homelessness and provide readers with more than one view of the problem. The multiple focus also increases the possibility that the reader will identify with at least one of the subjects.

You will want to point out that Hull makes no editorial comments. He does not cite statistics that indicate the severity of this problem or argue that the problem should be solved in a certain way or even that it needs to be solved. He merely tells these men's stories in graphic detail and lets the stories and descriptions speak for themselves. Students should begin to understand that narration and description are powerful forms of persuasion.

So How Did I Get Here? *Rosemary L. Bray*

Whereas Hull's essay describes the helpless poverty of the homeless, Bray's essay focuses on the institutionalized poverty of welfare. And yet, in the wake of belligerent attacks on the welfare system and even on those it supports, Bray argues persuasively that welfare is, or has been, the source of survival and of ultimate success for many who are eventually able to "get off welfare." Be sure that students understand that Bray's primary purpose is persuasive even though she employs narrative throughout.

Bray begins her essay by attacking head on the stereotypical view of the welfare family. Ask students how Bray's family as she describes it differs from the stereotypical welfare family. Also, ask students which view they have previously held of those on welfare. (*Note:* This essay would also be an excellent one to teach in conjunction with Unit Two: Self with Family.)

The **Before You Read** EXAMINE section points out several vocabulary words that may be unfamiliar to your students. Other words with which students may have difficulty are *mercurial* (4), *adamant* (7), *patriarch* (8), and *parochial* (15).

The final writing assignments allow students to choose between (1) writing a persuasive essay supporting or criticizing the welfare system, and (2) answering Bray's central—and somewhat ironic—question, "So how did I get here?" You might encourage half of your students to respond to the first assignment and the other half to respond to the second assignment. For peer reading groups, have students first meet with students who wrote on the same topic; then for more objectivity and sharing of ideas, mix the groups.

Nobody Ever Died of Old Age   *Sharon R. Curtin*

This reading selection is the first of two essays that focus on aging in our society. If students at first seem reluctant or uninterested in this subject, help them make a closer connection with the reading by asking each of them to think about an older person—perhaps a grandparent or a neighbor—whom they know personally and to write about this person in a journal entry.

Also point out the importance of the elderly in our society as a whole by reminding students that as the "baby-boomer" generation continues to age, the elderly are going to represent a larger and larger portion of our society. Ask students to think not only about the positions that the elderly hold in their families and in society (**Before You Read** THINK) and about the problems that they face (**After You Read** WRITE), but also about the challenge that society as a whole faces in using the talents and providing for the needs of this group, which is growing from a minority to a majority. Indeed, the first challenge may be for our society to learn to value age as many other societies already do, to replace modern prejudices toward the aged with age-old respect. As Curtin makes clear in the reading selection, our society is currently oriented primarily toward youth; not only do we not want to grow old ourselves, we do not even want to be reminded of the process of aging.

At some point in your discussion, focus on Curtin's title "Nobody Ever Died of Old Age." At first, students may think this is a ridiculous statement, but point out the increasing life span and specific problems, such as Alzheimer's disease, that lead to the deaths of people who are older. Some of your students may want to share experiences they have had with loved ones stricken with Alzheimer's disease—perhaps in free journal entries, as these experiences are often personal and painful.

After narrating the poignant incident in the park about the distance between older people and younger people, Curtin reminisces about her early experiences with older people who were her friends or family members and laments that members of the current generation often do not have these rich experiences. Several other essays in *Interactions* provide these experiences vicariously by focusing on relationships with older people. See, among other possibilities, Angelou's "Liked for Myself" and Maynard's "Generations."

We Don't Want to Grow Old   *Karla·Cole (student)*

This student essay by Karla Cole is an excellent complement to the previous selection by Curtin. A baby-boomer herself, Cole expresses the ambivalent but changing feelings this generation has about aging.

Although Cole's use of the phrases "growing up" and "growing old" may at times be confusing to your students, the interplay of ideas associated with these terms which Cole develops in her essay is thought-provoking. In effect, she argues that baby-boomers were, and perhaps still are, rather immature and spoiled and that their refusal (or inability) to grow up is directly related to their deliberate attempt to avoid growing older—or at least to avoid the appearance of it.

You may want to discuss with your students some of the methods of essay and paragraph development that Cole uses: comparison of older and younger generations (paragraphs 3–4); analysis of the past causes (the idealism and sense of betrayal of the sixties and seventies, the influence of the media); analysis of baby-boomers' attitudes (paragraphs 5–7); and analysis of the effects on baby-boomers' lives (paragraph 8).

The essay assignment at the end of the lesson asks students to argue whether or not it is wise to try to look, feel, and act young even as one ages. Whatever position students take, they may wish to consider the impact the media have had on the assumption that youth must be maintained. Refer students to paragraphs 8 and 9 of Cole's essay. Students will, of course, be able to add their own media examples of the idealization of youth.

CRITICAL THINKING AND WRITING ASSIGNMENTS

The **Exploring Ideas Together** section provides students with practice in the critical thinking skills of evaluating (ranking problems in question 1), comparing (questions 2 and 3), and analyzing (question 4). Most of these assignments use informal writing activities to encourage students to share ideas.

The **Writing Essays** assignments also involve students in critical thinking. Various assignments require students to use problem-solving strategies, to write persuasively, and to write for specific audiences. In addition to writing essays, students are asked to write a report and a letter to an editor.

Because the issues in this unit are more other centered and thus more complex than subjects for writing in previous units, you may want to allow students more time to complete their final essay assignment. For example, you need to build in time for students to research their topics through personal interviews or library work. And, as always, you should allow ample time for revision and editing of student writing. By this time in the semester, students should have become increasingly effective in peer revision and editing groups.

UNIT SIX
Self with Environment

This unit focuses on the reader's relationship to the environment. The selections in this unit not only allow students to explore their relationship to their natural environment but also encourage them to think about serious environmental issues. The unit begins with a series of descriptive "weather reports," two poems, a short story, and a fable. The remaining selections, however, are informative or persuasive essays.

Throughout, we have tried to maintain a balanced view of environmental issues, presenting selections that articulate different viewpoints. In several instances we have deliberately paired selections that express opposing viewpoints.

Before assigning the introduction to this unit, you might ask your students to brainstorm about the topic of environment. How do they define their environment? What does the environment include? What is their relationship to the environment? Then, as they read the introduction, they can compare their definitions and interpretations with ours.

Weather Reports   *Kathleen Norris*

We chose this selection as the first for this unit because it clearly establishes the connection between the environment and the self. However, it is difficult to classify in that it is not an essay or an article or a story but has elements of all these genres. Norris includes these brief, reflective pieces which she calls "Weather Reports" between the chapters of her book *Dakota: A Spiritual Geography*. Read in sequence, these reports form a poetic narrative of a year she spent in a small North Dakota town. Encourage the students to read these reports both individually, much as they would a poem, and collectively, as they would a story. Then they can come to some conclusions about what this year was like for the author, about what she learned about the place and herself.

Wild Geese   *Mary Oliver*

Like the previous reading selection, this one sets the tone for this unit, establishing the idea that human beings and nature constitute a "family."

54

You will probably want to read the poem aloud to your students as well as encourage them to read it silently. To help your students understand the poem, focus on the different images and allusions Oliver includes, especially the images of the penitent crawling through the desert, the sun and rain moving across the land, and the geese flying "high in the clean blue air." Ask students to explore some of the following issues: How do humans "relate" to their environment? How does our environment teach us or communicate with us? What does it mean to be a member of "the family of things"? What obligations do we have to the environment if we are members of the same family?

Song of the Sky Loom   *Native American (Tewa)*

This Native American chant is an appropriate selection with which to begin or end your study of the environment, because it portrays the ideal of a culture in total peace and harmony with its environment. In fact, you may want to have your students reread this poem at the conclusion of the unit.

After you discuss the **Before You Read** THINK and EXAMINE questions with your students and give them an opportunity to write their journal entries, read the poem aloud. Only an oral reading can give this chant the dignity and power that was an essential part of its composition. Later, you may want to have students prepare a choral reading. Have the entire class read the first and last lines in unison, with individual readers taking turns with the lines in the middle.

Ask students to speculate about the nature of the gifts that this ancient people brought the Earth and Sky. Perhaps these gifts were sacrifices of maize or other grains. Then use the **After You Read** THINK questions to expand your discussion into modern times. Ask students, for example, what gifts they can give Mother Earth and Father Sky today. Help students to see also that the poem—especially the metaphor of the "garment of brightness" —describes many gifts that the Earth and Sky have given to humankind.

The Gift   *Louis Dollarhide*

Whereas "Song of the Sky Loom" focuses on the gifts of sunlight and rain, birds and grass that nature gives to humankind, this story focuses on a gift that a human being gives to a creature of nature. Before students read the story, ask them to predict its contents from the title. After students have read the story, discuss with them the symbolic as well as the literal qualities of the ham that the woman gives the panther. Continue with the **After You**

Read EXAMINE questions, asking students to underline elements of personification in paragraph 4 (the house shuddered, creaked, and groaned as it "struggled up from the clay," and then it complained).

You may also want to discuss the style of this story with your students, pointing out that Dollarhide uses many effective modifiers, especially verbs used as modifiers. Point out a few of these to your students: "*Huddled* on the bed,she was . . . *Staring* into the dark, she eased . . . *Shivering*, she pulled back on the bed . . . The *lulling* constant sound . . . the *penetrating* chill. . . ." Then ask students to imitate some of these sentences, or provide them with kernel sentences that can be combined according to these patterns.

The **Before You Read** THINK and WRITE assignments give students an opportunity to recall prior experiences in which they—like the woman in the story—have felt threatened by their environments. After this initial assignment, however, you can direct your discussion in one of two directions. If you want to focus on the story itself, you can review literary elements of conflict, climax, and perhaps even denouement with your students and have them analyze the external and internal conflicts in the story. If you want to focus on responses outside the story, you can have students speculate about the understanding and behavior of animals. Perhaps students have observed closely the behavior of a pet or another animal and can make some comparisons between their observations and the actions of the panther in the story. In either case, ask students to comment about the conclusion, perhaps about why the storm ceases at the same moment the cat finishes its meal and leaves the stranded house.

A Fable for Tomorrow   *Rachel Carson*

"A Fable for Tomorrow" is rich in instructional possibilities. The title of Carson's book *Silent Spring*, as well as this individual selection, offers possibilities for discussion. You might ask students, for example, if the environment described in the first paragraph is a totally "silent spring." After the students note the sound of the barking foxes, you might ask what could silence this barking before you explore the positive, even poetic, imagery in the first two paragraphs.

The **As You Read** section provides students with clear purposes for reading, but you might involve them in active prediction by reading the first eight paragraphs orally to the class, stopping when you reach the final paragraph. As recognized by Walter Ong, Thomas E. Farrell, and others, occasional oral readings like this are pedagogically effective because basic writing students are often oral learners. (See *A Sourcebook for Basic Writing Teachers*, ed. Theresa Enos, New York: Random, 1987, pp. 27–55.)

After your students have discussed the implications of Carson's mythical fable, making their own guesses about the causes of the destruction, have them read the final paragraph *carefully*; ask them the questions in the EXAMINE section, and lead them to an understanding of how its expository style differs from the narrative-descriptive style of the fable itself. You might also want to discuss how Carson effectively combines these styles to achieve her purpose of illustrating the harmful effects of pesticides. (*Note:* Although many students will guess that pesticides could have caused the blight described in the fable, others may need clues from you and from the introduction.)

Finally, you may want to take class time for students to read their own "fables for tomorrow" aloud in small groups. These readings may be part of a peer review process, a final "presentation," or both.

Down with the Forests   *Charles Kuralt*

Just rereading our questions in the THINK section of "Down with the Forests" made us feel guilty about the amount of paper we have used in writing this textbook—numerous copies of articles, a first draft, a revised draft, a copyedited draft, page proof, and the final pages! If you as the instructor answer the last question in the section honestly in front of your students, you are likely to have an open and productive discussion of the topic. You might even try to save a few sheets of paper in class by writing the four-column list on the board or having students work in groups, with one person in each group serving as a recorder, rather than having each person use a separate piece of paper. If students really get involved in this topic, you can make purpose and audience truly meaningful for them if they actually send their letters or memoranda to your college newspaper or administration to try to get a conservation or recycling program started.

Dice or Doves?   *Cindy Camburn (student)*

This student essay includes the writer's own experiences as well as the results of her research. Because most students find it difficult to combine these two different forms of evidence, the essay provides them with a useful model. It is also a good model essay because it focuses on a very limited, local environmental problem rather than a very large, abstract problem such as waste disposal or acid rain. Camburn succeeds largely because her argument is limited to something she knows about first hand. She is not learning about the environmental problems on the coast by reading other sources; rather she is using her written sources to add other voices to her argument.

You can also use this essay to provoke discussion about the important question of whether economic or environmental issues should be valued more. Should we protect the environment at the expense of people's economic security? Or is environmental security as important as economic security? Are environmental and economic issues always an either/or proposition? Or can we make decisions that protect both our environment and our economic security?

Waste   *Wendell Berry*

This essay combines concrete description with abstract analysis of causes that are at the very root of our nation's problem with waste. And Berry places the blame for these problems squarely on us—on himself, on you, on me, and on all readers of the essay.

Because this essay introduces several complex ideas, you may want to approach it by moving from the concrete to the abstract. Discuss the specific items of trash listed by Berry, and then allow students to discuss their own lists of trash, perhaps in small groups. Then you might focus on Berry's statement that "as a country person," he is "on the bottom end of the waste problem." Ask students whether they think more trash is produced and stored in the city or in the country, requiring support for their opinions. Then move to some of the important moral and abstract questions that Berry raises in his essay: Do businesses deliberately create "waste" for a profit? Are consumers as well as sellers guilty of greed? of laziness? Of what "greater and graver problem" is waste a symptom? What human damage results from the waste in our society?

You may want to give different assignments to different students in your class. To students who are still having difficulty conceptualizing in their writing, assign the WRITE assignment in the textbook, which is very specific and concrete (explain what you can do personally to decrease the problem of waste). To your more advanced students, assign a writing (journal, paragraph, or brief essay) based on the EXAMINE questions or on one of the questions at the end of the preceding paragraph. Ask these students to explore reasons why we have become a "throw-away society."

America's "Garbage Crisis": A Toxic Myth   *Patricia Poore*

In this essay, which is a good example of persuasive discourse, Poore begins by focusing the reader's attention on the garbage crisis and then states that it is not true that garbage disposal is a crisis. Be sure that your students understand the effectiveness of this common rhetorical strategy—presenting an idea that is commonly accepted and then arguing that the common perception is erroneous.

Poore uses several other effective rhetorical strategies. First, she states her thesis clearly in her introduction (" . . . contrary to the rhetoric of some environmentalists, garbage is not a serious environmental hazard") and again in her conclusion (" . . . it is foolish and extremely wasteful to expend so much effort . . . on garbage"). Then she carefully refutes opposing arguments. One of her main counterarguments is that garbage disposal is not a moral issue but a management issue. Another is that recycling actually costs money that could be devoted to "schools, libraries, health clinics, and police."

Although it is difficult to engage students in a lively discussion of garbage, they may respond with some interest to Poore's argument that recycling is not the best way to deal with the problem of waste disposal. They may also be interested in Poore's suggestion that environmentalists have known this for some time but continue to emphasize recycling because it makes people feel that they are doing something worthwhile and enlists them in the cause.

What's Best for the West?   *David Diamond*

This essay allows students to view the issue of land use in the West from the neutral perspective of Diamond, who provides an informative overview of the issue. If this topic is one that some of your students find interesting and know something about, you might want to let them engage in a debate. You could divide the class into two groups with students in each group assuming different functions—some researching, others writing, and still others presenting the oral arguments.

Is a Lab Rat's Fate More Poignant than a Child's?   *Jane McCabe*
We Must Find Alternatives to Animals in Research   *Roger Caras*

Because these two articles are so closely related, we chose to present them in one lesson. In teaching these readings, be sure your students understand that although the authors are writing about the same topic, their purposes are quite different. With your help, students should be able to predict from the article titles and from the readings themselves that McCabe will use an emotional appeal (*pathos*) to convince her readers that animal research to find treatment or cures for human illnesses should be continued and that Caras will use a more objective, logical appeal (*logos*) to argue that animals should not be used in research on human illness. Thus, the primary purpose in each article is persuasive.

A closer look at the details and examples used by McCabe and Caras confirms that the former appeals primarily to her reader's emotions and the latter appeals to his readers' reason and emotion. For example, the beneficiaries of animal research described by McCabe are her nine-year-old daughter, who suffers from cystic fibrosis (paragraph 1), and the "youngsters fighting cancer, rare genetic illnesses [and] immunological diseases" (paragraph 6) who are residents of Children's Hospital at Stanford University. In contrast, the beneficiaries discussed by Caras are those "millions of people" who have "elect[ed] to smoke and expose themselves to the risks of cancer and heart disease" (paragraph 3). Similarly, the examples of research that McCabe lists focus on the products that have lessened her daughter's suffering and prolonged her life (paragraph 5), whereas the example that Caras gives is the mistreatment of chimpanzees in a research situation that provides a "lack of social interaction [that] is nothing less than cruelty" (paragraph 6), according to Jane Goodall.

Although we do not focus on audience in our questions, you might also ask students how various audiences (parents, scientists, animal rights supporters) will respond to the selections. If students write a persuasive letter on animal research, remind them to consider their audience and purpose carefully before they decide on their appeal and supporting examples.

CRITICAL THINKING AND WRITING ASSIGNMENTS

The second and third activities under **Exploring Ideas Together** involve your students in dialogic thinking—considering both sides of an issue. Either activity may be expanded into a classroom debate, but be sure that students realize that in a debate—indeed, in any effective persuasive discourse—they must be as knowledgeable about the opposing side as about their own.

The assignments for **Writing Essays** provide clear topics for writing, but you will also want to have students think further about their purpose and audience. For example, assignments 2 and 4 lend themselves to the vital purpose of convincing "the people" to change their actions, either to create the ideal tomorrow described in the product of assignment 2 or to avoid the environmental nightmare that is the subject of assignment 4. Remind students that a persuasive essay, like the one required for assignment 5, must be directed toward a specific audience if it is to be effective, and work with students to select and analyze their specific audiences.

UNIT SEVEN
Self with Technology

This unit focuses on an individual's relationship with technology. Students may at first resist the idea of relating to something as abstract as technology, protesting that they do not relate to machines the same way they do to people. This objection provides you with an opportunity to discuss with them how we use words such as *relate* to mean more than one thing. You may want to begin your discussion of this unit by brainstorming with your class about ways in which a person's relationships with machines are and are not like relationships with people.

The focus of this unit is, however, slightly broader than just individual relationships with machines. Several of the readings also suggest the complications of living in a society that is increasingly characterized by technology. The extent to which we are dependent on technology and the major role it assumes in our daily lives shape our culture to a significant degree. Thus, this unit not only explores the love/hate relationship we have with machines but also encourages students to think about how technology helps define our society.

In addition to the reading selections on technology in general (such as "At the Electronic Frontier" and "The Beep Goes On"), a number of the readings focus on the same form of technology. Thus, the readings by Nora Ephron, Marie Winn, and Amy Waldman focus on forms of technology related to television. The essays by Dave Barry, Mary Lord, and Deborah Tannen all focus on computer technology. If your time is limited, you may want to select one or the other of these groups rather than trying to include both. Or you could let students choose the form of technology that interests them more and read just those reading selections that focus on it. Students could then summarize the readings in the group they selected and report on them to the class.

At the Electronic Frontier   *Miguel Algarin*

This poem serves well as an introduction to the unit because it focuses so specifically on what it means to live in an age of technology. Students may find it strange to read a poem that includes the names of specific brand products, radio stations, and stores. So your discussion may need to focus initially on how these allusions function in the poem. You can help your students see how these specific details ground the poem in a certain time and place.

This discussion can then expand to a consideration of what readers expect a poem to be like and how Algarin's poem contrasts with those expectations. The conflict between what readers expect and what the poem delivers is one of the ways in which the poet communicates the idea that everything in our culture, even our poetry, is affected by our passion for technology.

Further discussion might focus on the word *frontier*. Again, you can contrast traditional ideas about frontiers with the way in which Algarin uses the term in his poem. Students can brainstorm individually or collaboratively about the ways in which the western frontier, the space frontier, and the electronic frontier are alike and different. You may want to use the term *analogy* in connection with this comparison, pointing out how an appropriate analogy lends added dimensions to a poem like this one.

Finally, you may want to focus on what it means to be a "child of the Electronic Frontier." What does it suggest if a person defines himself or herself in relation to technology? How does technology shape who we are, how we live, and what values we have? Are all people who live now equally affected by technology? Is Algarin suggesting that the electronic frontier has created a generation of "children," or is he merely suggesting that certain individuals can be defined in this way?

Living with My VCR   *Nora Ephron*

"Living with My VCR" focuses on the new technology that enables home viewers to tape television programs for later viewing. Although some of your students may not own VCRs, most of them will at least be familiar with movie videos and will thus understand in general how VCRs work. This essay introduces the idea that some people have a love-hate relationship with machines. Their fascination with machines, often with the technology of the machine rather than what it actually does, is complicated by their resistance to the control that machines exert on their lives.

The author describes the VCR in fairly technical ways, but students will probably have no difficulty with the terminology. (Students may, in fact, understand it better than you do.) Encourage them to be aware of how many new terms have entered our vocabularies because of this new technology, and point out that each new form of technology expands our vocabularies in similar ways.

The essay ends inconclusively, and students may find this lack of closure rather disturbing. You may want to discuss with them why tidy endings are not always appropriate and why Ephron chose to end her essay in this way.

Television Addiction   *Marie Winn*

No subject is likely to be more familiar to your students than television. Most of them are far more expert than their teachers concerning both what television offers and the technology involved. But they are often less aware of the effects that television has on both individual viewers and society as a whole. This article focuses on the effects of television on individual viewers, arguing that excessive viewing is, in fact, a form of addiction.

Your discussion can focus on this analogy. Encourage students to analyze the analogy to determine if it is appropriate. Just how is an addiction to television similar to other types of addiction? How is it different? Are all addictions harmful? What evidence does Winn present to support her argument? How is the analogy itself a type of argument?

Students should have fairly strong views, both pro and con, on this issue. You may want to let them debate the issue in small groups before discussing it as a class. Some students are reluctant to speak out before the entire class but will participate in small group discussions.

Technology and the Hearing Impaired   *Tammy Holm (student)*

This student essay is not wildly exciting but is thoughtful and informative. It will probably serve better as a model than as a stimulus for discussion. However, the central idea—that technology both helps and hurts people, in this case, hearing-impaired people—is one that should generate some discussion.

After the students have discussed this issue, you may want to point out how the author introduces her thesis clearly and then develops it with a great deal of information. Students need to understand why writers whose purpose is to inform usually include a very clear, explicit statement of their thesis and why any thesis, stated or unstated, needs to be supported and developed.

Although in some ways this is a "model" essay in that it is focused, clear, organized, and well developed, you may also want to discuss with your students how the writer could have made the essay more interesting. Students can also speculate on who the intended audience is and whether the essay is appropriate for this audience. Because the essay seems to be written for a general audience, are the explanations too technical? What other points

might the author have included? For example, would the essay have ben
stronger if she had developed more fully the idea that technology causes
some hearing impairment? What if she had begun with the idea that
technology helps the hearing impaired, but had focused primarily on how
technology can cause hearing impairment? What if she had told of a case
(even a hypothetical case) in which a particular individual's hearing was hurt
or helped by technology?

Lonely Hearts, Classy Dreams, Empty Wallets   *Amy Waldman*

Although this essay does *not* include an explicit thesis statement, you can
point out to students that Waldman's unstated but implied thesis is that
television networks that prey on the lonely are acting irresponsibly if not
unethically. You may want to discuss with your students how Waldman
makes her thesis clear without actually stating it.

This essay includes a great deal of information, but the information is
not very technical. The information is also reinforced by a strong emotional
element that is created by the author's description of the "actual" people
who have been victimized by home shopping networks. Students can discuss
not only the issue of whether networks should take advantage of people who
are lonely but also whether authors should use emotion to persuade readers.
You may want to point out that the use of emotion (*pathos*) by speakers and
writers is at least as old as Aristotle and that most effective arguments do
include emotional as well as logical arguments.

ERROR ERROR ERROR   *Dave Barry*

If students have not had some experience using computers, they may not see
the humor in this essay. You might introduce the essay by talking about
some of the frustrations associated with computer use. But all students
should be able to appreciate Barry's personification. You may want to lead
the discussion toward more serious computer issues, such as the depersonalizing effect they have had, the potential of artificial intelligence, our growing
dependence on access to computerized information, and the ways in which
computers are used to invade our privacy.

However, you may just want to have fun with this one. For example,
you could divide students into groups and let each group write a brief essay
or scenario in which they personify a certain machine.

Getting a Degree by E-Mail   *Mary Lord*

This essay is primarily informative. Its purpose is to inform readers about a new way to take college courses. One of the ways the author explains the new online programs is by comparing them to correspondence courses, with which most people are familiar. You may want to point out to your students that one of the basic ways in which writers explain a new concept is by comparing and contrasting it to a similar concept that is known or familiar. The writer also compares online courses to other forms of "distance learning." And underlying all of this information about new courses is an implicit comparison between them and the traditional course in which both students and instructors are present in the same classroom. Students can debate the pros and cons of these new forms of learning.

You may want to point out to your students that in the last five paragraphs of this article, the author's purpose shifts from informing to instructing/advising. Help students see the subtle shifts in tone and point of view that signal this change in purpose.

Students might have fun constructing a futuristic scenario in which students attend college without leaving their homes—or even their bedrooms.

Gender Gap in Cyberspace   *Deborah Tannen*

Tannen has earned a reputation as an authority on gender differences in communication styles. In this article she focuses on the differences in the way males and females use e-mail. Be sure all of your students have a basic understanding of e-mail and how it works before they read the essay. You may want to begin your discussion by asking students how communicating electronically differs from communicating in other ways. If no one in your class has had this electronic experience, you can explain that e-mail seems to lie somewhere between written and oral communication. Although it is written, it is much less formal and more interactive and immediate than is most written communication. In fact, most people who use e-mail seem to engage in it as they would a conversation. They are more likely to use slang and to be elliptical and less likely to correct errors than people usually are when they write.

At some point you will also want to discuss with your students their perceptions of the differences between male and female communication styles. Tannen's basic argument in all of her books and articles is that there are significant differences between the ways in which males and females communicate. She believes these differences reveal much about basic differences between males and females and also account for traditional male dominance in the workplace.

Finally, you and your students can speculate about how e-mail may affect communication in the future.

The Beep Goes On   *Carol Orlock*

Like the essay on VCRs by Nora Ephron, "The Beep Goes On" expresses the author's love-hate relationship with machines. However, instead of focusing on a single machine, Orlock discusses the general effect of machines on our society and even on the future. She is not entirely optimistic.

Students can keep a list of the machines Orlock approves of and those she disapproves of as they read, but they can also make lists of the machines they like and dislike. Encourage them to think about machines and the role they assume in our society. How do machines shape our society? What effect do they have on us as individuals and on the society in which we live? Students can brainstorm about both positive and negative effects.

Several words in this selection may be difficult for your students. An alternative or additional **As You Read** activity could be for students to circle the words that cause them difficulty while they are reading. After students have tried to determine the meaning of these words from context, you might make a class list and then define these words with your students.

CRITICAL THINKING AND WRITING ASSIGNMENTS

The **Exploring Ideas Together** suggestions for Unit Seven provide students with a variety of options—from collaboratively composing a technical description of a simple machine to discussing the different effects technology has on individuals and society as a whole. All of the suggested activities encourage students to view technology objectively and to evaluate its effects, both good and bad, critically.

Most of the final writing assignments for Unit Seven are rather challenging, requiring students to analyze their own attitudes toward technology, to argue that males are more fascinated with machines than females, and to explore the effects of machines (or a single machine) on society. Two of the assignments, however, are less demanding, depending primarily on personal experience or imagination rather than on analysis, evaluation, and argument. Question 1 asks them to write an imaginative narrative describing what a typical day in their lives would be like if the machines on which they depend were suddenly destroyed or rendered inoperative. Question 2 asks students to write a humorous essay about a frustrating experience with machines. You may want to ask your students to do one of these assignments as a journal entry. Or students can do one of these essays and then one of the more analytical writing assignments.

UNIT EIGHT
Self with Heroes

The focus of *Interactions* at first shifted outward from the self to the relatively close circle of family, friends, and mates. The emphasis then moved even further from the self, to work, society, the environment, and machines —or the technological elements of the environment. The focus of this final unit is a dual one, at first moving outward and upward to our heroes—to those people we look up to and admire—and finally returning to rest on the original self—on each individual's ultimate potential as a heroic person.

We hope that the questions for freewriting and discussion stimulate your students to get involved with the topic of male and female heroes—to compare ideas about what a hero is or is not, perhaps even to argue a bit about the topic. Here are some other questions you might ask your students:

- Why do we need heroes? What function do they play in a society?
- Do we have true heroes in our society today? Why or why not?
- How has your image of a male or female hero changed since you were a child? From your conversations with older people and your reading, do you think society's idea of a hero has changed? If so, how?

Although question 10 in the introduction will probably be the most difficult for your students, encourage them to think about themselves as heroes. Tell them that the last reading in the unit will return to this idea.

Larger than Life   *Phil Sudo*

The activities that accompany this reading provide several opportunities for group interaction. Have students compare their lists of heroes, explaining why they selected each. This activity should prepare them to consider Phil Sudo's definition of a hero and to write their own in the final WRITE assignment.

Other possibilities for interesting discussions can be found in the **After You Read** THINK and EXAMINE questions. Encourage students to consider how our perceptions of heroes differ at different times and in different cultures and to react to the charge that "our heroes are too one-sided." Ask students to review their earlier lists of heroes to see how many women and minorities they listed.

If you wish to discuss the style of this reading, you might focus on the parallel structure in paragraphs 10 ("Thwarting a robbery, rescuing a drowning man, pulling a child from a burning house"), 12 ("'It is an ideal which I hope to live for and to achieve. But if needs be, it is an ideal for which I am prepared to die'"), and 15 ("Look around you, at your friends, your family, your school").

The final WRITE assignment allows students to synthesize their independent thinking and ideas they have derived from group discussions to write their own definitions of a hero.

I Have a Dream   *Martin Luther King, Jr.*

Ask students not only to identify King's purpose as stated in the first paragraph of "I Have a Dream" but also to explain why he stated this purpose so explicitly. After students have identified King's persuasive purpose, ask them whom he was trying to persuade. Was he trying to persuade other blacks or the predominantly white government and society that had, as far as its black citizens were concerned, "defaulted on this promissory note" of the Constitution and Declaration of Independence?

To emphasize the oral qualities of King's speech, read part or all of it aloud to your students. Or, better, play a recording of King making the speech. Then ask students if the essay is more effective in spoken or written form. If they have heard the speech, students will be better able to analyze King's use of repetition and parallel structure. For example, he emphasized the idea of *freedom* by repeating this word twenty-five times, he used *justice* or *injustice* ten times, he said *dream* ten times, and he referred to *brother* or *brotherhood* five times. Other important words in the speech are *equality*, *opportunity*, and *dignity*. You may want to point out that in the 1960s the word *negro* was used more frequently than *black* or *African-American*.

Before students read Gwendolyn Brooks's poem memorializing King, which appears in the **After You Read** apparatus, ask them to write one word that, in their opinions, best describes King, his major goal, or his major accomplishment. Then compare their word choices with that of Brooks: *Justice*. You will certainly want to discuss King as a modern hero, as the term is defined by Phil Sudo and poetically interpreted by Brooks. Discuss with your students also King's personal "gifts," or heroic qualities.

Before students write their prose poems about King, you might explain that the phrase "prose poem" is an *oxymoron*, or two words that contradict one another. Help students to define both *prose* and *poetry*. Then brainstorm in class or in small groups not only about how King's was a prose poem but also about King's other gifts, or his legacy, and then share ideas. The assignment to write a prose poem can be adapted for a group project—for either small groups or the entire class writing the poem together.

For alternate writing assignments, students could write essays about King as an American hero or expand their journal entries about their personal dreams for America into essays.

Extraordinary People   *Herbert Buchsbaum*

Martin Luther King, Jr.'s "I Have a Dream" speech should help prepare students for this reading. The names and countries of the three heroes described in "Extraordinary People" will probably be unfamiliar to your students (we have provided maps in the **After You Read** section), but you can help students view these individuals in the same context as King—as culture heroes who express "the ideal of a group, in whom all human virtues unite." The fact that these heroes represent countries from all over the world—Guatemala in Central America and Tibet and Myanmar in Asia—emphasizes the universality of heroism and its qualities. In discussing the **After You Read** EXAMINE questions, you might quote John Donne's statement that "no man is an island" to illustrate that our very humanity binds us all together and that human cruelty or kindness in one part of the world ultimately affects all the world.

Give students the opportunity to describe in their journals the qualities that they feel should be present in winners of the Nobel Peace Prize and to share their ideas with one another. Students will probably list qualities such as concern and love for fellow human beings, the courage to express their beliefs, and the willingness to give their lives for their beliefs and their people. Certainly these qualities, whether listed by your students or not, are shared by all true heroes. If students have not identified these qualities before reading the selection, they will certainly find these characteristics in the three extraordinary people described by Buchsbaum. To aid students in summarizing the article, ask them to take notes as they read of specific qualities of each of the three individuals and to use these notes to help them draw conclusions about what these heroes all have in common.

If your students keep up with current events, they will enjoy writing a letter nominating an individual for the Nobel Peace Prize. Be sure that they understand that this is a world prize and that individuals nominated must have made some contribution to their country or their world—not just to their families or communities. If you make this assignment, you will probably need to allow students time to research the topic in the library and in the media.

The Nobel Peace Prize itself was instituted by Alfred Bernhard Nobel, a Swedish chemist who, ironically, invented dynamite and then suffered from guilt because of the deaths his invention caused. In his will he specified that the interest from a $9 million endowment would be used to ward annually five prizes in physics, chemistry, physiology or medicine, literature, and peace. The first prizes were awarded in 1901. In some years, a particular prize has not been awarded because a worthy recipient was not found. Others who have won the Nobel Peace Prize are Theodore Roosevelt, Woodrow Wilson, Albert Schweitzer, Mother Teresa, Nelson Mandela, and F. W. de Klerk.

On Heroes and the Media   *Jean Picker Firstenberg*

To emphasize the importance of the media in forming heroes, you might ask students to list as many heroes as they can think of and then to circle those that became heroes to them through the influence of the media. For an interesting aside, you might ask students to compare the number of female heroes in their list with the number of male heroes.

Depending on your time and interest, you might pursue the fact that society and the media highlight very few female heroes. For example, when we were trying to think of examples of heroes for the **Before You Read** WRITE section, we had great difficulty coming up with female heroes created by the media. The only examples that came readily to mind were Superwoman and the Bionic Woman, but the television shows based on these female heroes are hardly current.

Although "On Heroes and the Media" is quite readable, even for developmental students, it does include several rather difficult words. Thus, you may want to spend some time discussing *incarnation* (2), *wrought* (4), *venal* (5), *preempt* (8), *imbuing* (12), and other words that your students identify as problems. Additional discussion possibilities include comparing Firstenberg's definition of the antihero with students' own definitions and defining "visual literacy" in relation to "verbal literacy." Ask students whether our society is more visually literate or verbally literate.

The **After You Read** WRITE assignment focuses on heroes of recent movies and news items because your students are more likely to be familiar with these recent heroes than with those from previous decades. This assignment also encourages students to compare these more recent heroes with both the traditional hero and the antihero—and perhaps to evaluate modern society's view of the hero. In writing this essay, students may be able to use the lists they wrote in their earlier journal entries, or you could design an alternate writing assignment in which you ask students to write a paragraph or an essay comparing one or more heroes with one or more antiheroes.

Lenny Skutnik—Accidental Hero   *Richard Shereikis*

Before you assign "Lenny Skutnik—Accidental Hero," you should know that the next reading—"The Man in the Water"—focuses on the same air disaster. Thus, you may want to assign the two readings together.

The unusual title of this selection is a good starting point for discussion. Ask students to interpret the original title as given in the **Before You Read** EXAMINE section and then to read the selection to see if their interpretation fits. Before assigning the entire reading, you might even read the first paragraph aloud and then ask if anyone in the class happens to remember the name Lenny Skutnik. We have provided several questions to guide students' reading, but in this lesson we have not specifically told students to underline or write in the margins because we believe that by this time they should be marking their text on their own without specific instructions to do so. However, you may want to have students read this selection in class and observe their reading processes. If students are not interacting in writing with the text, you may want to remind them once again of the value of doing so.

The text itself is rich in possibilities for analysis and discussion. In fact, the simple questions we provide in the **As You Read** section are only a few of the questions students can explore. You might have students formulate additional questions, or you might ask them additional questions—either before or after they read. Here are some possibilities:

- Does Lenny look, or act, like a typical hero?
- Do his previous actions or lifestyle in any way suggest that Lenny has the makings of a hero?
- How is Lenny like the traditional hero? How is he unlike the traditional hero? Would you call him an "antihero" or an "ordinary hero"?
- What is the difference between a hero and a celebrity? What makes Lenny a hero? What makes him a celebrity? Which is more important to him?

The writing assignment that we suggest after the reading is also only one of many possibilities. The reference in paragraph 10 to the letters Lenny receives after his heroic act suggests another good informal assignment. That is, students could write an imaginary letter to Lenny, or, better, they could write a real letter to a "hero" who has been in the news more recently. If you wish to give your students a more complex assignment that requires them to go back into the text as well as into their own minds, you can have them write an essay comparing heroism and celebrity. In their essays, they can use support from their reading as well as from their own observations and personal experiences.

The Man in the Water   *Roger Rosenblatt*

Because "The Man in the Water" focuses on the same disaster described by
Shereikis and because Rosenblatt makes brief references to Lenny Skutnik,
it makes an excellent companion piece to the preceding reading. Again, the
title is a good place to begin discussion—perhaps comparing this title to
Shereikis's title, as suggested in the THINK section.

Because of its complex moral and philosophical probing, Rosenblatt's
essay requires a thoughtful, critical response from your students. Therefore,
after you have previewed the first paragraph of the essay with your students,
encourage them to read and reread the essay before discussing it. You might
point out that Rosenblatt provides clues to his thesis and purpose in his title
and in the question that concludes the first paragraph. Also encourage students to underline statements that they believe are important to Rosenblatt's
thesis and to write their own reactions—and questions—in the margins.

After students have read the essay, you might begin discussion with the
questions suggested in the **After You Read** section, or you might begin with
the questions and reactions students formulated during their reading. We
suggest that in addition to discussing the conflict between nature and human
nature and the universality of the man's actions, you draw students'
attention to Rosenblatt's statement in paragraph 8:

> Yet whatever moved these men to challenge death on behalf of their
> fellows is not peculiar to them. Everyone feels the possibility in
> himself. That is the abiding wonder of the story. That is why we
> would not let go of it. If the man in the water gave a lifeline to the
> people gasping for survival, he was likewise giving a lifeline to those
> who observed him.

Ask students if they believe that under the same circumstances they
would have acted as the man in the water did. We introduced the idea of the
heroic possibilities within ourselves—of ourselves as heroes—at the beginning of this unit and will return to it in the final selection.

Fall of the Legends   *Mike Lupica*

One reason why we included in this unit Mike Lupica's essay on the fall of
sports legends is that freshman students are often very interested in and very
knowledgeable about sports figures. Another reason why we included the
essay is that people—especially young people—often put sports figures at the
top of their personal lists of heroes. Discussing this essay with your students
will give you an opportunity to explore with them why sports figures are
often considered heroes, or at least role models, and whether or not this
view is valid.

It is not necessary for students to recognize all of the names of sports figures given in the essay, nor is it necessary for them to agree with Lupica's opinions about which sports legends have fallen off the pedestal (Simpson, Tyson, Johnson, Jordan, Rose, Koufax, Harding, and so forth) or which have stayed on the pedestal (Clemente, Mays, Mantle, and so forth). What is important is that students consider the qualities that legitimately belong to a true legend or hero—in or out of the world of sports. Indeed, Lupica seems to admire Mantle not so much for his baseball prowess, great as that was, but for his courage in facing personal problems such as alcoholism and in thus becoming a role model. In commenting on those legends who have fallen off the pedestal, Lupica believes that we as fans must also take responsibility for the fall of the legends because we demand too much of our sports heroes. According to Lupica, Mantle (who died in 1995) has remained on the pedestal partly because he is an athlete from a past time when the media were not so intrusive on the lives of famous sports figures.

The final writing assignment in this lesson asks students to write about a sports hero who has remained "on the pedestal" as an individual as well as a sports star. Subjects of essays should vary widely, with students in your own classroom disagreeing, for example, about whether or not Magic Johnson fell off the pedestal because of his promiscuity or remained (or climbed back) on it because of his honesty in admitting that he had the HIV virus and because of his courage and strength in returning to basketball and playing successful.

Heroines and Role Models   *Maxine F. Singer*

This selection focuses specifically on female heroes—on heroines and role models. You may want to begin by asking students to write brief informal definitions of *hero*, *heroine*, and *role model*. After writing their definitions, students should have less difficulty completing their lists in the **Before You Read** WRITE section. These preparations, in turn, should lead directly to the final WRITE assignment of comparing a contemporary heroine with a contemporary female role model.

The circumstances of this essay (really a speech) provide you with an excellent opportunity to reinforce the concepts of purpose and audience. Remind students that the selection was originally presented at Barnard College (a women's college) as a commencement address. Ask students to discuss, or write about, the specific purposes that Singer must have had in mind as she gave this address to her audience. Then ask students to evaluate the essay on the basis of the purposes they identified.

Mother Teresa and Her Endless Fight   *Ellen Goodman*

If students have read Jon D. Hull's essay "Slow Descent into Hell" from Unit Five, you might explain that Mother Teresa has spent her life battling poverty like that shown in that essay and that she has been awarded the Nobel Peace Prize for her efforts.

After students write their journal entries listing actions that individuals and government could take to reduce world poverty, have them share their ideas in small group sessions. You might even encourage students to send some of their best ideas to local, state, or national officials.

Goodman's column, written in journalistic style with short paragraphs, provides a vivid character sketch of Mother Teresa. Ask students to underline descriptive phrases and dialogue that help them to "know" this remarkable woman. This activity should help prepare students to write their essays classifying Mother Teresa as a hero rather than a role model, as based on Singer's definitions. (Most students will probably classify her as a hero, primarily because of her self-sacrificing nature.)

For a more challenging writing assignment, adapt the **After You Read** EXAMINE section into an essay assignment, asking students to think about the economic connections between peace and war. You may help students by giving them a few examples of places like Somalia, where poverty has caused war, and war has caused poverty. Encourage students to research this assignment.

Having Our Say   *Sarah and A. Elizabeth Delany*

The question of heroes and role models is also relevant to the reading selection by Sarah Delany and A. Elizabeth Delany, from *Having Our Say*, which the sisters co-authored when both were over one hundred years old. (The particular excerpt that we printed was authored by Elizabeth, or "Bessie," Delany.)

In the Preface to the Delanys' book, Amy Hill Hearth (to whom the sisters told their story) reports that Bessie was only the second black woman to practice dentistry in New York, and Sadie was the first black person ever to teach domestic science on the high school level in New York City public schools. In the 1950s the Delanys were "in the vanguard of middle-class black Americans who integrated the suburbs," and in the 1960s "they cheered from the sidelines as the civil rights movements flourished, praying and worrying about younger relatives who were getting caught up in the protests." (xii–xiii)

Sharing some of this background information might help students to decide whether Bessie is a role model or a hero—defined by Singer as one who is "known for courage and nobility of purpose, thereby uplifting our own ambitions out of narrow, self-centered concerns." Depending on the definitions they use, of course, students should be able to support Bessie Delany as a hero or a role model or both.

For example, readers can view the speaker of the following quotation as a hero or a role model: "I thought I could change the world. It took me a hundred years to figure out I *can't* change the world. I can only change Bessie. And, honey, that ain't easy, either." Likewise, the Delanys' declaration in the Preface—that their story is not "meant as 'black' or 'women's' history, but American history. It belongs to all of us" (xiii)—can be viewed as the statement of heroes or role models.

Although we placed this reading selection in the unit on heroes, it would also fit nicely in Unit Five: Self with Society, for it focuses on education, racial prejudice, and graceful aging.

Selena: Dreaming of You   *Ilan Stavans*

Ask students what they remember about Selena and her death. If you have several Hispanic students in your class, this question should give them the opportunity to talk about an individual who was important to much of the Hispanic community. Also, use your Hispanic students as resource persons to pronounce and further explain not only the Hispanic words in the article but also the culture that is described.

Before students read, ask them to each classify Selena as a hero, role model, celebrity, or even idol. Then review with your students the definitions of these terms discussed by earlier writers. For example, quoting Michael Lesy, Sudo laments the fact that the term *hero* has "become confused with 'celebrity,' 'role model,' and 'idol'"; Firstenberg suggests that whereas worthiness creates heroes, fame creates celebrities; Shereikis quotes Daniel Boorstin, who stated, "The hero created himself" through some great deeds, but "The celebrity is created by the media"; and to Singer "a heroine is distant while a role model's proximal reality encourages too close scrutiny and a destructive mimicry of both public and private behavior." After students read the selection, remind them of these definitions and ask them again to classify Selena as a hero, role model, celebrity, idol, "symbol" (see **After You Read** THINK), or some combination of these and to support their classifications, orally or in writing.

Both of the comparison assignments at the end of the reading selection require critical thinking. The second assignment also requires some outside research.

You and your students might be interested to know that this essay was published in the November 20, 1995, issue of *The New Republic* and that

Ilan Stavans has written a book, *The One-Handed Pianist and Other Stories*, scheduled for publication by The University of New Mexico Press.

A Hero's Journey: Neil Armstrong's Walk on the Moon
Thomas Talley (student)

The introduction to Talley's essay provides Joseph Campbell's important description of the hero and the hero's quest. Remind students that Jean Picker Firstenberg, whose essay "On Heroes and the Media" they read earlier in the unit, also relies on Campbell's ideas about the hero.

The essay itself focuses on Neil Armstrong as an American hero, but the prereading activities ask students to think of other individuals—heroes—who could compare with Armstrong in heroic courage and importance. Opinions will differ, but students could begin with historical figures such as Columbus or Cabeza de Vaca and work forward to more modern figures such as Colin Powell.

In discussing Armstrong's quest, however, Talley doesn't focus as much on his physical quest as on the knowledge, or "gifts," that he brought back to humankind. To Talley, Armstrong "brought back the power to change humanity's belief about itself." Talley's description of Armstrong as a hero—especially his last few paragraphs—provides you with an excellent opportunity to ask students to compare Armstrong with Martin Luther King. Remind students that Brooks discussed the "gifts" that King gave to his people just as Talley discusses the "gifts," or boons, that Armstrong brings to humanity. Explore also the idea that both of these men took inner journeys as well as outer journeys.

The last writing assignment asks students to consider the effect that Armstrong's heroic journey has had on us today. Ask students to think carefully about the effect that the space program and the walk on the moon has had on their lives, even though they probably take for granted these extraordinary occurrences from the past. Although most students in your classroom will be too young to remember Armstrong's walk on the moon, Talley himself—who is in his fifties—remembers the experience well. If you have older returning students in your class, ask them to describe how they felt as they first watched the moon walk—and use the success of Talley's essay to encourage them about their future academic success!

Christa McAuliffe: An Ordinary Hero
Mike Pride

Mike Pride's tribute to Christa McAuliffe follows naturally after Talley's tribute to Neil Armstrong, and the two essays provide many opportunities for comparison. Here are just a few of the many areas of comparison you and your students can discuss:

- Armstrong was a scientist and trained astronaut; McAuliffe was a teacher and housewife.
- Armstrong participated in the space program when it was new and all Americans were excited about it; McAuliffe participated in the program after Americans had begun to take space travel for granted.
- Talley describes Armstrong's journey as a quest; Pride describes McAuliffe's journey as an odyssey.
- Armstrong lived to complete his mission successfully; McAuliffe died just as her mission was getting started;
- Armstrong was a man; McAuliffe was a woman.

You may even want to substitute for the final assignment in the textbook an essay comparing Armstrong with McAuliffe.

The reading selection contains a variety of other possibilities for discussion and writing, many of these ideas extensions of topics discussed in previous selections. Thus, you can continue your focus on the contrast between heroes and role models. Or you can focus on the "ordinary hero" that is suggested by the title. Discuss carefully the idea of an ordinary hero as (1) a person who *seems* ordinary but who, at a moment of great challenge, takes extraordinary action (Lenny Skutnik, the man in the water, and so forth); or as (2) someone whose apparently quiet and ordinary life, upon closer inspection, takes on more heroic qualities than had at first been apparent (the Delany sisters, Christa McAuliffe). Ultimately, then, even ordinary heroes become extraordinary. Explain to students that the poem by Robert Hayden that they will read next also focuses on an ordinary, but extraordinary, hero.

Those Winter Sundays   *Robert Hayden*

You are no doubt familiar with (in fact, you have probably taught) "Those Winter Sundays." If your class is up to an introductory discussion about the various ways to approach literature, this wonderful poem is an excellent subject. Certainly, it can be read according to a new critical approach that does not seek to go outside the words on the page; however, such an approach is likely to result in a misreading of the phrase "chronic angers" (line 9), which even our advanced students have often read as angers between the father and the son. Thus, the biographical information that Hayden's stepfather and stepmother often quarreled helps prevent a major misinterpretation here. In addition, students can hardly read this poem without becoming emotionally involved with it and, in many cases, applying the poem to their personal lives. This latter way of reading is called "reader response." No doubt Hayden would have approved of such a way of reading his poem; he has said that he could not read it aloud without becoming emotional about his stepfather.

The information and questions provided in the textbook encompass all three of these approaches. The introduction provides biographical information, the THINK and WRITE activities demand a personal response from your students, and the EXAMINE activities force students to analyze the text of the poem (diction, imagery, and so on) using a new critical approach. Thus, students are interacting with the actual text of the poem as well as with their own experiences and memories.

A Song of Greatness (from the Chippewa)   *Mary Austin*

When we were looking for readings for this unit, we were excited to find "A Song of Greatness." We felt that it would make an excellent conclusion not only to the unit but also to the entire book, for it clearly relates the concept of "hero" to the concept of "self." Thus, this poem brings your students' personal journey through *Interactions* full circle back to its beginning.

In addition to the questions, activities, and assignments suggested in the text itself, you may want to focus more fully on the idea of stories, and how stories about family and heroes can strongly influence the developing self. You might even have students discuss or write journal entries about the influence of one or more specific stories on their lives. Students may be reluctant to share their personal evaluations and heroic aspirations with other class members, but they will probably be happy to read their "songs of greatness" in small groups.

CRITICAL THINKING AND WRITING ASSIGNMENTS

Even though not all of the **Exploring Ideas Together** assignments involve writing, each one requires group members to think critically through classification or analysis. And any one of these activities could be used as the basis for a writing assignment. Thus, students could write a summative essay categorizing the heroes about whom they have read; they could write a personal response to heroes or antiheroes in film; they could write an essay analyzing the relationship between a hero and a celebrity in selected readings; or they could write a persuasive analytical essay arguing for or against the idea that we live in "an age without heroes." If you decide to use any one of these assignments as a prompt for writing, consider assigning a collaborative essay so that group participation and learning can continue through the writing process.

In selecting assignments from **Writing Essays**, you will probably want to assign a more personal topic to classes or students who still have trouble with abstractions. For example, assignments 3 and 7 call for personal essays about a woman or an ordinary person whom the student considers heroic. More advanced classes and students can handle the persuasive essay required in assignment 1 (nomination of a person for a Medal of Valor); assignment 4 (argument for positive or negative effects of media on our perceptions of heroes); or assignment 5 (argument for or against a sports figure or entertainer as a true hero). Assignment 2 requires students to do outside research, whereas assignment 6 requires students to return to the text to compare the heroism of Lenny Skutnik and "the man in the water." Again, we suggest that you limit your assignment to one essay and that you remind students to revise, edit, and proofread their essays carefully.